RELIGIOUS INVENTIONS

STUDIES IN CHRISTIANITY AND JUDAISM

Series editor: Richard S. Ascough

The Studies in Christianity and Judaism series publishes volumes dealing with Christianity and Judaism in their formative periods, with special interest in studies of the relationships between them and of the cultural and social contexts within which they developed.

The series is sponsored by the Canadian Corporation for Studies in Religion whose constituent societies include the Canadian Society of Biblical Studies, Canadian Society for the Study of Religion, Canadian Society of Patristic Studies, Canadian Theological Society, Société canadienne de théologie, and Société québécoise pour l'étude de la religion.

1 Sacred Ritual, Profane Space
The Roman House as Early Christian Meeting Place
Jenn Cianca

2 The Christian Moses
Vision, Authority, and the Limits of Humanity in the New Testament and Early Christianity
Jaeda Calaway

3 Recovering an Undomesticated Apostle
Essays on the Legacy of Paul
Edited by Christopher B. Zeichmann and John A. Egger

4 Honouring Age
The Social Dynamics of Age Structure in 1 Timothy
Mona Tokarek LaFosse

5 The Authentic Paul
Critical Scholarship and the Making of a Christian Book
Gregory Fewster

6 Religious Inventions
Ancient Mediterranean Practice and the Study of Religion
Edited by William Arnal and Erin K. Vearncombe

Religious Inventions

Ancient Mediterranean Practice and the Study of Religion

Edited by

WILLIAM ARNAL

and

ERIN K. VEARNCOMBE

McGill-Queen's University Press
Montreal & Kingston · London · Chicago

ISBN 978-0-2280-2445-3 (cloth)
ISBN 978-0-2280-2446-0 (paper)
ISBN 978-0-2280-2447-7 (ePDF)
ISBN 978-0-2280-2448-4 (ePUB)

Legal deposit second quarter 2025
Bibliothèque et Archives nationales du Québec

Printed in Canada on acid-free paper that is 100% ancient-forest-free, containing 100% sustainable, recycled fibre, and processed chlorine-free.

This book has been published with the help of a grant from the Federation for the Humanities and Social Sciences, through the Awards to Scholarly Publications Program, using funds provided by the Social Sciences and Humanities Research Council of Canada.

Funded by the Government of Canada | Financé par le gouvernement du Canada | Canada | Canada Council for the Arts | Conseil des arts du Canada

We acknowledge the support of the Canada Council for the Arts.

Nous remercions le Conseil des arts du Canada de son soutien.

McGill-Queen's University Press in Montreal is on land which long served as a site of meeting and exchange amongst Indigenous Peoples, including the Haudenosaunee and Anishinabeg nations. In Kingston it is situated on the territory of the Haudenosaunee and Anishinaabek. We acknowledge and thank the diverse Indigenous Peoples whose footsteps have marked these territories on which peoples of the world now gather.

Library and Archives Canada Cataloguing in Publication

Title: Religious inventions: ancient Mediterranean practice and the study of religion / edited by William Arnal and Erin K. Vearncombe.

Names: Arnal, William E. (William Edward), 1967- editor | Vearncombe, Erin K., editor

Series: Studies in Christianity and Judaism; 6.

Description: Series statement: Studies in Christianity and Judaism; 6 | Includes bibliographical references and index.

Identifiers: Canadiana (print) 20240512251 | Canadiana (ebook) 20240512359 | ISBN 9780228024453 (cloth) | ISBN 9780228024460 (paper) | ISBN 9780228024484 (ePUB) | ISBN 9780228024477 (ePDF)

Subjects: LCSH: Church history—Primitive and early church, ca. 30-600. | LCSH: Judaism—History—Post-exilic period, 586 B.C.-210 A.D. | LCSH: Mediterranean Region—Religion—History—To 1500.

Classification: LCC BL687 .R45 2025 | DDC 200.93—dc23

This book was designed and typeset by Marquis Interscript in 11/14 Bembo. Copyediting by Joanne Richardson.

McGill-Queen's University Press
Suite 1720, 1010 Sherbrooke St West, Montreal, QC, H3A 2R7

Authorized safety representative in the EU: Mare Nostrum Group BV, Mauritskade 21D, 1091 GC Amsterdam, the Netherlands, gpsr@mare-nostrum.co.uk

In Memory of Stephen G. Wilson
1942–2020

Contents

SECTION FOUR: COMPARISON

Figures and Tables

FIGURES

TABLES

RELIGIOUS INVENTIONS

I

Religious Inventions: Introduction

William Arnal and Erin K. Vearncombe

The following collection represents the results of a six-year seminar on early Christianity, early Judaism, and the study of religion, undertaken by the Canadian Society for Biblical Studies (CSBS) from 2015 to 2021. The seminar was first proposed at the 2014 CSBS annual meeting at Brock University by Stephen G. Wilson, who coordinated the seminar for the 2015, 2016, and 2017 meetings, and successfully applied for a three-year renewal. The seminar was then coordinated by William Arnal and Erin Vearncombe in 2018, 2019, and – with 2020 skipped because of the COVID pandemic – 2021. The principal aim of the seminar (on which see Steve's original proposal, appended at the end of this introduction) was to explore how our thinking about Roman-era Christianity and Judaism could be enhanced, changed, or supplemented by framing our inquiry as part and parcel of the academic study of religion. Would doing so generate new kinds of questions? Would it preclude or de-centre other, more traditional, kinds of questions? Would certain kinds of data and arguments be foregrounded?

At first glance, such a project could appear to be something of a nothing-burger. After all, the writings of, say, the New Testament, or of the Mishnah, are religious writings, and so in studying them, in whatever way, we are necessarily studying religion. How is the ostensible project of this seminar in any way distinctive? But in fact it is far from obvious that the idea of *religion*, and the framework of the academic study thereof, serves as the basis – or even should serve as the basis – for academic analysis of the surviving writings of Roman-era Judaisms and Christianities. One's angle of view, one's tacit or explicit disciplinary context, provides certain motivations for studying a given set of data, and this shapes the kinds of questions that those data are imagined to answer as well as what kinds of answers are deemed satisfactory or persuasive. As mere data, ancient texts like the Gospel of Matthew, or Paul's first letter to the Corinthians, or the *Apocalypse of Baruch*, or tractate *Demai* of the Mishnah can be used as evidence of any number of things. First and foremost, the field of "*biblical* studies," the traditional home of much scholarly analysis of both the New Testament and the Hebrew Bible, is in origin and essence an exploration of *canonical* literature, that is, literature that a particular religious tradition – Christianity – has deemed authoritative (in one fashion or another) for religious understanding. This assumption in turn dictates a fundamentally hermeneutical approach to such texts: as repositories for correct religious information – what God is like, how people should behave, and so on – canonical documents need to be *understood*, as fully and as accurately as possible. Failure to understand them correctly has consequences: false doctrine, bad ethics, and so on. Thus, while an enormous and sophisticated apparatus of literary and even historical techniques has been applied to canonical texts by believers since the nineteenth century, the point of these techniques, including the so-called "historical-critical method," has been to illuminate the meaning of texts whose importance is grounded in religious commitments. The persistence of egregious canonical bias – not simply the act of ignoring non-canonical works but also the enormous effort invested in establishing such writings as late, derivative, or fraudulent[1] – is a reflection of how deeply this particularistic confessional framework is embedded in our field. Now, there is nothing particularly wrong with religious people seeking to understand the writings they claim as holy. But this is in itself a religious activity; indeed, something very much akin to divination or bibliomancy.[2] As such, it should not be of any particular interest to those who do not share the same confessional commitments. Moreover, in such approaches, there can be a rather circular reasoning, or a kind of inversion of the text's authority: one decides in advance, by virtue of their religious commitments, what can and cannot be true, and then imposes that certainty on the texts.

Another potential approach to our texts, one with a firmer place among the disciplinary norms of the humanities and social sciences, is the historical: the texts can be viewed as evidence, in one fashion or another, of past events and, thus, serve as data that allow us more fulsomely to reconstruct certain events of the Roman-era Mediterranean. If we adopt a rather broad definition of "history," as inclusive of cultural norms, art and literature, and social structures, perhaps a historically oriented approach would be the ideal for those coming at our body of textual data from the study of Classics. Texts like 1 Corinthians or the Mishnah are indeed products of the Graeco-Roman world, written in the period and location of the ancient Roman Empire. It only makes sense, then, that we can read them as sources of information for the society, culture, and doings (both quotidian and extraordinary) in much the same way we might likewise read Tacitus. Such an approach can, however, at times be ham-handed. If our texts are simply read as straightforward and factual accounts of events that took place – i.e., that ancient Jews did in fact observe the sabbath in such-and-such a way (per the Mishnah) or that Paul really did preach the gospel at the Areopagus – then we run into two major (perhaps insurmountable) difficulties. The first is that the texts we have are often more prescriptive than descriptive, offering a sense of what their authors – who may in fact have occupied minority and even idiosyncratic positions within the larger group – wish had been the case rather than what actually was the case. Even texts that aim to recount history are fatally dependent on the accuracy of their sources. A second problem concerns the actual historical impact of many (most?) of the events recounted in our literature. Even if we could piece together an accurate portrait of the deeds or teachings of the historical Jesus, for example, we would only have sketched out a life of an obscure Galilean who made little to no historical impact in his own lifetime, someone peripheral to the religious movements of first-century Judaism, and someone of little moment in the great events of the Galilee and Judea in the first century. To put it bluntly, the figure of Jesus is not a historical figure in the writings that discuss him (as they are not history books and their interest in him is not historical) and was not historically significant in either his religious or his political context. In any case, a historical approach need not suffer from these kinds of defects. The texts of interest to us are historical documents in the sense that they attest to the ideas, to the culture, and (perhaps only indirectly) to the society out of which they emerged. That society – notwithstanding a pervasive and usually unspoken tendency to isolate and insulate Jewish and Christian texts (and at the earliest stages of Christian literature, no distinction between the two is possible) from their "ambient culture"[3] – *was* Graeco-Roman. Judaism and Christianity were among the permutations – in Heidi Wendt's language, "ethnicizing" ones – of Hellenistic and Roman religion. And so recent scholarship has significantly advanced our understanding that early Jewish and Christian literature *was* Graeco-Roman literature, operating with similar kinds of stylistic conventions, similar kinds of tradents, and similar social and ideological constraints.[4] Likewise, comparison of the kinds of figures who appear in ancient Jewish and Christian literature with broader types and patterns of behaviour in the Roman world has yielded extraordinary results.[5]

But if religion is the rubric under which we study this literature, a whole host of different questions arises as well as a number of distinctive constraints or tendencies.[6] Perhaps the most remarkable tendency is the inherent comparative orientation of such a framework. "Religion," after all, is normally used as a high-level and quite abstract category, specific to no one culture or epoch. It draws together practices – ritual, discursive, and otherwise – from the entire breadth of human cultures and the entire depths of human history.[7] If we are to speak of ancient Jewish or Christian ideas and behaviours as *religious* ideas and behaviours, we are *inherently* claiming that they are meaningfully and substantially akin to ideas held by and behaviours typical of societies and cultures geographically and temporally far distant from the Mediterranean world of two thousand years ago. This comparative interest should incline us, then, to explore our data in search of *general patterns of human behaviour*. In other words, what is specific and unique to ancient Judaism and Christianity, what is incomparable, comes to be of less interest to the religionist than what is shared with other cultures, periods, and traditions. One need not engage in specific and explicit acts of comparison with other religious forms from different cultures – though it helps. But a comparative orientation can be manifest, too, in simply identifying specific ancient Jewish or Christian practices with broader and more abstract categories: concepts like magic, sacrifice, literate specialists, costly signalling, economic exchange, and so on.

Of course, there is a danger here, too. If one is not careful, it is easy to mistake the particular for the universal (a danger particularly marked for a hegemonic tradition like Christianity) and impose the specificities of one culture or one religious tradition onto another that in fact lacks those features. Indeed, some scholars of religion have claimed that *religion* itself is just such an imposition, a creation of the modern West that therefore does not apply to non-Western (e.g., Hinduism) or non-modern (e.g., ancient Judaism and Christianity) systems of belief and practice,[8] or, even worse, represents a technology of domination.[9] This debate is reflected in several of the chapters in this volume, especially those in the opening section. Similarly, there is a considerable scholarly literature proposing that the concept of *magic* is a Western concept inherited from the Greco-Roman world and then imposed universally.[10] And a core technique of the study of religion – comparison, considered by the chapters in section 4 of this volume – has often been used invidiously as a mechanism for highlighting the supposed defects or lacunae of positions other than one's own.[11] On the other hand, any academic approach to anything will always be in a process of taking stock of its conceptual apparatuses, so critical discourses on elements of the academic study of religion should be an encouraging, rather than a discouraging, sign. And the advantages of this approach, it seems to us, outweigh the dangers. Among those advantages is the way that the academic study of religion tends to place emphasis less on texts, and the interpretation thereof (a foible of "biblical studies" discussed above), and more on practice, ritual, and concrete social roles, an insight reflected in the chapters gathered in this volume in the section entitled "Undoing Text" *and* in the section entitled "Practice and Identity." Another substantial advantage of approaching ancient Judaism and Christianity as religion is that its implicitly comparative orientation is somewhat estranging of our subject matter and, as such, can help lead us away from conclusions or approaches we would find farcical when applied to other traditions. Consider, for example, the ink that has been spilled on demonstrating the inherent inferiority (including chronological inferiority) of "heretical" and other non-canonical expressions of Christian thought in antiquity.[12] Yet how laughable we would find a Western scholar who devoted him- or herself to arguing that, say, the Vedānta school is in all ways superior to the Vaiśeṣika or the Chārvāka; or who explored the ethical deficiencies of weak ḥadīth. The framework of religious studies is hardly perfect, but it can help us develop a more rigorous, and more even-handed, understanding of the world of antiquity as reflected in ancient Jewish and Christian materials; *and*, it is worth stressing, the application of this framework to antiquity can *also* itself contribute to our broader understanding of religion writ large.

Although each year of the seminar had a specific theme or issue to tie the papers together, the organization of the chapters in this book does not reflect a strictly chronological approach; rather, the chapters are organized according to their relevance to the themes – as discussed above – that seem to surface from an explicitly *religion*-oriented study of ancient Judaisms and Christianities. The first group of chapters explicitly discusses the salience of the concept of "religion" itself for making sense of ancient data. In chapter 2, Christine Mitchell demonstrates the complex interconnectedness of religion with empire, politics, and mixed cultural influences among Judeans in Achaemenid Egypt, a constellation of practices and institutions emerging from the tension between imperial authorities and colonial subjects. In chapter 3, John Kloppenborg's meticulous review of the identity language used by Christians in the first two centuries demonstrates that first-century followers of Jesus were more inclined to describe themselves in terms suggestive of scholastic than of cultic identity. But in the second century, the use by outsiders of the term Χριστιανοί implied political partisanship, and the newly interpellated "Christians" responded with a corrective emphasis on cultic identity and more distinctively religious virtues. In chapter 4, Stanley Stowers argues not only for the salience of religion as a "robust social kind" but as a complex one, one that exhibits several distinct types or modes. The letters of Paul are his primary example, and he stresses the ways in which making use of Paul as data can illuminate our understanding of religion, and not just the other way around. What all three chapters share, notwithstanding their divergent views and subject matters, is not only an explicit interest in applying – or testing the application of – the idea of religion to ancient data but, especially, an emphasis on the complexity of religion as a category or construct and a self-consciousness about the concept's analytic utility. As Willi Braun states in his chapter 5 response to the papers, "biblical studies are religious studies indeed" (89).

Section 2 of the volume is entitled "Undoing Text." The point here is not so much to question the stability or reality of any given text (say, the Gospel of Mark) as a stable text, either on theoretical or historical grounds – though there are certainly grounds for making arguments of this sort. Rather, the point is simultaneously to recognize *and* to express misgivings about the centrality of textual data for our enterprise – the study of Judaism and Christianity in antiquity. Again, the contrast between "*biblical* studies" and "*religious* studies" is crucial. It remains true that the majority of our data comes from textual sources; but it is not true that, if understanding religion is to be our desideratum, mere exegesis – which, ironically enough, can tend to occlude the material nature of textuality itself and replace real, concrete and specific realities with ideal ones – will suffice. All of the chapters in this section, therefore, use textual data as their primary point of departure but treat textuality as itself something in need of exploration, the ways that texts are both used and are read as strategies for refiguring conceptions of the world or for dealing with social realities. In chapter 6, Heather Macumber explores the tendentious exclusion of heavenly figures from biblical books such as Ezekiel and Revelation from the broader category of "monsters." In chapter 7, Esther Guillen explicitly delves into the question of how texts and textuality are used in the Gospel of Matthew. In chapter 8, Matthew Mitchell explores the complexity of the relationship between texts and imagined social contexts, emphasizing the difficulties involved in using hypothetical or otherwise non-extant texts to make inferences about unattested "communities" and stressing that the Gospel of the Hebrews is really no *text* at all. In chapter 9, Jason Yuh analyzes the Epistle of Barnabas's textual strategies for dealing with social objectives. In chapter 10, Erin Vearncombe explores the textualization of trauma as a coping strategy for the author of the Gospel of Mark in the face of disaster. In his chapter 11 response, Daniel Smith observes that, despite interventions such as these, we continue to be bound by the limitations imposed on us by the nature of our data.

Section 3, entitled "Practice and Identity," is organized around the principle that the study of religion is not simply the study of *ideas* but is also and especially, among other things, a study of *practices*, including practices that bear directly on identity, including ethnic identity. Since shared practices are one important feature of shared identities, it seemed appropriate to bring these two themes together. All of the chapters in this section deal straightforwardly with identity – Jewish identity especially – or with specific religious practices. In chapter 12, Adele Reinhartz addresses problems and complexities associated with a wide variety of posited identities in antiquity (religious and otherwise) and explores the problem of hybrid identities as raised especially by postcolonial theorists. She concludes that we should not inhibit ourselves by excessive fears about misnaming ancient identities but must be clear and specific about our reasons for preferring particular terms and conceptions. In chapter 13, William Arnal explores the ways a specific type of practice – healing – can be presented in different ways (miraculous, or magical) depending on the context and the assessment of the healer. Similarly, in chapter 14, Ryan Schroeder explores the practice of divination, that is, oracular consultation of divinities, and the ways in which this practice has been differentially categorized by scholars in evaluative ways. The biblical – which is to say scribal – emphasis on spontaneous prophecy has obscured the degree to which deliberate oracular consultation was actually practised in Israelite religion. Kimberley Stratton's chapter 15 traces the development of a distinctively Christian identity in antiquity to the exigencies of the Bar Kochba Revolt of 132–135 CE. John Van Maaren, in chapter 16, models the various ways ethnic boundaries are constructed, and he applies these to the *Book of Jubliees*, arguing that this text models ethnic identity on essentially the grounds of "race," in opposition to the Hasmonean effort to define Jewishness in national terms. In chapter 17, Jack Lightstone looks at how diaspora Jews, after the 70 CE destruction of the Jerusalem temple, actively re-read scriptural materials in order to fabricate new sets of shared practices, which, in their turn, fabricated a durable Jewish identity. In her chapter 18 response, Alicia Batten notes that all of the chapters in this section reinforce the close connection between practice and identity.

The fourth and final section of the book appears under the rubric of "Comparison." It is appropriate that comparison receive some dedicated and extensive attention since there is a case to be made that if the field of religious studies has any methodological integrity at all it is to be found in the practice of comparison. And, as already noted, "religion" itself is an inherently comparative concept. The chapters in this final section of the book are all explicitly concerned with comparison, whether conceived in a very precise way or sketched more broadly in terms of general patterns of human behaviour. Heidi Wendt's chapter 19 takes the scholarly construct of "freelance religious expertise" and applies it to Chinese spirit mediums, arguing that the ethnographic evidence for the latter fits the framework Wendt uses elsewhere to analyze the ancient Roman world, emphatically rejecting claims of incommensurability between cultures. In chapter 20, Jennifer Otto argues that exclusive comparison of Alexandrian Christian exegetical traditions as witnessed by, for example, Clement, with Philo, excludes a wide range of both parties' actual interlocutors, including Pythagoreans, Platonists, Stoics, and others. In this case, comparison poorly undertaken has distorted our understanding. In chapter 21, Rebecca Runesson focuses on a very precise question of comparison. She explores one dimension of the by now well-founded comparison between early Christ groups and the voluntary associations of antiquity. Focusing on ancient ideals about benefaction, Runesson concludes that elite literary sources are less appropriate comparanda for ancient Christianity than is the inscriptional evidence. Colleen Shantz's chapter 22 directly tackles the issue undergirding any informed effort at comparison: the question of human universals versus cultural specificity. Obviously, if it really *is* "culture all the way down," there is not much point comparing one cultural phenomenon to another (unless they are genetically related). Shantz argues, by contrast, that while culture is obviously a factor in human behaviour, so is biology. Finally, in chapter 23, Giovanni Bazzana expresses misgivings about universal categories, but generalizing categories such as spirit possession can allow for effective and illuminating comparative work. Maia Kotrosits, in her chapter 24 response, stresses that there is very little agreement among these chapters on just how, and how extensively, comparison can and ought to be undertaken, but at least one point of convergence is that all of the authors "are worried by the prospects of knowledge production after modernity" (403).

* * *

On 23 January 2020, after a distinguished career of teaching and research as a professor of religious studies at Carleton University, and of service to the field, including extensive service to the Canadian Society of Biblical Studies, Steve Wilson died. The editors wish to take this opportunity to acknowledge once again that the seminar represented by this collection was conceived, organized, and begun by Steve Wilson. Steve was an indefatigable proponent of the critical study of religion, a major force in the Canadian biblical studies "scene," and a past president of the CSBS. He was a bon vivant, thoroughly and profoundly affable, and simultaneously sharply and thoroughly intellectual. If you saw Steve at a conference, you knew that before long you would be ensconced in a dark bar somewhere with a pitcher on the table. But over that pitcher, you would be having an intense conversation about canonicity, or religious experience, or voluntary associations. We lost Steve prematurely, and we wish to remember him by dedicating this collection to his memory.

APPENDIX: STEPHEN G. WILSON'S ORIGINAL PLAN FOR THE SEMINAR

The following sketch was discussed at the annual meeting of the CSBS, Brock University, 2014.

1. First, a comment on the reason for this session: it is to gauge the level of interest in starting a new seminar on a theme that is of great interest to me but about which I know relatively little. It springs form a conversation with Bill Arnal, Zeba Crook, and Willi Braun (there may have been others too) in Victoria last year when the idea was floated. They all responded with enthusiasm, but each of them had reasons for not taking a lead, so they suggested I do it instead – which is odd, since they know more about the subject than I do. I nevertheless agreed to open a discussion and, if there is sufficient interest, to help organize a seminar for the annual meetings.

2. There is a biographical element to this too. I came to Canada in 1971 precisely with the aim of teaching Christian origins in a religion program, as distinct from the theology departments that were almost all that were on offer in the UK at that time, and in one of which I had taken my degrees. This worked out well, providing a happy home for me to pursue my interests without the pressures of confessional (i.e., Christian) conformity. At the same time it became increasingly obvious over the years that the material I studied and the way I studied it bore little relationship, indeed was largely irrelevant, to what else was going on in the department. The disjunction was increasingly uncomfortable, and it was largely my problem, not theirs. In more recent years, too, I've tossed around the idea of writing a book on early Christianity as religion to see how different it would look from standard surveys of the field. So far it has remained little more than a vague idea, in part because I had other projects on the go and in part because I didn't really know where to start. I'm not alone in this, since I know that Zeba Crook has contemplated something along these lines too. My hope is that this seminar will sharpen and shape the idea enough that someone else (or perhaps a collective) will write it!

3. Early Christianity is a natural place to begin for many of us, but the study of early Judaism is equally open to the same questions and, I suspect, poses similar problems. Graeco-Roman religions would of course fall within our remit, and there may well be Hebrew Bible scholars who would find the topic congenial. Liaison with interested members of the Canadian Society

for the Study of Religion (CSSR) and the Canadian Society of Patristic Studies (CSPS) could be very fruitful too. But first we need to get started and clear a bit of the preliminary brush.

4. This seminar would not be the first to explore these issues. The most sustained attempt to move in a similar direction was the Society of Biblical Literature (SBL) seminar entitled "Redescribing Christian Origins," run by Ron Cameron and Merrill Miller (1995–2003), followed since 2007 by a seminar entitled "Redescribing Early Christianity," which focuses on the second century and beyond. Currently one of the conveners of this seminar is Bill Arnal. I note too that Bill and Russ McCutcheon have recently published a brilliant and provocative book called *The Sacred Is the Profane: The Political Nature of Religion*, which raises many issues that could be discussed further in a new seminar. A CSBS seminar would overlap to some extent with the ongoing SBL seminar – which would be no bad thing – but it would no doubt develop its own agenda, reflecting the interests of our members. There are also things we have studied in other successful CSBS seminars that could have been, and perhaps still will be, included in a seminar of this nature – I think of religious rivalries, voluntary associations, travel and religion, human memory and the transmission of early Christian material, all of which resulted in important publications. How they might look when revisited in the context of a somewhat broader agenda, and one that is methodologically more self-conscious, is an interesting question.

5. At some point, earlier rather than later, we will have to discuss the contentious term "religion." Some see it as a modern Western, post-Enlightenment, colonialist concept used to distort and denigrate other cultures and religions that have no equivalent concept or terminology. They want to toss it overboard as being either too constricting and overbearing or too broad to be of any use. At this point I'm not convinced that the term is terminally useless, but we will need to take a look at the fascinating debates outside our field in the broader field of religious studies. And that means that from the outset we will not be working with one fixed and well-understood concept (religion) and another that is inchoate (Christian origins) but with two that are equally indeterminate. This whole debate might be old hat to some but, I suspect, news to others in the field of Christian origins.

6. It is quite widely accepted that a consistent trait in the study of religion has been the explicit or inadvertent use of Christian concepts to describe and even construct other religious traditions. The chief culprit here is

probably the concept of belief or faith, so influential that it has become commonplace to speak of religions as beliefs or faiths (the Hindu faith, the Jewish faith) as if that was all – or at least the most important thing – that could be said about them. Donald Lopez, in a chapter in Mark Taylor's book *Critical Terms in Religious Studies*, exposes all too clearly the hegemonic and restrictive nature of this tendency.

One way to look at this seminar is to see it as a way of shifting our attention to the way in which these same later Christian concepts can distort accounts of Christianity's own early tradition too – sometimes, it is true, with the collusion of the documents themselves (the NT does speak quite a bit about belief) but sometimes because we are too complicit and too lazy to work outside conventional agendas set by the very documents that we study.

7. This points to another important component: we will need to reflect on the dominant narratives of early Christian groups, historical and ideological, in the NT or outside of it, that have set the agenda of those studying them. Too often we become slaves to their priorities, their narratives, their concepts. We need to stand back and critically appraise them, not in their terms but in terms of our own devising, ways that we consciously choose and that do not necessarily conform to the way they present or understand themselves. In this sense, it can be argued, the insiders' view, the view of the early Christian authors (and most of the useful evidence is in texts), has no privileged position. And thus out of the window too, perhaps, would go all variants of the phenomenological approach to religion (Cantwell Smith, Eliade, et al.) – though this, of course, remains to be seen.

8. How could we otherwise characterize such an approach? One way would be to follow Willi Braun who, in his thoughtful essay in the Jonathan Z. Smith Festschrift (*Introducing Religion*, ed. Willi Braun and Russ McCutcheon, 2007), makes a lucid case for a firmly *anthropocentric* approach to religious studies in general and to Christian origins studies in particular. Here the study of Christian origins would consist of the study of a human phenomenon rooted firmly in this world. It would eschew "supernatural" beings (gods/spirits/demons etc.) as explanatory or causal factors on the human stage and focus on how and why humans make claims about such beings in the first place.

"There is no religion in itself apart from people who do things that either they or religion scholars call 'religious'" (Braun). Bill Arnal, in his recent book, makes the related claim that: "The bundles of behaviour we call religion, and the entities they imagine, are part of the broader and ordinary phenomenon of human imagination." On this view, since the religious claims and behaviours of people are the only things accessible to us, the study of religion is inevitably anthropocentric. This is a thesis that I find attractive, indeed self-evident, but not everyone will. It would be rewarding to give it an airing and consider its implications.

9. Bruce Lincoln from Chicago came to Carleton last year to lecture and I was chatting to him about the proposed seminar. Off the cuff he suggested two approaches. First, to apply familiar categories of religious studies to Early Christian material (e.g., myth, ritual, sacrifice, identity, religious experience – a thorny one!). This is perhaps the most obvious approach but could still be immensely fruitful if the categories themselves and the way they have been used are subjected to critical analysis. How would an account of Christian origins look if the categories came from outside, from the broader field of religious studies? What would be highlighted and what neglected? Many of the familiar themes would, I suspect, be relegated and unfamiliar ones elevated. The second, he said, would be to look at Early Christian data to see what it might contribute to the broader understanding of religions – a fascinating option and one which, to my knowledge, has been taken up only by Bill Arnal in his recent publications. To take one of his examples: What can we learn about the unpredictable evolution of religious movements in general from the unexpected and surprising transformation of Christianity from despised and insignificant cult to imperial religion (to use a host of loaded terms)? Read him and see.

10. Broadly speaking, I see the seminar combining two related elements. First, it will have a theoretical/methodological thrust in which familiar categories, concepts, and theories of Christian origins and evolution are interrogated, problematized, revised, and reapplied (or abandoned). Second, it will take a fresh look at the data of Christian Origins in the light of these reflections and perhaps, in the best of all worlds, throw light back on those widespread human behaviours that we loosely call "religion." Some, like the brilliant Jonathan Z Smith, can do both in the same essay. Most of us will never match him on our own, but perhaps in partnership with others we can achieve the same end.

11. A final word: obviously, the concerns of such a seminar will be more pertinent to some members of the society than to others. I would hope the issues would be of general interest, but they are particularly pressing for those working in a religious studies program. One by-product might be a fresh understanding of how the study of Christian origins can be defended in the

context of a secular university – a variant of the same question faced by religion programs in general. Another might be a consideration of pedagogy. For example, how would an introduction to Christian origins look if it was analyzed and presented as one religion like any other? How would this differ from the standard introductory courses currently on offer? In my experience, designing an undergraduate course is one of the best ways to clarify and distill one's thoughts. So, to return to a point made above, perhaps we could collectively sketch out an introductory textbook that takes seriously the issues discussed in the seminar. Richard Ascough has already mentioned a source of funding we might explore if we pursue this.

If there is sufficient interest we could hold one session in 2015 to scout out the territory and set a longer agenda. Three or four papers, circulated ahead of time and discussed in detail, would set us up well for the following years.

NOTES

1 Simply compare the number of commentaries, since, say, 1980, on the Gospel of John with those of the Apocryphon of John. For a good example of how the very idea of fraudulence is deployed against non-canonical literature, see Mark Goodacre, *Thomas and the Gospels* (Grand Rapids, MI: Eerdmans, 2012), who accuses the author of Thomas of "plagiarism" (a claim he does not make in connection with the Gospel of Matthew's use of Mark, for example). Likewise, see the strenuous (if vain) efforts of Stephen C. Carlson, *The Gospel Hoax: Morton Smith's Invention of Secret Mark* (Waco: Baylor University Press, 2005) to establish "Secret Mark" as a "hoax"; for an even-handed assessment of Carlson's work, see Geoffrey S. Smith and Brent C. Landau, *The Secret Gospel of Mark: A Controversial Scholar, a Scandalous Gospel of Jesus, and the Fierce Debate over Its Authenticity* (New Haven: Yale University Press, 2023). A rather ironic example of canonical bias can be found in James Crossley and Robert J. Myles, *Jesus: A Life in Class Conflict* (Alresford, Hampshire: Zero Books, 2023). In this work, the Gospel of Thomas – a text whose contents would have done much to support the authors' perspective – is dismissed as late and secondary. Also late and secondary, they claim, is the Gospel of John. Yet John is nonetheless used freely to reconstruct details of Jesus's life or of a Jesus movement, whereas Thomas is not used at all.

2 For the practice of bibliomancy in antiquity, see Jennifer Eyl, *Signs, Wonders, and Gifts: Divination in the Letters of Paul* (Oxford: Oxford University Press, 2019).

3 The language of "ambient culture" is used, for example, in Harold Attridge, "Early Christianity," in *Religions of the Ancient World: A Guide*, ed. Sarah Iles Johnston (Cambridge: Belknap Press of Harvard University Press, 2004), 237.

4 Exemplary are Kendra Eshleman, *The Social World of Intellectuals in the Roman Empire: Sophists, Philosophers, and Christians* (Cambridge: Cambridge University

Press, 2012); Heidi Wendt, "Christians as and among Writer-Intellectuals in Second-Century Rome," in *Christian Teachers in Second-Century Rome*, ed. H. Gregory Snyder (Leiden: Brill, 2020), 84–108; and Robyn Faith Walsh, *The Origins of Early Christian Literature: Contextualizing the New Testament within Greco-Roman Literary Culture* (Cambridge: Cambridge University Press, 2021).

5 Exemplary are Eyl, *Signs, Wonders, and Gifts*; and Heidi Wendt, *At the Temple Gates: The Religion of Freelance Experts in the Roman Empire* (Oxford: Oxford University Press, 2016); but also the weighty and ongoing research on early Christian *ekklēsiai* and Greaco-Roman voluntary associations. Among the latter, see, for example, Philip A. Harland, *Associations, Synagogues, and Congregations: Claiming a Place in Ancient Mediterranean Society* (Minneapolis: Fortress Press, 2003); Richard Ascough, *Early Christ Groups and Greco-Roman Associations: Organizational Models and Social Practices* (Eugene, OR: Cascade Books, 2022); Richard Last, *The Pauline Church and the Corinthian Ekklesia: Greco-Roman Associations in Comparative Context* (Cambridge: Cambridge University Press, 2016). Maren R. Niehoff, *Jewish Exegesis and Homeric Scholarship in Alexandria* (Cambridge: Cambridge University Press, 2011), explores the impact of Homeric scholarship and its techniques on Philo of Alexandria.

6 For a more extended consideration of this question, see William Arnal, "The Origins of Christianity within, and without 'Religion': A Case Study," in *The Sacred* Is *the Profane: The Political Nature of "Religion,"* William Arnal and Russell McCutcheon (Oxford: Oxford University Press, 2012), 134–70, cited by Steve in the appendix to this chapter. See also William Arnal, "What Branches Grow Out of This Stony Rubbish? 'Biblical' Contributions to the Study of Religion," *Studies in Religion* 39, no. 4 (2010): 549–72; and William E. Arnal, "A Parting of the Ways? Scholarly Identity and a Peculiar Species of Ancient Mediterranean Religion," in *Identity and Interaction in the Ancient Mediterranean: Jews, Christians, and Others –Essays in Honour of Stephen G. Wilson*, ed. Zeba A. Crook and Philip A. Harland (Sheffield: Sheffield Phoenix Press, 2007), 253–75.

7 We leave aside for the moment the question – one explored in several of the chapters of this volume – whether this universal application of the concept of religion is accurate and appropriate. The point here is that the term is not normally used to refer to any one specific tradition but, rather, to gather together a variety of different cultural practices.

8 Perhaps the sharpest and clearest summation of this position vis-à-vis Roman antiquity is that of Brent Nongbri, *Before Religion: A History of a Modern Concept* (New Haven: Yale University Press, 2013), who, notably, nonetheless supports the utility of "religion" as an etic concept. See also Carlin A. Barton and Daniel Boyarin, *Imagine No Religion: How Modern Abstractions Hide Ancient Realities* (New York: Fordham University Press, 2016).

9 In different ways, see Timothy Fitzgerald, *Discourse on Civility and Barbarity: A Critical History of Religion and Related Categories* (Oxford: Oxford University Press, 2007); and Tomoko Masuzawa, *The Invention of World Religions; or, How European*

Universalism Was Preserved in the Language of Pluralism (Chicago: University of Chicago Press, 2005).

10 See, for example, Kimberly B. Stratton, *Naming the Witch: Magic, Ideology, and Stereotype in the Ancient World* (New York: Columbia University Press, 2007), who is also a contributor to this volume.

11 The classic statement on this matter is, of course, Jonathan Z. Smith, *Drudgery Divine: On the Comparison of Early Christianities and the Religions of Late Antiquity* (Chicago: University of Chicago Press, 1990). See too William E. Paden, *Religious Worlds: The Comparative Study of Religion* (Boston: Beacon Press, 1994).

12 As a particularly dismal example, see Larry Hurtado's blog post entitled "Ancient 'Gnostics': Intellectuals? Not Really!" at https://larryhurtado.wordpress.com/2014/02/22/ancient-gnostics-intellectuals-not-really/.

SECTION ONE

Religion as a Category of Study

The three chapters in this section each explore the salience and applicability of the concept of "religion" to ancient data. Chapter 2 focuses on political factors in the construction of a Judean form of religion in Achaemenid Egypt. Chapter 3 explores the shift in Christian self-designations, from more scholastic terminology in the first century to more cultic language in the second, documenting how Christianity came to describe itself in religious terms. Chapter 4 argues for a robust, but complex, model for understanding religion as a "social kind" and shows how this category illuminates – and is illuminated by – the letters of Paul. A response to these contributions (chapter 5) concludes the section.

2

Inventing Religion in Elephantine: Judaeans and Egyptians under Persian Hegemony

Christine Mitchell

Around the year 475 BCE, an anonymous author wrote to a family member named Hoshaiah in Yeb, known to us now as Elephantine. Elephantine was a Judaean garrison of the Achaemenid Persian Empire in Upper Egypt, located at modern-day Aswan.[1] It was a quick note, written in Aramaic on a potsherd and probably transported from the town of Syene, on the Nile's bank, to Yeb, a town on an island in the Nile River immediately opposite Syene. In this note, our unknown correspondent asks after a number of family concerns, sends some instructions, and concludes with, "Send word to me when you are doing Pesach [אמת תעבד{ו}ן פסחא]. Do send word of the baby's welfare."[2] The note suggests that the author knew roughly when Pesach (Passover) would occur, but that the day or time of day was not known. From the note, we may conclude that if there was a calendrical day named Pesach at Yeb, there was a certain flexibility about when the ritual was carried out, at least in the family context.

A couple of generations later, in 419 BCE, a certain Hananiah wrote to his "brother Yedaniah and his colleagues" of the Judaean garrison at Yeb.[3] In this carefully composed formal letter, written according to standard Achaemenid imperial scribal conventions, Hananiah reports the measures commanded by the satrap Arshama and the king Darius II regarding the Festival of Unleavened Bread. While the name of the festival is not preserved in the fragmentary text, the letter is concerned with a time when leaven (חמיר) should not be eaten. This letter is usually called the "Passover Letter" in publication, even though the word *pesach* does not occur in the preserved text. This designation is due to the striking similarities of the letter to, although not exact correspondence with, the Pesach legislation in Exodus, Leviticus, and Deuteronomy. In the text from 475 BCE, we have a family-oriented observance of flexible date or time; in the text from 419 BCE, a publicly decreed observance of fixed date and time.

What might have led to this shift in observance? It might be due to the differing genres or contexts of the texts: a family note versus an imperial proclamation. In that case, we would not be able to state that there was a development through time but simply differing contextual manifestations of the same festival. The two kinds of observance might have been held concurrently. Nevertheless, the very specific decrees of the imperial proclamation suggest an attempt to override any other traditions or regulations of the Festival of Unleavened Bread.

It is also possible that the two festivals were not conflated at Yeb and that the two texts each refer to a different festival. Conflation of Pesach and Unleavened Bread is not a foregone conclusion, particularly because there is no mention, or space in these writings to mention, anything about a lamb sacrifice. If we have two different festivals here, Unleavened Bread was being regulated but Pesach may have still been a more flexibly observed festival. The biblical conflation of the two festivals is what became known as "Passover." This biblical conflation has been the lens through which, until very recently, almost all of the scholarship has read the text from 419 BCE, right down to its common designation as the "Passover Letter."

There has been some considerable amount of scholarship on the "Passover Letter," beginning with William R. Arnold; the most influential being that of Bezalel Porten, whose interpretations inform what follows here.[4] Most of this scholarship considers how the many lacunae in this fragmentary document might be filled, especially in comparison with the aforementioned biblical texts. There are also considerations of a peculiar stipulation or two; it is important to note, though, that the peculiarity exists only in comparison with the biblical texts, as if the biblical texts represent the norms from which all other stipulations deviate. One such stipulation is clear despite the lacunae: the letter forbids the drinking of beer during the festival, although there is no such proscription in the biblical texts.[5]

Another topic of scholarly discussion is the (so-called) problem of why the focus is on Unleavened Bread rather than Pesach. Some authors have discussed the possible background to the letter in this context. Since the Yaho-worshipping community at Yeb seems to have had some practices not attested in biblical texts (such as veneration of the deities Anat-Yaho and Eshem-Bethel), the usual conclusion is that Hananiah was relaying an order for the community to become more orthodox and orthoprax. Although not stated in any way in the letter, it is often assumed that Hananiah's instructions came in some way from the Jerusalem temple of YHWH, and the letter is taken as evidence for Jerusalem's increasing control over the worship of YHWH among Judaeans, no matter their location or whether they named their deity Yahweh, Yaho, Yahu, or Yah. The other, later, letters in the archive – especially those written to describe the destruction of the Yaho temple in 410 BCE, which are addressed in part to Jerusalem – are lurking behind this reading of Hananiah's letter. The clear discussion in Gard Granerød's *Dimensions of Yahwism in the Persian Period* (2016) spells out these assumptions in greater detail.[6]

All of the above discussion would be appropriate scholarly hypothesizing and reconstruction, except that Hananiah's letter quite explicitly names the basis for his instructions: the Achaemenid Persian king Darius and his satrap Arshama. The Yaho temple's priests appealed some years later, in 407 BCE, to Achaemenid governors for support of their quest to rebuild their destroyed temple, and the authorization for the rebuilding ultimately came from the Persian satrap Arshama.[7] These appeals to authority by the Judaeans are appeals to governmental authority, not to religious authority. They are not appealing to the priests in Jerusalem. The letter that suggests that appeals were made first to the priests in Jerusalem also notes that those priests did not answer; hence the appeal to governmental rather than to temple authorities.[8]

The veneration of Yaho at Yeb (Elephantine) provides one of two examples of the construction of religion in the Achaemenid Empire that I discuss in this chapter. The other is the veneration of the Egyptian ram-god Khnum, also at Elephantine. Taking my lead from David Chidester's recent work on imperialism and religion,[9] and Bruce Lincoln's careful attention to religious discourses,[10] I argue that what we have in the so-called "Passover Letter" of Hananiah is a pursuit of a definition of Judean religion through an imperial discourse. Since the Persians are widely viewed as having been tolerant of the religious practices of their subjects and as having been laissez-faire in their government, my argument runs counter to much established biblical scholarship. The evidence of Achaemenid bureaucracy that we have does not support this scholarly rhetoric, which is based largely on the biblical texts of Isaiah and Ezra Nehemiah. In fact, as Christopher Tuplin notes, the evidence from Egypt, Persepolis, and Bactria shows the tendency of Persian administrators to obsessively micro manage the affairs under their charge.[11] Even given our meagre evidence – a few texts, most fragmentary, and some archaeological evidence of the floor-plan of the Yaho temple[12] – it is startling how much the Achaemenid administration was involved in the definition of Yaho-veneration at Yeb.

Turning to the Khnum temple and its community at Elephantine, our evidence for the Achaemenid Persian period temple is even spottier than is that for the Yaho temple. The Hellenistic-era temple complex expansions have obscured our reconstruction of the Persian-period temple. The

26th Dynasty (Saite, pre-Persian) temple seems to have been in use until massive alterations began under Nectanebo II (mid-fourth-century BCE). This Saite-Persian temple complex included a new enclosure wall that abutted the main access street of the town, a chapel built by the Saite king Psamtik II, and a separate building to the south, whose function is unknown (Seidlmeier et al. 2015; 2016).[13] However, even before the fourth-century expansion, the Khnum complex was significantly larger than the Yaho complex that was immediately next to it, and they were separated only by the main access street, known from the papyri as the "Street of the King" (figure 2.1).

Recent analysis of the archaeology of Egypt has shown that while Darius I (522–486 BCE) sponsored significant construction and refurbishing projects, his successors did not. Temple building was an important part of the Egyptian ideology of kingship.[14] Similarly, in Babylon under Achaemenid rule, the king did not participate in the New Year's Festival at the Esagila temple.[15] On the other hand, the evidence from the Persepolis administrative texts (admittedly largely from the reign of Darius I) indicates that contributions were made to a number of mostly Iranian deities. However, Ahuramazda, the deity central to Achaemenid royal ideology, did not even receive the greatest number of contributions.[16] The implications of the Persepolis evidence have not been fully explored, but when added to the other evidence it seems likely that the Achaemenids were committed only to participation in Persian religious rituals and expectations. Based on the evidence from outside Persia, the Persians' famous toleration looks more like neglect. Was this neglect of Babylonian and Egyptian traditions associated with kingship accidental or intentional? That is, were the Achaemenid kings simply not interested in those traditions (because the size of their empire precluded participation in every region's traditions), or were they actively not participating as part of a broader strategy of discourse about kingship? We may never know, as our evidence for any Achaemenid's thought processes is non-existent. But while the Achaemenid kings did not participate, their administration's actions had in some cases, as an end result, the reconfiguration of a group's religion while under imperial control.

Bruce Lincoln's definition of religion is a helpful index to show how the Achaemenids configured religion at Yeb. Lincoln's definition of religion encompasses four "domains": discourse, practice, community, and institution. Discourse pertains to concerns that "transcend the human, temporal, and contingent" and "claims for itself a similarly transcendent status."[17] Practices are connected to discourses, seeking to shape human and other-than-human subjects in ways consistent with the discourse. Community is made up of individuals who construct themselves and their relationships with others

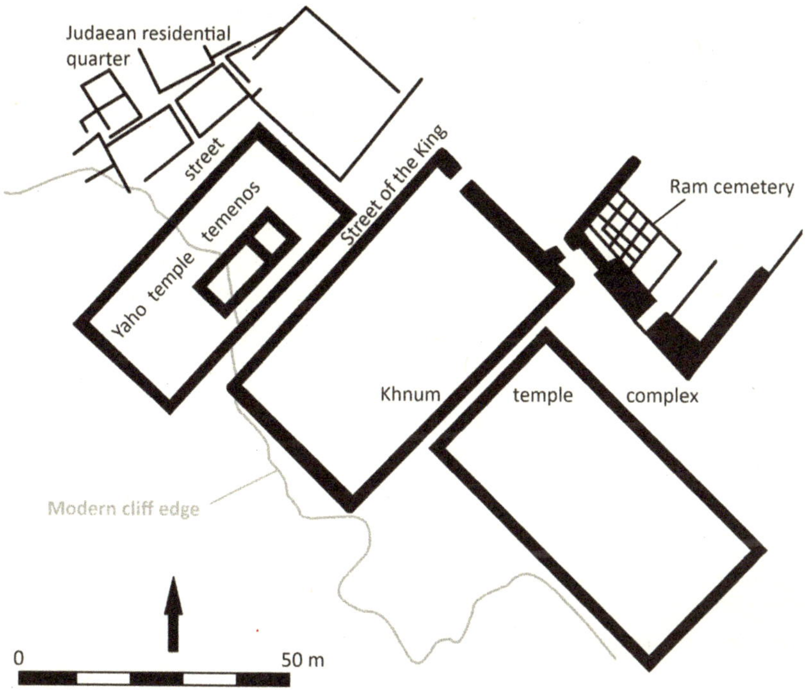

2.1 Persian-period Yaho and Khnum temple complexes at Elephantine

through common discourses and practices.[18] Finally, and very importantly for my argument, a religion involves "an institution that regulates religious discourse, practices, and community, reproducing them over time and modifying them as necessary, while asserting their eternal validity and transcendent value."[19] These are overlapping domains: for example, discourse is lived out in practices, while institutions require a community (or communities). Religion requires all these domains (at a minimum, Lincoln says), thus ensuring that personal preferences or individual practices do not meet the threshold.[20] I would argue, however, that particular religions might emphasize one or more of these domains over another (discourse for modern Protestant Christians, for example). For ancient religions, our evidence for the various domains may be skewed through the accidents of preservation, and we should not conclude that what is preserved (largely discourse) is what was most important to the ancient religious individuals and groups.

What distinguishes these domains as pertaining to religion, as opposed to some other lifeway or ideological interest, is the focus on the transcendent. While Lincoln's definition is meant to be inclusive of religion that is not specifically focused on a deity or deities, in the context of the Persian-period eastern Mediterranean, the transcendent bears the name of one or more deities, more often than not tied to a particular geographic location and its associated ethnos. There is some evidence that groups saw the deities of other groups as functionally similar to their own.[21] Intriguingly, the correspondence of the Judaean community at Elephantine may suggest a certain transcendence of the transcendent, at least in nomenclature: in their letter to the Persian governor of Judaea,[22] they refer to the "God of Heaven" (אלה שמיא), whose blessings they invoke for the governor.[23] With respect to Lincoln's definition, then, I define the transcendent as being a deity, deities, or divine epithet.

DISCOURSE

In the case of the Judaean community at Yeb, we have no datable records pertaining to the Yaho temple or any religious apparatus of the community prior to Hananiah's letter of 419 BCE. There is no evidence for any texts resembling the texts of the Jerusalem corpus (i.e., the texts that later became "the Bible"), but there were at least two substantial Aramaic texts in the community's archive: the Tale and Sayings of Ahiqar[24] and Darius's Bisitun proclamation translated into Aramaic,[25] both of which likely date as copies from well before 419 BCE, based on the physical evidence of the scrolls and the dates of the other documents found on them. I have recently argued that both copies date from about 450 BCE and that they served as part of the curriculum for an Aramaic-language scribal school located in the Yaho temple.[26] The cluster of datable texts in the archive from after 419 BCE is largely centred on the period 410–399 BCE, the time of the temple's destruction and the efforts to rebuild it. Those texts include Achaemenid officials in prominent roles, both as agents of destruction and as granters of rebuilding.

Unlike the Yaho priesthood, the Khnum priesthood wrote in Demotic, not in Aramaic, even when corresponding with Persian officials for whom Aramaic was the language of administration. Compared with the reasonably extensive preserved archive of the Yaho temple, there are few published documents from the Khnum temple. In the years 493–492 BCE, two letters were exchanged between a group of *wab*-priests[27] and the Achaemenid satrap Pherendates (Old Persian: Farnadata?) about the appointment of the administrative priest whom the *wab*-priests had selected.[28] This position, while senior, was not the chief priest of the temple; the *wab*-priests' letter suggests that they had selected the priest from among themselves. The satrap's response is noteworthy for several features:

1 He alludes to the characteristics and past behaviour of two *wab*-priests.
2 He describes the characteristics and behaviour of individuals suitable to be selected as the administrative priest: "a great man … there being nothing he has let fail," suggesting that competence as well as status was relevant to him.
3 He states that the selection of the priest will be "in accordance with that which Pharaoh Darius has ordered," which might refer to general instructions (such as those found at the end of the Aramaic version of the Bisitun inscription),[29] or to specific instructions about this priesthood; either way, it is the authority of Darius that is invoked.
4 He indicates that he, the satrap, will make the appointment. Like his later counterpart Arshama, Pherendates shows a tendency to micro-manage and invokes Persian royal authority.

Because of a later letter,[30] we know that the *wab*-priests' selection ultimately became the administrative priest. A document from 487 BCE shows that payment for appointment even as a regular *wab*-priest was routine, and in that year the payment was made to an office controlled by an official with a Persian name (Farnava).[31] A set of documents from 460 BCE shows that the priests could make agreements among themselves without satrapal approval, or at least such satrapal approval has not been preserved.[32] It was the appointment of priests, both major and minor appointments, that was the satrap's concern, and such appointment required payment to the Persian-controlled treasury.

While the Khnum priests called Khnum "the Great God," Pherendates called him "the Lord of Elephantine." For a Persian, only the Persian god Ahuramazda was the "Great God." By responding in this way, the Persian satrap Pherendates disciplined the Khnum priests, even if they did not realize they were being disciplined. In this case we can see that the Judaean community had adapted better to the Achaemenid conventions by referring to their god Yaho simply as "the god in heaven" (above) or even as "the god who is in Elephantine."[33]

The other documents that are pertinent to the discourses of the Khnum temple community are the ones that come from the Yaho temple archives. While they do not preserve the discourse of the Khnum temple adherents themselves, with some caution we can suggest what the discourse could have been. The documents demonstrate a long-running animosity between the priests of Yaho and the priests of Khnum (from 419 BCE to 410 BCE, and perhaps later). This animosity culminated in the destruction of the Yaho temple by the Achaemenid Persian authority, ostensibly at the instigation of the Khnum priests. The excavator of the Yaho temple has suggested that the cause was the Yaho temple's infringement on the main access road into the town as the second stage of the Yaho temple was built with the enclosure wall moved inward. The motivation for the Persian commander Vidranga to destroy the Yaho temple complex could simply have been to widen the access road, although the destruction of the cella and the looting of the complex seems a bit excessive for such a purpose.

But what could have been the Khnum-priests' motivation? One of the Yaho temple letters mentions that "Khnum has been against us from the time of Hananiah,"[34] indicating a fairly recent onset of hostilities, perhaps related to some building activities that blocked the road. The correspondence unwittingly suggests that the Khnum priests had taken the lessons of Darius as expressed in DB Aram to heart: they were reporting the errors of others to the appropriate authorities.[35] The Khnum priests, having seen the error(s) of the Yaho community, reported this error to Vidranga, who took appropriate disciplinary action.[36]

Hananiah, presumably a priest as he called the other priests his "brothers," provided instruction on the Festival of Unleavened Bread to the Judaean Yaho-worshippers. However, Hananiah claimed as his authority not the deity or a more senior priest but, rather, the king and the satrap. We may compare biblical texts, especially Deuteronomy, shown as divinely warranted. In fact, at Yeb the deity never came into the question. The discourses of Hananiah "transcend[ed] the human, temporal, and contingent" to return to Lincoln's model: although the commands may have been rooted in pragmatic concerns as discussed above, these commands were expressed as an eternal truth, "claim[ing] for itself a similarly transcendent status."[37] The two extended narrative texts of the Yaho temple archive claimed similarly transcendent status: the Tale and Sayings of Ahiqar, situated in a time and place long gone, proclaimed universal truths in its instruction; the Darius proclamation at Bisitun, while situated in a very specific time and place, included a portion of text not found in the inscription at the site of Bisitun, a text that oriented the proclamation to a much broader audience. The copy of Ahiqar was a palimpsest: the first text on the scroll was likely erased before 450 BCE for the scroll's reuse. That original text was a governmental shipping record for 475 BCE, which may suggest a governmental site for the scroll's reuse. It has been proposed that the copy of Darius's proclamation at Yeb was prepared for the centenary of the proclamation – that is, for 421 BCE – but given the dates on the verso of the scroll, it seems probable that the copy had been prepared considerably earlier than that, and thus it is more likely that the text had been at Yeb for some time.[38]

All four texts (Hananiah's instructions, Ahiqar, Darius's proclamation, Pherendates's instructions) assert royal authority – not divine authority – and insert Achaemenid interests into the religious discourse. In his letter to the Judaean governor Bagavahya, Yedaniah tried to accuse Vidranga and the priest of Khnum of fostering lies and disorder, which suggests an internalization of Achaemenid imperial ideology. Perhaps he was also accusing Vidranga of not listening to both sides in accordance with DB Aram.

PRACTICES

There are legitimate military and administrative reasons for Darius and Arshama to have been interested in the regulation of the Judaean Yaho Festival of Unleavened Bread. The Judaean community at Yeb was made up of a troop of mercenary soldiers and their families, and, as the staff of the garrison, they held an important position in border control and internal security.[39] It would thus be critical for the government of the satrapy and the Empire that their festival and temple-observance days be set well in advance so that alternative arrangements could be made for staffing the garrison and its functions. The Judaean community's cultic practices had a direct impact on the regulation of the satrapy and on the Empire as a whole. We know something of the satrap Arshama's obsession with micro-management in the corpus of texts that preserves some of his orders about the management of his estates.[40] So if Hananiah claimed that Arshama and Darius commanded what he was conveying, we can assume that they did indeed command it.

The enigmatic bribery letter in which prominent Judaeans promised a significant contribution to the satrapal treasury (one month's worth of grain) in exchange for permission to sacrifice at their Yaho temple includes the promise to only sacrifice grain and incense; that is, to not sacrifice animals.[41] While again this is usually read by modern scholars as a step towards recognizing the centrality of the YHWH temple in Jerusalem, it is much more likely to have been a concession to the temple next door, the temple of the ram-headed god Khnum.[42] Regardless of the reason for the end of animal sacrifices at the Yaho temple at Yeb, ultimately it was the Achaemenid authorities who determined what the appropriate sacrifices to Yaho at Yeb would be.

Hananiah's instructions were about nothing but practices, as were the temple reconstruction texts, with their focus on sacrifice, and the ultimate concession to forego animal sacrifice. These practices did not necessarily benefit the Judaean community or enhance the community's relationship with the deity Yaho, especially the elimination of animal sacrifice. Rather, these practices were about "producing proper human subjects" of Persian imperialism.[43] From this perspective, the much lamented delay in the rebuilding of the Yeb temple of Yaho, whose destruction had been undertaken by a junior Achaemenid official, was an effective disciplinary practice, forcing the community to submit to imperial authority over the community's worship practices. The priest Yedaniah's claim that the satrap Arshama knew nothing about the actions of his underling Vidranga cannot stand uncontested, given Arshama's propensity for micro-management discussed above. Thus Yedaniah's strategy of blaming Vidranga alone and accusing him of having been suborned by the priests of Khnum was a tactical error: it would have been better to have admitted guilt immediately and submitted to discipline, and might have resulted in a faster rebuilding of the temple. The time for listening to both sides (as Darius enjoined in several texts, including DB Aram) was past, probably three years past. Yedaniah's recounting of the practices of lament undertaken by the community did not include an admission of guilt; we might compare the penitential psalms that were being composed in Judah at this time and that did include a confession of sin. The Khnum priests' ability to convince Vidranga (if he indeed needed convincing) shows that they had already accepted imperial authority over the community's practices, as shown in their acceptance of imperial authority over priestly appointments. We should also recall that we do not know if or how the Khnum priests were disciplined for being part of the conflict with the Yaho priesthood; they very well may have been.

COMMUNITY

The clearest evidence for the construction of a community of Yaho-venerators is in the so-called Collection List.[44] This is a roll call of the community of Yaho. Collin Cornell argues persuasively that this list, in which dozens of named individuals are recorded as having donated two shekels of silver, records the silver being collected to replace the cult statues in the Yaho-sanctuary.[45] Approximately 40 percent of the names whose gender can be determined (by the use of "son of/daughter of" in the patronymic) were women. As such, we can be assured that the list reflects a wide cross-section of the community, and the temple community was open to both men and women.

We do not know what texts or precepts this community adhered to in any detail, but they practised both Pesach and Unleavened Bread, Sabbath observance, and swearing oaths by Yaho. They engaged in a sacrificial cult in a purpose-built temple. Despite all of this, it is important to remember that the community was most strongly and commonly identified by its status as garrison (חיל) and and its individuals as members of a century (מאה) or troop (דגל) of that garrison. The community had an imperial rather than an ethnic or religious basis. The fragmentary evidence from the Khnum temple does not allow us to reconstruct that community even in a limited way.

INSTITUTION

Finally, we come to Lincoln's idea of institution in the context of religion: religion includes "an institution that regulates religious discourse, practices, and community, producing them over time and modifying them as necessary, while asserting their eternal validity and transcendent value."[46] "Institution" in this context was not the Yaho temple or its priesthood but the Achaemenid administration. Even the Collection List, which superficially was a roll call of supporters of the temple, was a product of the imperial administration: it was necessary to collect the "donations" because the community itself presumably had to pay for rebuilding and refurnishing its temple even though the temple had been destroyed by the Achaemenid administration. In sum, the imperial construction of Judaean religion at Yeb was pervasive and all-encompassing. The Achaemenids constructed the Judaean religion in such a way that it served imperial interests over Judaean interests.

CONCLUSIONS

While on one level the Achaemenids were not involved with local religions, especially as local royal ideology pertained, on another level they were intimately involved with local religions. The cases of the Judaean Yaho and Egyptian Khnum communities suggest that there was a strategy involved and that the Achaemenids were actively defining religion in order to fulfill the purposes of imperialism. Much as the nineteenth-century project of comparative religions was both a product of and contribution to European imperialism, the Achaemenid project of religious regulation was a product of imperialism and contributed to Achaemenid imperial rule.

This brings us, in the end, to those Achaemenid imperial interests. In the imperial rhetoric and iconography as expressed in the Persian heartland, the earth-empire was composed of a couple of dozen lands-peoples, all coming together in peace to bring their tribute to the Great King. All of their diversity was a sign of the goodness of creation in its original harmony of design. Disorder, on the other hand, was a sign of the Lie and the rupture of that primordial order. The Empire was a place of order and law. Whoever was at fault, the Judaeans or the priests of Khnum, in Achaemenid eyes their conflict was a manifestation of the Lie and a rupture of Order. They had to be disciplined; their diversity of religions brought back into peace. The Achaemenids after Darius I may not have "neglected" their religious obligations (as seen by, for example, the priests of Babylon), they were honouring the diversity of discourses, practices, communities, and institutions as long as there was Order. They therefore constructed "religion" not in a way that involved them in its day-to-day or year-to-year practice but in a way that placed all discourse, practices, and community in subjection to the institution of imperialism.

NOTES

1 The designation of the community at Elephantine is a fraught topic in scholarship. The community members designate themselves as "Yehudi" or occasionally as "Aramaean." Using the designation "Jew" has led to consideration of the community only in terms of its conformity to "orthodox" Judaism of the Persian period as described in biblical texts (especially Ezra-Nehemiah, and particularly with respect to Torah-conformity). However, using the designation "Judaean" has the potential of isolating this community from other groups who used the same ethnos-designation. Because I am considering the community in its Persian-period Egyptian context and alongside Egyptian Khnum-worshippers, I settle on "Judaean"; thus, Judaean Yaho-worshippers. For a thorough discussion, although with the opposite conclusion, see Karel van der Toorn, *Becoming Diaspora Jews: Behind the Story of Elephantine* (New Haven: Yale University Press, 2019), x–xi. I have also found Adele Reinhartz's work helpful in thinking through these issues, although I am translating *yehudi* and not *ioudaios*. See Adele Reinhartz, "The Vanishing Jews of Antiquity," *Marginalia Review* (24 June 2014), https://themarginaliareview.com/vanishing-jews-antiquity-adele-reinhartz/.

2 Bezalel Porten and Ada Yardeni, *Textbook of Aramaic Documents from Ancient Egypt*, 4 vols (Jerusalem/Winona Lake, IN: Hebrew University/Eisenbrauns, 1986–99), D7.6. I follow their dating for the ostracon. Porten and Yardeni's *Textbook* is conventionally abbreviated as *TAD*, and this chapter follows this standard abbreviation. See also Gard Granerød, *Dimensions of Yahwism in the Persian Period: Studies in the Religion and Society of the Judaean Community at Elephantine*, BZAW 488 (Berlin: De Gruyter, 2016), 112, for the emendation from 2 fem. pl. to 2 masc. pl. form on the assumption of scribal error – the addressee is a man. Yet perhaps the fem. pl. form is correct, and it was addressed to the women of the household. Names were not always limited in use to one gender. Translations from Aramaic my own.

3 *TAD* A4.1.

4 William R. Arnold, "The Passover Papyrus from Elephantine," *Journal of Biblical Literature* 31 (1912): 1–33; Bezalel Porten, *Archives from Elephantine: The Life of an Ancient Jewish Military Colony* (Berkeley: University of California Press, 1968), 128–33.

5 Porten, *Archives from Elephantine*, 33, notes that the much later Mishnah does forbid the consumption of beer during Passover. The key, in both the case of Elephantine and the case of the Mishnah, is that beer is fermented and "rises" the same way leaven raises bread.

6 Granerød, *Dimensions*, 165–82.

7 The memorandum preserved in TAD A4.9 and the petition in TAD A4.10 do not specifically name Arshama as the authority figure. However, since the memorandum suggests the argument was being made before Arshama, the logical conclusion is that he was the official who made the authorization. See Granerød, *Dimensions*, 220–3, and James D. Moore, "Who Gave You a Decree? Anonymity as a Narrative Technique in Ezra 5:3, 9 in Light of Persian-Period Decrees and Administrative Sources," *Journal of Biblical Literature* 140 (2021): 69–89, specifically 83–6, for discussions of these documents. I am persuaded that, contrary to the older arguments, the memorandum in TAD A4.9 is not an authorization by the Jerusalem and Samaria governors but simply a recommendation on their parts to the appropriate authority in Egypt.

8 TAD A4.7/4.8.

9 David Chidester, *Empire of Religion: Imperialism and Comparative Religion* (Chicago: University of Chicago Press, 2014).

10 Bruce Lincoln, *Theorizing Myth: Narrative, Ideology, and Scholarship* (Chicago: University of Chicago Press, 1999); Lincoln, *Holy Terrors: Thinking about Religion after September 11* (Chicago: University of Chicago Press, 2003); Lincoln, *Discourse and the Construction of Society: Comparative Studies of Myth, Ritual, and Classification*, 2nd ed. (Oxford: Oxford University Press, 2014).

11 Christopher J. Tuplin, "The Fall and Rise of the Elephantine Temple," in *Aršāma and His World*, vol. 3, *Aršāma's World*, ed. Christopher J. Tuplin and John Ma (Oxford: Oxford University Press, 2020), 350.

12 Stephen G. Rosenberg, "The Jewish Temple at Elephantine," *Near Eastern Archaeology* 67 (2004): 4–13.

13 Stephan Johannes Seidlmeier et al., "Report on the Excavations at Elephantine by the German Archaeological Institute and the Swiss Institute from Autumn 2014 to Spring 2015" (Deutsches Archäologisches Institut, 2015), www.dainst.org; Stephan Johannes Seidlmeier et al., "Report on the Excavations at Elephantine by the German Archaeological Institute and the Swiss Institute from Autumn 2015 to Summer 2016" (Deutsches Archäologisches Institut, 2016), www.dainst.org.

14 Damien Agut-Labordère and Gilles Gorre, "De l'autonomie à l'intégration. Les temples égyptiens face à la couronne des Saïtes aux Ptolémées," *Topoi* 19, no. 1 (2014): 28–31.

15 Caroline Waerzeggers, "Babylonian Kingship in the Persian Period: Performance and Reception," in *Exile and Return: The Babylonian Context*, ed. Jonathan Stökl and Caroline Waerzeggers (Berlin: De Gruyter, 2015), 197–9; Amélie Kuhrt, "Babylonia from Cyrus to Xerxes," in *The Cambridge Ancient History*, vol. 4, *Persia, Greece and the Western Mediterranean, c. 525 to 479 BC*, ed. John Boardman, N.G.L. Hammond, D.M. Lewis, and M. Ostwalt, 2nd ed. (Cambridge: Cambridge University Press, 1988), 112–38.

16 Wouter F.M. Henkelman, "The Heartland Pantheon," in *A Companion to the Achaemenid Persian Empire*, vol. 2, ed. Bruno Jacobs and Robert Rollinger (Hoboken, NJ: Wiley Blackwell, 2021), 1221–42.

17 Lincoln, *Holy Terrors*, 5.

18 Ibid., 6–7.

19 Ibid., 7.

20 This proviso is more important for dealing with modern phenomena such as individual spirituality or "spiritual but not religious."

21 Mark S. Smith, *God in Translation: Deities in Cross-Cultural Discourse in the Biblical World* (Grand Rapids, MI: Eerdmans, 2010).

22 *TAD* A4.7/4.8.

23 Gard Granerød, "YHW the God of Heaven: An Interpretatio Persica et Aegyptiaca of YHW in Elephantine," *Journal for the Study of Judaism* 52 (2020): 1–26.

24 *TAD* C1.1.

25 Ibid., C2.1.

26 Christine Mitchell, "Berlin Papyrus P. 13447 and the Library of the Yehudite Colony at Elephantine," *Journal of Near Eastern Studies* 76 (2017): 139–47.

27 *Wab*-priests were responsible for bringing offerings in both Egyptian temple and mortuary contexts. Members of this low-level priesthood did not have access to the innermost areas of temples but carried out other ritually important actions. See Emily Teeter, *Religion and Ritual in Ancient Egypt* (Cambridge: Cambridge University Press, 2011), 20–1.

28 Bezalel Porten, *The Elephantine Papyri in English: Three Millennia of Cross-Cultural Continuity and Change*, 2nd rev. ed. (Atlanta: SBL Press, 2011), C1–2.

29 Abbreviated as DB Aram; here col. xi, ll. 64-73: "[Thus says Darius the king: Whoever yo]u are O King who will be after me, do not be a friend to a man who lies, or to [lawbreakers]. Guard yourself from great lies. [A servant] who lies, [do not support him]. [Very much] make known how you act and of what sort your behaviour is. [Let not that be good before you which one] may say [in] your [ea]r. Hear what one may say openly. [Moreover, let not that be good before you which a nobleman may d]o; observe also that which a poor man may do. For yourself too [... nor in] your wellbeing be insecure ... [... Tell the truth] to [the people. Do not conceal] it. [If] you do not conceal (it), Ahuramazda will b[less you and your descendants will be] numerous and your days will be longlasting. But if you do conceal (it), Ahuramazda will c[urse you and you will have no descendants]." Trans. from Mitchell, "Berlin Papyrus," 142. See also *TAD* C2.1.

30 Porten, *Elephantine Papyri*, C3.

31 Ibid., C35.

32 Ibid., C29.

33 *TAD* A4.7/A4.8. Porten and Yardeni read the repeated phrase אגורא זי יהו אלהא זי ביב in this letter as "the temple of Yaho the god which is in Elephantine," thereby emphasizing the temple-building, but it could as easily be read as "the temple of Yaho the god who is in Elephantine," thereby emphasizing the deity. The reference in one of the deeds of sale to יהו אלהא שכן יב "Yaho the god who dwells in Elephantine" (*TAD* B3.12) suggests that the reading of "god who is" is preferable. That is, the god was present in his dwelling-place in Elephantine.

34 *TAD* A.3.

35 Cf. note 27, above.

36 Some of the texts suggest long-running conflict that involved the earlier discipline of Yaho adherents, to which they did not submit. For example, one letter tells of members of the community who had been imprisoned as a result of some kind of protest action (*TAD* A4.4).

37 Lincoln, *Holy Terrors*, 5.

38 Mitchell, "Berlin Papyrus."

39 I am grateful to Jason Silverman for pointing this out to me.

40 *TAD* A6.1-16. See also Christopher J. Tuplin, "Aršāma: Prince and Satrap," in *Aršāma and His World*, vol. 3, *Aršāma's World*, ed. Christopher J Tuplin and John Ma (Oxford: Oxford University Press, 2020), 3–72.

41 *TAD* A4.10.

42 Cf. Granerød, *Dimensions*, 140–7.

43 Cf. Lincoln's definition of religious practice: the goal of practice "is to produce a proper world and/or proper human subjects, as defined by a religious discourse to which these practices are connected." See Lincoln, *Holy Terrors*, 6.

44 *TAD* C3.15.

45 Collin Cornell, "Cult Statuary in the Judean Temple at Yeb," *Journal for the Study of Judaism* 47 (2016): 1–19.

46 Lincoln, *Holy Terrors*, 7.

3

Second-Century Constructions of Christianity

John S. Kloppenborg

In a provocative 2006 essay, Edwin Judge asked, "was Christianity a religion?"[1] His point was that when one sets the documentary records of Christianity in the first century beside what is known of the ancient cults of Jupiter, Athena, Isis, Sarapis, and Mithras, Christianity did not look much like a "religion." It is of course well known that the term "religion" is itself problematic when it is used to refer to a complex of beliefs, creeds, rituals, and ethical stances oriented to the cult of a deity or deities and as conceptually distinct from such aspects of culture as politics, economics, or aesthetics. Understood in this way it is not an ancient term but probably an invention of the sixteenth century.[2] *Religio* and *religiosi* in antiquity referred, respectively, to rituals and to scrupulous persons. The opposite of *religio* was not secularism but *superstitio*, the excessive or immoderate performance of a rite.[3] In the plural *religiones* meant "rituals" and not, as it has come to mean, the array of constellations of beliefs, creeds, ritual practices, and ethical postures that we now call "world religions." The latter notion was likely the result of the colonial encounter of Europeans with non-Western cultures, when colonizers found it useful to categorize the people they encountered by synthetic constructions of "religion" analogous to the European construction. Needless to say, these other "religions" were inevitably judged to be inferior to Christianity.

The colonial construction of "religion" had a distorting effect on the understanding of the practices of the colonized. It privileged the doctrinal and confessional contents of colonial pieties and often ignored the importance of rituals. This segregated the resulting synthetic constructions from other realms of local cultures, so that one could speak of Hinduism or Buddhism as though they were conceptually distinct from South and East Asian domestic practices, politics, commerce, and art. Multiple divergent local expressions were synthesized into grand unities, called "-isms." Edwin Judge puts the point thus:[4] "Having formulated the concept [of religion], British and other enterprise [sic] exported it to India first, where the unsuspecting sages were just as surprised to learn that they enjoyed a religion called Hinduism as the 'Hellenists' under Julian in the fourth century had been to find themselves put into a quasi-ecclesiastical straitjacket."[5] Judge's point also implies that the export of post-Enlightenment constructions of "religion" onto antiquity would have had the same distorting effect that the export of Protestant understandings of "religion" had on the pious practices of India, Burma, and other colonial regions. The idea of "early Christian religion" is not only retrojection of the *taxon* of "religion" onto antiquity but it also had another role: to create fictive continuities between then and now, where it has played a critical role in the wars of religion, encouraging one to assess the truth and validity of more contemporary expressions of Christianity against a hypothetical construction of *Urchristentum*.

Judge's point is more pungent still. "It is hard to see," Judge argues, "how anyone could seriously have related the phenomenon of Christianity to the practice of religion in its first-century sense."[6] To be sure, the early Christ movement had some of the features of cults, for example, an entrance ritual, a common meal, hymns and prayers addressed to the deity. Judge's point, however, has to do with how "Christianity" *looked* to others – in effect how the next door neighbours of Christ groups could have perceived them. It lacked the apparatus typically associated with the cults of other deities: statues, temples, altars, priesthoods, and bloody sacrifices. I add that it also lacked the vocabulary typical of cultic groups, notably θρησκεία, and εὐσέβεια, missing from the earliest texts of the Jesus movement, including Paul. As I note, these critical terms appear only in the second century.[7]

The second comment is by William E. Arnal in an essay on the "invention" of Christianity in the second century.[8] Arnal was concerned with the category "Christian origins" and how it has functioned to collect the "scattered, distinct, and theologically unrelated documents that happen to appear in the New Testament" into a single discursive unity, and then to posit a strong continuity between the first century and the second.[9] Against this, Arnal argues that the origins of Christianity are to be found not in the first century but in the second, with the collection of Paul's letters, the appending of the Pastorals, the composition of Luke-Acts – which combined an account of the life of Jesus with a life of Paul – and the reactions to Marcion's combination of the *euaggelion* with the *apostolikon*: "If ... what we really want to explain are the origins of Christianity, we should not do so by looking at the origins and concomitant mythmaking of the earlier New Testament writings, but by looking at how these writings came to be collected together, shaped, and claimed as formative and ancestral."[10]

Arnal's proposal, that "Christianity" began with the second century, inverts the long-standing notion of *Urchristentum*, a discursive construct that, as its name suggests, conveyed the notion of an original and authentic form of the Jesus movement that could be employed as the measure of all that came thereafter. Arnal writes, "The claim is not that a diverse first-century Jesus-movement came to be overshadowed by a coherent second-century Christianity. It is, rather, that a number of first-century documents came to be re-imagined, and conceived as ancestral, by a variety of different second-century (and later) efforts to establish a Christian conceptual identity. That process of identity formation, of course, never came to a conclusion or ceased to be contested. The process did not end in the second century; but, I am claiming, it did begin then."[11] The notion of *Urchristentum* has recently come under some criticism because it implies a discursive unity where none can be established, and because of the normative role that is has played in the past. Some have rejected the term in favour of *frühes Christentum*. Markus Öhler, for example, points out how odd it is to speak of *Urchristentum* when one would hardly speak of *Ur-Mithraismus* or *Ur-Judaismus*.[12] Schnelle rightly notes that *Urchristentum* falsely imputes a unity in theological views to the first century.[13] Even those who choose to retain the term have usually stripped it of its normative role.[14] Arnal's proposal goes further: the notion of an originary "Christianity" is not a first-century notion but a second-century construct.

FIRST-CENTURY TERMS OF IDENTITY

Judge is of course right that first-century forms of the Christ movement lacked temples, altars, and sacrifices and, indeed, much more. When we examine the literature of early Christ groups, what is striking is also the almost complete lack of terms typical of Greek and Roman cultic associations, at least in the first century.[15] Moreover, instead of adopting the identity terms that were broadly legible as cultic terms, Christ followers used a mixture of idiosyncratic terms as well as terms that were not obviously those of cultic associations,[16] such as those in the following list:

1 Adherents of the Jesus movement were routinely known as οἱ ἀδελφοί,[17] a term that continued to be used as an identity term well into the third century.[18]

The term ἀδελφοί was widely used as an identity term among Judaeans but mostly in contexts that were intended to be read by other Judaeans (e.g., 2 Macc 1:1) rather than as a term that non-Jews were expected to understand. It is true that "brothers" are found in a small number of occupational guilds,[19] and they are only slightly more common in a few cultic associations. The devotees of Jupiter Dolichenus were known as *fratres*,[20] and the devotees of Theos Hypsistos were known as ἀδελφοί or εἰσποιητοὶ ἀδελφοί (adoptive brothers, i.e., of the god).[21] Thus, the term ἀδελφοί was not completely illegible to others, even if it was not the most common of identity terms.

Not all cultic associations had special terms for their devotees.[22] But many did. And when they did, they used terms very different from those of Christ groups: θεραπευῦται, θιασῶται/θιασῖται, μύσται, συνθύται, συνκλίται, συνοδεῖται, *coliti,* or *cultores* or by a name derived from the god and ending in -ασταί or -ισταί (e.g., Διονυσιασταί, Ἀμφιεραϊσταί, etc.).

> 2 The nominalized participle οἱ πιστεύοντες or adjective οἱ πιστοί are also attested in the first century and serve as titles for Christ followers rather than simply as functional descriptions.[23]

In those cases, they should be rendered as "those-who-trust" or "those who are loyal" rather than as "the believers" since the latter immediately implies for modern readers that belief in propositions was at stake rather than the embrace of a relationship of loyalty or trust (with the deity).[24] The term οἱ πιστεύοντες is in fact rather idiosyncratic. While *fidelis* occurred in a titular sense in the naming of several legions (e.g., *VII Claudia Pia Fidelis*), οἱ πιστεύοντες (τῷ θεῷ) has no parallels as a self-designation in Graeco-Roman cultic groups.[25] Πιστεύω + τῷ θεῷ is frequently attested in Delphic manumission inscriptions (^{3} 100×) in the formula καθὼς ἐπίστευσε/-αν τῷ θεῷ τὰν ὠνάν, where the god in question is Apollo. But here πιστεύω means "to entrust [the sale to the god]," that is, that the god acts as a fictive guarantor of the manumission, which is represented as a sale.

Teresa Morgan ventures that it should not be surprising that Christ followers identified themselves in this way since various Judaean groups also adopted monikers that identified them as distinctive among Judaean: Pharisees ("the abstemious, pure"), Ζηλωταί, *Haverîm*, *Hakamîm*, etc.[26] Yet, the earliest occurrences of the term among Christ groups is in 1 Thessalonians (1:7; 2:10, 13), addressed to non-Jews, who can hardly have been expected to understand the special linguistic uses of sectarian groups in Palestine. Once πιστεύω entered use, however, it persisted in later Christian epigraphy as a term of identity.[27]

3 As is well known, Luke uses the idiosyncratic term ἡ ὁδός as a technical term for the Christ movement in Acts.

The term is unattested outside of Acts, and even within Acts it appears mainly in editorial sections. This raises the possibility that it is Luke's creation.[28] It is now common to suggest that the term might show the influence of the use of Isa 40:3 and הדרך at Qumran.[29] The trope of two roads was of course common in Greek moral education – the choice of Herakles and Cebes's Tablet, for example. There is no evidence, however, of philosophical groups using "the Road" as an identity term, and the term did not persist as an identity term after Luke.

4 Q, the synoptic gospels, John, the Gospel of Thomas, the Apocryphon of James, the Apocryphon of John, and other early documents use μαθηταί as a designation for Jesus's followers. Acts applies the same term to Christ followers in general and, importantly, uses the term absolutely ("the disciples"), as if it were a title.[30]

The choice of the term is noteworthy since, up to the second century CE, it overwhelmingly belonged not to the semantic field of the cultic associations but to those of philosophy, rhetoric, medicine, and apprenticeship, where it has to do with learning. The title is particularly salient for the Gospel of Thomas, whose framing indicates that it was oriented to the acquisition of knowledge.[31]

Devotees of a god were not usually known as μαθηταί.[32] Philo twice refers to θεοῦ μαθηταί; however, in neither instance does it have the sense of a devotee of the deity but, instead, of someone who is instructed in a skill or discipline by a teacher.[33] Dio Chrysostom uses the idea of "disciples of god" in the same way when he refers to good kings as τοῦ θεοῦ τούτου μαθητάς τε καὶ ζηλωτάς (1.38). Again, what is in view is not devotion to Zeus but learning and emulating his mode of governance. The same sense of "learners" is carried by the Hebrew term *talmidîm* (students), with which the μαθηταί of the Gospels are commonly connected.[34] The term implies that rabbinic circles are comparable to philosophical groups, oriented to the principal activity of acquiring knowledge associated with those groups.

5 Finally, the most common collective designation for Christ groups was not any of the commonly used collectives for cultic associations, such as θίασος, κλίνη, κοινόν, συναγωγή, συμβίωσις, συνέδριον, σύνοδος, *coetus,*

> *collegium, corpus, sodalitas,* or *sodalicium*. A few Christ groups used the term συναγωγή.[35] The majority of Christ groups used the rather unparalleled term ἐκκλησία.[36]

Richard Last makes the important observation that some collective terms already imply the nature of the collective. Ἔρανος and ἐρανισταί carry with them the implication that a group was a credit association. Such terms as θίασος, θεραπευται, θιασῶται/θιασῖται, μύσται, and *cultores* immediately imply a cultic orientation. Συνεργασία naturally suggests that the group in question was organized around an occupation, while πλατεῖα and γειτνίασις imply spatial aspects of associations that were organized at the level of the street or neighbourhood.[37]

Ἐκκλησία, by contrast, belongs most closely to the lexical register of a civic decision-making body.[38] Paul and later writer sometimes add a city ethnic, a toponym, or a regional ethnic.[39] It is, however, only the addition of a secondary element that made the cultic orientation clear: ἡ ἐκκλησία τοῦ θεοῦ τῇ οὔσῃ ἐν Κορίνθῳ (1 Cor 1:2) or ἡ ἐκκλησία τοῦ θεοῦ ἡ παροικοῦσα Ῥώμην (1 Clem. 1.1).

The variety of choices of first-century authors to characterize members of the Jesus movement as ἀδελφοί, οἱ πιστεύοντες, and as μαθηταί in place of the more obvious terms connected with cultic activities and the use of the underdetermined ἐκκλησία as the collective give some encouragement to Judge's view that few would have connected the Jesus movement with "the practice of religion in its first-century sense." The frequent characterization of Christ-followers as μαθηταί indeed might add some heft to Judge's view of early Christians as a scholastic community.[40]

Notwithstanding Judge's observations that the Christ movement lacked the obvious apparatus of cultic associations, it is of course true that cultic practices and vocabulary were not far from the imagination of Christ groups. Paul's letters are full of quasi-oracular disclosures; his understanding that the initiation ritual is a symbolic death is not entirely unlike the initiation ritual sketched in Apuleius's *Metamorphoses* (Book 11); and the language of mystery is present (1 Cor 2:7; 15:51; Rom 11:25). The meal ritual of Christ groups, like those of Sarapiastai, imagined the deity to be present as a host. Prayers and communal songs addressed to the deity were associated with the common meal.

Some Christ assemblies employed an array of cultic vocabulary in a metaphorical sense. Paul described his own devotion with the verb λατρεύω (Rom 1:9) and the Philippian gift as a θυσία, "sacrifice" (Phil 4:18); he encouraged the Roman Christ followers to consider themselves as offering a θυσία ζῶσα as suitable λατρεία (Rom 12:1). The author of Hebrews employs a rich vocabulary of altars, sacrifice, and priesthood throughout, and the author of the Apocalypse imagines actions taking place in a heavenly temple that have an effect on the earth. Christ groups of the first century, nevertheless, failed to adopt the most obvious semantic markers of cultic associations (or any of the other common associative groups in antiquity). Some of their identity terms were highly idiosyncratic – the Road, the "Trusters in God," "the Learners," and "the Assembly" – even if they shared fictive family language with a few other cultic associations.

It is fair to say that most scholarship on Christ groups in the first century has taken it as self-evident that Christ followers were comparable to other cultic groups, honouring a deity. Robert Wilken, however, reminds us that "we would expect the self-understanding of the Christians to differ from the impression of them which was held by outsiders. Yet on many points we have, quite uncritically, accepted the Christian view of things and dismissed the views of their contemporaries."[41] This is in effect to notice, with Judge, that much of the language typical of cult associations is missing in first-century Christ groups, in spite of the fact that Christ groups seem to have positioned themselves in the context of the ancient marketplace of cults.[42] Already in 1 Thessalonians Paul characterizes Christ followers as having made a choice between idols and the true and living God. In 1 Cor 8–10, Paul argues that a primary consideration of the Corinthian Christ group should have to do with positioning members vis-à-vis other so-called gods. And Romans 1:19–32 begins with an argument that the true nature of deity should have been evident from reflection on creation and human culture, anticipating the arguments that would be invoked in the second century to the effect that the reverencing of other gods, especially their images, amounts to a failure of rationality.

THE CONSOLIDATION OF IDENTITY IN THE SECOND CENTURY

The second century was the occasion for important terminological transitions. Some of these terms were likely the imposition of others on Christ groups and were eventually normalized and adopted by them; others were developed from within. Both, nevertheless, have an impact on how Christ groups understood themselves and were understood by others. The most obvious example of a name imposed by others is Χρ(η)ιστιανός, which began to appear towards the end of the first century or the beginning of the second, depending on the dating of 1 Peter, Acts, and the Didache. As is well known, the term Χριστιανός appears in only a few texts, none of them especially early:

1 1 Pet 4:14–16: If you are reviled for the name of Christ (ἐν ὀνόματι Χριστοῦ), you are blessed, because the spirit of glory, which is also the spirit of God, rests on you. For let not anyone suffer as a murderer or thief or malefactor or a busybody. But if you (suffer) as a *Christianos*, do not be ashamed, but glorify God with his name.
2 Acts 11:26: And it happened that for an entire year they met with the ekklēsia and taught a great many people, and it was first in Antioch that the disciples were first known as *Christianoi*.[43]
3 Acts 26:28: Agrippa said to Paul: Are you so soon persuading me to become a *Christianos*?
4 Didache 12.4: If he (the visitor) does not have a trade provide (for him) according to your understanding, lest as a *Christianos* he lives among you in idleness.

Acts 11:26 implies that the name was coined in the early 40s and claims that it was Antiochene in origin.[44] The date seems unlikely, and although Antioch is a possible locale, it is not the most obvious one. The name Χριστιανός is a Latinism, as most commentators have recognized.[45] Had the coinage been in Greek, it would have been Χριστιασταί, analogous to the Σαραπιασταί or one of the numerous -ασταί names; or Χριστιεῖοι, in analogy to the Ἀρτεμείσιοι, devotees of Artemis (I.Neapolis 44.13–16; Neapolis, Italy; 194 CE), the Ἀπολλωνιεῖοι, the followers of Apollonios of Tyana,[46] and the Ἐπικούρειοι, the followers of Epicurus.[47] An equally likely Greek name would have been οἱ περὶ Χριστόν (cf. οἱ περὶ τὸν Διόνυσον) or οἱ τοῦ Χριστοῦ (e.g., 1 Cor 15:23; Gal 5:24). The -ιανος suffix, however, points to Latin-speaking circles.[48] Analogous names are well attested and normally indicate the partisans or supporters of the person whose name served as the root: Πομπηιανοί;[49] Καισαριανοί;[50] *Caesariani*;[51] *Augustiani*;[52] *Neroniani*;[53] *Othoniani*;[54] *Vitelliani*;[55] *Flaviani*;[56] and Ἡρωδιανοί (Mark 3:6).

Several factors support the view that Χρ(η)ιστιανοί was a term coined by outsiders: the name "Christ partisans" places Christians in a landscape defined by other kinds of political partisanship instead of other associative forms; and the formation presupposes that "Christ" was understood as a proper name rather than as a title.[57] It is still possible that the coinage occurred in Antioch, in Latin-speaking circles, but locations in the Latin West such as Rome seem a priori more likely.[58] Many suppose that the name, like *Augustiani*, was originally used in a derogatory sense.[59] Sometime after 59 CE Nero had created the *Augustiani* from among ambitious *equites*, whose only role seems to have been to applaud Nero's various public performances. The term disappeared from use after Nero, and the histories of Suetonius, Tacitus, and Dio treat the *Augustiani* as pathetic sycophants. If Χρ(η)ιστιανοί was coined in imitation of Nero's group as Mattingly once suggested,[60] it might have had the sense of "Christ lackeys."[61] Some even suggest that it carried a hint of subversion.[62] Haenchen objected to the latter point, arguing that Luke would hardly have used so unfavourable a term when he takes so much care elsewhere to underscore the goodwill that Χριστιανοί had among Roman authorities.[63] Haenchen's objection is cogent, but only if one puts the composition of Luke early. But by the time that Luke wrote in the second century, the term Χριστιανοί had been "normalized," regardless of whether it began as a term of disapprobation, still less whether it implied subversion. Brent Shaw, moreover, makes the important point that, irrespective of when (and why) the term was first coined, the critical issue is when Roman officials became aware of it.[64] Clearly, that was only at the time of Trajan and Hadrian.

Of course, Suetonius (*Nero* 16.2) and Tacitus (*Ann.* 15.44.2) refer to *Chrestiani* and *Chrestus/Christus* in their descriptions of the events of Nero's principate.[65] Both show confusion about the proper name of the supposed founder, whether it was *Chrestus* or *Christus*. Suetonius describes the *Chrestiani* as purveyors of a new and noxious superstition (*superstitio nova ac malefica*). Tacitus echoes Suetonius's characterization of the group as a superstition (*exitiabilis superstitio*) but dwells on their crimes (*flagitia*), which, he says, were what caused the masses to hate them. He recycles the accusation of μισανθρωπία routinely hurled at Jews,[66] but he is completely uninterested in the cultic activities of the Χριστιανοί, if indeed he knew any of them. The *-iani* suffix of the name suggests that, for both Suetonius and Tacitus, *Chrestiani* were some sort of political faction with dangerous and anti-social practices. It is telling that Pliny, writing at the same time as Suetonius and Tacitus – he was a younger colleague of both – concedes that he knew nothing of *Christiani* prior to interrogating them in Bithynia, although he does seem to know that they could not be compelled to sacrifice (*Ep.* 10.96.5). This is telling because both he and Tacitus served as junior senators under Domitian. If much had been known about *Chr(e)istiani* during the 90s, they would certainly have known this. But Pliny knew nothing of the *malificae* that Suetonius *Nero* 16.2 claims or the *flagitia* that Tacitus attributed to *public knowledge* in the 60s. This raises the possibility, suggested recently by Shaw, that in writing their accounts of Nero in the 60s, Suetonius and Tacitus imported names and characterizations that were only current much later, in the 110s.[67] This does not preclude the possibility that the name *Chr(e)istiani* had been coined about the time of Nero, but it does suggest that knowledge of the Christ movement was less widespread among the curial class than has hitherto been assumed.

As is clear, *Chrestiani*, however and wherever it was coined, would have suggested that *Chrestiani* were a political faction. This is likely what piqued Pliny's interest in them. Unlike Suetonius and Tacitus, however, Pliny had the occasion to inquire into the practices and beliefs of the *Christiani* (*Ep.* 10.96). He had learned from his interrogation that they had an array of cultic practices – hymns, prayers, beliefs about their hero, regular meetings, and meal practices – practices that are comparable to those of numerous other cultic associations about which Pliny surely knew.[68] But Pliny's interest lay in dispelling the suspicion that they constituted a *hetairia* (faction). Hence, his interrogation involved requiring suspected Christians to sacrifice to images of the emperor and the gods of Rome, and he offered Trajan the assurance that the *Christiani* had complied with his ban on *hetairiae* (*Ep.* 10.96.7). It is significant that, in his letter to Trajan, he reports having discovered through the interrogation of *ancillae* (female servants) facts about the nocturnal meetings (*ante lucem*), a *carmen*, a *sacramentum*, and the meal (*cibum*). As Robert Grant observes, the constellation of these terms shows that Pliny had in mind Livy's description of the Bacchanalia in Book 39.8, 15, 18.[69] Yet as he invokes each of these key terms associated with the (supposedly) notorious cult of Bacchus, he asserts that the nocturnal meetings were abandoned, that the *carmen* is simply a hymn to Christ as god (not an incantation), that the *sacramentum* was hardly a conspirator's oath, and that the meal was of harmless food. Hence, his verdict: *Christiani* were only infected by a *superstitio prava et immodica*. This is at once a statement that they looked like a cultic association with stupid beliefs and that, their name notwithstanding, they were not a *factio* or *hetairia*.

Trajan's rescript also focused on the issue of political disloyalty. It is worth noting that *Ep.* 10.97 concerns only how *former Christians* can convincingly demonstrate loyalty – he sidesteps the element in Pliny's diagnostic procedure that involves a *supplicatio* to the emperor – and speak only of *supplicando dis nostris* (supplication of our gods).[70] His advice to Pliny on those who are Christian is ambiguous: on the one hand those who (continued to be?) accused and convicted are to be punished; but on the other, they were not to be sought out (*conquirendi non sunt*, 97.2), nor should anonymous accusations be countenanced. This suggests that Pliny had satisfied Trajan that there was no real threat of conspiracy and that Pliny's moderate way of dealing with the matter accorded with Trajan's own values of allowing room for repentance.

While ἐκκλησία was underdetermined as a term of identity and hence needed to be qualified by a secondary term (τοῦ θεοῦ, *vel sim*), the etic term Χριστιανοί posed a different problem for Christ groups. Left untouched and unqualified, it would have implied that Christ followers constituted a faction comparable to the other *-iani* groups. It is perhaps for this reason, or perhaps owing to the odd absence of terms belonging to cultic registers, that in the second century the discursive constructions of "Christianity" began more intentionally to qualify it by focusing on its identity as a cultic association. This was not without its liabilities; but it also left *Christiani* less exposed to the suspicion of political partisanship.

What terms would offer the clearest signs of cultic orientation? In the early Augustan period, Dionysius of Halicarnassus offered accounts of the arrangements that first Romulus, then Numa, made for the appropriate worship of the gods (*Roman Antiquities* 2.18.62–3). These are instructive for the key institutions and values that Dionysius understood to constitute the basis for an ideal state and for the vocabulary that he used to describe those cultic practices. The key goals of the state were to cultivate piety (ευσέβεια), the goodwill (εὔνοια) of the gods and in the people, moderation (σωφροσύνη), justice (δικαιοσύνη), and nobility in war (γενναιότης) (2.18). This began by ensuring the proper worship of the gods and genii (τὰ περὶ τὰ θεῖα καὶ δαιμόνια σεβάσματα) (2.18). It is hardly a coincidence that Dionysius's list of civic values bears a strong relationship to Augustan ideology.[71]

When he came to Numa, Dionysius enumerated the elements that went into arranging the care of the gods (τὰ θεῖα). These included the building of altars and temples, the appointing of priests, and enacting forms of worship (θρησκεία), purifications, and other services (θεραπεῖαι) and honours (τιμαί) for the gods, all as expressions of the great piety (εὐσέβεια) of the Romans. In connection with Numa's initiatives Dionysius even provides a tale of Romulus's post-mortem appearance to a shepherd, announcing that he had been divinized (2.63). Again, the connections with Augustus are inescapable. Christ groups lacked temples, sacrifices, and altars, and also lacked the vocabulary associated with cultic associations and cultic activities. Paul (in Philippians and Romans) and Hebrews had already developed a vocabulary of metaphorical temples, sacrifices, and altars. They had also adopted the term ἀδελφοί, used widely by Judaeans, and by a small number of cultic associations as a marker of membership. These discursive strategies would have to be expanded if *Christiani* were to be seen as more than a group of partisans of *Chrestus*.

In what follows I pay special attention to second-century literature that is ostensibly addressed to outsiders – Aristides, Justin, Diognetus, Athenagoras – and writings that clearly have the opinions of outsiders in view (1 Peter). Three strategies are evident: the first is to borrow the apparatus of Roman cults but to use it metaphorically; the second is to show that the vocabulary that belongs to cultic registers was imported; and the third, as I suggest at the conclusion of this chapter, is that the first and second were connected in order to underscore the harmlessness of Christians.

METAPHORS OF THE CULT

The author of 1 Peter seems to be aware of a situation in Bithynia very much like that of the *Christiani* that Pliny encountered (whether or not 1 Peter was written before or after Pliny's letter to Trajan). Part of the problem was that Χριστιανός was both underdetermined as a cultic term and was in danger of being construed solely as a term of partisanship. Hence, the author engaged in the metaphorizing strategy of Paul and Hebrews, claiming that his addresses were a "spiritual *oikos*" and a "holy priesthood" that offers "acceptable spiritual sacrifices" to God (1 Pet 2:5, cf. 2:9: βασίλειον ἱεράτευμα). He also holds out the hope that, in spite of their being excoriated as malefactors (κακοποιοί), the observation of Christians' good deeds would win eventual approval. Καλὰ ἔργα (2:12) here should be understood as deeds and activities that would publicly be coded as beneficial rather than as harmful to the public good, and thus win public approbation. The scenario imagined by the author of 1 Peter thus resembles that described by Pliny: Christians were accused of being malefactors and were persecuted owing to those public accusations. 1 Peter of course imagines a rosy outcome: not simply that Christians are dismissed as infected by a depraved superstition, but, eventually, that they are praised for their good deeds. 1 Pet 2:13, 17, moreover, counsels not only submitting to the emperor and his governors but honouring the emperor (τὸν βασιλέα τιμᾶτε) – just the kind of gesture that Pliny required, designed to demonstrate that the *Christiani* were not a political faction.[72]

There is nothing in the paraenetic sections of 1 Peter on slaves (2:18–25), women (3:1–6), husbands (3:7), and general conduct (3:8–4:11) that would trouble the likes of Pliny any more than he was troubled by their oath (*sacramentum*) to repay debts and not to commit any crime (*scelus*) or adultery.[73]

THE VOCABULARY OF CULTS

As I note above, what is striking about the lexicon of first-century Christ groups is the almost complete absence of terms in the lexical register of the cult of the divine: εὐσέβεια, σέβομαι, and θεοσέβεια; θρησκεία and θρησκεύω (and *cultores*); and θεραπεία, θεραπεύω, and θεραπευτής. It is only in the second century that such cultic language begins to appear with greater density, thus characterizing Christ groups less as political factions and more as cultic associations.

Εὐσέβεια, for example, is one of the most fundamental values of Greek society, appearing as early as the various versions of the *Sayings of the Seven Sages*, which usually placed Θεὸν σέβου as the first, or as one of the first, ethical imperatives, along with the other fundamental values of honouring parents, assisting friends, honouring oaths, and obeying the law.[74] Although the verb σέβομαι and the nouns εὐσέβεια and θεοσέβεια are common in Greek literature, in the LXX, and other second Temple Jewish writings,[75] they are entirely missing from the writings of Christ groups in the first century. Paul uses σεβαζόμαι in Rom 1:25 but only to describe false piety. By contrast, these lexemes are richly attested in the second century: in Acts, the Pastorals, 1 Clement, the Apology of Aristides, Justin, Diognetus, and Athenagoras.[76] The effect of these terms is to mark or reinforce Christ groups as having a primary orientation to the cult of the deity. Since εὐσέβεια is also closely tied to ethical conduct, it is unsurprising to find repeated insistence on the moral character of Christians.

Aristides, for example, begins his explanation of the Χριστιανοί by positioning them clearly in the company of other cults (*Apol.* 1), but he emphasizes the distinctive character of their worship σέβομαι and their strong ethical code (*Apol.* 15). Justin likewise underscores the piety of Christians along with their innocence of any crimes. Indeed, "insofar as one can judge from their name by which we are accused, we are the most excellent (χρηστότατοι)," again playing on the Chrestus/Christus confusion (*1 Apol.* 4.1).

The situation is more complicated with the noun θρησκεία, the verb θρησκεύω, and the substantivized participle θρησκεύοντες owing to their potential pejorative nuances. The noun has been erroneously rendered as "religion" in biblical translations – erroneous because it implies far too much about the scope of the term. Θρησκεία means, variously, "rite," "worship," "cult," "devotion," "piety," or "service" (to a god or a superior such as a ruler), but it can also refer to the particular scruples or prohibitions that are entailed in the adoption of the cult of a god.

Whereas εὐσέβεια is uniformly coded in a positive way, the same is not true of θρησκεία. It appears over 550 times before the end of the fourth century, and its usages generally fall into one of three groups: (1) what might be called an "ethnographic" use,[77] where the term is used simply to refer to cultic practices and scruples of some *ethnos* or group, without the author explicitly or implicitly offering an evaluation of those practices; (2) a pejorative use whereby the term is associated with idols, demons, irrational persons, or anti-social postures; and (3) an approving use, especially in reference to the θρησκεῖαι with which the author is associated.

The sole occurrence of θρησκεία in the literature of first-century Christ groups is Col 2:18, where the author speaks disparagingly of the θρησκεία τῶν ἀγγέλων. Neither the verb nor the participle, θρησκεύοντες, appears.

The earliest occurrences of the noun are in Herodotus (2.18, 37, 64) and Aristodemos (FGrH 2a, 104F), where θρησκεία is used ethnographically.[78] Boyarin, however, suggests that θρησκεία came to be used by many Greek writers as a "near-synonym of δεισιδαιμονία" (superstition) and originated from the encounter of those who used θρησκεία of their own cults (the third usage) and Greek commentators (Strabo and Plutarch) who perceived these as "wild and extravagant and oriental."[79]

Wisdom of Solomon provides the first occurrences of the word group in the LXX, where Wisdom 14 uses the verb (14:17) and the noun (14:18, 27) of the worship of images. There is nothing in the author's use of θρησκεία by itself to imply something pejorative; it is rather the context, in which the author not only treats this kind of worship as indicative of a failure of reason but also as the beginning, cause, and end and goal of evil (παντὸς ἀρχὴ κακοῦ καὶ αἰτία καὶ πέρας, 18:27). Yet it should be noted that several Judaean writers from Alexandria tend to use θρησκεία rather than, for example, λατρεία, when describing irrational practices that do not constitute true piety.[80] As Van Henten shows, however, Philo and Josephus use the term positively of Judaean practices and descriptively of other cultic practices without a negative judgment.[81]

As Boyarin shows, the difference between the "ethnographic" or neutral use of θρησκεία and the approving and pejorative usages has to do with the view of piety. The practices associated with piety exist on a sliding scale: when those rites, inhibitions, and scruples – θρησκεῖαι – are appropriate, moderate, and informed, they accord with piety; but excesses move θρησκεία in the directions of either superstition or atheism and impiety.

Boyarin illustrates this understanding with Plutarch *Conj. praec.* 140D, where Plutarch advises that a wife should only "fear and know" (σέβεσθαι … καὶ γιγνώσκειν) the gods of her husband and avoid "overwrought devotions" (περίεργοι θρησκεῖαι) and "foreign superstitions" (ξέναι δεισιδαιμονίαι).[82] Soranus advised against having a midwife who is superstitious and inclined to "popular θρησκεία" since this would inevitably interfere with the appropriate care of the infant.[83] Plutarch's account of the circumstances of Alexander's birth claims that Olympia participated in Orphic and Dionysiac rites similar to those of Thracian women, and he then volunteers Θρῆσσαι as an etymology of θρησκεύειν, which, he says, refers to "immoderate (κατάκοροι) and overwrought ceremonies (περίεργοι ἱερουργίαι)" (*Alexander* 2.8).[84]

Boyarin sees that same tendency to represent θρησκεία as tending towards superstition in Antiochus's comment to Eleazar in 4 Macc 5:7: "you do not seem to me to be a philosopher (φιλοσοφεῖν), holding (as you do) the devotion of the Judaeans (τῇ Ιουδαίων χρώμενος θρησκείᾳ)." He suggests that θρησκεία *simpliciter* was coded in a negative way; it is not Judaean practices per se that makes Eleazar's practice a θρησκεία but, rather, his irrational scruples and his willingness to die for them that qualifies it as a θρηκσεία.[85]

As Boyarin points out, Philo has the same notion of a sliding scale of piety, poised between excess and neglect. True εὐσέβεια is a balance that "produces a knowledge of the θεραπεία θεοῦ" (*Spec.* 4.147). Δεισιδαιμονία, however, is the excessive or immoderate practice of a cult – similar to the Roman notion of *superstitio* – while ἀσέβεια is the product of the exaggerated effort to avoid superstition and that, in doing so, misses piety altogether. Plutarch says much the same thing in *Superst.* 171F: "some, fleeing superstition, fall into atheism, harsh and stubborn, thus overleaping true εὐσέβεια which lies between them." But despite Boyarin's effort to place θρησκεία near the superstitious end of this spectrum, neither Philo nor Plutarch mentions θρησκεία in these contexts. In *Det.* 21 Philo appears to treat θρησκεία as having to do with empirically visible actions that can mask a lack of underlying εὐσέβεια; but in *Legatio* 232, 298 Philo treats θρησκεία (in relation to the Temple) as entirely positive.

As the citation from Dionysius of Halicarnassus cited above indicates, θρησκεία and θρησκεύω are routinely used approvingly, except when qualified by an adjective, adverb, or adverbial expression that signals otherwise. Josephus uses the noun 91× and the verb 23×, attributing θρησκεία to Abraham (*Ant.* 1.122–4), David (*Ant.* 7.341), Josiah (*Ant.* 10.53), and Mattathias (*Ant.* 12.271).[86] Barton and Boyarin argue, rightly, that there is no hint of the "sliding scale" in his use of θρησκεία.[87] At Ant. 6.90 Josephus uses θρησκεία as a synonym for εὐσέβεια, and at 8.279 it is the antonym of ἀσέβεια. They argue that θρησκεία is semantically equivalent in Josephus to νόμος, which he uniformly codes as positive: "Thrēskeia, for Josephus, is clearly greater (semantically) than thus 'cult' but represents the entire array of human obligation toward God, including then all the things that Josephus identified as part and parcel of nomos: piety, fellowship [koinōnia], good order of government."[88]

In the most comprehensive treatment of the history of the use of θρησκεία before Barton and Boyarin, Laurence Foschia shows that the noun first meant "regulated ritual" (Herodotus 2.18) but that, by the Hellenistic period, had come to mean "all the rites required by a cult."[89] Confirming what Boyarin would later argue, these requirements, as Robert had shown, were comprehensive, even including the singing of hymns.[90] Foschia, moreover, adduced numerous instances in which θρησκεία was associated with εὐσέβεια. This is already clear from the citation of Dionysius of Halicarnassus (above) but is reinforced by rich epigraphic evidence that paired θρησκεία and εὐσέβεια or the adverb εὐσεβῶς.[91] Given Roman understandings of the efficacy of cultic practices, the convergence of the piety with θρησκεία is fully intelligible. Foschia argues: "Le culte paraît être envisagé dans ce cas précis comme la réunion de deux notions, d'une part la piété, de l'autre la pratique exigée par cette piété, le rituel, l'ensemble des gestes requis et réglementés, gestes qui viennent en complément de la piété."[92] All this is to suggest that, at least by the Roman period,[93] and probably in the late Hellenistic period, θρησκεία *simpliciter* was usually understood as the practices required by the cult of the gods[94] and was treated positively and as the equivalent of εὐσέβεια, especially when it referred to one's own cult.[95]

As Foschia observes, the use of θρησκεία *simpliciter* or the cognate verb in the literature of second-century Christ cults is not as common as εὐσέβεια. Nevertheless, Christian authors in the second century use the term to characterize the Christ followers as participating in a cult. 1 Clem 45.7, in a section that repetitively argues that the righteous were not persecuted by the pious, Clement uses the phrases οἱ φοβούμενοι τὸν θεόν in parallel with οἱ θρησκεύοντες τὴν μεγαλοπρεπῆ καὶ ἔνδοξον θρησκείαν τοῦ ὑψιστου, "those who worship the great and glorious worship of the Most High" and again in parallel with οἱ ἐν ὁσίᾳ καὶ ἀμώμῳ προθέσει δουλεύοντες τῷ θεῷ, "those who with a holy and unblemished purpose serve God." He concludes (62.1) by stating that his letter concerned matters τὰ ἀνήκοντα τῇ θρησκείᾳ ἡμῶν, where θρησκεία evidently compasses worship, ritual, and piety.

The letter of James famously epitomizes "pure and undefiled θρησκεία" not as a set of scruples or even cultic practices but instead in relation to ethical attitudes towards "orphans and widows" – persons in Israelite discourse who are consistently treated as the objects of divine solicitude (Jas 1:26–8). This is not quite the same strategy as that seen in 1 Peter, where "Christians" are to be known for their καλὰ ἔργα (understood as publicly visible actions), but it underscores the καλὴ ἀναστροφή to which Christ followers aspire (Jas 3:13). In the larger framework of James, θρησκεία is a set of practices that aims at self-control – James explicitly mentions control of speech. Thus, James's view of θρησκεία approaches that of Philo, who likewise stresses Stoicizing virtues of self-control as constitutive of piety.[96] And, like Philo, James is aware that devotion can mask hypocrisy and that the only genuine θρησκεῖαι are "those of the soul that offers the only sacrifice, the bare truth" (*Det.* 19–21).

The letter to Diognetus, which is framed as an exposition of the piety of *Christianoi*, leaves no doubt that *Christianoi* comprise a cultic group, comparable with (and superior to) other cults. The opening paragraph establishes that *Christianoi*, a term that it uses fourteen times, have a distinctive piety (θεοσέβεια), a god that they obey (τίνι τε Θεῷ πεποιθότες), and devotees (θρησκεύτοντες) of that god who are not infected by δεισδαιμονία (Diognetus 1). The content of what follows maintains the focus on cultic matters and cultic vocabulary: the irrational worship (σεβεῖν, 2.7) and worship (θρησκεύειν) of others; the similarities and especially the differences between Χριστιανοί and Judaeans, both of whom have a mode of worship (λατρεία, θρησκεία) and exhibit reverence for the divine (σεβεῖν), but Judaeans exhibit superstitious practices that manifest foolishness rather than true piety (θεοσέβεια) (3.1–4.6). Diognetus here appears to embrace Philo and Plutarch's notion of a sliding scale of εὐσέβεια/θρησκεία, such that superstition is not its opposite but, rather, an excessive or irrational version of εὐσέβεια/θρησκεία.[97]

As if Diognetus has in mind the aspersions that were cast at *Christianoi* as misanthropes and, even worse, as engaging in cannibalism, licentious sex, and incomprehensible cultic practices,[98] he insists on the utter ordinariness of *Christianoi*: they are not distinct in any way. Their language, locale, customs, and marriages are like those of others, although they refrain from exposing children. They participate in civic life, have common meals (but not communal sex), they obey laws, love all, and are ἀγαθοποιοῦντες (ch. 5 passim). The obvious intent of Diognetus's account is, on the one hand, to place *Christianoi* solidly in the context of other devotional cults and, on the other, to obviate any of the suspicions that had been cast on them.[99]

The adoption of θρησκεία/θρησκεύω by Christ groups as self-descriptions continued in the later second century and well into the third and fourth. Foschia notes that θρησκεία is often accompanied by the adjectives ἅγια, καθαρά, and ἀληθινή or even the superlatives ἁγνοτάτη, δικαιοτάτη, παναγεστάτη, σεβασμιωτάτη.[100] With this routine appearance of these terms it is clear that the Christ cult is positioned among the cults of the gods and, by the late third century, as a competitor to all of them.

The third set of lexemes associated with the cult of the gods includes θεραπεία, θεραπεύω, and θεραπευτής. These, perhaps curiously, are among the last items of cultic vocabulary to be adopted by Christ groups. The reasons for the slow adoption are not clear.

Θεραπεία and θεραπεύω have a very broad set of connotations – service, care, attendance, worship (service of the gods), and medical treatments. As "service to the gods/god," θεραπεία became common from the fifth century BCE onward, and the nature of ἡ θεραπεία τῶν θεῶν is the subject of Plato's *Euthyphro*. Later the Stoics would define εὐσέβεια as ἐπιστήμη θεῶν θεραπείας.[101] It is perhaps surprising that the LXX uses θεραπεία so sparingly; it refers to a cultic assembly twice (Joel 1:14; 2:15), while the verb appears several times with the meaning of "to worship" or "to serve [God]."[102] The notion of "service to the God," however, is very common in Philo and Josephus. Philo credits Moses with "a perfect knowledge (ἐπιστήμη) of the proper way to serve (θεραπεία) God" (*Mos.* 2.5) and takes over the Stoic definition of piety.[103] Josephus says much the same of Moses in *Ant.* 3.212.

Θεραπεία in the sense of service to God is missing from the first-century literature of the Christ cult, appearing only in the sense of "healing." The verb appears at Acts 17:25. In the second century, the noun rarely appears meaning "worship" except in a few places where it refers to the worship of demons and false deities.[104] Perhaps unsurprisingly, by the time of Clement of Alexandria, θεραπεία has become part of the vocabulary of Christians, and Clement even adopts a version of the Stoic definition of piety, adapting it to his focus on *paideia*: "Now piety (θεοσέβεια) is instruction, being the learning of the service of God (θεοῦ θεραπείας), and training in the knowledge of the truth, and right guidance which leads to heaven."[105]

It is perhaps also surprising that the noun, θεραπευτής was not adopted by Christ followers. The term appears very frequently in Philo, not only as a generic term for those who worship the Judaean God but also,[106] of course, as the name for a particular set of worshippers in Egypt.[107] Θεραπευταί was a common designation of devotees of Isis and Sarapis but is also attested for the cuts of the Pure Aphrodite, Sabazios, and Zeus.[108] A likely Latin equivalent is *cultores*, extremely well attested in Latin inscriptions and in practically every part of the empire. These include, inter alia, *cultores* of Jupiter OM, the Unconquered Sun (Mithras), Diana and Antinoüs, Mars, Minerva, Isis and Sarapis, Silvanus, and various Celtic and Germanic deities.[109] *Cultores* are also associated with the imperial house.[110]

The earliest uses of *cultores* in relation to Christ groups are found especially in North Africa, first in the mid-third century in Cyprian, who speaks frequently of *dei cultores*,[111] and in the early fourth century in Lactantius's *Diuinae Institutiones*.[112] It is in the fourth century that the first funerary monuments begin to appear using *cultor*, including a famous a funerary inscription attributed to Pope Damasus, from the cemetery of Priscilla, via Salaria Nova (Rome, late IV CE), which refers to two deceased martyrs as *cultores domini*.[113]

WHAT WAS TO BE GAINED?

In spite of some unevenness in the adoption of the cultic lexicon, second-century Christ groups promoted themselves as genuinely cultic groups, either by claiming that they had the fixture of cults – priests, altars, temples, sacrifices – though deployed only in metaphorical ways, or by incorporating the cultic lexicon of piety, reverence, worship, service (to the god), and related terms. Under the aegis of this cultic lexicon, the undetermined and ambiguous language of the first century could now find a place in discursive constructions that were properly cultic. Devotion to Christ now belonged to the categories of τὸ θεοσεβές and θρησκεία; and the good deeds of Christians were understood to flow from their εὐσέβεια, which, in turn, as Clement would claim, flowed from their knowledge of θρησκεία. Lingering doubts created by the *-iani* suffix should be dispelled by constant representation of second-century Christ followers as pious, devoted to the cult of their deity, and uninfected by superstition – or so Christ followers of the second century could hope.

These efforts to reconceive the Christ cult by making its cultic textures clear can be seen as serving several purposes. As I suggest, the moniker *Christiani*, coined by outside observers, carried with it the danger of being apprehended as a ἑταιρία or political faction – a danger no less ominous in the time of Hadrian or Antoninus Pius or Marcus Aurelius than it had been during Trajan's principate.

Rome had a long and complex history of attempts at (or perceptions of) political subversion. The most infamous example was the Bacchanalia conspiracy of 186 BCE, which resulted in the execution and exile of many members of a Dionysiac group alleged to be acting against the interests of the state.[114] In the late Republican period there were several laws and *senatus consulta* enacted outlawing or restricting the formations of groups. Unfortunately, the text of those *leges* is not extant, and it is far from clear how they were actually implemented. There are several inscriptions in which associations in Italy refer to having gained permission to meet under the provisions of the *lex Iulia*, but other contemporary groups failed to cite such permission, perhaps because the law was not applied to groups that served public interest (*res publica*) or because application of the law differed from one locale to another.[115] Similarly, the formula from the *senatus consultum* (probably from the time of Hadrian) that is quoted in CIL 14.2112 (*quibus ex s*[*enatus*] *c*[*onsulto*] *coire licet*) and alluded to in several other inscriptions is neglected in other inscriptions of comparable groups.

There is no evidence of a systematic application of restrictions on the formation of clubs and associations in Asia or Egypt, in spite of sporadic suppression of certain groups, which are best interpreted as police action rather than the application of a policy on meetings.[116] Nevertheless, there seems to have been a provision that permitted cultic groups to assemble *religionis causa* without the need for explicit senatorial approval, provided that they did not violate the provisions of the *S.C. de collegiis*.[117] As Bendlin observes, even if this ruling was in effect before the time of Severus, *religionis causa* was notoriously underdetermined, which "permit[ted] the political authorities to define its scope and limit its applicability to those associations they have declared lawfully constituted, regardless of whether the primary raison d'être is or is not religious."[118] All of this meant that it was in the interests of Christ groups to *look* as much as possible as a cultic group that might be allowed under the terms of the *S.C. de collegiis*, understanding of course that the vagaries of the formulation of the *S.C.* meant that suppression was still possible. Hence, Christ groups not only imported language that belonged to the linguistic registers of cultic activities and identity but also stressed the politically harmless nature of their activities and, as 1 Peter even ventures, the public utility of their way of life.[119]

NOTES

1 E.A. Judge, "Was Christianity a Religion?," in *The First Christians in the Roman World: Augustan and New Testament Essays*, ed. James R. Harrison, WUNT 229 (Tübingen: Mohr Siebeck, 2008), 404–9.

2 Wilfred Cantwell Smith, *The Meaning and End of Religion*, with a foreword by John Hick (San Francisco: Harper and Row, 1978), 50. See also Jonathan Z. Smith, "Religion, Religions, Religious," in *Critical Terms for Religious Studies* (Chicago: University of Chicago Press, 1998), 269–84; Brent Nongbri, *Before Religion: A History of a Modern Concept* (New Haven, CT: Yale University Press, 2013); Carlin A. Barton and Daniel Boyarin, *Imagine No Religion: How Modern Abstractions Hide Ancient Realities* (New York: Fordham University Press, 2016).

3 See Cicero, *Nat. d.* 2.71–2.

4 Whether "Hinduism" was invented by the British or whether there was already some notional unity to diverse Indian practices prior to European colonialism has been contested. There is, however, less doubt that the term "Hinduism" is a British coinage, as is the imposition of the category of "religion" upon the peoples of India. See Timothy Fitzgerald, "Who Invented Hinduism? Rethinking Religion in India," in *Rethinking Religion in India: The Colonial Construction of Hinduism*, ed. Esther Bloch, Marianne Keppens, and Rajaram Hegde (London: Routledge, 2010), 114–34.

5 E.A. Judge, "Was Christianity a Religion?," 407 (originally published in *Society for the Study of Early Christianity Newsletter* 56 [2006] 4–7). On the "invention" of world religions, see Tomoko Masuzawa, *The Invention of World Religions, or, How European Universalism Was Preserved in the Language of Pluralism* (Chicago: University of Chicago Press, 2005).

6 E.A. Judge, "The Social Identity of the First Christians: A Question of Method in Religious History," *Journal of Religious History* 11, no. 2 (1980): 212 (reprinted as pp. 117–35 in E.A. Judge, *The Social Distinctives of the Christians in the First Century* [ed. D.M. Scholer; Peabody, MA: Hendrickson, 2008]). See, more recently, Martin Ebner, *Die Stadt als Lebensraum der ersten Christen*, Das Urchristentum in seiner

Umwelt, Das Neue Testament Deutsche – Ergänzungsreihe 1 (Göttingen: Vandenhoeck & Ruprecht, 2012), 130 and Cilliers Breytenbach, "Comparative Philology and History of Religion: Analogies and/or Genealogies," in *Von Texten zu Geschichten: Aufsätze zur Konzeption und Geschichte der Wissenschaft vom Neuen Testament*, WUNT 448 (Tübingen: Mohr Siebeck, 2020), 69–78.

7 Both appear in the second century: θρησκεία (Jas 1:26, 27) and εὐσέβεια (Acts 3:12; 1 Tim 2:2; 3:16 4:7; 4:8; 6:3; 6:5–6, 11; 2 Tim 3:5; Tit 1:1; 2 Pet 1:3, 6–7; 3:11).

8 William E. Arnal, "The Collection and Synthesis of 'Tradition' and the Second-Century Invention of Christianity," *Method and Theory in the Study of Religion* 23, no. 3 (2011): 193–215.

9 Ibid., 194.

10 Ibid., 202 (emphasis in original).

11 Ibid.

12 Markus Öhler, *Geschichte des frühen Christentums*, UTB 4737 (Göttingen: Vandenhoeck & Ruprecht, 2018), 15. For others who reject *Urchristentum* as a conceptual category, see Stefan Alkier, *Urchristentum: Zur Geschichte und Theologie einer exegetischen Disziplin*, Beiträge zur historischen Theologie 83 (Tübingen: Mohr Siebeck, 1993).

13 Udo Schnelle, *Die ersten 100 Jahre des Christentums 30–130 n.Chr.: Die Entstehungsgeschichte einer Weltreligion*, 2. Auflage, Uni-Taschenbücher 4411 (Göttingen: Vandenhoeck & Ruprecht, 2016), 25–6, rejects the term because of its normative implications and because it prejudges the issue of whether *frühes Christentum* (his preference) was a unitary movement or a diverse set of formations that might have been in conflict with each other.

14 See Gerd Lüdemann, "Das Urchristentum I," and "Das Urchristentum II," *Theologische Rundschau* 65, nos. 2 and 3 (2000): 129; Dietrich-Alex Koch, *Geschichte des Urchristentums: ein Lehrbuch: Das Römische Reich und die hellenistische Kultur als Lebensraum des frühen Christentums in den ersten zwei Jahrhunderten*, 2. korrigierte und erweiterte Auflage (Göttingen: Vandenhoeck & Ruprecht, 2014).

15 In what follows I shall treat Acts, 1 Peter, and James as late first-century or, more likely, second-century compositions. The most compelling argument for a late dating of Acts has now been advanced by Steve Mason, who has shown that Luke knew (and used) Josephus's *Antiquities*, which is fairly securely dated to 93/4 CE. This implies that Acts cannot be any earlier than the very end of the first century CE. See Steve Mason, "Josephus a Source for Luke-Acts?," in *On Using Sources in Graeco-Roman, Jewish, and Early Christian Literature*, ed. Joseph Verheyden, John S. Kloppenborg, Geert Roskam, and Stefan Schorn, BETL (Leuven: Peeters, 2022), 199–246. See earlier, John S. Kloppenborg, "Luke's Geography: Knowledge, Ignorance, Sources, and Spatial Conception," in *Luke on Jesus, Paul, and Christianity: What Did He Really Know?*, ed. Joseph Verheyden and John S. Kloppenborg, Biblical Tools and Studies 29 (Leuven: Peeters, 2017), 110–11, for other indications that Luke's topographical knowledge of Jerusalem derives from Josephus.

1 Peter offers less purchase for secure dating, but the similarity of the conditions presupposed by the letter and what Pliny describes in his letter to Trajan (*Ep.* 10.96–7) suggests a date early in the second century, perhaps just before Pliny's letter in the early 110s.

Since James appears to know 1 Peter and owing to striking lexical affinities with 1 Peter and Hermas and its very late appearance both in the East and the West, a date in the early second century is most plausible. See Dale C. Allison, *A Critical and Exegetical Commentary on the Epistle of James*, ICC (New York: Bloomsbury, 2013), 29 (100–120 CE); John S. Kloppenborg, *James*, New Testament Guides (London: T&T Clark, 2022), 26–36 (first half of the second century).

16 See also Paul R. Trebilco, *Self-Designations and Group Identity in the New Testament* (Cambridge: Cambridge University Press, 2012).

17 1 Thess 4:10; 5:26; 1 Cor 8:12; 2 Cor 9:3, 5; Rom 16:14; Col 4:15; 1 John 3:14; 3 John 5,10; Acts 15:1, 32, 36; 16:40; 17:6; 21:7; 22:5.

18 For example, 1 Pet 2:17; 5:9; 1 Clem 2.4; Aristides, *Apol.* 15.7; Athenagoras, *Leg.* 32; Lucian, *Perigr.* 13; I.Perinthos 167.1, 4–5 (after 212 CE): Αὐρ(ήλιος) Φιλιππιανὸς χρ(ιστιανὸς) ἐποίησα ...εἰ δέ τις τολμήσει ἕτερον βαλεῖν | | δώσει τοῖς ἀδελφοῖς Χ φ; I.Perinthos 168.1, 5–6 (after 212 CE) [Αὐ]ρ(ήλιος) Φιλοκύρις χρ(ιστιανὸς)... παρακαλῶ | | [δὲ] τοὺς ἐμοὺς ἀδε[λ] | [φο]ὺς προνοεῖν; Yotam Tepper and Leah Di Segni, *A Christian Prayer Hall of the Third Century CE at Kefar 'Othnay (Legio): Excavations at the Megiddo Prison 2005* (in collaboration with Guy Stiebel; Jerusalem: The Israel Antiquities Authority, 2006), 34 = SEG 56:1899: Γαϊανὸς ὁ καὶ Πορφύρι(ο)ς (ἑκατοντάρχης) ἀδελφὸς ἡμῶν φιλο | τειμησάμενος ἐκ τῶν ἰδίων *vvv* | *vacat* ¿ ἐψηφολόγησε· Βρούτι(ο)ς ἠργάσετ[ο].

19 Members of a guild of Selgian stone cutters in Western Rough Cilicia, I.CiliciaBM II 180, 201 b.28, 29 (Lamos, central Rough Cilicia, before 69 CE) were known as ἀδελφοί. The term might also have designated business partners in P.Tor. Choach. 12.1.11 = UPZ II 162 (Thebes, 117 CE): Χονοπρῆν καὶ τοὺς τούτων ἀδελφούς, a group of funerary workers. See Peter Arzt-Grabner, "'Brothers' and 'Sisters' in Documentary Papyri and in Early Christianity," *Rivista Biblica* 50 (2002): 185–204.

20 CCID 373.5, 11 (Rome, 212–250 CE); CCID 377 = 382 (Rome, 212–250 CE); CCID 274 (Pannonia Superior, 201–250 CE): *fratres* devoted to Jupiter Dolichenus.

21 ἀδελφός: CIRB 104.10–11 (Pantikapaion, 200–250 CE); εἰσποιητοὶ ἀ̣δ̣ελφοὶ: CIRB 1281.5 (Tanais, 210–227 CE); CIRB 1283.6 (Tanais, 228 CE); CIRB 1284.6 (Tanais); CIRB 1285.6 (Tanais, 210–234 CE); CIRB 1286.1 (Tanais, 210–234 CE); IK Sinope 117 (Sinope, I–II CE) ἀγαθῆι τύχηι | vac | θεῷ Ὑψίστῳ | Α̣ἴλιος Θρεπτίων | | Ποντιανὸς Σεου | ρος Μάκερ οἱ | ἀδελφοὶ εὐξάμενοι; I.PrusOlymp 115 (Prusa ad Olympum [Bithynia], late II ce), on which see Walter Ameling, "Ein Verehrer des θεὸς Ὕψιστος in Prusa ad Olympum (I.K. 39, 115)," *EA* 31 (1999), 105–8, (SEG 49.1796). P.Lond.VII 2193.14 = GRA III 199 (Philadelphia, 69–58 BCE?), a *lex collegii* from an Egyptian Zeus Hypsistos group, refers to the collective as a φράτρα.

22 Thus Judith M. Lieu, *Christian Identity in the Jewish and Graeco-Roman World* (Oxford: Oxford University Press, 2004), 250.

23 1 Thess 1:7; 2:10, 13; 1 Cor 1:21; 14:22; Gal 3:22; Rom 3:22; 4:11; 2 Thess 1:10; Heb 4:3; 1 Pet 2:7. See Teresa Morgan, *Roman Faith and Christian Faith: Pistis and Fides in the Early Roman Empire and Early Churches* (Oxford: Oxford University Press, 2015), 235–41. In Acts οἱ πιστεύοντες usually appears in Lukan editorial comments (2:44; 4:32; 5:14; 19:28) but is found in speech at 21:20, 25, and 22:19.

24 Ryan S. Schellenberg, "Οἱ Πιστεύοντες: An Early Christ-Group Self-Designation and Paul's Rhetoric of Faith," *New Testament Studies* 65, no. 1 (2019): 33–42 agrees that οἱ πιστεύοντες is a title but argues that in Galatians and Romans the πίστις root is mobilized in his argument against "works."

25 Lucian, *Alex.* 38 mentions an announcement prior to Alexander of Abonoteichos's performance of the mysteries: Εἴ τις ἄθεος ἢ Χριστιανὸς ἢ Ἐπικούρειος ἥκει κατάσκοπος τῶν ὀργίων, φευγέτω· οἱ δὲ πιστεύοντες τῷ θεῷ τελείσθωσαν τύχῃ τῇ ἀγαθῇ. (If any atheist or Christian or Epicurean has come to spy on the rites, let him flee, and let those who trust the god perform the mysteries for good fortune.) Here οἱ δὲ πιστεύοντες τῷ θεῷ is not a group name but a description of the characteristics of the celebrants.

26 Morgan, *Roman Faith*, 238.

27 For example, I.Klaudiopolis 44 (Klaudiopolis, III CE): τοῖς ἁγνοτάτοις καὶ | θεῷ πιστεύσασιν Μάρ. [Αὐ.] | Δημητριανῷ | ...καὶ τῇ γλυκυτάτῃ | μητρὶ (ηλίᾳ) Παννυχίδι Αὐρ(ηλία); IG XIV 2346 (Venetia): Αὐρ(ηλία) Μαξ̣ει | μειανὴ τ̣έκνῳ | Ἀσκληπιοδότῃ | γ‹λ›υκυτάτῳ, | | πιστεύσα‹ν›τι | εἰς θεόν....

28 Acts 9:2[E]; 18:25[E], 26[E]; 19:9[E], 23[E]; 22:4[S]; 24:14[S], 22[E] ([E] = editorial; [S] = Sondergut).

29 S. Vernon McCasland, "The Way," *Journal of Biblical Literature* 77, no. 3 (1958): 222–30; Craig S. Keener, *Acts: An Exegetical Commentary* (Grand Rapids, MI: Baker Academic, 2012), 1626–7 and those cited by Keener.

30 Heinich Karpp, "Christennamen," *Reallexikon für Antike und Christentum* 2 (1954): 1115. Of the seventeen uses of ⲘⲀⲐⲎⲦⲎⲤ in Gos. Thom., only three (12, 18, 99) use the term absolutely. All the rest use ⲚⲈϤⲘⲀⲐⲎⲦⲎⲤ *vel sim.*

31 See especially William E. Arnal, "How the *Gospel of Thomas* Works," in *Scribal Practices and Social Structures among Jesus Adherents: Essays in Honour of John S. Kloppenborg*, ed. William E. Arnal et al., BETL 285 (Leuven: Peeters, 2016), 261–80, who observes that "the techniques that the redactor [of Thomas] uses to deliberately obscure its content and message force the reader not simply to recite the text, or to hear it once, but to slow down and *study* the text" (271, emphasis in original).

32 The verb μανθάνω appears, for example, in *Poimandres* (CH I.1, 1–3): Τί βούλει ἀκοῦσαι καὶ θεάσασθαι, καὶ νοήσας μαθεῖν καὶ γνῶναι; – (2) φημὶ ἐγώ, Σὺ γὰρ τίς εἶ; – Ἐγὼ μέν, φησίν, εἰμὶ ὁ Ποιμάνδρης, ὁ τῆς αὐθεντίας νοῦς· οἶδα ὃ βούλει, καὶ σύνειμί σοι πανταχοῦ. (3) – φημὶ ἐγώ, Μαθεῖν θέλω τὰ ὄντα καὶ νοῆσαι τὴν τούτων φύσιν καὶ γνῶναι τὸν θεόν. Here too the point is not devotion to Poimandres but learning from him.

33 Philo, *Sacr.* 7: those who have abandoned human instruction become "well-formed disciples of God" (μαθηταὶ δὲ εὐφυεῖς θεοῦ γεγονότες); *Sacr.* 79: God causes sprouts of self-taught wisdom to spring up in the "follower, or a friend, or a disciple of God" (τὸν γὰρ θεοῦ φοιτητὴν ἢ γνώριμον ἢ μαθητήν).

34 Karl H. Rengstorf, "μανθάνω, καταμανθάνω, μαθητής, κτλ.," *Theological Dictionary of the New Testament* 4 (1967): 390–461, especially 442–4; Karpp, "Christennamen," 1115.

35 The use of συναγωγή to mean "meeting" or "assembly" is found at Jas 2:2; Ignatius, *Pol.* 4.2; Hermas, *Mand.* 11.9, 13, 14; *Acta Petri* 9. Συναγωγή as the name of a Christ group is still unusual: Justin may use συναγωγή as a name at *Dial.* 63.5; Eusebius, *Hist.eccl.* 7.9.2: where συναγωγή appears to be the name of the group (πιστὸς νομιζόμενος ...τῆς συναγωγῆς μετασχών, "supposed to be faithful (and) participating in the *synagogē*." I owe these references to Ralph Korner, *per litt.*

36 As Ralph Korner shows (*The Origin and Meaning of* Ekklēsia *in the Early Jesus Movement* [AJEC 98; Leiden: Brill, 2017], 53–68), ἐκκλησία is only unequivocally attested as the *name* of a cultic association among Christ groups. Korner (pp. 129–35) thinks that Philo (*Virt.* 108) uses ἐκκλησία to refer to an "assembly" designed in initiate Egyptian proselytes, but it is unclear from Philo's formulation (καλεῖν τε εἰς ἐκκλησίαν καὶ μεταδιδόναι λόγων θείων) that the term is used as a title rather than "to invite (them) to assemble and to share in divine revelations." There are three instances in which cultic associations employ ἐκκλησία as the term for their assembly: ID 1519 (Delos, 149/48 BCE); IG XII,6 133 (Samos, II BCE); and Louis Robert, *Le Sanctuaire de Sinuri près de Mylasa* (Mémoires de l'institut français d'archéologie de Stamboul, 7, Bibliothèque archéologique et historique de l'Institut français d'archéologie d'Istanbul 8; Paris: Éditions de Boccard, 1945), no. 73 = Louis Robert, "Décret d'une syngeneia carienne au sanctuaire de Sinuri," *Hellenica* 7 (1949), 59–68 (Sinuri [Caria], 350–344 BCE). This corrects my earlier view in John S. Kloppenborg, "Edwin Hatch, Churches, and *Collegia*," in *Origins and Method: Towards a New Understanding of Judaism and Christianity: Essays in Honour of John C. Hurd*, ed. Bradley McLean, JSNTSup 86 (Sheffield: JSOT Press, 1993), 231.

37 Richard Last, "*Ekklēsia* Outside the LXX and the *Dēmos*: The Titles of Greco-Roman Associations and Christ-Followers' Groups," *Journal of Biblical Literature* 137, no. 4 (2018): 970.

38 George H. van Kooten, "Ἐκκλησία τοῦ θεοῦ: The 'Church of God' and the Civic Assemblies (ἐκκλησίαι) of the Greek Cities in the Roman Empire: A Response to Paul Trebilco and Richard A. Horsley," *New Testament Studies* 58, no. 4 (2012): 522–48.

39 ἡ ἐκκλησία Θεσσαλονικέων (1 Thess 1:1), ἡ ἐν Ἐφέσῳ ἐκκλησία (Rev 2:1), or αἱ ἐκκλησίαι τῆς Γαλατίας (Gal 1:2). For the term, see Mogens Herman Hansen, "95 Theses about the Greek 'Polis' in the Archaic and Classical Periods. A Report on the Results Obtained by the Copenhagen Polis Centre in the Period 1993–2003," *Historia* 52, no. 3 (2003): 257–82. The term does not imply that the region was united socially or ethnically.

40 E.A. Judge, "The Early Christians as a Scholastic Community," *Journal of Religious History* 1 (1960–61): 4–15, 125–37.

41 Robert Louis Wilken, "Collegia, Philosophical Schools and Theology," in *The Catacombs and the Colosseum: The Roman Empire as the Setting of Primitive Christianity*, ed. Stephen Benko and John J. O'Rourke (Valley Forge, PA: Judson Press, 1971), 269. See also Judith M. Lieu, "The Forging of Christian Identity and the Letter to Diognetus," in *Neither Jew nor Greek? Constructing Early Christianity*, Studies of the New Testament and Its World (Edinburgh: T&T Clark, 2003), 171–89.

42 For the notion of a marketplace of cults, see Andreas Bendlin, "Looking beyond the Civic Compromise: Religious Pluralism in Late Republican Rome," in *Religion in Archaic and Republican Rome and Italy: Evidence and Experience*, ed. Edward Bispham and Christopher Smith (Edinburgh: Edinburgh University Press, 2000), 115–35, 167–71 (notes).

43 By the Hellenistic period the verb χρηματίσαι meant "to go by the name of," "to be given a title," or "to assume a title." The context of Acts 11:26 leaves it unclear whether the verb has a passive meaning ("they were first given the name 'Christianoi' [by others]") or whether it means "they first styled themselves as Christianoi." See Christopher P. Jones, "Epigraphica," *Zeitschrift für Papyrologie und Epigraphik* 139 (2002): 108–11.

44 While Χριστιανούς is the majority reading, Χρηστιανούς is the reading of א* 91. *Chrestiani* is probably also the original reading in Tacitus, *Ann.* 15.44.

45 Elias J. Bickerman, "The Name of Christians," *Harvard Theological Review* 42, no. 2 (1949): 116–18; Karpp, "Christennamen," 1132; Harold B. Mattingly, "The Origin of the Name 'Christiani,'" *Journal of Theological Studies* n.s., 9, no. 1 (1958): 26–37; Justin Taylor, "Why Were the Disciples First Called 'Christians' at Antioch? (Acts 11, 26)," *Revue Biblique* 101, no. 1 (1994): 75–94; John H. Elliott, *1 Peter*, AB 37B (New York: Doubleday, 2000), 789 and others.

46 Philostratus, *Vita Apol.* 4.14; 8.21: Ἀφίκοντο δ' αὐτῷ κἀξ Ἰωνίας οἱ ὁμιληταὶ πάντες, οὓς ὠνόμαζεν Ἀπολλωνιείους Ἑλλάς... (All his disciples from Ionia also came to see him, whom the Greeks called 'Apollonieioi'....)

47 For example, Chrysippus, Frag. 307.5; 376.2; 687.5; 708.1; Poseidonius, Frag. 290c; 400a.

48 Thus Erik Peterson, "Christianus," in *Miscellanea Giovanni Mercati*, Studi e Testi 121 (Vatican City: Biblioteca Apostolica Vaticana, 1946), 355–72 and others.

49 Appian, *Bell. civ.* 3.11.82; cf. Tacitus, *Ann.* 4.34 reports that Augustus referred to Livy as a "Pompeianus" for his favourable depiction of Pompey.

50 Appian, *Bell. civ.* 3.18.91.

51 *Bell. Africum* 14, 24, 52, and so on.

52 Suetonius, *Nero* 25.1; Tacitus, *Ann.* 14.15; Cassius Dio 61.20.

53 Suetonius, *Galba* 20.2.

54 Tacitus, *Hist.* 1.34; 2.42.

55 Ibid., 1.70; 2.15–44 passim; 3.12–84 passim.

56 Ibid., 3.6–82 passim.

57 Alfred Firmin Loisy, *L'évangile selon Luc* (Paris: Emile Nourry, 1924 [repr. Frankfurt: Minerva, 1971]), 470.

58 Antioch: Loisy, *Luc*, 469; E.A. Judge, "Judaism and the Rise of Christianity: A Roman Perspective," *Tyndale Bulletin* 45, no. 2 (1994): 363; Richard I. Pervo, *Acts* (Hermeneia; Minneapolis: Fortress Press, 2009), 295 (most likely Rome but Antioch is possible). A very small number of early Latin inscriptions are extant from Antioch on the Orontes, including a dedication to Vespasian and Titus (AE 1934, 248); a milestone (AE 1983, 927, 75 CE); and several funerary dedications: to a Xvir stlitibus iudicandis (CIL 3.14165; 18–20 CE); to a tribune from Legio II Augusta (AE 1938, 177); to a tribune from Legio X Fretensis (AE 1940, 170); and a second-century funerary dedication to a legionary (CIL 3.6047).

59 Mattingly, "Origin of the Name 'Christiani'"; Judge, "Judaism and the Rise of Christianity," 363; Tim Hegedus, "Naming Christians in Antiquity," *Studies in Religion* 33, no. 2 (2004): 177; Elliott, *1 Peter*, 790–1; Keener, *Acts*, 1850. Karpp ("Christennamen," 1132) points out that Χρηστός (which both Suetonius and Tacitus assumed to be the name) was a common slave name and that, hence, Χρηστιανοί meant "partisans of a Chrestus, a slave."

60 Thus Mattingly, "Origin of the Name 'Christiani.'"

61 Elliott, *1 Peter*, 791.

62 Karpp, "Christennamen," 1132: "Der Name christianus schließt daher von Anfang an eine zur Verurteilung ausreichende politische und moralische Schuld ein"; so Peterson, "Christianus," 364–7.

63 Ernst Haenchen, *The Acts of the Apostles: A Commentary*, trans. Bernard Noble and Gerald Shinn (Oxford: Basil Blackwell, 1971), 367–8n3.

64 Brent D. Shaw, "The Myth of the Neronian Persecution," *Journal of Roman Studies* 105 (2015): 88–92.

65 Suetonius, *Nero* 16.2 [composed in the 110s or 120s]: [Nero] likewise inflicted punishments on the *Chrestiani*, a sort of people who held a new and impious superstition (*genus hominum superstitionis nouae ac maleficae*). Tacitus, *Ann.* 15.44.2 [written in the mid-110s or early 120s]: Consequently, to get rid of the report, Nero fastened the guilt and inflicted the most exquisite tortures on a class hated for their abominations, called *Chrestiani* by the populace (*quos per flagitia invisos vulgus Chrestianos appellabat*). Christus, from whom the name had its origin, suffered the extreme penalty during the reign of Tiberius at the hands of one of our procurators, Pontius Pilatus.

66 On *odium humani generis*, see Diodorus Siculus 34–35.1.2: τὸ μῖσος τὸ πρὸς τοὺς ἀνθρώπους, and Tacitus, *Hist.* 5.1: *adversus omnes alios hostile odium*.

67 Shaw, "Myth of the Neronian Persecution," 89.

68 Benedikt Eckhardt, "Who Thought That Early Christians Formed Associations?," *Mnemosyne* 70, no. 4 (2017): 300–2, argues that Pliny's statement (*Ep.* 10.96) that the Christians of Bithynia stopped meeting after (*post*) Pliny issued an edict

concerning Trajan's *mandata* to disband *hetairiae* does not imply that either Pliny or Christians regarded Christ groups as *hetairiae*. *Hetairia* is negatively marked in 10.96 and especially in 10.34 where Trajan famously forbade the formation of a *collegium fabrorum* in Nicomedia for fear that sooner or later it would become a *hetairia*. The same negative marking of the noun is seen in I.Eph 215.7–8: "I [the praefect] forbid the bakers to assemble 'faction-like' (κατ' ἑταιρίαν) or that their leaders be emboldened." Eckhardt's conclusion, however, that Pliny did not see Christians "on par with other associations" is belied by the fact that Pliny mentions Christ groups and *hetairiae* in the same breath, just as Trajan saw the danger of a regularly constituted *collegium fabrorum* (of which there were plenty in Rome) becoming a faction. The praefect of I.Eph 215 likewise saw the danger of the bakers (a common trade guild) acting κατ' ἑταιρίαν. Perception of danger is perspectival. While it is true that neither Pliny nor the Christians equated Christ groups with ἑταρίαι, and while it is likely that the ἀρτοκόποι did not regard themselves as a ἑταρία, it seems clear that Trajan and the praefect of I.Eph. 215 saw enough family resemblances to be worried.

69 Robert M. Grant, "Pliny and the Christians," *Harvard Theological Review* 41, no. 4 (1948): 273–4.

70 Dietrich-Alex Koch (*per litt.*) suggests that Trajan's rescript promotes his image as one of *moderatio* and *modestia*, including his reluctance to accept cultic veneration along with the gods (see Pliny, *Panegyricus* 52.1–2). This is a clear contrast with his predecessor Domitian.

71 See *Res Gestae* 34.2: "And for this merit of mine, by a senate decree, I was called Augustus and the doors of my temple were publicly clothed with laurel and a civic crown was fixed over my door and a gold shield placed in the Julian senate-house, and the inscription of that shield testified to the virtue, mercy, justice, and piety (*virtus, clementia, iustitia, pietas*), for which the senate and Roman people gave it to me." See further Richard Hunter and Casper C. de Jonge, "Introduction," in *Dionysius of Halicarnassus and Augustan Rome: Rhetoric, Criticism and Historiography*, ed. Richard Hunter and Casper C. de Jonge, Greek Culture in the Roman World (Cambridge: Cambridge University Press, 2019), 14: "On a more general level, Dionysius' interest in the religious life and morality of the early Romans and his emphasis on virtues like piety, justice and moderation (εὐσέβεια, δικαιοσύνη, σωφροσύνη) have been understood as resonating with the Augustan program of moral reform."

72 See, for example, Elliott, *1 Peter*, 501; Paul J. Achtemeier, *1 Peter: A Commentary on First Peter* (Hermeneia; Minneapolis: Fortress Press, 1996), 188. Nothing, however, in the grammar of 1 Pet 2:17 suggests that τὸν βασιλέα τιμᾶτε is meant to be read ironically or in some qualified sense, in comparison with πάντας τιμήσατε, τὴν ἀδελφότητα ἀγαπᾶτε, or τὸν θεὸν φοβεῖσθε. For a contrasting view, see Warren Carter, "Going All the Way? Honoring the Emperor and Sacrificing Wives and Slaves: 1 Peter 2:13–3.6," in *A Feminist Companion to the Catholic Epistles and Hebrews*, ed. Amy-Jill Levine and M. M. Robbins (London: T&T Clark, 2004), 14–33.

73 Similarly, Lieu, "Forging of Christian Identity," 182.

74 August Friedrich Wilhelm Mullach, *Fragmenta Philosophorum Graecorum* (Paris: Firmin Didot, 1860), 215–17.

75 Σέβομαι: LXX: 26×; Aristeas: 4×; Philo: 8×; Josephus 30×; εὐσέβεια: LXX; 57× (46× in 4 Macc); Aristeas: 9×; Philo: 162×; Josephus: 101×; εὐσεβής: LXX 33×; Philo: 17×; Josephus: 35×; θεοσέβεια: LXX: 7×; Philo: 9×; Josephus: 1×.

76 Σέβομαι: Acts 13:43; 16:14; 17:4; 18:7, used to characterize Christ followers; Aristides *Apol.* 2.2; 7.4; 15.3; Justin, *1 Apol.* 7×; Ps-Clementine *Hom.* 44×; *Rec.* 3×; Kerygma Petri 7×; Theophilus, *Ad Autolycum* 9×; σεβαζόμαι: Aristides, *Apol.* 12.7; εὐσέβεια: Acts 3:12; 1 Tim 2:2; 3:16; 4:7, 8; 6:3, 5, 6, 11; 2 Tim 3:5; Tit 1:1; 2 Pet 1:3, 6, 7; 3:11; 1 Clem. 1.2; 11.1; 15.1; 32.4; 2 Clem. 19.1; Ps-Clementine, *Hom.* 11×; *Epistula de virginitate* 7.1; 9.3; Justin, *Dial.* 13×; *1 Apol.* 3×; Athenagoras *Leg.* 4×; *De resurrectione*: 3×; Theophilus *Ad Autolycum* 3.9; εὐσεβής: Acts 10:2, 7; 2 Pet 2:9; 1 Clem: 3.2; 50.3 2 Clem 19.4; Ps-Clementine, *Hom.* 23× *Epistula de virginitate* 2.8.1; Aristides, *Apol.* [Pap. Lond. 2486].36; Justin, *Dial.* 6×; *1 Apol.* 3×; θεοσέβεια: 1 Tim 2:10; 1 Clem. 20.4; Ps-Clementine, *Hom.* 29×; *Rec.* 1; Justin, *Dial.* 5×; Athenagoras, *Leg.* 1×; Diognetus: 1.1; 3.3; 4.5, 6; 6.4; Theophilus *Ad Autolycum* 3×.

77 This is my term. Boyarin uses the term "neutral" (Barton and Boyarin, *Imagine No Religion*, 143).

78 Barton and Boyarin, *Imagine No Religion*, 128–9, treat as disapproving Herodotus's usage in 2.18, where he notes that Libyans were not sympathetic to the Egyptian θρησκεία which forbade the consumption of beef, and his comment at 2.36 that Egyptians were "the most excessively (θεοσεβέες δὲ περισσῶς) god-fearing of all humans." But they concede that at 2.64 Herodotus approves of the Egyptian θρησκεύοντες who did not have intercourse in temples, nor did they enter temples after intercourse without washing. ristodemus's comment on the scruples of Spartan θρησκεία is without any evaluative comment.

79 Daniel Boyarin, "Thrēskeia in 4 Maccabees," in *Sibyls, Scriptures, and Scrolls: John Collins at Seventy*, ed. Joel Baden, Hindy Najman, and Eibert Tigchelaar (Leiden: Brill, 2017), 200; Barton and Boyarin, *Imagine No Religion*, 123–7. See earlier, J.C.A. Van Herten, "θρησκεία Ἐυλαβεία, Ἱκέτης: Bijdrage tot de kennis der religieuze terminologie in het Grieks" (D.Litt thesis, Rijks Universiteit de Utrecht, 1934).

80 For example, Wis 11:15; 14:17, 27; *Or. Sib.* 8.380, 394; Philo, *Det.* 21; Philo, *Spec.* 1.315; Theophilus *Ad Autolycum* 2.1. See also Ps-Clementine, *Hom.* 2.33; 9.7; 10.22; *De virginitate* 1.3.4; Celsus, Ἀληθὴς λόγος. 3.17 (over-the-top and superstitious θρησκείαι).

81 Jan Willem van Henten, "θρησκεία in Philo and Josephus: Cult, Worship, Virtue, or Religion?" *Studia Philonica Annual* 32 (2020): 137–56.

82 Boyarin, "Thrēskeia," 211, citing Plutarch, *Conjugalia praecepta* 140D: ἀνὴρ νομίζει σέβεσθαι τῇ γαμετῇ καὶ γιγνώσκειν μόνους προσήκει, περιέργοις δὲ θρησκείαις καὶ ξέναις δεισιδαιμονίαις ἀποκεκλεῖσθαι τὴν αὔλειον. A wife ought not to make friends of her own but to enjoy her husband's friends in common with him. The gods

are the first and most important friends. Therefore, it is seemly for a wife to fear [σέβεσθαι] and to know only the gods that her husband honours [νομίζει] and to shut the outer door against all περιέργοις δὲ θρησκείαις and ξέναις δεισιδαιμονίαις.

83 Soranus 1.4.7: "She [the midwife] will be without superstition (ἀδεισιδαίμονα) so that she will not overlook what is advantageous (τὸ συμφέρον) because of a dream or omen or some customary mystery or popular (βιωτικὴ) θρησκεία."

84 A similar false etymology is attested in the Scholia to Euripides (Sch. Alc. 968 ed. Schwarz): πρῶτος Ὀρφεὺς μυστήρια θεῶν παραδέδωκεν· ὅθεν καὶ θρησκεία τὸ μυστήριον καλεῖται, ἀπὸ τοῦ Θρᾳκὸς Ὀρφέως (Orpheus first handed over the mystery of the gods, whence the mystery is called θρησκεία after the Thracian Orpheus), cited by Boyarin, "Thrēskeia," 215.

85 Boyarin, "Thrēskeia," 222; Boyarin, *Imagine No Religion*, 149.

86 See Steve Mason, "Judean War 2: Translation and Commentary," in *Flavius Josephus, Translation and Commentary*, ed. Steve Mason, 1B (Leiden: Brill, 2008), 30n260: "Josephus also favours a noun that integrates 'divine worship, ritual, cult, and piety' (*thrēskeia*) and its cognate verb 'to worship.' Though rarely used by non-Judaean writers the word group had some currency among other Judaean authors before Josephus picked it up. He found it singularly convenient for his claims about the Judaean disposition toward piety and worship."

87 Barton and Boyarin, *Imagine No Religion*, 163–77.

88 Ibid., 163.

89 Laurence Foschia, "Le nom du culte Θρησκεία, et ses dérivés à l'époque impériale," *L'Hellénisme d' époque romaine. Nouveaux documents, nouvelles approches (Ier s. a.C. – IIIe s. p.C.): Actes du colloque international à la mémoire de Louis Robert, Paris 7–8 juillet 2000*, ed. in Simone Follet, De l'archéologie à l'histoire (Paris: Éditions de Boccard, 2004), 15–35. See earlier, Van Herten, "θρησκεία Ἐυλαβεία, Ἰκέτης" and, more recently, Barton and Boyarin, *Imagine No Religion*. For the formula ἐτέλεσε πάντα τὰ περὶ τὴν θρησείαν τῆς θεοῦ, see IG XII,5 140.4–5 (Parion, III BCE) and IGRR IV 451 = IvP 525.2–3: εὐσεβῶς πᾶσαν θρησκείαν | ἐκτελέσασαν τῇ θεῷ.

90 On I.Stratonikeia 1101 = LSAM 68, see Louis Robert, *Études anatoliennes: Recherches sur les inscriptions grecques de l'Asie mineure*, Etudes Orientales 5 (Paris: Éditions de Boccard, 1937 [repr. Amsterdam: A.M. Hakkert, 1970]), 522–3.

91 SEG 44:1227.21–22 (Mopsuestia, ca 85 CE) in a letter of Sulla confirming a grant of asylum to a temple of Isis and Sarapis: τὰς θεραπε[ίας ποιού] | μενον εὐσεβεστάτας καὶ ἱεροπρεπέ[στατα τὰ τῶν] | θεῶν τείμια; I.Labraunda 61 (Labraunda, III CE) in a grant of asylum: ὡς πρό[κει]ται ταῖς θρησκείαις καὶ εὐσεβείαις τοῦ | θεοῦ; IGRR IV 451.13–14 (Pergamon, 217–218 CE) in an honorific decree for a priestess of Athena: εὐσεβῶς πᾶσαν θρησκείαν | ἐκτελέσασαν τῇ θεῷ; TAM V,1 490.2–4 (Hamadiya [Lydia], 159–160 CE): honorific decree for a priestess: οἱ καταλουστικοὶ ἐτείμησαν διά τε τὴν ἰς [τοὺς] | θεοὺς εὐσέβειαν καὶ θρησκείαν καὶ τὴν πρὸς π[άντας] | ἀνθρώπους φιλοκάγαθίαν; BE 1906, 14.6 (Aphrodisias) in a decree for a high priest; [πᾶ]σαν εὐσεβῆ θρησσκείαν εἰσενήνεκται; I.Stratonikeia 1101 = LSAM 69.6–7, 13: τῆς | δι' ὑμνωδίας προσόδου

καὶ θρησκείας εὐσεβεῖν αὐτούς ... 13 τάξιν καὶ θρησκείαν καὶ εὐσέβιαν τῶν θεῶν; I.Stratonikeia 15.8 (Stratonikeia, I CE): ποιεῖται πρὸς αὐτὸν εὐσέβειαν καὶ θρησκείαν; I.Stratonikeia 14.4–5 (Stratonikeia, late II CE): [ἐπεὶ διὰ τὸ πανηγύρεσ]ι καὶ μυστηρίοις θρησκεύεσθαι καὶ | [εὐσεβεῖν; I.Stratonikeia 174.9 (Stratonikeia, I/II CE): συνευσέβησεν κα[ὶ] συνεθρήσκευσεν τὸν θεὸν; Bean-Mitford, Journeys 1964–68 30,12(b).15–17 (Kotenna, Pamphylia, II CE): τὴν θρησκείαν δὲ τὴν πρὸς | τὸν θεὸν εὐσεβῶς καὶ φιλο[τείμως] | πάντοτε θρησκεύσας.

92 Foschia, "Le nom du culte Θρησκεία," 19, with reference to M. Linder and John Scheid, "Quand croire c'est faire: Le problème de la croyance dans la Rome ancienne," *Archives de sciences sociales des religions* 38, no. 1 (1993): 47–61.

93 In Claudius's letter to the Alexandrians (P.Lond.VI 1912.85–6; Alexandria, 41 CE), the Alexandrians are warned μηδὲν τῶν πρὸς θρησκείαν αὐτοῖς νενομισμένων | τοῦ θεοῦ λυμαίνωνται (to spoil none of their [the Jew's] customary practices for the *thrēskeia* of their god).

94 Ethnographic uses (i.e., referring to the practices of others, without a pejorative implication): Acts 16:5; Lucian, *Sacr.* 10; Antoninus Pius, *Epistula ad commune Asiae* 17; Celsus, Ἀληθὴς λόγος 3.5; 5.25 (of the Jews, who observe a θρησκείαν, ὁποίαν δή, πάτριον δ' οὖν); Chariton, Callirhoe 7.6.6 (reverence); Herodianus, *Ab excessu divi Marci* 3.10.3; 3.11.4; 4.2.2; 4.8.7; 5.3.3, 9; 5.7.2 (but Herodian in this passages describes θηρσκεία as often hypocritical); Cassius Dio, *Historiae Romanae* 49.22.5 (speaking of the excess θρησκεία of Jews during the first revolt); *Acta Scillitanorum Martyrum* §12; Sextus Empiricus *Pyrrhoniae hypotyposes* 3.220, 222, 226 (the latter where θρησκεία is contrasted with τὰ ἀσεβή); Aelianus, *De natura animalium* 10.28.3; Clement of Alexandria, Strom. 6.4.35.

95 Philo, *Fug.* 41; *Leg.* 232, 298; *Oracula Sibyllina* 8.485; Dionysius of Halicarnassus, *Antiquitates Romanae* 2.63.2; Josephus, passim; Dio Chrysostom Or. 12.25; Cassius Dio, *Historiae Romanae* 26.87.1; 45.30 and the epigraphic examples cited by Foschia.

96 For example, Philo, *Sacr.* 21–32 associates multiple virtues with ἀρετή and εὐσέβεια, including σωφροσύνη, and ἐγκράτεια and in *Sacr.* 37 argues that piety is only achieved along with devotion: εὐσέβεια καὶ ὁσιότης ἀγαθά, ἀλλ' οὐκ ἄνευ θεραπείας θεοῦ τυχεῖν αὐτῶν δυνάμεθα, θεραπεία δὲ τοῖς ἐν πόνοις φιλοτιμίαις συνέζευκται, "Now piety and holiness are goods, but we are not able to achieve these without devotion to God, and devotion is linked to zeal for hard labour."

97 Diognetus 3.1 concedes that, in worshipping one God, the Judaeans are right (καλῶς θεὸν ἕνα τῶν πάντων σεβεῖν καὶ δεσπότην ἀξιοῦσι φρονεῖν) but characterizes sacrifices, kasruth, and sabbath observance as superstitious.

98 See Philip A. Harland, *Dynamics of Identity and Early Christianity: Associations and Cultural Minorities in the Roman Empire* (London: Continuum, 2009), 172–6, with reference to Pliny, *Ep.* 10.96.7; Justin, *1 Apol.* 1.26.7; Eusebius *Hist. eccl.* 5.1.3–5.2.8; Minucius Felix, *Octavius* 8.3; 9.2–4; Tertullian, *Apol.* 8.2.

99 Lieu, "Forging of Christian Identity," 186, also points out the paradox of claiming to be a "third race" with virtually no distinguishing features.

100 Foschia, "Le nom du culte Θρησκεία," 24–5.

101 Chrysippus (*Fragmenta logica et physica*, frag. 1017); *Fragmenta moralia* 608; D.L. 7.64; Arius Didymus, *Liber de philosophorum sectis* 65 and elsewhere. Philo (*Sacr.* 37) takes the same view: εὐσέβεια καὶ ὁσιότης ἀγαθά, ἀλλ' οὐκ ἄνευ θεραπείας θεοῦ τυχεῖν αὐτῶν δυνάμεθα, θεραπεία δὲ ταῖς ἐν πόνοις φιλοτιμίαις συνέζευκται (piety and holiness are goods, but without service to God we are not able to attain them, and service [to God] must be joined to zeal for labours).

102 LXX θεραπεύω, to worship: Isa 54:17; Dan 7:10; Prov 14:17; 19:6; 29:26; 1 Esdr 1:4; Jdt 11:17; Tob 1:7; Sir 35:16; Ep Jer 25, 38.

103 Det. 55, 56: τὴν εὐσέβειαν λέγωμεν εἶναι θεοῦ θεραπείαν.

104 Justin *1 Apol.* 12.5; *Martyrium sanctorum Carpi, Papyli et Agathonicae* (BHG 294) 1, 13, 14, 15 (*tris*), 17 (*bis*).

105 Clement of Alexandria, *Paed.* 1.7.53.

106 Philo, *Leg.* 3.135; *Sacr.* 13, 118, 127; *Det.* 160; *Post.* 182; *Plant.* 60; *Ebr.* 69, 126; *Migr.* 124; *Congr.* 105; *Mos.* 2.135, 149; *Spec.* 1.309; Virt. 185; *Praem.* 43.

107 Philo, *Contempl.* passim.

108 θεραπευταί: Isis and Sarapis: IG XI,4 1062 (Delos); IG XI,4 1215 (Delos, late III BCE); ID 1417 (Delos, 155/54 BCE); ID 2077 (Delos, 119/8 BCE); ID 2079 (Delos, 115/4 BCE); I.Aeg.Thrace E182 (Thrace, II BCE); I.Aeg.Thrace E212 (Thrace, II/I BCE); IMT Kyz Kapu Dağ 1542 (Kyzikos [Mysia] I BCE/I CE); IMT Kyz Kapu Dağ 1799 (Kyzikos [Mysia]); SEG 39:229 (Athens, I CE); IvP II 338 (Pergamon, Imperial period); Isis, Sarapis, Harpokrates: ID 2081 (Delos, 94/3 BCE); Pure Aphrodite: ID 2222 (Delos, 110/9 BCE); ID 2229 (Delos, 112/11 BCE); ID 2240 (Delos 96/5 BCE); ID 2628 (Delos, 108/7 BCE); SEG 35:887 (Delos, 107/6 BCE); Sabazios: SEG 29:1205 = IK Estremo oriente 235 (Sardis [Lydia], 367/6 BCE); Zeus: Sardis 7,1 22 (Sardis [Lydia] 100 BCE); SEG 46:1529 (Sardis [Lydia] I/II CE).

109 *Cultores Iovis Optimi Maximi*: CIL 8.23326 (Africa proconsularis, late I CE/II CE); CIL 3.1602 (Magyarpeterd [Dacia], 201 CE); AE 2000, 1253 (Sarmizegetusa [Dacia], mid II–mid III CE); *cultores Iovis*: AE 1934, 66 (Hippo Regius [Africa proconsularis]; *cultores Iovis Heliopolitani Berytenses*: CIL 10.1634 (Puteoli, 115–116 CE); *cultores dei Solis*: IDR 3,2 484 (Sarmizegetusa [Dacia], III CE); *cultores dei Solis Invicti Mithrae*: CIL 11.5737 = CIMRM 1 688 (Sentinum [Umbria / Regio VI], III CE); *cultores Cererum*: CIL 8.4847 (Africa proconsularis); *cultores Dianae et Antinoi*: CIL 14.2112 (Lanuvium, 135 CE); *cultores Dianae et Mercuri*: ILAlg 2.1 2085 (Castellum Celtianum [Algeria], I–mid II CE); *cultores Fortunae*: AE 1979, 424 (Mogontiacum [Germania superior], late II–early III CE); *cultores Herculis*: CIL 11.1159 (Velleia Romana [Aemilia / Regio VIII] 131–170 CE); CIL 9.1681 (Beneventum [Apulia et Calabria / Regio II]); CIL 3.1339 = IDR 3,3 73 (Micia [Dacia], mid II–mid III CE); CIL 11.1449 (Pisa [Etruria / Regio VII]); *cultores Liberi*: CIL 9.459 (Venosa [Apulia et Calabria / Regio II], II CE); *cultores Martis Aug(usti)*: AE 1959, 172 (Mactaris [Africa proconsularis]); *cultores Mercuri*: CIL 13.4037 (Treveri [Belgica]); CIL 7.1069 (Blatobulgium [Brittania], late I–II CE); CIL 7.1070 (Blatobulgium [Brittania], late I–II CE); *cultores Minervae*:

CIL 11.1906 (Cortona [Etruria / Regio VII], III CE); *cultores Deae Sandraudigae*: CIL 13.8774 (Texuandri [Germania inferior]); *cultores deorum Serapis et Isidis*: RICIS 1, 113/1008 (Philippi [Macedonia], I–III CE).

110 *Cultores Larum et imaginum Aug(usti)*: CIL 8.17143 (Africa proconsularis); *cultores Victoriae Aug(us)torum* (i.e., Septimius Severus and Caracalla): ILS 8914 (Africa proconsularis, 196 CE) (i.e., Septimius Severus and Caracalla); *cultores domus Augustae*: CIL 8.21825 (Volubilis [Mauretania Tingitana], 157–158 CE).

111 Cyprian, *Ep*. 67.6 74.8; *De bono patientiae* 3.35; *Ad Quirinum* 3.14; *De mortalitate* 10; *Ad Demetrianum* 12, 17, 20, 21; *De habitu uirginum* 2.285 (*templorum cultores*).

112 Lactantius, *Diuinae Institutiones* 2.15.3; 5.1.6; 5.11.19; 7.26.27 (where Lactantius addresses Constantine on behalf of the *cultores dei*). As Karpp, "Christennamen," 1121 points out, Lactantius juxtaposes and contrasts the *cultores dei* with *deorum cultores* (2.1.6; 3.30.9; 4.4.5–6; 4.28.11; 5.10.15; 5.12.13; 6.13.13). Lactantius invokes the traditional Latin distinction between *religio* and *superstitio* in his explanation of the *deorum cultores*: sed quia deorum cultores religiosos se putant, cum sint superstitiosi, nec religionem possunt a superstitione discernere nec significantiam nominum exprimere (because those who worship the gods think themselves to be scrupulous, because they are superstitious they are not able to distinguish *religio* from *supersitio*, nor to explain the meaning of the terms) (4.28.11).

113 ICUR 9.24829 = ILCV 1957: Qui natum passumque deum repertisse paternas | sede atque iterum venturum ex aethere credit | iudicet ut vivos rediens pariterque sepultos | martyribus sanctis pateat quod regia caeli | respicit interior sequitur si praemia Chr(ist)i | cultores domini Felix pariterque Philippus | hinc virtute pares contempto principe mundi | aeternam petiere domum regnaque piorum | sanguine quod proprio Chr(ist)o meruere coronas | his Damasus supplex voluit sua reddere vota. (He who believes that God was born and suffered, regained his paternal home, and will come again from heaven, to judge both the living and those who those resting in sepulchers, understands that the inner reaches of the kingdom of heaven lie open to the holy martyrs, if he seeks to obtain the rewards of Christ. The *cultores* of the Lord, Felix and Philippus equally so, well matched in courageous disdain for the prince of the world, secured an everlasting home and the kingdom of the pious, because of their own blood they earned the crowns of Christ. To these, Damasus, a suppliant, wanted to repay his vow.) See also ILCV 2477a (Africa proconsularis) *Naucelius | pauperu(m) amator | cultor dei*; CIL 8.9585: (Mauretania Caesariensis): *cultor verbi*; CLEHisp 75 (Baetica, late IV–early V CE): *Pascentius ama|tor dei cultorque*.

114 A copy of The *S.C. de Baccanalibus* is available in a bronze tablet in Vienna: CIL 1^2 581.

115 See Jinyu Liu, "Local Governments and Collegia: A New Appraisal of the Evidence," in *A Tall Order: Writing the Social History of the Ancient World. Essays in Honor of William V. Harris*, ed. Jean-Jacques Aubert and Zsuzsanna Várhelyi, Beiträge zur Altertumskunde 216 (München and Leipzig: K.G. Saur, 2005), 285–316.

116 See Ilias Arnaoutoglou, "Roman Law and *Collegia* in Asia Minor," *Revue internationale des droits de l'antiquité* 49 (2002): 27–44; John S. Kloppenborg, *Ptolemaic and Early Roman Egypt* (vol. 3 of *Greco-Roman Associations: Texts, Translations, and Commentary*; contributions by Richard S. Ascough, et al., BZNW 246 (Berlin: Walter de Gruyter, 2020), 10–12.

117 D 47.22.1 (from Marcian, time of Severus): Sed religionis causa coire non prohibentur, dum tamen per hoc non fiat contra senatus consultum, quo illicita collegia arcentur. (To assemble for religious purposes is, however, not forbidden if, by doing so, no act is committed against the *senatus consultum* by which unlawful societies are prohibited.)

118 Andreas Bendlin, "Associations, Funerals, Sociality, and Roman Law: The *Collegium* of Diana and Antinous in Lanuvium (CIL 14.2112) Reconsidered," in *Aposteldekret und antikes Vereinswesen*, ed. Markus Öhler, WUNT 280 (Tübingen: Mohr Siebeck, 2011), 225. On the applicability of the s.c., see Pierangelo Buongiorno, "Riforme in tema di liceità dei collegia fra Augusto e gli Antononi," paper presented at the colloquium *La Città greco-romana: Modelli possibili per lo sviluppo dei Centre contemporanei* (Potenza: Università della Basilicata, October 2019).

119 I would like to express my thanks to Joseph Verheyden, Dietrich-Alex Koch, Matt Calhoun, Sarah Rollens, Cilliers Breytenbach, Ralph Korner, Dennis R. MacDonald, Judith Lieu, Henk Jan de Jonge, David Balch, Carl Holliday, Lars Rydbeck, Jan Willem van Henten, Dieter Roth, and Jan Bremmer for many comments and suggestions. The errors, of course, are my responsibility.

4

Theorizing Historical Moments of Religion: Paul and His Followers

Stanley Stowers

Fortunately, most of the affected areas in the academy have moved past the dark days of domination by doctrines reputedly from poststructuralism and postmodernism but having roots in German Idealism and Neo-Kantianism. Along with some areas of literary studies, the study of religion in the academy has been slower than the rest of the university to repudiate those doctrines. I agree with those who think that these postisms once had a salutary effect on awakening hidebound and uncritical areas of the academy, including the study of religion, but that they did not have the intellectual resources to underwrite positive work. In my estimation two states of affairs now prevail. Persuasive arguments have been made against the claims that "religion" is only ideological, that it only has utility as a modern Western notion, that it is only a feature of our linguistic usages, and that it cannot refer to anything that is real or outside of our minds and language.[1] Almost every area in the natural sciences, the social sciences, and many areas of the humanities have decisively renounced these sad legacies of idealism and antirealism. I argue that, like racism, economic recession, feudalism, language (*la langue*), oligarchy, and so on, religion is a real entity theorized in modern attempts at knowledge that typically does not need to be named or recognized by the societies in question to exist. Such discovered – not invented – social kinds are the very basis for the modern sciences, social sciences, and humanities.

I argue that religion forms a robust social kind. "Social kind" refers to a way of theorizing social entities in the mainstream philosophy of the sciences, the social sciences, and other areas. Two complementary approaches to social kinds have dominated: epistemic and ontological or constitutive. I do not elaborate on these here but only note that I presuppose that religion can be justified and theorized as a real entity in the world through both approaches. In my own theorization of these as applied to ancient Mediterranean religion,

I argue that four interactive sub-kinds exist.[2] On this view, religion consists of patterns of imagined human exchange with gods and non-evident beings given relative stability by human cognitive propensities and other material conditions. Historically, the most important material condition has been cognition situated in an agricultural environment. The question I raise here asks how the instances of religiosity evidenced in the letters of Paul can be theorized. Can study of the letters be a contribution to the study of religion? I can only offer the briefest outline of an answer, providing selected aspects of the theory and limited discussion of some evidence.

The sub-types of religion result from three basic inquiries: the first charts the way that human cognitive propensities promote the imagination of gods and non-evident beings; the second asks about the environments that shape those propensities; and the third asks how social practices connected to religion cluster and form networks of practices and larger social formations. The definition and ontology of religion emerges from these inquiries. The types are not mutually exclusive, and individuals and social formations can exhibit more than one mode at one time. Indeed, they are usually interactive but still tend to maintain some integrity. The cognitively and socially most basic of the types, upon which the second and third types depend, is the religion of everyday social exchange. The second, for convenience, I call "civic religion," the religion of cities, kingdoms, priestly aristocracies, and similar formations controlled by elites who shape religion according to their interests as the self-proclaimed guardians of the religion of the whole population in question. The third mode arises from competitive and highly interactive fields of semi-independent literate religious experts who write, interpret, and teach complex texts, such as narratives and law.

The religion of everyday social exchange features approachable deities and similar non-evident beings such as local gods, the beloved dead, the familiar heavenly bodies, angels, demons, ghosts, divinized humans, spirits, vaguely identified agents, "high gods" imagined as local, and many others. Participants believe that these beings affect their lives in personally relevant and tangible ways, such as giving humans the offspring of animals and plants, children, weather, health and illness, help and hindrance with the contingencies of life, and so on. Humans in turn want to build and maintain positive long-term relations with the beings most relevant to their lives. Humans intuitively feel that many of these normally unseen beings that are most relevant to life are naturally open to alliances and even to entering into complex practices of human-like social exchange, but with key differences from humans in that these beings can see what people are doing while the reverse is not normally the case. Many of them have very great powers and abilities. Such beings who inhabit the world of cause and effect behind the scenes of everyday life normally do not need the gifts that people offer to them, but they take pleasure in them and in sharing human pleasures, in acts and relationships of honour, of gratitude and recognition. Some ancients thought of these beings as serving under a high ruling god, but that did not eliminate the everyday and local qualities intrinsic to this religiosity. Any approach that treats the ancients as if they lived in our disenchanted world with a distant theoretical god rather than in a day-to-day environment filled with palpably present but normally unseen beings is, I would argue, a massive distortion. This type of religiosity does not require cities, temples, priests, books, or literacy, but it can exist in and alongside these formations. Three sorts of practices are central to the religion of everyday social exchange: divinatory practices, prayer, and kinds of exchange ideally based on gift-giving. We moderns can scarcely imagine the importance of divinatory practices and their constant role in everyday life.[3]

In the second mode – civic religion – divinatory practices were also important and deemed essential for the life of cities but, in contrast to the mundane religion, usually occurred in highly controlled contexts (such as public animal sacrifice) belonging to aristocrats and elites (such as established oracles and specialist diviners or prophets). Unlike the certain pronouncements and clear messages of the literate experts with their world of texts, these divinatory messages usually came in modest signs and traces or in dreams and visions. Also, unlike the experts, the practitioners of mundane religiosity treated knowledge about the moods and intentions of gods as usually limited and often, but not always, difficult to determine with regard to the conduct of everyday coping – a kind of epistemological modesty. Households, farms, workshops, neighbourhoods, and the activities of daily coping and common life-courses were the premier sites of everyday religion. The ubiquitous and most well known way of communicating with gods was prayer, and prayer often accompanied the giving of gifts to gods, which was the centre of the imagined social relation of reciprocity between unequals.

The central sites of religious production in civic religion were temples and similar "sacred" spaces with associated practices related to calendars of festivals, processions, spectacles and entertainments for the gods, and so on. This religion entailed the sacralization of time that punctuated lives with special religious days. Temples collected, redistributed, and consumed mostly agricultural goods produced on land centred on households. Civic religion thus tied itself structurally to the agricultural economy and the religion of everyday social exchange. It also enforced a structural opposition in that temples and sacred spaces had to be free from the pollution of childbirth, death, and other pollutions intrinsic to the lives of households and families. When someone prayed a votive in a civic temple – "If my crops flourish, I will give you a sheep" – mundane religion connected with civic religion. If the god fulfilled the request, the person would offer the animal at an altar with a civic priest perhaps getting the animal's hide and some meat. Of course, the farmer did not have to go to a civic temple in order to carry out a votive exchange, and civic temples were often not open to the general public.

The production of the semi-autonomous literate religious experts consisted of intellectual practices related to literate forms of cultural production. The expert's products were writings; textual techniques; learned interpretations; position-takings about what is true, just, and good; narratives; forms of teaching and transmitting knowledge; all taking form from existing literary and literate traditions. Such production, in contrast to that of civic religion and everyday religion, was separate from the agricultural economy and its products. The writer's study could be anywhere and writings could circulate anywhere. A kind of *atopia* characterized the dynamics of the mode, together with a complex cultural economy. Experts accrued social capital rewarded in various often non-obvious ways. While mundane religiosity sprang from intuitive cognition as extensively studied in the cognitive sciences,[4] as did much of civic religion, the literary experts depended heavily upon reflective and rationalizing thought that was not intuitive and was difficult to acquire and hold without the technical and social machinery of high literacy. The relative stability of the social kind known as religion only happens when the imagination of exchange relations (e.g., reciprocal gift giving, obedience/reward) with gods comes about, partly due to the shaping of a particular environment.

Most scholarship on Paul's letters seeks to describe his thought or theology. Some approaches emphasize his biography, with admittedly limited evidence. Much of this writing seeks to detail precursors of, influences on, and social or cultural contexts for his thought and biography. The individuals and assemblies addressed in the letters also receive analysis, usually in terms of how well they took to Paul's "gospel" or as bits of social history. None of these standard approaches can add much if anything to our understanding of what religion is and how it works in particular historical moments. Towards these latter aims, I propose beginning with the environments for the religiosities of Paul and his addressees. If we can find a particular pattern of exchange with gods significantly shaped by an environment, we will bring to light a historical instance of religion. My thesis holds that, just as the environment that sustained the religion of everyday social exchange and civic religion was the ancient agricultural economy, so the sustaining environment for the formation of Christianity was the field of literate and intellectualist cultural production in which "mind goods" replaced agricultural goods in patterns of reciprocity and other exchanges with the gods.

Elsewhere I discuss a field of literate intellectualist activity for the early Roman Empire,[5] but Kendra Eshleman provides a rich trove of detail about that field with an insightful analysis of its dynamics in *The Social World of Intellectuals in the Roman Empire: Sophists, Philosophers, and Christians*.[6] She writes about how these categories were highly contested forms of claimed identity on the part of those competing in the same world of intellectual production. That field's approach to identity formation, Eshleman states:

> equates group membership with attendance and full participation in the group's defining activities. As a result, each group's boundaries were continuously reasserted and renegotiated through decisions about which persons to admit and which to exclude. The implicit notion that the "circle of sophists" or the worldwide church was coterminous with those participating in classrooms, declamations, or worship services around the Empire is obviously fantastic. Attendance at those activities was not and could not be restricted to group members, however defined, nor for the most part would our subjects have wanted it to be, especially on the narrower conceptions of expert status.[7]

The central structure of the field consisted of the expert in some area of knowledge who, for convenience, I call "the teacher," surrounded by a circle of those who were or who aspired to be experts. The circle ranged from "students" to peers of the teacher. A more variable and shifting number of consumers of the discourses, writings, discussions, performances, and rites of the teacher and their circle consisted of individuals who did not aspire to become experts but were attracted to (some of) the teacher's products. Whereas associations typically had a relatively fixed number of members (seen in the many surviving lists), social formations in the field formed variably around the leadership and "performances" of teachers. The teacher, circle, and non-expert insiders partly defined themselves by patterns of recognition. What other teachers did *x* teacher and the circle recognize as legitimate? This question was the basis for networks of communication, for the exchange of writings and other products. These dynamics also make sense of why sophists, philosophers, and Christian experts attempted to contest and control the organization of their field niches by constructing lines of succession back to founding teachers.[8] The whole structure was obviously unstable and driven by competition for the prestige that gave social and even economic capital to the experts.

Our sources for the field in the Hellenistic age and the early empire have come down to us in a highly distorted way as the literature preserved and transmitted by literate Christians and the classicizing movement ("Second Sophistic"): those who won. Most of the "lower literature," "unorthodox," and writings from ethnic subfields (e.g., Lydian, Judean) has been lost. But we have enough evidence to envision a large complex field with a variety of interacting subfields. Sophists, philosophers, and Christian experts (eventually mostly clergy and bishops) differed from those in other areas of expertise (e.g., astrology, medicine) in that the areas of knowledge to which they aspired were broad, even aiming at being comprehensive (history, cosmology, the nature of the gods, rites for the gods, literature, classical Greek culture, traditional Judean writings, morality, ideal sociality, futurism). Experts, for instance, did not treat "the Greek Bible" as narrowly about something called religion but, rather, as a divinely produced compendium of knowledge about the world.

Perhaps the most important large-scale dynamic of the field was its tension between actors on the one side, who were largely independent of institutional location and legitimacy, and those on the other side, who were not – a semi-autonomous pole and a less autonomous pole both of which varied by degree on various scales. The poles shaped the field in that the sides partly defined themselves against each other. The most autonomous would be like the Cynic philosopher who had no possessions and rejected marriage, traditional religion, and conventional social roles and obligations, much like Jesus in the Synoptic Gospels and Q.[9] The Cynic life aimed to be free of social positions of the household and city, including the religion of everyday social exchange and civic religion, with their inherent norms and obligations.[10] The true Cynic was only to be guided by knowledge regarding the true nature of God, who was demeaned by gift-giving, statues, and temples.[11] Zeno the Stoic had none of those rites and objects in his ideal city (Diogenes Laertius 7.33). Later Stoics said that the true beliefs about the divine were the preserve of the wise but that traditional rites could be understood as symbols of those truths. Most Judeans who wrote in Greek adopted a philosophical God that they read into their holy writings and, like the philosophers, made connections with morality and immorality.[12]

Christians adopted this semi-autonomous-pole stance against the traditional norms already pioneered by the Judean writers, and they equated philosophical notions about gods with the concepts of idolatry, the moral depravity of society, and anti-superstition – that is, with opposition to civic religion and the practices of everyday religiosity. Sophists, as in Philostratus's "Second Sophistic," celebrated and defended the traditional religion of cities and Greek ethnicity, attacking the more independent philosophers as charlatans and radicals. Those on the opposite pole said that thinkers like the sophists had sold out to power, vanity, wealth, and convention. Still Philostratus, like his fellow sophist Lucian, could also idealize autonomous pole philosophers – in the former's case, telling the story of Paul's itinerant contemporary, Apollonius of Tyana.

If the patterns of exchange with gods and non-evident beings conceived in intuitive ways (e.g., human-like, local, palpable, approachable) central to the existence of the everyday religion and civic religion involved reciprocal gift-giving utilizing goods from farm and field, then what kind of exchange characterized the literate experts? The details and degree of distance from conventional views of religion promoted by literate experts was great, but several positions are illustrative, including the following.[13] There can only be one God in charge of the universe, the top and final power and organizing principle or being. Immortal gods do not need or find pleasure in petty human gifts such as food, drink, entertainment, or even praise. Cultic acts are kinds of bribery that only dishonour gods/God. God's nature is to be invisible, and physical representations degrade the respect due to him (philosophical aniconism).[14] God is not in a particular physical place. God's true nature is distorted by treating him as human-like, with a body, emotions, the need to travel, and on and on. God has ordered the universe to favour the good, the true, and the just. Humans can only respect God and his nature by being morally good and seeking truth. Proper exchange with God only involves mind goods, which were created to foster these principles. God rewards those whose entire lives follow what is good.

Intellectuals developed such ideas in numerous ways and to various degrees made accommodations with traditional conceptions. The field debated such ideas through writings and speeches. Even sophists sometimes resorted to allegorizing traditional views and valorized more conservative philosophers as products of Hellenic civilization.[15] Paul, I believe, like many Judean intellectuals, struggled to balance the views that he found compelling or confirmed by holy writings (e.g., idolatry, aniconism, God's moral order and perfection) with the highly anthropomorphic and morally questionable depictions in much traditional scriptural and Judean writing. He certainly valorized mind goods for his gentiles.

With this breezy sketch of the field as the environment shaping a religiosity distinct from but interacting with mundane religiosity and civic religion, we can ask whether the letters of Paul bear evidence of those field dynamics. First Thessalonians chapter 2 is a good place to begin. In a celebrated but greatly understated article, Abraham Malherbe shows how Paul positioned himself among others as a teacher in that part of the letter.[16] I go over some of his striking evidence in order to show that it cannot simply be coincidental. Highlighting details also makes the standard approach to 2:1–12 look absurd. Although the letter trumpets Paul's highly positive relation to "the Thessalonians," who had turned from idols to the true God to await Christ's return (1:9–10), the verses in chapter 2 supposedly show that these same people had accused him of being "useless"; afraid to enter "the struggle" like a serious teacher; only willing to speak with those who already agreed with him; having the goal of deceiving them to get money, fame, and sexual gratification by using flattery; lacking courage and boldness in speaking with the result that his teaching work was in vain. This is mirror reading gone wild.

Malherbe focuses on Dio Chrysostom's (40–c. 120 CE) Discourse 32 at Alexandria but points out that the literary versions we now have of speeches given at Tarsus (33), Olympia (12), and Celaenae (35) also show him attempting to define himself in their *proemia* as a certain type of speaker or philosopher over against others. Dio should be of great interest for a number of reasons. He was a famous sophist but claimed that exile had awakened him to the life of an itinerant Cynic philosopher. Thus he represents the interaction of the two opposing poles of the field. His life also crosses the boundary of the mythic and magical age of the New Testament into the second century, a boundary that historians must seek to treat critically.[17] One mythic theme about the first century tells of an intellectually and culturally virginal movement in which the power of the gospel message sprang not from human wisdom but directly from God through illiterate apostles of Jesus, himself ambiguously literate, and Paul, who disdained human wisdom. Only in the second century did Christian thinkers corrupt this innocence by courting philosophy in order to make the faith intellectually respectable.

In an antithetical style (32.11–18), Dio enumerates several types of philosophers, especially Cynics, to whom he contrasts his approach. First, he is not like resident philosophers who served select patrons and households (32.8) instead of teaching more broadly. They are "useless," like athletes who will not *join in the contest*. Second, there are lecture hall philosophers who only teach selected students who have already agreed to accept the message, such as Musonius, Epictetus, and Demonax. Eshleman shows how teachers in the field worried over these issues.[18] Again, Dio thought that such teachers had opted out of the *contest* to help humanity. Third are those belonging to the type of Cynic satirized by Lucian. They flatter people in order to collect money instead of speaking with the *frankness* that people need. Their motivations are *money, fame, and sensual pleasure*. Fourth are the would-be philosophers who are hard to distinguish from sophistic-like orators. Their entertainment speeches are *empty* and *vain*, having no substance. They do not *benefit* their audiences. The fifth type is the famously harsh Cynic who confuses true *frankness* with railing against humanity's sinfulness. Elsewhere (Or. 77/78.42) Dio expands his criticism of this harsh type of teacher and contrasts blanket castigation of human evil with *admonition*, which involves *frank criticism* and *gentleness*. In the latter combination, the teacher adapts his methods to individual needs and conditions. Malherbe then shows that various types of philosophers and sophists discussed these issues and that some used the image of the *gentle nurse*.

For the sake of efficiency and clarity, I simply italicize the English translation of the striking number of key Greek words and concepts that Dio and Paul share, and share in the course of making the same points. Readers can find the Greek terms in the Malherbe article. Paul did not fear the *violence* of the audience; his teaching was not *in vain*, but he spoke with *frankness* (1 Thess 2:2). He is engaged in a great *contest* (or *struggle*), here using a favourite Cynic term. Paul does not teach to *deceive* or out of *error* (2:2–3). He was not motivated by *impurity* or *guile*. He did not act from *greed* or seek human *reputation* or to *flatter* his audiences (2:5–6). Both Dio and Paul claim that their teaching is divinely directed (2:4). Rather than simply being *harsh*, Dio says that the teacher should adapt to the condition of each individual and be gentle as a nurse. Paul writes that he worked with each person individually (2:10) and was *gentle as a nurse* not *harsh* (2:7).

Chapter 2 does not find Paul defending himself against a long list of charges against him by the Thessalonians but shows him describing his teaching ideal, which he claims characterizes his preaching to those people. He draws this sketch in a way that shows his embeddedness in the field of intellectualist and moralistic expertise. The large number of substantive, linguistic, and rhetorical similarities that Malherbe demonstrates with Dio and other figures in the field cannot be accidental. Paul and his audience were highly conscious of the field of literate experts. Placing Paul in the field of contestation undermines our intuitive but anachronistic categories of Judaism, Christianity, and Paganism, which we habitually use exclusively to make sense of Paul and his letters. Recognition of Paul's high level of self-consciousness expressed rhetorically regarding his manner and method as a teacher, and his expectation that those he is addressing would share the concerns, opens the theological blinds covering his cultural location and the primary mode of his religiosity.

THE LETTERS AND FEATURES OF THE FIELD

In the briefest way, I reinforce my claims by noting some features of the letters that reflect the intellectualist field. When later in the second century Celsus looks at the Christian movement his eyes see numerous contending schools of thought, with circles of teachers, students, and non-expert followers. He describes these self-proclaimed experts and their followers as would-be but woefully inept philosophers whom he compares to low-class and poorly educated Cynics (e.g., Origen, *Cels.* 3.12).[19] Celsus was a Platonist philosopher partly shaped by the "Second Sophistic." The very fact that he spent so much time learning about Christian groups and considered the movement worthy of refutation shows that he saw it as attempting to contend in the field of intellectualist expertise. Otherwise, he would have had no reason to write a major work against it. I enumerate major field features as suggested by Celsus.

1 The driving force of the field and of the formation of Christianity was composed of experts in areas of knowledge (scripture, God's plans, desired behaviour, Christ's effects and plans, evil), usually with circles of peer experts, "disciples," and followers "consuming" the teachings and practices of the experts without wanting to become experts themselves. The expert/non-expert divide was a key social feature of the field. Circles spawned networks connecting like-minded experts. Paul's companions and fellow workers, such as Barnabas, Silvanus, Prisca, Apollos, Timothy, and Titus, were peers in Paul's circle. Paul's so-called churches or Christ-gatherings consisted of non-expert consumers of Paul's goods.
2 The goods of these circles were cast in terms of true knowledge. Knowledge about the gods, their roles in human life, and how to act towards them were central truths among philosophers, sophists, and the Christ movement. By way of contrast, truth and the explicit formulation of true knowledge was not important in everyday and civic Mediterranean religiosity. The wife, son, master, and slaves of a Roman household did not focus on discussion of the true nature of the house's Lares, or what ancient book authorized their rites, or what was the "real" underlying meaning of those mundane practices. Their religiosity was not characterized by the messages of contending teachers who had broken into sects, each arguing a different truth about the Lares.

3 The social processes of seeking knowledge and truth, including of the good, the just, and sometimes the beautiful, entailed the social dynamics of competition. Teachers with circles and non-expert followers constantly fractured, formed, and reformed around claims of possessing the genuine truth. The field consisted of competing teachers and circles that sometimes attempted networking with or condemning others. All of the letters except Philemon contain attacks on or criticisms of teachers and/or teachings that Paul views as competing with his teachings.

4 A high degree of self-authorization characterized the field. The authorizing practices and institutions for becoming a modern professional – for example, teacher, doctor, lawyer – begin in first grade and end in advanced professional education, and involve various accrediting and disciplining organizations. In antiquity, one might appeal to one's teacher or a lineage of teachers, but there were no certifying institutions until the late antique consolidation of the Church hierarchy. The teacher had to argue for her or his own credentials. Such rhetoric characterizes speeches and writings from the field. First Thessalonians 2:1–12 finds Paul in one of his many arguments about his credentials. He is somewhat odd in that, given the chance to establish a succession from Jesus through the apostles to himself, he refuses. Rather, God was his teacher (1 Cor 1:18–2:16; Gal 1:11–2:10).[20] His message and his knowledge come directly from God, Christ, and God's *pneuma* (poorly translated as "spirit"). He argues that direct revelations, his teachings, his methods, and his powers provide evidence to legitimize him as a teacher. Figures in civic religion – such as a Judean priest in the Jerusalem temple, or a priestess of Artemis, or a mother in everyday religion who tended household Lares – did not need self-authorization.

5 The stance of the intellectualist experts entailed critique of traditional religion. Because the field traded in truth claims and true propositions rather than simply involving what one's ethnicity, city, or family did to achieve their practical and local goals (such as good crops, health, and prosperity), truth about the gods was typically contrasted with falsehood about them. While sophists on the more conservative pole of the field held up the ideal of a classical Greek (or Roman) past as the measuring stick, philosophers tended to argue that the religion of everyday social exchange and the city was fundamentally wrong.[21] Philosophical critique of the religion of everyday social exchange has

come down to us moderns distortedly packaged as the critique of superstition, and the critique of civic religion has come down as the criticism of the poets (myth) and of anthropomorphizing the divine. Judean intellectuals writing in Greek claimed to have found these critiques in their traditional writings and developed versions that scholars have long seen echoed in the letters of Paul and other Christian writings.[22]

6 Social kinds endure through time and get socially reproduced because they possess relatively stable clusters of cognitive, social, and environmental features. At the centre of the cluster for religion one finds some sort of imagined exchange with gods and other non-evident beings. In the ancient Mediterranean and much of the world, animals and agricultural goods, seen as given by the gods, were the most important gifts offered back as food offerings. The field, with its urban practices, broke from the agricultural environment's imagining of exchange with the divine. In the religiosity of the literate experts, especially on the less conservative pole, true exchange required different conceptions of the gods, which entailed offering mind goods instead of agricultural and other mundane goods. Paul, for instance, after excoriating the non-Judean peoples for false iconic worship (supposedly of the creation instead of the creator) and the ensuing moral depravity (Rom 1:18–32), caps off the worship theme in Romans 12:1–3. The gifts that God wants are cognitive and moral: "Offer your bodies as a living animal offering (*thusia*), holy and well-pleasing to God which is your rational worship. And do not be structured by this age, but be transformed by the renewal of your mind so that you might test for what is the will of God." Mind goods have replaced agricultural goods.

7 The field and the Christ movement took a social form that possessed a division between experts (later the clergy) and insider non-experts (the laity), each with differing relations to the religion of everyday social exchange and its intuitive religiosity. Mundane religiosity did not simply disappear from Christianity but remained an area of contestation that conditioned the relation of experts to non-expert insiders.[23] The expert identity was inherently totalizing. Truth applies everywhere all of the time. There were no part-time sophists, philosophers, or Christian experts in the sense that other domains of life could be allowed equal value. For a Philostratus, a Zeno, a Paul, an Ignatius, or a Tertullian their identity as a purveyor of their particular truth and domain of knowledge trumped all other claims

on them. The expert on the more autonomous pole of the field was, in theory, always to teach and live by the non-intuitive intellectualizing doctrinal mode of religiosity.

8 The experts typically write about the non-expert Christ followers (our only sources for them) in this way: they are God's people and are to live lives totally dedicated to the truth, but many are false followers, defectors, and fail to live up to that total commitment. Critical scholarly reading of this rhetoric shows that non-experts often did not accept "following the truth" as totalizing, and they adapted many practices advocated by the experts to their own local and intuitive religion of everyday social exchange.[24] The Corinthian acceptance of the man in 1 Corinthians 5:1–5 and the practices of baptism for the dead (1 Cor 15:29) and speaking in tongues may possibly have been their own practices interpreted according to their own religiosity. And as Paul seems to indicate (e.g., 1 Cor 5:1, 6), they probably did not feel like they had to follow his strictures or interpretations. Such resistance might have been multiplied when the interested non-experts formed (or had previously formed) themselves into an association.[25] The patronage by non-experts that supported freelance and clerical life was both a necessity and a genuine and an oft-expressed existential threat to the autonomy of the experts.[26]

I bring this discussion to a conclusion by saying a bit more about three areas of evidence for the field dynamics in the letters: competition, self-authorization, and Paul's non-expert followers. In view of their length, the letters spend many words arguing for the legitimacy of what we can roughly characterize as his teaching methods, although, in a way, this is closely connected with his message.

Several books have been written about the opponents mentioned and implied in Paul's letters.[27] Scholars have viewed these books as the key to reading the letters because the conditions of the conflicts between Roman Catholics and Protestants in the sixteenth and seventeenth centuries have been read into the letters, with Paul usually taking the Protestant side. This history so naturalized battles over theological slogans that it seemed the right thing to find some Reformation-era theological position behind each opponent mentioned or supposedly implied in the letters. Placing Paul in the field of literate and intellectualist competition provides a much needed antidote to this anachronism. Eshleman, for instance, in *The Social World of Intellectuals*, handily shows that the same dynamic of splintering into competing groups, circles, and networks characterized philosophers and sophists. This can be said for other areas of literate knowledge, such as medicine, juristic learning, and astrology.

I limit myself to two points: the opponents given some substantive description in Paul's letters are Judean, from a Judean subfield, but his writing also possesses a more general ethos of field-like competition. Philippians 1:14–18 presents a good example of this last point: "Some proclaim Christ from envy and strife, but others from goodwill ... some out of selfish ambition, not from pure motives, but thinking to increase my suffering in prison." Paul thinks of competition as the context of his work. And the competitors, or at least the ones relevant to the letters, are other Judeans who are fellow experts in the knowledge and truth of the Christ movement. He expects that other literate experts will have different views that might well be convincing to his non-expert "students": "If someone comes preaching another Jesus different from the Jesus we preached, or you receive a different *pneuma* (spirit) from what you received, or another good message to which you did not assent, you accede all too easily (2 Cor 11:4)."

In addition to conflict over issues of message, matters of teaching methods and motives loom large. The major issue among philosophers, and sometimes sophists, regarding how teachers should finance themselves haunts many pages of the letters.[28] Paul defends his taking of money and support and calls certain opponents "peddlers of God's word" (2 Cor 2:17). Skill in speaking ability relative to competitors also looms large and is sometimes connected with educational credentials.[29] 1 Corinthians begins (1:10–17) with Paul bemoaning affiliations with various teachers, including Cephas and Apollos, that cause divisions among the non-expert followers. Everyone should just be loyal to Christ, which seems to mean being loyal to Paul's teaching and leadership. Paul contrasts himself as a purveyor of God's wisdom to human wisdom and eloquent oration (1:18–2:5). This highly allusive rhetoric makes concrete identification of the teachers that Paul is opposing impossible, but he makes them sound like practitioners of philosophy and sophistic rhetoric. Some commentators have thought that Apollos is the target.[30]

As noted above, we possess much evidence of a vigorous and extensive subfield of Judean literary production that had strong connections to the main philosophical and sophistic field of Greek writing. The Judean attack on "idolatry," false ideas about God, and immorality was highly developed in classical Greek genres.[31] Paul's letters and other early Christian literature show clear connections to this arena of intellectualist production. But a basic principle of intellectualist competition applies: the most vigorous debates and competitive activities arise with those who are closest to one's own positions. The socially elite figures who made up the so-called Second

Sophistic, even when writing about religion, were too distant from a Paul or an Apollos to be direct competitors. The same would probably be the case for someone like Philo of Alexandria. But a peer of Paul's in the Christ movement who was not in Paul's circle and had different ideas about methods and the message would have been a competitive threat. These are the kind of opponents seen in the letters.

Paul begins his self-authorization as a teacher in 1 Thessalonians 2 by noting the suffering and mistreatment that he had endured (2:2). Nevertheless, he and his fellow workers taught with boldness, used frank speech, and considered their enterprise to be "a great competitive contest" (2:2). He then continues: "For our appeal does not come from impure motives or deceit" (2:3). Paul is claiming that his willingness to endure suffering proves his motives as a teacher and legitimizes his activity and character. This appeal to sufferings and the endurance of hardships forms a major characteristic of philosophical discourse in Paul's era, and the use of hardship lists is an important rhetorical feature. Paul's letters abound with such rhetoric, the lists of and appeals to his sufferings.[32] One famous example must suffice. In 2 Corinthians, chapter 11, Paul contends against people he calls "false apostles," "super apostles," and boasting false apostles (11:5, 13) in an explosion of emotional rhetoric. "Apostle" here does not mean one of Jesus's twelve disciples as the writer(s) of Luke and Acts later tried to make it.[33] "Apostle" means one who is or claims to be an expert teacher in the Christ movement marked by the itinerant travel characteristic of that field. Evidently at least some of the Corinthians had been giving a hearing to other teachers and had not committed themselves to Paul and his teachings. Without institutional mechanisms for inclusion and exclusion, rhetorical power and personal arm twisting were the means for group formation around particular teachers. In the hardship list (2 Cor 11:22–9), like certain kinds of philosophers, Paul makes a case for his greater authenticity and virtues of endurance.

> Are they Hebrews? I am also. Are they Israelites? I am too. Are they seed of Abraham? So am I. Are they servants of Christ? As out of my mind, I am talking over the top – I am a better one: with far greater labors, far more imprisonments, with innumerable beatings, and often at death's door. Five times I received from the Jews the forty lashes less one. Three times I was beaten with rods. Once I was stoned. Three times I was shipwrecked, with a night and a day on the deep; on frequent journeys I was in danger from rivers, from bandits, from my own people, from non-Judeans, in the city, in the wilderness, at sea, from false brothers; in labor and toil, in many nights without sleep,

> hungry and thirsty, often without food, cold and naked. And apart from the external things, I am under daily pressure because of my anxiety for all the gatherings. Who is weak, and I am not weak? Who stumbles, and I am not indignant?

CONCLUSIONS

The way that we moderns think about religion, with doctrines, educated professional clergy, long-term plans of salvation, official moral teachings, true religion of the heart and mind, and so on, should not be generalized. Those assumptions about religion have a history and that kind of religion had beginnings. But the beginnings in the ancient Mediterranean did not result from the intervention of the simply new and unique. That religiosity was the result of social and cultural dynamics with long histories in the Mediterranean and west Asia. In the case of Christianity, and similarly in patterns of religiosity across China and South Asia, the religiosity developed by freelance literate experts eventually acquired institutional power that limited the autonomy of the experts and gave institutionally empowered experts the ability to rule entire populations of non-expert insiders.

The letters of Paul display the earliest evidence for Christ followers with social characteristics in that freelance mould – but again, not as detached and novel. The field of intense competition about truth and knowledge crossed boundaries that we designate as Greek, Judean, Roman, and Christian. One might say that the freelance field dynamics ran wild in the Christian case. The movement was also thoroughly embedded in cultures inhabited by everyday religiosity and the religion of cities and peoples in two major ways, the first negative. For the Christ movement, with its organization around intellectualistic practices developed from the Judean subfield and the more autonomous pole of philosophy, truth, and knowledge, took a form antithetical to the everyday religiosity and civic religion of the ancient Mediterranean and West Asia. Part of its constitution was that it was not the other. The Christian movement declared a culture war on the religious heart of ancient Mediterranean society. Second, the central structure of the movement maintaining a boundary between expert and non-expert members produced a dynamic of tension, sometimes instability, a two-level ethos, and constant accommodation to aspects of intuitive religiosity on the part of the experts. These dynamics arose largely from the difference between the difficult doctrinal religiosity taught by the experts and the intuitive religiosity of the non-experts. The letters of Paul are already witness to the social dynamics of a distinctive but not unique religiosity featuring the exchange of "mind goods" that would characterize Christianity, but with resistance from the everyday religion of the non-expert followers well evident.

NOTES

I offer this piece in gratitude for Steve Wilson in recognition of his deep generosity and pioneering leadership.

1 For example, Kevin Schilbrack, *Philosophy and the Study of Religions: A Manifesto* (Oxford: Wiley Blackwell, 2014); Stanley Stowers, "The Ontology of Religion," in *Introducing Religion: Essays in Honor of Jonathan Z. Smith*, ed. Willi Braun and Russell T. McCutcheon (London: Equinox, 2008), 434–49. A further development of my theory is found in my *History and the Study of Religion: The Ancient Mediterranean as a Test Case* (Oxford: Oxford University Press, 2024).

2 Stanley Stowers, "The Religion of Plant and Animal Offerings versus the Religion of Meanings, Essences and Textual Mysteries," in *Ancient Mediterranean Sacrifice: Images, Acts, Meanings*, ed. Jennifer Knust and Zsuzsanna Varhelyi (New York: Oxford University Press, 2011), 35–56; Stowers, "Why Expert versus Non-Expert Is Not Elite versus Popular Religion: The Case of the Third Century," in *Religious Competition in Late Antiquity*, ed. Nathaniel DesRosiers and Lilly C. Vuong (Atlanta: Society of Biblical Literature, 2016), 139–53; Stowers, "Why 'Common Judaism' Does Not Look like Mediterranean Religion," in *Strength to Strength: Essays in Honor of Shaye J. D. Cohen*. ed. Michael L. Satlow (Providence: Brown Judaic Studies, 2018), 235–55; Stowers, "Locating the Religion of Associations," in *Re-Making the World: Christianity and Categories – Essays in Honor of Karen L. King*, ed. Taylor G. Petrey (Tübingen: Mohr Siebeck, 2019), 301–24.

3 Jennifer Eyl, *Signs, Wonders, and Gifts: Divination in the Letters of Paul* (New York: Oxford University Press, 2019), 46–85.

4 David Slone, *Theological Incorrectness: Why Religious People Believe What They Shouldn't* (New York: Oxford University Press, 2004).

5 Stowers, "Religion of Plant and Animal Offerings"; Stowers, "Expert versus Non-Expert"; Stowers, "Common Judaism"; Stowers, "Religion of Associations." See also Heidi Wendt, *At the Temple Gates: The Religion of Freelance Experts in the Roman Empire* (New York: Oxford University Press, 2016).

6 Kendra Eshleman, *The Social World of Intellectuals in the Roman Empire: Sophists, Philosophers and Christians* (Cambridge: Cambridge University Press, 2012), 259.

7 Eshleman, *Social World of Intellectuals*, 259.

8 Eshleman, *Social World of Intellectuals*, 179–87, 191–210, 243–57.

9 John L. Moles, "Cynic Influence upon First-Century Judaism and Early Christianity?," in *The Limits of Biography*, ed. B. McGing and J. Mossman (Swansea: Classical Press of Wales, 2006), 89–116.

10 William D. Desmond, *The Greek Praise of Poverty: Origins of Ancient Cynicism* (Notre Dame: University of Notre Dame, 2006).

11 P.R. Bosman, "Traces of Cynic Monotheism in the Early Roman Empire," *Acta Classica* 51 (2008): 1–20.

12 Emma Wasserman, "Philosophical Cosmology and Religious Polemic: The 'Worship of Creation' in the Writings of Philo of Alexandria and the Wisdom of Solomon," *Journal for the Study of the Pseudepigrapha* 31 (2021):6–28.

13 Harold Attridge, "The Philosophical Critique of Religion under the Early Empire," *Aufsteig und Niedergang der römischen Welt* II.16.1 (1978): 45–78; Bosman, "Traces of Cynic Monotheism"; Wasserman, "Philosophical Cosmology and Religious Polemic."

14 One type is seen in Antisthenes: "God is not known with an image, is not seen with the eyes, resembles no one" (*SSR* 7 Fr. VA 181 G [Gabriele Giannantoni, *Socratis et Socraticorum Reliquae*, 4 vols., Naples, 1990]). Translations are my own.

15 Lucian provides an excellent example. He excoriates most Cynics and other philosophers but holds up Nigrinus the Platonist and Demonax the Cynic as ideal philosophers.

16 Abraham Malherbe, "'Gentle as a Nurse': The Cynic Background of 1 Thess ii," *Novum Testamentum* 12, no. 2 (1970): 203–17.

17 William Arnal, "The Collection and Synthesis of 'Tradition' and the Second Century Invention of Christianity," *Method and Theory in the Study of Religion* 23 (2011): 193–215.

18 Eshleman, *Social World of Intellectuals*, especially 21–66.

19 Joseph R. Hoffman, *Celsus: On the True Doctrine: A Discourse against the Christians* (Oxford: Oxford University Press, 1987), 70; cf. 89–97.

20 Stanley Stowers, "The Dilemma of Paul's Physics: Features Stoic-Platonist or Platonist-Stoic?," in *From Stoicism to Platonism: The Development of Philosophy 100 BCE–100 CE.*, ed. Troels Engberg Pedersen (Cambridge: Cambridge University Press, 2017), 231–53.

21 Attridge, *Philosophical Critique of Religion.*

22 Wasserman, "Philosophical Cosmology and Religious Polemic."

23 There is now much scholarship on the tendency of non-expert religious people to turn expert thought in unorthodox intuitive directions (e.g., Slone, *Theological Incorrectness*).

24 Stanley Stowers, "Kinds of Myth, Meals and Power: Paul and the Corinthians," in *Redescribing Paul and the Corinthians*, ed. Ron Cameron and Merrill P. Miller (Atlanta: Society of Biblical Literature, 2011), 105–50; Caroline Johnson Hodge, *"My God and the God of This House": Christian Household Cult before Constantine* (University Park: Pennsylvania State University Press, forthcoming); Éric Rebillard, *Christians and Their Many Identities in Late Antiquity* (Ithaca: Cornell University Press, 2012); Ramsay MacMullen, *The Second Church: Popular Christianity: AD 200–400* (Atlanta: Society of Biblical Literature, 2009).

25 John S. Kloppenborg, *Christ's Associations: Connecting and Belonging in the Ancient City* (New Haven: Yale University Press, 2019).

26 Eshleman, *Social World of Intellectuals*, 77–8, 92, 97–8, 100–2, 113–22.

27 For bibliography and critical discussion, see Wendt, *At the Temple Gates*, 168–74, especially 171n99.

28 Eshleman, *Social World of Intellectuals*, 48, 51, 81, 83, 117–18, 122; Wendt, *At the Temple Gates*, 179–89; E.P. Sanders, *Paul: The Apostle's Life, Letters, and Thought* (Minneapolis: Fortress Press, 2015), 140–4, 183–4.

29 Sanders, *Paul*, 246.

30 Ibid., 240–9.

31 Sean Adams, *Greek Genres and Jewish Authors: Negotiating Literary Culture in the Greco-Roman Era* (Waco: Baylor University Press, 2020).

32 I cannot get into this large topic but refer readers to John T. Fitzgerald, *Cracks in an Earthen Vessel: An Examination of Catalogues of Hardships in the Corinthian Correspondence* (Atlanta: Scholars Press, 1988).

33 Sanders, *Paul*, 99–100.

5

Response: Religion as a Category of Study

Willi Braun

In a learned and charming essay Tomoko Masuzawa sets out "to consider the dominant paradigm that governs our customary thinking about religious diversity today, or what I am inclined to call more generally the pluralist regime for organizing and regulating difference."[1] Prefacing her analysis of "how this regime may have come into prominence in the course of the last few centuries" is this modern example:[2]

> Observers of the academic scene in the United States pertaining to the study of religion would doubtless recognize a curiously twinned structure of the field, represented by two learned societies that seem to couple and decouple on various occasions, engage and disengage regularly, and not infrequently quarrel. These two bodies, the American Academy of Religion (AAR) and the Society for Biblical Literature (SBL), are not symmetrical either in size or in scope. As with any deeply entrenched division of long standing, moreover, they do not agree on the nature of the difference that divides them. That said, one way of characterizing this division that might be deemed relatively uncontroversial may be that the former organization claims or aspires to be global and pluralistic in the coverage of the subject, whereas the latter is essentially monocentric, if not also centripetal, in the sense that it is focused on a particular legacy, namely, the biblical – broad, expansive, and diversified though it may be within itself.[3]

The reasons for this estrangement are likely multiple. Masuzawa's accounting of the panoramic of the troubled entanglement and estrangement between biblical studies and the general study of religion is undoubtedly correct, even if incomplete. It may also be that the two old fields of study cannot convincingly articulate "the difference that divides them" and hence are unable to negotiate an end to it. Then, too, the term "religion" marks a modern concept that has its own histories that do not continuously proceed from some ancestor of the concept of religion in antiquity. Modern religion is a precipitate of the secularization of higher learning, which took place in the early modern period. Religion, it is claimed, cannot be used without qualification as the sum designation for what early Christians believed and practised. Doing so risks inventing unwarranted equivalencies between now and then and, more insidiously, drawing genealogical lines between an imagined original Christianity (*Urchristentum*) and modern Christianities – with many resulting iniquities (see John Kloppenborg's chapter in this volume). And so biblical scholars are in the main not interested in the study of religion writ large.

All this is true, but it does not mean that religion should not be used as a designation or as a name given to a range of human practices in the ancient Mediterranean and Near East, nor does it mean, especially, that biblical studies are not religious studies. Although biblical studies predate, and thus are ancestral to, the general study of religion, this is not an argument for the isolation of biblical studies from religious studies, nor from the humanities and social sciences in the modern university. On the contrary, the synergy between the two fields has been well documented.[4] For example, Julius Wellhausen drew on comparative Semitic philology, his specialized field, to make lasting contributions to biblical studies and the study of Islam. Similarly, William Robertson Smith "used the same philological learning to write classical theoretical works that are still influential on contemporary students of religion."[5] So, despite the long and detailed "definitional casuistry" surrounding the term,[6] it forms the disciplinary horizon for biblical studies and studies of the religions of Mediterranean antiquity and west Asia. "Biblical studies are religious studies."[7] This is both an acknowledgment and a mandate for biblical scholars and scholars in the general study of religion. The three scholars in this section of the book at least implicitly take Smith's claim that "biblical studies are religious studies" for granted – with varied but equally remarkable results.

Christine Mitchell's chapter, entitled "Inventing Religion in Elephantine: Judeans and Egyptians under Persian Hegemony," theorizes by means of demonstration what can be achieved with religion in a particular historical and social moment. The story very briefly goes as follows. In the fifth century BCE in Persian-period Egypt on an island in the Nile was the town of Yeb (known to us as Elephantine). It was a garrison town of the Achaemenid Persian Empire. The Judaean group at Yeb consisted of mercenary soldiers (and their families), tasked with internal town security and border control. There is some evidence of rituals performed that identify the group as Judean – "a family-oriented observance [of Pesach] of flexible date or time" (21); by Persian imperial decree, the celebration of a Festival of Unleavened Bread at a fixed date and time, which may have been designed to override by conflation the Pesach celebration; a temple and priesthood dedicated to the deity Yaho; keeping of the Sabbath; swearing oaths by Yaho. Next to the Yaho temple on the "Street of the King" stood the Egyptian Khnum temple and its devotees at Elephantine. It was larger than the Yaho complex, but less is known of its history, usage, and community practices.

How was religion "invented" at the two temples at Elephantine? To answer this question, Mitchell uses David Chidester's *Empire of Religion*, a material history of the study of religion on the colonial frontiers in Africa, in order to examine how knowledge and practice of religion was produced in the various mediations between imperial, colonial, and indigenous forces. This provides her with analogies for the construction of religion in the contest between royal, imperial interests, and the colonial subjects in Elephantine. Then, she relies on Bruce Lincoln's polythetic model of religion. In this model, religion, so often a fuzzy and broad category, is a human social and political performance rather than something consisting of personal and interior qualities.[8] It is a vehicle primarily for imposing legitimacy and authority on moral and aesthetic preferences that constitute a group as a group and a culture as a culture.[9] Lincoln's definition of religion allows Mitchell to use it as a model of analysis of the evidence concerning the relations between the Yeb communities and the Achaemenid imperial authorities. At the level of discourse – communication and instructions – the Achaemenids asserted royal authority and "insert[ed] Achaemenid interests into the religious discourse" (29). Imperial authority in various ways was used to regulate the community's worship practices and in the appointment of priests. "In sum," writes Mitchell, "the imperial construction of Judaean religion at Yeb was pervasive and all-encompassing" (31). The Achaeamenids constructed religion "in a way that placed all discourse, practices, and community in subjection to the institution of imperialism" (32). Mitchell's chapter is a great example of looking at even a very fragmentary set of material evidence from antiquity through a theoretical apparatus that disaggregates religion to more precisely and cogently see its working in a particular historical context. The chapter is also a fine example of what questions to ask of the evidence she investigates. Assuming that all discourse is at some level an exercise in persuasion, who is doing the persuading and with what means?

To whom is it directed? And what are the consequences if the persuasion should succeed or fail?[10]

In "Second-Century Constructions of Christianity," John Kloppenborg sets out to document with dazzling drudgery (divine, of course) and thoroughness the change of self-defining terms by Christ believers from the first to the second century. He prefaces the enterprise with several cautions. The first one arises from Edwin Judge's question, "was Christianity a religion?" In agreement with Judge and recent scholarship on the history of the term "religion," Kloppenborg disavows the term as descriptive of early Christ believers and of cultic practices in antiquity generally. Kloppenborg writes, "The idea of 'early Christian religion' is not only retrojection of the *taxon* of 'religion' onto antiquity but it also had another role: to create fictive continuities between then and now, where it has played a critical role in the wars of religion, encouraging one to assess the truth and validity of more contemporary expressions of Christianity against a hypothetical construction of *Urchristentum*" (37). Also deriving from Judge is the question how "Christianity" would have been perceived by members of the cults of other deities, lacking, as it did, "the apparatus typically associated with the cults of other deities" (37). Earliest Christ groups lacked not only statues, temples, bloody sacrifices, and so on but also "vocabulary typical of cultic groups," for example, θρησκεία and εὐσέβεια, which appear in the Christian documentary record only from the second century (37). Finally, taking an assist from William Arnal's ground-breaking argument that "original Christianity" did not begin in the first century, but with second-century attempts to synthesize first-century "traditions" into an imagined Christian identity, Kloppenborg sets aside the oft-criticized conceptual category *Urchristentum* as an expression of "an original and authentic form of the Jesus movement that could be employed as the measure of all that came thereafter" (38).

The expanse of Kloppenborg's chapter is then devoted to an exhaustive examination of first-century terms of identity and second-century semantic markers of Christianity. He notes that, in the first century, "Christ followers used a mixture of idiosyncratic terms as well as terms that were not obviously those of cultic associations" (38). Among those routinely used was "brothers," a familial term that continued to be used into the third century. Another self-ascription was the nominal participle οἱ πιστεύοντες (those who trust, or those who are loyal) to a deity.[11] In Q, the Synoptics, John, and Thomas (and other texts) μαθηταί (disciples, apprentices, learners) is a frequent self-designation. This, together with the "rather unparalleled term ἐκκλησία" (41) as the dominant collective self-designation, suggests that Christ followers of the first century tended to think of themselves in school terms or, in Judge's terms, a "scholastic community" (41). All this is not to say that first-century Christ devotees displayed no cultic qualities, as Kloppenborg notes, but that they prevailingly "failed to adopt the most obvious semantic markers of cultic associations" (42), and "that much of the language typical of cult associations is missing in first-century Christ groups" (42).

In the second century Kloppenborg notes "important terminological transitions" that had "an impact on how Christ groups understood themselves and were understood by others" (42). He notes the appearance of the term Χριστιανοί, a term likely coined by outsiders to mark political partisanship, the "Christ partisans," suggesting that the term "Christ" was taken as a proper name instead of a title (43). Kloppenborg shows that the term *Christianoi* was problematic for Christ groups; left unqualified the name implied that Christ followers were a political faction. Thus, the name was intentionally qualified "by focusing on its identity as a cultic association" (46). When he asks about terms that "offer the clearest signs of cultic orientation" (46), Kloppenborg, focusing on second-century literature ostensibly addressed to outsiders, identifies several strategies of amplifying Christ groups' cultic leanings. He finds metaphorical usage of cult terms (spiritual *oikos*, holy priesthood, spiritual sacrifices) designed (especially in 1 Peter) to distance "Christians" from the view that they might be political factions. Then he demonstrates that, in the second century, Christians began to import cultic language with greater density to portray Christ groups as cultic associations and not political factions. This is when the terms εὐσέβεια and θρησκεία appear, which "Christian authors of the second century use ... to characterize the Christ followers as participating in a cult" (51). Combined with the use of other terms, Christ groups had moved rather decidedly into the realm of legitimate cults of the gods, "and by the third century, as a competitor to all of them" (52).

Kloppenborg provides an exhaustive ethnographic description from an internal or emic point of view, or from the native point of view, across a century and a half of time. He makes it clear that the modern category of religion is neither descriptively nor analytically helpful in talking about early Christ groups; indeed, the history of scholarship has shown that the anachronistic use of the term has been harmful. Edwin Judge's question, "was Christianity a religion?" is allowed its point but not its vocabulary – indeed, in large part Kloppenborg's chapter is an answer to the question. Also to be noted is Kloppenborg's care in translations of Greek and Latin terms in order to rid them of modern theological meanings. While there is no doubt about the appropriateness of avoiding anachronisms in our terms and concepts, properly qualified, there is much to be gained in Bruce Lincoln's polythetic definition of religion, as Christine Michell shows, or Stan Stowers's ontological definition of religion. Both are eminently useful for comparing religion across history and cultures, and so religion's utility for studying ancient religions goes beyond a dismissible modern Western idea.

This is in so many ways a foundational chapter for further study of the transition of the early Christ groups from the first century to the second and later centuries. For example, Kloppenborg, acknowledging Judge, notes that there is some "heft" to seeing the early Christians as a scholastic community. Then, one may recall the observation of Peter Brown on the later Christian attraction to the older model of the διδασκαλεῖον: "Small study-circles were the powerhouses of the second and third centuries. The extraordinary intellectual ferment of the period is unthinkable without them."[12] It might be useful, among other things, to identify the transitions from a first-century model of Christ schools to the second-century Christ groups and their intellectual and scholastic activities.

Stanley Stowers's "Theorizing Historical Moments of Religion: Paul and His Followers" looks at Paul and his followers in order to determine if they belong to a specific, determinable "social kind" that can appropriately be applied to the ancient Mediterranean context. Foundational for his argument that "religion forms a robust social kind" (69) is religion's ontology. Very simply put, the claim that religion is ontological is the counter-idealist claim that religion exists as a real entity as a subset of the social in the world.[13] As such, religion does not need to be invented to exist. Stowers emphatically renounces views that religion "is only ideological, that it only has utility as a modern Western notion, that it is only a feature of our linguistic usages, and that it cannot refer to anything that is real or outside of our minds and language" (69). As a social kind, then, "religion consists of patterns of imagined human exchange with gods and non-evident beings given relative stability by human cognitive propensities and other material conditions" (70).

He identifies three types or modes of religion as a result of three kinds of inquiries: What are the human cognitive propensities that promote the imagination of gods and other non-evident beings? What environments shape those propensities? How are social practices connected to religion clusters? The types are to some extent heuristic. They are not exclusive of each other, and social formations can exhibit more than one type. The first type is the religion of everyday social exchange, which features a range of non-evident beings. Importantly, this form of religiosity does not require cities, temples, or literacy. A second religiosity Stowers calls "civic religion," the religion of cities, kingdoms, priestly aristocracies, and the like that shaped and guarded religious practices according to elite interests. The third type is the product of "competitive and highly interactive fields of semi-independent literate religious experts who write, interpret, and teach complex texts, such as narrative and law" (70).[14] These experts engaged in "intellectual practices related to forms of cultural production" (72). Importantly, their production was not dependent on the other two modes of religiosity, though it interacted with them, often competitively, but outside or on the margins of established orders such as priesthoods or institutions. Their "study could be anywhere and their writings could circulate anywhere" (72). Stowers extensively discusses the characteristics, the field marks, say, of the field of literate and intellectualist cultural production,[15] and argues that it was the "sustaining environment for the formation of Christianity" (72) just as the ancient agricultural economy was the sustaining environment for the religion of everyday social exchange and civic religion.

His chapter focuses on Paul as an illustrative example. Noting that none of the standard scholarly approaches to Paul and his letters "can add much if anything to our understanding of what religion is and how it works in particular historical moments" (72), little is lost and much can be gained by placing Paul and his addressees into a particular pattern of exchange with the gods that characterized the social field of literate and intellectual production. It is not possible here to provide even a thumbnail sketch of the results of this shift in the study of Paul. I highlight only some of the major results of his theory and how this guides Pauline studies. First, Paul is here radically dislodged from mainstream Pauline studies and recontextualized within the competitive social world of the independent literate experts. Second, Stowers reorganizes the Mediterranean world in such a way that the exhausted "religions" classifications – Judaism, Christianity, Gnosticism, Pagan, and other subcategories – are no longer of primary theoretical or analytic use. This is not to say that "ethnic coding" was not a technique used by free-lance intellectuals, including Paul.[16] Third, Stowers's reclassification of ancient Mediterranean religions into "social kinds" replaces the under-theorized "religions of the ancient Mediterranean." Fourth, Paul and his addressees are here placed within the domain of religious experts, in competition with other such experts but also entangled with the fields of everyday social exchange and civic religion. Fifth, as Stowers demonstrates, aspects of Paul's letters can best be explained in terms of that competition. In all, he shows that Paul's letters can indeed be theorized in a new way that can be foundational for novel and exciting studies. He also wonders if the study of Paul and his letters can contribute to the study of religion. I want to note that this is the first time in recent history that a biblical scholar has asked the question and made a remarkable attempt to answer it positively. Reading the three chapters here summarized allows stating with emphasis that "biblical studies are religious studies" indeed!

NOTES

1 Tomoko Masuzawa, "Striating Difference: From 'Ceremonies and Customs' to World Religions," *Republic of Letters* 3, no. 3 (2014): 1–25. PDF available at ROFL_v4_Masuzawa_0428_final.pdf. Accessed 29 September 2012.

2 Ibid., 1.

3 Ibid.

4 For example, Jonathan Z. Smith, "Religion and Bible," *Journal of Biblical Literature* 128, no. 1 (2009), 5–27.

5 Ibid., 6.

6 Rogers Brubaker, *Ethnicity without Groups* (Cambridge: Harvard University Press, 2004), 7, 11.

7 Smith, "Religion and Bible," 9.

8 The components or domains of Lincoln's model are: (1) a discourse that claims its interests transcend the human, temporal, and contingent, and that claims for itself similar transcendent status; (2) practices that are structured by that discourse; (3) a community that constructs its identity with reference to the discourse and its attendant practices; (4) an institution that regulates discourse, practices, and community. See Bruce Lincoln, "Culture," in *Guide to the Study of Religion*, ed. Willi Braun and Russell T. McCutcheon (New York: Cassell, 2000), 416. For an illustrative example of how to adapt this model to ancient and post-ancient religions, see Bruce Lincoln, "Epilogue," in *Religions of the Ancient World: A Guide*, ed. Sarah Iles Johnston (Cambridge: The Belknap Press of Harvard University Press, 2004), 659–65.

9 See Lincoln, "Culture," 416: "What religion does – and this, I submit, is its defining characteristic – is to invest specific human preferences with transcendent status by misrepresenting them as revealed truths, primordial traditions, divine commandment and so forth."

10 See Bruce Lincoln, "How to Read a Religious Text: Reflections on Some Passages of the Chāndogya Upaniṣad," *History of Religions* 46 (2006), 127–39.

11 Kloppenborg notes that *hoi pisteuontes* should not be translated as "the believers," which implies belief in a proposition rather than "the embrace of a relationship of loyalty or trust" (39).

12 Peter Brown, *The Body and Society: Men, Women and Sexual Renunciations in Early Christianity*, Lectures on the History of Religions NS 13 (New York: Columbia University Press, 1988), 104.

13 "A good account of religion's ontology would be an antidote for what one might call naive idealism," writes Stowers in "The Ontology of Religion," in *Introducing Religion: Essays in Honor of Jonathan Z. Smith*, ed. Willi Braun and Russell T.

McCutcheon (London: Equinox, 2008), 434. Ontology in Stowers's work is not a metaphysical ontology. "Ontology can be an anti-essentialist project" (434), as is his.

14 For an analogous model of three types of religiosities in Mediterranean antiquity, see Jonathan Z. Smith, "Here, There, and Anywhere," in *Relating Religion: Essays in the Study of Religion* (Chicago: University of Chicago Press, 2004), 323–39.

15 For greater detail and more extensive argument, see Stowers's other work (listed in the bibliography of his essay), along with Kendra Eshleman, *The Social World of Intellectuals in the Roman Empire: Sophists, Philosophers and Christians* (Cambridge: Cambridge University Press, 2012); and Heidi Wendt, *At the Temple Gates: The Religion of Freelance Experts in the Early Roman Empire* (Oxford: Oxford University Press, 2016).

16 See Wendt, *At the Temple Gates.*

SECTION TWO

Undoing Text

The five chapters in this section all struggle, in their different ways, with textuality as a real social phenomenon. The data for each paper are predominantly textual, but instead of treating text as an ideal object that stands on its own content, texts are treated as active creations and interventions into a complex social world. Chapter 6 looks at the way celestial beings in biblical texts (Ezekiel, Revelation) are – or are not – classified as "monsters." Chapter 7 explores the self-conscious use of texts as divinatory instruments by the author of the Gospel of Matthew. Chapter 8 explores the references to the "Gospel of the Hebrews," a "text" we do not actually possess, to argue for caution in making links between non-extant texts and hypothetical communities. Chapter 9 links textual strategies with social objectives in the *Epistle of Barnabas*. Chapter 10 explores textualization as a strategy for processing trauma by the author of the Gospel of Mark. A response to these contributions (chapter 11) concludes the section.

6

Monsters, Hybridity, and Text: A Cautionary Tale

Heather Macumber

By their very nature, monsters are indefinable creatures that break boundaries by regularly containing opposing spectrums in one body. The quest to understand the monstrous has expanded greatly in the last few years, as reading texts for their monsters has moved from the periphery to the centre.[1] This chapter employs monster theory as a critical lens to read a culture and their texts through their monsters.[2] As a discipline, it naturally lends itself well to comparative studies of monsters from all over the world and a variety of different time periods. Scholars working on monsters in ancient Jewish and Mediterranean cultures cast a wide net by drawing into conversation traditions from Egypt, Mesopotamia, Ugarit, and Greece. This type of comparative work brings great opportunity but is also fraught with tension. Or as Bruce Lincoln remarks, "comparison is never innocent."[3] The tendency to privilege biblical material as unique is prevalent, often elevating it over other cultures.[4] Comparisons are self-selected and often represent both the overt and unacknowledged biases of the interpreters.[5] This is of particular concern when approaching hybrid divine beings in biblical texts when those most closely associated with the heavenly sphere are excluded from the category of the monstrous by interpreters.[6] Finally, the tendency to over-generalize is always present, noting similarities while dismissing differences that complicate one's analysis.[7] These issues have plagued comparative work in biblical studies, and I propose they also apply to the examination of monsters.

With these cautions in mind, I contend that a clearer understanding of the multiform body in the ancient Mediterranean world illuminates similar fantastic composite creatures in biblical texts. This chapter focuses on the hybridity of the living creatures/cherubim of Ezekiel and John's Apocalypse as indicative of their participation in the category of the monstrous despite their heavenly origin. Interpreters of Revelation have often categorized composite bodies differently depending on whether they are predetermined as "good" or "evil" mainly based on their appearance and cosmic origin. Hybrid creatures that originate in heaven receive labels such as wondrous and good while their counterparts in the abyss or cosmic sea are deemed ugly, demonic, and/or evil.[8] Select examples of composite creatures from the ancient world confirm interpreters' views that the monster is evil and deformed when only more malevolent models are used. Popular monsters include the Ugaritic Lotan, Babylonian Tiamat, and Greek Typhon, all of which bolster understandings of hybridity as a sign of impurity and malignance. However, ancient monsters cannot be contained to such a limited paradigm as they act either benevolently or malevolently depending on the context or the myth in question. One could posit that some creatures act more impartially, like Cerberus, who, though fierce and dangerous, simply fulfills a function to guard a boundary against invaders (Hesiod, *Theog.* 767–74). After examining the ambivalence of the hybrid monstrous form, this chapter assesses how more benevolent hybrid Greek figures like Pegasus and Cheiron challenge assumed binaries governing treatments of the monstrous and present an alternative to current understandings of biblical hybrid beings.

THE AMBIGUITY OF MONSTERS

Monster studies is sweeping in scope as it encompasses numerous fields, historical periods, and an enormous range of media, including literature, film, epigraphy, and art. In contrast to traditional forms of biblical studies, it is less interested in drawing on lines of influence or origins. Rather than primarily seeking genealogical comparisons or relationships, it is self-aware with regard to its own intellectual exercise. Monster theory seeks to read the body of the monster as a way of understanding a culture, viewing the monster as a cipher or a symbol.[9] The term "monster" immediately presents a challenge as its Latin root *monstrum* is related both to *monere*, meaning, "to warn," and *monstrare*, meaning "to demonstrate."[10] These definitions are subsequently projected both backwards and forwards upon cultures regardless of their own localized ways of identifying and labelling the monstrous. This is true of Greek literature in which a variety of terms are used to indicate a monster, including: *teras* (something that is unnatural), *pelor* (unnatural bulk or excess), and *therion* (wild beasts), among others.[11] However, a term like *teras* also functions more broadly to indicate deformity (as in births), marvels, omens, and it can even signify nonsense.[12] In other instances that lack specific linguistic referents, one might only discover a monster via the horror or awe experienced upon its arrival. A multiplicity of descriptors and designations for fantastic creatures likewise characterizes the Hebrew Bible, which results in conflicting ideas of what constitutes a monster.[13] Although one scholar has recently stated: "Other divine beings – angels – are guilty of category violation," he concludes that they "are not strictly monsters."[14] The wide range of terminology and lack of specific marker for the monstrous complicates identification, leaving it up to the interpreter to decide who is included or excluded from the category.

Monsters are essentially "the other," and they challenge the boundaries of the human world either in their physical bodies or abilities to move across time and space. Etymological studies of the term *monstrum* also preserve their ambiguous character as signs or warnings rather than simply reducing them to an "evil" being.[15] This nuance is not always apparent in studies of fantastic biblical creatures as an artificial boundary is traditionally maintained between the "good" divine beings and the "evil" entities.[16] Identifying Daniel's beasts (Dan 7) or John's dragon (Rev 12) as monsters is commonplace; however, making room for heavenly creatures like angels or cherubim in the category of the monstrous is considered more suspect. A deep divide remains for some interpreters between creatures found in heaven and those that originate in the abyss or cosmic sea, despite their similarly composite presentations. This partly rests on the assumption that monsters are associated with chaos and disorder, whereas gods are the bringers of order. Yet Ezekiel's cherubim are identified neither as good nor as evil; instead their primary role is to serve the heavenly realm as guardians and conduits of the divine.[17] The rogue cherub of Ezek 28 is a reminder that their destructive potential always remains a threat.[18] Furthermore, it is the living creatures of Revelation, along with the Lamb, that initiate much of the chaos of the Apocalypse by calling on the four riders who inaugurate a series of disasters on earth (Rev 6:1–8). Though the term "judgment" might be employed as a means of legitimating the violence, it is not possible to divorce the living creatures from the disorder experienced by the arrival of the four riders. Both in Ezekiel and Revelation, the cherubim/living creatures partake in traditional monstrous categories as hybrid and liminal beings that act as a warning against trespassing cosmic boundaries.

ABJECTING THE UGLY AND GROTESQUE

Hybrid bodies are one key indicator of the monstrous. Other features include the ability to metamorphosize between states, the tendency to be supersized, and a penchant for taboo eating habits. Each of these markers is an example of boundary breaking, whether it be the crossing of species in one body or the ability to morph between liminal zones and states.[19] Despite efforts to definitively analyze and categorize the monstrous, it should be recognized that monsters by their very nature challenge such attempts. Hybrid beings perceived as disgusting are the easiest to stamp with the label of the monster. Their composite bodies typically include components of phobic animals (e.g., serpents, wild animals, insects) and are presented as predatory towards humans or the divine order.[20] The language of horror and abjection is employed by interpreters who view the monster through the lens of impurity and category violation. The unsettling Dragon and hybrid beasts in Rev 12–13 fit into this narrative as they pose a threat to John's community and the heavenly regions.[21] Their otherness is reinforced by their indescribable bodies, and their origin in the cosmic sea places them squarely in the familiar role of the antagonistic sea monster.

However, the opposite is also true – that anomalies can amaze rather than disgust. One might be more familiar with the abjected monster that is relegated to the abyss or the sea, but numerous fantastic beasts are revered and maintain a central position. Scholars that solely approach hybridity with the mindset that it implies a failure or a lack of wholeness are not adequately accounting for hybridity in the divine beings that they privilege. For example, the composite nature of the living creatures of Ezekiel is acknowledged, but they are traditionally placed in different categories from other hybrid beings. Daniel L. Smith-Christopher labels the beasts of Dan 7 as "mixed monsters" and Ezekiel's living creatures as "amazing figures," arguing that the latter differ too much to be considered monstrous.[22] His main criterion for this differentiation is that the features of these "amazing figures" are usually accompanied with descriptions of precious stones, fire, or metals.[23] While the living creatures are associated with burnished bronze (Ezek 1:7), Smith-Christopher does not account for their other perplexing hybrid components, which incorporate a human form with wings, human hands, and straight legs that end in soles like a calf (Ezek 1:5–12). The strangeness intensifies as the creatures also have four faces and later are closely associated with wheels that contain eyes all around (Ezek 1:15–21; cf. 10:9–14). Their connection with the divine throne room has effectively domesticated them despite the accepted status of their ancient Near Eastern and Mediterranean equivalents as monsters.[24]

A common justification for the exclusion of heavenly composite figures from the category of the monstrous is an appeal to the binary of chaos versus order. The monster is assumed to be a chaos creature whose body is an incomplete and disordered confusion of elements. Smith-Christopher alludes to this binary in his reflections on monster theory:

> Finally, is it wandering too far under the influence of postcolonial and Monster Theory to wonder if mixed creatures suggest phenomena literally *opposed to God's creation and authority?* Is this why they are monstrous? God created regularity and discrete creatures – and we have seen that peace is even represented on occasion as these same discrete creatures returning to an Eden-like *created coexistence. Mixing is thus thought to be "counter-creational"?* Perhaps it is a threat because it is a violation. This may further suggest why it is contrasted against other amazing creatures in the same literature, but creatures that are on "our side." *However, "our" creatures are never mixed, they simply display features of value like precious stones, or power, like fire!*[25]

Hybridity is viewed as a violation and a challenge to the assumed orderliness of creation – leaving little room for the equally terrible and wondrous aspect of the monster. This line of reasoning is followed by some Revelation scholars who also exclude John's living creatures from the category of the monstrous. James L. Resseguie draws firm boundaries, stating: "Whereas the demonic creatures signify God's creation in total rebellion from its creator, the four living creatures symbolize God's creation in complete harmony with its creator."[26] In this sense, the monstrous is only equated with those creatures deemed opponents of the heavenly realm, effectively muting equivalent monstrous beings aligned with God. Hybridity in this scheme is treated differently depending on the predetermined view of the interpreter regarding their valuation of the divine creature in question. Thus, the same criterion of hybridity problematically signifies both chaos (i.e., anti-creation) and order (i.e., harmony with creation) rather than serving as a common indicator of the monstrous regardless of the text or interpreters' interests.

ASSUMPTIONS: WHOLENESS VERSUS HYBRID

The root of this binary division between fantastic hybrid beings rests partially on Mary Douglas's "holiness/wholeness paradigm," derived from Leviticus.[27] The external completeness or perfection of an animal or individual is considered a reflection of their status as holy.[28] Douglas's work is influential in the study of the monstrous as it, too, emphasizes the crossing of boundaries – especially concerning issues of disgust and impurity. Her axiom "Hybrids and other confusions are abominated" functions for many interpreters as an obvious invective of the monstrous body that rejects normal boundaries.[29] This holiness/wholeness paradigm is adopted by scholars to read the composite bodies of monsters, particularly those deemed malevolent.[30] However, Douglas's appropriation of this model to the divine world is not as clearly delineated, and she acknowledges the ambivalent position of biblical cherubim in Israel's cosmogony.[31] The sharp boundaries one expects from Douglas's paradigm are further complicated by the paradox of finding typically unclean items sacralised in ritual: "Then suddenly we find that one of the most abominable or impossible is singled out and put into a very special kind of ritual frame that marks it off from other experience. The frame ensures that the categories which the normal avoidances sustain are not threatened or affected in any way. Within the ritual frame the abomination is then handled as a source of tremendous power."[32] Douglas is not speaking about divine bodies specifically but signalling the perplexing elevation of that which is often abjected in sacred contexts. This echoes her statement elsewhere regarding monsters: "They can be judged very auspicious. Alternatively, they can inspire horror, aversion, disgust."[33] In this instance, Douglas's nuance provides an opportunity to explore the paradoxical alignment of the abhorrent with the sacred, whether this is part of a religious ritual or descriptive of divine bodies.

In her discussion of dirt "as matter out of place," Douglas acknowledges the persistent existence of anomalies when societies develop systems of classification.[34] An effective way to neutralize the threat of difference is to rename it, thereby reducing its power to disturb.[35] Although the cherubim and living creatures thoroughly fulfill the characteristics of a monster, they are regularly renamed with descriptors like "amazing"[36] or simply "divine."[37] This domestication of the cherubim is accompanied by a tightening of the binary between order and chaos. If monsters are only associated with impurity in this system, then the cherubim's close connection with the divine throne room is aligned with order – specifically, that of creation. This assumed equation of nature with "the pure and uncontaminated" is questioned by Margrit Shildrick who notes that it is equally "deeply disruptive and uncontrollable."[38] For instance, a sense of horror mixed with awe is not uncommon upon witnessing aspects of nature that challenge notions of it as orderly. In her book, *Pilgrim at Tinker Creek*, Annie Dillard records a "monstrous and terrifying" experience when she witnesses a water bug drain the innards out of a frog until its skin was "formless as a pricked balloon."[39] A similar unsettling quality of nature is highlighted in God's elevation of Leviathan and Behemoth in the book of Job as extraordinarily dangerous but beautiful monsters (Job 40–1). These beings are unexpectedly not removed from nature but retained "as astonishing presences in the cosmos."[40] Thus, their very category-breaking nature is a catalyst to expand a narrow understanding of how chaos is incorporated into the created world.

POSSIBILITIES: HYBRIDITY RECONSIDERED

Rather than automatically assuming hybridity implies "disgust" or "evil," this section adopts the suggestion of J.Z. Smith to "redescribe" through comparison with examples drawn from Greek literature.[41] Arguments that hybrid beings are "counter-creational" leave little room for exploring the monstrous body of the cherubim traditionally deemed benevolent. Rather than emphasizing the sharp distinction between hybrid creatures based either on their location (heaven/abyss/sea) or perceived character (benevolent/malevolent), the use of monster theory levels the playing field. This is not a genealogical endeavour aiming to draw direct connections between any of these Greek deities to composite creatures in ancient Jewish texts; instead, the goal is to understand more broadly how hybridity is portrayed in the ancient world, especially in the Greco-Roman texts, to counteract recent approaches to hybridity in biblical material. Specifically, I investigate two examples of divine beings, Pegasus and Cheiron, that, despite their obvious hybridity, are viewed either positively or ambivalently. These two characters, one subservient and the other a deity, demonstrate an alternate perspective on the hybrid and monstrous body.

Hybridity as a means of describing Greek gods is prevalent in both texts and art, especially painted pottery. Examples of deities include the river god Acheloos (man-faced bull), Triton the sea god (human and fish), Cheiron the centaur (human and horse), Glaukos (merman), Pan (human and goat), and Proteus (merman), among others. On vases, more familiar goddesses like Artemis, Athene, and Nike, though mainly humanoid, are also depicted as winged. In addition to hybridity as a fixed state, other deities can also shift between human and animal states through the process of metamorphosis.[42] Not least of these includes Zeus, who frequently transforms into a bull, a swan, or even a shower of gold in his relationships with human women (Ovid, *Metam.* 6.103–13). Numerous heroes, like Heracles, Perseus, and Achilles, are the offspring of mortals and gods, themselves hybrids and extraordinary humans.[43] Additionally, hybridity is a common characteristic of creatures typically labelled as monstrous, including: the Gorgons, the Sphinx, the Sirens, the Minotaur, and the god Typhon. Scholars from various disciplines have noted the discomfiting closeness of gods and monsters despite tendencies to exclude benevolent divine beings from the label of the monster.[44] This thin (or non-existent) line between god and monster is reminiscent of J.Z. Smith's identification of the "proximate other," in which difference is noted most prominently between "near neighbours."[45] He further notes that difference involves "a hierarchy of prestige ranking," reinforcing the fact that comparison is not a neutral enterprise.[46]

Even within the same divine family, the older generation of the Titans are remembered negatively as deformed and threatening hybrids, while the newer Olympians are found in more familiar anthropomorphic representations. Similar distinctions are maintained between fantastic hybrids, as the Chimaera is considered more "frightening" than Pegasus "because lions and snakes are more dangerous than horses."[47] This differentiation embedded in the texts privileges the perspective of the new Olympians, who overthrow the earlier generation of "monstrous" gods. To adopt the stance of the narrator uncritically continues the "othering" of the older deities while ignoring or missing the monstrosity of the favoured Olympians. Despite the largely anthropomorphic character of the Olympians, there is slippage in the texts as their "otherness" cannot be completely concealed. In the *Homeric Hymn to Aphrodite* (168–95), the goddess Aphrodite initially hides her divinity from Anchises until she reveals and overwhelms him with her "unearthly beauty, superhuman stature, and a kind of radiance or luminescence."[48] The typical response to unveiled encounters with Greek deities is astonishment, but, unfortunately, direct divine interaction can also be deadly, as experienced by Semele.[49] Zeus's metamorphosis into a dizzying array of animals (i.e., man-bull, lion, panther, serpent) during intercourse with Semele shields her from his overwhelming and dangerous divinity (Nonnus, *Dion.* 7.319–43). Semele, persuaded by a disguised Hera, reproaches Zeus for hiding his true nature and is consumed by fire upon touching his thunderbolt (Apollodorus, *Bibl.* 4.3; Nonnus, *Dion.* 8.286–406). Without the buffer of Zeus's metamorphosis, there is nothing to protect her from the danger of contact with the divine.[50]

Beyond the otherness of both malevolent and benevolent Greek deities, a wide variety of fantastic creatures appear in subordinate roles. These are often composite creatures who are described as malicious and set up as opponents of the heroes (e.g., Scylla, Charybdis, Chimaera). However, other hybrid creatures (e.g., Pegasus, hippocamps, centaurs, etc.) fulfill a more ambivalent status as servants or allies of the gods and heroes. Pegasus, a hybrid winged horse, might initially be an unexpected candidate for the category of the monster. The origins of this divine horse are varied, ranging from the offspring of Medusa and Poseidon (Ovid, *Metam.* 6.119; Hyginus, *Fab.* 151) to an expanded account of his birth emerging from the blood of Medusa's severed head (Hesiod, *Theog.* 280; Ovid, *Metam.* 4.786). In either tradition, Pegasus is the product of Poseidon, a favoured deity, and the gorgon Medusa – a feared and reviled hybrid "monster." Although Pegasus is remembered as a benevolent creature that aids the Greek heroes, it is originally portrayed as a wild beast (Pindar, *Ol. Ode* 13.63) until tamed by Bellerophon to help him kill the Chimaera (Hesiod, *Theog.* 325). A trace of this divine horse's wild nature and danger is preserved in traditions that attribute Bellerophon's death to Pegasus, who throws him off on their flight to the heavens (Pindar, *Isth.* 7.44; Nonnus *Dion.* 11.142). Pegasus is not the only hybrid horse that aids the Greek deities: the hippocamp (half horse/half fish) is used as a mount by Nereids, and in some traditions hybrid horses pull the chariot of Poseidon.[51] The hippocamp also shares features with the *ketos* (the sea monster) and sometimes is given wings.[52] Despite their hybrid appearance, neither Pegasus nor the hippocamp are considered deformed or evil. The comparison between the hippocamp and the cherubim is particularly apt since both serve either as a mount or pull the chariot of a deity (2 Sam 22:11; Ps 18:11; Ezek 1:5–21; 10:1–22). In both cases, the proximity and subordination to the favoured deity mitigates their monstrous appearance in ways that other composite creatures are not afforded.

Cheiron the centaur, part human and part horse, is another example of a hybrid being that proves helpful in reassessing the basic characteristics of the monster. Centaurs as a group were known as wild and drunken creatures that lived on the outskirts of civilization. Their violent tendencies were memorably displayed in their attack on the wedding of Pirithous and Hippodameia, which caused lasting enmity between the centaurs and humans (Homer, *Od.* 21.330–40; Ovid *Metam.* 12.210). In contrast to other centaurs, with their less than stellar reputations, Cheiron is the wise teacher who guides the heroes through adolescence to adulthood. His roster of pupils includes many celebrated Greek heroes, such as Achilles, Jason, and Heracles, who come to his cave to receive instruction and guidance. Although Cheiron also lived outside of civilization, his isolation is viewed positively and he was considered as a deity worthy of receiving worship at local shrines. According to Emma Aston, "So a hybrid, for all its animal part, does not have to stand for the wild, the uncultivated, but can be essentially the reverse, a guarantor of human progress."[53] Cheiron's positive assessment as a half-animal god stems partly from his close associations with the human world and his role as teacher and mentor. Despite efforts to corral the hybrid monster into the category of the malevolent and evil, the prevalence of hybridity across the spectrum of Greek deities and creatures pushes against these artificial boundaries.

CONCLUSION

The diversity of hybrid forms in Greek literature presents an alternative to binary thinking regarding hybridity. There are multiple examples of malevolent composite figures, but there is also room for the extraordinary hybrid monster. Debra Ballentine cautions that the modern interpreter should be self-aware enough not to internalize the bias of the ancient author regarding figures associated with "chaos."[54] This is especially relevant to the study of hybrid divine beings and the ways that the label of "monster" is either applied or denied. Although it is common to see the monster as that which is repudiated or feared, this definition remains far too narrow considering the overwhelming hybridity of Greek deities and creatures. Moreover, the so-called benevolent characters are often just as dangerous and lethal as their "monstrous" counterparts. Monsters are essentially indefinable as they surpass simple binaries – thus forcing a reconsideration of the lines that separate human/animal, earthly/divine, and even good/evil. In the end, little separates the marvellous from the aberrant: it is simply a matter of perspective and a recognition of the human tendency to domesticate the monstrosity of their favoured divine figures.

NOTES

1 Jeffrey Jerome Cohen, "Monster Culture (Seven Theses)," in *Monster Theory: Reading Culture*, ed. Jeffrey Jerome Cohen (Minneapolis: University of Minnesota Press, 1996), 3–25; Timothy K. Beal, *Religion and Its Monsters* (New York: Routledge, 2002); Noel Carroll, *The Philosophy of Horror: Or, Paradoxes of the Heart* (New York: Routledge, 2003); Stephen T. Asma, *On Monsters: An Unnatural History of Our Worst Fears* (Oxford: Oxford University Press, 2009); David D. Gilmore, *Monsters: Evil Beings, Mythical Beasts, and All Manner of Imaginary Terrors* (Philadelphia: University of Pennsylvania Press, 2012); Brandon R. Grafius, *Reading the Bible with Horror*, Horror and Scripture (Lanham: Lexington Books/Fortress Academic, 2019).

2 Cohen, "Monster Culture," 3.

3 Bruce Lincoln, *Apples and Oranges: Explorations in, on, and with Comparison* (Chicago: University of Chicago Press, 2018), 25.

4 For a challenge regarding the use of the "unique" as a category, see J.Z. Smith, *Drudgery Divine: On the Comparison of Early Christianities and the Religions of Late Antiquity* (Chicago: University of Chicago Press, 1990), 36–7.

5 Lincoln, *Apples and Oranges*, 25; Stephen L. Young, "'Let's Take the Text Seriously': The Protectionist Doxa of Mainstream New Testament Studies," *Method and Theory in the Study of Religion* 32 (2020): 328–63.

6 I explore this issue with regard to Revelation and its presentation of hybrid and liminal creatures in Heather Macumber, *Recovering the Monstrous in Revelation*, Horror and Scripture (Lexington Books/Fortress Academic, 2021).

7 J.Z. Smith, "In Comparison a Magic Dwells," in *A Magic Still Dwells: Comparative Religion in the Postmodern Age*, ed. Kimberley C. Patton and Benjamin C. Ray (Berkeley: University of California Press, 2000), 40–1; Lincoln, *Apples and Oranges*, 25–33.

8 Leonard L. Thompson, *The Book of Revelation: Apocalypse and Empire* (New York: Oxford University Press, 1990), 77–8; James L. Resseguie, *Revelation Unsealed: A Narrative Critical Approach to John's Apocalypse*, Biblical Interpretation Series 32 (Leiden: Brill, 1998), 103–5, 117, 129–30; G.K. Beale, *The Book of Revelation: A Commentary on the Greek Text*, New International Greek Testament Commentary (Grand Rapids: W.B. Eerdmans, 1999), 329–30, 491–505; Craig R. Koester, *Revelation: A New Translation with Introduction and Commentary*, Anchor Yale Bible 38A (New Haven: Yale University Press, 2014), 367–9, 464, 473; Wilfrid J. Harrington, *Sacra Pagina: Revelation* (Collegeville: Liturgical Press, 2017), 80.

9 Cohen, "Monster Culture," 4.

10 Émile Benveniste, *Le Vocabulaire des institutions indo-européennes*, vol. 2: *Pouvoir, droit, religions* (Paris: Éditions de Minuit, 1969), 255.

11 Emma Aston, *Mixanthrôpoi: Animal-Human Hybrid Deities in Greek Religion*, Kernos Supplément 25 (Liège: Centre International d'Étude de la Religion Grecque Antique, 2011), 33–4.

12 Fiona Mitchell, *Monsters in Greek Literature: Aberrant Bodies in Ancient Greek Cosmogony, Ethnography, and Biology*, Routledge Monographs in Classical Studies (London: Routledge, 2021), 8–9.

13 Daniel Smith-Christopher, "A Postcolonial Reading of Apocalyptic Literature," in *The Oxford Handbook of Apocalyptic Literature*, ed. John J. Collins (Oxford: Oxford University Press, 2014), 188–94.

14 Ryan S. Higgins, "The Good, the God, and the Ugly: The Role of the Beloved Monster in the Ancient Near East and the Hebrew Bible," *Interpretation* 72, no. 2 (2020): 139.

15 Benveniste, *Vocabulaire*; C. Moussy, "Esquisse de l'histoire de Monstrum," *Revue Des Études Latines* 55 (1977): 345–69.

16 Smith-Christopher, "Postcolonial Reading," 188, uses "mixed monsters" and "amazing figures" to draw distinctions between creatures.

17 Lena-Sofia Tiemeyer, "Zechariah's Spies and Ezekiel's Cherubim," 104–27, in *Tradition in Transition: Haggai and Zechariah 1-8 in the Trajectory of Hebrew Theology* (New York: T&T Clark, 2008), 110–11.

18 Dale Launderville, "Ezekiel's Cherub: A Promising Symbol or a Dangerous Idol?," *Catholic Biblical Quarterly* 65, no. 2 (2003): 165–83; Tienmeyer, "Zechariah's Spies," 117–22.

19 Carroll, *Philosophy of Horror*, 44–8.

20 Ibid., 48–52; Gilmore, *Monsters*, 178–80.

21 Heather Macumber, "The Threat of Empire: Monstrous Hybridity in Revelation 13," *Biblical Interpretation* 27, no. 1 (2019): 107–29.

22 Smith-Christopher, "Postcolonial Reading," 188.

23 Ibid., 188, 195.

24 William Foxwell Albright, "What Were the Cherubim?," *Biblical Archaeologist* 1, no. 1 (1938): 1–3; F.A.M. Wiggermann, "Mischwesen A," 8.222–44, in *Reallexikon Der Assyriologie Und Vorderasiastischen Archäologie* (Berlin: de Gruyter, 1994).

25 Smith-Christopher, "Postcolonial Reading," 195 (emphasis in original).

26 Resseguie, *Revelation Unsealed*, 130; cf. Koester, *Revelation*, 464.

27 I am adopting the terminology "holiness/wholeness paradigm" from Saul M. Olyan, *Social Inequality in the World of the Text: The Significance of Ritual and Social Distinctions in the Hebrew Bible*, Journal of Ancient Judaism Supplements 4 (Göttingen: Vandenhoeck & Ruprecht, 2011), 187.

28 Mary Douglas, *Purity and Danger: An Analysis of Concepts of Pollution and Taboo* (London: Routledge and K. Paul, 1996), 51–4.

29 Ibid., 53.

30 Carroll, *Philosophy of Horror*, 31–5; Gilmore, *Monsters*, 18–19; Safwat Marzouk, *Egypt as a Monster in the Book of Ezekiel*, Forschungen zum Alten Testament 2.76 (Tübingen: Mohr Siebeck, 2015), 126–7.

31 Mary Douglas, *Implicit Meanings*, in *Mary Douglas: Collected Works*, vol. 5 (New York/Philadelphia: Routledge/Taylor and Francis, 2002), 282n4.

32 Douglas, *Purity and Danger*, 164.

33 Douglas, *Implicit Meanings*, 257.

34 Douglas, *Purity and Danger*, 38–9.

35 Ibid., 29.

36 Smith-Christopher, "Postcolonial Reading," 188, 195.

37 Thompson, *Book of Revelation*, 77.

38 Margrit Shildrick, *Embodying the Monster: Encounters with the Vulnerable Self* (London: SAGE, 2002), 11.

39 Annie Dillard, *Pilgrim at Tinker Creek* (New York: Harper Collins, 1974), 8.

40 Rebecca Raphael, "Things Too Wonderful: A Disabled Reading of Job," *Perspectives in Religious Studies* 31, no. 4 (2004): 419.

41 J.Z. Smith, "What a Difference a Difference Makes," in *"To See Ourselves as Others See Us": Christians, Jews, "Others" in Late Antiquity*, ed. Jacob Neusner, Ernest F. Frerichs, and Caroline McCracken-Flesher, Scholars Press Studies in the Humanities Series (Chico, CA: Scholars Press, 1985), 52–3. It should be noted that this choice is to a degree arbitrary as examples of hybridity from Mesopotamia or Ugarit would be equally valid for comparative purposes.

42 This shape-shifting ability is a type of hybridity that Carroll, *Philosophy of Horror*, 45–8, labels fission.

43 Jenny Clay, "The Generation of Monsters in Hesiod," *Classical Philology* 88, no. 2 (1993): 116.

44 Beal, *Religion and Its Monsters*, 1–3; Richard Kearney, *Strangers, Gods, and Monsters: Interpreting Otherness* (New York: Routledge, 2002); Gilmore, *Monsters*, 9–10; Emma Aston, "Part-Animal Gods," in *The Oxford Handbook of Animals in Classical Thought and Life*, ed. Gordon Lindsay Campbell (Oxford: Oxford University Press, 2014), 374.

45 Smith, "What a Difference," 15.

46 Ibid.

47 Mitchell, *Monsters in Greek Literature*, 7.

48 Aston, *Mixanthrôpoi*, 314.

49 Ibid.

50 Richard Buxton, *Forms of Astonishment: Greek Myths of Metamorphosis* (Oxford: Oxford University Press, 2009), 158–9.

51 Daniel Ogden, *The Dragon in the West: From Ancient Myth to Modern Legend* (Oxford: Oxford University Press, 2021), 98–100.

52 Ibid., 98n32.

53 Aston, "Part-Animal Gods," 379–80.

54 Debra Scoggins Ballentine, *The Conflict Myth and the Biblical Tradition* (New York: Oxford University Press, 2015), 186–7.

7

As It Was Written: The Gospel of Matthew as a Symbolic Artifact

Esther Guillen

In the ancient Mediterranean, texts had value that was (1) separate from their content and/or (2) enhanced their content. Having something *written* would impart authority, and performative use of this written text would communicate sacred authority, close association with the author(s), and close association with the text's protagonists. The author(s) – who may have also been the public reader(s) – of this text would be imbued with the symbolic value of the text itself.[1] For those persons who used the biography of Jesus traditionally designated the "Gospel according to Matthew" as their primary liturgical and historical text, and probably most persons living in first- and second-century Mediterranean societies, there would have been a "symbolic value" to a written text.[2] The attributed-value model of textual value imagines text as an artifact, which is valuable not only for the information contained within the text but also for the symbolic value of texts themselves as well as for the symbolic value of the memorialized creator of a particular text and the context in which the text is used or read aloud.[3] This text is valuable not only for the information contained therein, its *inherent* value, but also for what the text symbolically represents: its *attributed* value. Attributed value can also be found in the sources used in composition, the way that those sources are treated by the author(s), the register used (such as formal or informal), the aesthetic and visual properties of the text, and the language in which the text is written.

"Writing is not a neutral and autonomous medium."[4] This statement should come as no surprise to scholars of religion, both in our vocations as scholars and in our fields of study. Writing has magical properties: an essay, finely written, takes on the value of the writer herself, and a paper rejected can lead us to question our capabilities as scholars. While the value imbued in ancient documents was, of course, different from that for modern scholars, the completed whole of the document was no less symbolic of the author's abilities and authority. The New Testament gospels have been studied extensively. We have asked them what can be learned about the historical figure of Jesus; what they can teach us about early Christian, Christ-follower, and Jesus-follower theology; and what we can glean of the nature of these groups. Each of these fields has been primarily concerned with the words contained in the text: the stories that the particular narratives tell. While I address the contents of the book of Matthew in order to show the value that was placed on texts in the ancient Mediterranean, I am more concerned with the book as an *artifact* rather than as a narrative.

Matthew's biography of Jesus is a deeply literary text. Evidence of Matthew's literary aspirations is twofold: first, their use of two written sources for their gospel narrative and, second, their reliance on and reference to the Septuagint. When Matthew wrote their account of the life of Jesus they used Mark and Q as written sources. In this Matthew is not unique: Luke also used Mark and Q and is more faithful to Q's sequence than is Matthew. However, Matthew's alterations of Q can be used as evidence of their literary goals and beliefs. For Matthew the textual sources available are not "scripture," but they are valuable because they are written. Of course, not all written texts would convey the same symbolism or value; a narrative of a messiah would not be viewed in the same way as a tax list, nor would a curse inscribed on lead have the same symbolic value as an association inscription on stone. What we can say is that, in the ancient Mediterranean, writing something down did give it value, and the written word had power. Arguments have been made that the earliest Christians did not view their texts as symbolic or valuable because they wrote them on codices. The argument follows that, if the text was valuable, they would have used a scroll.[5] If one imagines that all so-called sacred texts were written in scroll format, and that all pragmatic texts on codices, and that a text can only be either sacred or pragmatic, then this argument would have weight. However, binaries such as sacred/pragmatic, prestige/practical, and even scroll/codex are not particularly helpful for imagining the ancient world. Why must it be either sacred or pragmatic? I would argue instead for gradations of symbolic value and that pragmatic concerns can still be within the realm of the sacred.

Distinctions between binary categories such as *prestige* versus *pragmatic* and *sacred* versus *profane* serve little purpose in examinations of the ancient world.[6] What we now imagine to be a sacred concern may have been for a Hellenistic person quite practical. For example, a trader asks for an oracle before setting out on a voyage; a student looks for a sign in the *Iliad* for whether they passed an examination; I flip a coin to decide whether to drive or walk to the grocery store. Matthew's use of the prophetic texts in the Septuagint falls, I believe, within this gradation of sacred and pragmatic, as do the later uses of the gospels by early Christians in Egypt. The gospels took on magical properties in mid- to late antiquity in Egypt, and the opening lines were employed as protective texts on papyrus amulets.[7] The written word was, for the earliest Christians, a source of conveyed information, a sign of status and identity, and a magical tool for protection and to propitiate the divine.

While we cannot know whether Matthew's source copy of the Septuagint conforms to the version now available, the evidence is fairly strong that Matthew was less free-handed when copying prophetic sources than when copying Mark or Q (see table 7.1). Matthew uses γέγραπται seven times in their gospel to refer to Septuagint verses. One is independent Matthean and found in the infancy narrative, two are Markan in origin, and four are sourced from Q. Matthew's "quotation" in the infancy narrative is a combination of Micah 5:2 and 2 Samuel 5:2.

Matthew's use of the Septuagint is here similar to the scribe of *4QpaleoExod*[m]. Both have taken material from one book of the writings and supplemented it with material from another book.[8] Judith Sanderson writes that when copying prophecy or revelation, it appears that the "words of revelation were treated with more care than the form and structure." A scribe could easily take material from other books, or other locations in the same book, and add it together to produce the required narrative or message. While it may be easy to judge Matthew deficient in their knowledge of the Israelite and Jewish writings when they make "mistakes" such as that found in 2:5, it may be that they are simply following an established procedure for creating use-specific copies of other texts. Matthew's use of Mark and Q is less wooden, however.[9] Matthew elaborates and edits these sources much more than they do their Septuagint prophecies. John Kloppenborg uses this evidence to identify the social location of the gospel writers as non-elite and states that Matthew and Luke's use of Q "approximates the practices of the *librarius* or archivist/scribe."[10] The *librarius* was a skilled copier, whose goal was a text free from errors: a verbatim transcription.[11] The archivist/scribe was someone "whose role included both simple transcription and a degree of genuine composition."[12] This is in keeping with Matthew's gospel production. Matthew uses both Mark, Q, and the Septuagint, but not in the same way. Matthew's independent transcriptions from the Septuagint are more faithful to the (assumed) source text than their transcriptions of Mark and Q.[13] The two Septuagint quotations that come from the Markan source are found at 21:13 and 26:31. Matthew 21:13 is a composite of Isaiah 56:7,

Table 7.1
Sources for Matthew 2:6

Matthew 2:6	*Micah 5:2*	*2 Samuel 5:2*
"And you, Bethlehem, in the land of Judah, are by no means least among the rulers of Judah; for from you shall come a ruler who is to shepherd my people."	But you, O Bethlehem of Ephrathah, who are one of the little clans of Judah, from you shall come forth for me one who is to rule in Israel, whose origin is from of old, from ancient days.	For some time, while Saul was king over us, it was you who led out Israel and brought it in. The Lord said to you: "It is you who shall be shepherd of my people Israel, you who shall be ruler over Israel."

Jeremiah 7:11, and Zechariah 14:21, in a similar manner to that found in 2:5 (see table 7.2). At 21:13 and 26:31, however, Matthew has directly quoted Mark, without additions. It appears from this that Matthew believed the quotations in these two locations were sufficient to fulfill the prophecies as found in the writings.

Matthew's twelfth fulfilment formula uses another composite quotation. In this narrative Matthew has Jesus request "a donkey tied, and a colt with her" (21:2) from his disciples. This story is Markan in origin, but Matthew adds a prophetic fulfilment that combines Isaiah 62:11 and Zechariah 9:9.

In Mark, Jesus rides on "a colt that has never been ridden" and Luke reproduces the Markan version almost verbatim.[14] Matthew, however, is concerned with Mark's seemingly unliteral transcription of the essence of the prophecy, and while we cannot know whether Matthew saw Mark's narrative as prophetic, something triggered this use of prophecy for Matthew. There are two issues worth noting about Matthew's use of the Zechariah prophecy: first, that they have added it to Mark's Jerusalem entry narrative, and, second, that they sacrifice plausibility for verbatim prophetic fulfilment. Matthew is not concerned that in their version Jesus implausibly rides two donkeys at once; where Mark is content with the essence of prophecy, Matthew requires *verbatim agreement*. I address the second issue first, and then discuss Matthew's literary aspirations and bibliomantic use of the prophecy. In Matthew, Jesus rides two animals into Jerusalem. While the image of Jesus straddling two donkeys at once is rather amusing, it seems a somewhat uncomfortable and impractical way to travel. We do not know whether Matthew was using the Septuagint or a Hebrew version of the writings. Matthew does not reproduce the Greek text verbatim (see table 7.4) but does reproduce the additional colt, which is found in both the Hebrew and the Greek.

Table 7. 2
Sources for Matthew 21:13

Matthew 21:13	*Isaiah 56:7*	*Jeremiah 7:11*	*Zechariah 14:21*
My house shall be called a house of prayer; but you are making it a den of robbers	for my house shall be called a house of prayer for all peoples	Has this house, which is called by my name, become a den of robbers in your sight?	And there shall no longer be traders in the house of the Lord of hosts on that day.

Table 7.3
Sources for Matthew 21:5

Matthew 21:5	*Isaiah 62:11*	*Zechariah 9:9*
Tell the daughter of Zion, Look, your king is coming to you, humble, and mounted on a donkey, and on a colt, the foal of a donkey.	The Lord has proclaimed to the end of the earth: Say to your daughter Zion, "See, your salvation comes."	Lo, your king comes to you; triumphant and victorious is he, humble and riding on a donkey, on a colt, the foal of a donkey.

Table 7.4
Matthew 21:5 and MT/LXX parallels

Matthew 21:5 (Greek)	*Zechariah 9:9 (Hebrew)*	*Zechariah 9:9 (Greek)*
Ἰδοὺ ὁ βασιλεύς σου ἔρχεταί σοι πραΰς καὶ ἐπιβεβηκὼς ἐπὶ ὄνον καὶ ἐπὶ πῶλον υἱὸν ὑποζυγίου.	הנה מלכך יבוא לך צדיק ונושע הוא עניורכב על־חמור ועל־עיר בן־אתנות:	ἰδοὺ ὁ βασιλεύς σου ἔρχεταί σοι, δίκαιος καὶ σῴζων αὐτός, πραΰς καὶ ἐπιβεβηκὼς ἐπὶ ὑποζύγιον καὶ πῶλον νέον.

While this is interesting from a grammatical and source-critical viewpoint, it does not tell us much about Matthew's literariness or their appeal to the Matthean intended audience. For this, we must look at their choice of adding the prophetic quotation at all. Part of this was likely Matthew's desire to convince a Jewish audience of Jesus's messianic status. By adding the fulfilment formulas, Matthew explicitly links Jesus to the Israelite and Hebrew writings, and assigns him the position of *Jewish* messiah. This is, of course, already present in Q, and Mark to a lesser extent, but it is not until Matthew that the synoptics take on this particular *textual* messianic characteristic. In Matthew's version, that Jesus is the Jewish messiah is flagged by specific verbatim fulfilment of the writings. For Matthew, it is much more important that Jesus fulfill the written prophecy than that what he do be realistically

Table 7.5
Mark 15:34

Mark 15:34	*Matthew 27:46*	*Psalm 22:2*
Ἐλωΐ ἐλωΐ λεμὰ σαβαχθάνι;	Ἠλὶ ἠλὶ λεμὰ σαβαχθάνι;	אלי אלי למה עזבתני
Eloi, eloi, lema sabachthani	Eli, Eli, lema sabachthani	Eli, eli, lama azavtani

possible. Mark has Jesus fulfill the prophecy implicitly, but Matthew requires explicit fulfilment of the text *as it is written*.

Matthew's use of Mark's crucifixion narrative displays the same requirement. In Mark's narrative, Jesus calls out from the cross in Aramaic, but Matthew, who reproduces much of Mark's crucifixion story, replaces the Aramaic with a transliteration of the Hebrew. As above, Mark does not require Jesus to fulfill prophecy to the exact word but only in essence. Matthew, however, is using the writings in an oracular sense: for Jesus to be the Jewish messiah, they must use the words as they are written in the Jewish texts. This is also evident in Matthew's temptation narrative, at 4:4. The source for this narrative is Q; Mark has a much shorter version, two verses to Matthew's eleven, and Q's thirteen.[15] In this pericope there are four quotations from the writings, three of which Matthew reproduces verbatim from Q. The fourth, which is actually the first quotation, Matthew reproduces verbatim, but with an addition.

The quotation is from Deuteronomy 8:3, and whether Matthew is quoting from the Septuagint or the Hebrew writings is here unimportant. What is of interest is that Matthew takes the quotation from the Q source and adds to it.[16] As with the two examples above, Matthew takes a perfectly serviceable source and changes it because it does not exactly conform to the prophetic writings they require Jesus to fulfill.[17] Matthew's oracular use of the writings is analogous to the oracles from Delphi. The Pythia acted as a vessel for the words of the god,[18] as the writings did for the words of the Hebraic god, and in the case of the Pythia, the oracles were used verbatim, as Matthew requires them to be. This is seen in Herodotus, who recounts Croesus's interaction with the Delphic oracle in *The Histories* in 1.46–51. Croesus sent emissaries to enquire of a number of oracles whether he should resume the campaign against the Persians, and at 1.47.1, Herodotus tells us that Croesus told his emissaries to *write down* the answer given by the oracles and bring the writing to him. This shows that the written account – the verbatim words – of the prophecy were needed and not just the essence, or gist, of the oracle.

Table 7.6
Matthew 4:4 and Q

Matthew 4:4	*Q 4:4*
Οὐκ ἐπ' ἄρτῳ μόνῳ ζήσεται ὁ ἄνθρωπος, ἀλλ' ἐπὶ παντὶ ῥήματι ἐκπορευομένῳ διὰ στόματος θεοῦ.	Οὐκ ἐπ' ἄρτῳ μόνῳ ζήσεται ὁ ἄνθρωπος.
The person does not live by bread alone, but on every word coming from the mouth of God.	The person does not live by bread alone.

Matthew's readers adopted their oracular use of the writings in their Septuagint form. Justin Martyr, who quotes from Matthew, was attempting to solve a hermeneutical problem of the Jewish scriptures: whether they were to be read as law or as prophecy. This relationship between the Jewish writings and the gospels, which at times reject the written law, was problematic for Justin and his contemporaries, and it is evident that Justin's use of the Matthean gospel allowed for a prophetic reading of the Jewish writings that reconciled the contradictions. Justin Martyr, as a literate cultural producer himself, is a prime candidate for the category of Matthew's intended audience, and I am convinced that the influence of Matthew's readings and use of the Jewish writings are here evident in the texts produced by Justin.[19] Justin would have read Matthew in its original language, Greek, and takes care to authorize the prophetic and oracular nature of the Septuagint. In chapter 31 of the *First Apology* Justin modifies the legend of the *Letter of Aristeas* to include divinely authorized translation not just of the Law but of all of the "prophetic writings."[20] In this way Justin follows, and authorizes, Matthew. If, like Mark, Justin had been content that Jesus fulfilled the *essence* of the prophecy, there would be no need for the Greek version of the writings to be divinely authorized: the translation would not change the meaning, and therefore the Hebrew would suffice. However, Justin, like Matthew, requires a *word agreement* for prophetic fulfilment, and therefore the Greek translation must have prophetic weight.[21]

In the Gospel of Matthew, the author performs a form of scribal activity. As noted above, Matthew displays a scribe/archivist quality in their use of Mark, Q, and the Septuagint, though they appear to have a more theological goal in their use of the Septuagint than in the use of their other two sources. We often call Matthew an "author," but this is not strictly true. Matthew does display some *scribere* qualities in their independent material,[22] but much of the gospel is not their own creation. The book of Matthew is a combination of contemporary and scriptural sources, and material of Matthew's own invention, and their use of sources both verbatim and paraphrased identifies them not as an *author*, as we would imagine it, but as a *performative author*. Matthew performs *scribere* activity, when much of what they are actually doing is *describere* with additions. Matthew tells their reader – repeatedly – that they have evidence for Jesus's messianic nature and that this evidence is from a written source: the Israelite/Hebrew writings.

Matthew also displays a level of respect for the "scribes" that is not evident in either Mark or Luke. Matthew uses γραμματεύς twenty-two times in their gospel, where Mark has twenty-one uses and Luke fourteen. The number of times this noun is used, though, is not what is interesting but, rather, the times that Matthew either removes or adds reference to the scribes in material from either the double or the triple tradition. In the double tradition, Matthew refers to the scribes eight times, and we can be reasonably certain that these are Matthean additions as in these eight locations Luke does not refer to the scribes.[23] These additions are split equally between positive and negative allusions to the scribes, but it is worth noting that all of the negative allusions appear in the pericope where Jesus denounces the actions of the scribes and Pharisees, and the negative occurrences are bracketed with positive allusions. This pericope opens with Matthew acknowledging the authority of the scribes: "The scribes and the Pharisees sit on Moses' seat; therefore, do whatever they teach you and follow it" (23:2–3 NRSV). Following this, Matthew denounces not the authority of the scribes but their practices: they teach correctly but do not follow their own teaching, they are concerned with outward purity but not inward, and they worry about tithes but not the more important aspects of the Law. This narrative is closed with a positive reference, where the scribes are grouped with the sages and prophets, two groups that Matthew gives great value to throughout their gospel. The reference is found at 23:35: "Therefore I send you prophets, sages, and scribes, some of whom you will kill and crucify, and some you will flog in your synagogues and pursue from town to town" (NRSV).

As a contrast, Matthew omits reference to the scribes in nine locations where they have used Mark as their source. Eight of these are positive omissions, and one, at 17:14, is neutral.[24] The eight positive omissions fall into three categories: questioning of Jesus, Jesus questioning the scribes, and responsibility for the crucifixion. At 9:11 and 9:34 (Mark 2:16 and 3:22) Matthew keeps reference to the Pharisees and adds reference, respectively, in pericopes that specifically challenge Jesus's acts of eating with tax collectors and casting out demons. At Mark 11:27 (Matt. 21:23) the scribes are grouped with the high priests and the elders, and come to challenge Jesus's authority to teach and heal, and at Matthew 22:34 and 22:42 the opposition between Jesus and the scribes over the Law that is found in Mark is replaced with a disagreement between Jesus and the Pharisees. The most telling omissions, however, come in the story of the arrest and crucifixion of Jesus. In these pericopes Mark again groups the scribes with the high priests and elders, and Matthew removes this reference. In essence, Matthew removes responsibility for the crucifixion from the scribes in these three verses and places it with the elders and the high priests.[25]

In their independent material, Matthew refers to the scribes only twice, once with positive allusions and once with negative. In 2:4 the scribes are shown as knowledgeable of the prophetic writings in that Herod asks them where the messiah will be born, but at 5:20 the scribes, with the Pharisees, are insufficiently righteous to enter the Kingdom. From the evidence, it appears that this second reference can be grouped with the negative allusions found in the double tradition material; Matthew does not accuse the scribes of being insufficiently educated, or knowledgeable of the Law, but, rather, their actions disqualify them from the Kingdom. As well, their lack of righteousness is even worse because of their familiarity with the Law: the scribes should know better. The reference at 2:4 fits with that at 23:2 and 23:34, where the scribes are authoritative and classed with prophets and sages. Matthew's additions, omissions, and independent references to scribes show their respect for this profession and their high valuing of scribal activities.

Matthew's intended audience would have seen literariness as an example of elite-ness. Literacy-rate estimations of the ancient Mediterranean range from 3 to 10 percent,[26] which even at the higher end is quite low compared to the modern world. However, this does not mean that non-literate persons were unaware of literate culture. Texts were performed, either at the pre-publication stage, where writers could receive feedback and guidance from a small group of friends, where both poetry and prose would be given in a *recitatio* prior to publication,[27] or after publication in public readings. As well, any information that needed to be conveyed to a large group of people would be read aloud in a public space.[28] Public and semi-public readings were not just performances of reading ability, they were also performances of writing ability: performance of *production* of cultural materials. Justin Martyr tells us that readings were performed during the assembly of Christ-followers and that they read aloud the prophets and the "memoirs of the apostles."[29] These texts would be understood to be composed by the prophets, apostles, or those close to them, and their performance by literate members of the assembly would create an association between the performers and the prophets and the apostles. As well, the literate members of the assemblies would gain status by means of public readings. I propose here that the cultural framework within which Matthew's intended audience would exist was one of limited engagement with literacy for the urban majority and full literacy for only the educated elite. Limited engagement with literacy assumes that a person is able to identify simple written words, such as those needed to identify goods in a marketplace or signs identifying occupation. Full literacy assumes that a person can both read a *scriptio continua* text and write more than a simple accounting (e.g., write a letter or copy a poem or other literary text with understanding). Of course, literacy in the ancient world should not be understood as a binary; rather, I am proposing that these are two locations on a continuum of literacy and that persons may not have fallen along this continuum in an obvious way. A merchant or tax collector, who we might imagine to have the limited engagement with literacy required for their occupations – writing lists, keeping accounts – may instead have had full-literate aspirations or abilities.[30] Education was highly valued in the non-elite classes.[31] If we imagine the Matthew-group as non-elite, as we must, we can say that education was likely valued by this group and that it was used both as a signal of elite-ness and as a method to increase social prestige. As well as an effective status-elevating mechanism, books conferred social capital on their owners.[32]

Kloppenborg shows that books came to be symbolic of Christian identity in the mid- to late second century. I am not arguing that Matthew was influenced by this; even the mid-second century is much too late for the composition of Matthew.[33] However, I do argue that the gospel of Matthew *contributed* to this identity formation. Papyrological evidence tells us that Matthew was widely copied in Egypt. There are more surviving copies of Matthew than of the other synoptics combined, and while this does not tell us definitively that Matthew was more widely used in the first centuries after its composition, as evidence of Markan or Lukan materials may simply be lost or not yet discovered, the fragmentary evidence we do have suggests that Matthew was widely popular in this period. It is likely that part of Matthew's appeal was the kind of literary nature they represented. For the early Christians, the ability to produce texts was important; they desired their heroes to be seen as producers of culture, not just consumers. For example, 2 Timothy 4:13 exhorts Timothy to bring "the cloak that I left with Carpus at Troas, also the books, and especially the parchments."[34] In this instance, the authenticity of 2 Timothy is not in question, and this letter may actually serve as a better example of the importance of literary production as a pseudo-Pauline letter than as an authentic composition of Paul's. If Paul had written this letter, then his request for his books and parchment would be a banal detail, but as it is a pseudepigraphal letter, we can assume that this request serves a particular purpose. Here I agree with Kloppenborg that the request is meant to show Paul as literate. The goal is to "advance the claim that Paul is a *literate* agent, who is able to *use and read* from books and to write his own notebooks."[35] Kloppenborg stresses the ability to read and use, but I would like to suggest that Paul's ability to *write* is more important for the author of 2 Timothy. The author requests the books (τα βιβλία) but especially the parchments (μάλιστα τας μεμβράνας). This is the key point for the author of 2 Timothy – that Paul is a literate cultural producer.

The concept of "literate cultural producers" was developed by Stanley Stowers as a modification of Harvey Whitehouse's theory of two modes of religiosity, the doctrinal and the imagistic. While the binary classifications necessitated by Whitehouse's theoretical model are problematic, a modified form of this theory can be extremely helpful for both creating taxonomies of religion and as a thinking-assist when imagining religions in antiquity.[36] Stowers's adaptation is that, rather than drawing a firm line between modes of religion, each mode should be thought of as permeable, and a religious practitioner thought of as able to move between one mode and another. In addition, Stowers has developed four modes, though only one, that of the "literate cultural producers," is addressed here.[37] Persons in this mode had status because of their ability to produce texts, and the dissemination of these texts allowed for widespread networks of literate cultural producers, even though their numbers were limited in their own geographical locations.[38] I am convinced that persons who acted in this mode would place value on *other* written texts as well as on their own productions, and this is why I locate Matthew in this mode.

Stowers's modes of religion should not be imagined as firm categories but, rather, as attractor positions that allow scholars to think about religious experts in helpful ways. The theory should not be imagined monothetically: Matthew does not belong *only* in the mode of literate cultural producer because they write and appeal to literary authority in the Septuagint but, rather, because they straddle mode 2 and mode 4 (see figure 7.1). Matthew's intended audience would likely do similarly: they would be interested in Matthew as a literate cultural producer, but their appeal to institutional authority in the writings would enhance their own authority and status.[39]

If we imagine Matthew in the mode of literate cultural producer who appeals to traditional textual authority through Jesus's prophetic-writing fulfilment, then we can see the inherent value of Matthew as a *written text*.

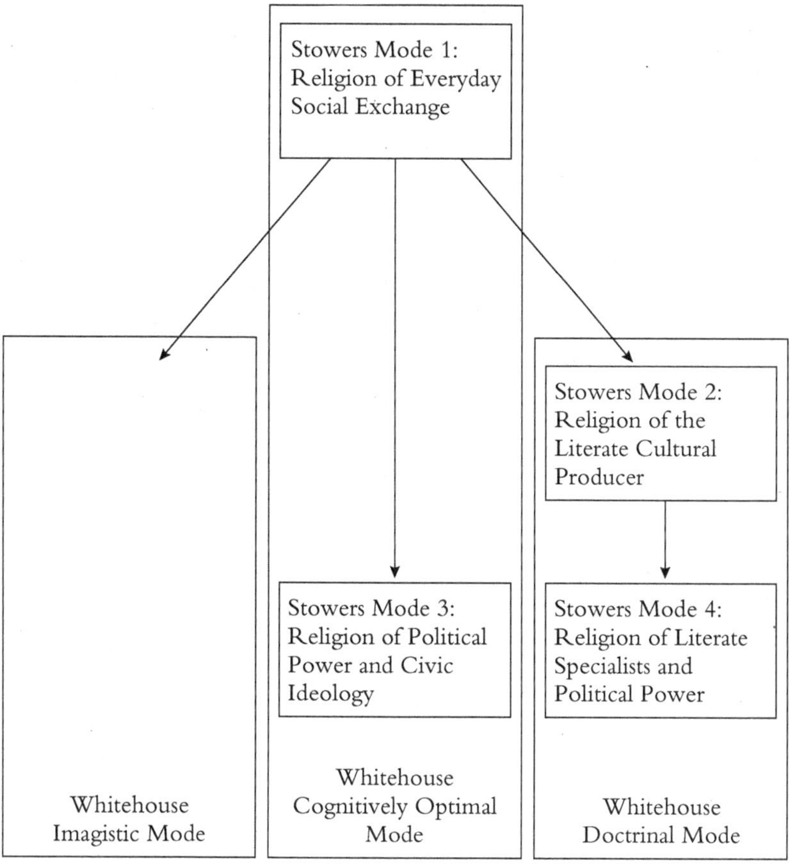

7.1 Daniel Ullucci's comparison of Stowers and Whitehouse

As Kloppenborg notes, this is most definitely not an isolated phenomenon. Luke goes to great lengths to locate his heroes – Paul and the other apostles in Acts – as literate persons able to quote freely from both the Torah and Greek philosophical and rhetorical writings.[10] Like the writer of Second Timothy, Luke's Paul is a literate, and literary, hero. While Matthew does not ask their characters to embody the same literary nature as Luke, by displaying and performing literariness himself Matthew promotes those values to their readers. Matthew's reliance on written sources, and their veneration of the written word as seen in the prophetic fulfilments, tells us that Matthew saw texts as symbolic objects, with attributed value beyond the information contained in them, and that they wrote for an intended audience that would imagine the same.

APPENDIX I: PROPHETIC QUOTATIONS AND THE USE OF ΓΡΑΜΜΑΤΕΎΣ

Table 7.7
Matthean references to the "writings" and prophetic quotations

Verse		*Source*	*Reference*	
1:23	FF1	Matthew	Isa 7:14	
2:6	FF2	Matthew	Mic 5:2, 2 Sam 5:2	
2:15	FF3	Matthew	Hos 11:1	
2:18	FF4	Matthew	Jer 31:15	
2:23	FF5	Matthew	Unknown	
3:03	FF6	Mark	Isa 40:3	
4:4		Q / Matthew	Deut 8:3	Matthew adds to the quote
4:6		Q	Ps 91:11–12	
4:7		Q	Deut 6:16	
4:10		Q	Deut 6:13	
4:15–16	FF7	Matthew	Isa 9:1–2	
8:17	FF8	Matthew	Isa 53:4	Pericope is Markan, quote is Matthew
11:10		Q	Mal 3:1	
12:17	FF9	Matthew	Isa 42:1–4	
13:14–15	FF10	Matthew	Isa 6:9	Pericope is Markan, quote is Matthew
13:35	FF11	Matthew	Ps 78:2	Pericope is Markan, quote is Matthew
21:5	FF12	Matthew	Isa 62:11, Zech 9.9	Pericope is Markan, quote is Matthew
21:13		Mark	Isa 56:7, Jer 7:11, Zech 14:21	
21:42		Mark	Ps 111:22–3	ταῖς γραφαῖς
26:24		Mark	Son of Man	
26:31		Mark	Zech 13:17	
26:56	FF13	Mark		αἱ γραφαί
27:9	FF14	Matthew	Zech 11:13 (loosely)	
27:46		Mark	Ps 22:11	Matthew changes quote from Aramaic to Hebrew

Table 7.8
Matthean additions of γραμματεύς to Q

8:19	Scribe calls JC "teacher"	Positive: locates scribes among JC's followers
12:38	Scribes call JC "teacher"	Positive: locates scribes among JC's followers
23:2	Scribes on the seat of Moses	Positive: Gives scribes authority
23:13	Woe to you	Negative: They say but do not do
23:23	Woe to you	Negative: Concerned with tithes but not the more important aspects of the Law
23:25	Woe to you	Negative: Outward purification, but not inward
23:27	Woe to you	Negative: Outward beauty, but not inward
23:29	Woe to you	Negative: Descendants of prophet-murderers
23:34	Scribes grouped with prophets and sages	Positive: Scribes, prophets, and sages required to be persecuted in order to bring about the Kingdom

Table 7.9
Matthean omission of γραμματεύς from Mark

9:11	2:16	Keeps Pharisees	Positive: Scribes in negative light in Mark S Q's JC activities
9:34	3:22	Replaces with Pharisees	Positive: S Q's JC activities
17:14	9:14		Neutral
21:23	11:27	Keeps elders and high priests	Positive: S Q's JC authority
22:34	12:28	Replaces with Pharisees	Positive: S Q's JC knowledge of the Law
22:42	12:35	Replaces with Pharisees	Positive: JC Q's S knowledge of the Law
26:3	14:1	Replaces with elders	Positive: Matt. removes S responsibility for the plot to arrest JC
26:47	14:43	Keeps elders and high priests	Positive: Matt. removes S responsibility for arrest of JC
27:1	15:1	Keeps elders and high priests	Positive: Matt. removes S responsibility for the crucifixion

Table 7.10
Independent Matthean uses of γραμματεύς

2:4	Positive: With the high priests shown as knowledgeable of the prophetic writings
5:20	Negative: With the Pharisees have insufficient righteousness to enter the Kingdom

NOTES

1 Throughout I use the gender and number neutral pronoun "they" and the name "Matthew" to refer to the author(s) of the text I am examining. This should not be understood as a definitive statement of singular or plural authorship; I do not ascribe to the community-production model of Gospel authorship, but because of constraints of evidence, we cannot state firmly that the author was a single person. Use of the name "Matthew" to designate the author(s) should be read in the same manner. While possibly autobiographical elements contained in the text are presented in the masculine, this is not definitive proof that the author(s) were male, though if these elements are taken as autobiographical, then the author(s) have presented themselves in that way. I have chosen the neutral "they" rather than the specific "her" or "him" to reflect the current impossibility of knowing the gender or the number of the author(s). There is, of course, strong evidence for female scribal activity in the ancient world, though this evidence centres on a slightly later period than the earlier dates for the composition of the text I am examining and shows more that girls and women were employed as copyist-scribes rather than as composer-scribes as described by Matthew's biography of Jesus. For a full discussion of the role of women scribes in the transmission of early Christian literature, see Kim Haines-Eitzen, *Guardians of Letters: Literacy, Power, and the Transmitters of Early Christian Literature* (Oxford: Oxford University Press, 2000).

2 Rosalind Thomas, *Literacy and Orality in Ancient Greece*, Key Themes in Ancient History (New York: Cambridge University Press, 1992), 74.

3 My use of "artifact" to refer to the text of the Gospel of Matthew is intended to signal my understanding of the Gospel as a physical object rather than as a repository for a narrative. I here act as an archeologist of an imagined artifact and attempt to describe the value of the object *as an object* without the benefit of an actual artifact to hold and study. My thinking is related to the language Matthew uses to describe the text they have created. Matthew 1:1 describes the following narrative as the "book" (βίβλος) of the genesis of Jesus Christ. By their use of "book" I argue that Matthew intends to associate the narrative with the Judean writings, but the author also tells us that they conceive of the text as a bounded, physical object, both a record of the (mythologized) life of Jesus of Nazareth and a symbolic artifact that confers value through its materiality.

4 Ibid., 74.

5 G.H.R. Horsley, "Classical Manuscripts in Australia and New Zealand, and the Early History of the Codex," *Antichthon* 27 (1993): 60–85.

6 Jennifer Eyl, *Signs, Wonders, and Gifts: A Study of Divination and Reciprocity in the Letters of Paul* (Oxford: Oxford University Press, 2019), 50.

7 Theodore S. de Bruyn and Jitse H.F. Dijkstra, "Greek Amulets and Formularies from Egypt Containing Christian Elements: A Checklist of Papyri, Parchments, Ostraka, and Tablets," *Bulletin of the American Society of Papyrologists* 48 (2011): 194.

8 References to "the writings" refer to the Hebrew Bible in either Hebrew or Greek. When the Greek version is intended, "Septuagint" is used. I have chosen this terminology to avoid the use of "scripture" and to reflect Matthew's language in the gospel.

9 John S. Kloppenborg, "Variation in the Reproduction of the Double Tradition and an Oral Q?," *Ephemerides Theologicae Lovanienses* 83, no. 1 (2007): 74.

10 Ibid., 78.

11 Ibid., 62.

12 Ibid., 78.

13 I say "assumed" because we cannot, of course, know the actual form of the Septuagint Matthew was using. Ancient texts were hardly fully reliable in their sameness: lazy scribes, overzealous use of memory in copying, and different versions of the Greek source text would all contribute to the variations we now see in Matthew's prophetic transcriptions.

14 Cf. Mark 11:2 – Ὑπάγετε εἰς τὴν κώμην τὴν κατέναντι ὑμῶν, καὶ εὐθὺς εἰσπορευόμενοι εἰς αὐτὴν εὑρήσετε πῶλον δεδεμένον ἐφ' ὃν οὐδεὶς οὔπω ἀνθρώπων ἐκάθισεν·λύσατε αὐτὸν καὶ φέρετε. (Go into the village ahead of you, and immediately as you enter it, you will find tied there a colt that has never been ridden; untie it and bring it.) – with Luke 19:30 – Ὑπάγετε εἰς τὴν κατέναντι κώμην, ἐν ᾗ εἰσπορευόμενοι εὑρήσετε πῶλον δεδεμένον, ἐφ' ὃν οὐδεὶς πώποτε ἀνθρώπων ἐκάθισεν, καὶ λύσαντες αὐτὸν ἀγάγετε. (Go into the village ahead of you, and as you enter it you will find tied there a colt that has never been ridden. Untie it and bring it here.)

15 James M. Robinson, Paul Hoffmann, and John S*.* Kloppenborg, ed., *The Sayings Gospel Q in Greek and English* (Minneapolis: Fortress Press, 2002), 79–81.

16 James M. Robinson, Paul Hoffmann, and John S. Kloppenborg, eds, *The Critical Edition of Q*, Hermeneia (Minneapolis: Fortress Press, 2000), 26.

17 There are three other similar instances, at 8:17, 13:14–15, and 13:34, where Matthew adds quotations from the writings to Markan pericopes. At 8:17 Matthew adds a quotation from Isaiah 53:4, at 13:14–15 a quotation from Isaiah 6:9, and at 13:35 the quotation is from Psalm 78:2.

18 Hugh Bowden, *Classical Athens and the Delphic Oracle: Divination and Democracy* (Cambridge: Cambridge University Press, 2005), 25.

19 There is evidence in the *Dialogue with Trypho* and the *First Apology* that Justin Martyr was reading Matthew as an authoritative source for the sayings of Jesus and for narratives of Jesus's infancy and life. For a detailed analysis, see Leslie L

Kline, "Harmonized Sayings of Jesus in the Pseudo-Clementine Homilies and Justin Martyr," *Zeitschrift Für Die Neutestamentliche Wissenschaft Und Die Kunde Der Älteren Kirche* 66, nos. 3 and 4 (1975): 223–41; and Arthur J. Bellinzoni, *The Sayings of Jesus in the Writings of Justin Martyr* (Leiden: Brill, 1967).

20 *Apology in Behalf of Christians* 31.1–5, in Justin Martyr, *Justin, Philosopher and Martyr: Apologies*, ed. Denis Minns and Paul Parvis, Oxford Early Christian Texts (Oxford: Oxford University Press, 2009), 163–7.

21 Giving the Greek translation of the prophets divine authority also solves the virgin-birth problem. I imagine that this would have been a contentious issue for the prophetic-fulfilment camp, and the idea appears to have been important to the early Church fathers. By authorizing the Septuagint, Justin effectively authorizes *parthenos* over *almah*.

22 This term is borrowed from Cicero: *describere* describes the act of copying, while *scribere* is to compose. See Kloppenborg, "Variation in the Reproduction of the Double Tradition," 78.

23 John S Kloppenborg, *Q Parallels: Synopsis Critical Notes and Concordance* (Sonoma, CA: Polebridge Press, 1988), 216.

24 In 17:14 (9:14 in Mark) scribes are part of a large crowd that neither Matthew nor Mark displays in either a positive or a negative light. I have therefore identified this omission as neutral.

25 Matthew does not, however, remove all responsibility from the scribes. At 26:57 Jesus is taken to the house of Caiaphas, where earlier only the elders and high priests had gathered but here the scribes are included, and, at 27:41, the scribes join the chief priests and elders in mocking Jesus on the cross.

26 John S Kloppenborg, "Literate Media in Early Christ Groups: The Creation of a Christian Book Culture," *Journal of Early Christian Studies* 22, no. 1 (2014): 27.

27 Harry Y. Gamble, *Books and Readers in the Early Church: A History of Early Christian Texts* (New Haven: Yale University Press, 1995), 204–5.

28 Most people in the ancient Mediterranean would also have been familiar with literary culture from public inscriptions, which were a common method of both communication and data storage, and from contact with libraries, booksellers, public notices, and, of course, tax and census records. See Kloppenborg, "Literate Media," 27.

29 *Apology on Behalf of Christians* 67.3 in Justin Martyr, *Justin, Philosopher and Martyr: Apologies*, 258–9.

30 As an example, we have papyrological evidence from the "house of Socrates," a tax collector in Roman Karanis who we would expect to have only practical literary skills but who appears, from the papyrological remains found, to posses greater literary goals and aspirations. See Peter van Minnen, "House-to-House Enquiries: An Interdisciplinary Approach to Roman Karanis," *Zeitschrift Für Papyrologie Und Epigraphik* 100 (1994): 237–49.

31 Raffaella Cribiore, *Gymnastics of the Mind: Greek Education in Hellenistic and Roman Egypt* (Princeton: Princeton University Press, 2005), 249–50; Beryl Rawson,

"Family and Society," in *The Oxford Handbook of Roman Studies*, ed. Alessandro Barchiesi and Walter Scheidel (Oxford: Oxford University Press, 2010), 619.

32 The uniquely Christian evidence of books as status elevators and prestige-conferring items is from a slightly later period. "The *traditio legis* motif typically shows Christ flanked by Peter and Paul, handing either a scroll or a book to one of the disciples." This is seen on sarcophagi from the fourth century onward. See Kloppenborg, "Literate Media," 31.

33 The date of composition of the gospel is here important only for general context, and I am comfortable assuming a range of 70–110 CE.

34 This translation of 2 Tim 4:13 is from Kloppenborg, "Literate Media," 32.

35 Ibid., 33 (emphasis in original).

36 Eyl, *Signs, Wonders, and Gifts*, 45.

37 For a complete discussion of the four modes, see Stanley Stowers, "The Religion of Plant and Animal Offerings versus the Religion of Meanings, Essences, and Textual Mysteries," in *Ancient Mediterranean Sacrifice*, ed. Jennifer Wright Knust and Zsuzsanna Varhelyi (Oxford: Oxford University Press, 2011), 9–24.

38 Ibid., 41.

39 Daniel Ullucci further modifies the theory of modes of religiosity, creating a theory that is a hybrid of Whitehouse and Stowers. Ullucci suggests that three modes – rather than Whitehouse's two or Stowers's four – are most helpful in creating a typology of religious experts. As well, Ullucci focuses his theory on experts only, in order to acknowledge the vast differences between the "formulations of religious experts" and the realities of religious activity for most persons in the ancient Mediterranean. See Daniel Ullucci, "Toward a Typology of Religious Experts in the Ancient Mediterranean," in *"The One Who Sows Bountifully" Essays in Honor of Stanley K. Stowers*, ed. Caroline Johnson Hodge, Saul M. Olyan, Daniel Ullucci, and Emma Wasserman (Providence, RI: Brown University, 2013), 96.

40 Kloppenborg, "Literate Media," 35.

8

Would You Know a Jewish Gospel if You Saw it? Ignatius, Jerome, Eusebius, and the Search for the Hebrew Gospel

Matthew W. Mitchell

Christian interest in Jewish literature has always been apologetic or polemic rather than historical.[1]

"Jewish Christianity" was not discovered by historical analysis. It was invented as a humanistic reclamation of Christian myth.[2]

This gospel [the Gospel of the Hebrews] is at least as old as, and probably older than, the synoptic gospels of our canon; that it issued from the common early gospel tradition, and so may be a source of, or at least a concomitant of, our canonical Matthew and Luke.[3]

Sometimes profound insights are hidden in observations that, at a first glance, seem to be statements of the obvious. In an essay on the apparent liminal canonical status of the *Gospel of the Hebrews* in Eusebius' *Historia Ecclesiae*, Petri Luomanen draws a seemingly banal conclusion about Eusebius of Caesarea's ambivalence about the gospel and the curious element of his mentioning of the text as "an example of a text whose canonical status was not perfectly clear": "The main reason why Eusebius placed the 'Gospel of the Hebrews' in the second category in his list of canonical writings was that it was referred to by writers he understood to be trustworthy transmitters of the apostolic tradition ... it was no longer a real option for the writers within the 'mainstream,' but Eusebius, who had carefully reviewed the writings of his predecessors, could not dismiss it out of hand because it was referred to by esteemed teachers of the apostolic faith."[4] That Eusebius is largely focused on carefully examining and cataloguing his predecessors in a work such as the *Church History* is a trifle obvious, perhaps, but Luomanen has hit upon something important that I return to below. He is not the first scholar to note, however, that Eusebius seems more concerned with who champions a book than with the book's contents. "What determined his attitude towards the canonicity of a New Testament work was almost exclusively its use by the churches or by Christian writers such as Irenaeus, Clement of Alexandria, or Origen."[5] This has not been emphasized enough, however, as attention has focused more on the vagueness with which Eusebius seemingly draws distinctions between the New Testament's canonical and non-canonical books (Revelation, famously, occupying a place in two categories).

The notion of a "margin" or liminality to the canon Eusebius writes of has been a bit of a puzzle to modern scholars produced by Protestantized cultures; not that it existed (as it clearly did), but how to comprehend its structure.[6] As Bruce Metzger observes, "what seems at first reading to be a straightforward account, on closer analysis leaves one perplexed."[7] Éric Junod's statement two decades later is virtually identical: "À la première lecture, cette célèbre notice du livre III frappe par son caractère systématique. Pourtant plus on l'examine, moins on est sûr de bien comprendre les classifications d'Eusèbe!"[8] In a more wide-ranging assessment that attempts to clarify the confusion, François Bovon writes that scholars need to take account of the long-standing practice of Christians to divide books "not into two but into three categories: the most authoritative were considered canonical; those deprived of any authority were rejected and called apocryphal; and those that had some authority, that is, those that were considered profitable or useful, comprised a third category."[9] This presentation by Bovon, though helpful, also requires some additional reflection. First, however, it is necessary to touch briefly upon the general issue of Jewish Christianity and the often conflated issue of its gospels.

JEWISH CHRISTIANITY AND ITS GOSPELS

As many scholars have noted, "Jewish Christian" as a category is difficult to define, if it is not, in fact, meaningless.[10] Perhaps this is unsurprising given that simply putting together two terms that are individually the subjects of complex histories and scholarly disputation is likely not to give rise to a self-evident meaning.[11] Summaries of scholarship abound, especially in books with dissertation-style lit reviews, but the general trends are pretty clear.[12] "Jewish Christian" seems to emerge, in part at least, as a modern attempt to more accurately and generically describe groups known to the Church

Fathers that did not fit their emergent notions of "orthodox" Christian belief. Additionally, in modern New Testament scholarship (meaning F.C. Baur in this instance), "Jewish Christianity" serves as a descriptor of Torah-observant Jesus-belief, contrasting to non-observant gentile Christianity.[13] Thus there are multiple masters being served by this terminology: in Baur's case an emergent grappling with the understanding of what we now think of axiomatically as the historical development of a Jewish sect into a non-Jewish religion. Whether viewed as a gradual or a rapid "Gentilization," a sudden versus a slow "parting of the ways," it does not matter (Baur is simply anchoring this shift in the New Testament rather than gradually throughout late antiquity). In later scholars (e.g., Daniéliou or Schoeps), there is an attempt to find systematic theological and organizational principles behind the seemingly bewildering number of groups in the literature (Elkasites, Ebionites, Nazoreans), extending throughout the pre-Nicene era even into the rise of Islam.[14] Jewish Christianity's ultimate destiny in Schoeps's view is "a paradox of world-historical proportions, viz., the fact that Jewish Christianity indeed disappeared within the Christian church, but was preserved in Islam and thereby extended some of its basic ideas even to our own day."[15]

When several things are happening all at once, and connections are being made across broad sweeps of texts, centuries, and alleged historical groups, sometimes it is necessary to pause and survey what is happening (e.g., the energy expended on defining "Jewish Christian" as if other categories are more self-evident or unproblematic[16]). We must first acknowledge that we are stuck with the basic issues that most of us first encountered as students. We really only know of "Jewish Christians" indirectly through the texts that reference them and their writings. However, the interpretation of the texts upon which we are reliant is fraught with pitfalls – from our own inevitable importing of questions into our readings to the biases and reliability of the material upon which we are focused and dependent. Generating new questions and meanings is naturally central to almost any document worth studying, especially narrative documents with characters and thematic layering, but it poses problems in the quest for basic historical inquiry. Petri Luomanen's 2012 *Recovering Jewish-Christian Sects and Gospels* is aptly named,[17] inasmuch as we are "excavating" as much as we are "reading." Andrew Gregory makes a similar distinction between viewing these writings as "texts" or "sources."[18]

To oversimplify, Baur's openness to non-canonical writings like the *Pseudo-Clementines* was predicated upon a sort of theological thematic decoding of a continuity between those materials and the anti-Pauline elements from the earliest New Testament evidence. In this regard, as in so many respects,

Baur's approach sets a kind of template for later scholarship, and one can, of course, draw a line of influence through to much more recent scholarship.[19] That Baur's categories of Pauline Christianity and Jewish Christianity are now viewed, fairly or not, as "invidious fabrications" does not alter their impact.[20] The largest variation is really how much continuity one sees behind the various groups whose theology we reconstruct from the materials at hand, and how much continuity there is between the New Testament materials and the next three or four centuries. In some cases there is a high degree of optimism about the ability of scholars to identify later materials with much earlier groups or vice versa.[21] As our volume's honoree Stephen Wilson notes, for Jewish Christian groups, though the "evidence is slight, and often late and tendentious[,] [y]et the fascination ... exerts a considerable pull."[22] The basic problem for all scholarship, however, remains the one that Taylor notes: "If one can trace Jewish roots in any given text, this does not necessarily mean that a text is Jewish-Christian."[23] If this is true for any given text, clearly it is a *qal vahomer* for the "Jewish Christian gospel" tradition, the *Gospel of the Hebrews* included. Scholars, of course, have long been aware of these difficulties.[24] Andrew Gregory lists the questions a scholar must ask about any so-called Jewish Christian gospel:

> The first is the question of what is a gospel, and which early Christian texts should be considered as such. The second pertains to the narrower but no less complex problem of what is meant by "Jewish-Christianity," and what it might mean to refer to a gospel or indeed to any other text as Jewish-Christian. This raises the question as to the grounds on which it is appropriate for the historian to differentiate between and to classify such early Christian gospels as are extant. Is it on the basis of their postulated provenance and authorship, on the manner of their subsequent transmission and reception, on their perceived theological outlook or on differences in their literary form?[25]

Luomanen's efforts to avoid the methodological pitfalls Gregory outlines involves the search for "Jewish Christian indicators" over other clues, though the difference seems one of a matter of degree only.[26]

Yet how does one dovetail these cautionary notes with the extravagant claims made for "the Hebrew Gospel" or "the *Gospel of the Hebrews*" in particular, and the Jewish Christian Gospel tradition more generally? As to the groups who presumably utilized these texts, a lack of knowledge has not been dissuasive: "We know little for sure about the developments in any early Christian communities. It is therefore an impossible task to trace the origins of a sect like the Ebionites to the Jewish-Christian groups of the first century that just happen to be known to us. *This has not stopped anyone from trying.*"[27] The confidence with which speculations are built rests upon a gospel tradition that has either *three* or *one* gospels, none of which are currently extant beyond fragmentary quotations. Yet the *Gospel of the Hebrews* holds a "peculiar interest and fascination" that has meant its being proffered as a vehicle to provide a new slant on the synoptic problem,[28] for example, serving as the source behind one or the other of the gospels, either as a competitor to Q or as some other possible unrecognized but nonetheless identifiable source. For example, Luke 1:1 could refer to the Hebrew Gospel itself or a source held in common with the Hebrew Gospel.[29] This is clearly the position of James R. Edwards (in *The Hebrew Gospel and the Development of the Gospel Tradition* and elsewhere), who argues for a replacement of the Q source with the Hebrew Gospel.[30] Andrew Gregory, though more cautious, thinks the *Gospel of the Ebionites* should be reflected in the Nestle-Aland apparatus (Gregory 2005).[31]

These implications of the *Gospel of the Hebrews* for understanding the Synoptics were raised in the nineteenth century,[32] and in the 1930s and 1940s it was even proposed that the *Gospel of the Hebrews* was the inspiration for the *Toledoth Yeshu* (or was perhaps the object of a parody of an earlier recension of it[33]), could help in understanding perplexing rabbinic Aramaic idioms,[34] and of course (!) preserved traces of or an acquaintance with the Semitic original of Matthew as per Papias.[35] Many of these connections are tantalizing and occasionally even seem logically coherent or compelling. But the more exciting the connections, the more one needs to verify that coherency and plausibility are appropriate to the evidence being presented. So I now turn to the alleged appearance of the Jewish Christian *Gospel of the Hebrews* in the writings of Ignatius of Antioch.

THE *GOSPEL OF THE HEBREWS* AND IGNATIUS

That Ignatius of Antioch bears witness to this particular document is based upon the explicit testimony of Jerome. Now, this has been written about fairly extensively, so I rely on summarizing as much as is possible, but the textual basis of this testimony requires some examination.[36] To make clear the connection with Edwards and similar theories of the Hebrew Gospel's significance: Jerome's assessment of Ignatius's knowledge of this particular document presents a witness to the document's circulation *in the early second century*, which lays a firmer foundation for claims such as Lukan dependency upon it,[37] or identification with this text as either the lost Semitic original of Matthew or an ancestor of that document. The Ignatian passage in *Smyrneans* runs as follows:

> For I know and believe [Ἐγὼ γὰρ καὶ μετὰ τὴν ἀνάστασιν ἐν σαρκὶ αὐτὸν οἶδα καὶ πιστεύω] that he was in the flesh even after the resurrection. And when he came to those who were with Peter, he said to them, "Reach out, touch me and see that I am not a bodiless daimon [Λάβετε, ψηλαφήσατέ με καὶ ἴδετε ὅτι οὐκ εἰμὶ δαιμόνιον ἀσώματον]." And immediately they touched him and believed, having been intermixed with his flesh and spirit. For this reason they also despised death, for they were found to be beyond death. And after his resurrection he ate and drank with them as a fleshly being, even though he was spiritually united with the Father. (*Smyrn.* 3.1–3)

Eusebius comments on this passage in the *Church History* with the statement that he simply does not know the origin of this saying. "And the same man writing to the Smyrnaeans, used the following words: I do not know whence he took them [οὐκ οἶδ᾽ὁπόθεν ῥητοῖς συγκέχρηται], with regard to Christ, saying: But I know and believe that he was in the flesh after the resurrection. And when he came to Peter and those with him he said to them, Take me and feel me and see that I am not a demon [Lake: 'phantom'] without a body and immediately they touched him and believed" (Eus. *Church History* 3.36.11). Jerome, of course, attributes this phrase to the *Gospel of the Hebrews*:

> Leaving from there [Smyrna] he wrote to the Philadelphians and Smyrnaeans and separately to Polycarp recommending the Antiochaean Church to him. In this he bore also witness to the gospel which I have recently translated, in respect of the person of Christ saying: "I indeed saw him in the flesh after the resurrection and I believe that it was he [in qua et de evangelio, quod nuper a me translatum est, super persona Christi ponit testimonium dicens: 'ego vero post resurrectionem in carne eum vidi et credo, quia sit'], and when he came to Peter and those who were with Peter, he said to them: 'Behold, touch me and see me how that I am not a demon without a body [quia non sum daemonium incorporale],' and straightway they touched him and believed." (*De vir. ill.* 16)

There are several reasons that scholars are so optimistic about Jerome's identification of this quotation in *Smyrneans*, but chief among them is that there are multiple references to a Jewish Christian gospel called the *Gospel of the Hebrews*, so that, on the surface, there may not be any good reason to doubt the identification. Putting it another way: a quotation from a seemingly well-known, apparently widely circulated text is identified by a prominent linguist and biblical exegete. Additionally, Jerome claims that this reference derives from a text he has personally encountered and has even translated.[38]

Of course, as has been pointed out by many scholars, the mystery around Jerome's confidence is all the more puzzling when taken in combination with Eusebius's lack of recognition. Jerome claims not only to have personal knowledge of the *Gospel of the Hebrews* but that a copy of the *Gospel of the Hebrews* was in the library at Caesarea, which seems to have been the case for some time (going back to Origen). Yet while Eusebius certainly had the Ignatian materials available to him (likely "the seven letters" with Polycarp's *Philippians* attached[39]), and while he is aware of the *Gospel of the Hebrews*, he does not recognize this quotation.[40]

There are, of course, numerous small details that are striking. Pier Beatrice places great emphasis upon Jerome's "I saw and believe" (vidi et credo versus the "I know and believe" of the Greek texts [οἶδα καὶ πιστεύω]) as an authentic reading rather than as a misreading or a conflation of some sort. Of course, as Beatrice notes, that Origen apparently attributed this odd saying ("bodiless demon") to another work (the *Doctrina Petri*) altogether requires explanation as well.[41] The reading "vidi" is important for the alignment Beatrice makes between the Petrine attribution of Origen and Jerome's attestation to the *Gospel of the Hebrews* (though Origen is not only quoting the line to contest the authenticity of its source, this passage only comes to us via Rufinus's translation). J.B. Lightfoot sees both an issue with Jerome's knowledge of Ignatius (being dependent upon Eusebius) and possible contamination for this reading via a similar passage in Luke 24:39.[42] It is equally possible that some slips of the pen or eye could lead to confusion between εἶδον, οἶδα, and vidi (they are, oddly, etymologically connected).[43] What one makes of Jerome's attribution seems to be more dependent upon one's sense of Jerome's reliability than anything else. Jerome clearly, however, equates the *Gospel of the Hebrews* (and the *Gospel of the Nazoreans*) with the Aramaic original of Matthew (i.e., Jerome thinks there is one Semitic/Jewish gospel[44]).

This may seem like it is hardly solid ground upon which to demonstrate a connection between Aramaic Matthew and the *Gospel of the Hebrews*, yet the scholarly literature abounds with claims of Jerome as either sturdily reliable or dubious, largely consonant with the view of the Hebrew Gospel the scholar wishes to advance. This is either the recognition of a now lost text from a great scholar or a mistake made in the middle of a work that is "self aggrandizing" and is "a clumsy, incomplete, and pompous first attempt" at cataloguing Christian writers.[45] *De viris illustribus* is "inevitably derivative," "propagandistic history," which only shows Jerome's knowledge of Eusebius to be "uncritical" and demonstrates that, "through sheer carelessness, he misunderstood or mistranslated him."[46] Timothy C.G. Thornton notes more broadly that Jerome's enthusiastic references to a Semitic gospel seem to fade away over time, and he describes the situation as one of "academic embarrassment" as Jerome gradually realized that he either misunderstood what he had seen or had been misled (similar to modern scholars perhaps who cease mentioning things about which they have been wrong).[47] After all, "no Christian Father after Jerome says anything about the presence of a copy of Matthew's original 'Hebrew' Gospel in the library at Caesarea."[48] Yet we are still left with Eusebius not recognizing a quotation from a work that he writes about elsewhere, so that to value Jerome's testimony may be seen to diminish Eusebius's reliability. However, as I and others note, the use of *any* written material in Ignatius is a notoriously difficult topic, and there are other ways to approach Jerome, Ignatius, and the Hebrew Gospel.[49]

First, a list of the questions that seem to be raised by this one alleged quotation in *Smryneans*, beginning with Ignatius:

1 Is Ignatius "quoting" an unknown variant of a gospel, an unknown gospel (Hebrew Gospel), or some kind of testimony document? Keep in mind that this quotation looks quite a bit like Luke 24:39. Or …
2 Is Ignatius "quoting from memory" or is he imprecisely recalling something that he had heard proclaimed, recited, or read? This would make far more sense in the context of the Ignatian correspondence.

Given that Eusebius does not know the source of the quotation, but Jerome is quite certain:

3 Is Jerome correct that the quotation occurs in the Hebrew Gospel (not that it follows that Ignatius knows it from the same place)?
4 If he is he mistaken about the source of the quotation, why does he sound so confident as to his attribution?
5 But if he is correct, what does the absence of any such identification by Eusebius mean? Eusebius does not, after all, merely let this phrase pass without comment but pointedly states he does not know its source.

If Jerome is correct *and* Ignatius knows it from the Gospel:

6 Does this mean that Ignatius uses what later Christian writers fairly clearly consider a "Jewish" gospel? Albeit in Greek, and without quoting it as such? This would of course raise further questions about whether Ignatius considered this document as "Jewish." Ignatian scholarship has long assumed some sort of Jewish or Jewish Christian opposition in the letters, but usually this is because Ignatius is seen as "the product of a line of development which goes directly back to Paul and to his law-free gospel" versus "Jewish Christian opposition" in a Baurian schema.[50] But we would need to rethink our sense of Ignatius, at any rate.
7 Does this mean the *Gospel of the Hebrews* is early? Ignatius is writing in the early second century, but he is writing in Greek, so does this mean that this gospel is not only early but already translated and available? But what became of the original version, then, if it was already in Greek among the Syrian Christians of the early second century?
8 Could Jerome be half-right only? For example, the quotation is like one he has seen in a gospel he *thinks* is the *Gospel of the Hebrews*, but he is wrong about the gospel, not the quotation (as had been pointed out in the nineteenth century, even if one assumes an Aramaic original for Matthew, this does not mean that any later gospel text encountered in Aramaic is the original Matthew[51]).
9 Perhaps another "half-right" solution: the quotation is like one in the *Gospel of the Hebrews*, which he has seen, but Ignatius knows it from elsewhere (whether written or not), which explains Origen's attribution to a Petrine document. That is, the *Gospel of the Hebrews* either shares a common source with both Ignatius and the *Kerygmata Petrou/Doctrina Petri* or Ignatius knows the latter, which is the ultimate source for the *Gospel of the Hebrews* (making it later, not early).

This sketch leaves me exhausted. But as to follow the question a bit further would mean asking about Eusebius's knowledge and not Jerome's reliability, the last question would then be whether we have evidence that Eusebius simply does not know this gospel as well as Jerome. This brings us back to Eusebius's view of the *Gospel of the Hebrews*, and the article of Luomanen I mention at the start of this chapter,[52] but there are a few points to clarify first. As I do not think that Ignatius is best understood through the lens of "quoting" a written gospel, and it is pretty clear that Ignatius is concerned with creating a boundary line between what he (at least) calls "Judaism" and "Christianity" (*Magn.* 8.1; 9.1; 10.1; 10.3; *Phil* 6.1; 8.2), there is really not much point in exegesis that results in talking about Ignatius "quoting a Jewish Christian gospel." There is not much point, really, in talking about Ignatius quoting any written document. Ignatius is far more concerned with personal authority and a claim to the authority and traditions of the apostles than he is to any written text, even the ones we are certain about him using, such as 1 Corinthians, which he never "quotes": "I will repeat in simpler terms that there is every indication that 1 Corinthians is used, but not cited, by Ignatius because *1 Corinthians* is not an authority. The language of 1 Corinthians, however, *has authority* because it is Paul's. This point should not be misunderstood, since it seems to ignore an obvious association or a simple shorthand manner of saying that Paul's writings have authority because they are written by Paul. This is undoubtedly so, but Paul is not used as a written text."[53] This view of Ignatius makes perfect sense in light of the role played by *agrapha*, especially during the second century, a period in which distinctly Christian writings are being circulated as apostolically authoritative but not really Scripture.[54] They are "not holy texts but the records of living memory."[55] Even the very title of a text like the *Didache* is, in Helmut Koester's view, "an attempt to give material substance to the hitherto undefined authority of the apostles."[56] So if none of the questions above are going to be answerable, what can the Ignatian connection to the Hebrew Gospel help us with?

Let us start with a different approach, as I think it is likely represented in Ignatius, Eusebius, and Jerome: the issue is not the theology of the book but the theological identity and lineage of the person using the book. Second-century Christians, after all, inherited a written authority (the Jewish Bible) that, although it was read by other groups, was authoritatively understood through a distinct line of interpretation (the "gospel") that traced itself back to Jesus and, in the case of Ignatius, was overseen by an *episkopos* whose authority depended upon this connection. Apostolic tradition is reliable and authoritative because of the authority of those who originated and curated it, which is the rationale for the Ignatian overtures to Pauline language, and likely all the traditions in Ignatius that generations of scholars have thought "sound like" Matthew or Luke, including the "bodiless demon." This is different from *scripture* in this era as the apostolic authority of a tradition and its transmission may be in a written form but is not dependent upon or conceived of as a text:[57] "authority was accorded not to these books directly, but more obliquely."[58] For Ignatius, to Judaize or keep the sabbath negates the authority of what one teaches (*Magn.* 8–10), while the identity of "circumcised" or "foreskinned" is not as important as whether they "profess Jesus" or "expound Judaism" (*Phil* 6.1–2). Of course, the famous passage at *Philadelphians* 8.1–2 seems to uphold the authority of the bishop and a Christocentric interpretative tradition over the written authority of the Old Testament.[59] Parallels have been drawn with the development of the notion of rabbinic lineages, especially among those interested in the textualization of oral traditions,[60] but the implication here is simple enough: there are no "gospel quotations" to find in Ignatius, but Ignatius provides an apostolic authentication and anchor for Jerome to solidify his views (Semitic language originals being of special interest to Jerome and his view of the canon[61]). For the modern scholars who seek the Hebrew Gospel, Ignatius provides an authenticating early witness to the circulation of a gospel and, alongside Jerome, a textual continuity with fourth-century Jewish Christians. Edwards represents this pattern nicely in all its (in my view) wrongheadedness: "Four reputable witnesses in the early church – Ignatius, Origen, Eusebius, and Jerome – " quote something like Luke 24:39 without attributing it to Luke, indicating that "thus already, already in Ignatius's day the Hebrew Gospel of Matthew was recognized as an authority preserving an authentic saying of the resurrected Lord."[62] This is, of course, not even backwards but wholly misunderstands "authority" in the Ignatian correspondence. As a cautionary note on scholarly enthusiasm, it should be remarked upon here that not only was the authority of the *episkopos* the ultimate issue at stake in the famous nineteenth-century denial (F.C. Baur!) and affirmation (J.B. Lightfoot!) of the authenticity of the Ignatian corpus, this very passage has been equally touted as proving the lateness of the Ignatian writings. That is to say, the parallels may be indicators not of an early Hebrew Gospel but of a much later date for the Ignatian corpus.[63]

APOSTOLIC LINEAGE AND "THE CANON"

There is evidence that Ignatius's understanding of apostolic legitimation through both a chain of authentic transmission and the legitimacy of the person using or interpreting a writing rather than the writing itself is pervasive and ongoing. The third and fourth centuries are not the second, of course, but the force of apostolic lineage and orthodox spiritual ancestry continues and is actually the animating force behind the *de viri illustribus* and the *Church History*. Also, of course, the New Testament in the fourth century is established as a written text, a collection of *books with authors* (who are, of course, apostles). But Eusebius lists the books of the New Testament, and the *Gospel of the Hebrews* among them, not according to their theologies, but according to *who uses them*. Now, the complexity of the Eusebian list requires more comment below, but for the moment note that at *Church History* 3.25 there are:

1 books used by all Christians (*homologoumena*);
2 books used by some, but not all Christians;
3 the books "put forward by heretics."

The books put forward by heretics have *no support* among "real" Christians, demonstrated by the fact that nobody among those who belong "to the succession of the orthodox ever thought it right to refer to in his writings." Books used by all, books used by some, and books used only by heretics. That is, although Eusebius knows that books have authors, styles, and contents, we know the books by who uses them, not by what they say.

This, of course, is not at all how modern scholars approach these texts. I would formulate the difference as follows: (1) the Modern scholar: text betrays belief system of group or belief system can be articulated from the text. "Text says x, thus group/community that believed x produced and used it." (2) Eusebius: text is x because x group uses it. "X group uses it, therefore it is x text and must say x." Eusebius was, among other things, a librarian and textual critic. He does not think that texts do not need scholarly care or occasionally correction. For Pamphilus (and thus his successor, Eusebius), the biblical and religious writings collected at Caesarea were often in need of correction and restoration. In this context it is not the changing of an apostolic text by a scholar that makes it suspicious but, rather, changing something without noting it, which is the activity of a heretic.[64] The text is known as reliable not because it is simply what it is but by the reliability of the person and community who use it, and by the authority of the people who have transmitted it. Eusebius lists the *Gospel of the Hebrews* not because he knows it well (or not) but because it is valued by a group of people who, however marginal to his understanding of the Church, are "Christian."

Thus also in the case of Jerome, whatever one may think of a development in his thought or a weakness in his comprehension; his statements about the Jewish Christian gospel make perfect sense from this approach. Jerome thinks the Aramaic/Semitic gospel is plausible because of the (apostolic) belief that Matthew wrote in Aramaic, but it is credible because *it is used by a community he thinks of as Jewish but also acceptably Christian*. Whether or not he is correct in any or all details, his (and Eusebius's) understanding of "a Jewish Christian gospel" is pretty straightforward: it is the one used by a group he thinks of as Jewish Christians. Jerome's writings really only attest that he encountered a group he thought of as sufficiently Christian to give its book credence, although he may "simply be repeating the origin myth surrounding the group whose gospel he encountered,"[65] or at least accommodating/assimilating it to the origin myths of his own tradition. There is an unfortunate side effect to noting this state of affairs, of course. No amount of theoretical tweaking of the terms "Jewish," "Christian," and "gospel" will allow us to encounter a Jewish Christian gospel defined thus.[66] The "bodiless demon," after all, is Jewish Christian (Jerome), heretical (Origen), or simply unknown (Eusebius), but it only really matters because it is, whatever else it is, Ignatian.

To trace the lineage of apostolicity and personal authority further, the Latin translator Rufinus later translates the *Church History* with some tweaking of the Eusebian canon list (which ultimately may have its roots in Origen's writings) to reflect his reality: *The Gospel according to the Hebrews* is still listed on the margins, but Revelation has moved away from it. Edmon Gallagher observes that this is not a sign of Rufinus being inept or inaccurate in his translation of Eusebius. Although he "adapts" the discussion of Scripture to the "fifth-century context, after the boundaries of the canon had become more firm,"[67] this is not a sign of unreliability. It is more likely the work of a careful translator working with the text of an author perceived to be orthodox, and in need of updating and correction, as Eusebius and Pamphilus themselves had done.

More explicitly, and on the same point, Catherine Chin observes of Rufinus's treatment of Origen's writings that this hermeneutic of *authentication via the person* is an integral aspect of scholarly work:

> Rufinus addresses the problem of textual change over time most directly in the preface to his *Apology for Origen* and in the short treatise at the end of the work, generally known as *On the Adulteration of the Works of Origen* … The argument of Rufinus's work is relatively straightforward: *whatever appears heretical in the works of Origen is likely the result of interpolations by heretics.* As evidence, Rufinus adduces a list of other Christian writers of unimpeachable orthodoxy, such as Clement of Rome, Athanasius, and Hilary of Poitiers, whose works have from time to time also been tampered with. He further quotes at length a letter of Origen's that complains of unreliable copies of his work in circulation. On strictly text-critical grounds, the argument (as Jerome would later point out) is weak, but it is of interest because it relies on *three basic assumptions: first, the instability of texts given the mechanics of late ancient book production; second, the presumption of authorial consistency, so that the same author cannot be both orthodox and heretical*; and third, the

> more general notion that textual corruption necessarily occurs over time, and that it is the task of later readers to restore a text to its original condition.[68]

The same themes emerge in Rufinus, apparently. Revelation is no longer on the margins for the Latin Church and thus Eusebius needs updating, and Origen is known to be an orthodox authority not simply because of what his writings say but because of the persons who have used his writings. In summary, modern scholars have properly become self-aware about the methodological traps that terms like "Jewish" and "Christian" contain. Yet much of the scholarship on the Jewish-Christian gospel traditions has focused on sophisticated technical and philological discussions to the exclusion of simple questions such as: Can a text be considered Jewish because it contains particular elements, characteristics, or language? Or is such a definition of "the text" not ultimately (pre)determined by one's categorization of the group or person using it?

It may be that most telling is the avoidance of an even simpler question I seek to raise, which is that reconstructing hypothetical communities through and with their reconstructed, hypothetical documents is not a meaningful activity. The grounds upon which we would or could recognize a Jewish Christian gospel, absent both Jewish Christians and their gospel, is, dare I say it, incorporeal, and dependent solely upon resurrection via scholarly imagination.

A SEEMINGLY UNNECESSARY PHILOLOGICAL APPENDIX: THE EUSEBIAN "CANON" LIST AT *CHURCH HISTORY 3.25* AND *THE GOSPEL OF THE HEBREWS*

At the outset I mention Bovon's proposed three categories of books in Christian tradition (canonical, apocryphal, and good for the soul), paired with Luomanen's attempt to sketch out Eusebius's view of the *Gospel of the Hebrews*. Luomanen, like many scholars,[69] thinks that there are also three categories of writing for Eusebius in his listing at *Church History* 3.25: accepted, disputed, and heretical. However, confusion abounds with the Eusebian categories (the more one examines them, seemingly, as Metzger and Junod claim), in part because he seems to operate with a degree of permeability within the category of "disputed" books but also because his terminology is varied and "manque parfois de rigeur dans les classifications qu'il opère et dans leur designation."[70] Problematic is his use of one of the "adjectifs classique de la critique littéraire," νόθος,[71] usually rendered as "spurious." Νόθος is applied to Revelation and the *Gospel of the Hebrews*, among others, and seems to many commentators to form a subgroup of the disputed. Gallagher, in his study of how these categories occur in Rufinius's Latin transmission of Eusebius, observes that "Eusebius here divides Christian literature into three categories of books: the ὁμολογούμενα (universally acknowledged), the ἀντιλεγόμενα (disputed), and the heretical books, to which Eusebius does not here assign a title, though he later will call them παντελῶς νόθα, 'completely spurious' (3.31.6). Problematically he has already used the word νόθος in 3.25 to describe the ἀντιλεγόμενα in such a manner that in that passage νόθος constituted either an alternative name for the ἀντιλεγόμενα or the name of a sub-category of the ἀντιλεγόμενα."[72] Kalin thinks that there is not much to be gained from examining the terminology as, in the end, "if there is a difference, it is not substantial."[73] Carriker makes a slightly different, but similar, assessment in surveying the likely contents of the Eusebian library. The issue is less with Eusebian terminology and more with the fact that he has two different categorization schemas, which results in a mixture of categories. "Eusebius' system of classifying NT writings at HE III.25 is somewhat confusing because Eusebius actually divides his texts into two overlapping categories: orthodox and unorthodox works on the one hand and, on the other, canonical (accepted as well as disputed) and uncanonical works."[74] This model comes from Metzger's *Canon of the New Testament*, which explains the "peculiar position" of the "spurious" books like *Gospel of the Hebrews* as "orthodox but uncanonical" and lays out a pictorial representation to make things clearer (table 8.3).[75] A.D. Baum further argues that a three-columned approach works better, assuming that Eusebius has three schemas, not just two: "Rezeption, Kanonizität, and Authentizität" (table 8.2).[76] Gallagher's examination of Rufinus's categories derived from Eusebius also helpfully includes a chart (see table 8.1, next page).

Luomanen notes that Eusebius placing the *Gospel of the Hebrews* in the "spurious" category (*Church History* 3.25), which he views as part of the Eusebian list of *antilegomena*, indicates its marginality.[77] However, explaining something by noting it belongs to a poorly understood category that may be one thing or may be something else does not much clarify things.

But instead of counting categories, let us assume some of the terms are fairly clear: ὁμολογούμενα (universally acknowledged) and the ἀντιλεγόμενα (disputed). Now, ἐνδιάθηκος and οὐκ ἐνδιάθηκος seem to function as more formal categories ("Testamentary"?), a word whose use seems to "début avec Origène et se termine avec Eusèbe,"[78] but which is understandable as a step towards later terminology like "canon": (1) books used by everyone with no objections; (2) books used by some, though there have been objections. At the very end of the discussion are the books *not* used, except by heretics, which deserve no real mention other than for dismissal.

Table 8.1
Eusebius and Rufinus

Eusebius h.e. 3.25	*Rufinus*
ὁμολογούμενα	About which no doubt ever existed (*de quibus nulla umquam prosus exstitit dubitation*)
Gospels, Acts, Paul, 1 Peter, 1 John, Apocalypse of John	same books minus Apocalypse of John
ἀντιλεγόμενα ("disputed")	About which some doubted (*de quibus a nonnullis dubitatum est*)
James, Jude, 2 Peter, 2–3 John	same books plus Apocalypse of John
Νόθα	About which there is total doubt (*de quibus quam maxime dubitur*)
Acts of Paul, Shepherd of Hermas, Apocalypse of Peter, Ep. Barnabas, Didache, Apocalypse of John, *Gospel according to the Hebrews*	same books minus Apocalypse of John

Source: Adapted from Edmon L. Gallagher, "Origen via Rufinus on the New Testament Canon," *New Testament Studies* 62, no. 3 (2016): 461–76.

Table 8.2
Assessments of NT canonical works

Die Bücher der apostolischen Zeit	Der Kanon der Kirche: Rezeption	Kanonizität	Der kritische Kanon: Authentizität
Mt Mk Lk Joh Act Paulinen [Heb] 1Joh 1 Petr (Apk)	ὁμολογούμενος	ἐνδιάθηκος	[γνήσιος]
Jak Jud 2Petr 2Joh 3Joh ActPaul Herm ApkPetr Barn Did (Apk) EvHebrv	ἀντιλεγόμενος	οὐκ ἐνδιάθηκος	
EvPetr EvThom EvMath ActAndr ActJoh *etc.*	[ἀμνημονούμενος]		νόθος

Source: Adapted from A.D. Baum, "Der neutestamentliche Kanon bei Eusebios (*Hist. eccl.* III,25,1–7) im Kontext seiner literaturgeschichtlichen Arbeit," *Ephemerides Theologicae Lovanienses* 73, no. 4 (1997): 305–48.

Table 8.3
Eusebius, according to the schema of Bruce M. Metzger.

Book types, all orthodox unless struck through:

1. Canonical
   a. Recognized (*homologoumena*)
   b. Disputed (*antilegoumena*)
2. Uncanonical
   a. Spurious (νόθα)
   b. ~~Fictions of heretics/unorthodox~~ (παντελῶς νόθα)

Source: Bruce M. Metzger, *The Canon of the New Testament: Its Origin, Development, and Significance* (Oxford: Clarendon Press, 1987), reorganized.

ΝΌΘΟΣ

This organization then leaves us only with the category of the "spurious," in which Eusebius places the *Gospel of the Hebrews*. As mentioned above, confusion stems from Eusebius's seemingly inconsistent use of the term and his placement of Revelation in both the ὁμολογούμενα and as νόθος. Occupying two categories would, one would think, make something disputed. Eusebius, despite stating that heretical writings do not belong, later describes the writings of the heretics as, among other things, "wholly spurious" (παντελῶς νόθα) in 3.31.6. Though an adverb is present, of course, "il n'empêche qu'Eusbèbe brouille son message."[79]

Three problems exist: one is that Eusebius may not be wholly consistent either in his usage or with what he thinks of these books. A second problem is with the English terminology. The third problem is the study of words without attention to the particles, adverbs, and terms surrounding them. Now, νόθος is often rendered as "spurious," and the lexicons will render it as "bastard," or "baseborn." These terms, or even the term "illegitimate," carry little meaning to many contemporary English speakers, I suspect. The base meaning of νόθος in classical Greek is as an opposite to γνήσιος (genuine) and refers to parentage and lineage. To be accurate, a child of a citizen father and a non-citizen mother is νόθος, while a child of two citizen parents is γνήσιος. In some cases being the child of a παλλακίς/παλλακή may have been less of a disadvantage than others, but it was never the same as being the child of a "legal" citizen-wife. This distinction obviously depended greatly upon the family and the *polis* in question and the era in which one was living. The analogous application to matters of "legitimate" books, worship, or doctrine is obvious; but the technical meaning of the term remains present. Now, being "illegitimate" in terms of one's parentage is not necessarily a mark of pride or a compliment, at least in contrast to the legitimate child, but we are helped by remembering that many references to νόθος are acknowledged not with shame (although I have no doubt this was sometimes the case) but simply as a statement of fact. One *can* still be a member of the family, in this sense, but one is simply never of a pure lineage or licit relations. To be clearer, one can walk around the *agora*, and participate to some extent in the life of the *polis*, even though one is not necessarily allowed into the *ekklêsia*. Aristophanes plays the term for laughs in *The Birds* as Herakles discovers he is (of course) νόθος, not having been listed by his father ἐς τοὺς φράτερας (1650–69), and thus cannot inherit legally.

Rather than make a full survey here, it is enough to note that the term's basic meaning does not shift much over the intervening years. Thesaurus Linguae Graecae occurrences indicate Eusebian use of the term predominates mostly in passages reproduced from Philo. Philo often contrasts γνήσιος with νόθος, usually in reference to notions like "beauty," "piety" (i.e., legitimate versus illegitimate), or the like. He preserves the classical legal meaning, however, referencing how Abraham left all to Isaac and not to his "bastards and to the spurious reasonings of concubines" (νόθοις καὶ πλαγίοις τῶν παλλακῶν λογισμοῖς, *Sacr.* 43.3), and noting that Joseph appears tending sheep with brothers who were νόθοι, not γνήσιοι, even in appearance as a means of contrast (as the Bible mentions their mothers rather than their father [*Deus* 121]). The same terms apply to the contrast of Ishmael and Isaac (*Sobr.* 8–9). Josephus uses the term in its technical sense, generally (e.g., *J.W.* 1.26.2: Aliphaz son of Esau had five γνήσιοι, but Amalek was not one [γὰρ νόθος ἦν ἐκ παλλακῆς]; cf. *A.J.* 2.4; 5.233; *J.W.* 2.89; 5.443). The New Testament itself uses the term in Hebrews to describe how being God's υἱός means accepting his παιδεία, while not accepting it renders one νόθος (Hebrews 12:8). υἱός here evidently supplants γνήσιος as the contrast, for obvious reasons.

It is easy to see how νόθος becomes a term of art in ancient literary criticism (Galen allegedly wrote a volume on the γνησιῶν and νοθῶν of Hippocrates). It is a statement of ancestry or parentage, literary or real (Junod: "paternité littéraire douteuse"); it does not automatically mean that a book could not be read or even loved. The act of reading would not, however, change the birth certificate or its place in the will (to mix the metaphor a bit). The *Gospel of the Hebrews* is cherished by one group that is odd but clearly acceptably orthodox; its apostolic ancestry is dubious so that, while it may be read, it can never occupy the licit place of unquestioned writings. This is far different from being heretical, of course. Eusebius can doubt the lineage of a text but not its use by a particular group nor that it has been used or referenced by authors of apostolic integrity. Thus with not only the Hebrew

Gospel but with all the books seen as νόθος. The *Shepherd*, *Epistle of Barnabas*, the *Didache of the Apostles*, Acts of Paul, and Revelation are all somehow slightly illicit in their origin or lineage, but they are valued by members of the community (in some cases far outstripping "canonical" books in actual usage among early Christians). Thus books of the heretics do not even rightly belong to this category (ὅθεν οὐδ᾽ἐν νόθοις αὐτα κατατακτέον, 3.25.7).

Revelation falls confusingly into place as either accepted, with no objection, or else it is of illicit origins. This would normally be, one would think, a matter of debate, but the conditional phrasing may be a clue to this puzzle. Eusebius earlier states that Revelation's status among the ὁμολογούμενα or as νόθος is a live debate "up to now" (ἔτι νῦν, 3.24.18) and then observes each of its potential classifications with a conditional clause (εἰ γε φανείη … εἰ φανείη, 3.25.4). Eusebius states that all the books he describes as νόθος might well have been among the ἀντιλεγόμενα, or perhaps might be yet (ταῦτα δὲ πάντα τῶν ἀντιλεγομένων ἄν ἐιη, 3.25.6). The lack of any conditional moods with the ἀντιλεγόμενα or the other ὁμολογούμενα, taken alongside his indication that this is an ongoing debate, with Revelation yet to have its status settled, and that, in theory, future legitimation would move this book (and perhaps others?) into the ἀντιλεγόμενα, might then also mean that the ἀντιλεγόμενα had been objected to by some but currently were not. This is not a necessary reading of the Greek, but it explains Revelation being in two places and certainly accords with Rufinus's later moving of Revelation from both its conditional categories and into one corresponding with the ἀντιλεγόμενα (see table 8.1). The *Gospel of the Hebrews*, of course, has not moved. Nor, for that matter, does Eusebius indicate that there is any doubt about other writings such as the *Shepherd* not being illegitimate.

The phrasing in 3.25.6, ταῦτα δὲ πάντα τῶν ἀντιλεγομένων ἂν εἴη, could be taken to mean "these all [i.e., everything listed after the ὁμολογούμενα' would be the ἀντιλεγόμενα." But this fails to explain Revelation not simply being among the straightforward ἀντιλεγόμενα (i.e., why put it in two categories if it really is only a subset of a category designed to encompass contested works). But this line may also mean "these all [i.e., the books designated as illegitimate] *might be* among the ἀντιλεγόμενα, *but* we have necessarily made a list nevertheless." This understanding would mean that these books designated as "illegitimate" are not listed as ἀντιλεγόμενα for an additional reason. Eusebius also wants to list them to "fully distinguish" between them and the other books.

We now hit upon an issue that is beyond simply stacking and collating nouns, adjectives, and adverbs, inasmuch as Eusebius subtly makes use of particles in the subsequent clauses, favoring τε … καί but also μὲν … δέ and variations thereof, in what is quite a complex sentence.[80] Kalin makes much of his use of καί in one line, but there is more going on than that.[81] The sentence is a result clause with an optative (and complementary infinitive) governed by the verb πεποιήμεθα (we have made a list [κατάλογον πεποιήμεθα], so that we might have the capacity to know [ἵν' εἰδέναι ἔχοιμεν]).

> ταῦτα δὲ πάντα τῶν ἀντιλεγομένων ἂν εἴη, ἀναγκαίως δὲ καὶ τούτων ὅμως τὸν κατάλογον πεποιήμεθα, διακρίνοντες τάς τε κατὰ τὴν ἐκκλησιαστικὴν παράδοσιν ἀληθεῖς καὶ ἀνωμολογημένας γραφὰς καὶ τὰς ἄλλως παρὰ ταύτας, οὐκ ἐνδιαθήκους μὲν ἀλλὰ καὶ ἀντιλεγομένας, ὅμως δὲ παρὰ πλείστοις τῶν ἐκκλησιαστικῶν γινωσκομένας, ἵν' εἰδέναι ἔχοιμεν αὐτάς τε ταύτας καὶ τὰς ὀνόματι τῶν ἀποστόλων πρὸς τῶν αἱρετικῶν προφερομένας …

The articles and nouns in the participial phrase beginning with διακρίνοντες bracket a τε … καί … καί phrase: "*distinguishing the* [both in Church tradition, as well as true, and also recognized] *writings*" from "*the* [otherwise contrary to them (καὶ τὰς ἄλλως παρὰ ταύτας)] *writings*." The description of the τὰς ἄλλως παρὰ ταύτας is constructed with another μὲν … δέ clause (with an adversative): "The contrary writings: those not testamentary, on the one hand, yet contested [οὐκ ἐνδιαθήκους μὲν ἀλλὰ καὶ ἀντιλεγομένας]; but on the other hand nonetheless known among most ecclesiastics [ὅμως δὲ παρὰ πλείστοις τῶν ἐκκλησιαστικῶν γινωσκομένας]." We then reach the purpose clause, with another τε … καί: "So that we might possess the capacity to know both these [ἵν' εἰδέναι ἔχοιμεν αὐτάς τε ταύτας]; and also those writings presented by heretics, in the name of the apostles [τὰς ὀνόματι τῶν ἀποστόλων πρὸς τῶν αἱρετικῶν προφερομένας]." The difficult element to understanding this sentence is noting the antecedents of all the various "this-es" and "these-s," and trying to clarify what is being linked or compared in the various clauses.

But let us assume this structure, for the sake of argument. ταῦτα δὲ πάντα and τούτων refer to the illegitimate books, and they could be (but are not) listed as ἀντιλεγόμενα. Τὰς γραφὰς and τὰς ἄλλως παρὰ ταύτας then refers to a balancing of the ὁμολογούμενα and all the other Christian writings (τὰς ἄλλως παρὰ ταύτας). Then the μὲν … δέ clause that follows is explicating the τὰς ἄλλως παρὰ ταύτας as the ἀντιλεγόμενα and illegitimate: "those that are, on the one hand, non-testamentary but yet still ἀντιλεγόμενα, and those that are, on the other hand, nonetheless known to the ecclesiastics." Then the result clause's αὐτάς τε ταύτας goes back to the τὰς ἄλλως παρὰ ταύτας, while balancing with the heretical books with a τε … καί. The meaning would be something like: "All these spurious books could be classed as ἀντιλεγόμενα, but we have made a list, so that, in addition to distinguishing the ὁμολογούμενα from the ἀντιλεγόμενα, we are also able to know how to distinguish effectively these [readable ἀντιλεγόμενα and much loved spurious writings] from the writings of the heretics." Confusing books worth reading with those that are heretical is not on, and Eusebius does not want any confusion. Given that the heretical books also use apostolic names, he is at greater pains to list things, causing him to create a vague category that could be collapsed into another, but is worth detailing to avoid the writings of the heretics. Why then does he use νόθος elsewhere of the books of the heretics? Again, the context of 3.31.6, with additional balance clauses and adverbs, makes it clear that the heretical writings have no claims at all, either of lineage, usage, or even literary style. We could, at a stretch (although it is not really necessary), also make this passage keep the distinctions just made between accepted, disputed, unclear lineage, and heretical. Eusebius has given us the facts concerning "the sacred writings left us, as well as [τε … καί]: a) the ἀντιλεγόμενα, and b) those nonetheless used openly [μὲν … δέ]." He has also informed us of those writings that are "*completely illegitimate as to lineage* [παντελῶς νόθων], as well as [τε … καί] being foreign to our apostolic orthodoxy."

THE EUSEBIAN CATEGORIES

1 Agreed without objection;
2 objected to (but likely no longer);
3 illicit (unapostolic, or unclear claims to apostolicity) but read by Christians;
4 heretical books (νόθος in an absolute sense; to push the metaphor, they are the children of a hostile alien[ξένη] not a respected or beloved concubine [παλλακίς]).

I do not think Eusebius is establishing firm categories the way we moderns would like, but he does seem to want to be clear about the distinctions between the writings used by the church and those used by the heretics. This seems to be the main reason for his distinguishing the "spurious" from the *antilegomena*. It might actually be easier to think of them as follows:

1 ὁμολογούμενα: (ἀνωμολογημένας γραφάς);
2 τὰς ἄλλως παρὰ ταύτας (γραφὰς): a) the once-disputed ἀντιλεγόμενα; b) books whose lineage is νόθος;
3 τὰς πρὸς τῶν αἱρετικῶν προφερομένας [γραφάς].

NOTES

In which we do not find the Hebrew Gospel but yet solve its place in the New Testament canon of Eusebius.

1 George Foot Moore, "Christian Writers on Judaism," *Harvard Theological Review* 14, no. 3 (1921): 197.

2 Matt Jackson-McCabe, "The Invention of Jewish Christianity in John Toland's *Nazarenus*," in *The Rediscovery of Jewish Christianity: From Toland to Baur*, ed. F. Stanley Jones, History of Biblical Studies 5 (Atlanta: Society of Biblical Literature, 2012), 90.

3 W.R. Schoemaker, "The Gospel according to the Hebrews," *Biblical World* 20, no. 3 (1902): 202.

4 Petri Luomanen, "On the Fringes of Canon: Eusebius' View of the 'Gospel of the Hebrews,'" in *The Formation of the Early Church*, ed. Jostein Ådna, WUNT 183 (Tübingen: Mohr Siebeck, 2005), 266.

5 Geoffrey Mark Hahneman, *The Muratorian Fragment and the Development of the Canon*, Oxford Theologic Monographs (Oxford: Clarendon Press, 1992), 138.

6 See Annette Yoshiko Reed, "The Afterlives of New Testament Apocrypha," *Journal of Biblical Literature* 133, no. 2 (2015): 401–25; Reed, "The Modern Invention of 'Old Testament Pseudepigrapha,'" *Journal of Theological Studies* 60, no. 2 (2009): 403–36. See more generally Lee Martin McDonald and James A. Sanders, ed., *The Canon Debate: On the Origins and Formation of the Bible* (Peabody: Hendrickson, 2002).

7 Bruce M. Metzger, *The Canon of the New Testament: Its Origin, Development, and Significance* (Oxford: Clarendon Press, 1987), 204.

8 Éric Junod, "D'Eusèbe de Césarée à Athanase d'Alexandrie en passant par Cyrille de Jérusalem: de la construction savante du Nouveau Testament à la clôture ecclésiastique du canon," in *Le canon du Nouveau Testament: Regards Nouveaux sur l'histoire de sa Formation*, ed. G. Aragione, É. Junod, E. Norelli (Geneva: Labor et Fides, 2005), 175.

9 François Bovon, "Beyond the Canonical and the Apocryphal Books, the Presence of a Third Category: The Books Useful for the Soul," *Harvard Theological Review* 105, no. 2 (2012): 125–37.

10 Joan E. Taylor, "The Phenomenon of Early Jewish-Christianity: Reality or Scholarly Invention?," *Vigiliae Christianae* 44, no. 4 (1990): 314–15. See also the special issue of *Jewish Quarterly Review* from 2009, especially Natalie B. Dohrmann, "Name Calling: Thinking about (the Study of) Judaism in Late Antiquity," *Jewish Quarterly Review* 99, no. 1 (2009): 1–5; Daniel Boyarin, "Rethinking Jewish Christianity: An Argument for Dismantling a Dubious Category (to Which Is Appended a Correction of My *Border Lines*)," *Jewish Quarterly Review* 99, no. 1 (2009): 7–36; Megan Hale Williams, "No More Clever Titles: Observations on Some Recent Studies of Jewish-Christian Relations in the Roman World," *Jewish Quarterly Review* 99, no. 1 (2009): 37–55; and Martha

Himmelfarb, "Judaism in Antiquity: Ethno-Religion or National Identity," *Jewish Quarterly Review* 99, no. 1 (2009): 65–73.

11 This is not really different from "identity" terms in *any* era (Israelite, Judean, Canadian, American), which emerge and evolve with a wide variety of associations and meanings, sometimes fairly rapidly, but it can be especially complex in cases in which groups are closely connected to one another. As has been noted, early separation at the level of "theological reflection" may not reflect any real separation at the level of "religious practice" (e.g., Wolfram Kinzig, "'Non-Separation': Closeness and Co-operation between Jews and Christians in the Fourth Century," *Vigiliae Christianae* 45, no. 1 [1991]: 27–53, 27).

12 Joshua Ezra Burns, *The Christian Schism in Jewish History and Jewish Memory* (New York: Cambridge University Press, 2016), 1–100; Simon Claude Mimouni, *Early Judaeo-Christianity: Historical Essays*, trans. Robyn Fréchet (Leuven and Walpole: Peeters, 2012), 27–53; Matt Jackson-McCabe, ed., *Jewish Christianity Reconsidered: Rethinking Ancient Groups and Texts* (Minneapolis: Fortress Press, 2007).

13 On Baur, see Mimouni, *Early Judaeo-Christianity*, 31n26; cf. Hans Joachim Schoeps, *Jewish Christianity* (Philadelphia: Fortress Press, 1969), 9–13. On earlier predecessors such as John Toland, see the introduction in Oskar Skarsaune and Reidar Hvalvik, ed., *Jewish Believers in Jesus: The Early Centuries* (Peabody: Hendrickson, 2007).

14 Richard Bauckham, "The Origin of the Ebionites," in *The Image of the Judaeo-Christians in Ancient Jewish and Christian Literature*, ed. Peter J. Tomson and Doris Lambers-Petry, WUNT 158 (Tübingen: Mohr Siebeck, 2003), 162–81; Jean Daniélou, ed., *The Theology of Jewish Christianity: A History of Early Christian Doctrine before the Council of Nicaea*, vol. 1 (Chicago: Regnery, 1964).

15 Schoeps, *Jewish Christianity*, 140.

16 See Terence L. Donaldson, "Gentile Christianity as a Category in the Study of Christian Origins," *Harvard Theological Review* 106, no. 4 (2013): 433–58.

17 Petri Luomanen, *Recovering Jewish-Christian Sects and Gospels*, VC Supplements 110 (Leiden and Boston: Brill, 2012).

18 Andrew Gregory, "Hindrance or Help: Does the Modern Category of 'Jewish-Christian Gospel' Distort Our Understanding of the Texts to Which It Refers?" *Journal for the Study of the New Testament* 28, no. 4 (2006): 387–413.

19 Petri Luomanen, "Where Did Another Rich Man Come From? The Jewish Christian Profile of the Story about a Rich Man in the '*Gospel of the Hebrews*' (Origen, *Comm. in Matth.* 15.14)," *Vigiliae Christianae* 57, no. 3 (2003): 244–6; David Lincicum, "F.C. Baur's Place in the Study of Jewish Christianity," 137–66, in Jones, ed., *Rediscovery of Jewish Christianity*.

20 Burns, *Christian Schism*, 100.

21 For example, Michael Goulder, "Hebrews and the Ebionites," *New Testament Studies* 49, no. 3 (2003): 393–406. More widely ranging is Goulder, *St. Peter vs. St. Paul: A Tale of Two Missions* (Lousville: Westminster John Knox, 1995). Goulder stands apart in that he does not look to reconstructed or fragmentary documents.

22 Stephen G. Wilson, *Related Strangers: Jews and Christians 70–170 CE* (Minneapolis: Fortress Press, 1995), 143.

23 Taylor, "Phenomenon of Early Jewish-Christianity," 317.

24 A.F. Klijn, *Jewish-Christian Gospel Tradition*, VCSup 17 (Leiden: Brill, 1992); Klijn and G.J. Reinink, *Patristic Evidence for Jewish-Christian Sects*, NovTSup 36 (Leiden: Brill, 1973).

25 Gregory, "Hindrance or Help," 388.

26 Luomanen, "Where Did Another Rich Man Come From," 268–9:

The study of *indicators* of Jewish-Christian profiles examines the following types of questions: 1) Are characteristically Jewish practices such as circumcision, the Sabbath and purity laws observed? 2) Are characteristically Jewish ideas – Yahweh as the only God, the Temple as Yahweh's abode, the Torah – maintained? 3) What is the pedigree of the group/person? 4) What is the role of Jesus in the worship and ideology of the community? Is Jesus considered as a Jewish prophet or is he more a divine being, worshiped as Kyrios, an equal to God? 5) Is baptism in the name of Jesus (or triune God) an entrance rite to the community? 6) The analysis of the above (and other pertinent) issues will always be connected to the question of their role in the social interaction within the community as well as their function in border-marking towards outsiders.

Cf. Luomanen, "Ebionites and Nazarenes," 81–118, in Jackson-McCabe, *Jewish Christianity Reconsidered*, 84.

27 Taylor, "Phenomenon of Early Jewish-Christianity," 321 (emphasis added).

28 A.S. Barnes, "The Gospel according to the Hebrews," *Journal of Theological Studies* 6, no. 23 (1905): 356.

29 As a source for Luke, see Christian-Bernard Amphoux, "L'évangile selon les hébreux: Source de l'évangile de Luc," *Apocrypha* 6 (1995): 67–77; James R. Edwards, "The *Gospel of the Ebionites* and the Gospel of Luke," *New Testament Studies* 48, no. 4 (2002): 568–86. On a common source with Luke, see Pierson Park, "A Proto-Lukan Basis for the Gospel according to the Hebrews," *Journal of Biblical Literature* 59, no. 4 (1940): 471–8.

30 James R. Edwards, *The Hebrew Gospel and the Development of the Gospel Tradition* (Grand Rapids: Eerdmans, 2009), 36–62.

31 Andrew Gregory, "Prior or Posterior? The *Gospel of the Ebionites* and the Gospel of Luke," *New Testament Studies* 51, no. 3 (2005): 344–60.

32 Rudolf Handmann, *Das Hebräer-Evangelium*, TUGAL 5.3 (Marburg, 1888), 127–42; Edward Byron Nicholson, *The Gospel according to the Hebrews: Its Fragments Translated and Annotated with a Critical Analysis of the External and Internal Evidence Relating to It* (London: C. Kegan Paul and Co., 1879).

33 So Harris H. Hirschberg, "Simon Bariona and the Ebionites," *Journal of Biblical Literature* 61, no. 3 (1942): 171–91.

34 Luitpold Wallach, "The Textual History of an Aramaic Proverb (Traces of the Ebionean Gospel)," *Journal of Biblical Literature* 60, no. 4 (1941): 403–15.

35 Michael J. Kok, "Did Papias of Hierapolis use the *Gospel according to the Hebrews* as a Source?" *Journal of Early Christian Studies* 25, no. 1 (2017): 29–53. Kok answers in the negative and suspects Eusebius is responsible for ascribing an unsourced Papian story of a "sinful woman" to this gospel.

36 For example, Matthew W. Mitchell, "Bodiless Demons and Written Gospels: Reflections on 'The Gospel according to the Hebrews' in the Apostolic Fathers," *Novum Testamentum* 52, no. 3 (2010): 221–40, contra Pier F. Beatrice, "The *Gospel according to the Hebrews* in the Apostolic Fathers," *Novum Testamentum* 48, no. 2 (2006): 147–95. See also Charles E. Hill, "Ignatius, 'the Gospel,' and the Gospels," in *Trajectories through the New Testament and the Apostolic Fathers*, ed. Andrew F. Gregory and Christopher Tuckett (New York: Oxford University Press, 2005), 267–85; Gregory, "Prior or Posterior."

37 Amphoux, "L'évangile selon les hébreux," 69–71.

38 Klijn, *Jewish-Christian Gospel Tradition*, 16–19.

39 See Andrew Carriker, *The Library of Eusebius of Caesarea*, VCSup 67 (Leiden: Brill, 2003), 215–17, 233–4.

40 Noting that the view that the *Gospel of the Hebrews* was "certainly in the library at Caesarea" depends, in part, on Jerome's testimony. See Carriker, *Library of Eusebius*, 233.

41 Klijn and Reinink, *Patristic Evidence*, 124–5.

42 Mitchell, "Bodiless Demons," 230–1; J.B. Lightfoot, *The Apostolic Fathers Part II: Saint Ignatius and Saint Polycarp*, 2nd ed. (London: Macmillan, 1889), 2:295–7.

43 Technically οἶδα is a perfect form of the same verb, which initially was more clearly related to the "vid" root [ἔϝιδον].

44 See Klijn, *Jewish-Christian Gospel Tradition*, 86–7.

45 Colin Whiting, "Jerome's *De viris illustribus* and New Genres for Christian Disputation in Late Antiquity," in *Shifting Genres in Late Antiquity*, ed. Elton Hugh and Geoffrey Greatrex (Farnham: Ashgate, 2015), 51.

46 J.N.D. Kelly, *Jerome: His Life, Writings and Controversies* (New York: Harper and Row, 1975), 175, cited in Whiting, "Jerome's *De viris illustribus*," 41. See the literature reviewed in ibid., 41–3nn1–7.

47 Timothy C.G. Thornton, "Jerome and the 'Hebrew Gospel according to Matthew,'" *Studia Patristica* 28 (1993): 118.

48 Thornton, "Jerome and the Hebrew Gospel," 122. See also Thomas M. Tanner, "A History of Early Christian Libraries from Jesus to Jerome," *Journal of Library History* 14, no. 4 (1979): 407–35; Anthony Grafton and Megan Williams, *Christianity and the Transformation of the Book: Origen, Eusebius, and the Library of Caesarea* (Cambridge: Belknap Press, 2006).

49 For a fuller discussion of alleged quotations in Ignatius, see Matthew Mitchell, "In the Footsteps of Paul: Scriptural and Apostolic Authority in Ignatius of Antioch," *Journal of Early Christian Studies* 14, no. 1 (2006): 27–45.

50 Paul J. Donahue, "Jewish Christianity in the Letters of Ignatius of Antioch," *Vigiliae Christianae* 32, no. 2 (1978): 92.

51 Nicholson, *Gospel according to the Hebrews*, 107–10.
52 That is, Luomanen, "On the Fringes of Canon."
53 Mitchell, "Bodiless Demons," 236 (emphasis in original).
54 John Barton, *Holy Writings, Sacred Text: The Canon in Early Christianity* (Louisville: Westminster John Knox, 1997), 79–105.
55 Barton, *Holy Writings*, 79.
56 Helmut Koester, *Ancient Christian Gospels: Their History and Development* (Philadelphia: Trinity, 1990), 32.
57 Barton, *Holy Writings*, 99–100.
58 Ibid., 105.
59 See Mitchell, "In the Footsteps of Paul," 36–40.
60 Azzan Yadin-Israel, "'For Mark Was Peter's *Tanna*': Tradition and Transmission in Papias and the Early Rabbis," *Journal of Early Christian Studies* 23, no. 3 (2015): 337–62.
61 See Edmon L. Gallagher, "The Old Testament 'Apocrypha' in Jerome's Canonical Theory," *Journal of Early Christian Studies* 20, no. 2 (2012): 213–33.
62 Edwards, *Hebrew Gospel*, 55.
63 For example, M. Vincent, "'Ich bin kein körperloses Geistwesen': Zum Verhältnis von κέρυγμα Πέτρου, 'Doctrina Petri,' διδασκαλία Πέτρου und IgnSm 3," in *Der Paradox Eine: Antignostischer Monarchianismus im zweiten Jahrhundert*, ed. R.M. Huber, VCSup 50 (Leiden: Brill, 1999), 242–55 and 258–9.
64 Grafton and Williams, *Christianity and the Transformation of the Book*, 190–1.
65 Mitchell, "Bodiless Demons," 240.
66 My colleague Rebecca Krawiec drew my attention to similar issues among scholars of the Nag Hammadi materials: "a particular challenge, however, for analyzing their importance is the lack of information for the context of the texts themselves: who wrote, read, and copied them?" This challenge has made some question whether any of the groups alleged to be behind them ever even existed. See Rebecca Krawiec, "Review of Hugo Lundhaug and Lance Jenott, *The Monastic Origins of the Nag Hammadi Codices*," *Journal of Late Antiquity* 10, no. 1 (2017): 291–4.
67 Edmon L. Gallagher, "Origen via Rufinus on the New Testament Canon," *New Testament Studies* 62, no. 3 (2016): 463–4.
68 Catherine M. Chin, "Rufinus of Aquileia and Alexandrian Afterlives: Translation as Origenism," *Journal of Early Christian Studies* 18, no. 4 (2010): 636–7 (emphasis added). Thanks to my colleague Rebecca Krawiec for this reference.
69 See Everett Kalin, "New Testament Canon of Eusebius," 386–404, in McDonald and Sanders, *Canon Debate*.
70 Éric Junod, "Les mots d'Eusèbe de Césarée pour désigner les livres du Nouveau Testament et ceux qui n'en font pas partie," 341–53 in *Eukarpa: Études sur la Bible et ses exégètes en hommage à Gilles Dorival* (Paris: Cerf, 2011), 341.
71 Junod, "Les mots d'Eusèbe," 348.
72 Gallagher, "Origen via Rufinus," 464.

73 Kalin, "New Testament Canon," 394.
74 Carriker, *Library of Eusebius*, 232.
75 Metzger, *Canon of the New Testament*, 205.
76 A.D. Baum, "Der neutestamentliche Kanon bei Eusebios (*Hist. eccl.* III,25,1–7) im Kontext seiner literaturgeschichtlichen Arbeit," *Ephemerides Theologicae Lovanienses* 73, no. 4 (1997): 346.
77 Luomanen, "On the Fringes of Canon," 265.
78 Junod, "Mots d'Eusèbe," 351.
79 Ibid., 349.
80 At this point, Eusebius will demonstrate his Greek is less the "a semester of seminary New Testament Greek staring at John" variety, and much more "boarding school Attic composition."
81 Kalin, "New Testament Canon," 395.

9

Do as I Say Not as They Do: Social Construction in the *Epistle of Barnabas* through Canonical Interpretation and Ritual

Jason N. Yuh

INTRODUCTION

Scholars have not yet expounded on the importance and rationale of "the somewhat strangely" phrased metaphor found in the *Epistle of Barnabas*: the circumcision of hearing.[1] In part, that is because the significance of this metaphor does not directly contribute to the theological outlook or background of Barnabas, which are topics that have largely preoccupied Barnabas scholarship.[2] Yet not only is this metaphor significant, but its significance lies in its social and communal implications.

To explore the social and communal implications, I draw upon interdisciplinary research on canon and ritual. Canon is a set of fundamental principles that simultaneously shapes and is shaped by the identity of a community, while rituals are the embodiment of these principles that, inter alia, differentiates the group from outsiders while also structuring internal, hierarchical distinctions. Research in these areas has independently demonstrated that canon and ritual are fundamental elements of any group, and I employ these concepts to explain how Barnabas attempts to fulfill these fundamental elements through the circumcision of hearing.[3] More specifically, I argue that an examination of the metaphor illuminates how Barnabas sought to persuade his fledgling community to adhere uncompromisingly to his teachings by offering a new canon (or canonical interpretation, i.e., an interpretation that is asserted to be revelatory and therefore authoritative).[4]

Two features of Barnabas require discussion. First, it is because canon is indispensable for communities in general that Barnabas finds himself in a precarious argumentative stance: he seeks to refute "Jewish" traditions by using "Jewish" writings.[5] Barnabas is unable to offer a new canon, so he offers a new canonical interpretation or γνῶσις (knowledge) that can only be perceived when one's hearing is circumcised. Second, Barnabas's repudiation against most rituals once again leaves him in a tenuous situation when reflecting upon the fundamental role that rituals play for social groups. Upon closer analysis, however, various elements of the epistle are best explained when considering select concepts from ritual theories: Barnabas regards his hearers as fragile neophytes in the ambiguous phase of liminality. It is through the circumcision of hearing that Barnabas addresses both of these fundamental aspects of group formation, thereby quickening his hearers to become τὸν λαὸν τὸν καινόν (the new people) of God (Barn. 5:7; 7:5).[6]

Owing to the theoretical richness of canon and ritual, my study can also serve as a methodological template to examine the dynamics of other communal groups beyond the one that Barnabas sought to establish and maintain. The most pertinent areas of research are the formation of early Christian identities and the contentious topic of early Jewish-Christian relations. Although the methodology and conclusion of this study are primarily concerned with the social dimensions of Barnabas, I do not intend to undermine the importance of the theology of Barnabas; rather, I intend to supplement, or perhaps even clarify, the theological outlook of Barnabas.

CANONICAL INTERPRETATION

Barnabas's Need for Canonical Interpretation

Reidar Hvalvik observes that one of the key themes for Barnabas is his struggle for scripture. From a historical standpoint, the struggle is intense for the obvious reason that both Christ-devotees and Jews based their norms on the same sacred texts. For Barnabas, this struggle was acutely difficult as he (unlike Marcion) maintained a high regard for the Hebrew scriptures and (unlike Justin Martyr, Origen, or Tertullian) contended that there was always only one people and covenant of God.[7] Thus, Barnabas distinguishes his authoritative γνῶσις by denouncing the way that various strands of Judaism have understood these scriptural texts.[8] Whether it is animal sacrifices (ch. 2; chs. 7–8), fasting (ch. 3), circumcision (ch. 9), dietary laws (ch. 10), the Sabbath (ch. 15), or the temple (ch. 16), the root of the problem is not what these sacred texts say about these things (e.g., 9:4; 10:1); rather, the problem is that the sacred texts have been understood literally, a problem that is so egregious that it is of demonic influence (9:4).[9]

Canon as a Prerequisite for Group Identity

In order to appreciate more fully Barnabas's predicament in this regard, it is helpful to note that there is an inextricable – and inevitable – connection between canon and group formation, as recently established by numerous scholars from varying areas of study.[10] For the purpose of this study, canon operates simply as a finite set of basic principles (or convictions, axioms, core narratives) that plays an authoritative role for, and is shaped by, a group.[11] The very existence of a canon – its inception, maintenance, relevance, and interpretation – is thus predicated upon its group. However, the inverse is equally true: the very existence of a group is predicated upon its canon. A group cannot be considered as such unless its individual members share at least some common principles that they perceive as normative or canonical. Canon, however, does not entail fixity or precision. Especially in a discipline in which canon is often conflated with the Bible or distorted by "bibliographic" concepts, it is critical to make a distinction between a theoretical canon that was functional based on communal reception/practice and an anachronistic canon that assumes ideas that skew our perspective on this ancient period.[12] In this chapter, canon is used only in the former sense.

Closely related to the critical role that canon plays within a community is the need for interpreters.[13] These interpreters are individuals within a community whose interpretations of what various principles mean and how they can be applied are considered to be authoritative or canonical. As Jan Assmann remarks, "In this way interpretation becomes the central principle of cultural coherence and identity. The normative and formative impulses of cultural memory can only be gleaned through the incessant, constantly renewed textual interpretation of the tradition through which identity is established. Interpretation becomes the gesture of remembering, the interpreter becomes a person who remembers and reminds us of a forgotten truth."[14] If the identity of a group is established through "renewed" interpretations of sacred traditions and/or texts, then this explains the social reasons behind why Barnabas, and many other early "Christian" writers, would have been so preoccupied with scriptural texts. The stories of Jesus compelled individuals to create these contemporary interpretations. Those who agreed with these interpretations eventually formed their own subgroups. As differences of interpretations became intolerable, the need for a subgroup to become its own group necessitated a change in canon – or, in Barnabas's situation, the interpretation of scripture.[15]

Thus, Barnabas attempts to create and/or sustain a community by offering new interpretations of writings that were deemed authoritative or normative at the time. This delicate balance meant that Barnabas could not introduce new texts that were explicitly about Jesus but, rather, was required to interpret Jesus into the existing sources that were already authoritative.[16] In other words, Barnabas needed "to develop exegetical procedures that [would] allow the canon to be applied without alteration or, at least, without admitting to alteration."[17] For instance, Barnabas construes covenantal faithfulness as being grounded not upon physical practices but upon true γνῶσις, which enables one to "know the commandments in an upright way" (10:12). In other words, the problem with "them" is that they have misunderstood scripture; hence, the solution is the right interpretation of scripture through the disclosure of Barnabas's γνῶσις.[18] Consequently, this interpretation becomes the new "canon" around which Barnabas's group can form. Borrowing the terminology of J.Z. Smith, Barnabas is assuming the role of the group's "hermeneute."[19]

Barnabas as the "Hermeneute" with Γνῶσις

By virtue of having τελεία γνῶσις (perfect knowledge) and his desire to disseminate it, Barnabas establishes himself as the group's "hermeneute" from the outset (1:5), a point which he strongly and proportionally develops throughout the letter. Barnabas assumes his pedagogical role and his possession of τελεία γνῶσις in virtually every chapter (e.g., 1:5, 8; 4:6; 6:9; 7:1; 8:2; 9:7, 9; 10:11; 12:3, 8; 14:4; 15:5; 16:7, 8; ch. 17; 18:1), and he implicitly reinforces this role with the concentrated integration of Jewish traditions into his arguments.[20]

There is also evidence that Barnabas is writing in response to contemporaneous events, prompting him to write with urgency (e.g., 1:5, 8; 2:1, 10; 4:1–2, 6, 9–10; 16:4, 5). Γνῶσις in this way works as the cipher that allows Barnabas and his hearers to make proper sense of what is currently transpiring (1:7; 5:3). Barnabas is therefore assuming "the indigenous theologian's task," the task to interpret and apply Jewish sacred traditions to the specific circumstances and concerns of his community.[21] Once again, a canon is not a canon unless it is being animated within the triangular relationship between itself, interpreter, and listener.[22]

Even the Two Ways tradition (Barn. 18–21), which concludes the epistle, is portrayed as another form of teaching (from the lemma διδαχή; 18:1). Moreover, the way of the righteous is described as a way of γνῶσις (19:1; 21:5–6).[23] Therefore, more than any other role, Barnabas presents himself as the "hermeneute" who has divine γνῶσις, which legitimizes not only his truth claims but also his efforts to create simultaneously a new community and a new canon.[24] However, Barnabas's γνῶσις is controversial, and there are indications that his hearers might not accept parts of it.[25] It is thus the circumcision of hearing that provides his hearers the requisite ability to properly understand and believe his teachings.

The Need for the Circumcision of Hearing

Our analysis of Barnabas's circumcision of hearing (8:7; 9:3; 10:12; 16:10; see also 11:11) begins with the possible influences behind the metaphor.[26] Although the combination of "circumcision" and "hearing" (οὐκοῦν περιέτεμεν ἡμῶν τὰς ἀκοάς [he circumcised our hearing], 9:3; see also 10:12) does not occur in any prior writing, the underlying concept can be traced to Jeremiah 6:10 (LXX: ἀπερίτμητα τὰ ὦτα αὐτῶν [their ears are uncircumcised]).[27] Additionally, this metaphor would not have been uncommon in Hellenistic Judaism: "This type of approach [linking disobedience with hearing] was extended especially to the thought of life ...in the Judaism represented by Philo – circumcision of the understanding (ear, heart) thus became prime for him [Philo]."[28] Kraft is right to group "ear, heart" together because nowhere does Philo actually combine (un)circumcision with ears or hearing. However, Philo does make a cryptic reference to the circumcision of the eyes.[29] The faculties of seeing and hearing are often coupled together for Philo as they are "the lordliest of the senses" (*Spec.* 1.193) or the philosophical senses (*QG* 3.5).[30] So, although the exact phrase is not found in Philo's extant writings, the general notion is certainly there. Perhaps more indicative of a Hellenistic influence on Barnabas is how Philo famously rebukes those who "repeal the law laid down for circumcising" (*Migr.* 92). This would imply that within Philo's circles, which likely included other Hellenistic Jews who had the penchant for allegorizing, there were those who would have understood circumcision in the same way as did Barnabas. If it were not for the historical distance between Philo and Barnabas, it would be reasonable to presume that Philo was speaking of Barnabas.[31]

All four of the allusions to the circumcision of hearing are placed at pivotal positions within Barnabas's overall argument (8:7, 9:3; 10:12; 16:10). As mentioned earlier, Barnabas opens his letter with his claim of divine γνῶσις (1:5), which he demonstrates by reproving one Jewish practice after another. Hence, 1:1 to 8:6 is more or less a denunciation of Jewish ancestral customs. Such a radical assertion might raise the question for his hearers: How can so many practising Jews, who have been perceived as being faithful to the covenant based on these specific practices, be so misled? According to Barnabas, such insights are "obscure to them, because they have not heard (ἤκουσαν) the voice of the Lord" (8:7). This, of course, raises yet another question: If scriptural insights are "obscure to them" fundamentally "because they have not heard the voice of the Lord" (8:7), then what enables Barnabas and his hearers to hear properly? Barnabas attempts to answer this question in the ensuing argument on circumcision proper (ch. 9). Thus, 8:7 has two functions. Barnabas simultaneously concludes his previous arguments (1:1–8:6) while introducing his next argument on the circumcision of hearing (ch. 9).[32]

Barnabas provides a rather facile answer: the Lord "circumcised (περιέτεμεν) our hearing (ἀκοάς), that once we heard (ἀκούσαντες) the word we might believe" (9:3), thereby affording them eternal life (9:2). Circumcision of hearing is, therefore, the critical difference between "us" and "them" as indicated by the ἵνα clause with the subjunctive form of πιστεύω (I believe) ("that once we heard the word we might believe" [ἵνα ἀκούσαντες λόγον. πιστεύσωμεν ἡμεῖς]; see 11:11 for a similar correlation). Just as literal circumcision was the sign of the covenant, so is the epistemological circumcision that Barnabas is advocating. Barnabas substantiates his assertion by including a cluster of scriptural citations (9:1–5),[33] refuting hypothetical counterarguments (9:6–7), and generously disclosing his most "reliable lesson," which explains why Abraham and his household were nevertheless circumcised (9:8–9).

Although Barnabas introduces a new topic in the next chapter (i.e., dietary laws in ch. 10), his argumentative strategy is consistent. That is, people fail to acknowledge his γνῶσις concerning dietary laws because their hearing has not been circumcised (10:12). The syntactical repetition of ἵνα followed by a subjunctive verb ("that we may understand these things" [ἵνα συνιῶμεν ταῦτα]) that we read in 9:3 reinforces the causal significance of this circumcision. Furthermore, referring to the circumcision of hearing at this juncture reveals that the relevance of the metaphor is not limited to his discussion of literal circumcision (ch. 9). This is precisely how Clement of Alexandria, whose work has been considered "the best commentary on Barnabas,"[34] later cites this metaphor in his own discussion on true knowledge (*Strom.* 5.8.51.6 cites Barn. 10:12).[35] Indeed, Clement makes the connection between knowledge and the circumcision of hearing by including the accompanying subjunctive clause, ἵνα συνιῶμεν ταῦτα.[36] As we saw in 8:7, the metaphor not only explains the erroneous practices of chapters 1–8 but also the dietary laws of chapter 10.

Circumcision of hearing, therefore, allows an individual to hear truly. This, then, enables one to have proper understanding (10:12),[37] the ability to believe (9:3), and the privilege of everlasting life (9:2). All of these effects are assumed in Barnabas's discussion regarding one of the primary themes of the letter, the temple.[38] Barnabas assumes that those who have access to the true temple are those who have proper understanding of and the ability to believe God's "word of faith ...the wisdom of his upright demands, the commandments of the teaching" (16:9). Moreover, the "imperishable temple" (16:9: τὸν ἄφθαρτον ναόν) assumes that such inhabitants have everlasting life. What transpires at this temple is "a 'gnostic' reading of Scripture" that is made possible only through the circumcision of hearing, otherwise such a "reading" would be "obscure to them" (8:7).[39] Hence, when Barnabas describes this interaction, the emphasis is on speech and hearing: "For the one who longs to be saved looks not merely to a person but to the one who dwells and speaks in him. For he is amazed at him since he has never heard (ἀκηκοέναι) him speak these words from his mouth nor even ever desired to hear (ἀκούειν) them" (16:10).

Chapter 16, however, is not exclusively about the temple. It is the natural culmination of the preceding arguments about the people (ch. 13), the covenant (ch. 14; also ch. 4), and the Sabbath (ch. 15). Rather than "they" who practise the literal interpretations of scripture (ch. 13) on the Sabbath (ch. 15) under the assumption of their broken, nullified covenant (ch. 14; also ch. 4), it is "we" who will celebrate the true Sabbath (i.e., the eighth day, 16:6), in the spiritual temple in which God's voice is directly heard (16:10). In this way, the image of the spiritual temple is a convergence of both of these social principles: canonical interpretation (i.e., the voice of God in 16:10) and ritual (i.e., the eighth day in 16:6).[40] Hence, the distinction between the two, as is further demonstrated below, is merely heuristic.[41]

In sum, the circumcision of hearing is a motif that plays the prerequisite role for the theme that governs the whole epistle: τελεία γνῶσις, which is referenced as Barnabas's only competitive advantage against his rival teachers. Without this circumcision, Barnabas's claim to γνῶσις is meaningless. As we have seen with the emphasis on canon, Barnabas's failure to convince others of his canonical interpretation is his failure to create his own community. However, Barnabas's metaphor is not merely an analogy because the metaphor plays a critical role in other parts of the letter. More specifically, it functions as some sort of a ritual for Barnabas and should therefore be understood in the same way in which "they" believed that physical circumcision was the seal of their covenant (9:6).[42] Circumcision of hearing is therefore the initiatory rite of the covenant for Barnabas and his hearers (8:7; 9:3). As Peter Richardson and Martin B. Shukster note: "The covenantal sign of Christian exegesis is the true circumcision."[43] Consequently, this metaphorical ritual is critical for Barnabas and his hearers, compelling a closer investigation into the relationship between the epistle and rituals in general.

RITUALS

Deconstruction or Destruction of Rituals?

For most, if not all, of the Jewish communities of Second Temple Judaism, rituals were particularly important. Shaye J.D. Cohen argues that religion in the ancient world was not primarily based on faith or dogma but, rather, on practices, commandments, acts, and other customs. Accordingly, the boundary lines between Jews and gentiles were drawn mostly on differing observances.[44] Cohen continues: "For the polytheists of the Greco-Roman world, the most characteristic features of Judaism were, aside from circumcision, the observance of the Sabbath and the abstention from pork."[45] This description is corroborated by the oft-quoted texts from writers like Juvenal (*Sat.* 14.96–106), Suetonius (*Dom.* 12.2), and Tacitus (*Hist.* 5.5.1–2). If one, like Barnabas, seeks to destroy this strand of Judaism, then one must attack its foundational practices – or, in this context, rituals.[46] That Barnabas does so is readily apparent even at a cursory skim of the letter. This has led Geoffrey D. Dunn, following Pierre Prigent, to suggest that perhaps Barnabas is more anti-cultic than anti-Judaic.[47] Barnabas can be seen as one who deconstructs Judaism, but his opprobrium against rituals cuts both ways. If Barnabas deconstructs Judaism and its rituals, then in what ways does he (ironically) advance his own ritual(s)? Is it possible for Barnabas to create a community that is devoid of any ritual?[48]

Rituals and Social Distinctions

According to most ritual theorists, the answer is negative. Rituals are needed for group identity because they address the group's need for social and ideological distinctions. Concerning the former, Richard Jenkins argues that group identity is reducible to (1) demarcating external boundaries to distinguish the group from the other as well as to (2) defining internal hierarchies to create group roles. Jenkins locates rituals as the means that allow groups to make these necessary external and internal distinctions – distinctions that can be categorized as social.[49]

Although Barnabas appears to reject rituals when compared with most groups of Judaism at this time, he is clearly attempting to generate these external and internal differences that are not only integral for group formation but also accomplished through rituals. Efforts to differentiate externally and internally recur throughout the epistle through Barnabas's "us-and-them" language along with the frequent reminders of his pedagogical role (1:5, 8;

4:6; 6:9; 7:1; 8:2; 9:7, 9; 10:11; 12:3, 8; 14:4; 15:5; 16:7, 8; ch. 17; 18:1). Circumcision of hearing is able to make both of these social distinctions. Externally, circumcision is a covenantal sign that separates "us" from "them." Internally, if Barnabas is the one with true γνῶσις that his recipients need to hear, then he is clearly setting his role apart from the rest of the group.[50] Hence, we see that not only does circumcision of hearing function as a ritual because of its repeated references with causal implications (i.e., more than a mere analogy) but also because it creates the social distinctions that every group needs.

Rituals and Ideological Distinctions

Groups also need to create ideological distinctions. This point has already been mentioned in the above discussion on canon, but what has not been underscored is the role that rituals play in this regard. It is often quoted that "Ritual is, above all, an assertion of difference," but it is important to recognize that, in the fuller context of this quotation, the difference is more ideological than social – or, as J.Z. Smith describes it, what we are looking at is the "'gnostic' dimension to ritual."[51] Smith's reference to "gnostic" is significant as it implies that rituals have the ability to convey some kind of knowledge. Thus, we see more clearly the intricate relationship between canon and ritual. In other words, groups are formed around principles, as prescribed by their canon, that are expressed and understood through rituals. Rituals, therefore, "are more likely to serve as the foundation ...of the community's identity"[52] as they are "a powerful and visible embodiment of the abstraction of collective identity."[53]

This convergence between canon and ritual that is required for communal identity is what makes the metaphor of the circumcision of hearing an apt one. To put it simply, ears and hearing would correlate with the gnostic or canonical dimension, while circumcision would correlate with the ritualized dimension. This suggests that Barnabas is not rejecting rituals in their entirety but only certain types. Because circumcision of hearing has epistemological or hermeneutical implications, it satisfies Barnabas's need for some kind of a ritual and provides an explanation of why some people have not fully submitted to his teachings. More specifically, what is examined below is how Barnabas perceives his hearers now that their ears have been circumcised. On the one hand, the purpose of their circumcision was for them to be able to believe and to understand (9:3; 10:12); on the other hand, Barnabas continually implies that his hearers do not yet truly believe and understand, even though it appears that this circumcision took place in the past. In fact, it is because of this delicate tension that this metaphorical ritual is most suitably described as circumcision.[54]

The Tension of Barnabas's Hearers

According to Barnabas, the baseline for proper believing and understanding is found in the prophets – such as Moses (4:8; 10:1; 14:3), David (12:10; 13:10), and Abraham (9:8; 13:7) – and, unsurprisingly, himself (1:4, 5; 6:5; 17:1–2). Such unqualified attribution of knowledge and faith is not given to his hearers. Although Barnabas writes that "a great faith and love dwell within [them]" (1:4), he continues in the next line that he had "hastened ...to send [them] a brief letter, that [they] may have perfect knowledge to accompany [their] faith" (1:5). Elaborating further on their faith, Barnabas mentions that it "will be of no use to us if we do not stand in resistance" (4:9). In other words, though his hearers have a degree of knowledge and faith, Barnabas later reveals that "'perfect knowledge' is lacking."[55] Barnabas still believes that it is urgent for them to increase their knowledge and faith, and, as it currently stands, their faith is vain unless they are able to stand in resistance.

In other instances, Barnabas claims that "we" have the true understanding. Despite the rhetoric, what he really means is that only he himself is presently privileged with this wisdom. This is most evident when he makes the claim that "the Master has made known to us what has happened and what now is" (1:7); however, the ensuing verse makes a counter-claim as Barnabas has the need to "show a few matters to [them]" in order that they "will gladden [their] hearts in the present circumstances" (1:8). There are, additionally, scattered references to what is currently transpiring, and, in each of these references, Barnabas finds the need to explain the significance of these events (e.g., 5:3; 6:19; 8:7; 16:4, 5). Similarly, Barnabas expresses gratitude to the Lord because he has "placed the wisdom and knowledge of his secrets within us" (6:10). Their wisdom and knowledge, however, are nonetheless lacking, as he later makes explicit (ch. 17). This point is also implied throughout the entire letter: citation after citation, and explanation after explanation, only cement the current wisdom and knowledge of Barnabas, not that of his hearers.

Barnabas also expresses urgency – or even uncertainty – about his readers' ability to understand and believe, despite his allusions to the circumcision of hearing. Though circumcision is intended so that they might understand and believe, nowhere does Barnabas actually state that they are presently understanding and believing (with the exception of 16:7).[56] The mood for all of the verbs related to understanding and believing, when referring to the recipients, is either subjunctive or infinitive and is not used to convey the present reality of the recipients – though 3:6 is an indicative of πιστεύω, this is in the future tense.

Barnabas does, however, use similar verbs in the imperative mood or in conjunction with ὀφείλω (I ought). Barnabas uses the verb μανθάνω (I learn) nine times, seven of which are used in the second person imperative (e.g., 5:5; 6:9; 9:7, 8; 14:4; 16:2, 7).[57] The verb ὀφείλω is also used frequently (2:1, 9, 10; 4:6; 6:18; 13:3), but what is significant about Barnabas's usage is how it is supplemented with an epistemological verb, usually αἰσθάνομαι (I am aware).[58] On the one hand, these imperatival expressions imply, to a certain degree, Barnabas's confidence that his hearers can fulfill what is being requested of them; on the other hand, these expressions imply the need for Barnabas to be particularly pointed in his teachings, as if to sear them into their minds.

There are still further indications that the recipients are not fully understanding what Barnabas has to say, namely, his rhetoric. The rhetoric is used in two ways: (1) Barnabas postures himself as one who is humble and genuine, and (2) he positions himself as one with superior knowledge. In the former, such rhetoric is often employed to accompany one of his (many) injunctions for the recipients to accept his teaching. Followed immediately after one of these injunctions that they "should understand," he softens the tone by saying, "I am asking you this as one who is from among you and who loves each and every one of you more than my own soul" (4:6). Just a few verses later, he says, "I hasten to write, as your lowly scapegoat. Therefore, we should pay close attention here in the final days" (4:9). Almost verbatim, Barnabas adds: "I am a lowly scapegoat for your love" after he expresses his desire for them to "understand" (6:4; also 1:8). When considering only this first use of his rhetoric, it is tempting to conclude that Barnabas has doubts about his own teachings and γνῶσις.

However, Barnabas's first rhetorical strategy should be balanced by, if not interpreted through, his claims that he possesses superior knowledge. That is, Barnabas's self-perception is more likely to be the one of a wise teacher than of a lowly scapegoat. In fact, Barnabas mentions frequently that his teachings have already been revealed previously (e.g., 1:7; 3:6; 5:3; 6:7, 12; 7:1; 11:1), so the fact that his hearers fail to understand fully is not an indictment on his part. But Barnabas does not put the blame solely on his hearers. After one of the more strained interpretations offered by Barnabas (i.e., his usage of the *nomina sacra* in 9:8), he is compelled to further substantiate his creative assertion by writing: "No one has learned a more reliable lesson from me. But I know that you are worthy" (9:9). Here, Barnabas is saying two things that correspond to his twofold rhetorical strategy: his teachings are reliable and his recipients are worthy. It is likely that Barnabas is more convinced of the former than of the latter. For instance, Barnabas also mentions twice that he is holding back on his superior teaching because he is afraid that his hearers will not be able to understand: "I am writing to you in very simple terms, that you may understand" (6:5; also 17:2). Are these indications that Barnabas doubts the ability of his hearers to understand his teachings? Or is Barnabas concerned that his hearers are unwilling to agree with his γνῶσις? If so, then how can we reconcile these possibilities with the fact that the hearing of his hearers has already been circumcised (9:3; 10:12)?

Circumcision Producing Liminality

Such a paradox corresponds to Victor Turner's model of liminality.[59] Turner developed this notion within the context of Arnold van Gennep's threefold phase of rites of passage (i.e., separation, margin/liminality, and aggregation).[60] Based on his studies on the Ndembu tribe of Zambia, Turner observed that, after initiatory rites such as circumcision, neophytes are placed in a fragile phase that is marked by the kind of inconsistency that has been outlined above. Turner observes that, "in some boys' initiations, newly circumcised boys are explicitly likened to menstruating women."[61] The neophytes in this transitory phase are thus "neither living nor dead from one aspect, and both living and dead from another. Their condition is one of ambiguity and paradox, a confusion of all the customary categories."[62]

In the context of Barnabas, we see that though Barnabas regards circumcision as already "performed" in the past, there is no evidence that his hearers have reached their final phase of aggregation – the ability to believe and understand properly. This is not because Barnabas doubts his own teaching. Nor is it because his hearers are unwilling to listen or unable to understand. When considering how initiatory rites typically create a state of liminality, the likelier explanation for why Barnabas writes the way that he does is because he is aware of the recipients' vulnerable state. They are impressionable to both Barnabas's own teachings and to the deleterious teachings of others (2:9, 10; 4:6, 14; 16:1).[63] In short, Barnabas is certain of the truthfulness of his own teachings but, because of the initiatory condition of his hearers, he makes a concerted effort to ensure that they are able to understand and believe his teachings.[64] Turner's observations are once again pertinent: "The arcane knowledge or '*gnosis*' obtained in the liminal period is felt to change the inmost nature of the neophyte, impressing him, as a seal impresses wax, with the characteristics of his new state. It is not a mere acquisition of knowledge, but a change in being. His apparent passivity is revealed as an absorption of powers which will become active after his social status has been redefined in the aggregation rites."[65] Once again, we see the connection between ritual and gnosis, but we also gain a new perspective on what was previously observed about Barnabas's choice of verbs, especially in the imperatival sense. In essence, Barnabas is seeking to impress his hearers "as a seal impresses wax." Hearing the epistle should not be understood as "mere acquisition of knowledge, but a change in being," which finds its consummation in τὸν λαὸν τὸν καινὸν of God (5:7; 6:19; 7:5). As Barnabas is quite forthcoming that the purpose of his writing is "that you may have perfect knowledge" (1:5: ἵνα μετὰ τῆς πίστεως ὑμῶν τελείαν ἔχητε καὶ τὴν γνῶσις), it is significant that, towards the end of the letter, he writes, "we maintain that our knowledge is now perfect" (13:7: ἀπέχομεν τὸ τέλειον τῆς γνώσεως ἡμῶν).[66] The placement of these two statements and their syntactical agreement indicate Barnabas's hope that he had impressed "arcane knowledge or '*gnosis*'" upon his neophytes.

CONCLUSION

For Barnabas, his means of initiating the members of his community is through the circumcision of hearing (8:7; 9:3; 10:12; 16:10). This circumcision enables his hearers to deconstruct past interpretations, interpretations that will bring "error in through the backdoor" (2:10) so that they can orient themselves around Barnabas's canonical interpretation. In this way, the circumcision makes external distinctions between "us" and "them" as well as an internal distinction (i.e., Barnabas is the possessor of γνῶσις while his hearers are dependent upon him). Despite these distinctions, there is still ambiguity as Barnabas's hearers are not yet able to fully grasp his γνῶσις because they are in the vulnerable state of liminality wherein the present circumstances are difficult to discern (1:8). Hence, Barnabas writes in such a way as to impress his "arcane knowledge and '*gnosis*'" onto his hearers,[67] leading them to become τὸν λαὸν τὸν καινόν of God, which will not be fulfilled until the "eighth day" (6:19; 15:7–9; 16:8–9).

This chapter therefore seeks to make a significant contribution to scholarship on both the *Epistle of Barnabas* in particular and on group dynamics and early Jewish-Christian relations in general. At the most granular level, the allusions to the circumcision of hearing are shown to be placed at key points within the letter (8:7; 9:3; 10:12; 16:10). By illustrating the critical importance that this metaphorical ritual has in the text, I address a lacuna in the scholarship on the epistle as sustained analysis on this matter has been wanting. More broadly, I offer a richer picture of the liminality of the community that Barnabas was attempting to construct and maintain. While Ferdinand R. Prostmeier is generally correct to assert that "the anti-Judaism of Barn *is* inner-Christian polemics," much of the social analysis on the letter has focused on the intergroup dynamics, namely, its relation to "Judaism."[68] I, on the other hand, reconstruct the fragile dynamics from a more intragroup standpoint.[69] Concerning the impact on the general area of early Jewish-Christian relations, the methodological approach taken in this chapter – which provides a more theoretical articulation of the key constituents of a communal group, that is, canon and ritual – presents analytical constructs to help explore this contentious topic in new and penetrating ways.

Finally, the utilization of cross-cultural and interdisciplinary studies allows modern (and mostly Western) scholars to see the rationale behind the oddities that have been well expressed in Barnabas scholarship. By interpreting the letter along more conceptually thoughtful formulations on canon and ritual, it has been argued that what Barnabas was attempting to do is not different from what takes place in every communal group even in our present societies. Within the convergence of canonical interpretation and ritual performance, certain aspects of the strangeness of Barnabas begin to fade away. Even in modern times, blockbuster hits in the entertainment industry promise either a glimpse into the future or a privileged perspective into the past.[70] It is likewise difficult to decide which question is most frequent at the water cooler: "How was your weekend?" or "Do you have any plans this weekend?" Outside of our modern, Western culture, familial lineage is critical, as is one's posterity. For Barnabas, this tension "betwixt and between" interpreting the past and creating a future is vital not only for his theology but also for the power of his rhetoric:[71] his assertions are persuasive because they generate claims where "such possibilities cannot be realized"[72] – at least in this world. Traditionally accepted interpretations of the past must be overhauled with Barnabas's new γνῶσις – another example of how "the crucial issue is not history but hermeneutics."[73] On the other hand, Barnabas concedes that contemporaneous circumstances present paradoxes to his γνῶσις, but this is only because his community is still in the liminal state. It is also because he and his community have not yet experienced their new creation status (6:19), and because the true Sabbath is on the always-future eighth day (15:7–9), and because the temple is still being built (16:8–9), and so on.[74] In the interim, Barnabas and his community can find refuge in the fact that "Texts construct a world," a world that "authors and readers already inhabit and experience as 'reality.'"[75] Where "our knowledge is now perfect" (13:7) and where "God truly resides within our place of dwelling – within us" (16:8). In other words, where "the imagined ceases to be imaginary."[76]

NOTES

This chapter originally appeared in *Harvard Theological Review* 112, no. 3 (2019): 273–95. Reprinted with permission from HTR and Cambridge University Press. I am thankful for the helpful feedback of Warren C. Campbell, Terence L. Donaldson, Gregory P. Fewster, and John S. Kloppenborg. Above all, I thank my wife, Jeanie L. Yuh, for her overall support.

1 So James N. Rhodes, *The Epistle of Barnabas and the Deuteronomic Tradition: Polemics, Paraenesis, and the Legacy of the Golden-Calf Incident*, WUNT 2/188 (Tübingen: Mohr Siebeck, 2004), 59, regarding Barn. 9:1–3. Though very little has been written on the circumcision of hearing, the exceptional strangeness of the overall text itself has been well documented. See, for example, Philipp Vielhauer, *Geschichte der urchristlichen Literatur: Einleitung in das Neue Testament, die Apokryphen und die Apostolischen Väter* (New York: de Gruyter, 1975), 612; James Carleton Paget, *The Epistle of Barnabas: Outlook and Background* (Tübingen: Mohr Siebeck, 1994), 1; Jörg Frey, "Temple and Identity in Early Christianity and in the Johannine Community: Reflections on the 'Parting of the Ways,'" in *Was 70 CE a Watershed in Jewish History? On Jews and Judaism before and after the Destruction of the Second Temple*, ed. Daniel R. Schwartz and Zeev Weiss (Boston: Brill, 2012), 463; Ruth A. Clements, "Epilogue: 70 CE After 135 CE – The Making of a Watershed?," in *Was 70 CE a Watershed in Jewish History? On Jews and Judaism before and after the Destruction of the Second Temple*, ed. Daniel R. Schwartz and Zeev Weiss (Boston: Brill, 2012), 522; and Stephen G. Wilson, "Gentile Judaizers," *New Testament Studies* 38 (1992): 610. This strangeness has led to a negative view on the text (e.g., John Lawson, *A Theological and Historical Introduction to the Apostolic Fathers* [New York: Macmillan, 1961], 198), which has created the perception that the epistle "is not really worthy of the range of critical approaches applied to texts such as the NT" (Ken Derry, "One Stone on Another: Towards an Understanding of Symbolism in the *Epistle of Barnabas*," *Journal of Early Christian Studies* 4 [1996]: 515–28, 516). English translations and verse references of the *Epistle of Barnabas* are from Bart D. Ehrman, "Epistle of Barnabas," 1–84, in *The Apostolic Fathers*, vol. 2, *Epistle of Barnabas* (Cambridge: Harvard University Press, 2003).

2 There is a recent trend in exploring the social dimensions of this epistle: Michael Kok, "The True Covenant People: Ethnic Reasoning in the Epistle of Barnabas," *Studies in Religion* 40 (2011): 81–97; Julien C.H. Smith, "The Epistle of Barnabas and the Two Ways of Teaching Authority," *Vigiliae Christianae* 68 (2014): 465–97; Derry, "One Stone on Another," 528. The emergence of these studies is indebted to the works of James Carleton Paget and Reidar Hvalvik as they remedied the prevalent view that Barnabas is merely a mindless motley of sources (Paget, *Epistle of Barnabas*; Reidar Hvalvik, *The Struggle for Scripture and Covenant: The Purpose of the Epistle of Barnabas and Jewish-Christian Competition in the Second*

Century, WUNT 2/82 [Tübingen: Mohr Siebeck, 1996]). Last, the social-scientific approach taken in this study functions as a response to Burton L. Mack's challenge for a "redescription of Christian origins" that is "firmly anchored in a social and cultural anthropology, capable of sustaining a conversation with the humanities" (Burton L. Mack, "On Redescribing Christian Origins," *Method and Theory in the Study of Religion* 8 [1996]: 247–69, 254).

3 Recent utilization of canon and ritual as conceptual tools to analyze the communal aspects of early Christianity can be seen in Daniel Stökl Ben Ezra, "Weighing the Parts: A Papyrological Perspective on the Parting of the Ways," *Novum Testamentum* 51 (2009): 168–86; Risto Uro, *Ritual and Christian Beginnings* (Oxford: Oxford University Press, 2016). Through these tools, I am merely offering suggestive possibilities to what Barnabas was attempting to accomplish with his letter, especially with his use of the circumcision of hearing metaphor, while acknowledging that a misapplication of these tools could obscure some of the important distinctions of specific contexts.

4 For an example in the Dead Sea Scrolls, see Hanne von Weissenberg and Elisa Uusimäki's study on how the interpretations of the Maskil and the pesharim are portrayed as equally revelatory and authoritative as texts that are later known to be biblical (Hanne von Weissenberg and Elisa Uusimäki, "Are There Sacred Texts in Qumran? The Concept of Sacred Text in Light of the Qumran Collection," in *Is There a Text in This Cave? Studies in the Textuality of the Dead Sea Scrolls in Honour of George J. Brooke*, ed. Ariel Feldman, Maria Cioată, and Charlotte Hempel, STDJ 119 [Leiden: Brill, 2017], 21–41. See also Philip S. Alexander, "Textual Authority and the Problem of the Biblical Canon at Qumran," in *Is There a Text in This Cave? Studies in the Textuality of the Dead Sea Scrolls in Honour of George J. Brooke*, ed. Ariel Feldman, Maria Cioată, and Charlotte Hempel, STDJ 119 [Leiden: Brill, 2017], 42–68).

5 I use terms such as "Jew" and "Jewish" rather than "Judaean" (Anders Runesson, "Inventing Christian Identity: Paul, Ignatius, and Theodosius I," in *Exploring Early Christian Identity*, ed. Bengt Holmberg [Tübingen: Mohr Siebeck, 2008], 64–70).

6 See also Smith, "Epistle of Barnabas," 468. Note the textual variant for 5:7 from the defective manuscripts of G (11th century and later).

7 For example, Barn. 4:6. See Rhodes, *Epistle of Barnabas*, 178–82; Hvalvik, *Struggle for Scripture*, 91–2.

8 In older scholarship, a distinction was made between two kinds of γνῶσις in the epistle (e.g., Hans Windisch, *Der Barnabasbrief* [Tübingen: Mohr, 1920], 307–9; Robert A. Kraft, *The Apostolic Fathers: A New Translation and Commentary*, ed. Robert M. Grant [New York: Nelson, 1964], 3:22–7). For a detailed summary of this view, see Paget, *Epistle of Barnabas*, 46–49. I am following more recent studies by interpreting γνῶσις as conveying the same meaning throughout the epistle (e.g., Jonathan A. Draper, "Barnabas and the Riddle of the Didache Revisited," *Journal for the Study of the New Testament* 17 [1995]: 89–113, 95; Hvalvik, *Struggle for Scripture*, 84–6).

9 Although there are portions of the text where these sacred texts are to be understood literally – for example, Daniel C. Ullucci, *The Christian Rejection of Animal Sacrifice* (New York: Oxford University Press, 2012), 97. For a dedicated study on 9:4, see James Carleton Paget, "Barnabas 9:4: A Peculiar Verse on Circumcision," *Vigiliae Christianae* 45 (1991): 242–54.

10 Pertaining to early Christianity in particular, see Guy G. Stroumsa, "Early Christianity – A Religion of the Book?," in *Homer, the Bible, and Beyond: Literary and Religious Canons in the Ancient World*, ed. Margalit Finkelberg and Guy G. Stroumsa (Leiden: Brill, 2003), 153; Christoph Markschies, "The Canon of the New Testament in Antiquity," in *Homer, the Bible, and Beyond: Literary and Religious Canons in the Ancient World*, ed. Margalit Finkelberg and Guy G. Stroumsa (Leiden: Brill, 2003), 192; David Brakke, "A New Fragment of Athanasius's Thirty-Ninth Festal Letter: Heresy, Apocrypha, and the Canon," *Harvard Theological Review* 103 (2010): 47–66. Another article by Brakke, published nearly thirty years ago, merits special mention as it is perhaps the earliest study to explore the "social and political implications" of the concept of canon (David Brakke, "Canon Formation and Social Conflict in Fourth-Century Egypt: Athanasius of Alexandria's Thirty-Ninth 'Festal Letter,'" *Harvard Theological Review* 87 (1994): 396). It also rates attention for its application of Jonathan Z. Smith's cross-cultural findings (ibid., 416). At a more general level, see Jonathan Z. Smith, *Imagining Religion: From Babylon to Jonestown* (Chicago: University of Chicago, 1982); Miriam Levering, "Introduction," in *Rethinking Scripture: Essays from a Comparative Perspective*, ed. Miriam Levering (Albany: SUNY, 1989), 5; Margalit Finkelberg and Guy G. Stroumsa, "Introduction: Before the Western Canon," in *Homer, the Bible, and Beyond: Literary and Religious Canons in the Ancient World*, ed. Margalit Finkelberg and Guy G. Stroumsa (Leiden: Brill, 2003), 5; Markschies, "Canon of the New Testament," 178; Guy G. Stroumsa, *Hidden Wisdom: Esoteric Traditions and the Roots of Christian Mysticism*, rev. ed. (Boston: Brill, 2005), 88; Aleida Assmann, "Canon and Archive," in *Cultural Memory Studies: An International and Interdisciplinary Handbook*, ed. Ansgar Nünning, Astrid Erll, and Sara B. Young (New York: de Gruyter, 2008), 100.

11 Similar to Finkelberg and Stroumsa's notion of "foundational texts" ("Before the Western Canon," 5).

12 On textual pluriformity and the lack of fixity in early Judaism, see Alexander, "Textual Authority"; Judith H. Newman, *Before the Bible: The Liturgical Body and the Formation of Scriptures in Early Judaism* (Oxford: Oxford University Press, 2018). On anachronistic assumptions in studies related to canon, see Eva Mroczek, *The Literary Imagination in Jewish Antiquity* (New York: Oxford University Press, 2016). On the distinction between a theoretical and an anachronistic canon, see Stephen B. Chapman, "Collections, Canons, and Communities," in *The Cambridge Companion to the Hebrew Bible/Old Testament*, ed. Stephen B. Chapman and Marvin A. Sweeney (New York: Cambridge University Press, 2016), 35–6; Alexander, "Textual Authority," 51.

13 This touches upon the inseparable relationship between canon and hermeneutics as seen across different cultures, such as the Neoplatonists, Rabbinic Jewish communities (Finkelberg and Stroumsa, "Before the Western Canon," 6–7), and religious groups of ancient Rome (Mary Beard, "Ancient Literacy and the Function of the Written Word in Roman Religion," in *Literacy in the Roman World*, ed. Mary Beard, et al., JRASup 3 [Ann Arbor: University of Michigan, 1991], 53–8, though Beard's emphasis is on written texts and not canon per se). See also Stroumsa's observation (*Hidden Wisdom*, 79–91; Stroumsa, *The Making of the Abrahamic Religions in Late Antiquity* [New York: Oxford University Press, 2015], 31–2) concerning the parallel between the Mishnah and the New Testament.

14 Jan Assmann, *Religion and Cultural Memory: Ten Studies* (Stanford: Stanford University Press, 2006), 43. Assmann grounds these assertions primarily in evidence from ancient Egyptian culture and, interacting with Leo Oppenheim, ancient Mesopotamian culture. Assmann's statements are even more relevant for the "textual communities" of early Christianity (Judith Lieu, *Christian Identity in the Jewish and Graeco-Roman World* [Oxford: Oxford University Press, 2004], 28–9). See also Smith, *Imagining Religion*, 49; Harald Welzer, "Communicative Memory," in *Cultural Memory Studies: An International and Interdisciplinary Handbook*, ed. Ansgar Nünning, Astrid Erll, and Sara B. Young (New York: de Gruyter, 2008), 285–98. For an example in early Judaism, see note 5 above.

15 For example, George W.E. Nickelsburg, "Revealed Wisdom as a Criterion for Inclusion and Exclusion: From Jewish Sectarianism to Early Christianity," in *"To See Ourselves as Others See Us": Christians, Jews, "Others" in Late Antiquity*, ed. Jacob Neusner and Ernest S. Frerichs, (Chico: Scholars Press, 1985), 73–92. However, Shaye J.D. Cohen places the emphasis on the temple and on who is the true Israel (Shaye J.D. Cohen, *From the Maccabees to the Mishnah* [Louisville: Westminster John Knox, 2006], 119–66). But even topics concerning the temple and true Israel would have been based on competing interpretations of scripture (ibid., 129).

16 Some scholars suggest that there were "foundational texts" that were authoritative over most Jewish communities during this time (Bruce M. Metzger, *The Canon of the New Testament: Its Origin, Development, and Significance*, rev. ed. [New York: Oxford University Press, 1997], 2) or that "by the end of the first century CE there was a canon that most Jews accepted" (Timothy H. Lim, *The Formation of the Jewish Canon* [New Haven: Yale University Press, 2013], 180). The point, however, is that Barnabas relies heavily on Jewish sources and very little on Christian ones (Metzger, *Canon of the New Testament*, 58–9; James Carleton Paget, "Paul and the Epistle of Barnabas," *Novum Testamentum* 38 [1996]: 359–81). For a detailed study of Barnabas's source, see Paget, *Epistle of Barnabas*.

17 Smith, *Imagining Religion*, 50. See also Bernard M. Levinson's helpful nuances to Smith's theoretical model: the exegetical innovation is hidden and the canon does not need to be closed (*Legal Revision and Religious Renewal in Ancient Israel* [Cambridge: Cambridge University Press, 2008], 15–18).

18 Draper, "Barnabas and the Riddle of the Didache", 95; Hvalvik, *Struggle for Scripture*, 85.

19 Smith, *Imagining Religion*, 48. While canon and group formation can be understood within the conversation concerning the relationship between "social formation and mythmaking," this chapter does not attempt to explore the "social logic" of this epistle. For a short summary of this conversation, see Ron Cameron and Merrill P. Miller, "Conclusion: Redescribing Christian Origins," in *Redescribing Christian Origins*, ed. Ron Cameron and Merrill P. Miller (Atlanta: SBL Press, 2004), 513–15.

20 On the inextricable connection between Barnabas and Jewish traditions, see Daniel Stökl Ben Ezra, who notes that Barnabas represents "the text best informed about the Temple rite [of Yom Kippur]" and is therefore a "goldmine o Jewish traditions" (Daniel Stökl Ben Ezra, "Fasting with Jews, Thinking with Scapegoats: Some Remarks on Yom Kippur in Early Judaism and Christianity, in Particular 4Q541, Barnabas 7, Matthew 27 and Acts 27," in *The Day of Atonement: Its Interpretations in Early Jewish and Christian Traditions*, ed. Thomas Hieke and Tobias Nicklas, Themes in Biblical Narrative [Boston: Brill, 2012], 173–4). Also, James D.G. Dunn suggests that, other than 1 Clement, the Epistle of Barnabas uses the Hebrew scripture more heavily than any other early Christian writing at this time (James D.G. Dunn, *Neither Jew Nor Greek: A Contested Identity*, vol. 3, *Christianity in the Making* [Grand Rapids: Eerdmans, 2015], 550–69). See also Pierluigi Lanfranchi, "Attitudes to the Sabbath in Three Apostolic Fathers: Didache, Ignatius, and Barnabas," in *Jesus, Paul, and Early Christianity: Studies in Honour of Henk Jan De Jonge*, ed. Rieuwerd Buitenwerf, Harm W. Hollander, and Johannes Tromp (Leiden: Brill, 2008), 243–60; Tim Hegedus, "Midrash and the Letter of Barnabas," *Biblical Theology Bulletin* 37 (2007): 20–6; L.W. Barnard, "The 'Epistle of Barnabas' and Its Contemporary Setting," *Aufstieg und Niedergang der römischen Welt* 2.27.1 (1993): 159–207.

21 Smith, *Imagining Religion*, 46, 51.

22 See also Assmann, "Canon and Archive," 100.

23 See also Hvalvik, *Struggle for Scripture*, 86.

24 See also Smith, "Epistle of Barnabas," 486–9

25 Ibid., 488; Hvalvik, *Struggle for Scripture*, 53. I show later in this chapter that the uncertainty lies not in the content of Barnabas's teaching but in the condition of his hearers.

26 Though the idea of hearing is also found in 12:8, these four verses are primarily examined because they all convey the notion of differentiation that is also seen in the literal circumcision. For instance, these verses not only include the idea of hearing, but they (or their respective contexts) also imply the covenantal implications of circumcision (e.g., 9:6) by making a contrast between those who hear and those who do not hear. On the other hand, 12:8 only references the notion of hearing without making a distinction between those who are in and out of the covenant. A lexical search would also return references such as 7:3

and 13:2, but the sense of ἀκούω (I hear) in these are idiomatic and should not be taken in a technical way (e.g., "consider this"). Also, 9:3's circumcision of hearing is actually placed in 9:4 in some editions (e.g., Michael W. Holmes, ed., *The Apostolic Fathers: Greek Texts and English Translations*, trans. Michael W. Holmes, rev. ed. [Grand Rapids: Baker, 2007], 406).

27 The LXX translation is from the author, but all other scriptural translations are from the NRSV. Note that Jer 6:10 is later cited by Acts 7:51 (ἀπερίτμητοι καρδίαις καὶ τοῖς ὠσίν [uncircumcised in heart and ears]). Also, there are instances of "circumcision" and "hearing" in Herodotus, but these are not related to circumcision in the Jewish cultic sense (e.g., *Hist.* 2.162.5: περιταμεῖν προστάξαι αὐτοῦ τά τε ὦτα καὶ τὴν ῥῖνα). One qualification is important: Prigent and Kraft see two additional references to circumcision of hearing in Barn. 9:1 (following P and L rather than S and H). The first additional reference is not a quotation, but the second would be from Jer 4:4. Even if one favours P and L, Prigent and Kraft (Pierre Prigent and Robert A. Kraft, ed., *L'Épître de Barnabé*, SC 172 [Paris: Cerf, 1971], 142n2) acknowledge that the linguistic metaphor would not have originated from Jer 4:4: "the citation is strongly reworked to better fit the collection."

28 Kraft, *Apostolic Fathers*, 3:106. Note that Kraft interprets the letter in general as a collection of pre-existent sources. As indicated in n4, this assumption has been rightly qualified. Hvalvik, *Struggle for Scripture*, 330, writes that "the author's material is traditional; his use of the material, however, is often original" as the letter in general discloses a coherent purpose, namely, the right interpretation of scripture (ibid., 102–36) and the distinction between two peoples or ways (ibid., 137–57). See also Carleton Paget, *Epistle of Barnabas*, 2:258–60; "Barnabas 9:4."

29 "And when the mind is circumcised and contains only necessary and useful things, and when at the same time there is cut off whatever causes pride to increase, then with it are circumcised the eyes also, as though they could not (otherwise) see" (*QG* 3.47). All texts and translations of Philo's writings throughout are from Philo, *On the Confusion of Tongues. On the Migration of Abraham. Who Is the Heir of Divine Things? On Mating with the Preliminary Studies*, trans. F.H. Colson, G.H. Whitaker, Loeb Classical Library 261 (Cambridge: Harvard University Press, 1932); *On the Decalogue. On the Special Laws, Books 1-3*, trans. F.H. Colson, Loeb Classical Library 320 (Cambridge: Harvard University Press, 1937); *Questions on Genesis*, trans. Ralph Marcus, Loeb Classical Library 380 (Cambridge: Harvard University Press, 1953); *Questions on Exodus*, trans. Ralph Marcus, Loeb Classical Library 401 (Cambridge: Harvard University Press, 1953).

30 Philo typically groups seeing and hearing together (*Migr.* 103, 119; *Spec.* 1.29, 337, 342), which are inferior to "the rational" faculties of "mind and speech" but higher than smell and taste (*QG* 3.5). Hearing, however, is secondary to seeing (*Migr.* 49–52; *QG* 3.32, 59). The next closest writing to the circumcision of hearing or ears by Philo besides *QG* 3.47 would be: "For he who listens with the tips of his ears is able to get (only) a somewhat vague perception of what is said, while to him who listens carefully the words enter more clearly and the things

heard travel on all the paths so that they form his mind with deep impressions, as if (it were) wax, lest it easily become stupid and (the impressions) leap away" (*QE* 2.13). However, in this quote, he is not suggesting that the tips of the ears need to be circumcised. Last, it should be noted that Barnabas's metaphor differs in significant ways from Philo's famous treatment on circumcision (*Spec.* 1.1–11). Whereas Barnabas's focus on his metaphorical circumcision is primarily hermeneutical, Philo's is more diverse (e.g., healing from "anthrax or carbuncle" [1.4], cleanliness [1.5], "fertility of offspring" [1.7], "the excision of pleasures" [1.9]) and presupposes the literal practice of circumcision (so Barclay 1998, 538–40).

31 See also Paget, "Paul and the Epistle of Barnabas," 378; "Barnabas 9:4," 245. Additionally, the broad Hellenistic influence may have in part inspired Barnabas to view the entirety of the Jewish law figuratively. To continue Philo's quotation, there were certainly those in Philo's circle that neglected "the sanctity of the Temple and a thousand other things" (*Migr.* 92). Heikki Räisänen, *Jesus, Paul and Torah: Collected Essays* (Sheffield: JSOT, 1992), 149–202, suggests that certain strands within Hellenistic Judaism were not only abandoning their hopes for the physical restoration of the temple but possibly eschewing the practice of literal circumcision. See also Daniel R. Schwartz, *Studies in the Jewish Background of Christianity*, WUNT 60 (Tübingen: Mohr Siebeck, 1992), 10–19.

32 Failing to trace how 8:7 is connected to the previous chapters, and ultimately to the very beginning of the letter, is one of the reasons the circumcision of hearing has not received sustained analysis up until now. Most commentators see 8:7 as merely an introduction to ch. 9, which is concluded with 10:12 (e.g., Paget, *Epistle of Barnabas*, 149; Hvalvik, *Struggle for Scripture*, 184). However, Julien Smith, "Epistle of Barnabas," 477–89, sees that it is also connected to 3:6, while still being used to transition into ch. 9. Though not explicit, Rhodes, *Epistle of Barnabas*, 59, implies what I am arguing, that the "main point" is the "capacity to understand and respond appropriately to the divine will," which are ideas that have been introduced from the very beginning of the letter. See also Klaus Wengst, *Tradition und Theologie des Barnabasbriefes*, Arbeiten zur Kirchengeschichte 42 (Berlin: de Gruyter, 1971), 78; Ferdinand R. Prostmeier, *Der Barnabasbrief*, Kommentar zu den Apostolischen Vätern 8 (Göttingen: Vandenhoeck & Ruprecht, 1999), 352–3.

33 Robert A. Kraft, *The Epistle of Barnabas: Its Quotations and Their Sources* (Ph.D. diss., Harvard University Press, 1961), 43. To be exact: "9:1–3 alone contains eight short quotations concerning 'hearing' and 'ears.'"

34 Kraft, *Apostolic Fathers*, 3:45. Clement's high regard for Barnabas has been well documented: James Carleton Paget, *Jews, Christians and Jewish Christians in Antiquity* (Tübingen: Mohr Siebeck, 2010), 95n23, notes that Clement explicitly cites Barnabas eight times in the *Stromateis*. See also Klaus Wengst, *Didache (Apostellehre); Barnabasbrief; Zweiter Klemensbrief; Schrift an Diognet*, ed. Klaus Wengst, Schriften des Urchristentums (München: Kösel, 1984), 106; Ehrman, "Epistle of Barnabas," 3, 7.

35 References to the *Stromateis* follow Otto Stählin, ed., *Clemens Alexandrinus*, vol. 2, Griechischen christlichen Schriftsteller (Berlin: Akademie-Verlag, 1960).

36 Clement's epistemological usage of this metaphor is all the more remarkable when considering that his extant writings reveal his overarching concern with knowledge (Eric Osborn, *Clement of Alexandria* [Cambridge: Cambridge University Press, 2005], xiii, 1–4; Andrew C. Itter, *Esoteric Teaching in the Stromateis of Clement of Alexandria* [Leiden: Brill, 2009], 81). Interestingly, scholars have used ritualized language to describe how the pursuit of knowledge is one of the primary purposes of the *Stromateis*, for example, "to initiate souls into the true philosophy of Christ and to have knowledge of the first principle of the universe" (Itter, *Esoteric Teaching*, 109); "the initiation into true gnosis" (Louis Roberts, "The Literary Form of the 'Stromateis.'" *Second Century* 1 [1981]: 211–22, 213). That this chapter (*Strom*. 5.8) is specifically concerned with knowledge is apparent by noticing how Clement uses even the barbarians as examples of ones who employ the use of symbols (5.8.44.1, 45.1) and how he cites Theognis 35–36 (5.8.52.4) and Isa 1:3 (5.8.54.1).

37 For the same analysis on 9:1–3, see Prostmeier, *Barnabasbrief*, 352–3.

38 On the temple being one of the primary themes of Barnabas, see Rhodes, *Epistle of Barnabas*, 81; Stephen G. Wilson, *Related Strangers: Jews and Christians, 70-170 C.E.* (Minneapolis: Fortress Press, 1995), 131–6; Richardson and Shukster, "Temple and Bet Ha-Midrash," 17–32.

39 Prigent and Kraft, "Épître de Barnabé," 195n2, translation by author.

40 Though Richardson and Shukster, "Temple and Bet Ha-Midrash," also interpret 16:10 as a critical verse, representing the convergence of the two major themes of the letter, they see the themes as being different (i.e., the temple and the *birkat ha-minim*); however, their argument for the rebuilding of the temple by Nerva is tenuous. They base it on Nerva's coin, which does not necessarily have to mean what they suggest, and they also base it on the historically suspicious account of *Gen. Rab.* 64.8. See also Emil Schürer, *The History of the Jewish People in the Age of Jesus Christ (175 BC–AD 135)*, ed. Géza Vermès and Fergus Millar (Edinburgh: T&T Clark, 1973), 1:535 (though Richardson and Shukster acknowledge this and also cite texts from the *Megillat Ta'ani*). For a recent analysis of Richardson and Shukster's hypothesis, see Paget, *Epistle of Barnabas*, 15–17; concerning Richardson and Shukster's suggestion of the *birkat ha-minim*, recent research has questioned the direct influence that the *birkat ha-minim* had on "Christians" in the Diaspora cities, for example, Jonathan Bernier, *Aposynagōgos and the Historical Jesus in John: Rethinking the Historicity of the Johannine Expulsion Passages*, Biblical Interpretation Series 122 (Leiden: Brill, 2013), 40–1 – though Richardson and Shukster place the provenance of Barnabas in Syria. However, Richardson and Shukster's observations of Barnabas responding to the *birkat ha-minim* via his exegesis can also be explained through the arguments proposed in this study.

41 Scholarship on early Christianity has also mentioned, but not explored, this connection, for example, Stroumsa, "Early Christianity," 165, 172; *Making of the*

Abrahamic Religions, 39; Brakke, "Canon Formation and Social Conflict," 403, 408. See Newman, *Before the Bible*, for this exploration in early Judaism.

42 The argument is not that this metaphor was an actual ritual that took place in a social context but that it addresses the most primary communal needs that are typically addressed by rituals. In short, it functions as a ritual. See the next section for more details.

43 Richardson and Shukster, "Temple and Bet Ha-Midrash," 29.

44 Of course, Cohen, *Maccabees to the Mishnah*, 51–2, does not mean to say that the Jews did not have any faith or beliefs. George W.E. Nickelsburg, *Ancient Judaism and Christian Origins: Diversity, Continuity, and Transformation* (Minneapolis: Fortress Press, 2003), 60, says that the difference between "Jews" and "Christians" was "christological"; however, he does say that "For Jews, the right life was bound up with the observance of the Torah." See also Daniel Boyarin, *Border Lines: The Partition of Judaeo-Christianity* (Philadelphia: University of Pennsylvania, 2004), 10.

45 Cohen, *Maccabees to the Mishnah*, 65. However, see Cohen's more detailed treatment that assesses circumcision, language, and social mechanisms, particularly in the setting of Diaspora Jews, where he concludes: "the diaspora Jews of antiquity were not easily recognizable, if, indeed, they were recognizable at all" ("'Those Who Say They Are Jews and Are Not': How Do You Know a Jew in Antiquity When You See One?," in *Diasporas in Antiquity*, ed. Shaye J.D. Cohen and Ernest S. Frerichs [Atlanta: Scholars Press, 1993], 39). J.Z. Smith, "Fences and Neighbors: Some Contours of Early Judaism," in *Approaches to Ancient Judaism: Theory and Practice*, ed. by William Scott Green (Missoula: Scholars Press, 1978), 2:1–25, also argues that circumcision was not reliably a central mark for a Jew since many other groups, especially the Egyptians, were also circumcised (Barn. 9:6) – Smith rather sees that the association to the synagogue was the most prominent marker based on funeral inscriptions.

46 By rituals, I am referring to sacrifices, fasting, circumcision, and Sabbath; I am not arguing that abstention from pork – though Barnabas addresses this (10:3) – should be considered a ritual.

47 Geoffrey D. Dunn, "Tertullian and Rebekah: A Re-Reading of an 'Anti-Jewish' Argument in Early Christian Literature," *Vigiliae Christianae* 52 (1998): 140; Pierre Prigent, *Les Testimonia dans la christianisme primitif: L'épître de Barnabé I-XVI et ses sources* (Paris: Gabalda, 1961), 29–83.

48 In 11:11, Barnabas does make a reference to baptism, but it is difficult to see if this is performed in a way that would make this ritual different than that from Jewish traditions.

49 Richard Jenkins, *Social Identity*, rev. ed. (New York: Routledge, 2008), 169–83. For more on the latter point, see Catherine Bell, *Ritual Theory, Ritual Practice*, rev. ed. (New York: Oxford University Press, 2009), 102.

50 For a discussion of the student-teacher emphasis in early Christianity, particularly in Egypt (the likely provenance of Barnabas), see Brakke, *Canon Formation and Social Conflict*, 400–3. Brakke is influenced by Hans von Campenhausen,

Ecclesiastical Authority and Spiritual Power in the Church of the First Three Centuries, trans. J.A. Baker (London: Black, 1969), 195–211, who reconstructs the student-teacher emphasis primarily through Clement of Alexandria because there is no other textual evidence on this topic, though he does mention Barnabas (ibid., 192–5). I would contend, however, that the student-teacher emphasis can be traced earlier to Barnabas himself, when examining the circumcision of hearing motif through canon and ritual, especially considering the close relationship between Barnabas and Clement (at least on ideological grounds).

51 Jonathan Z. Smith, *To Take Place: Toward Theory in Ritual* (Chicago: University of Chicago, 1987), 109.

52 David Manier and William Hirst, "A Cognitive Taxonomy of Collective Memories," in *Cultural Memory Studies: An International and Interdisciplinary Handbook*, ed. Ansgar Nünning et al. (New York: de Gruyter, 2008), 251.

53 Jenkins, *Social Identity*, 77.

54 This point does not take away from the more obvious reason Barnabas phrased this metaphorical ritual as circumcision, which is to subvert the literal practice of circumcision.

55 Wengst, *Tradition und Theologie*, 113.

56 There is a total of eight instances of πιστεύω and six of them are used with the recipients as the subject (7:2; 9:3; 16:7; implied subject, 3:6; 6:3; 7:2). There is a total of seven instances of συνίημι (I understand); the recipients are the subject of three of these instances (4:6; 6:5; 10:12).

57 By contrast, the New Testament does not use μανθάνω in the second person imperative in any of the epistles. This form of the verb is only found in Jesus's sayings (Matt 9:13, 11:29, 24:32; Mark 13:28). Perhaps it is only coincidental, but it is worth mentioning that these imperatives are used multiple times in the epistle's more controversial discussions of circumcision (ch. 9) and the temple (ch. 16), which strengthens Daniel Schwartz's hypothesis (*Jewish Background of Christianity*, 147–53) on how Hadrian's policies may have instigated the Bar Kokhba revolt. For an alternative view on this topic, see Giovanni Battista Bazzana, "The Bar Kokhba Revolt and Hadrian's Religious Policy," in *Hadrian and the Christians*, ed. Marco Rizzi, SKGEJ 30 (New York: de Gruyter, 2010), 85–110.

58 Interestingly, in 2:10 the supplementing verb is from the rare verb ἀκριβεύομαι or ἀκριβεύω (I pay strict attention).

59 Victor W. Turner, *The Forest of Symbols: Aspects of Ndembu Ritual*, rev. ed. (Ithaca: Cornell University Press, 1970), 93–111. An updated version of Turner's chapter can be found in Turner, *The Ritual Process: Structure and Anti-Structure*, rev. ed. (New Brunswick: Aldine Transaction, 2007).

60 Turner, *Forest of Symbols*, 94; Arnold van Gennep, *The Rites of Passage*, rev. ed. (New York: Routledge, 2010).

61 Turner, *Forest of Symbols*, 96.

62 Ibid., 96–7. See also Gen 34.

63 This explains why there are other instances in the letter where Barnabas does not view his hearers as full members of the group that he is trying to construct. Barnabas's thoroughly didactic explanations of why some of the "fundamental" practices of the other are misguided all imply that his hearers were tempted to engage in these practices, if not already engaged in them (e.g., sacrifice in 2:4–10, fasting in 3:1–5, circumcision in 9:6, and the Sabbath in 15:1–9; the need for Barnabas to distinguish his hearers from the other in 4:6; 13:1–7; 14:1–9). The notion of liminality also explains why Barnabas outlines the basics of salvation (17:1) yet insinuates that there is still more to learn (17:2). See also Derry," One Stone on Another," 528; Dunn, "Tertullian and Rebekah"; Janni Loman, "The Letter of Barnabas in Early Second-Century Egypt," in *The Wisdom of Egypt: Jewish, Early Christian, and Gnostic Essays in Honour of Gerard P. Luttikhuizen*, ed. Anthony Hilhorst and Geurt Hendrik van Kooten (Boston: Brill, 2005), 247–66; Lanfranchi, "Attitudes to the Sabbath."

64 This emphasis is therefore a nuance to the interpretations of Julien Smith and Hvalvik.

65 Turner, *Forest of Symbols* (emphasis in original).

66 Paget, *Epistle of Barnabas*, 165, regards the syntactical relationship as being "surely significant." See also Kraft, *Apostolic Fathers*, 3:23.

67 Turner, *Forest of Symbols*, 102 (emphasis in original).

68 Ferdinand R. Prostmeier, "Antijudaismus im Rahmen christlicher Hermeneutik: Zum Streit über christliche Identität in der Alten Kirche Notizen zum Barnabasbrief," *Zeitschrift für Antikes Christentums/Journal of Ancient Christianity* 6 (2002): 56 (emphasis in original). The intergroup emphasis can be seen in Derry, "One Stone on Another"; and Kok, "True Covenant People." Note, however, Kok's hypothetical qualification in ibid., 88.

69 While Julien Smith, "Epistle of Barnabas," does touch upon the intragroup dynamic, it is to focus mostly on the teaching authority – or, canonical interpretation – of Barnabas, whereas the present study is focused more on the liminality of Barnabas's hearers as well as on providing a sustained examination of the circumcision of hearing with more conceptual depth.

70 See also Marco Cinnirella, "Exploring Temporal Aspects of Social Identity: The Concept of Possible Social Identities," *European Journal of Social Psychology* 28 (1998): 227–48, on how social identity is usually based on the re-interpretation of the past as well as on the shaping of the future. For this similar, temporal concept, see Smith, *To Take Place*, 109–12.

71 Turner, *Forest of Symbols*, 96.

72 Smith, *To Take Place*, 109. From a cognitive-scientific standpoint on the power of religious claims, see Richard Sosis, "The Adaptive Value of Religious Ritual," *American Scientist* 92 (2004): 172.

73 Shaye J.D. Cohen, *The Beginnings of Jewishness: Boundaries, Varieties, Uncertainties* (Berkeley: University of California, 1999), 349.

74 One might view this reference to liminality to be different than the more hermeneutical one mentioned earlier in this chapter. A closer reading of the letter, however, suggests that this distinction does not exist for Barnabas since elsewhere he conflates the more eschatological or new-creational quality with the more hermeneutical or epistemological quality (Barn. 6:10–19; 16:6–9).

75 Lieu, *Christian Identity*, 61.

76 Jenkins, *Social Identity*, 177.

10

Witnessing Disaster: Mark's Gospel as a Monument to the Catastrophe of Jesus's Death

Erin K. Vearncombe

Pliny the Younger concludes his correspondence with the historian Tacitus about the disastrous eruption of Mount Vesuvius in 79 CE and the consequent loss of his uncle with a declaration concerning Pliny's status as a witness. He asserts, "I have described in detail every incident which I either witnessed myself or heard about immediately after the event, when reports were most likely to be accurate. It is for you to select what best suits your purpose, for there is a great difference between a letter to a friend and history written for all to read" (Omnia me quibus interfueram quaeque statim, cum maxime vera memorantur, audieram, persecutum. Tu potissima excerpes; aliud est enim epistulam aliud historiam, aliud amico aliud omnibus scribere).[1] Pliny differentiates between the work of the witness and the work of the historian in the formal description and presentation of monumental events. "I gave you an accurate report," Pliny says, "and now you can decide what you want to use and how you want to shape that report from here" – *tu potissima excerpes*, "you choose what is most important" or "you extract what best serves you."

Umberto Eco offers a different translation of *tu potissima excerpes*: "Now, Tacitus, it is you who must transform my honest report into a cultural monument"[2] This translation also differentiates the work of the witness from that of the historian. However, for Eco, Pliny is presenting the work of the historian as the construction of a monument. His report may be "honest," but it is not without intent. Eleanor Winsor Leach, in her article "The Politics of Self-Presentation: Pliny's *Letters* and Roman Portrait Sculpture," picks up the idea of a text as a cultural monument when she states that Tacitus's invitation to Pliny to write to him concerning the circumstances of his uncle's death during the Vesuvius eruption gave Pliny "the occasion to construct not only a monument for his uncle, but also one for himself."[3] Monuments abounded in the ancient Mediterranean, a highly visual culture dependent to a large extent on the visual rhetoric of the honorific statue and relief. What makes a *writing*, though, qualify as a monument? How does the act of writing monumentalize?

The idea of the act of writing or written object as cultural monument lends itself particularly well to an investigation of the structuring of a *reading culture*, a key concept drawn from William A. Johnson's essential work on reading practices in the Roman world. Starting from a place of "strangeness" – we cannot assume that ancient reading practices were the same as those in contemporary North America, or that the act of reading and the cultural meanings ascribed to reading were the same – Johnson asserts that reading must be interpreted in the language of culture, rather than just cognition: "I prefer to look at reading as not an act, nor even a process, but as a highly complex sociocultural system … reading is not simply the cognitive process by the individual of the 'technology' of writing, but rather *the negotiated construction of meaning within a particular sociocultural context*."[4] A reading culture, whether because of an approach to the act of reading or because of a central focus on a physical piece of writing, structures the sociocultural reality of a particular reading community, the people who gather around that writing, the people who *use* it. Writing of elite Roman reading practices, Johnson states, "the system is symbiotic, in that the focal text provides fodder for the community's activity (this is what they get together to do), while the interrogation of the text validates the community's sense of self-identity as *the educated*, able to derive special meaning from this exclusive text. The successful use of the text in this way both revalidates the text as worthy and recommends the community as suitable gatekeepers."[5] A piece of writing, when understood as part of the complex of a reading culture, works to establish and maintain the boundaries of group identity, structuring the physical activities of a reading community and the dispositions of that community in outlining both an approach to and an understanding of what qualifies as knowledge or knowing. A reading culture validates not only what is known or what is important to know but also *how* things are known. Written words, read in a culture or community, *do* things. Yet given the level of literacy in the ancient Mediterranean and the many different uses to which writings were put, I argue that it is more helpful to consider *use* rather than *reading* specifically. To present the situation more accurately: written words, *used* in a culture or community, *do* things.

Chris Keith recognizes that an easy substitution might also be made for Johnson's "*the educated*": "the church," or, perhaps, "the early Jesus movement."[6] Keith applies Johnson's work to what he calls "the first certain instance of the textualization of narrativized Jesus tradition," that is, the Gospel of Mark (hereafter GMark).[7] Keith is particularly interested in the importance of GMark as a cultural artifact that enabled and constructed identity in the early Jesus movement due to its material, physical form as well as to its content.[8] The written object that was GMark *did* things within a specific sociocultural context. This chapter builds upon Keith's interrogation of the oral/written tension in the interpretation of GMark's literary production. As both a written and a material artifact, GMark is still read for or in terms of its orality. Keith questions Paul J. Achtemeier's statement that the texts of the New Testament "are oral to the core, both in their creation and in their performance,"[9] as well as assertions by Joanna Dewey and Werner Kelber that privilege the "oral legacy" of early Christian written tradition, specifically GMark.[10] What does it mean to call written objects "oral"? Keith asks, "How could *writing a text on a manuscript* remain 'fundamentally' on the oral side of the so-called Great Divide? … how could such an act fail also to be 'textual'?"[11] Keith's questions inspire further thought about why GMark continues to be considered as fundamentally oral. How might GMark's narrative style be considered as written rather than oral? What are the consequences of shifting the focus from its supposed oral performance to written storytelling?

GMark's style can be meaningful when weighted towards the written. GMark as a piece of writing, the first "textualized" narrative of Jesus, produces a user as part of what I call a culture of *witness*, and a culture centred around the cultural artifact of the GMark as a *monument to disaster*. My essential starting point is Johnson: reading has a fundamental sociocultural dimension. It is both structured by and is structuring of culture, on a broader scale, and particular reading communities, or using communities, on a local scale. Similar to Pliny's witness to the death of his uncle, GMark's accomplishment with this written object is the creation of a cultural monument that tells a particular story of the disaster that was the death of Jesus. This monument enables the community using that monument to be both structured by that story and held responsible for that story, or for the epistemic world behind the story. GMark is the first textualization of the disaster of the death of Jesus, the first written witness. In reporting on the disaster, the writer develops a technology of written witness that both facilitates a transition from oral reportage to written tradition, as others have argued, and, as I argue here, creates a specific culture of disaster response through the use of written object as monument.

* * *

The language of witness brings with it a great deal of theological baggage. My interest here is not in what Bauckham would call "the Jesus of Testimony" but is, rather, in contemporary sociological theory of witnessing and trauma.[12] John Durham Peters provides the primary lens through which I view GMark; Peters theorizes witnessing as "an intricately tangled practice. It raises questions of truth and experience, presence and absence, death and pain, seeing and saying, and the trustworthiness of perception – in short, fundamental questions of communication."[13] Communication occurs in a triangle involving an agent who bears witness to a traumatic event, a textual witness that encodes the experience of the agent in a sort of speech-act, and an audience that witnesses and, in "witnessing," becomes somehow involved in the event. Witnessing involves positioning oneself relative to a situation of pain, trauma, or suffering, a position determined by location in space (presence/absence) and location in time (presence/absence). Peters writes:

> Of four basic types of relations to an event, three can sustain the attitude of a witness. To be there, present at the event in space and time is the paradigm case. To be present in time but removed in space is the condition of liveness, simultaneity across space. To be present in space but removed in time is the condition of historical representation: here is the possibility of a simultaneity across time, a witness that laps the ages. To be absent in both space and time but still have access to an event via its traces is the condition of recording: the profane zone in which the attitude of witnessing is hardest to sustain.[14]

This "attitude" is significant – essential – because it involves the implication of the witness in the event, the requirement to act. Witnessing implies responsibility.[15] Reporting does not.

The reading/using community of GMark is absent in both space and time from the events of Jesus's death. This double absence places the writing in the dangerous reporting zone where, as a historical event, the crucifixion may be interesting but not directly *engaging*. Listening or reading can be an act of pure consumption or more active interpretation. Witnessing, though, insists upon something more. It insists upon a certain "liveness," or "in being tied by simultaneity,"[16] as Peters writes. GMark is a witness first and foremost as it insists on this liveness or simultaneity. There are multiple ways in which the narrative makes Jesus's death meaningful, but GMark renders the death a *disaster* requiring *witness* not necessarily in the story itself (though the narrative mechanism of scriptural allusion certainly makes Jesus's death meaningful in relation to another reading/using culture/s) but in the way in which the story is told. The writing *does something* with words.

A primary means of shifting the narrative from historical record to witness is through the use of the historical present. GMark's narrative style is variously treated as an example of the writer's poor writing abilities or of the writer's so-called oral storytelling. Following Keith's refutation of the privileging of the oral, and rejecting assumptions about GMark's literary location, the use of the historical present and any speculation about intent does not interest me so much as does its effect. The *effect* of the historical present is the elision of the present with the past. Mark 1:29–31 offers a paradigmatic example of this elision: "And immediately, having come out of the synagogue, they went into the house of Simon and Andrew, with James and John. And the mother-in-law of Simon was lying in a fever, and immediately they tell him about her. And having come and taken her by the hand, he lifted her up; and immediately the fever left her, and she began to serve them" (Καὶ εὐθὺς ἐκ τῆς συναγωγῆς ἐξελθόντες ἦλθον εἰς τὴν οἰκίαν Σίμωνος καὶ Ἀνδρέου μετὰ Ἰακώβου καὶ Ἰωάννου. ἡ δὲ πενθερὰ Σίμωνος κατέκειτο πυρέσσουσα, καὶ εὐθὺς λέγουσιν αὐτῷ περὶ αὐτῆς. καὶ προσελθὼν ἤγειρεν αὐτὴν κρατήσας τῆς χειρός· καὶ ἀφῆκεν αὐτὴν ὁ πυρετός, καὶ διηκόνει αὐτοῖς). While only one example among many, Mark 1:29–31 illustrates the time shifting that occurs through verb tenses.

In the shifting between past and present, GMark operates similarly to another witness to disaster, Pliny's letter to Tacitus regarding his uncle's death. The Elder Pliny's death as a result of the eruption of Vesuvius in 79 CE must, like GMark, make sense of an apparent disaster, an "accidental" death that seemed to occur because Pliny was not paying close enough attention to his surroundings. The story is not one of heroism but of accident and tragedy. The discourse surrounding the story, however, works to accrue proper meaning to the death. The distinction between story and discourse relies on Umberto Eco's analysis of the letter: "the story (once it has been isolated by a reader in the form of a series of macro-propositions chronologically ordered) says something. However, the discourse says, if not something else, at least something more, in such a way that it is difficult to isolate the two levels clearly."[17] Tacitus the historian asked Pliny for a record of "facts" concerning the death of his uncle, and Pliny states, on the level of story, that he is, in fact, providing "just the facts": "You only wanted to hear about my uncle's death," writes Pliny, "so I'll stop myself before I say anything that is not of 'historical interest.'" These "facts," however, are wrapped up in what Eco calls

> a complicated gamut of discursive operations, mainly temporal shiftings in and out ... and a planned confusion between the subject of the speech act and the subject of the narrative utterance ... the *fabula* [story] does not only concern the world of events but also the epistemic worlds (or the propositional attitudes) of the characters, and these epistemic worlds continually overlap with the supposed epistemic world of the Model Reader (different propositional attitudes are thus *focalized* at the same moment). The final result is that the reader does not understand (provided he does not perform a metatextual analysis) *who* is speaking at a given moment.[18]

These temporal shiftings are accomplished through verb tenses that change from imperfect to present or from pluperfect to imperfect.

While Eco uses some complicated equations to make his point, the basic idea of the time-shifting verb tenses is that, in blurring the world of the reader (who knows who the Elder Pliny is and appreciates his significance) with the world of the disaster (where the Elder Pliny's death might be termed accidental at best, irresponsible and dishonourable at worst), it becomes impossible for the reader to interpret the events of Pliny's narrative apart from the reader's own epistemic world, in which the Elder Pliny "makes sense" in a particular way: he is honourable, he is heroic. The movement from past to present presses the reader into thinking of the Elder Pliny in the reader's present terms. The reader has access to knowledge that the Elder Pliny did not and is compelled to apply that knowledge to the facts of the story. Pliny's truth collides with the truth of the reader and, while not the truth of Pliny's uncle, his uncle sails into that truth as if he knew it all along, and himself calls the reader to be complicit in that truth. The world of the story and the world of the reader become the same; it is as if, Eco suggests, the reader looks into a mirror and sees the Elder Pliny reflected there.[19]

At the conclusion of his letter, Pliny calls the reader to return from past to present, as if he were not writing about the present: *finem ergo faciam*. "What a supreme lie!" Eco exclaims.[20] The letter is not a recording of facts meant for someone else, the historian, to memorialize; it is its own account for posterity, a cultural monument.[21] The facts are not speaking for themselves. As Eco argues: "Pliny's letter is a text which, as any other text, is not empirically addressed to an empirical addressee: it builds up, by a discursive strategy, the type of reader who is supposed to co-operate in order to actualize the text such as the Model Author (that is, the objective textual strategy) wants it to be. We can refuse to play the role of the Model Reader, as we are presently doing; but we must recognize the kind of reader that the text not only presupposes but also produces through the use of given linguistic strategies."[22] The temporal shift moves the reader back to the previous world, removing absence in time.

Both Pliny and GMark use writing as a socio-rhetorical tool to remove reader/user absence in time. The removal of absence requires a new attention to the witness of disaster, an attention necessitated by the simultaneity of a present event. Peters confirms that presence in time is essential to witnessing: "We have to keep up with the world because we are, in some complicated way, responsible to act in it, and we can only act in the present. We feel guilty about hurt people in the news, not in fiction films. Pain separates facts from fictions. Facts are witnessed, fictions are narrated."[23] GMark's Model Reader, or model reading/using community, may not have realized that they were observing the events of the past as witnesses. Shifting presents require the using community to observe and, in observing, to witness. GMark, as a "report" or media event of disaster, enables the formation of a using culture focused on what becomes a collective experience of witness.[24]

* * *

Peters points to a fundamental fallibility of witnessing: once experience is translated into discourse, direct access to that experience vanishes: "The forensics of the trial, the pains of the martyr and the memoirs of the survivor are all attempts to overpower the melancholy fact that direct sensory experience – from the taste of the pineapple to the pains of childbirth – vanishes when put into words and remains inaccessible to others except inasmuch as they claim to share similar experiences."[25] Lack of access in space or time makes all witnessing suspect as a "veracity gap" is created between the witness and the interpretation of the witness. If you have never eaten a pineapple, how can you tell if the description of the pineapple-eater of the pineapple's taste is true? Is it honest? Is it real? Peters suggests that different sociocultural moments have created different "devices" to compensate for this veracity gap, including the ancient Greek attempt to locate truth in bodily examination or torture.[26] Witnessing is connected to and expressed through bodies. Enslaved persons, in Greek ideology, were believed to be compulsive liars; if information was elicited from the body of an enslaved person through torture, however, this information was held to be reliable: "torture served as a cultural line dividing slaves, who respect only bodily pain, and citizens, who speak the logos in freedom. Since slaves supposedly lie compulsively, torture exposes the truth by extinguishing the power to invent … Torture enforces the claim that slaves are ruled by necessity (*anangkê*). A slave could not appear in court, but a slave's testimony obtained under torture was admissible as evidence."[27] Peters uses this example to highlight what he interprets as the strange etymological connection between torture and witnessing, and between the body and witnessing: as *basanos*, "touchstone" or a way to test pure gold, developed into "trial of genuineness" to "inquiry by torture," *parastatês* means both "one who stands by" and "testicle," while the Latin *testis* is both "witness" and "testicle." The language of witnessing has odd physical roots.

These roots are odd to a contemporary reader, perhaps, but they are not just a system of metaphors, as Peters suggests.[28] The connection between witnessing and the body is essential, particularly in understanding a written object like GMark. The ancient body is its own teller of truths in a couple of different ways. The process of speaking in GMark – telling, concealing, revealing – is a product of the ancient Mediterranean body. Language is a primary social phenomenon that requires embodiment either in writing or in speech. As a *material* system, language as speech is embodied in human physical action and reaction, in the movements of lips and tongue, in the use of the ears, in bodily gesture and in vision. As a *cultural* system, language is dependent upon particular, context-bound speech communities: "society and culture are communicatively constituted, and … *no* sphere of social or cultural life is fully comprehensible apart from speaking as an instrument of its constitution."[29] Language comes from socioculturally specific bodies. As Richard Bauman and Joel Sherzer state in *Explorations in the Ethnography of Speaking*, "the patterning of language goes far beyond laws of grammar to comprehend the use of language in social life … such organization inescapably involves the radical linking of the verbal and the sociocultural in the conduct of speaking."[30] The social means available to people – and here I include the body in the category of the social – condition what they can do with language. Because speech comes out of and from bodies, it will reflect the constitution of those bodies as bodies are socially and historically constructed. As Maude Gleason declares, "Narrative patterns can be as much sociocultural as they are literary,"[31] and in GMark, the narrative pattern traditionally associated with secrecy, when examined socioculturally, is shown to *reveal* much more than it *conceals*. The inconsistent leakage of information in GMark makes sense when this language is embodied. The ancient Mediterranean body was its own source of information, and as a leaky, permeable body, information, language, also leaked out accordingly. Control over this leakage implicated not only the self but social authority as well.

Two examples to help clarify this point: First, early in the second act of Terence's second-century BCE play, *The Eunuch*, the courtesan Thais asks her lover Phaedria if Parmeno, an enslaved person, can keep a secret, or "hold his tongue" (*potin est hic tacere*).[32] Parmeno responds in the affirmative: of course he can hold his tongue, but only if he hears the truth. He declares, "the truth that I hear, I'm silent upon, and retain it well; but if I hear what's false and without foundation, it's out at once; I'm full of holes, and leak in every direction. Therefore, if you wish it to be kept secret, speak the truth" (I.ii.25). Parmeno constructs his body as something permeable and porous, subject to uncontrolled seepage. Truth, though, seems to be something he can retain within the boundaries of his body. While the ancient Mediterranean body was something unstable, in constant need of social and spatial "fixing," the body is also, perhaps paradoxically, a communicator or revealer of truth. The body is its own source of information, manageable in part, but also dependent on its material realities. It is no scholarly secret that the ancient Mediterranean was a culture of visibility, of being "in the eyes" or under the constant gaze of others. "Being, in Roman culture," asserts Carlin Barton, "was being seen."[33] The body, at once both physical and social space, was something that demanded constant attention and practised presentation due to its constant "reading" in the eyes of others. Identifications could be won or lost, sustained or abandoned, through the body. The ancient body was part of its own reading culture, as it were.

The second example comes from GMark, where the truth leaks, not lies The dissemination of information in Mark relates to the bodies from which that information comes. Speech, visibility, and the boundaries of the body participate together in a phenomenon of leaks as a fundamental mode of communication. Leaks are not always predictable – sometimes information stays within boundaries, sometimes it does not. Sometimes Jesus's command to silence is obeyed, like a stopper in a bottle – the transfiguration scene is a good example here, Mark 9:9–10 – but sometimes it is not. There are lots of examples to list in this particular case, but 7:36–7 is a great one: "And he charged them to tell no one; but the more he charged them, the more zealously they proclaimed it. And they were astonished beyond measure." And sometimes the audience doesn't know whether or not a command was obeyed — Mark 5:41–3 is a good example here. Many miracles and healings in GMark are accompanied by such a command, but sometimes they are not. The nature of language prohibits speech from being handled in any kind of rigid, consistent manner. Could the leper of Mark 1:40–5 have attempted to keep his secret? In this case, the audience is told, or hears, "And he sternly charged him, and sent him away at once, and said to him, 'See that you say nothing to any one; but go, show yourself to the priest, and offer for your cleansing what Moses commended, for a proof to the people.' But he went out and began to talk freely about it, and to spread the news, so that Jesus could no longer openly enter a town, but was out in the country; and people came to him from every quarter." Surely, his body would have told the truth just through its relocation in public space. The truth about Jesus's body also gradually leaks out; total leak, the complete revelation of the meaning of Jesus's body, drives the entirety of the GMark story, ending with a broken, seeping body on the cross. GMark is not about concealment; leaking is essential to the purpose of the text.

The use of speech in relation to the body must be read as part of the politics of GMark. In the GMark story, the manipulation and control of communicative boundaries establishes worthy, meaningful bodies. We can read GMark's Jesus as part of a speech community – a speech culture? – a community based on, to quote Bauman and Sherzer: "the shared or mutually complementary knowledge and ability (competence) of its members for the production and interpretation of socially appropriate speech. Such a community is an organization of diversity, in so far as this knowledge and ability (i.e., access to and command of resources for speaking) are differentially distributed among its members; the production and interpretation of speech are thus variable and complementary, rather than homogeneous and constant throughout the community."[34] If the power to speak is differentially distributed – if it is a limited good, really – we can see that the circulation of words becomes a "way to define and limit access to control that one person hopes to gain over another person" or group, as Weiner asserts, a way to "penetrate or maintain a boundary between an individual and others."[35] Controlling speech gives one control over bodies – one's own body but also the bodies of others. In Mark 1:23–8, a man with an unclean spirit cries out to Jesus, "I know who you are, the Holy One of God." Jesus rebukes him, using the language of judgment and bodily punishment (ἐπιτιμέω), commanding that he be silent or be shut up as with a muzzle (φιμόω). The punishment for the unclean spirit is both silence and disembodiment. The result is an intact body with the authority to astonish the crowd: "With authority he commands even the unclean spirits, and they obey him." Jesus's fame spreads like a flood throughout Galilee. The one in control of words is also in control of bodies. In GMark, we see Jesus constantly negotiating this control, with regard both to his own body and to those of others.

To return to the main line of the argument: witnessing can be interpreted as having a bodily basis as the body provided its own kind of access to or window into truth. Truth was embodied. In case this thread still feels loose, my assertion in this section is that witnessing in the ancient world had a fundamental materiality, a materiality linking language to embodiment. We have to leave open the possibility that users of GMark could have linked the language of the writing to the activities and functions of their own bodies not simply as readers/users but also as embodiments of the same cultural processes of truth-telling and witness. The language of GMark itself could have affected the bodies of the using community. As a witness to the disaster of Jesus's death, the writing supplies the experience of that death, endowing that experience with meaning (or *monumentalizing* it) along the way, to the community that lacks the original.[36] The community becomes a bodily, physical witness via the written medium of GMark. This argument about witness must remain abstract, to a certain extent, given the profound differences between reading cultures/cultures using written things in the ancient eastern Mediterranean and our own reading cultures today.

* * *

This embodiment of witnessing is particularly significant given the absence of a body in the GMark reading community. GMark ends with a missing body and with the fear that results from this absence. GMark provides no closure for the experience of disaster. What can we do with a missing body? The writing monumentalizes Jesus's death both as text and as artifact. I want to return to Keith's work on the importance of the materiality of GMark and its essential contention that manuscripts gave ancient reading cultures "physical emblems of the community": material texts "functioned as cultural artifacts whose significance extended far beyond the content or tradition that they transmitted."[37] Extending Keith's argument, I suggest that the material GMark acted as a *monument*. Monuments, both public and therapeutic, speak to the politics of collective identity. Kirk Savage, in "Trauma, Healing, and the Therapeutic Monument," differentiates between the public monument and the disaster monument: where public monuments are about the reaffirmation of a discourse of social agency over and against a situation of powerlessness, the disaster monument, or therapeutic monument, seeks to "find collective purpose when the victims' own individual purpose has been violated or destroyed."[38] In the case of GMark, the monument could be public or therapeutic. As a public monument, GMark would work, in Kirk's language, to reaffirm "over and again the beneficial presence of human (more properly, male) agency in society. [Public monuments] told the stories of men who had acted decisively upon their world, by transforming it for the better or saving it from peril."[39] The visual commemorative culture in the Greco-Roman world lends itself most readily to the rhetoric of the public monument, certainly. Public monuments are honorific, meant not so much to console or produce personal meaning as to insist upon honour, heroism, or political triumph. They are didactic rather than therapeutic.[40]

Jesus's story may not easily be read in terms of heroism. GMark reinterprets Jesus's death in a way that can produce meaning for his model reading community, certainly, but the disaster of his death remains. GMark is better understood as Savage's therapeutic monument. For a community gathered around a missing body, a community potentially experiencing its own pain and trauma in a situation of persecution, a monument that works "to find collective purpose when the victims' own individual purpose has been violated or destroyed," to repeat Savage's definition, makes perfect sense.[41] The victim of pain or trauma is able to regain some sense of agency, or at the very least of meaning, through the material expression of trauma in a monument.

Maya Lin's Vietnam Veteran's Memorial and GMark's textualization of Jesus traditions seem to be very different material artifacts. Both, however, qualify as "monument." Richard S. Ascough has recently interpreted the Christian martyrdom accounts as a way to memorialize martyrs when the usual methods of memorialization – namely, epigraphic memorialization – were not available due to the absence of material remains. Ascough writes, "This absence of bodies would disrupt the culturally expected mechanisms for burial and memorialization. Given the importance of the latter for the living community, alternatives would have to be found … oral story telling followed (eventually) by writing on parchment replaces writing on stone to mark the presence of the dead among the living, and in so doing forging connections – 'identity' – within the group."[42] While the primary mode of memorialization after death in the Greco-Roman period involved writing on stone, writing on parchment or papyrus, while less permanent, perhaps, can be read as a reasonable substitute, especially if no other material location is available. A community could not gather around a relief or a stele, but they could still gather around a physical text and, through the text, establish a continuity with the past.[43] While Ascough discusses martyrdom accounts, there is no reason the same argument cannot be made about GMark.

* * *

This argument relies on Peters's sociological theory of witnessing. Peters discusses the "media" of witnessing and the performance of a "media event" around the witnessing of or to an event in a contemporary context, one dominated by television and the internet. GMark, however, can also be considered the performance of a media event in that GMark, too, offers "presence-at-a-distance." A written form allows GMark to achieve a presence-at-a-distance that orality cannot. Perhaps elements of its narrative style could be reproduced in speech, and certainly the narrative relies on the identification of speech patterns with the sociocultural bodies of GMark's model reading community. The written format, though, enables a deeper implication of the audience in the narrative. Whatever the writer's intentions, the written form of the story of Jesus's death was an accomplishment that enabled communal identification. Newsreels enabled Ronald Reagan to claim that he had witnessed the liberation of the concentration camps after the Second World War, when Reagan had never left the United States. Peters declares, "He believed in false presence: that he had really been there when he had only watched films. But presence-at-a-distance is precisely what witnessing a media event claims to offer … Media events studies seek the conditions in which the willing suspension of disbelief is justified. In media events, the borrowed eyes and ears of the media become, however tentatively or dangerously, one's own. Death, distance and distrust are all suspended, for good and evil."[44] As an act of witness, the GMark requires the active participation of the reader/reading community, as the communal body, in reading, is held responsible for the encounter, specifically the encounter with pain: the disastrous death of Jesus. The communal body makes sense of this death collectively as witnessing is also an act of making meaning: Pliny can no more present "just the facts" of his uncle's death than can the author of GMark; the very act of recounting a disaster involves the creation of a monument, the creation of collective purpose when that purpose is, in its time-shifted context, shown to be problematic or absent. GMark's format allows for a certain presence in space, in an absence in time, both through the narrative (the writing as writing) and through the medium (the writing as object). As a narrative, GMark can shift time. As an object, GMark can accumulate time. Peters discusses historicity, or historical authenticity, as follows: "If in visiting the Tower of London I am told that a block of wood is the one on which Henry VIII's victims were dispatched, I will act and feel differently than if I learn the block is a replica, even if it is physically identical or equally old. The block hovers in a limbo between reality and fake, its metaphysical status depending on something so slight as a caption. The caption 'real' ties it to a tradition of testimony passed across the generations, an accumulation of time that links the block historically to the event."[45] GMark is like Henry VIII's block of wood in that, present in space but absent in time, it accumulates the time of the reading community, read or experienced collectively, as is a memorial or monument. The relationship of GMark to a reading/using culture is that of cultural monument, a medium of witness that activates the community as possessors and producers of cultural knowledge.

NOTES

I am indebted to a former colleague in the Princeton Writing Program, Dr Timothy Recuber, for the "Witnessing Disaster" title; Dr Recuber taught a writing seminar on the topic based on his own sociological research. My inspiration for an examination of GMark as a witness to disaster came out of several conversations with Dr Recuber. I would like to formally thank Dr Recuber for introducing me to this fascinating area of sociological scholarship.

1 Text and translation of Pliny's letter to Tacitus (*Letters* 6.16) from the Loeb Classical Library edition: *Letters/Pliny the Younger; with an English translation by Betty Radice* (Cambridge: Harvard University Press, 1969).

2 Umberto Eco, "Portrait of the Elder as a Young Pliny," 123–36, in *The Limits of Interpretation* (Bloomington and Indianapolis: Indiana University Press, 1990), 124.

3 Eleanor Winsor Leach, "The Politics of Self-Presentation: Pliny's *Letters* and Roman Portrait Sculpture," *Classical Antiquity* 9, no. 1 (1990): 18. Leach cites Eco's essay in her article, though it is not clear if the language of "monument" comes from Eco.

4 William A. Johnson, "Toward a Sociology of Reading in Classical Antiquity," *American Journal of Philology* 12, no. 1 (2000): 603 (emphasis in original).

5 William A. Johnson, *Readers and Reading Culture in the High Roman Empire: A Study of Elite Communities* (Oxford: Oxford University Press, 2010), 202 (emphasis in original).

6 Chris Keith, "Early Christian Book Culture and the Emergence of the First Written Gospel," in *Mark, Manuscripts, and Monotheism: Essays in Honor of Larry W. Hurtado*, ed. Chris Keith and Dieter T. Roth (London: Bloomsbury T&T Clark, 2015), 28.

7 Ibid., 23.

8 See ibid., 28: "Books in these ancient communities were not merely carriers of content; they played a central role in helping their readers construct their identity and became emblematic of that identity."

9 Paul J. Achtemeier, "*Omne verbum sonat*: The New Testament and the Oral Environment of Late Western Antiquity," *Journal of Biblical Literature* 109, no. 1 (1990), 3–27, 19; quoted in Keith, "Early Christian Book Culture," 35.

10 Among others, Keith cites Werner H. Kelber, *The Oral and the Written Gospel: The Hermeneutics of Speaking and Writing in the Synoptic Tradition, Mark, Paul, and Q* (Philadelphia: Fortress Press, 1983); Joanna Dewey, "The Gospel of Mark as Oral Hermeneutic," in *Jesus, the Voice, and the Text: Beyond the Oral and the Written Gospel*, ed. Tom Thatcher (Waco: Baylor University Press, 2008), 72, 86; Joanne Dewey, "Textuality in an Oral Culture: A Survey of the Pauline Traditions," in *Orality and Textuality in early Christian Literature*, ed. Joanna Dewey. Semeia 65 (Atlanta: Society of Biblical Literature, 1995), 51.

11 Keith, "Early Christian Book Culture," 35 (emphasis in original).

12 Richard Bauckham, *Jesus and the Eyewitnesses: The Gospels as Eyewitness Testimony* (Grand Rapids: William B. Eerdmans, 2006).

13 John Durham Peters, "Witnessing," *Media, Culture and Society* 23 (2001): 707.

14 Ibid., 720.

15 Witnessing a disaster – not in person but through written media – makes the reader responsible, and the reader perhaps also has the expectation that this

responsibility should or will occur. Reading a "witness" account and then becoming a "witness" oneself involves a certain emotional or physical experience for the reader, it seems. Here I'm thinking of Jean-Jacques Rousseau's reaction to Voltaire's "Poem on the Lisbon Disaster." In 1756, Jean-Jacques Rousseau sent a letter to Voltaire regarding Voltaire's response to the earthquake in Lisbon in 1755. The earthquake resulted in the deaths of tens of thousands of people, due both to the earthquake itself and to the chaos after the event; the landscape of Lisbon changed not just from seismic activity but also from the activity of King Joseph I in the erection of gallows to hang looters in key areas of visibility. Rousseau's reaction to Voltaire's response, his "Poem on the Lisbon Disaster" (Poème sur le désastre de Lisbonne), amounts, essentially, to "How could you do this to me?!" Rousseau laments, "I expected from [the poem] more worthy evidence of the humanity that apparently inspired you to write it … you so burden the list of our miseries that you further disparage our condition. Instead of the consolations that I expected, you only afflict me further. It might be said that you fear that I don't feel my unhappiness enough, and that you are trying to soothe me by proving that all is bad." Rousseau to Voltaire, 18 August 1756, cited in J.A. Leigh, ed., *Correspondence complete de Jean Jacques Rousseau*, vol. 4, trans. R. Spang (Geneva, 1967), 37.

16 Peters, "Witnessing," 721.

17 Eco, "Portrait," 124.

18 Ibid., 128–9, (emphasis in original).

19 Ibid., 301.

20 Ibid.

21 Ibid., 124.

22 Ibid., 128.

23 Peters, "Witnessing," 722.

24 There are a number of other features of GMark that deserve attention in this context as well, including the use of irony, seams and summaries, and the focused attention on the end of Jesus's life.

25 Peters, "Witnessing," 711.

26 Ibid.

27 Ibid., 712.

28 Ibid.: "The explanation of this pervasive and odd system of metaphors is obscure, but one may conjecture that the testicles, as physical by-standers to the act of procreation, were thought witnesses of paternity or virility in Indo-European culture. That knowing first-hand should be associated with the testicles may suggest an ancient preference for the testimony of men over women."

29 Richard Bauman and Joel Sherzer, "Introduction to the Second Edition," xi–xxvii, in *Explorations in the Ethnography of Speaking*, 2nd ed., Studies in the Social and Cultural Foundations of Language (Cambridge: Cambridge University Press, 1989 [1974]), xi (emphasis in original).

30 Ibid., 6.

31 Maud W. Gleason, "Truth Contests and Talking Corpses," in *Constructions of the Classical Body*, ed. James I. Porter (Ann Arbor: University of Michigan Press, 1999), 288.

32 Literally, "is he able to keep silent," but the *holding of the tongue* is an apt translation. Cut-out tongues were described as quivering for their owners' mouths; Ovid, in the *Metamorphoses*, describes the tongue of Philomela, cut out to prevent her from accusing a tyrant of rape (6.560), as quivering "and, dying, [it] seeks out the tracks of its mistress," See Amy Richlin, "Cicero's Head," in *Constructions of the Classical Body*, ed. James I. Porter (Ann Arbor: University of Michigan Press, 1999), 204. See also Lucan, who depicts the cut-out tongue of Marius Gratidianus under torture also as quivering and "striking the empty air with mute motion" (2.181–82).

33 Carlin Barton, "Being in the Eyes: Shame and Sight in Ancient Rome," in *The Roman Gaze: Vision, Power, and the Body*, ed. D. Fredrick (Baltimore: Johns Hopkins University Press, 2002), 220.

34 Bauman and Sherzer, *Explorations*, 6.

35 Annette B. Weiner, "From Words to Objects to Magic: Hard Words and the Boundaries of Social Interaction," *Man* n.s., 18, no. 4 (1983): 691.

36 I am here paraphrasing Peters, "Witnessing," 709.

37 Keith, "Early Christian Book Culture," 37, 30.

38 Kirk Savage, "Trauma, Healing, and the Therapeutic Monument," in *Terror, Culture, Politics: Rethinking 9/11*, ed. Daniel J. Sherman and Terry Nardin (Bloomington: Indiana University Press, 2006), 111.

39 Ibid., 103.

40 Ibid., 106. In this context, Leach's linking of Roman portrait sculpture to Pliny's correspondence requires further discussion. Leach argues that Pliny understood literary and artistic portraits as "two forms of personal representation that he himself found meaningfully analogous" (Leach, "Politics," 15).

41 Savage, "Trauma," 111.

42 Richard S. Ascough, "Memorializing Martyrs and Negotiating Christian Identity," paper presented at the Afterlives of Violence conference, Kingston, Ontario, 16–18 September 2016, 1.

43 On "continuity" see Ascough, "Memorializing Martyrs," 23. See also Maia Kotrosits, *Rethinking Early Christian Identity: Affect, Violence, and Belonging* (Minneapolis: Fortress Press, 2015), 37.

44 Peters, "Witnessing," 717.

45 Ibid., 720.

11

Response: Undoing Text

Daniel A. Smith

The chapters in this section are collected under the heading of "Undoing Text," and I hope in this brief response to draw them together and explore some of the implications of their approaches and findings.[1] The past generation of scholarship on early Judaisms and early Christianities has rightly become increasingly sensitive to the fact that approaches privileging "text" also privilege singular, elite, and male (not to mention "canonical" and "orthodox") voices and views in understanding these movements. Recent (and welcome) attempts to circumvent this privilege have, for example, shifted their focus to the material culture of the ancient Mediterranean world so that other voices and views can be accessed. In her book *Archaeology and the Letters of Paul*, Laura Nasrallah "uses archaeological materials to consider specific, local contexts and the cities of the Roman Empire … [and to] focus not on the one, Paul, complicated and controverted as he admitted he was, but on the many," the *adelphoi* and those with whom they were in contact every day.[2] Even in dealing with material culture, however, scholars of early Judaisms and Christianities often turn to texts, as Nasrallah does in studying *defixiones* (lead tablets inscribed with curses) found at the sanctuary of Demeter and Kore in ancient Corinth – and in using their perspective on grief and loss to interpret aspects of 1 Corinthians.[3] Nasrallah's approach is welcome and refreshing. But can we completely undo our privileging of texts? And if we could, would that be a good thing?

Both Esther Guillen and Erin Vearncombe take a novel approach with the texts they analyze in their chapters: both are interested in the communal and cultural value of the gospels qua texts, that is, as things, once written and received, as artifacts. It is noteworthy, in connection with the tendency of our discipline to privilege singular, male authors of texts, that Guillen centres the discussion by referring to Matthew's "author/s" as they/them (126n1).

The possibility that Matthew's Gospel had symbolic value as a physical text for those who read and used it is intriguing, quite apart from (or maybe better, alongside of) its contents or ideas, or the access it purports to grant to foundational events, figures, and memories. This can be taken for granted with much later gospel-books, such as the Lindisfarne Gospels, due to their illuminations as much as to their ritual and liturgical usage; but Guillen has in mind the first production and reception of Matthew.

The text itself, its memorialized creator, and the context in which it is used or read can all be aspects of a text's symbolic value, argues Guillen. She pays close attention to Matthew's treatment of their sources, Mark and Q but especially the scriptural citations, and how Matthew's deployment of them creates Jesus as a "textual Messiah," that is, one who fulfills prophecies literally. One could contrast Mark's literary (rather than literal) approach of disclosing Jesus's messianic identity via the secrecy motif. Guillen is also interested in Matthew's author as a "literate cultural producer," linking this to their memorialization in or through the text, once produced and received, but more so to Matthew's scribal activity. Although early papyri manuscripts of Matthew, which outnumber those of other gospels, could indicate its continuing value as a "symbolic artifact," one wonders in the end whether Matthew's literary or even "biblical" qualities would have distinguished it in any measurable way from,[4] for example, Luke or Mark, which were also significant literary achievements. Were their authors not also "literate cultural producers" whose texts would have had symbolic value as physical objects?

Like Guillen, Vearncombe also touches on social and cultural aspects of writing and reading in the ancient world. In particular, Vearncombe's use of William A. Johnson and Chris Keith seems to connect the various aspects of composition – reception, reading, interpretation, valuation – as social acts in a way that would support Guillen's contention about the "symbolic value" of Matthew as a written text and physical object. Vearncombe also explores how Mark as text "produces a user as part of … a culture of *witness*, centred around the cultural artifact of the GMark as a *monument to disaster*" (185), emphasis in original). Using John Durham Peters's sociological theory of witnessing and trauma, she demonstrates that we can view Mark both as witness and as the means through which its audience becomes involved as witness in its collective experience of and through the gospel. In this regard, Mark's gospel functioned as "cultural artifact" with a significance beyond its contents, but, more than that, the material gospel acted as *monument*.

Following an analysis of Pliny the Younger's account (*Ep.* 6.16) of his uncle's death in the eruption of Vesuvius, and its "temporal shiftings" (Umberto Eco), Vearncombe argues that Mark similarly implicates its readers in its witness to the death of Jesus through the "liveness" and "simultaneity" of its narrative, especially its verbal constructions (186). According to Vearncombe, Mark as text (both as physical object and as that which constructs a reading community) "stands in" for the body of the absent Jesus and memorializes him not as hero but as victim, where no epitaph or epigraph was possible. Taking some cues from Mark and its Jesus, I would suggest that such an epitaph might echo those inscribed by parents mourning the untimely death of an infant or child,[5] particularly because these use the language of theft or removal to convey the pain of absence. Mark prepares the reader to expect, but also to experience and interpret – that is, to witness – the death of Jesus; yet the narrative focus on the absent Jesus, as well as his own predictions about the bridegroom going missing (Mark 2:20) and the shepherd being struck (14:27), situates the readers with those traumatized by his removal/absence (16:8) and awaiting his restored presence, which is both hope and threat (13:28–37).

By looking beyond the compositional/scribal strategies of authors of Matthew and Mark (while taking these strategies seriously!) to the import of these texts as cultural and symbolic artifacts, Vearncombe and Guillen decentre traditional readings of Matthew and Mark, which privilege the singular author and create space for their collective valuation in their continuing reception. Heather Macumber also seeks to dismantle the privilege often afforded to canonical texts in her application of monster theory to the hybrid "living creatures" of Ezekiel and Revelation. "Monsters are essentially 'the other,' and they challenge the boundaries of the human world" either through their hybridity or their liminality (101), but Macumber notes a (theologically motivated) unwillingness on the part of some scholars to think of "heavenly" creatures aligned with the God of the Bible, such as those just noted, as "monsters" or "monstrous" – despite clear indications of hybridity and/or liminality.

Unhelpful binaries, namely, "chaos-order" as aligned with "hybrid-whole" or "malevolent-benevolent," and the reactive binary "disgust-amazement," often complicate the issue when commentators assume that the positive side of each binary applies to "heavenly" creatures while negating the obviously "monstrous" attributes of such creatures. To counteract such approaches, Macumber reconsiders hybridity through redescription. Well known figures and beings from the literatures of antiquity, Macumber finds, are not uniformly malevolent simply because of their hybridity or monstrosity. What might we conclude about the living creatures of Ezekiel and Revelation, then, if we see them as monsters? A nonbinary approach to the question rightly refuses to put them on the side of "order" and "benevolence" (cf. the chaos they inflict in Revelation 6) despite their heavenly origin, precisely because they are terrifying and were intended to be. Macumber does not raise this point, but it seems that many scholars are apt to forget (or unwilling to acknowledge) that the authors of texts eventually canonized wrote out of their cultural milieux, not to mention their own imagination, and that the texts produced as a result – canonical or not – can and should be analyzed using the same tools as any other text.[6] This means that figures described therein can be profitably compared with any other figures using any methodology, which is Macumber's main point.

In his chapter, Matthew Mitchell analyzes something that scholars, ancient and modern, love to do with texts, namely, to classify them. Mitchell deals with two problems raised by the so-called *Gospel of the Hebrews*, long lost and known only through citation and reputation. First, ancient classifications of the text on canonical lists show it as neither canonical nor apocryphal. Apparently its lineage (in terms of its citation by early Christian authors of sound orthodox reputation) was more important to Eusebius in evaluating its "liminal canonical status" than its contents, which were scarcely accessible. Second, Mitchell also addresses the question of how and on what basis this fragmentary gospel can be described as "Jewish-Christian." Both these questions are exacerbated by the fact that we only have a few fragments of the *Gospel of the Hebrews* to analyze, and in some cases the attribution is insecure. Mitchell examines one such citation in great detail (with an exhaustive list of questions for which he apologizes): Jerome, *Vir. ill.* 16 refers to a fragment of a gospel he had recently translated (i.e., *Gos. Heb.*?) in which the just-risen Jesus contrasts his bodily presence to an "incorporeal daimon." We also know this saying from Ignatius, *Smyrn.* 3.2 (Eusebius, *Hist. eccl.* 3.36.11, says he does not know the origin of the saying), but it is also reputed to have been found in the *Kerygma Petrou*.

Enticing (and baffling) references such as these, and the fact that *Gospel of the Hebrews* is one of those once known but now lost texts, have given rise to numerous speculations about the *Gospel* and its relationships. Was it the putative Aramaic or Hebrew precursor of Greek Matthew to which both Papias and Jerome referred (Eusebius, *Hist. eccl.* 3.39.16; cf. Jerome, *Comm. Matt.* 12.13; *Vir. ill.* 2)? The lost *Gospel of the Hebrews* also converges with the lost Sayings Gospel Q in the recent work of David B. Sloan.[7] Here we have a situation (not all that uncommon in our field, ancient and modern) in which hypothetical texts are remade in order to do what scholars want them to do. Mitchell's conclusion with respect to both questions is appropriately measured: "The grounds upon which we would or could recognize a Jewish Christian gospel, absent both Jewish Christians and their gospel, is, dare I say it, incorporeal, and dependent solely upon resurrection via scholarly imagination" (143).

Finally, Jason Yuh explores issues related to canonical interpretation and the social and rhetorical function of a (metaphorical?) ritual in his chapter on the *Epistle of Barnabas*. Looking beneath textual production to discern social construction, Yuh examines Barnabas's self-positioning as expert hermeneut and mediator of *gnōsis* (a new canonical interpretation) and his deployment of the idea of "circumcision of hearing" (e.g., Barn. 9.3; a "ritual" having significant social implications). Barnabas sets out to refute Jewish traditions using Jewish writings, while claiming a perfect (authoritative, revealed) interpretive *gnosis* and therefore the right to interpret these authoritative texts. By this strategy, "Barnabas attempts to create and/or sustain a community," and also to legitimate its practices – or rather, its non-practising of Jewish rituals (159). But does Barnabas abandon ritual? The "circumcision of hearing" is "not merely an analogy … [but] functions as some sort of a ritual" (163). And do the lengths to which Barnabas must go rhetorically to convince his readers indicate that the ritual has failed? Yuh contends that the "circumcision of hearing" produces a liminal state for the intended recipients, which they must overcome (i.e., aggregation). One is reminded here of Paul's castigation of his readers for still needing milk when they should have moved on to "solid food" (1 Cor 3:2).

Yuh's analysis illuminates Barnabas's social objectives and how they are met through textual strategies. Mitchell discusses ancient and contemporary scholarly categorizations of a text that is not really a text but scattered fragments, rumours, and innuendoes. Macumber problematizes the favoured scholarly treatment – and exemption from the troubling category of "monster" – of "heavenly" figures whose uniqueness and holiness, by virtue of their association with the God of Ezekiel and Revelation, cannot be sullied with the category "monster." Guillen and Vearncombe both build upon the compositional and narrative strategies of their texts in order to think beyond the contents and ideologies of Matthew and Mark to their communal value as symbolic/cultural artifacts. Are we undoing texts and undoing the privilege granted them in our disciplines? In manifold ways, these chapters all demonstrate how we continue to be tied to the texts that provide the best evidence (even if that evidence is fragmentary, not to mention tendentious in various ways) of the social movements and formations we study. How would we know what Barnabas was up to without the epistle? Nevertheless, these chapters all provide welcome and refreshing interventions on the well studied texts they undertake to analyze.

NOTES

1 Parts of this response were previously presented at the Early Christianity, Early Judaism, and the Study of Religion Seminar of the Canadian Society of Biblical Studies, University of Regina, 27 May 2018. I am grateful for the opportunity to offer my small contribution to this volume dedicated to the memory of Professor Stephen Wilson, who initiated this seminar.

2 Laura Salah Nasrallah, *Archaeology and the Letters of Paul* (Oxford: Oxford University Press, 2019), 1.

3 Ibid., 167–76.

4 Ulrich Luz, "Intertexts in the Gospel of Matthew," *Harvard Theological Review* 97 (2004): 119–37.

5 Such as those compiled in Anne-Marie Vérilhac, *ΠΑΙΔΕΣ ΑΩΡΟΙ: Poésie funéraire* (Athens: Athenian Academy Press, 1978).

6 Recalling Benjamin Jowett's famous dictum: "Interpret the Scripture like any other book" (Benjamin Jowett, "On the Interpretation of Scripture," 330–433 in *Essays and Reviews* [London: John W. Parker and Son, 1860], 378), although, interestingly, Jowett's context required him to add that such inquiry will disclose to the interpreter the manifold ways in which "Scripture is unlike any other book" (ibid.).

7 David B. Sloan, "What If the Gospel according to the Hebrews Was Q?," paper presented at the Q Section of the Society of Biblical Literature annual meeting, Boston, MA, 2017, http://reconstructingq.com/gospel-of-the-hebrews.pdf.

SECTION THREE

Practice and Identity

The six chapters in this section explore the connection between shared practices and the construction of identity. Chapter 12 addresses the complexities of hybrid identities in antiquity. Chapter 13 shows how practices sometimes designated as "magic" shape and are shaped by multiple contexts. Chapter 14 looks at the distinction between prophecy and divination as presented in the Hebrew Bible. Chapter 15 explores the development of a distinctly Christian identity as a response to the Bar Kochba revolt. Chapter 16 looks at the way the *Book of Jubilees* offers a construction of "Jewishness" in opposition to Hasmonean national identity. Chapter 17 shows how Diaspora Jews actively reread their sacred texts to generate new forms of shared practice that would result in a durable Jewish identity. A response to these contributions (chapter 18) concludes the section.

12

"Hybridity," "Identity," and the Ancient Mediterranean World

Adele Reinhartz

In our present postmodern, postcolonial, transdisciplinary intellectual moment, the language of our field has become so contested that it can be difficult to talk about anything at all. No longer can we discuss first-century Judaism and Christianity – neither had been invented until centuries later.[1] Instead of Christians we refer to Christ-believers,[2] Christ-confessors, Christ-followers,[3] nascent Christians,[4] or, if we must, proto-Christians.[5] The Gnostics have disappeared,[6] and Jews are an endangered species, increasingly replaced by Judeans, whether they claim birth or residence in Judea or not.[7] And are the ordinary denizens of the Greco-Roman world pagans, gentiles, or polytheists?[8]

Even more problematic than the labels for ancient individuals or groups is the language that we use to talk about them and about their relationships with one another. We ponder the meanings and appropriate usage of terms like "ethnicity," "race," and "gender," and question whether things like religion, culture, and society really exist or are only remnants of our unenlightened pre-postmodern formation.[9] And can we still discuss communities or groups, or should we find some other vocabulary with which to discuss what happens when two or more people gather in some shared activity or set of beliefs?[10]

Our terminological concerns are due in some measure to the widened purview of our field, which has moved well beyond canonical and quasi-canonical sources such as the Hebrew Bible, New Testament, rabbinic and patristic literature, to encompass material objects, archaeological sites, inscriptions, papyri, as well as a broad range of ancient texts. They are also affected, I believe, by the tenor and events of our own times, including the mass migration of refugees from war, political oppression, economic crisis, the environmental crisis, the global pandemic, and, in light of all of the above, our own self-absorption as we try to find a language to describe ourselves.

In this chapter I discuss two contested terms – hybridity and identity – that have become ubiquitous in the study of antiquity as we have become more and more aware of the complex ways in which people understood themselves and interacted with one another. It is not only academics who ponder hybridity and identity. Here are the opening paragraphs of John Irving's novel, *Avenue of Mysteries*:

> Occasionally, Juan Diego would make a point of saying, "I'm a Mexican – I was born in Mexico, I grew up there." More recently, he was in the habit of saying, "I'm an American – I've lived in the United States for forty years." Or, in an effort to defuse the nationality issue, Juan Diego liked to say, "I'm a Midwesterner – in fact, I'm an Iowan." He never said he was a Mexican American … What Juan Diego always maintained was that, in his mind – in his memories, certainly, but also in his dreams – he lived and relived his two lives [the Mexican and the American] on "parallel tracks." A dear friend of Juan Diego's ...teased him about the so-called parallel tracks. She told him he was either a kid from Mexico or a grown-up from Iowa all the time. Juan Diego could be an argumentative person, but he agreed with her about that.[11]

The ancient people whose lives we discern in our extant texts and artifacts also frequently inhabited more than one world, whether in parallel tracks, sequentially, or as Juan Diego's friend put it, "all the time." I argue, however, that the way that we talk about these people reflects not so much their self-understanding as the vocabulary and ideas of our own cultural moment.

The basic dictionary definition of "hybrid" is "relating to or produced from parents of different species, varieties, or breeds."[12] This definition points to the primarily agricultural context in which the term was initially used, in which plants and animals were (and still are) bred for particular characteristics, such as beauty, colour, hardiness, or strength. As early as the eighteenth century, however, hybridity played a key role in the discussion of the "Great Chain of Being" – a system of classification according to which God stood at the top of the hierarchy, followed by angels, human beings, animals, plants, and minerals.[13] This debate had a biblical foundation in the creation stories of Genesis, but it was sharpened by racism and colonization, contexts within which white Europeans imposed their values and exerted power over others. Proponents of slavery, for example, had no difficulty in viewing Africans as a distinct species that occupied the border between the human and the animal (ape) categories of this Great Chain of Being.[14]

The debate on the place of non-white human beings initially hinged on the question of fertility: just as a mule, the hybrid between a horse and a donkey, is infertile, so too should the union of two different "species" of humans be infertile. According to this criterion, there should have been no question that Africans were just as human as white Europeans; mixed unions, if frowned upon, nevertheless occurred and the children of those unions were as capable of conceiving and bearing children as were any other offspring. Proponents of the opposite view, however, were not deterred by such common-sense evidence. Some claimed that infertility was not the only or even the most important criterion of difference; others argued that, while mixed couples could reproduce initially, their fertility would diminish through the generations.[15] The term "hybridity" itself implied that "humans of different races" were different species. Even once the notion of diminishing fertility was definitively refuted, the idea continued to have traction with regard to race, ethnicity, religion, and sexuality in scientific, legal, and socio-political discourse, with practical consequences – legal prosecution, eugenics, and worse – that continue to be felt in many countries around the world. Even from this very brief description, it is obvious that the cultural use of the term "hybridity" in the eighteenth century onwards was profoundly shaped, as noted, by racism and colonialism. It can hardly be surprising, for example, that European empires, whose leaders and elite were white, would set whites at the top of the human ladder and everyone else near or at the bottom.

POSTCOLONIAL DISCOURSE

In our own intellectual era, the term "hybridity" has been reclaimed, and transformed, in two different but overlapping directions. One such direction is found in postcolonial discourse, profoundly influenced by the work of Homi Bhabha. This direction entails a self-conscious transformation of that disparaging colonial usage into a positive term.

Homi Bhabha's writing is difficult to paraphrase; below, I quote a few relevant sentences from his 1994 book, *The Location of Culture*, in which he presents his understanding of hybridity in detail.

> Hybridity is the sign of the productivity of colonial power, its shifting forces and fixities; it is the name for the strategic reversal of the process of domination through disavowal (that is, the production of discriminatory identities that secure the "pure" and original identity of authority). Hybridity is the revaluation of the assumption of colonial identity through the repetition of discriminatory identity effects.

> It displays the necessary deformation and displacement of all sites of discrimination and domination. It unsettles the mimetic or narcissistic demands of colonial power but reimplicates its identifications in strategies of subversion that turn the gaze of the discriminated back upon the eye of power. For the colonial hybrid is the articulation of the ambivalent space where the rite of power is enacted on the site of desire, making its objects at once disciplinary and disseminatory – or, in my mixed metaphor, a negative transparency.[16]

Hybridity refers to an in-between state, a "Third Space" as a way of "conceptualizing an *inter*national culture, based not on the exoticism of multiculturalism or the *diversity* of cultures, but on the inscription and articulation of culture's *hybridity*."[17] "Colonial hybridity is not a *problem* of genealogy or identity between two *different* cultures which can then be resolved as an issue of cultural relativism. Hybridity is a problematic of colonial representation and individuation that reverses the effects of the colonialist disavowal, so that other 'denied' knowledges enter upon the dominant discourse and estrange the basis of its authority – its rules of recognition ...cultural differences are not simply *there* to be seen or appropriated."[18] Although postcolonial discourse emerged in the modern and postmodern eras, empires and colonies have been in existence since time immemorial, and the insights of postcolonial reflection have been applied in interesting ways to ancient empires and colonies as well.[19]

A postcolonial perspective can be particularly significant in the study of the Christian scriptures – the so-called Old Testament and New Testament – as these texts have been used to justify the colonial proscription of mixing among the nations and to support a hierarchical understanding of the relationships among various social groups. Although hybridity can in theory pertain to any type of identity marker – race, gender, ethnicity, and so on – it is mostly used with regard to ethnicity in biblical studies and studies of the ancient world, as, indeed, is the case in social-scientific studies of identity not focused on antiquity.[20] Kim Stratton, for example, states: "The insights of post-colonial theory enable us to better understand how the imperial cult contributed to the construction of hybrid identities: denizens of the colonized provinces felt at once to be members both of a large unified empire through their contacts with Roman imperial bureaucracy and emperor cult, and ethnically distinct members of their provincial communities, which continued age-old traditions and customs. Recent work on material culture brings to light subtle ways that individual families negotiated hybrid identities in local contexts."[21] Another example of such usage can be found in Warren Carter's chapter on postcolonial biblical interpretation in a collection called *New Meanings for Ancient Texts.* In this chapter, Carter explains that "various analyses have recognized that colonizer and colonized impact one another to create mixed or hybrid identities and cultural syntheses (so Homi Bhabha) and that dynamics of imitation, accommodation, elite benefit, mutual dependency, and transformation exist alongside resentment, resistance, and opposition."[22] In her analysis of 1 Peter, Jennifer Bird interacts with David Horrell, who, in her words, "suggests that we consider approaching this passage with the dynamics of resistance and hybridity in mind. Resistance is characterized by ambivalence ...and hybridity is what happens to people in that in-between space, where they embody the ambivalence of resistance and conformity. What is strikingly missing, however, is an assessment of the implications of this ambiguous, hybrid identity."[23]

SOCIOLOGICAL USE OF HYBRIDITY

While reliant on Homi Bhabhi's writings on hybridity, the examples that we have just looked at from the study of antiquity also illustrate the more general use of the language of hybridity simply to mean mixing. This usage is widespread in diverse fields and areas. Hybridity is often used in linguistics to refer to creolization, that is, the "mixture of two social languages within the limits of a single utterance."[24] It can also be used, for example, to describe cyborgs as a hybrid between human and machine.[25]

Most often, however, the term is used to refer to ethnicity, culture, and society. In these contexts the term's specific meaning is difficult to grasp because it is so vague. This vagueness has its advantages. As John Hutnyk notes, "hybridity is a usefully slippery category, purposefully contested and deployed to claim change. Strange then that the term can be so productive, from its origins in biology and botany, its interlude as the more weighty syncretism to its reclamation in work on diaspora by authors as different as Paul Gilroy, Stuart Hall, Iain Chambers, Homi Bhabha, and James Clifford. It is in the to and fro of these works especially that hybridity has come to mean all sorts of things to do with mixing and combination in the moment of cultural exchange."[26] But the term also creates a problem in that it frequently seems to presume that there exist "pure" cultures, ethnicities, and languages, which then become mixed or hybridized under certain circumstances.

This notion of purity is implied in the agricultural uses of the term as well as in the eighteenth century and later proscription of so-called miscegenation. As Stockhammer notes:

> The possibilities offered by the concept of hybridity are deeply rooted in its even more problematic counterpart: purity. This has

> long been neglected in postcolonial studies, which have unconsciously re-introduced the notion of purity into cultural studies. Hybridity can only exist in opposition to purity: if we speak of hybridity, we must accept the existence of purity. Every aim to transcend borders starts with the acknowledgement of those borders, confirming the existing of what needs to be overcome. Every discipline which argues about hybridity has to define what it understands to be pure. If nothing can be designated as pure, everything is hybrid and hybridity becomes a redundant term which might then be used in a metaphorical way for stimulating discussion, but not as a conceptual tool ...However, this perception of purity may not be useful for an epistemological approach, but deeply linked with xenophobia and racism.[27]

The presumption of the purity, or, at least, the existence of identifiably distinct ethnicities and cultures is evident in many uses of "hybridity" in the discussion of antiquity.[28] Todd Penner and Caroline Vander Stichele, for example, urge us not to "lose sight of the profoundly hybrid nature of early Christian oratorical discourse, ultimately reflecting a similar amalgam in Christianity itself, as it was shaped by both its Jewish and Greco-Roman heritages. It is exactly this combination of elements that, structurally speaking, creates the unique blend of rhetorical features that we find operative in both the early Christian material and the later Church homilies."[29] This quotation implies that two distinct and identifiable heritages – Jewish and Greco-Roman – existed in the period when early Christian material and later Church homilies came into existence. Whether we agree with this statement or not, some notion of purity seems to be at play in their understanding of the hybridity of early Christian discourse.

Annette Yoshiko Reed acknowledges this problem, at least indirectly: "If we can no longer presume that 'Jew' and 'Christian' were firmly established as mutually-exclusive religious identities by the close of the second century C.E., then we cannot also assume as a matter of course that the so-called 'Jewish Christians' of Late Antiquity were transgressing a clear-cut boundary between 'normative' Judaism and 'normative' Christianity or forging a hybrid identity based on universally accepted notions of 'Jew' and 'Christian.'"[30] The role of the "purity" assumption, however, is complex. On the one hand, Bhabha himself explicitly denies that hybridity implies antecedent purity. He sees hybridity as a liminal, in-between, third space that does not require essentialist claims for any antecedent identities: "Cultures come to be represented by virtue of the processes of iteration and translation through which their meanings are very vicariously addressed to – *through* – an Other. This erases any essentialist claims for the inherent authenticity or purity of cultures which, when inscribed in the naturalistic sign of symbolic consciousness frequently become arguments for the hierarchy and ascendancy of powerful cultures."[31] Further, he insists that hybridity is an ambivalent term that must therefore be distinguished from "an inversion that would suggest that the originary is, really, only an 'effect.' Hybridity has no such perspective of depth or truth to provide: it is not a third term that resolves the tension between two cultures, or two scenes of the book, in a dialectical play of 'recognition.'"[32]

On the other hand, even as we disavow any notion of racial or ethnic purity, an important move given the deployment of such notions in twentieth-century history, it is possible, and perhaps necessary, to acknowledge that boundaries and borderlines exist, even if they are porous and even if they are constantly being revised and redrawn. Philipp Stockhammer, for example, points to the usage of hybridity to mark the boundaries or borderlines between groups, noting: "Hybridity ...is often treated as a specifically postcolonial phenomenon and discussions have rarely overcome the narrow boundaries within this narrow field of study. In most other disciplines, the terms hybridity and hybridization are used to characterize phenomena which are easily detected as somehow 'borderline' but not so easily explained."[33]

Like Juan Diego, the main character in John Irving's novel, most people have a good sense of where they fit into various social, ethnic, cultural and other groupings, and where the boundaries lie that mark off these groupings from adjacent ones. This may well be the case even when one person's boundaries do not match up well, or at all, with those drawn by others in the same group. So, for example, I venture that most Jews today view the conviction that a particular historical personage is the messiah as being outside the boundaries of Judaism, yet one particular and relatively mainstream ultra-orthodox community believes that Rebbe Schneerson, who seemingly died in 1994, is the messiah, is still alive, and will return to bring salvation.[34]

The concept of boundaries is emphasized in numerous discussions of hybridity. Fredrik Barth, for example, whose 1969 book, *Ethnic Groups and Boundaries*, is often cited in discussions of ethnicity and hybridity, argues that the locus of study of ethnicity should focus primarily on the boundary and its markers rather than on the content. He also stresses the importance of self-ascription (one's own sense of belonging) and ascription (how one is seen by others).[35] The importance of boundaries, self-ascription, and a sense of belonging may get closer to the experience of the individual than the amorphous term "hybridity." On the other hand, hybridity, particularly in its postcolonial mode, has drawn attention to the larger social, historical, and political contexts within which boundaries and self-ascription function.

IDENTITY

Even more ubiquitous than "hybridity" is the term "identity." Indeed, it is rare to find a book that does not in one way or another claim to be addressing identity.[36] Numerous books and articles address the definitions and uses of "identity" as a category of analysis. A key article is that of Rogers Brubaker and Frederick Cooper, entitled "Beyond 'Identity,'" published in the journal *Theory and Society* in 2000.[37] The article engages in a trenchant critique of how this term is used in the social sciences and humanities, and provides some alternatives that in my view are worthy of consideration.

Brubaker and Cooper's main argument is that "the social sciences and humanities have surrendered to the word 'identity'; [and] that this has both intellectual and political costs; and that we can do better."[38] Brubaker and Cooper distinguish between the "hard" meaning of identity as a "singular, abiding, foundational sameness" and the "soft" meaning of identity as multiple, fluid, fragmented, and negotiated.[39] The "hard" meaning has justifiably been discarded, but the "soft" meaning is also problematic as a category of analysis. This is because:

> The prevailing constructivist stance on identity – the attempt to "soften" the term, to acquit it of the charge of "essentialism" by stipulating that identities are constructed, fluid and multiple – leaves us without a rationale for talking about "identities" at all and ill-equipped to examine the "hard" dynamics and essentialist claims of contemporary identity politics. "Soft" constructivism allows putative "identities" to proliferate. But as they proliferate, the term loses its analytical purchase. If identity is everywhere, it is nowhere. If it is fluid, how can we understand the ways in which self-understandings may harden, congeal, and crystallize? If it is constructed, how can we understand the sometimes coercive force of external identifications? If it is multiple, how do we understand the terrible singularity that is often striven for – and sometimes realized – by politicians seeking to transform mere categories into unitary and exclusive groups? How can we understand the power and pathos of identity politics?[40]

Brubaker and Cooper do not quarrel with those who use "identity" to describe practice; they acknowledge that, in everyday experience, we all engage in activities that express one aspect or another of our identity as we understand or construct it for ourselves. Rather, their concern is that, due to its imprecision and vagueness, "identity" cannot serve its desired purpose as an analytical category.

"Identity" was first introduced in the 1960s by social scientists such as Erik Erikson, Erving Goffman, and Peter Berger. From that point "identity" spread quickly into virtually all areas of the humanities and the social sciences, to be used in several different ways:

1 To describe the ground or basis of social or political actions, for example, by stressing how individual or collective action could be governed by "particularistic self-understandings rather than by putatively universal self-interest."[41]
2 To denote a fundamental and consequential sameness among members of a group or category. "In this usage, the line between 'identity' as a category of analysis and as a category of practice is often blurred."[42]
3 To refer to a core aspect of individual or collective "selfhood" or as a fundamental condition of social being, "to point to something allegedly *deep, basic, abiding, foundational*."[43]
4 To refer to the product of social or political action such as the development of "groupness" that makes collective action possible.[44]
5 To refer to "the evanescent product of multiple and competing discourses, 'identity' is invoked to highlight the unstable, multiple, fluctuating, and fragmented nature of the contemporary 'self.'"[45]

This list highlights the multiple meanings that "identity" has taken on and the different uses to which it has been put. Brubaker and Cooper question whether the term can still be useful once its core meaning – sameness – has been repudiated. Referring to the "weak" understanding of "identity," that is, the understanding that views identity as unstable, constructed, and multivalent, they comment that "the everyday sense of 'identity' strongly suggests at least some self-sameness over time, some persistence, something that remains identical, the same, while other things are changing. What is the point in using the term 'identity' if this core meaning is expressly repudiated?"[46] In other words, they are not questioning or challenging this "weak" meaning but simply wondering whether the term "identity" itself is useful once it is understood in this contingent way. This question allows them to move to their main point: the opening up of alternative terms and concepts to discuss the issues that are often grouped together under the vague category of "identity."

Identification and Categorization

The terms "identification" and "categorization" invite us to specify the agents that do the identifying without reifying the concept of "identity" as such. Modes of identification can include the relational (how we define ourselves in relation to other people or groups, for example, as a spouse, mother, grandmother, sister, daughter, friend) or the categorical (how we categorize ourselves, for example, as a professor, a Canadian, a woman, a Jew, a lover of books and music).[47] Within this latter context we can also distinguish between self-categorization and the identification of oneself by others, including powerful authoritative institutions, as in Nazi Germany (Jew or Aryan) or apartheid-era South Africa (White, Coloured, Black). Brubaker and Cooper comment: "The literature on social movements ...is rich in evidence on how movement leaders challenge official identifications and propose alternative ones. It highlights leaders' efforts to get members of putative constituencies to identify themselves in a certain way, to see themselves – for a certain range of purposes – as 'identical' with one another, to identify emotionally as well as cognitively."[48]

Self-Understanding and Social Location

Brubaker and Cooper define "self-understanding" as "a dispositional term that designates what might be called 'situated subjectivity': one's sense of who one is, of one's social location, and of how (given the first two) one is prepared to act ...[It] does not imply a distinctively modern or Western understanding of the 'self' as a homogeneous, bounded, unitary entity. A sense of who one is can take many forms."[49] As subjective categories, self-understanding and social locatedness must be understood in relation to each other: "both the bounded self and the bounded group are culturally specific rather than universal forms."[50] Nor do these terms imply sameness, as does "identity." Nevertheless, Brubaker and Cooper point out that their very subjectivity and auto-referentiality limit the possibility of critique and therefore may also limit the usefulness of these terms as analytical categories.[51]

Commonality, Connectedness, Groupness

Brubaker and Cooper use the terms "commonality," "connectedness," and "groupness" to designate "the emotionally laden sense of belonging to a distinctive, bounded group, involving both a felt solidarity or oneness with fellow group members and a felt difference from or even antipathy to specified outsiders."[52] Commonality and connectedness refer to the characteristics, attributes, values, or other types of connections that link people together; groupness refers to the feeling of belonging together, which may depend on commonality and connectedness but can also depend on other factors, such as a common experience (e.g., surviving a natural disaster or participating in some extraordinary event) or activity (e.g., choral singing creates a sense of groupness not only among the members of a specific choir but also among all who love the activity). Groupness does not require relational connectedness, but it does create "a powerfully imagined and strongly felt commonality."[53]

OBSERVATIONS

Concerns about the meanings, uses, and usefulness of the terms "hybridity" and "identity" are worth taking into account when we decide on the language and heuristic framework for our own studies of individuals and groups in the ancient Mediterranean world. Do they help or hinder our investigations? When we refer to someone as having a hybrid identity, are we celebrating the "Third Space" that they might inhabit between colonizer and colonized? Or are we lamenting the possibility that they have forfeited a part of a prior fixed identity in order to assimilate, accommodate, acculturate, or otherwise participate in the culture or cultures among whom they find themselves? And would our scholarly judgments about the hybrid identity of an ancient figure or group have been meaningful or even recognizable to the ones of whom we are speaking? If so, how do we know? If not, does it matter?

Given the problems that my brief survey raises, it is reasonable to ask whether we should abandon the terms "hybridity" and "identity" altogether. I would say not, as long as we are able to articulate how we are using them and why they are helpful to us. But are they essential? I would answer this in the negative as well. Although these terms are popular for our fields, the ideas that they express and the phenomena they describe have been of interest for much longer than that. In some cases, the older vocabulary may no longer be acceptable either conceptually or ethically. We no longer should or would use terms such as "mixed race," "mulatto," or "miscegenation." But other vocabulary may still prove useful for one purpose or another. In some circumstances, for example, what we now might refer to as hybridity may still be profitably described as syncretism. And I find it more helpful to think about Philo as a Hellenistic Jewish philosopher than as someone with a hybrid identity, though he certainly could be described that way.

The example of Philo raises an issue with both terms under discussion. As Brubaker and Cooper point out, the term "self-identification" provides room for considering the ways in which a group or an individual might identify themselves, but it falls short if we are seeking to categorize or define that group or individual alongside others. This distinction, which Brubaker and Cooper describe as subjective versus objective, also coheres with what anthropologists describe as emic and etic, from within and from without. I do not know whether Philo would have described himself as a Hellenistic Jew, though he may have described himself as an Alexandrian Jew. Similarly, I wonder whether others to whom we might ascribe hybrid identities would in fact have understood themselves in ways that resemble what we might mean by that description. This observation, like the critiques I have discussed, should not prevent us from using this language, but it underscores the primary point that I have gleaned from my own attempt to understand these terms: that by being clear and specific in our writing about our choice and usage of particular terms and interpretive frameworks, we will also become clearer in our own minds about how we are approaching our objects or subjects of study, and why.

NOTES

1 Daniel Boyarin, "Rethinking Jewish Christianity: An Argument for Dismantling a Dubious Category (to Which Is Appended a Correction of my *Border Lines*)," *Jewish Quarterly Review* 99, no. 1 (2009): 8, 13; Daniel Boyarin, *Judaism: The Genealogy of a Modern Notion* (New Brunswick, NJ: Rutgers University Press, 2019).

2 Mikael Tellbe, *Christ-Believers in Ephesus: A Textual Analysis of Early Christian Identity-Formation in a Local Perspective* (Tübingen: Mohr Siebek, 2009).

3 Mark T. Finney, *Honour and Conflict in the Ancient World: 1 Corinthians in Its Greco-Roman Social Setting* (London: T & T Clark, 2012), 1.

4 Daniel Boyarin, *Border Lines: The Partition of Judaeo-Christianity* (Philadelphia: University of Pennsylvania Press, 2004), 30.

5 Alan Saxby, *James, Brother of Jesus, and the Jerusalem Church: A Radical Exploration of Christian Origins* (Eugene, OR: Wipf and Stock, 2015), 95.

6 Ismo Dunderberg, *Beyond Gnosticism: Myth, Lifestyle, and Society in the School of Valentinus* (New York: Columbia University Press, 2008), 16–19.

7 Steve Mason, "Jews, Judeans, Judaizing, Judaism: Problems of Categorization in Ancient History," *Journal for the Study of Judaism* 38, no. 45 (2007): 457–512; cf. Adele Reinhartz, "The Vanishing Jews of Antiquity," *Marginalia*, 24 June 2014, https://themarginaliareview.com/vanishing-jews-antiquity-adele-reinhartz/.

8 Christopher P. Jones, *Between Pagan and Christian* (Cambridge, MA: Harvard University Press, 2014).

9 Denise Kimber Buell, *Why This New Race: Ethnic Reasoning in Early Christianity* (New York: Columbia University Press, 2005), 2.

10 Stanley K. Stowers, "On the Concept of 'Community' and the History of Early Christianity," *Method and Theory in the Study of Religion* 23, no. 3 (2011): 238–56; cf. Rogers Brubaker, *Ethnicity without Groups* (Cambridge, MA: Harvard University Press, 2004).

11 John Irving, *Avenue of Mysteries* (New York: Simon and Schuster, 2015), 1.

12 See https://www.merriam-webster.com/dictionary/hybrid.

13 Arthur O. Lovejoy, *The Great Chain of Being: A Study of the History of an Idea* (Cambridge, MA: Harvard University Press, 1936); Francis Oakley, *Omnipotence, Covenant and Order: An Excursion in the History of Ideas from Abelard to Leibniz* (Ithaca, NY: Cornell University Press, 1984).

14 Robert Young, *Colonial Desire: Hybridity in Theory, Culture, and Race* (London: Routledge, 1995), 6–8.

15 Young, *Colonial Desire*, 8.

16 Homi K. Bhabha, *The Location of Culture* (London: Routledge, 1994), 112.

17 Ibid., 38 (emphasis in original).

18 Ibid., 114 (emphasis in original).

19 Warren Carter, "Postcolonial Biblical Criticism," in *New Meanings for Ancient Texts: Recent Approaches to Biblical Criticisms and their Applications*, ed. Steven L. McKenzie and John Kaltner (Louisville, KY: Westminster John Knox Press, 2013), 97–116.

20 Andreas Wimmer, *Ethnic Boundary Marking: Institutions, Power, Networks* (New York: Oxford University Press, 2013); Eric P. Kaufmann, *Rethinking Ethnicity: Majority Groups and Dominant Minorities* (London: Routledge, 2004).

21 Kimberly Stratton, "Identity," in *The Cambridge Companion to Ancient Mediterranean Religions*, ed. Barbette Stanley Spaeth (New York: Cambridge University Press, 2013), 242.

22 Carter, "Postcolonial Biblical Criticism," 100–1.

23 Jennifer Bird, *Abuse, Power and Fearful Obedience: Reconsidering 1 Peter's Commands to Wives* (London: T&T Clark, 2011), 33.

24 Young, *Colonial Desire*, 18, quoting M.M. Bakhtin, *The Dialogic Imagination: Four Essays*, trans. Caryl Emerson and Michael Holquist (Austin: University of Texas Press, 1981), 358.

25 John Huntyk, "Hybridity," *Ethnic and Racial Studies* 28, no. 1 (2005): 80.

26 Ibid.

27 Philipp Stockhammer, "Questioning Hybridity," in *Conceptualizing Cultural Hybridization: A Transdisciplinary Approach*, ed. Philipp Stockhammer (Heidelberg: Springer, 2012), 1–2.

28 Gary Reger, "Ethnic Identities, Borderlands, and Hybridity," in *A Companion to Ethnicity in the Ancient Mediterranean*, ed. Jeremy McInerney (Malden: Wiley, 2014), 117.

29 Todd Penner and Caroline Vander Stichele, "Rhetorical Practice and Performance in Early Christianity," in *The Cambridge Companion to Ancient Rhetoric*, ed. Erik Gunderson (Cambridge: Cambridge University Press, 2009), 258.

30 Annette Yoshiko Reed, "'Jewish Christianity' after the 'Parting of the Ways': Approaches to Historiography and Self-Definition in the Pseudo-Clementines," in *The Ways that Never Parted: Jews and Christians in Late Antiquity and the Early Middle Ages*, ed. Adam H. Becker and Annette Yoshiko Reed (Minneapolis: Fortress Press, 2003), 202.

31 Bhabha, *Location of Culture*, 58 (emphasis in original).

32 Ibid., 13–14.

33 Stockhammer, "Questioning Hybridity," 1.

34 Samuel C. Heilman and Menachem Friedman, *The Rebbe: The Life and Afterlife of Menachem Mendel Schneerson* (Princeton, NJ: Princeton University Press, 2010).

35 Reger, "Ethnic Identities," 112.

36 For example, Miriam Taylor, *Anti-Judaism and Early Christian Identity: A Critique of the Scholarly Consensus* (Leiden: Brill, 1995); Judith Lieu, *Christian Identity in the Jewish and Graeco-Roman World* (Oxford: Oxford University Press, 2004); Adiel Schremer, *Brothers Estranged: Heresy, Christianity, and Jewish Identity in Late Antiquity* (New York: Oxford University Press, 2010); Matthew Thiessen, *Contesting Conversion: Genealogy, Circumcision and Identity in Ancient Judaism and Christianity* (New York: Oxford University Press, 2011); Carl S. Ehrlich, Anders Runesson, and Eileen M. Schuller, ed., *Purity, Holiness, and Identity in Judaism and Christianity: Essays in Memory of Susan Haber* (Tübingen: Mohr Siebeck, 2013); Tom Thatcher and Barry Schwartz, *Memory and Identity in Ancient Judaism and Early Christianity: A Conversation with Barry Schwartz* (Atlanta: Society of Biblical Literature, 2014); Yifat Monnickendam, *Jewish Law and Early Christian Identity: Betrothal, Marriage, and Infidelity in the Writings of Ephrem the Syrian* (Cambridge: Cambridge University Press, 2021).

37 The article is revised and reprinted in Brubaker, *Ethnicity without Groups*.

38 Rogers Brubaker and Frederick Cooper, "Beyond 'Identity,'" *Theory and Society* 29, no. 1 (2000): 1.

39 Brubaker, *Ethnicity without Groups*, 4.

40 Brubaker and Cooper, "Beyond Identity," 2000, 1.

41 Ibid., 6.

42 Ibid., 7.

43 Ibid. (emphasis in original).

44 Ibid.

45 Ibid., 8.

46 Ibid., 11.

47 Ibid., 14–15.

48 Ibid., 16.

49 Ibid., 17.

50 Ibid.

51 Ibid., 17–19.

52 Ibid., 19.

53 Ibid., 19–20.

13

Jesus, Paul, and the Geography of Magic

William Arnal

The anthropology of magic is a lot like the Nile River: long, voluminous – and filled with garbage. But it is especially like the Nile in having two main sources. Our Blue Nile is the approach of E.B. Tylor and J.G. Frazer, in which magic is distinguished from religion objectively: it has specific performative or cognitive features that mark it out from other kinds of actions. The White Nile stems from Émile Durkheim and Marcel Mauss. Here, magic is distinguished from religion on the basis of different social contexts and different social functions. For the purposes of this chapter, I adopt the latter view, following especially Mauss's definition of magic as, simply, unauthorized ritual. But even this definition needs to be qualified: since the social world is never monolithic or unitary, there can be no single canon, no Archimedean referee, to provide objective authorization. Rather, what we can say is that certain figures and types of activities are of contested or questionable authority. And the challenges can arise from any quarter: they are not limited to some objectively determined elites, nor are its targets limited to figures of some objectively determined margins. "Magic" refers to a fluid range of accusations, agents, and practices.

If we turn to the ancient world in which the New Testament writings were composed, and take a look at the individuals and the actions that tended to have accusations of "magic" thrown at them, what we find is that they have a tremendous amount in common with non-magical ritualism as well: formalized movements, non-ordinary uses of language, appeals to supernatural agents, use of supernatural assistants, linguistic and conceptual appeals to relevant "great tradition" religious motifs, a ritual performer with marked status, use of special materials, manipulation of objects, physical contact between performer and audience, and appeals to efficacy. The features that tend to accrue distinctively to "magic," that is, to *contested* ritual, are those that follow naturally from the fact of its being contested: secrecy, performance in "profane" space, and performance in contested social space. It seems to me that ancient "magic" is neither more nor less than simply ritual, but ritual which is somehow open to question, deauthorization, or conflicting assessments of its legitimacy.

In terms of how to interpret this ancient material, I follow the suggestions of Jonathan Z. Smith but as refined and applied especially by David Frankfurter, and now more recently by Heidi Wendt. They argue that the kinds of characters described as magicians in antiquity can be understood as mobile ritual specialists who served to effect a bridge between the (necessarily) static ritual centre of temple (and the traditions that undergird it) and the various localized and personal needs that could seem distant from the temple's (necessarily) fixed liturgies. It is precisely the mobility of these specialists, the absence of the total apparatus of the ancient temple, that allows their authority to be called into question; and called into question it very often was, with accusations of being cheats, quacks, jugglers, and the like. But this dismissal should not blind us to the reality that these individuals – philosophers, priests, scribes, healers, exorcists, and religious entrepreneurs[1] – may have functioned as integrative agents,[2] establishing connections between local and quotidian realities, on the one hand, and the grander ideologies invoked by civic or national institutions of temple and priesthood, on the other.

In the New Testament we encounter instances of the pejorative use of the language of magic in so far as the practices of some characters are deauthorized with the terminology of μάγος or γοής, or by associating them with the kinds of practices that such quacks and evil-doers were wont to do. These accusations are easy enough to understand. As David Aune notes, "In view of the general illegality of magic in the Roman empire, the accusation of magic is among other things a form of social control used by those within the dominant social structure to label and exert control on those in the ambiguous and unstructured areas of society."[3] Here the effect of such accusations is emphasized: calling someone else's ritual practice "magical" is an act of social control. Aune's view however is too limited. One need not have a dominant role in the social structure to employ this rhetoric. Harold Remus is more accurate when he emphasizes that such accusations can be, and are, exchanged between rival groups.[4] And the evidence of the New Testament bears this out. One of the more significant accusations of magic in the New Testament is directed at Jesus in the so-called "Beelzebul controversy," a story that appears with different emphases in Q 11:14–23 and in Mark 3:22–30.[5] Here Jesus comes under scrutiny as a potentially marginal social figure, and an effort at deauthorization is made against him by rivals. In the Markan version, Jesus is accused of demonic possession, of a piece with the accusation of insanity in verse 21 (ἐξέστη); but in Q's account, opponents claim that Jesus's exorcisms are made possible ἐν Βεελζεβούλ, that is, by his use of a supernatural assistant under the magician's control.[6] Here it is not difficult to see a straightforward attempt at delegitimation: Jesus is accused of undertaking what seems to be a positive act by invoking or controlling malign agents, an accusation that would resonate with the widespread perception that maleficent magic-workers do precisely this. Similar accusations are made in Acts, but this time are levelled by the narrator against rivals of the church. A Samaritan charismatic wonder-worker named Simon is accused of essentially the same thing that Jesus is accused of in Q: he is undertaking his ritualistic acts of power for selfish or malign purposes, or fraudulently, or both. All Acts needs to do to convey this is describe Simon's actions as "magic." Likewise Elymas bar-Jesus, a Jewish magician, is out-magicked by Paul, who renders him blind in Acts 13:6–12. Both villains have strong similarities in behaviour to our heroes, Jesus and Paul; but both are competing with the program Acts attributes to its heroes – they are deauthorized, quite simply, for being wrong. There is for the author no difference between a "magician" and a "false prophet," the latter term also being applied to Elymas (13:6: ἄνδρα τινὰ μάγον ψευδοπροφήτην Ἰουδαῖον). Both Simon and Elymas are figures very similar to Jesus: charismatic wonder-workers bringing the power of the Jewish God to bear in concrete, localized, and immediately present ways. They just happen to be wrong.

Acts similarly describes Paul's decommissioning of a girl with a spirit of prophecy (πνεῦμα πύθωνα), who engages in "soothsaying" in Acts 16:16–19. This story, interestingly, does not make use of the vocabulary of abuse associated with magic: the girl is not called a magician or sorcerer, for example. Her gift of prophecy is deemed to be legitimate, if perhaps derived from an ungodly source (the πνεῦμα exorcised by Paul in v. 18), in so far as she correctly identifies the status of Paul and his comrades as "servants of the Most High" (v 17).[7] Paul does not exorcise the girl's spirit as part of an overarching program of opposition to mantic or oracular practices but simply because she has become an annoyance (v. 18: he was διαπονηθείς). Acts 19, likewise, describes Paul and his retinue overcoming practices that the author characterizes, pejoratively, as "magical." After Paul has made an impressive showing in the city of Ephesus, Acts states that "a number of those who practiced magic arts [τὰ περίεργα, a word referring to waste of time, or superfluity, i.e., quacks] brought in their books together and burned them in the sight of all; and they counted the value of them and found it came to fifty thousand pieces of silver. So the word of the Lord grew and prevailed mightily" (Acts 19:19–20). Again, this is not so much a principled opposition to magic, either on the part of Acts' author or on the part of his characters, as it is a competitive notice. After all, just prior to this account, Acts 19:11–12 tells of Paul performing miracles that seem to involve precisely the kinds of mechanical actions predicated on contact, analogue, or action at a distance that so often (albeit unhelpfully) are understood as magic: "God did extraordinary miracles by the hands of Paul, so that handkerchiefs or aprons were carried away from his body to the sick, and diseases left them and the evil spirits came out of them."[8] Actions that, when Paul performs them are "miracles" (δυνάμεις), are "magic" (μαγεία) or even "over-wrought superfluities" (περίεργα) when others perform them.[9] Likewise, the Jewish exorcists of Acts 19 are described as engaging in *exactly* the same activity as Paul (and as Jesus, for that matter), but, since they are not authorized to do so, they fail. Acts is therefore describing a rivalry between its own heroes' program of access to divine power and those of their competitors. Paul and the boys so effectively provide what others could not that there was no longer any need for the population of Ephesus to even consider what these others had to offer, whether books of magic or the devotional products of silversmiths (19:24–27). In calling this latter material "magic," Acts is deauthorizing practices that are in fact identical to those of his protagonists, favouring one set of actors over another in a sea of competing practitioners.

In addition to accusations of magic (μαγεῖα), numerous activities occur in the New Testament that are magic-like. A woman is healed by touching Jesus's hem in Mark 5:27; others by Paul's apron in Acts 19:12. As I read these accounts, though, they are simply expressions of the idea that Jesus and Paul channel or communicate divine power,[10] which extends to their clothing or personal effects. The same idea can be found in the generic figure of the temple priest, who more "legitimately" functions as a channel of divine power and will.[11] These magical actions can be somewhat illuminated by appeal to the principles of contagion, action at a distance, and imitation: all features of magic but also features of ritual more broadly.

A more interesting and complex example is found in the miraculous healing described in Mark 7:32–36:[12] "They brought to him a man who was deaf and had an impediment in his speech; and they besought him to lay his hands upon him. And taking him aside from the multitude privately, he put his fingers into his ears, and he spat and touched his tongue; and looking up to heaven, he sighed, and said to him, 'Ephphatha,' that is, 'be opened.' And his ears were opened, his tongue was released, and he spoke plainly. And he charged them to tell no one." In this and other healing and exorcism stories, we encounter not all, but many, of the features that seem to characterize unauthorized ritual actions of the sort that are vulnerable to accusations of magic.[13] These features include: formalized movements; formulaic or non-ordinary types of speech; appeal to deity; arguably, the use of a magical assistant (the holy spirit); comment on the status of the practitioner; use of special materials; manipulation of objects; physical contact with the magician; evidence of efficacy; secrecy; and performance in contested social space.

The broad similarity between Jesus and (other) itinerant magicians, or the later spell-workers of the Greek Magical Papyri, has generated opposing scholarly responses. At the more obviously apologetic end of the spectrum are those who insist, on very thin grounds, that Jesus's activity has nothing in common with magic, as Walter Grundmann pronounces: "The NT miracles of Jesus have no connexion with magic, or with magic means and processes, like the majority of miracles outside the NT. The biblical concept of God forbids this."[14] While recent work is more subtle about it, we still encounter the claim that Jesus's activity, perhaps reminiscent of magic, is in some way set apart from it by virtue of its different ideological assumptions. Scholars will invoke some supposed feature of the worldview of Jesus (or his biographers) that is described as incompatible with a magical worldview, even if the activities in question are nearly identical. The criteria that exclude the possibility of a so-called magical worldview are invoked ad hoc; in this kind of special pleading, any individual characteristic of Jesus's activity or thought-world can be invoked to make such a distinction. We find an especially egregious instance of this in Howard Clark Kee's book on magic and the New Testament:[15] "To make historical judgments on the basis of arbitrary definitions or theological prejudices does not contribute to constructive inquiry. What [has been] ignored is that there is a fundamental difference between the apocalyptic worldview, which sees the cosmos as a place of struggle between God and his opponents, but which awaits the triumph of God and the vindication of his faithful people, and a magical view which regards the gods and all the other powers as fair game for exploitation and manipulation by those shrewd enough to achieve thereby their own ends."[16] John Meier does essentially the same thing, albeit with a different criterion of distinction: "it is fair to say that the context of many of these stories within a given Gospel is one of a personal religious relationship between Jesus and the recipient(s) of his miracles. At least implicitly, the context of miracles in the Gospels is one of faith, trust, or discipleship. At times, other motifs are added: the audience responds with worship and praise of God or Jesus; alternately, the recipient of the miracle becomes an unofficial missionary, spreading the news of Jesus' miracle to others."[17] Gerd Theissen, who quite brilliantly deconstructs the distinction between religion and magic, nonetheless re-erects that same distinction by appealing, as do Kee and Meier, to an ad hoc differentiating feature: "Magic is an individualistic reaction to social disintegration. The magician has no need to be integrated into society. He remains in the dark. It is quite different with the charismatic miracle-worker."[18] And Richard Horsley in his recent book on magic in the gospels makes much of the "fact" that the Greek Magical Papyri do not contain many healing or exorcism spells, whereas Jesus's behaviour is marked by these two activities. Horsley seems to have simply invented this "fact": by my quick count, there are at least six exorcism spells and dozens of healing spells in the Greek corpus of magical spells.[19]

Against such efforts to protect the New Testament or Jesus from the (apparently scandalous) imputation of magic, a number of rather bolder scholars have asserted that, in fact, Jesus *was* a magician. This claim is associated most strongly with Morton Smith,[20] but Wendy Cotter shows the numerous literary parallels between Jesus's healings and those of other miraculous/magical figures in the same period.[21] Harold Remus likewise emphasizes the similarities.[22] David Aune has contributed immensely to this discussion, dismantling many of the artificial barriers between "miracle" and "magic," while noting that "a great deal of theological flummery has been occasioned by the retroactive importation of later Christian notions of faith into the use of the notion by Jesus. Equally erroneous is the notion that faith played no part in Jewish or Graeco-Roman miracles."[23] But we may ask in all these instances, what is gained? Certainly, a very important gain is the extension of the range of comparative material for making sense of the tales about Jesus. If Jesus is, or is comparable to, a magician, then we can use texts like the Greek Magical Papyri, or accounts of "pagan" itinerant healers,[24] or even instances of magic drawn from completely different cultures,[25] to understand the dynamics of Jesus's activities, and that is surely a major step forward. But can we translate these similarities into substantive insights into the behaviour of Jesus, or Paul,[26] or the literary representations of their behaviour? I think we can.

The "magical" story from Mark 7:32–36 just discussed can be described in a way that neither shies away from the "magical" elements of the account nor, again, that sees as its goal merely establishing that Jesus was a "magician." First, the story deliberately and self-consciously describes a ritual performer whose authority is contested. One might even say that the "magical" elements of the story – direct bodily contact, secrecy, foreign words, application of spit – are there precisely to signal or set up the contested status of Jesus's authority. For the author of Mark, the story of Jesus is the story of a struggle over status: between Jesus and the more or less "official" leaders of the people. The latter can rely on institutional hallmarks of authority; pitted against them, Jesus draws his authority straight from the supernatural realm and its god.[27] Since contesting institutional authority is the issue here, since in fact it is a central structuring element of Mark's story, *of course* Jesus is unable to derive legitimacy from formal institutions or their functionaries. His authority therefore must be created in an ad hoc fashion, one that moves around the ordinary and formal mechanisms of religious authorization, and goes directly to the source of their authority, that is, again, the supernatural reality that underwrites the institutions in question. Mark's Jesus therefore is deeply characterized by his extra-institutional actions vis-à-vis a given supernatural reality and, thus, is necessarily a "magician." This is not due to the mechanical technologies he employs in healing; it is due, more broadly, to his renegade ritual activity, which in its turn dictates the "mechanical" technologies he employs. In light of this, we should think of Jesus – or rather the presentation of Jesus in Mark – not so much as a magician, after all, with the enormous baggage associated with that term, but as a mobile ritual specialist, that is, as a performer of religious ritual outside of the context of expected, predictable, and catholic formats. He is a functionary of deity, but a maverick functionary; not a priest, not operating in the temple or directly making use of its appliances, he nonetheless brings its God to bear on quotidian, local, personal problems.

Much of this presentation stems from location as well.[28] As a mobile ritual specialist, Mark's Jesus takes the temple's operations, or at least some of the functions of those operations, and brings them to bear on territory that is somewhat distant from the cultic centre itself. From Mark's narrative perspective, the absence of the temple is a function of distance: it is away in Judea, and Jesus is operating through Galilee, moving from one town to the next, through the countryside, around the lake, even in the wilderness, channelling the God of Israel directly for those who are somewhat physically remote from God's dwelling.[29] Also conceptualized spatially is the "distance" between God's activity, his kingdom, and the gentiles. Jesus moves into their "territories" as well, extending the ritual and effective reach of the God of the Jerusalem temple beyond the borders of Israel. With all of this in mind, Mark's portrayal of Jesus's Galilean opponents makes sense. The scribes and, anachronistically, the Pharisees oppose him at every point, including and especially calling out his lack of authority. In Mark 2:1–12 – the healing of the paralytic – these motifs come together nicely. Jesus responds to someone who has entered his private home in Capernaum by extending to his visitor one of the temple's primary functions, atonement: "your sins are forgiven" (2:5: ἀφίενταί σου αἱ ἁμαρτίαι), he says. Quite reasonably, scribes question his authority to do something like this. He responds, "magically," by asserting divine authorization – "the son of man has authority to forgive sins" (2:10: ἐξουσίαν ἔχει ὁ υἱὸς τοῦ ἀνθρώπου ἀφιέναι ἁμαρτίας) – and then proving it by performing a magical act of healing. Earlier, Mark makes a virtue of necessity in 1:22 by treating Jesus's self-authorization as a sign of greater authority than that possessed by the scribes and Pharisees (ἦν γὰρ διδάσκων αὐτοὺς ὡς ἐξουσίαν ἔχων καὶ οὐχ ὡς οἱ γραμματεῖς).[30] I think it is significant that these presentations focus on the *kinds* of figures who serve functions similar to that of Jesus and, hence, are his direct competitors. The Pharisees in particular operated as mediators of temple functions, especially those concerning purity. In this sense, the Pharisees were just as much magicians as Jesus; they too were a faction or group that took ritual aspects of the temple "on the road." This helps us make sense of Mark's burlesque of purity considerations: this is not a rejection of "Judaism" or even "dietary laws," it is a rejection of a competing modality of mobile ritualism.

The way that tension levels in Mark's gospel are organized in geographical terms also supports this interpretation. While Jesus experiences opposition from Pharisees and scribes from the very start, the general mood of the story is celebratory and positive until Jesus turns to Jerusalem. From this point forward, and especially after his arrival in Jerusalem, he is greeted with consistent hostility, and his own tone becomes more and more badgering, to the point that he is engaging in acts of direct violence (11:15–19), while active plots against him are being put into action (14:1–2, 10–11). The emphasis shifts from opposition from Pharisees (and scribes) to opposition from temple functionaries (and scribes); as always, Jesus returns the favour. By taking on a view of Mark's Jesus as a mobile ritual specialist, we can see the logic, and the novelty, of Mark's presentation. As long as Jesus remains in the Galilee, or the surrounding areas, he is not intruding on the temple's turf; he may not be clearly authorized to perform its functions, but his approach can be viewed as a kind of supplement to or extension of the temple's role. In Mark 1:44 this augmentative role is very clear: Jesus instructs a man he has healed of leprosy to "go and show yourself to the priest and make offering for your cleansing what Moses prescribed" (ὕπαγε σεαυτὸν δεῖξον τῷ ἱερεῖ καὶ προσένεγκε περὶ τοῦ καθαρισμοῦ σου ἃ προσέταξεν Μωϋσ). Jesus accords to the authorized ritual functionaries in charge of purity and sacrifice a role alongside his own. But as he moves towards Jerusalem, his stance becomes more and more aggressive, less an extension of the temple's range and more a replacement of it. Mark is able to conceive of such a replacement because of his temporal position, that is, looking back on the destruction of the Jerusalem temple in 70 CE.[31] From a post-70 perspective, seeking to replace the temple is not an outrageous, anti-social, or revolutionary act: it is a necessity. It only appears outrageous when narratively retrojected to a period in which the temple was still standing.

As I argue elsewhere,[32] the Gospel of Mark can be understood as an effort, like Josephus's *War*, to make intellectual sense of the loss of the house of his God. He does so in a double fashion, first, by retroactively portraying the loss of the temple as no loss at all because it had, in fact, already lost its significance long before.[33] But he also does so, second, by posing his own solution to this problem as preferential to another solution: that of mobile Pharisaic purity and their equally mobile teaching of the Law. Thus in addition to a narrative portrayal of Jesus as embattled with respect to his authority, we may also find the same self-understanding for whoever produced Mark: they viewed their program as one potentially denied authorization, in need of authorization, and having to compete – especially with Pharisaic models – for authority. Mark is invoking the standard utensils of ritual-competence claims in the Roman era for his protagonist, and for himself. Jesus performs "magic" in Mark as a signal, and as a result, of Jesus being a ritual specialist in the service of a specific God and in relationship with that God's "great tradition"; yet he nonetheless stands outside of the formal and unchallenged ritual forms by which that God's functionaries are authorized. In the case of Jesus, this is so in order for him to supplement, extend, and, yes, challenge those forms; in the case of Mark's author, it is because the formal structures of authorization are, post-70 CE, no longer there.

I speak here of extensions of authority, and of contests over it, rather than more baldly of marginality since it is not at all clear with respect to what Mark would be marginal. There is no objective standard against which to measure marginality in Mark's context: the society in question and its religions are simply too complex. Part of what places Mark in a questionably authorized position is probably that, at this point, there is no single authorized position, perhaps no authorized position at all. In light of this, we should not understand Mark as attempting to replace a temple apparatus – or worse, a "Judaism" – that is oppressive or insensible to the needs of common people. Rather, there is an effort here to localize and transfer temple functions, to embody them in a Galilean location perhaps, but certainly in a post-War and thus post-Temple context.

A similar reading can be offered – albeit very briefly – for the magical activity, as well as the critique of magic, that appears in Acts of the Apostles. Much of the activity in Acts that seems to us to be magic – and would have seemed so to hostile outsiders of the time as well – should really be understood as abbreviated encounters with deity and his agents. A deity's power is invested in his or her sacred places and in the holy items blessed by his or her chosen functionaries. In Acts, however, these authorized spaces are not available, and this is fundamentally because the story of Acts, somewhat as with Mark, is the story of an extension of authority. The author of Acts does everything he can to authorize and situate the divine power channelled by the Jesus movement:[34] he invents an official hierarchy and a mechanism of formal authorization, the laying on of hands, manifested by possession of the holy spirit. Even more striking, the roots of that hierarchy, the apostles, are very deliberately situated in the temple in Jerusalem, and it is to that temple that more distant agents like Paul return. Nonetheless, the temple's ritual reach is being expanded into new territory and to new people ("the nations") through the whole of Acts and so is continually in a state of struggling for legitimacy. In some instances, this involves God's power being directly accessed through his mobile agents or even, via the logic of contact, through their clothes or shadows. Since these particular agents of expansion are not the resident priesthood of a situated temple, but like contemporary philosophers are roving envoys of the divine truth, or priests of a not-yet-established system,[35] the divine power to which they have access can appear to be fundamentally unauthorized – or only incompletely authorized – in the social sphere. It thus appears to hostile outsiders, as well as to ourselves, as magical practice. And Acts of course is forced simultaneously to reject all other types of mobile ritualism, whether in the form of charismatic persons (8:11) or in the form of written liturgies (19:19), because they are in direct competition with his own project. Acts is, I think, quite self-consciously presenting an extension of the ritual space of the Jewish God, this time to the whole world, so of course his protagonists will be presented as mobile ritual specialists of contested authorization; this is why Acts contains such grossly magical dimensions and, at the same time, condemns in the strongest terms those who practise magic.[36]

If we follow David Frankfurter's work on the social operations of magical practices, we can view the activities described in Mark, or in Acts, not so much as revolutionary, nor again as irruptions of the little tradition over and against the great tradition, nor yet as the voice of the peasantry or "the people" against the elites.[37] Magic can have subversive, oppositional uses and intentions; and the threat of subversion is always present in any unregulated social, religious, or political activity. But this oppositional potential is less essential to the practice of magic than its local and localizing application of great tradition ideologies and institutions.[38] It is one of several vehicles by which the distance is bridged between the metropolis, the religion of "there," the great tradition, the temple, the function of collective sanctification, on the one hand; and on the other, the religion of not just of "here" but of "*right* here," the little tradition, the function of immediate sanctification as is so evident in, for example, the exorcisms of Jesus. As Frankfurter states, "religion takes places not according to a series of levels of sophistication but rather within the context of the village, the city, the district, in dialectic with broader frames of reference, like regional cults, national cults, and textual traditions and their interpreters."[39] We have in the New Testament an activity that smacks as much (or more) of Durkheim as of Marx, performances of integration as much as performances of opposition. The exorcisms, in particular, use an appeal to the God of the Jerusalem temple but apply his power right here in the Galilee, in our town, or even out in the bush. And they do so moreover to use that deity to reconstruct and reaffirm local relationships, to draw people back into the community, to repair breaches within it. That is to say, they do on a small scale precisely what the temple is there for on a large scale.

One final observation: I have barely mentioned the role of writing in magic. In the gospels and in Acts, the actions that we tend to associate with magic, and that would have been identified as such by hostile contemporary observers, do not generally involve writing. Jesus does not read magical spells from texts; and he certainly is not described as writing magical words, never mind preparing amulets or conveying spells to others (except perhaps in the textually dubious instance of John 8:6). Yet a connection can be made. David Frankfurter's brilliant work on deracinated Egyptian priests performing "magic" in the late Roman period has striking analogies to explorations of the role of village scribes in the composition of early gospel materials:[40] in both cases, changing political circumstances led to changed status for state functionaries and, therefore, to changes in behaviour.[41] We can imagine the resulting sorts of unofficial activities taken on by Egyptian priests or Galilean scribes in terms of deprivation; in terms of a loss of employment or status. But we can also view them as an effort to take advantage of opportunities – provided by a complex, cosmopolitan, and increasingly interconnected world – to extend their own expert reach. In so doing, they also extend the reach of state instruments into new environments.[42] It strikes me as extremely suggestive that, in both of these cases, the function or effect of such actions was mediative. It is here that I think Sarah Rollens's work on medial or "middling" figures in antiquity shows its wider applicability. Whether or not our Galilean or diaspora "magicians," or those who told their tales, had anything to do with scribes specifically, they were a form of active and creative intellectual; they were the middling figures theorized by Rollens, transferring and mediating the institutional instruments of governance to local applications. In the process, they generated innovations of ideology and practice, innovations that did not overthrow the Roman order but ensured its flexibility and capacity to accommodate change. The earlier stages of the sayings tradition, as observable in Q, and of the narrative tradition, as reflected in tales of Jesus's "magical" actions, reflect similar processes and circumstances: bridge-building for a celestial deity who was at the same time a deity of nation, village, and neighbourhood; and doing so in and through the complicated layers of a multi-ethnic, cosmopolitan social reality. Cast as villain and enemy of the state, the magician was infiltrating new spaces, and providing new layers of functionaries, for state and temple. He or she is the secret hero of the religious versatility of antiquity.

NOTES

1 This terminology was broached by Jonathan Z. Smith, "Here, There, and Anywhere," 323–39, in *Relating Religion: Essays in the Study of Religion* (Chicago: University of Chicago Press, 2004), 330; Jonathan Z. Smith, "The Temple and the Magician," 172–89, in *Map Is Not Territory* (Chicago: University of Chicago Press, 1978), 186. But it has since been picked up and applied by others in various ways. See Heidi Marx-Wolf, *Spiritual Taxonomy and Ritual Expertise: Platonists, Priests, and "Gnostics" in the Third Century C.E.* (Philadelphia: University of Pennsylvania Press, 2016), 113–14; and, especially, Stanley K. Stowers, "The Concept of Community and the History of Early Christianity," *Method and Theory in the Study of Religion* 23, no. 3 (2011): 238–56.

2 Cf. Richard A. Horsley, *Jesus and Magic: Freeing the Gospel Stories from Modern Misconceptions* (Cambridge: James Clarke and Co., 2015), 166, referring to the "interaction of healer and healed and supporters in village communities."

3 David E. Aune, "Magic in Early Christianity," 368–420, in *Apocalypticism, Prophecy, and Magic in Early Christianity* (Grand Rapids, MI: Baker Academic, 2006), 384.

4 Harold Remus, "'Magic or Miracle?' Some Second-Century Instances," *Second Century* 2, no. 3 (1982): 127.

5 Horsley, *Jesus and Magic*, 164, claims: "In the Gospels, moreover, Jesus is not accused of practicing magic."

6 See Harold Remus, *Jesus as Healer* (Cambridge: Cambridge University Press, 1997), 30: "Some scholars have suggested that as practitioners of 'magic' used spells and rituals to summon spirits into their service, perhaps entering a trance ('madness') as they did, so too did Jesus – or at least knowledge of such practices may have led to the charge that he 'had' a demon and used it to cast out demons."

7 This is also true of the demons that Jesus casts out, who correctly identify him as son of God, and so on.

8 Similarly, touching the clothing of the holy or powerful man in (fulfilled) hopes of a cure is described in Mark 5:27–29; and again in Mark 6:56 (par. Matt 14:36). Adela Yarbro Collins, *Mark: A Commentary*, Hermeneia – A Critical and Historical Commentary on the Bible (Minneapolis: Fortress Press, 2007), 282, notes that

Plutarch's *Life of Sulla* (35.4) has a very similar story: someone seeks out a bit of the "nap of his mantle" to partake of Sulla's good luck.

9 Remus, *Jesus as Healer*, 101, notes that, in Acts, "magical" powers are also used to *harm*: Acts 5:1–11; 9:3–9; 12:20–3; 13:6–11.

10 Something apparent, for example, in the instances in which God renders his people impervious to snakebites, as in Mark 16:18; Acts 28:23–6.

11 The distinction is nicely rendered by Gerd Theissen, *The Miracle Stories of the Early Christian Tradition*, ed. John Riches, trans. Francis McDonagh (Minneapolis: Fortress Press, 2007), 233: "More important is a second distinction between institutionalised, charismatic and 'technical' forms of miraculous activity. Healing sanctuaries and oracles are recognised institutions of social and religious life. Their legitimation is traditional and achieved by means of foundation legends ... This sort of legitimation is not available to individual prophets or miracle-workers. They are inspired. Their charisma is attached to their person and generally disputed by the public. Distinct from the charismatic is the 'technician': soothsayers and magicians exercise their activities as the result of a skill they have learned. They have a 'technical' legitimation and can transmit their skill without any consideration of persons."

12 There is a matching miracle story in Mark 8:23–26. The distinct feature of *this* story that seems to mark it for many as "magic" rather than "miracle," as a description of *technique* rather than divine intervention, is the fact that the action is unsuccessful the first time and has to be performed twice. But there is a very clear literary reason for this repetition: Mark is encouraging the reader to "look intently," and a second time, at Jesus's identity. See Collins, *Mark*, 391–2. She notes a fascinating parallel: an inscription from the Asclepium in Epidaurus, 2nd half of 4th cent BCE: "Alcetas of Halieis. The blind man saw a dream. It seemed to him that the god came up to him and with his fingers opened his eyes, and that he first saw the trees of the sanctuary. At daybreak he walked out sound."

13 With some changes, the same sorts of motifs can be found in Matthew, Luke, and John as well.

14 Walter Grundmann, *TDNT*, s.v. δύναμαι/δύναμις, v.2, 302.

15 For a critique of Kee's approach, see John Dominic Crossan, *The Historical Jesus: The Life of a Mediterranean Jewish Peasant* (New York: HarperCollins, 1991), 306. The irony is that Kee opens his arbitrary definition and his statement of theological prejudice by criticizing arbitrary definitions and theological prejudices.

16 Howard Clark Kee, *Medicine, Miracle and Magic in New Testament Times*, SNTSMS (Cambridge: Cambridge University Press, 1986), 114. Kee is referring to the earlier work of Hull (John M. Hull, *Hellenistic Magic and the Synoptic Tradition* [A.R. Allenson and SCM Press, 1974]), which argues that Luke-Acts is deeply influenced by Hellenistic beliefs about magic. For a critique of Hull's position, see Paul J. Achtemeier, "The Lucan Perspective on the Miracles of Jesus: A Preliminary Sketch," *Journal of Biblical Literature* 94, no. 4 (1975): 547–62.

17 John P. Meier, *A Marginal Jew: Rethinking the Historical Jesus*, vol. 2, *Mentor, Message, and Miracles* (New York: Doubleday, 1994), 542.

18 Theissen, *Miracle Stories*, 242. It is mean-spirited, perhaps, but not unreasonable, to quote back at Theissen his own comment (Theissen, *Miracle Stories*, 293): "The method of argument is always the same. The features modern theology finds undesirable are blamed on the period, while the positive ones are assigned to the credit of Christianity."

19 Horsley, *Jesus and Magic*, 164: "As they [scholars] gave further attention to motifs of magic in the miracle stories, they assumed that healing and exorcism loomed large in the practice of magic. With no critical review of the 'magical papyri,' however, they did not notice that healings and exorcisms were rare in the papyri and that the few references to exorcism exhibited features of having been borrowed from earlier Jewish and Christian traditions." It is difficult to see how Horsley came to this conclusion. Exorcism appears in the PGM in, among other instances, PGM 4.86–7; 1227–64; 85.1–6; 89.1–27; 94.17–21; and 114.1–14. For healing, the list is even longer: PGM 7.193–6; 197–8; 199–201; 201–2; 203–5; 207; 208–9; 209–10; 211–12; 213–24; 218–21; 260–71; 63.24–5; 26–8; 65.1–4; 4–7; 90.14–18; 91.1–14; 94.4–6; 7–9; 10–16; 22–6; 27–35; 36–8; 39–60; 95.14–18; 97.1–6; 15–17; 104.1–8; 106.1–10; 113.1–4; 115.1–7; 119b.4–5; 120.1–13; 122.51–5; 123a. 48–50; 53–5; 56–68; 128.1–12; 130.1–13; and, among the Demotic spells, PDM xii.21–49; xiv.554–62; 563–74; 574–85; 585–93; 594–620; 620–6; 935–9; 953–5; 970–7; 978–80; 981–4; 985–92; 993–1002; 1003–14; 1015–20; 1021–3; 1024–5; 1097–103; 1104–9. It is also notable that the exorcism spells often occur in the context of (other) healing spells, indicating that the distinction between healing and casting out demons is a very fragile one and may not exist for our sources at all. Horsley is correct, of course, to note the differences between the Gospels and the PGM: they come from different periods, different locations, and probably different sectors of society; and, perhaps more important, they represent different kinds of literary genres. This hardly means, however, that the two bodies of writing may not be compared to each other as long as these differences are kept in mind.

20 Morton Smith, *Jesus the Magician* (New York: Barnes and Noble, 1993).

21 Throughout Wendy Cotter, *Miracles in Greco-Roman Antiquity: A Sourcebook for the Study of the New Testament Miracle Stories* (London: Routledge, 1999). Oddly, she dismisses (177) the utility of magic for making sense of the miracles, essentially on terminological grounds: "there is no suggestion in any Christian material that magic was considered as anything but completely negative, no matter where it occurred. If our purpose is to interpret the intended meaning of the Jesus miracle stories, then, a suggestion of a magical power, such as was understood in the Greco-Roman world, is completely unsupported."

22 Remus, "Magic or Miracle" and *Jesus as Healer*.

23 Aune, "Magic in Early Christianity," 397. As noted above, Aune thinks that Christianity is a millenarian movement; what distinguishes him from, for

example, Kee, is that he sees this millenarianism as an explanation for "magic" in Christian origins, not as a prophylactic against it.

24 Remus, *Jesus as Healer*, 16: "Rather than setting Jesus as a healer apart from pagans (and Jews) of his day, these utterances in fact situate him firmly in a world that was convinced of the power of words."

25 For example, Mary Douglas, *Purity and Danger: An Analysis of the Concepts of Pollution and Taboo* (London: Routledge and Kegan Paul, 1966), 70–1, analyzes an episode in which a village healer extracts a tooth from the body of a sick man who has been marginalized in his village: "The back-biting and envy of the villagers, symbolised by the tooth in the sick man's body, was dissolved in a wave of enthusiasm and solidarity. As he was cured of his physical symptoms they were all cured of social malaise. These symbols worked at the psycho-somatic level for the central figure, the sick man, and at the general psychological level for the villagers, in changing their attitudes, and at the sociological level in so far as the pattern of social statuses in the village was formally altered and in so far as some people moved in and others moved away as a result of the treatment." It is of course quite reasonable to interpret Jesus's exorcisms in precisely the same way.

26 For baptism – a significant ritual performance in Paul's ἐκκλησίαι – as a magical act, see Morton Smith, *Clement of Alexandria and a Secret Gospel of Mark* (Cambridge, MA: Harvard University Press, 1973), 220–36. Even if one does not entirely subscribe to the way Smith defines magic, Paul is certainly a "magician" by the terms of the definition advocated in this chapter: he is a mobile ritualist of uncertain authorization. It is unfortunate that there is not space here to consider Paul under this rubric, but see now Jennifer Eyl, *Signs, Wonders, and Gifts: Divination in the Letters of Paul* (Oxford: Oxford University Press, 2019).

27 The battle is an interesting one: from Mark's perspective, Jesus has all the advantages as he is repeatedly and directly affirmed by God himself. But such direct affirmation in fact is indicative of a weakness: the structures by which such divine affirmation is normally indicated are all in the hands of his opponents.

28 I continue to be influenced by the intriguing discussion in Elizabeth Struthers Malbon, *Narrative Space and Mythic Meaning in Mark* (San Francisco: Harper and Row, 1986).

29 Note that Mark's John the Baptist is *exactly* the same kind of character, moving a ritual performance (baptism) whose function is identical to a temple function (forgiveness of sins) into non-sanctified space, and doing so as a self-authorized solo act. John is as much a "magician" as Jesus. This similarity in being unauthorized is cited by Jesus quite explicitly in Mark 11:27–30, and as a defence of his own authority: if you want to know how *I* am authorized, Jesus says, figure out how *John* was authorized.

30 It is notable, once again, how this assertion is buttressed with a "magical" action, in this case, an exorcism. 1:22 asserts Jesus's teaching *authority*; 1:23–6 describes a "magical" exorcism; 1:27 stresses the *authority* of Jesus to command demons.

31 See now, classically, John S. Kloppenborg, "*Evocatio Deorum* and the Date of Mark," *Journal of Biblical Literature* 124, no. 3 (2005): 419–50. In my understanding of Mark, I am drawing from, especially, Burton L. Mack, *A Myth of Innocence: Mark and Christian Origins* (Philadelphia: Fortress Press, 1988).

32 William E. Arnal, "The Gospel of Mark as Reflection on Exile and Identity," in *Introducing Religion: Essays in Honor of Jonathan Z. Smith*, ed. Willi Braun and Russell T. McCutcheon (London: Equinox, 2008), 57–67.

33 Josephus does something strikingly similar when he describes anticipatory omens of the temple's destruction, especially omens that imply God's abandonment.

34 In the case of Acts, one can *almost* feel comfortable calling them "Christians."

35 I do not mean "Christianity" but, rather, something like "the rites of the Judean God undertaken by Gentiles."

36 For the very thin line between wandering philosophers (or school-founders) and magicians, see, among many others, Ramsay MacMullen, *Enemies of the Roman Order: Treason, Unrest, and Alienation in the Empire* (Cambridge, MA: Harvard University Press, 1966), 95–127.

37 Again, it is on this point that I depart quite significantly from Crossan, *Historical Jesus*, especially 313–18, in which demonic possession is characterized as a reflection of "the almost schizoid position of a colonial people" (317). This may be so (although it is difficult to see why colonial domination must be the single cause of such a condition), but the actual causes of possession need not be related or coordinated with the causes for, or intentions behind, or contemporary interpretation of, exorcism. If anything, Jesus as exorcist *deprives* the "little tradition" of a source for its most radical objections to the status quo.

38 Cf. David Frankfurter, "Beyond Magic and Superstition," 255–84, in *A People's History of Christianity: Late Ancient Christianity*, vol. 2, ed. Virginia Burrus (Minneapolis: Fortress Press, 2005), 269: "it seems useful to begin to speak more of a local religion, embracing the concentric worlds of village, region, and district, than a popular religion, dependent on notions of 'elite' or 'educated' religion that tend to say more about the prejudices of the observer than the phenomenon observed."

39 Frankfurter, "Beyond Magic," 269. I want to reserve some possibility of making distinctions – albeit nuanced, detailed, and relational ones – between elite discourses and activities and non-elite.

40 On which see John S. Kloppenborg, "Literary Convention, Self-Evidence and the Social History of the Q People," in *Early Christianity, Q and Jesus (= Semeia 55)*, ed. John S. Kloppenborg and Leif E. Vaage (Atlanta, GA: Scholars Press, 1992), 77–102; William E. Arnal, *Jesus and the Village Scribes: Galilean Conflicts and the Setting of Q* (Minneapolis: Fortress Press, 2001); Sarah Rollens, *Framing Social Criticism in the Jesus Movement: The Ideological Project in the Sayings Gospel Q*, WUNT 2 (Tübingen: Mohr Siebeck, 2014); Giovanni Bazzana, *Kingdom of Bureaucracy: The Political Theology of Village Scribes in the Sayings Gospel Q*, BETL (Leuven: Peeters, 2014).

41 I quite deliberately refrain from erecting a distinction between political and religious functionaries.

42 Crossan, *Historical Jesus*, 303–4, claims that Jesus's use of magic served to *undermine* patronage relationships. Horsley, *Jesus and Magic*, 84–5, quite rightly criticizes this view, noting that anthropological studies of magic such as Bryan R. Wilson, *Magic and the Millennium: A Sociological Study of Religious Movements of Protest among Tribal and Third World Peoples* (New York: Harper and Row, 1973) have shown that magic operates within, and develops, relationships and networks of patronage.

14

Spontaneous or Solicited? A Methodological Problem in the Study of Ancient Near Eastern Prophecy as Divination

Ryan D. Schroeder

The question "*spontaneous or solicited?*" arises from a major shift in the way that scholars of ancient Israelite religion approach the categories "prophecy" and "divination." Throughout the nineteenth and most of the twentieth century, biblical scholars drew a sharp distinction between prophecy and divination. The theoretical separation of these two practices rested equally on biblical polemics against "foreign" divinatory practices (e.g., Deut 18:9–22; 1 Sam 15:22–3; Isa 2:6) and on the categorical distinction between "magic" and "religion" that pervaded the academic study of religion in its formative years. Early biblical scholars constructed an ideal image of the prophet as an inspired spokesman for God, someone compelled to speak whatever and whenever the deity had a message for his people. The great prophetic tradition of Israelite religion stood in stark contrast to the divinatory practices of the heathen, magic-oriented civilizations of the ancient Near East.[1] Whereas the other nations anxiously sought answers from the stars and using extispicy, Israel rested easy with the knowledge that Yahweh chose to reveal through his specially commissioned prophets.

By the end of the twentieth century, the purported divide between Israelite prophecy and pagan divination became increasingly difficult to maintain. First, the discovery and publication of cuneiform texts from the Old Babylonian kingdom of Mari (Tell Ḥarīri, in modern Syria) and from the Neo-Assyrian capital Nineveh (Kouyunjik, in modern Iraq) revealed that prophecy was not a uniquely Israelite phenomenon.[2] Rather, Israelite prophecy represents a local expression of a wider ancient west Asian oracular tradition. Second, from the 1980s onward, scholars interested in the social function of prophecy recognized that the prophetic roles described in the Hebrew Bible have close parallels in the divinatory practices attested across a range of cultures, both ancient and modern.[3] Like other forms of divination, prophecy provides humans with information from suprahuman sources. Accordingly, contemporary scholarship treats prophecy as one mantic modality among many.[4] Applying the label "divination" to prophecy has facilitated new ways of thinking about oracle giving in ancient west Asian societies, yet one aspect of the old construct still stands in need of re-examination: the spontaneity that has been associated with prophecy.

In this chapter, I first revisit early biblical scholarship's aversion to oracular consultations. Although the Hebrew Bible depicts numerous oracular consultations, modern scholars – armed with the distinction between "religion" and "magic" – have historically treated such depictions as unimportant in comparison with the spontaneous oracles of the so-called "classical" prophets. Next, I briefly review the evidence for oracular consultation in ancient Israel, with the help of a few scholars who have acknowledged in various ways the likelihood that oracles were regularly solicited. I then turn to the concept of "divination" and explain why inquiry should be considered integral to this category of human activity. Finally, I return to the idea of spontaneous prophecy and suggest that, although this was not the primary mode of Israelite oracle giving, it is not purely an invention of modern scholars.

THE STUDY OF RELIGION AND ORACULAR CONSULTATION IN ANCIENT ISRAEL

Even though the Hebrew Bible depicts numerous oracular consultations, early biblical scholars treated spontaneity as a defining characteristic of prophetic revelation and tended to regard the solicitation of oracles as an insignificant feature of ancient Israelite religion. It seems the Hebrew Bible's depictions of oracular consultations posed a threat to the ideal of spontaneous prophecy, and thus scholars posited a sharp division between the quasi-magical, divination-like oracular consultation and the spontaneous prophecy of Israelite religion.[5] Harry Orlinsky's treatment of oracle giving in the Hebrew Bible is illustrative. Orlinsky distinguishes between two distinct types of oracle giver in ancient Israel.[6] The classical prophets like Amos, Isaiah, and Jeremiah spoke unsolicited words from Yahweh, while the preclassical seer could be consulted to deliver suprahuman information.[7] Moreover, the seer was a magician of sorts, working miracles and telling fortunes for a fee. According to Orlinsky, the seer inhabited the earliest stages of Israelite history, playing an ever-diminishing role until he was ultimately replaced by the classical prophet. In sharp contrast, the prophet "unreservedly opposed divination and miracle-making in every form"; he did not predict the future but merely proclaimed Israel's covenant with God; and, unlike the seer, he received no remuneration for his revelations.[8]

The proclivity of early biblical scholars to cast aspersions on ancient oracular diviners cannot be disentangled from broader trends in the early study of religion. Rannfrid I. Thelle is probably correct in suggesting that the scholarly neglect of texts depicting oracular consultations results from the influence of a Protestant preference for the proclaimed "Word of God" over and against ritual practice.[9] At the same time, while the religious inclinations of modern scholars certainly contributed to the construction of spontaneous prophecy, a theoretical distinction between magic and religion also played a role. Significantly, Orlinsky's seer and prophet clearly echo figures in Max Weber's typology of religious authority. In *The Sociology of Religion*, Weber identifies three ideal "types" of religious expert, based on their social functions and ritual praxis: the priest, the magician, and the prophet.[10] The *priest*, for Weber, serves a religious constituency by maintaining on its behalf harmonious relations with the divine through formal, regular worship. He maintains "the continuous operation of a cultic enterprise" and receives consistent remuneration for services rendered to the community. His authority rests in the established, socially recognized office that he holds.[11] The *magician*, by contrast, is a self-employed practitioner of "magical" arts. Unlike the priest, the magician derives his authority from "personal gifts (charisma) made manifest in miracle and revelation."[12] Also unlike the priest, the magician works for private, paying clients as needs arise, and he coerces suprahuman beings into action.[13] Weber's *prophet* is a founder or reviver of a religion. Unlike priestly authority, prophetic authority derives not from any formal association with a cultic establishment but, rather, from personal charisma, or a unique "call" from the divine. At times, the prophet may perform authenticating miracles, like those of the magician. "Unlike the magician, however, the prophet claims definite revelations, and the core of his mission is doctrine or commandment, not magic."[14] In other words, the "proclamation of a religious truth" sets the prophet apart from the magician, who deals instead with practical, local, and temporary concerns.[15] And while priests maintain the cultic status quo, the prophet promotes radical social change, either by ostensibly returning to a long-lost religion or by founding an altogether new one. Finally, whereas the priest and the magician receive payment in exchange for their engagement with the suprahuman, the "typical prophet propagates ideas for their own sake and not for fees."[16]

Table 14.1
Weber's typology of religious authority

	Priest	*Magician*	*Prophet*
Activity	cult/worship	sorcery/magic	proclamation
Social sphere	official cult	private	public
Legitimization	established office	charisma/miracles	"call"/charisma/ miracles
Relation to suprahuman	worship	coercion	channel (of a message)
Time frame	regular/cyclical	occasional/ on demand	continual
Remuneration	employed	self-employed	non-remunerated
Expertise	traditional knowledge	traditional knowledge	revealed knowledge

Weber's typology (see table 14.1) is an influential modern attempt to classify the diverse social and religious phenomena of *particular* societies according to *universal* categories of human experience. This approach has been immensely popular in the study of religion, including the field of biblical studies.[17] Armed with scientific typologies and theoretical descriptions of social actors, early biblical scholars argued (or rather, presupposed) that the practice of eliciting oracles was *categorically* distinct from the work of the Hebrew prophet. When Orlinsky separates the seer from the Israelite prophet, he clearly has in view the kind of distinction that Weber draws between the magician and the prophet (see table 14.2).[18] Like Weber's magician, Orlinsky's seer plies a mantic/magical trade, offering oracles to paying customers outside the aegis of an official cultic institution. By contrast, the prophet, for Weber and Orlinsky alike, is an individualist who proclaims a divinely revealed message and shuns earthly reward. Although Weber's typology of religious authority remains a relevant analytic for the study of oracle giving and other forms of "religious" activity, it is not without problems.[19] Notably, the modern distinction between "magic" and "religion" is rooted in a thoroughly racist account of human evolution.

Influenced by European colonial encounters with so-called "savage" societies and a (mis)application of evolutionary theory to the study of human culture, early practitioners of religious studies imagined evolutionary timelines in which a period of "primitive" (i.e., New World, "Oriental," etc.) magic precedes superior, "civilized" (i.e., Christian/European) religion (which may, in turn, transition to a modern, "scientific" worldview).[20] Thus,

Table 14.2
Orlinsky's seer and prophet

Seer	*Prophet*
Induced ecstasy	Entered ecstasy spontaneously
Belonged to a professional guild	Was individualistic
Practised a learned craft	Had no (human) mentor
Received payment	Took no payment
Predicted the future ("fore-teller")	Opposed future prediction ("forth-teller")
Performed miracles	Performed no miracles
Was a "man of action"	Was a "man of words"

it is no surprise that many early biblical scholars made sense of Israelite prophecy in terms of a progression from "magic" to "religion." For example, in *Prophecy and Divination among the Hebrews and Other Semites* (1938), Alfred Guillaume describes the transition from "magician-prophets" to classical prophets using overtly Darwinian language: "Finding in the old ways means to secure a livelihood, [the 'magician-prophet'] took the line of least resistance. He never made the forward movement in religious evolution which would have carried him on to the higher plane of ethical monotheism … Biologically the organism must either perish or for ever remain inferior. Spiritually and morally the same may be said of men who fail to reach out to the highest truth which is available to them."[21] For Guillaume, Israel's pre-classical "magician-prophets" contented themselves with miracle working and oracle giving for hire. They *failed* to "reach out to the highest truth" and, like a maladaptive species, went extinct. Meanwhile, the classical prophets, by yielding only to the divine initiative, were "carried … on to the higher plane." Oracular consultation was a primitive, magical practice superseded by the unsolicited oracle giving of the more highly evolved, and thus "spiritually and morally" superior, classical prophets. In Guillaume's estimation, "the great moments of revelation came not at man's but at God's initiative," and this spontaneity was crucial for Israel's religious evolution.[22]

While Orlinsky expressly rejects the evolutionary approach reflected in Guillaume's work, he retains the hierarchy between religion and magic, associating spontaneous prophecy with the former and oracular consultation with the latter.[23] Orlinsky is explicit about the matter when he claims that classical prophecy "reflects a far more sublimated moral and religious experience, free from the least trace of magic."[24] That is to say, the Hebrew Bible's prophetic literature represents a religious experience "more sublimated" (i.e., elevated, lofty, exalted) than the base practice of eliciting oracles for anxious commoners. A similar approach appears when Yehezkel Kaufmann describes oracle giving as a spontaneous phenomenon in *The Religion of Israel from Its Beginnings to the Babylonian Exile* (1960).[25] For Kaufmann, Israelite prophets were utterly different from non-Israelite dispensers of suprahuman knowledge, for their revelation "was never cultivated or induced."[26] As for oracular replies to human queries in ancient Israel, these represent a divine concession that was eventually rendered obsolete by the full realization of classical prophecy.[27] This tendency to push oracular consultation to the periphery and to regard (spontaneous) "classical prophecy" as representative of authentic Israelite religion can be seen throughout early scholarship.[28]

By the end of the twentieth century, scholars of religion generally rejected such a dichotomous approach to magic and religion. Most recognize that the differences supposed to distinguish magical from religious ritual – if such exist – relate to perceptions of alterity, group boundaries, and socio-religious polemics more than they reflect the actual phenomena under investigation.[29] The fact that biblical scholars now classify prophecy as a form of divination is one consequence of this dissolution of the magic/religion binary. Nevertheless, even as prophecy is now studied as a form of divination, it has continued to be regarded as spontaneous. The idea that oracles are given on the deity's whim appears, for example, in the entry on "Ancient Near Eastern Prophecy" in *The Anchor Bible Dictionary*, which construes prophecy "as inspired speech at the initiative of a divine power."[30] More recently, it has again been suggested that prophets in ancient west Asia "had to wait until the deity chose to communicate with humans."[31] However, the spontaneous prophecy paradigm can be challenged on both empirical and theoretical grounds.

ELICITING ORACLES IN ANCIENT ISRAEL

Although modern scholars have tended to imagine prophecy as involving oracles given at the deity's initiative, some have acknowledged that oracles at times constituted answers to queries, or at least were given in response to prompts. Usually, the solicitation of oracles has been associated with cultic settings such as the Jerusalem temple. This idea informs Sigmund Mowinckel's claim that cultic prophecy underlies much of the material preserved within the biblical psalter. To be sure, Mowinckel assumes the spontaneity of prophecy, as illustrated by his characterization of the Israelite prophets as "Yahweh's messengers who stepped forward with concise, spontaneous, topical, brief messages from Yahweh in a concrete situation."[32] Yet he situates this spontaneity within the context of cultic ritual, asserting that "the *nebi'im* knew of technical means that could induce rapture. Its form is naturally a free, unsought, momentary inspiration."[33] Paradoxically, oracular speech could be simultaneously induced *and* spontaneous as part of the liturgical rites performed within the temple. While Mowinckel's arguments relating the psalms to cult prophecy met with criticism, the idea that oracle givers operated within cultic contexts finds strong support both in biblical texts depicting such an association and in cuneiform texts that locate oracle giving in Mesopotamian temples.[34]

While prophets' affiliation with temple ritual merely implies some form of solicitation, a few texts explicitly describe efforts to induce prophetic speech. Taking his inspiration from I.M. Lewis's classic study, *Ecstatic Religion: A Study of Shamanism and Spirit Possession*,[35] Jonathan Stökl notes that "intuitive" divinatory methods such as prophecy typically involve specific techniques that allow practitioners to enter altered states of consciousness (or "ecstasy").[36] Stökl then observes several potential techniques of this kind in sources for ancient Israelite and Mesopotamian oracle giving and concludes that "triggers were used at least by certain individuals and in certain contexts, be they historical or literary."[37] Stökl still emphasizes the (perceived) divine prerogative in the oracular process, insisting that individual diviners had no way of guaranteeing a divine response, and he hesitates to suggest that oracles were ordinarily solicited in ancient Israel.[38] Nevertheless, by drawing attention to "triggers" for ecstasy, Stökl observes that the mental states associated with intuitive divination such as oracle giving could indeed be induced.[39]

Another reason for thinking that oracles were solicited in ancient Israel is the comparative evidence. Oracular consultation is a conspicuous feature of the mantic mindscape of ancient Greek authors.[40] Historically, sources from the Aegean have played a minimal role in the comparative study of Israelite prophecy, but this is a consequence of artificial disciplinary boundaries more than a reflection of historical realities. The ancient Mediterranean was an interconnected world, and there is strong evidence of religious and mythological exchange.[41] In light of the consultation that features so prominently in ancient sources describing Greek oracular practices,[42] it would be surprising if Israelite oracle givers were not also consulted for information from the deity. More commonly, the comparative study of prophecy sets biblical sources alongside cuneiform records from Mesopotamia. The genres of these sources, however, make it difficult to discern the precise origins of individual oracles. In many cases, the oracles may have been solicited, yet the circumstances of their delivery are not preserved as part of the written record. This is the case both with the letters from Mari and the edited oracle reports from Nineveh. At the same time, when these texts are read without the assumption that prophecy is spontaneous, it becomes possible to see hints that these oracles were given in response to ritual activities and/or consultations.[43] Moreover, it is noteworthy that in one of the few extant Mesopotamian narratives featuring prophecy,[44] an exiled Esarhaddon prays in desperation for help from the gods and receives favourable oracles in response.[45] In short, the evidence for oracle giving from elsewhere in the ancient Mediterranean and west Asia hardly supports the idea that prophecy in the ancient world was thought to be divinely initiated.

Finally, the Hebrew Bible itself contains roughly thirty narratives in which an individual approaches a prophet specifically to put a question to the deity or receives an oracle promptly after praying to the deity.[46] Noting the presence of such texts, Thelle breaks from the tendency to view prophecy as a spontaneous activity. She concludes that fielding queries for anxious clients is not merely "a subordinate type of prophetic activity" in ancient Israel and insists that the biblical depictions of oracular consultation reflect the lived experience of biblical writers.[47] Thelle observes that such texts follow a "script" or "pattern," despite their "different narrative thrusts and various particular characterizations of prophets."[48] She argues that even though it is impossible to reconstruct specific oracular consultations, the repetition of this scenario in literary settings in the Hebrew Bible points to an underlying sociohistorical phenomenon, a divinatory institution known by Hebrew scribes.[49] In support of Thelle's contention is the fact that the biblical references to oracular consultation do not belong to a single strain of literary tradition or definite historical period of composition (e.g., priestly, Deuteronomistic, prophetic, monarchic, exilic, etc.). Moreover, the language used to depict oracular consultations in biblical literature varies considerably.[50] The many and diverse references to prophetic inquiries thus point to an understanding of the mechanics of oracle giving that was common to multiple generations of Hebrew scribes with diverse theological and ideological interests. Moreover, the literary and linguistic character of the stories of solicited oracles in the Hebrew Bible suggests that oracular consultation was part of the mantic mindscape of the scribes. In addition, while past research failed to recognize or dismissed such evidence as marginal to the phenomenon of prophecy, the notion that consultation was integral to the historical practice of oracle giving in ancient Israel makes perfect sense when prophecy is categorized as divination.

DEFINING DIVINATION, PRODUCING PROPHECY

The assertion of early biblical scholars that Israelite prophecy was a spontaneous phenomenon stands at odds with the new scholarly paradigm that categorizes prophecy as divination. "Divination" is an analytical tool used to classify and compare a range of phenomena occurring across cultural, geographic, and temporal boundaries. I understand the term "divination" to refer to *any human activity aimed at accessing information from suprahuman sources in order to navigate immediate concerns.* My own formulation is not unique in maintaining that some kind of inquiry is intrinsic to the category. For example, Barbara Tedlock writes that "divination is a way of exploring the unknown in order to elicit answers (that is, oracles) to questions beyond the range of ordinary human understanding."[51] In *The Encyclopedia of Religion,* Evan M. Zuesse describes divination as "the art or practice of discovering the personal, human significance of future or, more commonly, present or past events. A preoccupation with the import of events and specific methods to discover it are found in almost all cultures."[52] Walter Burkert eloquently proposes that "divination may be described as a quest for epiphany beneath a misty surface."[53] Elsewhere, divination is defined as "any ritual and its associated tradition performed in order to ask a more-than-human intelligence for guidance,"[54] and "as an inquiry of the unknown, a tactic for making time cohere, a grammar for turning uncertainty into certainty and a communal procedure for procuring a warrant for a choice."[55] Judging from these and other definitions and descriptions,[56] it seems that the phenomena typically denoted by the word "divination" involve an active pursuit of suprahuman knowledge.[57]

I suggest that inquiry is a typical element in formal definitions of divination because it belongs to the very logic of divination. Several assumptions about the world underlie mantic practices. First, there are suprahuman sources of information that can help humans facing challenging situations. Such sources typically are "culturally postulated super-human beings" like deities, ancestors, and so on,[58] though sometimes they may be non-personal forces.[59] The crucial point is that information exists in cosmic realms (the heavens, the underworld, etc.) that are ordinarily inaccessible to humans, yet certain living, human members of society are capable of accessing and conveying knowledge from these suprahuman sources.[60] Thus, divinatory specialists mediate suprahuman knowledge in a consultative process that often involves payment in exchange for services rendered. This set of assumptions constitutes the logic of divination and explains a pattern of social interaction that is widely attested across human societies.

In so far as the label "divination" assumes a deliberate pursuit of suprahuman information, its application to Israelite oracle giving severely disrupts the old ideal of spontaneous prophecy. By calling prophecy "divination," scholars assert that prophecy shares key properties with other mantic modalities, with the point of comparison being a transfer of suprahuman information to humans. Like astrology, extispicy, tarot, and ouija boards, prophecy is understood by its practitioners to provide knowledge from another realm. I am arguing, however, for a more specific *tertium comparationis* (i.e., common element[61]) linking together the various mantic modalities, including prophecy: an *active pursuit* of suprahuman information. The "prophecy-as-divination" paradigm thus invites a redescription of Israelite prophecy that takes seriously the evidence for oracular consultation. As Nissinen notes, "prophecy" itself is a scholarly construct, a product of an academic project aimed at *re*constructing conceptually the historical practice of oracle giving in ancient Israelite society.[62] The construct of prophecy continually changes with the discovery of new sources, comparanda, and interpretive paradigms. Within this project, biblical texts depicting oracular consultations can no longer be dismissed as marginal, fringe, or ancillary to a supposedly primary mode of prophecy that relied on the deity's initiative.

FURTHER REFLECTIONS ON "SPONTANEOUS" PROPHECY

It is tempting to draw on the title of this volume and claim that early biblical scholars "invented" the image of a Hebrew prophet spontaneously speaking for the god of Israel: a *religious invention* both in the sense that it is an invented ancient religious specialist and in the sense that it is an invention inspired by the religious predilections of modern scholars. However, the old ideal of spontaneous prophecy does have a basis in biblical texts that depict the deity initiating revelation. To be sure, oracles were both spontaneous and solicited in ancient Israel. However, it is notable that spontaneity is emphasized through stock literary devices: the "call narrative" genre and the formulaic expression "the word of Yahweh came to PN."[63] Also, an impression of spontaneity is conveyed when the prophetic books present oracles completely detached from the concrete circumstances surrounding their origins. Thus the fact that the prophetic books are heavily edited, *scribal* products of the early Second Temple period[64] is significant for evaluating the spontaneity of Israelite prophecy.[65] Nissinen helpfully distinguishes between ancient Hebrew prophecy (the historical practice of oracle giving in ancient Palestine/Israel) and biblical prophecy (the Hebrew Bible's literary *representation*[*s*] of Israelite oracle giving).[66] Evidently, the amplification of spontaneity in the Hebrew Bible reflects a scribal ideal more than it does historical reality.

I conclude by proposing just two possible reasons for the scribal amplification of spontaneous oracle giving. One reason assumes a theological motivation. Diana V. Edelman suggests that scribes came to favour prophecy over other forms of divination because, from their perspective, it provided a channel for a transcendent deity *to initiate communication* with his people. She writes: "It might be worth considering if historically, ecstatics ever gave oracles in response to questions; if they had only served as mouthpieces for the divine when it chose to communicate something spontaneously, then the choice of this particular medium of revelation could also have been motivated by a desire to emphasize that Yahweh, the sole god, could not be consulted, manipulated, or held to a revealed course of action."[67] I am arguing that oracles were indeed given in response to questions, yet Edelman's observation regarding the connection between unsolicited oracles and an elevated view of divine agency remains relevant. By (re)casting oracle giving as a spontaneous phenomenon, scribes imagined a deity who dictates for himself the terms of his engagement with humans. If a transcendent deity helps to explain why scribes came to represent prophecy as spontaneous, however, there is still room for a second explanation of a more terrestrial sort. All cultures of the east Mediterranean and west Asia engaged in divinatory activities that involved the consultation of experts. The idea that Israelite diviners received oracles primarily on their deity's initiative thus set an imagined Israel apart from other peoples. The Deuteronomic proscription against certain forms of divination implies that oracle-giving is Yahweh's chosen method for communicating with his people (Deut 18:9–21; notably, in v. 15, Yahweh promises to take the initiative in "raising up" a prophet within Israel). Spontaneity thus differentiated Israelite oracle giving from the sorts of divination practiced by "foreign" nations. By contributing to a sense of the uniqueness of Israel, "spontaneous prophecy" did much the same thing for ancient scribes, then, as it did for modern scholars. However, this idealized, scribal view of prophecy should no longer be confused with the practice of oracle giving on the ground in ancient Israel. Like other diviners, ancient Israelite prophets offered suprahuman information not on divine but on human initiative.

NOTES

I am grateful to Sara Milstein, Ehud Ben Zvi, Rob Cousland, and Rannfrid Thelle for providing thoughtful comments and suggestions that have improved the quality of this chapter. I take sole responsibility for any errors or oversights that remain.

1 For example, William Robertson Smith, *Lectures on the Religion of the Semites: Second and Third Series*, ed. John Day, JSOTSS 183 (Sheffield: Sheffield Academic Press, 1995 [1890–91]), 56–8.

2 Jean-Marie Durand, *Archives Épistolaires de Mari I/1. Vol. 1*, Archives Royales de Mari 26 (Paris: Editions Recherche sur les Civilisations, 1988); Simo Parpola, *Assyrian Prophecies*, State Archives of Assyria 9 (Helsinki: Helsinki University Press, 1997); Martti Nissinen, *Prophets and Prophecy in the Ancient Near East*, 2nd ed., Writings from the Ancient World 12 (Atlanta: Society of Biblical Literature, 2019).

3 For example, Robert R. Wilson, *Prophecy and Society in Ancient Israel* (Philadelphia: Fortress Press, 1980); Thomas W. Overholt, *Channels of Prophecy: The Social Dynamics of Prophetic Activity* (Minneapolis: Fortress Press, 1989); Frederick H. Cryer, *Divination in Ancient Israel and Its Near Eastern Environment: A Socio-Historical Investigation*, JSOTSup 142 (Sheffield: Sheffield Academic Press, 1994); Lester L. Grabbe, *Priests, Prophets, Diviners, Sages: A Socio-Historical Study of Religious Specialists in Ancient Israel* (Valley Forge: Trinity Press, 1995); Grabbe, "Ancient Near Eastern Prophecy from an Anthropological Perspective," in *Prophecy in Its Ancient Near Eastern Context: Mesopotamian, Biblical, and Arabian Perspectives*, ed. Martti Nissinen, SBLSS 13 (Atlanta: Society of Biblical Literature, 2000), 13–32.

4 For example, Anne Marie Kitz, "Prophecy as Divination," *Catholic Biblical Quarterly* 65, no. 1 (2003): 22–42; Eva Cancik-Kirschbaum, "Prophetismus und Divination: Ein Blick auf die Keilschriftlichen Quellen," in *Propheten in Mari, Assyrien und Israel*, ed. Matthias Köckert and Martti Nissinen, FRLANT 201 (Göttingen: Vandenhoeck & Ruprecht, 2003), 33–53; Martti Nissinen, "What Is Prophecy? An Ancient Near Eastern Perspective," in *Inspired Speech: Prophecy in the Ancient Near East – Essays in Honor of Herbert B. Huffmon*, ed. John Kaltner and Louis Stulman, JSOTSS 378 (London: T&T Clark International, 2004), 17–37; Nissinen, "Prophecy and Omen Divination: Two Sides of the Same Coin," in *Divination and Interpretation of Signs in the Ancient World*, ed. Amar Annus (Chicago: Oriental Institute of the University of Chicago, 2010), 341–51; Nissinen, *Ancient Prophecy: Near Eastern, Biblical, and Greek Perspectives* (Oxford: Oxford University Press, 2017); JoAnn Scurlock, "Prophecy as a Form of Divination; Divination as a Form of Prophecy," in *Divination and Interpretation of Signs in the Ancient World*, ed. Amar Annus, Oriental Institute Seminars 6 (Chicago: Oriental Institute of the University of Chicago, 2010), 277–316; Jason Radine, *The Book of Amos in Emergent Judah*, Forschungen Zum Alten Testament 45 (Tübingen: Mohr Siebeck, 2010); Jonathan Stökl, *Prophecy in the Ancient Near East: A Philological and Sociological Comparison*, Culture and History of the Ancient Near East 56

(Leiden: Brill, 2012); Stökl, "A Royal Advisory Service: Prophecy and the State in Mesopotamia," in *Enemies and Friends of the State: Ancient Prophecy in Context*, ed. Christopher A. Rollston (University Park: Eisenbrauns, 2018), 87–114; Esther J. Hamori, "The Prophet and the Necromancer: Women's Divination for Kings," *Journal of Biblical Literature* 132, no. 4 (2013): 827–43; Hamori, *Women's Divination in Biblical Literature: Prophecy, Necromancy, and Other Arts of Knowledge* (New Haven: Yale University Press, 2015).

5 Esther Hamori eloquently shows how the old distinction between prophecy and divination results from facile readings of certain tendentious biblical texts, on the one hand, and a scholarly division between religion and magic, on the other hand ("The Prophet and the Necromancer," 827–8; see also Ann Jeffers, *Magic and Divination in Ancient Palestine and Syria*, SHCANE 8 [Leiden: Brill, 1996]; Jeffers, "Interpreting Magic and Divination in the Ancient Near East," *Religion Compass* 1, no. 6 [2007]: 684–94; Jeffers, "Magic from before the Dawn of Time: Understanding Magic in the Old Testament – A Shift in Paradigm [Deuteronomy 18.9–14 and Beyond]," in *A Kind of Magic: Understanding Magic in the New Testament and Its Religious Environment*, ed. Michael Labahn and L.J. Lietaert Peerbolte [New York: T&T Clark, 2007], 123–32). Sarah Iles Johnston shows that early scholarship on Greek and Roman religion tended to place "divination" somewhere between "magic" and "religion" ("Introduction: Divining Divination," in *Mantikê: Studies in Ancient Divination*, ed. Sarah Iles Johnston and Peter T. Struck, Religions in the Graeco-Roman World 155 [Leiden: Brill, 2005], 1–28). While classicists associated divination more closely with magic, divination nevertheless failed to elicit quite the same negative evaluations.

6 H.M. Orlinsky, *Ancient Israel* (Ithaca: Cornell University Press, 1954), 143–8; [Leiden: Brill, 2005]; Orlinsky, "The Seer in Ancient Israel," *Oriens Antiquus* 4 (1965): 153–74.

7 Orlinksy, "Seer," 154–5.

8 Ibid., 156–8, 168. Orlinsky sets the distinction in bold terms: "the seer was the person to whom people came for advice, to help them in problems that a mere mortal, without special access to God, could not solve. For these services the seer was paid. One cannot imagine an Amos, or a Jeremiah, or a Deutero-Isaiah being approached thus and making a living in this manner" (156).

9 Rannfrid I. Thelle, "Reflections of Ancient Israelite Divination in the Former Prophets," in *Israelite Prophecy and the Deuteronomistic History: Portrait, Reality, and the Formation of a History*, ed. Mignon R. Jacobs and Raymond F. Person, Jr, Ancient Israel and Its Literature 14 (Atlanta: Society of Biblical Literature, 2013), 9, 23.

10 Max Weber, *The Sociology of Religion*, trans. Ephraim Fischoff (Boston: Beacon Press, 1993 [1922]), 20–31, 46–59.

11 Ibid., 28–30.

12 Ibid., 29.

13 Ibid., 28.

14 Ibid., 47.

15 Ibid., 54.

16 Ibid., 47–8.

17 Joseph Blenkinsopp, *A History of Prophecy in Israel*, 2nd ed. (Louisville: Westminster John Knox Press, 1996), 35; Steve Cook, "The Weberian Construct of Prophecy and Feminist Recuperative Criticism," in *Constructs of Prophecy in the Former and Latter Prophets and Other Texts*, ed. Lester L. Grabbe and Martti Nissinen (Atlanta: Society of Biblical Literature, 2011), 65–75.

18 Orlinsky makes no explicit reference to Weber in his treatment of the seer and the prophet, yet the striking similarities in Weber's magician and Orlinsky's seer, in contrast to the prophet, point to the shared theoretical assumptions of these scholars.

19 See, for example, Lars Kirkhusmo Pharo, "A Methodology for a Deconstruction and Reconstruction of the Concepts 'Shaman' and 'Shamanism,'" *Numen* 58, no. 1 (2011): 10–17.

20 See, for example, Edward B. Tylor, *Primitive Culture: Researches into the Development of Mythology, Philosophy, Religion, Art and Custom* (London: John Murray, 1871), 2:101–2, 327. One of the most influential articulations of this kind of schema appears in Sir James George Frazer's *The Golden Bough*, which was revised and expanded several times between 1890 and 1915 (see Sir James George Frazer, *The Golden Bough: A Study in Magic and Religion*, 3rd ed., 12 vols [London: Macmillan and Co., 1907–15]).

21 Alfred Guillaume, *Prophecy and Divination among the Hebrews and Other Semites: The Bampton Lectures 1938* (London: Harper and Brothers Publishers, 1938), 110–11, see also 57.

22 Guillaume, *Prophecy and Divination*, 94–7.

23 Orlinsky, "Seer," 170, writes, "divination nowhere developed into prophecy, no more than polytheism developed into monotheism … Divination was a common Ancient Near Eastern phenomenon; prophecy is a uniquely Israelite phenomenon, no less so than monotheism."

24 Orlinsky, *Ancient Israel*, 148, see also 146.

25 Yehezkel Kaufmann, *The Religion of Israel from Its Beginnings to the Babylonian Exile*, trans. Moshe Greenberg (Chicago: University of Chicago Press, 1960). The work was originally published in Hebrew as תולדות האמונה הישראלית: מימי קדם עד סוף בית שני in eight volumes between 1937 and 1956.

26 Kaufmann, *Religion of Israel*, 101. Like Orlinsky, Kaufmann rejects an evolutionary understanding of Israelite religion, yet he nevertheless describes prophecy as something that replaced earlier Hebrew mantic practices: "The clairvoyant, the 'seer,' possessing a personal charism, is replaced by the prophet, the servant of God. In place of the diviner and interpreter of signs appears the messenger of God who proclaims his will. This change is coeval with the monotheistic transformation of ancient Hebrew religion" (*Religion of Israel*, 215).

27 Kaufmann, *Religion of Israel*, 276–7.

28 For example, Georg Heinrich A. Ewald, *The Prophets of the Old Testament*, trans. J.F. Smith (Edinburgh: Williams and Norgate, 1875–1881), 1:7, 11, 19, 51, etc.;

Smith, *Religion of the Semites*, 55–8; Morris Jastrow, Jr, "Rô'ēh and Ḥôzēh in the Old Testament," *Journal of Biblical Literature* 28, no. 1 (1909): 42–56; Bernhard Duhm, *Israels Propheten* (Tübingen: Mohr Siebeck, 1916); George A. Barton, *Archaeology and the Bible*, 6th ed. (Philadelphia: American Sunday School Union, 1933), 521–4; Georg Fohrer, *History of Israelite Religion* (Nashville: Abingdon, 1972), 237; Burke O. Long, "The Effect of Divination upon Israelite Literature," *Journal of Biblical Literature* 92 (1973): 489–97; Siegfried Herrmann, *Ursprung and Funktion Der Prophetie Im Alten Israel*, Rheinische-Westfalische Akademie Der Wissenschaften 208 (Opladen: Westdeutscher, 1976); Menahem Haran, "From Early to Classical Prophecy: Continuity and Change," *Vetus Testamentum* 27, no. 4 (1977): 385–97.

29 For example, E.E. Evans-Pritchard, *Theories of Primitive Religion* (Oxford: Oxford University Press, 1965), 5–9, 108–12; Randall Styers, *Making Magic: Religion, Magic, and Science in the Modern World* (Oxford: Oxford University Press, 2004); Matteo Benussi, "Magic," *The Cambridge Encyclopedia of Anthropology* (2019), 1–16.

30 Herbert B. Huffmon, "Ancient Near Eastern Prophecy," in *The Anchor Bible Dictionary*, ed. David Noel Freedman (New York: Doubleday, 1992), 5:477. See also Jean-Marie Durand, "Les Prophéties Des Textes de Mari," in *Oracles et Prophéties Dans l'Antiquité: Actes Du Colloque de Strasbourg 15–17 Juin 1995*, ed. Jean-Georges Heintz, Travaux Du Centre Recherche Sur Le Proche-Orient et La Grèce Antiques 15 (Paris: De Boccard, 1997), 117–20; Abraham Malamat, *Mari and the Bible*, Studies in the History and Culture of the Ancient Near East 12 (Leiden: Brill, 1998), 84. Elsewhere, Huffmon concedes that in some cases oracles may have been given in response to specific queries, though he concludes that "many of the Ancient Near Eastern prophetic oracles were apparently initiated by the deity rather than being responses to a specific inquiry" (Herbert B. Huffmon, "The Oracular Process: Delphi and the Near East," *Vetus Testamentum* 57 [2007]: 449–60, 455–6).

31 Stökl, "Royal Advisory Service," 90.

32 Sigmund Mowinckel, *The Spirit and the Word: Prophecy and Tradition in Ancient Israel*, ed. K.C. Hanson (Minneapolis: Fortress Press, 2002), 36. These arguments appear originally in Sigmund Mowinckel, "The 'Spirit' and the 'Word' in the Pre-Exilic Reforming Prophets," *Journal of Biblical Literature* 53 (1934): 199–227; and Mowinckel, *Prophecy in Israel*, trans. James Schaff, SVAO (Philadelphia: Fortress Press, 1982 [1922]).

33 Mowinckel, *Spirit and the Word*, 114.

34 For example, John W. Hilber, "Psalm CX in the Light of Assyrian Prophecies," *Vetus Testamentum* 53 (2003): 353–66; Hilber, *Cultic Prophecy in the Psalms* (Berlin: Walter de Gruyter, 2005); Hilber, "Cultic Prophecy in Assyria and in the Psalms," *Journal of the American Oriental Society* 127 (2007): 29–40; Hilber, "Royal Cultic Prophecy in Assyria, Judah, and Egypt," in *"Thus Speaks Ishtar of Arbela": Prophecy in Israel, Assyria and Egypt in the Neo-Assyrian Period*, ed. Robert P. Gordon and Hans M. Barstad (Winona Lake: Eisenbrauns, 2013); Martti Nissinen, "The Ritual

Aspect of Prophecy," in *Prophecy and Its Cultic Dimensions*, ed. Lena-Sofia Tiemeyer, Journal of Ancient Judaism Supplements 31 (Göttingen: Vandenhoeck & Ruprecht, 2019), 101–14; Nissinen, *Ancient Prophecy*; Nissinen, *Prophets and Prophecy*; Lester L. Grabbe, "Cultic Prophecy *Déjà vu*," in *Prophecy and Its Cultic Dimensions*, ed. Lena-Sofia Tiemeyer, Journal of Ancient Judaism Supplements 31 (Göttingen: Vandenhoeck & Ruprecht, 2019), 39–49. From Greece to Mesopotamia to Judah, oracle givers in cultic sites experienced ecstatic mental states and spoke for the gods. Nissinen writes, "the huge time-span covering the Old Babylonian, Middle-Assyrian, Neo-Assyrian, Neo-Babylonian, and Seleucid period speaks volumes about the persistence of the presence of the prophets in Mesopotamian temples" (Nissinen, *Ancient Prophecy*, 222). According to Greek literary sources and epigraphic evidence, oracle giving took place in sanctuaries devoted to the purpose (Nissinen, *Ancient* Prophecy, 230–5, 280–2. See also Huffmon, "Oracular Process," 449–60).

35 I.M. Lewis, *Ecstatic Religion: A Study of Shamanism and Spirit Possession*, 3rd ed. (London: Routledge, 2003 [1971]).

36 Jonathan Stökl, "Ready or Not, Here I Come: Triggering Prophecy in the Hebrew Bible," in *Prophecy and Its Cultic Dimensions*, ed. Lena-Sofia Tiemeyer, Journal of Ancient Judaism Supplements 31 (Göttingen: Vandenhoeck & Ruprecht, 2019), 115–33.

37 Stökl, "Ready or Not," 133. For example, Stökl considers music (1 Sam 10:5–6, 10–13; 2 Kgs 3:11–15; nos. 51 and 52 in Nissinen, *Prophets and Prophecy*), ritual slaughter (Numbers 23–24; 1 Kings 18), sleep (Num 22:8–9, 19–20; 1 Samuel 3), and certain beverages (no. 17 in Nissinen, *Prophets and Prophecy*; see also no. 22). To these methods of inducing revelation, we might add self-mutilation, fasting, and/or ecstatic dance (1 Kgs 18:28–9; no. 122 in Nissinen, *Prophets and Prophecy*; see Nissinen, *Ancient Prophecy*, 182). Nissinen discusses additional potential triggers in Greek sources, including certain noises and, at least in the case of the Delphic oracle, subterranean fumes (*Ancient Prophecy*, 198).

38 Several of the texts that Stökl examines involve practical queries: Numbers 22 (perhaps also Numbers 23–4); 1 Samuel 28; 1 Kings 22 (//1 Chr 18:6); 2 Kings 3, 22; while others seem to involve states of ecstasy with no definite oracular speech (e.g., 1 Samuel 10, 1 Kings 18, Numbers 11). Although Stökl recognizes that music accompanies oracular speech in a number of biblical texts (e.g., Exodus 15, Judges 5, and in Levitical music in the temple in 1 Chron 25:1–8), he insists that music was "not used as the trigger of prophetic activity but as the expression of prophetic activity" (Stökl, "Ready or Not," 123); Stökl disagrees with Hilber's conclusion that the psalms reflect the practice of oracular speech in the Jerusalem temple (Stökl, "Ready of Not," 127).

39 Similarly, Edelman suggests that various kinds of intuitive diviner may have offered oracular responses to queries, though she also speculates that "ecstatics" may have "only served as mouthpieces for the divine when it chose to communicate something spontaneously" (Diana Edelman, "From Prophets

to Prophetic Books: The Fixing of the Divine Word," in *The Production of Prophecy: Constructing Prophecy and Prophets in Yehud*, ed. Diana V. Edelman and Ehud Ben Zvi [London: Equinox, 2009], 31–4, 48).

40 Richard Stoneman, *The Ancient Oracles: Making the Gods Speak* (New Haven: Yale University Press, 2011), 13–15.

41 For example, Peter Walcot, *Hesiod and the Near East* (Cardiff: University of Wales Press, 1966); Martin L. West, *Hesiod: Theogony; Edited with Prolegomena and Commentary* (Oxford: Clarendon Press, 1966); West, *The East Face of Helicon: West Asiatic Elements in Greek Poetry and Myth* (Oxford: Clarendon Press, 1997); Carolina López-Ruiz, *When the Gods Were Born: Greek Cosmogonies and the Near East* (Cambridge: Harvard University Press, 2010).

42 See Nissinen, *Ancient Prophecy*, 230–5, 281–2.

43 For more on the solicitation of oracles in ancient Mesopotamia, see Ryan D. Schroeder, *Let Us Go to the Seer! Prophecy, Scribal Culture, and the Invention of Hebrew Scripture*, Beihefte zur Zeitschrift für die alttestamentliche Wissenschaft 563 (Berlin: De Gruyter, 2025).

44 Nin A; no. 97 in Nissinen, *Prophets and Prophecy*.

45 For more on the inscription, as well as its relationship to the Neo-Assyrian oracle reports, see Parpola, *Assyrian Prophecies*, lxviii–lxi; Martti Nissinen, *References to Prophecy in the Neo-Assyrian Sources*, State Archives of Assyria Studies 7 (Helsinki: The Neo-Assyrian Text Corpus Project, 1998), 58–61; Nissinen, *Ancient Prophecy*, 104; Manfred Weippert, *Götterwort in Menschenmund: Studien zur Prophetie in Assyrien, Israel und Juda*, Forschungen zur Religion und Literatur des Alten und Neuen Testaments 252 (Göttingen: Vandenhoeck & Ruprecht, 2014), 27–9; Andrew Knapp, *Royal Apologetic in the Ancient Near East*, Writings from the Ancient World Supplement Series 4 (Atlanta: SBL Press, 2015), 301–35.

46 Gen 25:22–3*; Exod 18:15–16; 33:7–8*; Num 9:6–14*; 15:32–6*; Lev 24:10–23*; Judg 4:4–5*; 1 Sam 9:5–10; 28:6* (see also 1 Chr 10:10, 14); 2 Sam 24:10–15, 17–25* (see also 2 Sam 21:1); 1 Kgs 14:1–18; 22:5–28 (//2 Chr 18:4–27); 2 Kgs 1:2–5; 3:11–27; 8:7–15; 13:14–19; 19:1–7*//Isa 37:2–7; 2 Kgs 19:14–37*//Isa 37:14–38; 2 Kgs 20:2–6//Isa 38:6//2 Chr 32:24; 2 Kgs 22:12–20 (//2 Chr 34:19–28); Jer 21:1–7; 23:34; 37:3–10, 17*; Ezek 14:3–10; 20:1–3, 31; Zech 7:3; 1 Chr 21:7–11*; 2 Chr 20:1–19*. Thelle's list of oracular inquiries (indicated above with asterisks) is more limited (Rannfrid I. Thelle, "דרש את־יהוה: The Prophetic Act of Consulting Yhwh in Jeremiah 21,2 and 37,7," *Scandinavian Journal of the Old Testament* 12, no. 2 [1998]: 254), and Nissinen's list only includes royal consultations (*Ancient Prophecy*, 289–90).

47 Thelle, "Prophetic Act," 255.

48 Thelle, "Reflections of Ancient Israelite Divination," 17, 18.

49 Ibid., 14.

50 The closest we get to a standard phrase or literary formula is the use of the verb דרש (to inquire, consult), which commonly denotes an act of divinatory inquiry. However, this verb is sometimes used in idiosyncratic ways (e.g., Gen 25:22; 2 Kgs

3:11; Exod 18:15–16; 1 Kgs 14:1–18; 22:5–28; 2 Kgs 8:8–15) or not at all (e.g., Exod 33:7–8; Num 9:6–14; 15:32–6; Lev 24:10–23; Judg 4:4–5; 1 Sam 28:6; 2 Sam 24:10–15, 17–25; Jer 23:34; 37:17). In view of this linguistic variety, it seems unlikely that oracular consultation was merely a stock feature of an ancient Hebrew storytelling repertoire.

51 Barbara Tedlock, "Divination as a Way of Knowing: Embodiment, Visualisation, Narrative, and Interpretation," *Folklore* 112, no. 2 (2001): 189. See also Michael Loewe and Carmen Blacker, ed., *Divination and Oracles* (London: George Allen and Unwin, 1981), 1, 39, 63.

52 Evan M. Zuesse, "Divination: An Overview," in *The Encyclopedia of Religion*, 2nd ed. (Detroit: Macmillan Reference USA, 2005), 4:2369.

53 Walter Burkert, "Signs, Commands, and Knowledge: Ancient Divination Between Enigma and Epiphany," in *Mantikê: Studies in Ancient Divination*, ed. Sarah Iles Johnston and Peter T. Struck, Religions in the Graeco-Roman World 155 (Leiden: Brill, 2005), 36. Burkert goes on to write that "there are spontaneous epiphanies too," though he implies that such phenomena are distinct from divinatory activity ("proclamations of piety do not eliminate the risks and uncertainties of existence. The drive to 'know more' remains").

54 Patrick Curry, *Divination: Perspectives for a New Millennium* (London: Routledge, 2010), i.

55 Evan Heimlich, "Darwin's Fortune, Jonah's Shipmates and the Persistence of Chance," in *Divination: Perspectives for a New Millennium*, ed. Patrick Curry (London: Routledge, 2010), 145.

56 See, for example, George K. Park, "Divination and Its Social Contexts," *Journal of the Royal Anthropological Institute of Great Britain and Ireland* 93, no. 2 (1963): 195–6; Jean-Pierre Vernant, "Parole et Signes Muets," in *Divination et Rationalité*, ed. Jean-Pierre Vernant (Paris: Éditions du Seuil, 1974), 9–10; Radine, *Book of Amos*, 83–5; Kim Beerden, *World Full of Signs: Ancient Greek Divination in Context*, Religions in the Graeco-Roman World 176 (Leiden: Brill, 2013), 19–21; Thelle, "Reflections of Ancient Israelite Divination," 25.

57 Hamori's cautious definition remains ambivalent regarding elicitation, perhaps in order to ensure that "spontaneous prophecy" may remain in the category: "Divination, however, is an umbrella term, which I will define as a type of action culturally understood to allow acquisition of knowledge otherwise restricted to the divine realm, whether through technical skill (e.g., extispicy or other omen reading) or the divine granting of special direct communication (e.g., spontaneous prophecy and some dreams or dream interpretation)" ("Prophet and the Necromancer," 828; Hamori, *Women's Divination*, 4).

58 Melford Spiro, "Religion: Problems of Definition and Explanation," in *Anthropological Approaches to the Study of Religion*, ed. Michael Banton (London: Routledge, 1966), 96.

59 Emily Martin Ahern, *Chinese Ritual and Politics* (Cambridge: Cambridge University Press, 1981), 50.

60 Nissinen, *Ancient Prophecy*, 12.
61 Oliver Freiberger, *Considering Comparison: A Method for Religious Studies* (Oxford: Oxford University Press, 2019), 104.
62 Nissinen, *Ancient Prophecy*, 4–6.
63 Call narratives appear, for example, in Exod 3:4–6, 10; 1 Sam 3:2–14; Amos 1:2; 3:8; Isa 6:8; 7:15; Jer 1:5; Ezek 2:1–5.
64 Ehud Ben Zvi, "The Concept of Prophetic Books and Its Historical Setting," in *The Production of Prophecy: Constructing Prophecy and Prophets in Yehud*, ed. Ehud Ben Zvi and Diana V. Edelman (London: Equinox, 2009), 73–95; M.H. Floyd, "The Production of Prophetic Books in the Early Second Temple Period," in *Prophets, Prophecy, and Prophetic Texts in Second Temple Judaism*, ed. M.H. Floyd and R.D. Haak, LHBOTS 427 (London: T&T Clark, 2006), 276–97; Nissinen, *Ancient Prophecy*, 150–1.
65 The notion that prophetic books should be understood as distinctly scribal products is one of the outcomes of a debate in the 1980s and 1990s over whether we should regard the creators of these texts to be "prophets" or "poets." For convenient access to the debate, see the collection of articles from the *Journal for the Study of the Old Testament* by Auld, Carroll, Williamson, Overholt, and Barstad (Philip R. Davies, ed., *The Prophets: A Sheffield Reader*, the Biblical Seminar 42 [Sheffield: Sheffield Academic Press, 1996]). See also Lester L. Grabbe, "Poets, Scribes, or Preachers? The Reality of Prophecy in the Second Temple Period," in *Prophets, Prophecy, and Prophetic Texts in Second Temple Judaism*, ed. Michael Floyd and Robert D. Haak (New York: T&T Clark, 2003), 192–215; Radine, *Book of Amos*, 103–8; Sara J. Milstein, "'Who Would Not Write?' The Prophet as Yhwh's Prey in Amos 3:3–8," *Catholic Biblical Quarterly* 75 (2013): 441–5.
66 Nissinen, "What Is Prophecy," 31.
67 Edelman, "From Prophets to Prophetic Books," 48.

15

Trauma, Meaning-Making, and Christian Identity Formation in Justin's *Dialogue with Trypho*

Kimberly B. Stratton

In his influential monograph, *Related Strangers: Jews and Christians 70–170* CE, Stephen G. Wilson grapples with the complex factors that contributed to the eventual separation of Jews and Christians into distinct and all too frequently antagonistic communities.[1] Steve's work on this topic is recognized for its nuanced insights and ability to weave together an analysis of historical, theological, and apologetic materials, including a robust engagement with scholars of rabbinic literature. Steve resisted simple explanations for what he understood to be complex and multifaceted processes that involved divergent theologies, social and political forces, internal competition, and lived experience in communities around the Mediterranean. His book continues to be a touchstone for subsequent studies of early Jewish-Christian relations.[2]

The conversation around Christian identity formation and the so-called parting of the ways with Judaism continued in the first decade of this century, energized by an influx of postmodern theory, which led scholars to interrogate essentializing labels such as "heresy," "Gnostic," "Christian," and even "Jewish" in ways that echoed Steve's critical and probing use of these terms a decade prior. Judith Lieu, for example, opens her book on Christian identity with the very same question that I engage in this chapter,[3] namely, how, when, and why did Christians first begin to self-identify as Christian and not as something else? "Perhaps what is most striking about [the trial episode in the Martyrdom of Polycarp] is the way that the terms 'Christian' (Χριστιανός) and 'Christianity' (Χριστιανισμός) are used without comment or explanation. At what point in the century or more since the death of Jesus and the earliest preaching of his followers did this become possible? How would not only outsiders but also those who claimed the epithet 'Christian' have understood the label, and how did the sense of being a Christian emerge?"[4]

Her study adroitly identifies, and avoids, the pitfalls of earlier investigations of Christian identity formation (including her own) in noting the tendency to essentialize Christianity as a "self-contained phenomenon" or as "fundamentally isolable and explicable in its own terms."[5] Lieu questions the anachronistic conception of identity in post-Enlightenment terms and an over-reliance on elite textual productions by situating them, and the ideological work they did to construct Christian identity, within a broader context of embodied space, place, gender, memory, and racial analogies. Daniel Boyarin's landmark book, *Border Lines: The Partition of Judaeo-Christianity*, similarly avoids essentializing Judaism and Christianity as mutually exclusive identities. Instead, he sees Christianity as initially a dialect "among others within Judaism that eventually broke off to become a distinct language."[6] Boyarin posits a crisis of identity experienced by gentile converts to Christianity, who no longer participated in their natal rites and customs but also did not observe those of the Jews. They were betwixt and between, experiencing psychological pressure to draw boundaries and define a new identity for themselves.[7] Self-appointed border-guards – heresiologists – started patrolling the boundaries of this new entity by defining who/what was in or out. In the process, heresiologists also produced the category religion.[8]

Other studies of Justin's *Dialogue with Trypho* have broadened our critical understanding of the dialogic nature of identity formation that, as Andrew Jacobs describes, is never complete but always in conversation with an Other – heretical, pagan, or Jewish – who is both internalized and externalized.[9] Laura Nasrallah identifies the spatializing rhetoric of early Christian writers, such as Justin, who reconfigures centre and periphery in his presentation of Christians as both a universal people (ἔθνος) and the true Israel, inheritors of the covenant promises and holy city, Jerusalem.[10] Denise Buell interrogates "ethnic reasoning" implicit in Christian assertions of being a new race (γένος) despite claims to universalism.[11] In all these studies, Christian identity formation is fingered as the primary focus and objective of Justin's *Dialogue*.[12] Other studies have situated the *Dialogue* in the context of religious competition. Justin felt an urgent need to persuade either gentiles or Jews to convert to Christianity before it was too late.[13]

Benefitting from the rich insights of previous scholarship, I take a different tack in this chapter. Focusing on a close reading of the opening scene that sets the stage for Justin's conversation with Trypho – who claims to be a refugee from the Bar Kokhba revolt (132–136 CE)[14] – I interrogate the role of Roman violence in provoking the debate and contouring Trypho's questions and Justin's replies. I propose that theodicy – an attempt to explain and justify the failed revolt against Rome – constitutes the immediate context and impetus for this dialogue: logos theology, supersessionism, and even the construction of a distinct Christian identity arise in response to accusations from Trypho and his friends that non-law-abiding followers of Jesus violated the covenant and provoked God's anger. This line of inquiry also raises questions about the separation of Christianity from Judaism at this point in history and undermines the notion that "Christian" identity even existed at the time of the initial conversation with Trypho.[15] Certainly, by the time the *Dialogue* was written, towards the end of Justin's life, over twenty years of theological distillation and fermentation had ensued: the extant version of the *Dialogue* reveals a significantly more developed response to Jewish accusations as well as to internal debates, including especially the one with Marcion, as many scholars have argued.[16]

TERMINOLOGY

Before moving to my argument, I want to address the problematic minefield posed by nomenclature in a study of this kind, which discusses concepts and terms that only begin to appear in the texts we are studying. As much as possible I try to avoid anachronistic essentializing of Christianity and Judaism, recognizing that these entities did not yet exist in the sense that we understand them today. Following Malcolm Lowe and Steve Mason, I regard "Judean" to be the best translation for Ἰουδαῖος in most cases where it indicates geoethnic identity.[17] In Justin's *Dialogue,* however, Ἰουδαῖοι appears consistently in contradistinction to Χριστιανοί (72.14, 16; 77.22; 80.25, 29),[18] indicating that it is no longer functioning as merely a geoethnic identity marker but is a foil for Justin's construction of Christians as the true Israel and inheritors of the covenant. In this case, Ἰουδαῖοι expresses what we commonly understand to be a religious identification best translated as "Jews."[19] Similarly, I avoid using the term "Christian" to speak of followers of Jesus (whether Judean or gentile) in the first and early second centuries except to translate or interpret texts in which the term Χριστιανός/οί appears. To speak of Jesus followers as Christian prior to their own self identification with this label anachronistically retrojects later identities and ideologies onto groups of Jesus people, who, as many scholars have rightfully noted, lacked a coherent or systematic belief system and shared doctrines.[20] Buell notes with regard to Justin's *Dialogue* that "English translations frequently supply 'Christian' and 'Jew'" where they do not appear in the Greek, "giving the impression that these categories are clearer and more widely used than they actually are."[21] Den Dulk uses the term "Christ-faiths" to describe these early groups of Jesus followers.[22] Since Χριστός translates the generic Hebrew term for an anointed servant of God (משיח), I prefer to specify Jesus as that figure for his followers and, hence, in this chapter I use various locutions, such as Jesus people, Jesus followers, and Jesus believers, to identify groups that regarded Jesus to be the anticipated messiah in some capacity, whether as a revealer of higher mysteries, apocalyptic Son of Man, interpreter of the law, prophet, or divine Son of God. It also underscores more clearly that "Christian" was originally a term applied specifically to and embraced by certain (mostly gentile) believers in Jesus but was not a universal term for all Jesus people. The label "Jewish-Christian" is thus an anachronistic neologism, as Annette Reed demonstrates.[23]

"CHRISTIAN" ORIGINS

The term "Christian" first begins to appear as a self-designation in the early to mid second century.[24] William Arnal describes the second-century invention of "Christianity" through a collation of texts and ideas into a consolidated tradition as "a second-century museum," which showcases artifacts from the first century to produce a unified identity among disparate groups of Jesus people. This process generated "Christianity" via second-century interpretive and authorizing practices.[25] Arnal's apt museum metaphor reveals the creative interpretive labour that writers in the second century performed and the resulting sleight of hand that conceals their artifice from centuries of subsequent interpreters, who accepted the curated presentation of Christian origins as reality. Building upon Arnal's argument, this chapter understands Christian identity to be only just crystallizing in texts like Justin's *Dialogue with Trypho*. I focus on the production of Christian identity in the *Dialogue* in response to what I perceive to be a debate over Deuteronomic theodicy and meaning-making in response to Rome's brutal suppression of the failed Bar Kokhba revolt. I tie assertions of Christian difference and identity to arguments spawned by the disastrous outcome of the war.

Justin is illuminating in this regard: he uses the term "Christian" sparingly in the first half of the *Dialogue* (17.10; 35.2; 44.3; 47.19) and in contexts that indicate it functioned as a derogatory third-party designation. David Horrell confirms this observation; he proposes a judicial origin for the word "Christian" in Roman courts and argues that the shame of persecution engendered a desire to recuperate the name Christian from its derogatory connotations.[26] Building upon Horrell, I focus on the embrace of this formerly derogatory label to assert a new identity distinct from Ἰουδαιοί, following the failed Bar Kokhba revolt. Rather than finger Bar Kokhba's presumed persecution of Jesus people, or the rejection of YHWH as a failed god,[27] I look to trauma and its impact on social formations to understand how the disastrous war prompted disparate responses and attempts to restore coherence – in the process, sundering social bonds and fostering diverging socio-religious identifications.

TRAUMA, MEANING-MAKING, AND SOCIAL COHERENCE

Social psychologists Travis Proulx and Michael Inzlicht describe physiological discomfort – namely, autonomic arousal and neurocognitive activation – that occurs after a "meaning violation." A meaning violation is triggered when expectations based on prior experience or beliefs about the world are violated, resulting in disequilibrium, dissonance, imbalance, and uncertainty.[28] Proulx and Inzlicht identify five types of palliative behaviours that enable individuals to restore coherence and continue functioning in a world they believe to make sense and to be consistent.[29] War and violence shatter a sense of security and order, provoking significant crises of meaning that demand explanations or justifications to restore coherence in the world. Bar Kokhbah's defeat in 136 CE constituted such a trauma not only for the loss of life but for the utter destruction of Jewish cultural presence in the land of Judea, which distinguished this war from the first Judeo-Roman war (66–70 CE). Although the destruction of Jerusalem and the temple in 70 CE was tragic, it did not lack precedent and many scholars have argued that Judeans, including Josephus, anticipated that the temple would be rebuilt.[30] Archaeological evidence from the interbellum period (70–132 CE) shows that the region around Jerusalem was rebuilt and that Jewish life returned more or less to normal in the decades following 70 CE. This is not the case after 136 CE; material evidence shows widespread destruction and lack of cultural continuity in the decades and centuries following Roman suppression of Judea.[31] The social breakdown of Judean society following the fall of Betar was not only profound but also unprecedented.

The psychological dissonance this war provoked was equally profound: the failed Bar Kokhba rebellion defied expectations that God would vindicate Judea and restore the temple following its destruction as he had restored the temple following the Babylonian conquest of 586 BCE.[32] Thus historical precedent and prophecy heightened expectations with disastrous consequences, raising profound questions about theodicy in the war's wake: Why did God allow this to happen? A close reading of Justin's *Dialogue with Trypho* suggests that the original conversation was prompted by disagreements concerning the meaning and cause of the war.[33] I read Trypho's criticisms and Justin's

Christological and supersessionist assertions as attempts to redress the cognitive dissonance caused by the war's tragic outcome. Explaining the tragedy, I propose, aggravated tensions that already existed between many Judeans and certain groups of Jesus followers, especially those who did not observe the covenantal obligations that were believed to ensure the safety and security of Judea.[34]

Proulx and Inzlicht explain individual responses to trauma and the pressing psychological need to restore meaning and a sense of coherence after a tragedy. Gilad Hirschberger illuminates collective trauma, which he defines as a "cataclysmic event that shatters the basic fabric of society,"[35] echoing Arthur Neal's work, which similarly highlights the breakdown of social cohesion and shared meaning in the wake of national trauma.[36] These social-psychological insights into trauma and its reverberations help us understand that the failed Bar Kokhba rebellion provoked a crisis of meaning that fostered diverging explanations of the event and intensified divisions among various communities of Judeans, including gentile Jesus people.

Justin's *Dialogue with Trypho* preserves two competing explanations for the traumatic event and two different attempts at making it coherent: the tension between them exacerbates differences over questions of theodicy and adherence to the covenant that originate with the Pauline mission. The debate over Mosaic law in the *Dialogue*, thus, does not emerge spontaneously from a need to define an identity or refute a heresy but from an originary need to justify Roman victory and exonerate God for failing to redeem Jerusalem. This disagreement over meaning-making catalyzed a new identity – Christian. I want to emphasize that I do not posit a universal "parting of ways" that would essentialize Christians as a unified group at this time; rather, I want to explore how the need to explain and justify Roman victory within the framework of Deuteronomic theodicy contributed to the formulation of Christian identity. In the scholarly literature on Justin's theology, Christology, legal observance, and heresy hunting, meaning-making in response to trauma has been overlooked as a significant factor in the concretization of Christian difference and identity.

JUSTIN'S *DIALOGUE* AND THE FAILED WAR AGAINST ROME

Justin's *Dialogue with Trypho* is widely regarded as a pivotal text in what Boyarin describes as the "production of an independent Christianity." The text, however, is something of a Rorschach's blot, producing different interpretations of its purpose and intended audience depending on the orientation of each interpreter.[37] Scholars have read it as an attempt to construct discreet

Jewish and Christian identities,[38] to convince Jews that Jesus is the Christ (i.e., to convert them to Christianity), to convert pagan proselytes to Christianity instead of to Judaism, to convince Christians to stop observing Mosaic law (i.e., to stop Judaizing), or to counter demiurgical claims of Marcion and/or other so-called gnostics.[39] This chapter proposes a reading that I have not encountered elsewhere: that the original *Dialogue* (notwithstanding any subsequent accretions and their theological motivations) addresses questions of theodicy that arose in the wake of the failed Bar Kokhba revolt. More specifically, I argue that Justin's *Dialogue* responds to accusations that non-observant Jesus followers violated the covenant and caused the revolt to fail. Justin harnesses logocentric Christology and supersessionism to justify Roman victory over Judea and to blame Judeans for their own misfortune.[40]

The opening scene of the *Dialogue* sets the stage for Justin's debate with Trypho, who describes himself as a circumcised Hebrew fleeing the war in Judea (Ἑβραῖος ἐκ περιτομῆς φυγὼν τὸν νῦν γενόμενον πόλεμον, 1.15).[41] Scholars often dismiss the *Dialogue*'s mise-en-scène as fictionalized and focus instead on Justin's Christological excursus.[42] I regard the staging of this debate to be not only important for understanding the ensuing dialogue but also a realistic reflection of actual conversations between Judeans and Jesus followers in the wake of the Bar Kochba revolt.[43] It presents a significant historical witness to one factor that, I suggest, drove some Jesus followers to develop a distinct identity separate from Judeans at this time.[44] The main topics of the debate – covenant obligations, Jesus's status as the anticipated messiah, the identity of Israel, and the reliability of scripture – flow naturally from the opening discussion of theodicy in response to the failed war.[45] The need to restore coherence after the war transformed theoretical disagreements and differences into heated controversies upon which life itself seemed to hinge.

The opening passages of the *Dialogue* mimic Platonic dialogues, presenting Justin as a masterful Greek philosopher engaging an interlocutor in debate.[46] Justin is approached by Trypho, who says he recently escaped the war in Judea and is spending his days in Greece (1.15–16). Justin wears a philosopher's robe, which sparks a series of questions about theodicy as Trypho asks him to expound upon God's sole rulership (μοναρχίας) and divine providence (προνοίας, 1.20). Many scholars regard these questions to be directed against Marcion and other forms of what Den Dulk aptly labels "demiurgists" in an attempt to avoid the essentializing label "gnostic."[47] Given the ostensible context of the war Trypho's questions strike me as resoundingly authentic, especially following a second failed rebellion that destroyed Judaea and humiliated its god for a second time. Trypho expresses concern over God's power and justice, indicating a fear that God is either not actually in control of events or has forsaken his people in favour of Rome.[48] Similar questions followed the destruction of the second temple in 70 CE, as reflected in writings such as *4 Ezra* and *2 Baruch*, and were answered with messianic prophecies.[49] How much more so should these questions have presented themselves when redemption failed to materialize as predicted?

When Justin admits that he follows the "philosophy" of Jesus, the conversation abruptly turns to a critique of the Jesus movement: Trypho admonishes Justin for being deceived by false claims and for following men who are not worthy (ἢ λόγοις ἐξαπατηθῆναι ψευδέσι καὶ ἀνθρώποις ἀκολουθῆσαι οὐδενὸς ἀξίοις, 8.17–18). He asks what kind of salvation remains for someone who abandons God and places expectations in a man (καταλιπόντι δὲ τὸν θεὸν καὶ εἰς ἄνθρωπον ἐλπίσαντι ποία ἔτι περιλείπεται σωτηρία; 8.19–20). Trypho advises him instead to observe the covenantal laws of circumcision, the sabbath, feasts, and new moons – "absolutely, do all the things that are written in the law, and then likely you will receive mercy from God" (καὶ ἁπλῶς τὰ ἐν τῷ νόμῳ γεγραμμένα πάντα ποίει, καὶ τότε σοι ἴσως ἔλεος ἔσται παρὰ θεοῦ, 8.23–24). Trypho rejects the claim that Jesus is the Christ and accuses Justin of "accepting a profane account and fashioning a Christ for yourselves, for whose sake you are recklessly perishing" (ὑμεῖς δέ, ματαίαν ἀκοὴν παραδεξάμενοι, Χριστὸν ἑαυτοις τινα ἀναπλάσσετε καὶ αὐτοῦ χάριν τὰ νῦν ἀσκόπως ἀπόλλυσθε, 8.27–28).[50] Furthermore, his repeated emphasis on the connection between salvation and observance of the law provides insight into what I regard to be Trypho's primary concern: covenantal theodicy. Like Josephus and other Judeans who responded to the destruction of the temple in 70 CE, Trypho views the world through the lens of Deuteronomic theology, which ties national security to observance of God's law.[51]

Justin responds to these charges by asking Trypho to listen to his explanation of why, despite persecution, "we do not cease acknowledging him" (οὐδὲ παυσόμεθα ὁμολογοῦντες τοῦτον, 9.4–5). Trypho agrees to listen even as some of his companions laugh and insult Justin: one of them tosses out a remark (λόγον) about the war in Judea (ἐμβαλόντος τινὸς αὐτῶν λόγον περὶ τοῦ κατὰ τὴν Ἰουδαίαν γενομένου πολέμου, 9.20–21).[52] I focus on this "remark" because I regard it as an important key to understanding Justin's *Dialogue*: like an irritating grain of sand that provokes the formation of a pearl, Justin's *Dialogue* responds to this aggravating provocation and grows around it.

Unfortunately we do not know the precise contents of this λόγον because it is not quoted,[53] but from Trypho's prior criticisms and from Justin's immediate reply I surmise that it offered an account of the war that impugned certain followers of Jesus for abrogating Torah, angering God, and causing the rebellion to fail. If this speculation is correct, Justin's response makes greatest sense. In the very next sentence, Justin retorts: "And is there nothing else for which we are blamed, dear fellow, than this: we do not live according to the law, nor are we circumcised in the flesh like your ancestors, or observe the Sabbath like you?" (Μὴ ἄλλο τί ἐστιν ὅ ἐπιμέμφεσθε ἡμᾶς, ἄνδρες φίλοι, ἢ τοῦτο ὅτι οὐ κατὰ τὸν νόμον βιοῦμεν, οὐδὲ ὁμοίως τοῖς προγόνοις ὑμῶν περιτεμνόμεθα τὴν σάρκα, οὐδὲ ὡς ὑμεῖς σαββατίζομεν; 10.1–4). Justin then turns the blame back onto Judeans, asserting that God has forsaken *them* for killing Jesus:

> For the circumcision of the flesh from Abraham was given as a sign (σημεῖον) so that, being separated from all other nations and from us, you alone would suffer what you now justly endure (καὶ ἵνα μόνοι πάθητε ἃ νῦν ἐν δίκῃ πάσχετε): your ancestral lands are desolate, your cities are burnt, and all your fruits are devoured in front of you by strangers, and not even one of you may go up to Jerusalem ... And these things, in fact, happened to you fairly and justly (καὶ ὑμῖν οὖν ταῦτα καλῶς καὶ δικαίως γέγονεν). For you put to death the Just One ('Απεκτείνατε γὰρ τὸν δίκαιον) and his prophets before him, and now you disparage those who hope for him and the one who sent him – God, the all-powerful and creator of everything – whom many of you dishonor by cursing in your synagogues those who believe in the Christ. (Dial. 16.2–3)

Using the language of "we" and "you" to differentiate between Judeans and gentile Jesus followers, Justin baldly asserts that the recent defeat in Judea is proof that God rejected *you* for killing the Just One and transferred his covenant to *us* who constitute the true Israel.[54] The rest of the *Dialogue* is a lengthy attempt to demonstrate with scriptural proof-texts that Jesus supersedes the written law and is foretold in the scriptures.[55]

As I reconstruct it, the entire debate between Justin and Trypho over Jesus's status as the incarnate Logos evolves from an argument over who is to blame for the failed revolt. Justin and Trypho are engaged in a contest over meaning-making: their dialogue attempts to explain and justify dashed expectations that God/Jesus would overthrow Rome. By blaming Judeans for their own misery, Justin follows a long tradition in the writings of Josephus, Deuteronomy, and the prophets that justifies foreign military conquest of Judea and exonerates God for failing to uphold his end of the covenant.[56] Justin hijacks this ancient Judean strategy to preserve God's honour and faith in the covenant when he claims that God rejects Judeans and adopts gentile Jesus followers as the true Israel.

It is important to clarify here that I do not see this as a battle between Judaism and Christianity, as many scholars do.[57] Conflict over observance of covenantal law in this text does not cut along a Jewish/Christian binary but is part of an internal conversation among Judeans, which at this moment still includes *gentile* followers of Jesus.[58] In a manner that recalls conflicts between Paul and other apostles over circumcision (Gal 1:6–9, 2:11–14) or criticism against certain prophets in the Apocalypse of John over eating meat sacrificed to Greco-Roman deities (Rev 1:14, 20), Trypho charges that followers of Jesus claim to be pious (εὐσεβεῖν λέγοντες) but do not separate themselves from the nations and differentiate their way of living (κατ' οὐδεν αὐτῶν ἀπολείπεσθε, οὐδὲ διαλλάσσετε ἀπὸ τῶν ἐθνῶν τὸν ὑμέτερον βίον, 10.15–17).[59] Rather, at the risk of being cut off from God's people, they put their hopes in a man who was crucified and expect to obtain some good thing all the while openly despising God's covenant (τῆς διαθήκης εὐθέως καταφρονήσαντες, 10.18–25). This accusation frames the conversation in terms of covenantal theodicy: salvation depends on adherence to the law – apostasy leads to punishment and God's rejection (Josh 1:2–15; Judg 2:11–15).

STILL JUDEANS

Trypho's accusation that Justin and his compatriots anger God by putting their faith in a crucified saviour and ignoring the law at their peril signals his understanding that Jesus followers are members of the Judean community and subject to the covenant: they may be wrong about the messiah's identity and misguided, but Trypho insists that observance of covenantal law is incumbent upon them for divine protection and mercy as it is for all other Judeans.[60] Justin's argument that Jesus *replaces* the law refutes Trypho's assertion that covenantal obligations apply to Jesus followers. Significantly, Justin does not assert that Christians form a different religion at this point; instead he argues that Jesus *replaces* the law for all believers. Christianity is not being presented here as a separate religion – yet.

In fact, Justin reinforces the ambiguous status of Jesus people by using the labels "we" and "you" throughout the first half of the dialogue. Until chapter 63, Justin only uses the term "Christian" four times. In 17.10 "Christian" appears as a derogatory label applied by emissaries who, Justin claims, were sent from Jerusalem to condemn the "godless heresy of Christians" (αἵρεσιν ἄθεον Χριστιανῶν). At 47.19 he uses it to specify gentile believers in Christ, referring to two groups – "the Christians and the faithful" (Χριστιανοῖς καὶ πιστοῖς) – and denounces those Judeans who accept Jesus as the Christ yet compel gentile believers to observe Mosaic law. This group of Jesus followers upholds a viewpoint similar to the one I have attributed to Trypho: they regard the Jesus movement to be Judean and to fall under covenant regulations. The debate thus unfolds, at least initially, between two internecine camps, not two distinct religions.[61] Furthermore, the label "Christian" does not yet appear to apply to Judean Jesus followers.[62]

IDENTIFYING AS CHRISTIAN

Justin finally self-identifies as "Christian" in chapter 63 when he describes it as a unifying identity for all believers in Jesus as the Christ: "And above all, that the word of God speaks to those who believe in him, as being one soul, and one synagogue, and one church, as to a daughter, to the church that is called by his name (τῇ ἐξ ὀνόματος αὐτοῦ λεγομένῃ) and participates in his name – for we are all called Christians (Χριστιανοὶ γὰρ πάντες καλούμεθα), in like manner clearly the words proclaim, teaching us to forget the customs of our forefathers" (63.34–39). At the same time that he embraces this new identity, derived from the name of Christ, he also asserts that being Christian involves forgetting one's ancestral customs (τῶν παλαιῶν πατρῴων ἐθῶν ἐπιλαθέσθαι, 63.38–39). Thus, Justin resolves the ambiguous position of non-observant Christ followers vis-à-vis the law by constructing a new category – what we would consider to be a new religion, which encompasses *all* followers of Jesus. This step towards independence from Judaism accomplishes two things: as Boyarin points out, it resolves the identity crisis gentile Jesus people faced from being neither Jew nor Greek. It simultaneously rebutted charges of abrogating Torah and angering God.

CONSTRUCTING 'ΙΟΥΔΑΙΟΊ AS THE OTHER

Justin's changing nomenclature constructed Jew and Judaism as foils, part and parcel of the invention of Christian and Christianity. Justin only begins to use the term "Jews" (Ἰουδαῖοι) in chapter 72, where it functions oppositionally to identify those who crucified Jesus and redacted scriptural references that prove Jesus's identity as the Christ (72.14, 16). In hindsight, it is easy to retroject the terms "Christian" and "Jew" onto the opposing positions throughout the dialogue as most scholars (and translations) do, but, in fact, Justin does not use those terms or present the debate as anything other than an internal disagreement until nearly half way through the *Dialogue*. I understand this to indicate that these identities are being worked out in and through this debate and others like it that were taking place at this time in the wake of the second Judeo-Roman War. Furthermore, I propose that the failed revolt provided the context for and instigation of many of those debates just as it does here.

Scholars date the *Dialogue* towards the end of Justin's life (d. 163–67 CE) and certainly after he wrote the *First Apology*, which Justin cites in it.[63] The arguments Justin wields display highly developed Christology and supersessionist claims, both of which he supports with a profuse use of proof texts from the LXX.[64] The arguments Justin wields indicate a large degree of theological development and refinement that must have taken place in the years following the Bar Kokhba revolt and the difficult conversations that it generated.[65] Just as Plato often cast real people and events as characters and backdrops for his dialogues, Justin appears to have drawn on real characters and conversations to stage this Christological and supersessionist treatise. The accretion of theological arguments and proof texts over this period of time also helps to explain the seemingly disjointed and long-winded argumentation that is derided by some scholars.[66]

The gap in time between the original dialogue with a Judean refugee and the publication of Justin's logocentric diatribe may account for the disjunction in tone and tenor: the friendly atmosphere of the introduction does not permeate the rest of the dialogue, as scholars have noted.[67] It also may account for the introduction of the self-identifying label "Christian," which occurs relatively late in the *Dialogue*. Nomenclature used in the *Dialogue* thus appears to mirror the concretization of Christian identity that occurred during the period of its composition. When Justin uses "us" and "you" in the early chapters of the *Dialogue* to identify the two parties in the debate, he reveals the indeterminate status of gentile Jesus followers in the early second century. By the time Justin writes the *Dialogue* three decades later, the term "Christian" is well established. Consequently he begins to use it later in the *Dialogue* when Justin moves from dialogue to monologue and long explanatory excursuses with biblical proof texts. Justin's *Dialogue with Trypho* thus mirrors as well as participates in the project of self-definition that, I propose, was intensified by the need to respond to charges of abrogating God's law and causing the revolt to fail.

CONCLUSION

The absolute and brutal suppression of the Bar Kochba rebellion, I argue, instigated a search for meaning and an attempt to restore coherence to a worldview that had been shattered. When redemption failed to materialize as anticipated,[68] Judeans, including those who expected Jesus's imminent parousia,[69] searched for answers and pointed fingers of blame – this is what we see motivating the *Dialogue with Trypho*. The answers different groups found and the meanings they constructed to make sense of Rome's second victory over Judea constituted early steps on a path that, retrospectively, we know led towards an eventual separation between certain self-identifying "Christians" and other Judeans, who identified Jesus as the Messiah or not.[70] If, as I surmise, certain Jesus followers were being accused of causing God to punish Judea because they ignored ancestral laws upon which the nation's security depended, then they needed a rebuttal. In the process of levelling the same accusation against their accusers, "Christians" cemented their difference. This argument does not attribute Justin's position to all Jesus people at this time; it merely recognizes the *Dialogue* as an early salvo in what becomes a battle between two increasingly estranged camps that eventually concretize separate identities as Jews and Christians.[71] Justin's supersessionist claims thus counter Trypho's covenant theodicy.

This argument helps explain the "failed conversion" of Trypho that has preoccupied many scholars.[72] If we read Justin's *Dialogue* as a defence of the antinomianism of certain Jesus-followers, who are now asserting a distinct identity apart from Judaism, the unresolved parting of Justin and Trypho at the end signals a parting of ways for some Jesus people,[73] who staked their claim to this new identity – Christian. Converting Trypho was never the goal. Presenting a new identity, grounded in sacred scripture that resolved cognitive dissonance from the war and the ongoing conflict over observing Judean law was the primary objective.[74] Thus, in the process of making meaning and responding to trauma, two distinct religions were born.

This should not surprise us. Arthur Neal's work, *National Trauma and Collective Memory*, highlights the schismatic effects of trauma on social collectivities as they struggle to make meaning out of experiences that violate coherence. Social tensions and disagreements rupture into full blown fissures as different explanations and responses tear society asunder.[75] I wonder whether, without the tragedy of the failed Bar Kokhba revolt, gentile Jesus people could have remained within the capacious tent of Hellenistic Judaism indefinitely, or if they would have drifted off into their own sect without the amplification of conflict this crisis created. The answer to that question I believe lies in Roman persecution of gentile Jesus followers who rejected their natal obligations to revere Greco-Roman deities. But this is the topic for another work.

NOTES

1 Stephen G. Wilson, *Related Strangers: Jews and Christians 70–170 C.E.* (Minneapolis: Fortress Press, 1995).

2 Stephen G. Wilson, "Marcion and Boundaries," in *Crossing Boundaries in Early Judaism and Christianity: Ambiguities, Complexities, and Half-Forgotten*

Adversaries – Essays in Honor of Alan F. Segal, ed. Kimberly B. Stratton and Andrea Lieber, JSJSupp 177 (Leiden: Brill, 2016), 200–20. In this article Wilson nuances and expands upon some of his earlier arguments.

3 Judith M. Lieu, *Christian Identity in the Jewish and Graeco-Roman World* (Oxford: Oxford University Press, 2004).

4 Ibid., 1. Candida R. Moss, "On the Dating of Polycarp: Rethinking the Place of the *Martyrdom of Polycarp* in the History of Christianity," *Early Christianity* 1 (2010): 539–74, persuasively argues that the extant version of *The Martyrdom of Polycarp* dates to the third century.

5 Lieu, *Christian Identity*, 3. Lieu, *Image and Reality: The Jews in the World of the Christians in the Second Century* (Edinburgh: T & T Clark, 1996), treats the identities of Jews and Christians as far more distinct and defined than she does in her later book.

6 Daniel Boyarin, *Border Lines: The Partition of Judaeo-Christianity* (Philadelphia: University of Pennsylvania Press, 2004), 20.

7 Ibid., 16–17.

8 Ibid., 29. The "existential threat" of hybridity operated both ways, according to Boyarin: he sees the production of the Mishnah as a counter-move to draw boundaries of its own and define an orthodox Judaism in opposition to nascent Christianity.

9 Andrew S. Jacobs, "Dialogical Differences: (De-)Judaizing Jesus' Circumcision," *Journal of Early Christian Studies* 15, no. 3 (2007): 293–5.

10 Laura Nasrallah, "Mapping the World: Justin, Tatian, Lucian, and the Second Sophistic," *Harvard Theological Review* 93, no. 3 (2005): 309.

11 Denise Kimber Buell, *Why This New Race: Ethnic Reasoning in Early Christianity* (New York: Columbia University Press, 2005). See also Terence L. Donaldson, "'We Gentiles': Ethnicity and Identity in Justin Martyr," *Early Christianity* 4 (2013): 216–41; and Terence L. Donaldson, "'Gentile Christianity' as a Category in the Study of Christian Origins," *Harvard Theological Review* 106, no. 4 (2013): 433–58.

12 See also more recent publications that continue this line of inquiry: Nina E. Livesey, "Theological Identity Making: Justin's Use of Circumcision to Create Jews and Christians," *Journal of Early Christian Studies* 18, no. 1 (2010): 51–79; and Matthijs den Dulk, *Between Jews and Heretics: Refiguring Justin Martyr's* Dialogue with Trypho (London: Routledge, 2018), who situates the *Dialogue* in a heresiological context directed against "demiurgists" such as Marcion rather than against Jews.

13 Rodney Werline, "The Transformation of Pauline Arguments in Justin Martyr's *Dialogue with Trypho*," *Harvard Theological Review* 92, no. 1 (1999): 79–93, argues that Justin seeks to convert Jews like Trypho. So does Dulk, *Between Jews and Heretics*, 6. Erwin R. Goodenough, *The Theology of Justin Martyr: An Investigation Into the Conceptions of Early Christian Literature and Its Hellenistic and Judaistic Influences* (Amsterdam: Philo Press, 1968), 282, regards the matter of conversion

to be somewhat urgent as the parousia is imminently anticipated by Justin. Jon Nilson, "To Whom Is Justin's *Dialogue with Trypho* Addressed?," *Theological Studies* 38, no. 3 (1977): 539–40, argues that Justin strives to convert gentiles who were contemplating converting to Judaism or to convince "Christians" not to Judaize.

14 I am following the new date proposed for the end of hostilities by Werner Eck, "The Bar Kochba Revolt: The Roman Point of View," *Journal of Roman Studies* 89 (1999): 87–8.

15 Wilson, "Marcion and Boundaries," 217–18, similarly contextualizes both Marcion's rejection of Judaism and Justin's supersessionism in the context of the failed Bar Kokhba rebellion.

16 L.W. Barnard, *Justin Martyr: His Life and Thought* (London: Cambridge University Press, 1967), 23–4, and Timothy J. Horner, *"Listening to Trypho": Justin Martyr's* Dialogue *Reconsidered*, Contributions to Biblical Exegesis and Theology (Leuven: Peeters, 2001), similarly posit an original debate that was elaborated upon decades later.

17 Malcolm Lowe, "Who Were the ΙΟΥΔΑΙΟΙ?," *Novum Testamentum* 18, no. 2 (1976): 101–30; Steve Mason, "Jews, Judaeans, Judaizing, Judaism: Problems of Categorization in Ancient History," *Journal for the Study of Judaism* 38 (2007): 457–512, who notes that "religion" is equally problematic as a heuristic term. Adele Reinhartz, "The Vanishing Jews of Antiquity," *Marginalia: Deep Learning for a Digital Age*, 24 June 2014, argues forcefully for preserving the Jewish connection to translations of *Ioudaios*. Further discussion on both sides of the debate appears in Adele Reinhartz, Steve Mason, Daniel Schwartz, Annette Yoshiko Reed, Joan Taylor, Malcolm Lowe, Jonathan Klawans, Ruth Sheridan, and James Crossley, "Jew and Judean: A Forum on Politics and Historiography in the Translation of Ancient Texts," *Marginalia Review of Books*, 26 August 2014. Annette Yoshiko Reed in particular incisively probes problematic questions raised by scholarly taxonomy vis-à-vis ancient writings.

18 Except in 103.20 where it describes Herod as king of the Ἰουδαῖοι.

19 Justin only ever uses the plural term Ἰουδαιοί, and only towards the end of the *Dialogue* (beginning in chapter 72), when he also starts asserting his supersessionist theology more aggressively. Daniel Boyarin, *Border Lines: The Partition of Judaeo-Christianity* (Philadelphia: University of Pennsylvania Press, 2004), 17, argues that the concept "religion" is produced at this time through the invention of Christianity, which was independent of one's birth, language, and geographic location. Part and parcel of this process, Judaism is constructed as a foil. The modern conception of religion as a constellation of beliefs and practices discrete from a secular frame of action is the product of Enlightenment and colonialism. See, for example, Talal Asad, "The Construction of Religion as an Anthropological Category," in *Genealogies of Religion: Discipline and Reasons of Power in Christianity and Islam* (Baltimore: Johns Hopkins University Press, 1993), 27–54; Jonathan Z. Smith, "Religion, Religions, Religious," in *Critical Terms for Religious Studies*, ed. Mark C. Taylor (Chicago: University of Chicago Press, 1998),

269–84; Russell McCutcheon, *Manufacturing Religion: The Discourse on Sui Generis Religion and the Politics of Nostalgia* (New York: Oxford University Press, 1997); and Paula Fredriksen, "Divinity, Ethnicity, Identity: 'Religion' as a Political Category in Christian Antiquity," in *Comprehending Antisemitism through the Ages: A Historical Perspective,* vol. 3, ed. Armin Lange, Kerstin Mayerhofer, Dina Porat, and Lawrence H. Schiffman (Berlin: De Gruyter, 2021), 101–20, doi: https://doi.org/10.1515/9783110671995-006.

20 See Dulk, *Between Jews and Heretics*, 3–4, for a recent discussion.

21 Buell, *Why This New Race*, 206n13.

22 Dulk, *Between Jews and Heretics*, 1, 3, 10n19.

23 Annette Yoshiko Reed, *Jewish-Christianity and the History of Judaism: Collected Essays*, Texts and Studies in Ancient Judaism (Tübingen: Mohr Siebeck, 2018), xv.

24 James D.G. Dunn, *Neither Jew Nor Greek: A Contested Identity*, Christianity in the Making 3 (Grand Rapids: Eerdmans, 2015), 12–13. Identifying the earliest use of this term is difficult. Josephus uses it in the suspect *Testimonium Flavianum* where he refers to "the tribe of Christians" (τῶν Χριστιανῶν, 18.64). If this reference is authentic it dates use of the label to as early as 92 CE, decades before any other witness, including Pliny *Ep.* 10.96, Tacitus *An.* 15.44, or Suetonius *Nero* 16. Acts 11:26 states that the disciples were first called Christians in Antioch and uses the term again in the context of Paul's appearance before Agrippa (26:28). Convincing arguments have been made for dating Acts to the second century, thus raising questions about whether use of the term "Christian" in Acts reflects the historical period it describes or its own. See William Arnal, "The Collection and Synthesis of 'Tradition' and the Second-Century Invention of Christianity," *Method and Theory in the Study of Religion* 23 (2011): 195. Paul never uses the term himself in his letters (whether authentic or deutero-Pauline) and neither do the gospels or Revelation. 1 Peter 4.16 represents the only other appearance in the New Testament and it also dates to the early second century. See David G. Horrell, "The Label Χριστιανός: 1 Peter 4:16 and the Formation of Christian Identity," *Journal of Biblical Literature* 126, no. 2 (2007): 361–81. On dating Acts to the second century, see Burton L. Mack, *Who Wrote the New Testament? The Making of the Christian Myth* (San Francisco: HarperSanFrancisco, 1995), 45; Joseph B. Tyson, *Marcion and Luke-Acts: A Defining Struggle* (Columbia: University of South Carolina Press, 2006); and Richard I. Pervo, *Dating Acts: Between the Evangelists and the Apologists* (Santa Rosa: Polebridge Press, 2006).

25 Arnal, "Invention of Christianity," 199.

26 Horrell, "Label Χριστιανός," 380. See further discussion below.

27 See discussion in Wilson, *Related Strangers*, 2–11; and Wilson, "Marcion and Boundaries," 217–19.

28 Travis Proulx and Michael Inzlicht, "The Five 'A's of Meaning Maintenance: Finding Meaning in the Theories of Sense-Making," *Psychological Inquiry* 23, no. 4 (2012): 322.

29 These include assimilation, accommodation, and affirmation. See Proulx and Inzlicht, "The Five 'A's of Meaning Maintenance," 325–7.

30 Honora Howell Chapman, "What Josephus Sees: The Temple of Peace and the Jerusalem Temple as Spectacle in Text and Art," *Phoenix* 63, nos 1 and 2 (2009): 108n4; Martin Goodman, *Rome and Jerusalem: The Clash of Ancient Civilizations* (New York: Vintage, 2007), 427. I am currently writing an article on the importance of the Babylonian exile as a precedent and mythic paradigm for the events of 70 CE; restoration following the demise of the first temple inculcated hope that the second temple would be rebuilt within a similar time frame.

31 Boaz Zissu, "Interbellum Judea 70–132 CE: An Archaeological Perspective," in *Jews and Christians in the First and Second Centuries: The Interbellum 70–132 CE*, ed. Joshua Schwartz and Peter J. Tomson (Leiden: Brill, 2018), 28–29.

32 Marcel Simon, *Verus Israel : Étude sur les Relations Entre Chrétiens et Juifs dans l'Empire Romain, 135–425*, 2nd ed., Bibliothèque Des Écoles Françaises d'Athènes et de Rome (Paris: E. de Boccard, 1964), 24, regards the events of both 70 and 135 CE as parallel to the conquest of 586 BCE in being understood as divine punishment and inculcating hopes for a restored Zion. In contrast, I see a distinct difference in communal response to the conquests of 70 and 135. The first war prompted eschatological expectations for divine redemption on a sixty-five- to seventy-year time-frame following the paradigm of the Babylonian conquest. When that hope was dashed at Betar, meaning violation became acute: the biblical paradigm of discipline and restoration failed to apply.

33 I follow Horner, *Listening to Trypho*, in attributing some historical reality to the *Dialogue*, reflected in a kernel preserved in the early chapters of the work.

34 This description of the two groups strives to avoid essentializing either the Judean perspective or that of gentile/Pauline Jesus believers, many of whom observed at least some Judean customs and observances. See Wilson, "Marcion and Boundaries," 218–19. I am also trying to avoid anachronistic assumptions that there was at this time a single unifying set of ritual observances, although Andrea M. Berlin, "Jewish Life before the Revolt: The Archaeological Evidence," *Journal for the Study of Judaism* 36, no. 4 (2005): 417–70, argues for a shared a set of domestic practices that encoded a unified cultural/religious identity in Judea prior to 135 CE. Interestingly, the practices that she identifies in the material record do not map onto those mentioned by Trypho, who emphasizes observance of sabbath, new moons, and circumcision (8.21-24). Marc Hirshman, "Polemic Literary Units in the Classical Midrashim and Justin Martyr's *Dialogue with Trypho*," *Jewish Quarterly Review* 83, nos. 3 and 4 (1993): 377–8, illuminates this discrepancy: Trypho's list mirrors Isa 55:6 and 66:23 and not any knowledge of authentic Judean practice at this time. Hirshman regards Trypho as a foil throughout the *Dialogue*, whose job is to set up pins "for Justin to knock down" in his rejection of rabbinic Judaism. While I find Hirshman's readings of Justin, the Mekhilta, and Genesis Rabbah astute, he anachronistically treats Christianity

as a unified and coherent religious entity at a time when it was only just establishing itself as independent of Judaism.

35 Gilad Hirschberger, "Collective Trauma and the Social Construction of Meaning," *Frontiers in Psychology* 9 (August 2018): 1–14, 1, doi:https://doi.org/10.3389/fpsyg.2018.01441.

36 Arthur G. Neal, *National Trauma and Collective Memory: Extraordinary Events in the American Experience*, 2nd ed. (Armonk: M.E. Sharpe, 2005), 7, 10, 18–19.

37 Bishop Demetrios Trakatellis, "Justin Martyr's Trypho," *Harvard Theological Review* 79, nos. 1–3 (1986): 287–8, similarly notes the diversity of opinion on this text.

38 Boyarin, *Border Lines*; Daniel Boyarin, "Justin Martyr Invents Judaism," *American Society of Church History* 70, no. 3 (2001): 427–61; Livesey, "Theological Identity Making."

39 Dulk, *Between Jews and Heretics*; Benjamin L. White, "Justin between Paul and the Heretics: The Salvation of Christian Judaizers in the *Dialogue with Trypho*," *Journal of Early Christian Studies* 26, no. 2 (2018): 163–89.

40 Barnard, *Justin Martyr*, 165, proposes that Justin drew on "an earlier strand of millennial teaching" found in Revelation and Jewish tradition to answer the question, "what is to become of the ruined Jerusalem?"

41 Identifiable as the Bar Kokhba rebellion (132–135 CE). All translations of Justin's *Dialogue with Trypho* are my own based on the text of Miroslav Marcovich, ed., *Iustini Martyris Dialogus Cum Tryphone*, Patristische Texte und Studien (Berlin: Walter de Gruyter, 1997).

42 Goodenough, *Theology of Justin Martyr*, 88–90, dismisses the entire scene as a fictionalized and stereotyped depiction of the philosopher's quest; Trypho he regards as an idealized composite of Hellenistic and Palestinian forms of Judaism. Dulk, *Between Jews and Heretics*, 7, situates the *Dialogue* in the context of "internal Christian debate and conflict." He regards the introduction as having little relevance for the rest of the text. Boyarin, "Justin Martyr Invents Judaism," 457, and Dunn, *Neither Jew Nor Greek*, 134, also dismiss Trypho as a fictionalized straw man. Tessa Rajak, "Talking at Trypho: Christian Apologetics as Anti-Judaism in Justin's *Dialogue with Trypho the Jew*," in *Apologetics in the Roman Empire: Pagans, Jews, and Christians*, ed. Mark Edwards, Martin Goodman, and Simon Price (Oxford: Oxford University Press, 1999), 59–60, reads Trypho and the Greek setting as fictional but symbolically important for signalling Judaism's inferior status. See also Horner, *Listening to Trypho*, 15–32, who reviews scholarly opinion about Trypho before reconstructing Trypho's side of an original debate, which Justin has subsequently expanded upon.

43 Horner, *Listening to Trypho*, 15–32, attempts to reconstruct Trypho's side of an original debate upon which Justin later expanded to produce the *Dialogue*. See also Wilson, *Related Strangers*, 260–1. A.J.B. Higgins, "Jewish Messianic Belief in Justin Martyr's 'Dialogue with Trypho,'" *Novum Testamentum* 9, no. 4 (1967): 298–305, examines evidence for Jewish messianic beliefs and finds Justin's account mostly reliable and authentic in its presentation of Jewish attitudes and ideas.

Despite arguing that Trypho is a fictionalized "ideal" Jew and straw man, Goodenough, *Theology of Justin Martyr*, 92–5, finds that Trypho reproduces with remarkable accuracy Tannaitic teachings that appear in later rabbinic compilations.

44 See also Wilson, "Marcion and Boundaries," 216–19.

45 Although *Dial.* 1.15 suggests that the war is still ongoing, Justin's description of the situation in Judea and the ignominy of the Jews for killing the Just One indicates that they are discussing the war's aftermath. See also Barnard, *Justin Martyr*, 165, for the same conclusion. Oskar Skarsaune, *The Proof from Prophecy: A Study in Justin Martyr's Proof-Text Tradition: Text-Type, Provenance, Theological Profile*, NovTSup (Leiden: Brill, 1987), identifies these as prominent themes in the proof text that he argues Justin relied upon in his crafting of the *Dialogue*. My argument does not discount the existence or importance of such proof texts but proposes that Justin is citing scriptural proofs in response to criticisms directed at non-Torah-abiding Jesus people that were intensified and amplified by the tragic outcome of the Bar Kokhba rebellion.

46 Goodenough, *Theology of Justin Martyr*, 58–63, argues that the conversion narrative and description of passing through different philosophical schools follows literary convention; furthermore, Justin's critiques of each school are conventional and do not reflect the authentic insider knowledge of a former student. Barnard, *Justin Martyr*, 7–11, refutes Goodenough's position and argues that Justin's description of his philosophical education and conversion is biographical and interprets his theology in light of this pedagogical trajectory. Rajak, "Talking at Trypho," 63, emphasizes the power difference and negative stereotyping implicit in this symbolic presentation. Nasrallah, "Mapping the World," 287, 310, identifies the dialogue format as typical of the Second Sophistic movement, which deliberately sought to recapitulate the glory days of classical Greek *paideia*. She sees the narrative complicating any Jew/Greek binary as Justin also lays claim to "barbarian" scripture and a "barbarian" sacred centre – Jerusalem. Horner, *Listening to Trypho*, 73–84, rejects the argument that Platonic discourse is a model and instead situates Justin in the context of the Second Sophistic. Nilson, "To Whom Is Justin's *Dialogue with Trypho* Addressed?," 540, sees the esteemed valuation of philosophy as a way to appeal to gentiles by situating Christianity in recognizable terms.

47 Dulk, *Between Jews and Heretics*, 4. Because these questions direct the conversation towards contested theologies that distinguish between the god of the Hebrew scriptures and Jesus's god many scholars interpret them as staged. See note 42.

48 Wilson, "Marcion and Boundaries," 117, makes a similar argument. Barnard, *Justin Martyr*, 116, in contrast, situates the discussion of divine *pronoia* or providence in response to Stoic and Middle Platonism.

49 See Hindy Najman, *Losing the Temple and Recovering the Future: An Analysis of 4 Ezra* (New York: Cambridge University Press, 2014); Gwendolyn B. Sayler, *Have the Promises Failed? A Literary Analysis of 2 Baruch* (Chico: Scholars Press, 1984); Jacob Neusner, "Judaism in a Time of Crisis: Four Responses," *Judaism* 21/3, no. 83 (1972): 313–27; Jonathan Klawans, "Josephus, the Rabbis, and Responses

to Catastrophes Ancient and Modern," *Jewish Quarterly Review* 100, no. 2 (2010): 278–309. William Arnal, "Shipwrecked on a Desert Island: The Barren Isolation of 'Christian Origins,'" in *Worth More Than Many Sparrows: In Honour of Willi Braun*, ed. Patrick Hart and Sarah Rollens, Studies in Religion and Ancient Culture (London: Equinox, 2022), 70–84, sees these questions driving the Gospel of Mark.

50 Trypho's charge resonates with later rabbinic denunciations of Jesus and likely represents commonly held views at the time. See Wilson, *Related Strangers*, 186; Barnard, *Justin Martyr*, 47. Hirshman, "Polemic Literary Units," 371, in contrast, argues that Trypho's statements "reveal little or no intrinsically rabbinic material." Accusations against Jesus no doubt circulated long before rabbinic compilations and provide the context for the formulation of proof texts that Skarsaune, *Proof from Prophecy*, identifies as sources for Justin's arguments in the *Dialogue*.

51 Hirshman, "Polemic Literary Units," 372, notes that Trypho's participation is limited to the first half of the *Dialogue* (up to chapter 90) and is concentrated in 45–9, which address the ongoing relevance and force of the law. On Deuteronomic theodicy in response to 70 CE see Simon, *Verus Israel*, 21–3; Klawans, "Josephus, the Rabbis," 291–5; and Kimberly Stratton, "Religious Legitimation of Violence and the Restoration of Social Coherence: Jewish and Christian Responses to the Judeo Roman Wars (70–136 CE)," in *In Religiöse (De) Legitimationsansätze von Gewalt in der Antike*, ed. Johannes Breuer and Jochen Walter (Stuttgart: Franz Steiner-Verlag, 2023), 105-22.

52 The identity of these companions is the subject of debate. Some scholars argue that they are gentile proselytes to Judaism whom Justin seeks to dissuade and convert to Christianity instead. I see no strong evidence for this interpretation; the reference to circumcision in *Dial.* 23.3 could be an argument directed at the intended audience of the *Dialogue* – other Gentile Jesus people – whom Justin seeks to convince to remain uncircumcised. See also Dulk, *Between Jews and Heretics*, 40, 47n12, who reviews the different positions and proposes a similar argument.

53 This could be a deliberate omission or possibly due to a lacuna in the poorly preserved manuscript of Justin's *Dial.* See Marcovich, *Iustini Martyris Dialogus Cum Tryphone*, viii.

54 Judith M. Lieu, *Image and Reality: The Jews in the World of the Christians in the Second Century* (Edinburgh: T&T Clark, 2003), 109–10, notes the shift from the singular "I" and "you" in the opening scene to a collective "we" and "you" (plural) throughout the rest of the *Dialogue*, which Lieu, consequently, describes as a debate "between two groups, Christianity and Judaism." This conclusion is not necessary; I read "you" and "we" as different groups within a broadly conceived Judean tent that still contains gentile Jesus followers, who have not yet formulated a distinct identity as Christian.

55 For a rigorous analysis of Justin's use of scriptural proof-texts, see Skarsaune, *Proof from Prophecy*. On Justin's exegetical strategies to identify Christ followers with Israel and ethnic Judeans who reject Jesus with "the nations" in Isaiah, see

Matthew W. Bates, "Justin Martyr's Logocentric Hermeneutical Transformation of Isaiah's Vision of the Nations," *Journal of Theological Studies* 60, no. 2 (2009): 549–53.

56 Stratton, "Religious Legitimation of Violence," 111-12.

57 Nilson, "To Whom is Justin's *Dialogue with Trypho* Addressed?" 62. Lieu, *Christian Identity*, 82–83, when discussing this passage, describes Christianity and Judaism as fundamentally distinct; Wilson, *Related Strangers*, 258–9, sees the debate in terms of Jewish-Christian dialogue. Werline, "Transformation of Pauline Arguments," 81–2, essentializes the differences between the "church," which he claims is predominantly gentile at this point, and Judaism.

58 Trypho notes that the law of circumcision was commanded for extended members of the Judean community – resident aliens and slaves – who are not ethnically Judean (10.22–3), suggesting that gentile Jesus followers fall into this category. Donaldson, "We Gentiles," presents a subtle analysis of Justin's embrace of outsider status as a gentile, illuminating the process by which he constructs a new identity for gentile Christians as a distinct and separate race (γένος) and as the people (λαόν) prophesied to inherit the covenant. I suggest that this line of thinking represents a later stage in the production of the *Dialogue* and reflects Justin's later and more developed thinking on the subject.

59 See John W. Marshall, *Parables of War: Reading John's Jewish Apocalypse*, Studies in Christianity and Judaism (Waterloo: Wilfrid Laurier University Press, 2001), 127–31; and David Frankfurter, "Jews or Not? Reconstructing the 'Other' in Rev 2:9 and 3:9," *Harvard Theological Review* 94, no. 4 (2001): 403–25.

60 Other scholars have read the debate over circumcision and sabbath observance to indicate that Trypho's companions are non-Jewish proselytes, whom Justin hopes to convince with his arguments about Jesus's messianic status. I do not see evidence for this conclusion in the text; rather, I see the debate being generated by Trypho's commitment to Deuteronomic theodicy: salvation is tied to observance of the law even for followers of Jesus.

61 See also Dulk, *Between Jews and Heretics*, 40, who emphasizes the variety and lack of unity among Jesus followers.

62 Dulk, *Between Jews and Heretics*, 90n11, notes that "Justin's multiple references to the Christians as 'we gentiles' ...suggests that the group had a predominantly, or even exclusively, gentile character." This may be true for Justin's cohort, but other evidence points to communities of law-abiding Jesus people existing well into the fourth century CE. I suggest that it was specifically gentile Jesus people who embraced the term "Christian," and with it a new identity, while Judean Jesus people continued to see him within the scope of Judean messianic traditions. They had no need to embrace a new identity. Boyarin, "Justin Martyr Invents Judaism," 461, proposes relabelling the undifferentiated entity of Justin's time "Jewish-Christianity" to deconstruct "the binary opposition of two mutually exclusive entities." This label still anachronistically employs the term "Christian" *avant la lettre*. See also Reed, *Jewish-Christianity and the History of Judaism*,

xxiii-xxvii, who sees heuristic value in critically engaging this label, its scholarly history, and preconceptions.

63 Marcovich, *Iustini Martyris Dialogus Cum Tryphone*, 1. Horner, *Listening to Trypho*, 7, 62, gives 160 CE as the date for the final composition, which includes a record of the actual debate that occurred c. 135 CE.

64 Horner, *Listening to Trypho*, 40. Skarsaune, *Proof from Prophecy*, marshals evidence for a "kerygma source" that Justin drew upon to support his arguments against Trypho. See also Oskar Skarsaune, "Jewish Sources Used by Justin Martyr and Some Other Greek and Latin Fathers," in *Jewish Believers in Jesus: The Early Centuries*, ed. Oskar Skarsaune and Reidar Hvalvik (Peabody: Hendrickson, 2007), 379–416, for a summary. It consisted of selected passages from Hebrew scriptures with accompanying interpretations that Justin quotes largely verbatim. Skarsaune posits a Jewish Christian milieu for the origin of these texts.

65 Other scholars, such as Nilson, "To Whom," 541, similarly posit that the *Dialogue* is an expansion upon a real debate that occurred shortly after 135 CE. Horner, *Listening to Trypho*, 19–23, provides a useful summary and critique of their positions although I find his classification a little forced: most of the scholars he discusses would likely see their arguments crossing the borders that Horner constructs to classify them.

66 Goodenough, *Theology of Justin Martyr*, 87, describes the *Dialogue* as "astonishingly dull." Wilson, *Related Strangers*, 261, describes it as "lengthy," "rambling," and "tangential." Dulk, *Between Jews and Heretics*, 4–5, links these accretions to Justin's attack on various forms of Jesus-belief that he deems heretical in the first recorded attempt to delineate acceptable and unacceptable forms of Christianity – the term and concept of a singled codified doctrine conceived in the process.

67 Rajak, "Talking at Trypho," 60, 68, 70–1, notes the vitriolic tone and harsh condemnation of Jews that she says precludes proselytizing Judeans for conversion to Christianity. Notwithstanding Justin's attacks on Judeans, Trakatellis, "Justin Martyr's Trypho," notes the positive portrait of Trypho throughout the *Dialogue*. While some scholars dismissively attribute Trypho's good nature to his role as a straw man, enabling Justin's theological excursus, Trakatellis's argument presents a Trypho well in tune with Jewish interlocative tradition as reflected in rabbinic literature: he expresses an openness to different interpretations, a zeal for exploring scripture, and an ability to remain amicably unpersuaded at the end of a long debate. Dulk, *Between Jews and Heretics*, 64n11, argues that Justin's harsh anti-Jewish polemic is intended to address charges of "demiurgists," like Marcion, who capitalized on the misfortune of Judeans to prove that the biblical God was entirely separate from the god of Jesus. In other words, the Jews are a foil for "heretics" and not the actual target of Justin's *Dialogue*.

68 *4 Ezra* 11–13; *2 Baruch* 29–30; Rev 5:5; 12:10; 19:11; and y. Ta'anit 4.5:13 document messianic expectations during the interbellum period, leading up to the Bar Kokhba rebellion.

69 As Justin still apparently does. See discussion in Goodenough, *Theology of Justin Martyr*, 282–3.

70 This process of differentiation occurred to different degrees in different places and among different communities, leading scholars to invent terms such as "Jewish-Christian" to label the often disturbing hybridity of Jesus followers well after the first century CE. Such terms anachronistically essentialize Judaism and Christianity as discrete and opposing entities. See Reed, *Jewish-Christianity and the History of Judaism*, xvi-xx. The introduction to *The Ways That Never Parted: Jews and Christians in Late Antiquity and the Early Middle Ages*, ed. Adam H. Becker and Annette Yoshiko Reed (Tübingen: Mohr Siebeck, 2003), lays out the problem well. In that volume, see especially Annette Yoshiko Reed, "'Jewish Christianity' after the Parting of the Ways: Approaches to Historiography and Self-Definition in the Pseudo-Clementine Literature," in Becker and Reed, *Ways That Never Parted*, 188–231; David Frankfurter, "Beyond 'Jewish Christianity': Continuing Religious Sub-Cultures of the Second and Third Centuries and Their Documents," in Becker and Reed, *Ways That Never Parted*, 131–44; and Adam H. Becker, "Beyond the Spatial and Temporal *Limes*: Questioning the 'Parting of the Ways' Outside the Roman Empire," in Becker and Reed, *Ways That Never Parted*, 373–92.

71 Jesus people who do not follow Justin's line of thinking (perhaps still a majority) find themselves increasingly marginalized over the course of the century as Judaizers. Dulk, *Between Jews and Heretics*, 81–3, argues that blaming the Jews for the failed revolts against Rome responded to demiurgists, who rejected the Judean God as impotent. Justin thus recuperates God's honour at the cost of blaming Jews.

72 Horner, *Listening to Trypho*, 95; Dulk, *Between Jews and Heretics*, 4; Nilson, "To Whom," 539, argues that converting Trypho or Jews is not Justin's goal; rather he seeks to convince gentile proselytes to Judaism to become Christian instead. The stark anti-Judaism of the *Dialogue* furthers this goal by deprecating his competitor. Andrew Hofer, "The Old Man as Christ in Justin's 'Dialogue with Trypho,'" *Vigiliae Christianae* 57, no. 1 (2003): 9, also regards conversion to be the primary focus of the *Dial*.

73 Dulk, *Between Jews and Heretics*, 4.

74 Nilson, "To Whom," 539.

75 Neal, *National Trauma*, 18–19.

16

Jubilees and Jewishness in Hasmonean Judea: Linking Text and Context in the Study of Jewish Identity with the Help of Ethnic Studies

John Van Maaren

INTRODUCTION

What made one a Jew in antiquity and what did it mean to be one?[1] This question has received much attention and numerous answers in recent years: Jewishness[2] is variously labelled as an ethnicity,[3] a religion,[4] an ethno-religion,[5] and a national identity.[6] Changes in the meaning and function of Jewishness have also been identified: Shaye Cohen argues that there was a shift from ethnicity to ethno-religion towards the end of the second century BCE due to Hasmonean mimicry of Greekness, a label that had itself morphed from an ethnic category into a cultural designation;[7] Daniel Boyarin argues for the beginning of a religious definition in the fourth century CE during the Christianization of the Roman Empire.[8] Criticisms of the enterprise have noted that scholars too often work in binaries (e.g., *either* a religion *or* an ethnic group), emphasizing that the reality is more complex.[9] As the theses of Cohen and Boyarin illustrate, perceived changes in Jewishness are often attributed to macro-level political causes. However, existing studies of Jewishness have mostly relied on common sense for linking macro-level political developments to changes in how Jews understood their Jewishness. In a recent project I introduced a mechanism from the social sciences that I believe can usefully be applied to the study of Jewishness in antiquity.[10] After outlining a few salient parts of the model, I use the book of *Jubilees* as a case study to illustrate the model's usefulness.

THE ETHNIC BOUNDARY MAKING MODEL

In *Ethnic Boundary Making: Institutions, Power, Networks*, anthropologist-turned-sociologist Andreas Wimmer developed the first comparative analytic that explains changes in the form and function of ethnicity by "a cycle of reproduction and transformation composed of various stabilizing and transformative feedbacks."[11] The model is part of a focus in the last twenty years among sociologists of ethnicity on the mechanisms influencing ethnic identity construction, a tradition that traces its roots to Fredrick Barth's oft-cited volume, *Ethnic Groups and Boundaries: The Social Organization of Culture Difference*.[12] Wimmer's model addresses the stated need for more systemization of boundary processes.[13] As the only attempt at "systematically explaining the varying character and consequences of ethnic boundaries,"[14] it represents a unique resource for developing a more nuanced definition of Jewishness.

The full model is depicted in figure 16.1. The left side of the model represents macro-level factors influencing ethnic construction, especially political structures and boundary characteristics, while the right side represents micro-level factors influencing ethnic construction, especially how individual persons engage in the struggle over the meaning, location, and relevance of ethnic groups and boundaries in a contested social field.

While the entire model is useful for defining Jewishness in antiquity, this chapter focuses on three macro-level field characteristics (figure 16.2) that influence how individuals construct their identity: the institutional order, the distribution of power, and the networks of alliances. First, the institutional order influences whether persons will draw and emphasize ethnic boundaries rather than other types of boundaries, such as class or gender.[15] That is, the formal policies and the informal conventions of the ruling power provide incentives for persons to make and to emphasize certain types of boundaries. For example, if a ruling power aligns itself with a national ethnic group, it provides incentives for persons to emphasize their ethnic identity in order to be included among the national ethnicity. In the same way, groups excluded from the majority ethnic group also have incentives to organize along ethnic lines and gain recognition as a minority ethnic group. The institutional order, then, primarily influences *whether* ethnicity matters. For our purposes, the institutional order does not directly influence who was Jewish and what it meant to be Jewish, but it does provide a partial explanation for the salience of Jewishness and its long-term durability.

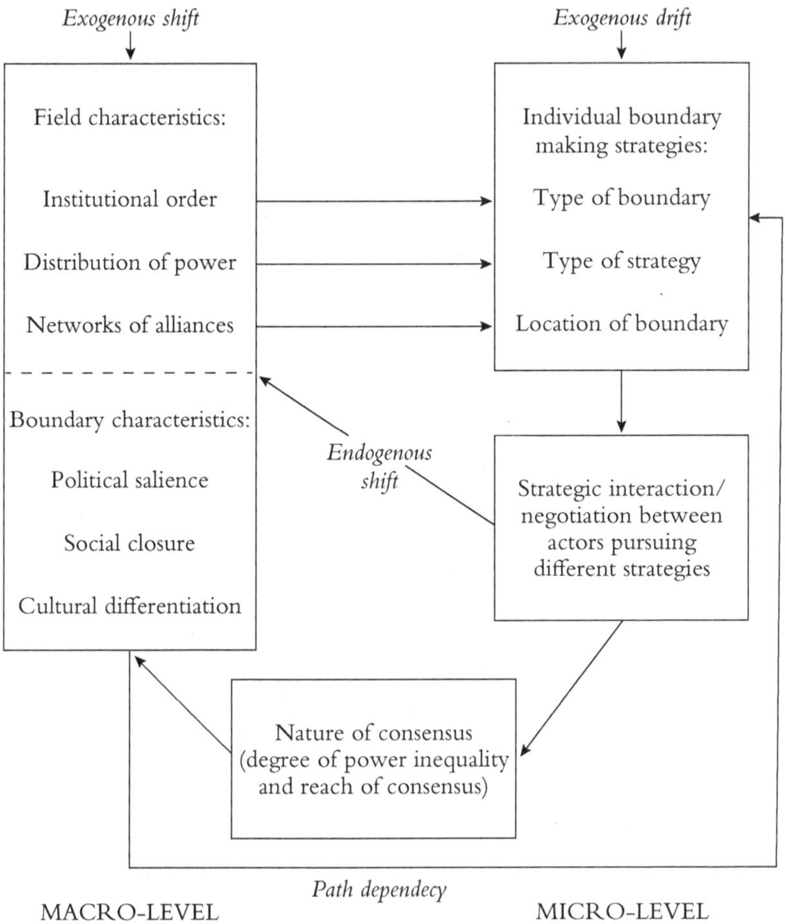

16.1 A processual model of the making and unmaking of ethnic boundaries

Second, the distribution of power between members of different ethnic groups influences the types of strategies that they attempt in the competition over the meaning, relevance, and location of ethnic boundaries.[16] A person's place in the hierarchy of boundaries influences their choice in two ways. First, persons will tend to interact in ways that allow them to claim an advantageous position in relation to individuals of other ethnic groups. Second, one's place in the ranked boundary system determines which resources are available to make one's preferred vision of the ethnic landscape relevant for others. Most obviously, those in control of the institutional power have a clear advantage in making their ethnic vision relevant for others, while those

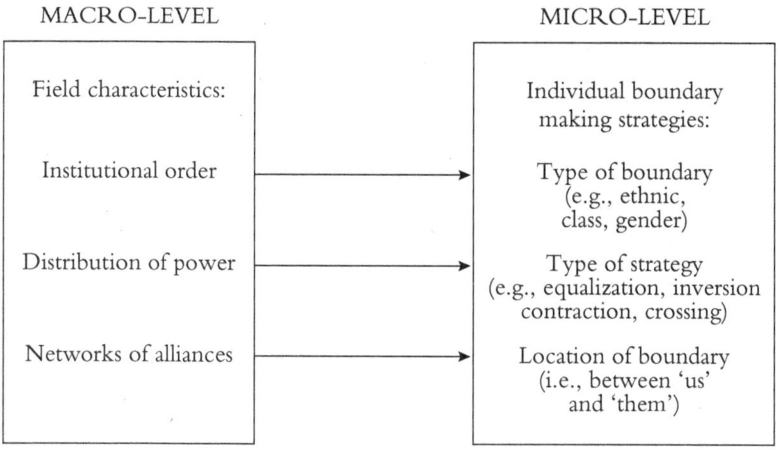

16.2 Field characteristics

excluded may resort to counter discourses, whether through text production or placing emphasis on a higher or lower level of ethnic identity, such as Jewish rather than Galilean, or vice versa.[17] For example, in the United States members of the white middle class may emphasize professional competence and achievement as criteria of moral and social superiority,[18] while some African Americans, in order to counter exclusion or stigmatization and invert the hierarchical black/white boundary, may emphasize the "hipness" of black culture.[19] The dynamics of power, then, primarily influence which strategies people will pursue. The various strategies are pursued by emphasizing or reworking some aspect of ethnicity and potentially modifying what it means to be Jewish. This will be illustrated below with the book of *Jubilees*.

Third, the extent to which the networks of personal relationships of state elites extend into various segments of the population will determine the location of the boundary between a national majority and the various ethnic minorities.[20] To use examples from the more recent past, when slavery was abolished in Brazil, Brazil's elite relied on ties that stretched into a middle class of mixed ethnic origins, and state elites attempted to integrate and mix these peoples. In contrast, when slavery was abolished in the United States, the middle class was nearly exclusively white, leading to an image of the nation as white.[21] In this way, the network of personal relationships of state elites influences the location of ethnic boundaries between a national majority and marginalized minority groups. These networks of personal relationships then can alter who is, and who is not, identified as Jewish by the ruling elite.

CASE STUDY: *JUBILEES* AND JEWISHNESS IN HASMONEAN JUDEA

The second part of this chapter uses *Jubilees* as a case study to illustrate the usefulness of the ethnic boundary making model for defining Jewishness. While people have proposed a number of different dates for *Jubilees*, I am convinced by Martha Himmelfarb's argument that the writer's interests in intermarriage, conversion, and especially the status of the descendants of Esau fit best with a date during the high priesthood of John Hyrcanus I (134–104 BCE).[22] This section first outlines the relevant field characteristics of Hasmonean Judea at the time of John Hyrcanus I and then examines how the writer of *Jubilees* engages in the strategic renegotiation of ethnic boundaries.

My understanding of the field characteristics of Hasmonean Judea at the end of the second century BCE are summarized in figure 16.3 and discussed below.

First, according to the ethnic boundary making model, the institutional frameworks influence whether ethnic categorization matters. In the case of Hasmonean Judea, the Hasmonean rulers aligned themselves with the Jewish people. This can be demonstrated from both archaeological and textual sources. First, the legends on all coins issued by John Hyrcanus I (as well as coins of all subsequent Hasmonean rulers) combine the name of the Hasmonean high priest with a reference to the Jews as a people group (היהדים חבר).[23] The Hasmonean choice of this joint designation communicates that they ruled "*for* and *with* the Jewish people."[24] Second, 1 Maccabees, a Hasmonean propagandist narrative, aligns the Hasmoneans with the Jews by presenting the Hasmoneans as saviours and legitimate leaders of the Jewish people.[25] Therefore, in Hasmonean Judea, including during the time of John Hyrcanus I, the institutional frameworks provide incentives for people to emphasize their Jewishness rather than other non-ethnic ways of grouping persons, and the importance of Jewishness, and ethnic identity more generally, is elevated in and around Hasmonean Judea.

Second, according to the ethnic boundary making model, the distribution of power provides incentives for persons to attempt to change the ethnic boundaries in specific ways and also restricts the types of ways a person can seek to change them. The Jews, aligned with the ruling Hasmoneans, formed a privileged majority at the top of the ranked boundary system in and around Hasmonean Judea. In addition, the available sources suggest that, at least through the high priesthood of Hyrcanus, the Hasmoneans sought to expel non-Jews from their expanding territory and to create a mono-ethnic, homogenous national majority.[26] Therefore, the distribution of power

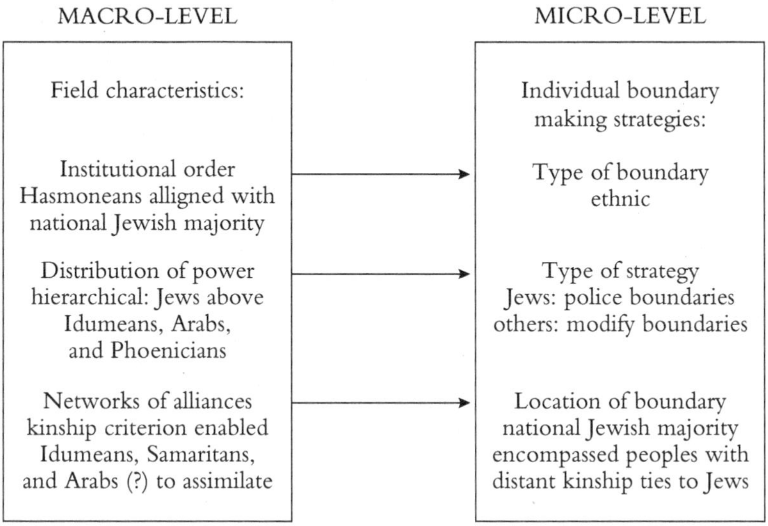

16.3 Hasmonean field characteristics

provided Jews incentives to police the Jew/non-Jew boundary and to prevent non-Jews from crossing the boundary and becoming Jewish. Among members of the Jews, only the elite Jews close to the Hasmonean rulers had access to official means of boundary making.

Third, the networks of personal alliances established by state elites determine the location of the boundary between the national privileged majority and the marginalized "other." In the case of the Hasmonean state there is insufficient data to relate the networks of alliances with the various people groups of Coele-Syria and Phoenicia to the boundaries of the national Jewish *ethnos*.[27] However, the attempt by John Hyrcanus I to incorporate Idumeans and Samaritans, but not Greeks, within their nation-building project finds a ready explanation within the ethnic boundary making model: the selection of Idumeans, identified as descendants of Esau, and Samaritans, tracing descent from Jacob,[28] suggests that the Hasmoneans employed a criterion of kinship through Abraham in their selection of those people groups who were included, most likely by force, to integrate into the national Jewish ethnic group.[29] According to the same genealogical criterion, Greeks, aligned with the Seleucid Greek Empire against which the Hasmoneans defined themselves, are conveniently excluded.[30]

It is worth noting at this point that the evidence suggests that the Hasmonean nation-building project seemed to retain the common proper name "the Jews" rather than shift the emphasis to a higher-level ethnic classification such as "Israel" or some more encompassing label that emphasized descent from Abraham. This is suggested by Josephus's later summary that "from this time on they [Idumeans] have continued to be Jews."[31] It is further supported by the earliest written evidence for official Hasmonean policy. The writer of 1 Maccabees uses "the Jews" and "Israel" apparently synonymously.[32] In the context within which most Jewish writers in antiquity use "the Jews" for descendants of the southern kingdom of Judah and so as a subcategory of larger "Israel," which encompasses those from both the southern and northern kingdom, the interchangeable use of "the Jews" and "Israel" suggests a strategy of nation building around the common proper name "the Jews."[33] In the categories of the ethnic boundary making model, this represents a boundary expansion of the category "the Jews" through incorporation of other peoples rather than boundary expansion through an emphasis shift from "the Jews" to "Israel" or through amalgamation into a new ethnic category that emphasized descent from Abraham.[34]

It has often been noted that Hyrcanus's incorporation of Idumeans within the Jews may have been based on kinship ties.[35] In addition, there is good reason to believe that Hyrcanus's destruction of the temple on Mount Gerizim was meant to reorient the Samaritans to the Jerusalem temple, and not to expel them from their land.[36] In contrast to the Greek cities of Samaria and Scythopolis, whose inhabitants Josephus expelled, and whose hinterlands show a significant population decrease,[37] regional surveys around Mount Gerizim and Shechem show no population decline,[38] indicating that Hyrcanus did not expel the Samaritans, a people group who claimed ancestry from Jacob. In contrast, there is no evidence that Hyrcanus enabled the Phoenician inhabitants of the conquered coastal cities to assimilate to the Jewish *ethnos*.[39] Further confirmation might be found in Josephus's note that Aristobulus incorporated the Itureans into the Jewish *ethnos*. The Itureans were likely an Arab tribe, and at least some Jewish texts from the time period (e.g., *Jubilees*) understand the Arab tribes as descendants of Ishmael and the other sons of Abraham.

In summary, then, during the high priesthood of John Hyrcanus, the field characteristics influenced the ethnic boundary system in the following way: the independence of the Hasmonean state created an autonomous political entity that aligned itself with the Jewish *ethnos*, thereby elevating the significance of drawing ethnic boundaries and privileging Jews over members of other ethnic groups. While earlier leaders of the Hasmonean dynasty expelled non-Jews from the expanding Hasmonean territory, John Hyrcanus sought to expand the location of the Jewish boundary by compelling members of ethnic groups with putative kinship ties to the Jews through Abraham to either cross the boundary and become Jews or to leave.

In the social field of Hasmonean Judea with the above field characteristics, *Jubilees* represents one particular vision of the ideal boundary system of Judea (figure 16.4). Anti-Hasmonean elements suggest that the writer is not aligned with the Hasmonean rulers.[40] Therefore, the writer lacks access to official means to make their ideal vision relevant for others and instead employs a *discursive* means of boundary making through rewriting the historical memories of the Jews. As someone without access to official means of boundary making, the writer has an incentive to police the Jew/non-Jew boundaries against boundary crossing by non-Jews in order to maintain privileged status. This policing of ethnic boundaries contrasts with Hasmonean boundary expansion.

Discursive *means* of boundary making use categorization and identification to present an ideal vision of the ethnic boundaries.[41] In contrast to the Hasmonean nation-building project centred around the Jewish *ethnos*, the writer of *Jubilees* consistently uses "Israel."[42] While the Israel/Greek boundary is only implicit in *Jubilees*, the writer directly addresses the Israel/Idumean and Israel/Arab boundaries. The writer associates the descendants of Esau with the present-day Idumeans,[43] and the descendants of Ishmael and Abraham's other sons with Arab people groups,[44] and has a special interest in each.[45] Most interesting for our purpose, the writer used eighth-day circumcision to identify members of Israel and to attempt to exclude Idumeans and Arabs. "Anyone who is born, the flesh of whose private parts has not been circumcised by the eighth day, does not belong to the people of the pact which the Lord made with Abraham but to the people [meant for] destruction ...Now you command the Israelites to keep this sign of this covenant ...For the Lord did not draw near to himself either Ishmael, his sons, his brothers, or Esau. He did not choose them [simply] because they were among Abraham's children, for he knew them. But he chose Israel to be his people" (15:26–30). The writer of *Jubilees* also attempts to counteract boundary crossing by promoting the holy seed ideology of the book of Ezra[46] and prohibiting exogamy.[47] The writer reinforces the boundary distinguishing Isreal from the nations by claiming that God has caused all other peoples to be governed by spirits that lead them astray.[48]

Interestingly, the logic of *Jubilees's* boundary contraction does not necessarily exclude Samaritans from Israel, although the writer never addresses their status directly. Based on the writer's criteria noted above, it is conceivable that they might have welcomed them if they accepted their claim to Israelite descent, rejected the idea that they had intermarried with the other people groups who were resettled in their ancestral homeland, and if they had practised circumcision on the eighth day. Ultimately, this is unknown,

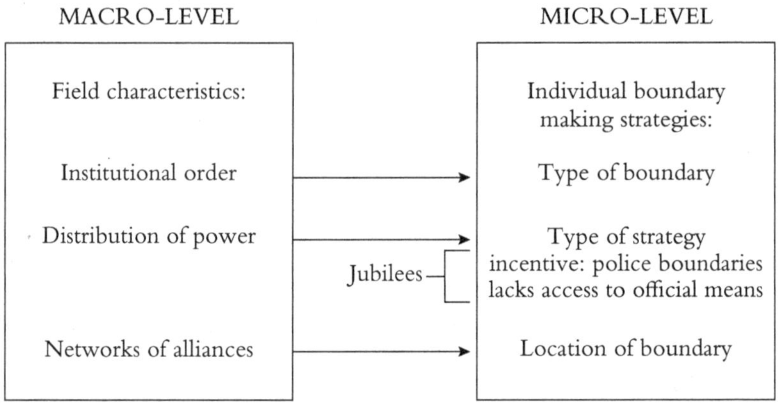

16.4 *Jubilees*'s strategies of boundary making

but it is at least possible that the writer objected to the Hasmonean incorporation of Idumeans and possible Itureans but accepted their attempt at the reorientation of the Samaritans to the Jerusalem temple cult.

The evidence from *Jubilees* can be compared with the strategies of the Hasmonean rulers and depicted by something like figure 16.5. Whereas the Hasmomean rulers sought to expand Jewishness by redefining it based on descent from Abraham, the writer of *Jubilees* emphasized Israel, excluding Idumeans and Arabs, while possibly including Samaritans. Still, the boundary of *Jubilees's* Israel excludes some persons who might otherwise claim Israelite descent (whether Samaritans or Jews) on the basis of either intermarriage or poorly timed circumcision, and so the boundary of Israel, for *Jubilees*, runs through those who would otherwise claim descent from the southern kingdom of Judah or the northern kingdom of Israel.

This can be filled out with other texts from the time period for a more complex understanding of types of boundary making strategies.[49] Further, the types of strategies reflect back on the type of boundary consensus and boundary characteristics. Even without incorporating other evidence for the time of John Hyrcanus, the evidence of *Jubilees* suggests a couple of things about the ethnic boundaries.[50] First, the writer of *Jubilees* and the Hasmonean rulers agree about the *relevance* of the Israel/nations boundary (i.e., the category "Israel" matters). Since *Jubilees* includes no Jew/nations boundary, it is easier here to talk about an Israel/nations boundary. Second, they disagree about who is a member of Israel (i.e., the *location* of the boundary separating Israel from other peoples). For *Jubilees* Israel includes those descended from Jacob apart from intermarriage with other peoples and who are circumcised

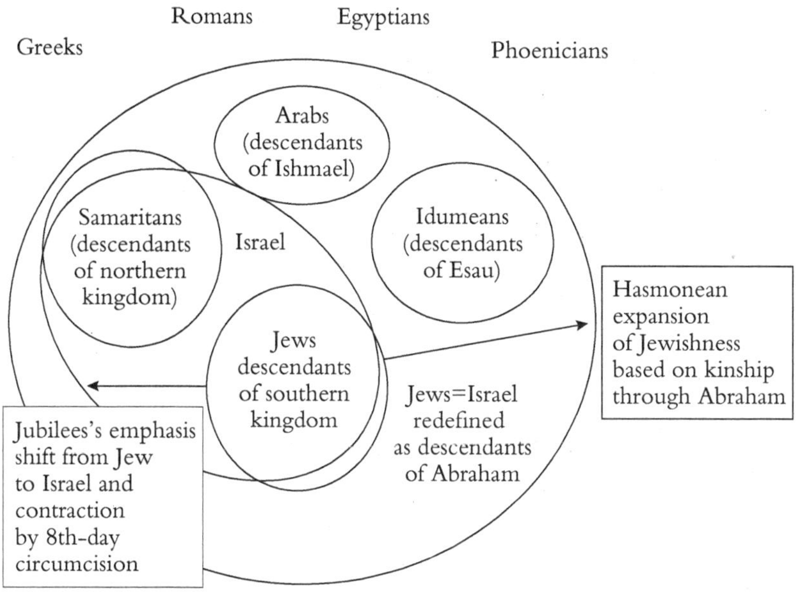

16.5 Competing ideal visions of Jewishness and its boundaries

on the eighth day. For the Hasmoneans – as seen through 1 Maccabees – Israel is equated with the Jews and is expanded to include those with putative descent from Abraham. This means that the boundary consensus is not *encompassing* but only *partial*. The lack of an *encompassing* consensus reflects on boundary characteristics and suggests, for example, that the accretion of additional cultural diacritics that marked Jews/Israel from others may have developed less smoothly. Third, the writer of *Jubilees* and the Hasmonean rulers also disagree about the significance of Jewishness (i.e., its *meaning*). The Jewishness of the Hasmonean rulers, as far as they identify the Hasmonean state as a Jewish state, can be designated "nationalism." The writer of *Jubilees*, who defines Israel in strictly genealogical terms, adopts a definition of that can be subcategorized (in modern parlance) as a "race."

CONCLUSION

What then, was Jewishness at the end of the second century BCE? It depends on whom you ask. For the Hasmonean rulers who attempted to expand the boundaries, it functions as a national identity. The writer of *Jubilees*, quite possibly in response to Hasmonean nation building, attempted to contract boundaries. These contrasting strategies of boundary making also influenced the ideal ethnic-configuration of Jewishness. In the case of *Jubilees* and the Hasmonean rulers, this is seen most clearly in different appropriations of genealogical descent and the sign of circumcision. Aspects that we commonly associate with the modern category "religion" are also employed by both the Hasmonean rulers and the writer of *Jubilees*, but these cannot so easily be separated from ethnic, political, and other factors in antiquity as well as today.

NOTES

1 The object of investigation is not the meaning of the *proper name* "Jew" (יהודי, Ἰουδαῖος, *Iudaeus*) but a group of people who used multiple proper names, including "Israel" (ישראל, Ἰσραήλ) and "Hebrew" (עברי, Ἑβραῖος) with sometimes different meanings and cultivated a *sense of solidarity* through shared *historical memories*, a link to a *common homeland*, and one or more elements of *common culture*, including language, religion, and customs. These six common elements of ethnic groups are outlined by John Hutchinson and Anthony D. Smith, "Introduction," in *Ethnicity*, ed. John Hutchinson and Anthony D. Smith (New York: Oxford University Press, 1996), 1–14. The choice of the English "Jew" here is pragmatic.

2 The use of the intentionally vague term "Jewishness" rather than "Judaism" is meant to disassociate the study from modern connotations of Judaism, which is sometimes understood in too strictly "religious" terms. Here I follow Shaye J.D. Cohen, *The Beginnings of Jewishness: Boundaries, Varieties, Uncertainties*, HCS 31 (Berkeley: University of California Press, 1990), 7–9. My interest is in the way that ancient Jews defined themselves, but I use modern categories heuristically. The model outlined below adopts a broad definition of ethnicity into which the ancient Jews fit nicely: "a subjectively felt belonging to a group that is distinguished by a shared culture and by common ancestry." The model understands designations like racial, ethno-religious, national, ethnosomatic, ethnoregional, and ethnolinguistic groups as subcategories of ethnicity (Andreas Wimmer, *Ethnic Boundary Making: Institutions, Power, Networks* [New York: Oxford University Press, 2013], 7–8).

3 For example, Steve Mason, "Jews, Judaeans, Judaizing, Judaism: Problems of Categorization in Ancient History," *Journal for the Study of Judaism in the Persian, Hellenistic and Roman Period* 38 (2007): 457–512.

4 For example, Shaye J.D. Cohen, "Religion, Ethnicity, and 'Hellenism' in the Emergence of Jewish Identity in Maccabean Palestine," in *Religion and Religious Practice in the Seleucid Kingdom*, ed. Per Bilde (Aarhus: Aarhus University Press, 1990), 204–23.

5 For example, Cohen, "Religion, Ethnicity, and 'Hellenism,'" 109–93.

6 For example, David Goodblatt, *Elements of Ancient Jewish Nationalism* (New York: Cambridge University Press, 2006).

7 Cohen, *Beginnings of Jewishness*, 109–39. Cohen follows Jonathan M. Hall (*Ethnic Identity in Greek Antiquity* [New York: Cambridge University Press, 1997] and *Hellenicity: Between Ethnicity and Culture* [Chicago: University of Chicago Press, 2002]) in his understanding of Greekness.

8 Daniel Boyarin, *Dying for God: Martyrdom and the Making of Christianity and Judaism* (Redwood City, CA: Stanford University Press, 1999).

9 Seth Schwartz, "How Many Judaisms Were There? A Critique of Neusner and Smith on Definition and Mason and Boyarin on Categorization," *Journal of Ancient Judaism* 2 (2011): 231.

10 John Van Maaren, *The Boundaries of Jewishness 200 BCE–135 CE: Power, Strategies, and Ethnic Configurations*, Studia Judaica (Berlin: De Gruyter, 2022); cf. Van Maaren, "Mapping Jewishness in Antiquity," *Journal of Ancient Judaism* 9, no. 3 (2018): 421–54.

11 Wimmer, *Ethnic Boundary Making*, 111.

12 Fredrik Barth, "Introduction," in *Ethnic Groups and Boundaries: The Social Organization of Culture Difference*, ed. Fredrik Barth (London: Allen and Unwin, 1969), 9–38.

13 Michèle Lamont and Virág Molnár, "The Study of Boundaries in the Social Sciences," *Annual Review of Sociology* 28, no. 1 (2002): 175.

14 Wimmer, *Ethnic Boundary Making*, 80.

15 Ibid., 90–3.

16 Ibid., 93–5.

17 The model acknowledges that persons may possess multiple ethnic identities and that these are arranged in a "hierarchy of nested segments" so that one's identity as a Galilean, or Idumean, does not exclude one from also identifying as a Jew (Wimmer, *Ethnic Boundary Making*, 23–5; cf. 139–73). This insight goes back to Michael Moerman, "Ethnic Identification in a Complex Civilization: Who Are the Lue?," *American Anthropologist* 67, no. 5 (1965): 1215–30. It was developed by the situationalist school, especially Judith Nagata, "What Is a Malay? Situational Selection of Ethnic Identity in a Plural Society," *American Ethnologist* 1, no. 2 (1974): 331–50; and Jonathan Okamura, "Situational Ethnicity," *Ethnic and Racial Studies* 4, no. 4 (1981): 452–65.

18 Michèle Lamont and Crystal Fleming, "Everyday Antiracism: Competence and Religion in the Cultural Repertoire of the African American Elite," *Du Bois Review* 2 (2005): 29–43.

19 Michèle Lamont and Virág Molnár, "How Blacks Use Consumption to Shape Their Collective Identity: Evidence from African-American Marketing Specialists," *Journal of Consumer Culture* 1 (2001): 31–45.

20 Wimmer, *Ethnic Boundary Making*, 95–7.

21 Anthony W. Marx, *Making Race and Nation: A Comparison of the United States, South Africa, and Brazil* (Cambridge: Cambridge University Press, 1999).

22 Martha Himmelfarb, *A Kingdom of Priests: Ancestry and Merit in Ancient Judaism*, Jewish Culture and Contexts (Philadelphia: University of Pennsylvania Press,

2006), 55, 72, 75. Cf. Eyal Regev, "Jubilees, Qumran, and the Essenes," in *Enoch and the Mosaic Torah: The Evidence of Jubilees*, ed. Gabriele Boccaccini and Giovanni Ibba (Grand Rapids: Eerdmans, 2009), 435–40; Michael Segal, *The Book of Jubilees: Rewritten Bible, Redaction, Ideology and Theology*, JSJSup 117 (Boston: Brill, 2007), 332.

23 John Hyrcanus I's coins explicitly associate him with the Jewish ἔθνος: יהוחנן כהן גדל וחבר היהדים. Some also describe him as the "head" (ראש) of the Jewish people: יהוחנן כהן גדל ראש חבר היהדים (George F. Hill, *Catalogue of the Greek Coins of Palestine [Galilee, Samaria, and Judaea]* [Bologna: A. Forni, 1965], 188–96; Eyal Regev, *The Hasmoneans: Ideology, Archaeology, Identity*, JAJSup 10 [Göttingen: Vandenhoeck & Ruprecht, 2013], 188–9, 193–6). Some have suggested חבר referred to a council that ruled jointly with John Hyrcanus I (e.g., Daniel Sperber, "A Note on Hasmonean Coin-Legends: Heber and Roš Heber," *Palestine Exploration Quarterly* 97 [1965]: 85–93; Baruch Kanael, "Ancient Jewish Coins and Their Historical Importance," *Biblical Archaeologist* 26, no. 2 [1963]: 38–62, 43–44). However, parallels with coins from Greek, Roman, and Phoenician cities, which often refer to citizens but never a ruling council, suggest that חבר refers to the Jewish people collectively and not a specific council or delegation. In addition, חבר more often refers to a general association rather than a council of delegates (Benedikt Eckhardt, *Ethnos und Herrschaft: politische Figurationen judäischer Identität von Antiochos III Bis Herodes I*, SJ 72 [Berlin: De Gruyter, 2013], 62–3).

24 Regev, *Hasmoneans*, 199 (emphasis in original).

25 John R. Bartlett, *1 Maccabees*, Guides to Apocrypha and Pseudepigrapha (Sheffield: Sheffield Academic, 1998), 33; Stephanie von Dobbeler, *Die Bücher 1–2 Makkabäer*, NSKAT 11 (Stuttgart: Katholisches Bibelwerk, 1997), 46.

26 However, unlike his predecessors, John Hyrcanus seems to have allowed some non-Jewish inhabitants of conquered areas to cross the boundary into the national Jewish *ethnos* (discussed below). John Hyrcanus's policy of forced expulsion represents a strategic *means* of *discrimination*. It is also in continuity with the policies of Jonathan and Simon. According to 1 Maccabees, Simon expelled the non-Jewish inhabitants of Joppa and Gezer and resettled them with Jews (1 Macc 13:11, 47–8). At Gezer, a destruction layer in the archaeological remains confirms Simon's conquest, and the presence of Miqva'oth in the resettlement layer corroborates 1 Maccabees' claim that the new inhabitants were Jews (Ronny Reich, "Archaeological Evidence of the Jewish Population at Hasmonean Gezer," *Israel Exploration Journal* 31, nos. 1 and 2 [1981]: 48–52, 49–51). Further confirmation is provided by thirteen boundary stones, written in Hebrew, demarcating Gezer's agricultural land from those of the surrounding areas, written in Greek (Ben-Zion Rosenfeld, "The 'Boundary of Gezer' Inscriptions and the History of Gezer at the End of the Second Temple Period," *Israel Exploration Journal* 38, no. 4 [1988]: 235–45). That under Jonathan and Simon the repopulation of Gezer was part of a wider policy of expelling non-Jews from Hasmonean territory and resettling it with Jews is confirmed by the destruction and abandonment of non-Jewish settlements within the province of Judea (Andrea M. Berlin, "Between Large

Forces: Palestine in the Hellenistic Period," *Biblical Archaeologist* 60, no. 1 [1997]: 2–51, 28), the settlement of new sites (Shim'on Dar, *Landscape and Pattern: An Archaeological Survey of Samaria [800 B. C. E. – 636 C. E.]*, BARIS 308 [Oxford: B.A.R., 1986], 2:816), and the disappearance of pottery produced outside of Judea (Berlin, "Between Large Forces," 29).

27 Eyal Regev nicely summarizes the state of our sources when he writes "a detailed history of the Hasmoneans' internal affairs, namely, their political institutions and their relationships with the people, cannot be written; the sources are too scarce, and are highly biased either for or against the Hasmoneans" (Regev, *Hasmoneans*, 12).

28 Two honorary inscriptions at Delos, dated to the second century BCE, nicely illustrate Samaritan ancestral claims. Each identifies the originator as an "Israelite" (ΙΣΡΑΕΛΕΙΤΑΙ/ΙΣΡΑΗΛΙΤΑΙ) who is distinguished from other Israelites by sending the temple tax to Mount Gerizim (ΑΡΓΑΡΙΖΕΙΝ) (Philippe Bruneau, "'Les Israélites de Délos' et La Juiverie Délienne," *Bulletin de Correspondance Hellénique* 106 [1982]: 465–504, 484; Magnar Kartveit, "Samaritan Self-Consciousness in the First Half of the Second Century BCE in Light of the Inscriptions from Mount Gerizim and Delos," *Journal for the Study of Judaism in the Persian, Hellenistic and Roman Period* 45, nos.4 and 5 [2014]: 449–70, 466–8).

29 According to the ethnic boundary making model's typology of strategic *means*, Hyrcanus I's conversion/expulsion alternative represents a strategic *means* of *coercion and violence* by *forced assimilation* (Wimmer, *Ethnic Boundary Making*, 70–2). For the forced circumcision of the Idumeans and perhaps Itureans, see Steven Weitzman, "Forced Circumcision and the Shifting Role of Gentiles in Hasmonean Ideology," *Harvard Theological Review* 92 (1999): 37–59.

30 The Hasmonean self-definition over and against Greekness is seen most clearly in the Judea-Rome dichotomy in 1 Maccabees (Kevin Lee Osterloh, "Judea, Rome and the Hellenistic Oikoumenê: Emulation and the Reinvention of Communal Identity," in *Heresy and Identity in Late Antiquity*, ed. Eduard Iricinschi and Holger M. Zellentin, TSAJ [Tübingen: Mohr Siebeck, 2008], 185). While a kinship through Abraham might have been used to exclude Greeks and others from incorporation into the Hasmomean nation-building project, it did not seem to keep them from using fictive kinship through Abraham for other diplomatic purposes (cf. 1 Macc 12:21).

31 *Antiquities* 13.9.1.

32 In his wide-ranging study of these terms, Jason Staples summarizes: "unlike the other texts we have examined so far, 1 Maccabees uses 'Israel' and 'Israelites' (apparently) interchangeably with 'Judaea' and *Ioudaioi*." See Staples, *The Idea of Israel in Second Temple Judaism: A New Theory of People, Exile, and Israelite Identity* (Cambridge: Cambridge University Press, 2021), 167.

33 This explanation differs from Staples, who argues that it is the use of "Israel" language in 1 Maccabees that needs to be explained. See Staples, *Idea of Israel*, 170–71. In the context of the incorporation of other peoples with more distant kingship ties, the retention of "the Jews" appears more significant.

34 Wimmer, *Ethnic Boundary Making*, 49–63. Cf. Van Maaren, *Boundaries of Jewishness*, 25.

35 Josephus notes that John Hyrcanus I pursued this strategic *mode* of *boundary expansion* through *nation building* in relation to the Idumeans, who were permitted to remain in their land as long as they were circumcised and observed the customs of the Jews: "Hyrcanus also captured the Idumaean cities of Adora and Marisa, and after subduing all the Idumeans, permitted them to remain in their country so long as they had themselves circumcised and were willing to observe the laws of the Jews" (*Antiquities* 13.9.1). Strabo, writing earlier (c. 27 CE), states that the Idumeans joined the Jews by choice (*Geography* 15.2, 34), but this is inconsistent with the destruction at Maresha. The archaeological record suggests that some Idumeans remained, but many left. Continued occupation is attested at the Idumean sites of Tel Ḥalif and Tel 'Ira (Berlin, "Between Large Forces," 31). New settlements are attested at Tel Sera' and Horvat Rimmon in Idumea, which were quite possibly settled by Jews (Eliezer Oren, "Ziglag: A Biblical City on the Edge of the Negev," *Biblical Archaeologist* 45, no. 3 [1982]: 155–66, 158). Many other sites show widespread destruction and abandonment. A destruction layer at Maresha around 112 BCE and the abandonment of its lower city indicate that at least some of the inhabitants left (Amos Kloner, "Mareshah [Marisa]," in *New Encyclopedia of Archaeological Excavations in the Holy Land*, ed. E. Stern [New York: Simon and Shuster, 1993], esp. 3.953). Tel Beer-Sheva was abandoned soon after John Hyrcanus I's campaign (Dan Barag, "New Evidence on the Foreign Policy of John Hyrcanus I," *Israel Numismatic Journal* 12 [1992]: 1–12, 6). Numerous other sites show evidence of destruction and abandonment. These include Khirbet er-Rasm, Tel Arad, Khirbet 'Uza, and possibly Lachish (Avraham Faust, Oren Ackerman, and Adi Erlich, *The Excavations of Khirbet Er-Rasm, Israel: The Changing Faces of the Countryside*, BARIS 2187 [Oxford: Archaeopress, 2011], 208, 252; Moshe Fischer and Oren Tal, "The Hellenistic and Roman Periods," in *Horvat 'Uza and Horvat Radum: Two Fortresses in the Biblical Negev*, ed. Itzhaq Beit-Arieh, Institute of Archaeology Monograph Series 25 [Tel Aviv: Tel Aviv University Press, 2007], 335). Evidence for an increased Idumean presence in Egypt suggests some immigrated to Egypt (Uriel Rappaport, "Jewish Religious Propaganda and Proselytism in the Period of the Second Commonwealth" [PhD diss., Hebrew University of Jerusalem, 1965], 79–80, 82).

36 Jonathan Bourgel, "The Destruction of the Samaritan Temple by John Hyrcanus: A Reconsideration," *Journal of Biblical Literature* 135, no. 3 (2016): 505–23.

37 Josephus reports that Hyrcanus completely destroyed the πολίς of Samaria and enslaved its inhabitants (*Antiquities* 13.10.3). The destruction of the recently constructed fort wall confirms this destruction (John Winter Crowfoot, Kathleen M. Kenyon, and Eleazar L. Sukenik, *The Buildings at Samaria*, Samaria-Sebaste 1 [London: Palestine Exploration Fund, 1942], 30). Regional surveys show a significant decline in population around the Greek cities where only seven of the twenty-six Hellenistic sites in the surrounding area continued into the

Roman period (Adam Zertal, *The Manasseh Hill Country Survey*, vol. 1, *The Shechem Syncline*, CHANE 21 [Leiden: Brill, 2004], 63).

38 See the regional surveys of the valley surrounding Shechem (Edward F. Campbell, *Shechem II: Portrait of a Hill Country Vale – The Shechem Regional Survey*, ed. Karen I. Summers, VSOR Archaeological Reports 2 [Atlanta: Scholars Press, 1991]), southern Samaria (Israel L. Finkelstein, Zvi Lederman, Shelomoh Bunimovits, and Ran Barkai, *Highlands of Many Cultures: The Southern Samaria Survey: The Sites*, Sonia and Marco Nadler Institute of Archaeology Monograph Series 14 [Tel Aviv: Institute of Archaeology of Tel Aviv University Publications Section, 1997], 907–19, 953–4), and the areas of the Shechem Syncline (Zertal, *Manasseh Hill Country*, 63).

39 Among the coastal cities there is evidence for the removal of some inhabitants and for Jewish reoccupation. After the destruction of Azotus, it was immediately reoccupied, and during the reign of Alexander Jannaeus it is listed among the cities in his possession (Jos., *Antiquities* 13.15.4), making it at least likely that these new inhabitants were Jews (Berlin, "Between Large Forces," 30–1). The predominance of Phoenician pottery not found at known Jewish sites indicates that the earlier inhabitants of Shiqmona were almost certainly non-Jews, and after the town's destruction it was not immediately reoccupied (Joseph Elgavish, "Pottery from the Hellenistic Stratum at Shiqmona," *Israel Exploration Journal* 26, no. 23 [1976]: 65–76, 65).

40 Most prominently, much of *Jubilees* is aimed against the calendar used by the Hasmoneans (Himmelfarb, *Kingdom of Priests*, 76–7).

41 Wimmer, *Ethnic Boundary Making*, 64–5.

42 Eth. አስራኤል ፡ The two uses of "Hebrew" (ዕብራዊ ፡) as a proper name simply reflect its use in Torah (39:10; 47:7; cf. Gen 39:17; Exod 2:7).

43 "The Edomites have not extricated themselves from the yoke of servitude which Jacob's sons imposed on them until today" (*Jub* 38:14, cf. 38:12). English translations are from James C. VanderKam, *The Book of Jubilees: Translated*, CSCO 511 (Lovanii: Peeters, 1989).

44 "Ishmael, his sons, Keturah's sons, and their sons went together and settled from Paran as far as the entrance of Babylon – in all the land toward the east opposite the desert. They mixed with one another and were called Arabs and Ishmaelites" (20:12–3). Latin includes "until the present" (*usque in diem hanc*) at the end (James C. VanderKam, *The Book of Jubilees: A Critical Text*, CSCO 510 [Lovanii: Peeters, 1989]).

45 The writer of *Jubilees* deliberately enhances their profile of Abraham's other sons and associates them more closely with the promises made to their father Abraham. This connection is made by the addition of a final testament of Abraham that is addressed to Ishmael, Isaac, and the sons of Keturah (in that order) and commands them to worship the Lord, keep his commandments, circumcise their sons, and avoid exogamy (20:2–10). In other words, Abraham commands all his sons to be observant Jews (Doron Mendels, *The Land of Israel*

as a Political Concept in Hasmonean Literature: Recourse to History in Second Century BC Claims to the Holy Land, TSAJ 15 [Tübingen: Mohr, 1987], 149) Further, in Genesis, Ishmael's reward for being Abraham's son is to become a great nation but not a *blessing* to all nations, which is reserved for Isaac and then Jacob (Gen 12:2–3; 17:19–20; 21:13; 26:4; 28:14). However, in *Jubilees*, all Abraham's descendants become a blessing to the nations. Abraham addresses all his sons when he states: "You will become a blessing on the earth, and all the nations of the earth will be delighted with you. They will bless your sons in my name so that they may be blessed as I am" (*Jub* 20:10). At the end of Abraham's life he celebrates the festival of weeks with both Ishmael and Isaac (*Jub* 22:1–9). Whereas the profile of Ishmael and his descendants is enhanced, the writer of *Jubilees* reworks the biblical stories that involve Esau to create a precedent and divine approval of Jacob's dominance over his brother Esau (Roger Syrén, "Ishmael and Esau in the Book of Jubilees and Targum Pseudo-Jonathan," in *The Aramaic Bible: Targums in Their Historical Context*, ed. Derek R.G. Beattie and Martin J. McNamara, JSJSup 166 [Sheffield: Sheffield Academic, 1993], 312–3). From the moment of the twins' birth, Jacob is called "perfect and upright" while Esau is "a harsh, rustic, and hairy man" (*Jub* 19:13; cf. Gen. 25:24–6). Jacob is not chosen arbitrarily, but because of his obedience and because of Esau's disobedience: the writer solves Isaac's inconvenient preference for Esau (Gen 25:28) by narrating how Abraham came to prefer Jacob after seeing Esau's behaviour (*Jub* 19:16) and then commended Rebecca's preference for Jacob (*Jub* 19:19). By the end of Isaac's life, he, like Rebecca and Abraham, has seen Esau's evil behaviour and has come to love Jacob more (*Jub* 35:13). When Jacob tricks Isaac and steals Esau's blessing, divine aid serves to guarantee the rightness of Jacob's deception (*Jub* 26:18). In addition, the curse that Esau receives in place of a blessing not only guarantees his descendants' servitude to Israel (Gen 27:39–40) but also promises destruction as a consequence of attempting to gain independence (*Jub* 26:33–4). Finally, Esau himself acknowledges the rightness of Jacob's favoured position (*Jub* 36:14) and agrees to live at peace with Jacob after Isaac's death (*Jub* 37:4). However, Esau breaks this promise when his sons convince him to rebel against Jacob (*Jub* 37:13). The ensuing conflict culminates with Jacob killing Esau (*Jub* 38:2), symbolizing Jacob's superiority over his brother and Esau's inability to keep the oath (*Jub* 37:17). This demonstrates that Esau, like the nations (*Jub* 35:31), has an evil inclination (*Jub* 35:9) and is unworthy of divine election. The narrative concludes by noting: "So they [Jacob's sons] made peace with them [Esau's sons] and placed the yoke of servitude on them so that they should pay tribute to Jacob and his sons for all time ... The Edomites have not extricated themselves from the yoke of servitude which Jacob's sons imposed on them until today" (*Jub* 38:12–4).

46 See especially Ezra 9:2. This point is argued in most detail by Christine E. Hayes, *Gentile Impurities and Jewish Identities: Intermarriage and Conversion from the Bible to the Talmud* (New York: Oxford University Press, 2002), 73–81.

47 Whereas in Exodus, Israel is prohibited from intermarrying only with the Canaanites (Exod 34:11–6), *Jubilees* extends this to all non-Jews: "Now you, Moses, order the Israelites and testify to them that they are not to give any of their daughters to foreigners and that they are not to marry any foreign women because it is despicable before the Lord" (30:11) (Hayes, *Gentile Impurities*, 73–81; Cana Werman, "Jubilees 30: Building a Paradigm for the Ban on Intermarriage," *Harvard Theological Review* 90 [1997]: 1–22).

48 "For there are many nations and many peoples and all belong to him. He made spirits rule over all in order to lead them astray from following him" (*Jub* 15:31).

49 I develop this more complete picture in Van Maaren, *Boundaries of Jewishness*.

50 Here I go beyond the aspects of Andreas Wimmer's model that I outline above in order to illustrate the usefulness of the model.

17

Scripture and the Social Formation of "Displaced" Religious Communities

Jack N. Lightstone

In memory of Stephen Wilson

THE ISSUES AT STAKE

Biblical Studies' Ambivalent Relations with the Academic Study of Religion

For anyone interested in the history of modern scholarship on biblical literature, a study of the relationship of the American Academy of Religion (AAR) and the Society of Biblical Literature (SBL) might prove valuable.[1] Viewed at the most external level, the two organizations have held their annual meetings at the same place on the same dates for most of the last forty-five years.[2] This has been done to facilitate participation in both conferences by scholars whose interests spanned the two organizations.[3] Yet I have often questioned the degree of mutual interest and influence between biblical scholarship and scholarship on religion. To what extent have these modern scholarly arenas actually overlapped, and how? How have they informed or failed to inform one another? Are there, or ought there be, subject areas in which these two arenas of scholarship legitimately operate separately, in relative isolation from one another? Are there areas where there should be much more dialogue and mutual influence? A comprehensive consideration of such questions is beyond the scope of this chapter. But in what follows, I hope to offer one illustration, a test case, of how issues undoubtedly central to the academic study of religion might lead one to consider biblical literature differently. The illustration draws on the history of early, so-called post-biblical Judaism in the Roman period in the Mediterranean basin, with a special focus on Jews and Judaism outside of the land of Israel, in the Greco-Roman diaspora.

That the Judaic biblical literature continued to be authoritative for Jews and Judaism inside *and* outside the land of Israel over the first half of the first millennium CE is a truism that borders on platitude. The biblical literature, it may be said, travelled with the Jews. It is commonly asserted that the biblical literature facilitated the travel of Jews without cataclysmic loss of a shared social and religious identity to host lands around the Mediterranean basin. To borrow the phraseology of Daniel Boyarin,[4] the Jewish biblical literature constituted "a travelling homeland." That said, many of the actual ways in which biblical scriptures played a role in these Jews' lives tend to be ways that typically elude the focus and methods of modern biblical scholars. This chapter is not so much a plea to change the field of biblical studies radically as it is an indication that the study of biblical literature ought not to be limited to the traditional range of questions.

Why Are Greco-Roman Diaspora Jews and Their Judaism a Compelling Test-Case?

Why focus on post-biblical Jews and Judaism, with special attention to Greco-Roman diaspora Jews? One reason is that there is nothing particularly special or unique about these Greco-Roman Jews and their Judaism, even after their texts have been removed – socially, culturally, temporally and/or geographically – from their original settings. The sacred texts of Christianity, Islam, Buddhism, and Hinduism (to name just a few) have, arguably, played similar roles. Consequently, much of what I have to say about Jews and Judaism ought to be meaningfully generalizable. Another reason for this focus goes back to my remarks about the relationship between the SBL and the AAR. It has never been clear to me where research papers on early post-biblical Judaism and its literature (including, sometimes, my own) are best placed in the conferences of these two organizations. I have often felt that such papers are viewed as somewhat peripheral to both organizations: almost too ancient and too biblical for the AAR, and almost too post-biblical and too focused on the study of religion for the SBL.[5] As an "in-between" phenomenon, this topical arena ought to be informative of how the questions, methods, and conceptual frameworks for the academic study of religion, the purview of organizations like the AAR (and the Canadian Society for the Study of Religion), might profitably expand those of biblical studies as normatively observed in organizations such as the SBL (and the Canadian Society for Biblical Studies).

This chapter presents specific evidence in support of a plea to expand somewhat the typical agenda of biblical scholarship. I should avow at the outset that such a plea is hardly new. It has previously been made by others, one of whom is among the acknowledged founders of the modern academic study of religion, as a distinct enterprise from theology, in North America, Wilfred Cantwell Smith.[6] Near the end of his long academic career, W.C. Smith wrote what he considered his capstone book, *What Is Scripture?* (1993). Smith therein intended to follow a scholarly line of inquiry, perceived by him to have been launched nearly a century earlier with the publication of Max Müller's multi-volume *Sacred Books of the East*, to understand the roles played by "canonical" sacred texts in the lives of adherents of the religious traditions of both the East and the West. By so defining his agenda, Smith sought, in essence, to liberate the category of "scripture" from the confines of traditional, often theologically based, Christian (and especially Protestant) biblical studies and exegesis, and focus on the role(s) canonical sacred texts play in the lives of religiously informed social formations. What makes a discussion of the place of the Judaic biblical literature in the collective lives of diaspora Jews so useful is the glaring and incontrovertible observation that most of the prescriptions and proscriptions of the most authoritative section of their biblical scriptures, "the Torah of Moses," are completely inoperable outside of the land of Israel.[7] These prescriptions and proscriptions are predicated on the existence and functions of a one and only one national temple of the God of Israel and on its associated personnel and institutions situated,[8] until its destruction in 70 CE, in the homeland "capital,"[9] Jerusalem.

This dependence on the homeland setting and on regular access to the Jerusalem temple in the performance of much biblically enjoined practice is nearly comprehensive in scope. No sabbath, new moon, or festival day could be appropriately or fully observed in accordance with the Torah's teachings without the temple. No purification processes were complete without it. Most of the instructions of the Torah about tithes and priestly gifts were irrelevant outside the land and without Jerusalem's temple. No expiation of one's sins was complete without sacrifices that could only be performed in the temple's precincts by its priestly caste. No supreme, universally authoritative judgment based on the Torah's teachings and laws could be made without appeal to the temple personnel. Nor could any final, universally recognized decree or interpretation of Torah law be issued by any other body. In effect, much of the Torah of Moses, popularly understood to have functioned as a "travelling homeland" for the Jews, was (or ought to have been) a "dead letter" (to mix metaphors) upon arrival in Greco-Roman diaspora Jewish communities, even before the temple's destruction by the Romans in 70 CE, let alone afterwards.

Yet, notwithstanding these observations, the Judaic biblical literature, and especially the Torah, remained the most authoritative text of diaspora Jews and (arguably) their most sacred possession. Why this should have been the case is no mystery. Much of the social, cultural, and political history of the Jews from the Achaemenid-Persian era to the Roman conquest was predicated on making an evolving scriptural literature, and especially the emerging text of the Torah, the basis for identities, roles, norms, and institutions. By the Roman era, diaspora Jewish communities could not jettison this basis without significantly undermining their identity and solidarity. And those diaspora Jews who did abandon (formal) allegiance to the Torah, like Philo of Alexandria's own nephew, soon thereafter "Romanized" completely.

So, *why* Jewish diaspora communities retained biblical scriptures and the Torah as core to their shared identity is not that compelling a question. Rather, the question that needs to be addressed is *how*? Given that so much of the prescriptions and proscriptions of the Torah are a dead letter upon arrival in a diaspora setting, precisely *how* did the biblical texts play their roles in forging a shared, religiously based diaspora-Jewish identity? We are confronted with a paradox. Diaspora Jews travelled with a sacred scripture, which (many would argue) facilitated settlement beyond their homeland but whose content was ill-suited to such displacement. Yet diaspora Jews made a rather sustainable go of it, based, they maintained, on loyalty to biblical scriptures, and this well before the Babylonian Talmud was composed, let alone espoused as authoritative.

Beyond the Stock Interests of Biblical Scholars: Some Methodological Guardrails

The majority of modern biblical scholars have typically focused their attention on a number of discrete questions, as W.C. Smith points out in the introductory chapter of *What Is Scripture*? My own list would highlight the following:

- Philological questions: What does the language of the biblical books mean in light of the lexicography and grammar of the Hebrew, Aramaic, and Greek dialects of their time and place of composition?
- Exegetical and interpretive questions: What is, and has been, the meaning of the text, both for its pre-modern and modern readers/interpreters?
- Literary-historical questions: How, when, with what sources, and by whose agency did the biblical books come to assume the literary form and language of their current states, and what might that tell us about

the communities that produced them and their antecedent social and cultural histories?

- Literary-analytical questions: What structural, formal, or rhetorical traits are exhibited in a biblical text, and what may one discern from these about the text's meaning to its original, intended audience?
- Closely associated social and cultural questions: What did these books' original framers mean to say and achieve in their respective social and cultural contents, and (reciprocally) how do those contexts help us better understand the meaning of these biblical texts?
- Questions about the process of "authorizing" or "canonizing" these texts: How, when, why, where, under what circumstances, and by whose agency did these texts and collections of them come to be deemed authoritative for the communities that came to revere them?[10]

While some modern scholars attend to the history of the interpretation of biblical literature, it is less common for biblical scholars who are not working in the field of theology to take an interest in interpretive histories of biblical texts for periods much beyond the texts' initial period of composition and reception. Thus papers on Philo's first-century interpretation of the Bible are far more likely to be found on the program of the SBL than, for example, presentations Rashi's eleventh-century commentary.[11]

On the basis of this (incomplete) list of typically pursued lines of inquiry, I conclude that one common feature unites most of them. It is the tendency to "stick close to home" when analyzing biblical literature. By "close to home" I mean an overriding interest in the (near-) original settings of biblical texts and of their antecedent component parts. I do not for a second challenge the value of pursuing these scholarly interests. Quite the contrary. The significant contribution of the modern, academic study of biblical literature stems from this focus on original settings and the scrutiny of antecedent sources. The results speak volumes and positively for the enterprise. My point, rather, is that such lines of inquiry will not help us understand many other, often-observed phenomena in which the biblical text is paramount for "lives lived together with others," as W.C. Smith would put it. It does not, for example, elucidate the meaning of the Bible's use in the inauguration of presidents of the United States or, as was once de rigeur, the swearing in of witnesses in trial proceedings. Nor do these types of inquiry help us understand the modern Orthodox Jewish practice upon entering a home of "kissing" the *mezuzah*, the box affixed to the right side of the doorframe containing a parchment on which are inscribed particular biblical verses. More typical modes of biblical studies make sense of none of these several, seemingly disparate, phenomena. By contrast, scholars of religion will recognize in such practices the use and veneration of the Bible (or its elements) as a holy object, relic, or talisman that makes the deity present in some fashion. So there are lessons to be learned from surveying some of the ways biblical scriptures supported the forging and legitimating of the religious and social identity of Greco-Roman diaspora Jewish communities. But before proceeding, a few methodological comments are in order.

First and foremost, this chapter focuses on shared group identity, not on individual identities. Philo, to name one Greco-Roman diaspora Jew, wrote much about the biblical scriptures. There is no denying that his personal identity as a Jew was tied to scripture, as he understood it. In his view, scripture, and especially the Torah, had a surface meaning and an equally intended deeper meaning. The latter was consistent with the Middle-Platonic and Stoic philosophies of Philo's era and, perhaps, with an emerging Middle-Platonic philosophical-religious mysticism.[12] That this deeper meaning of scripture relates to Philo's construction of his personal identity as a Jew is undeniable. What we cannot know is whether Philo's scripturally based identity was more widely characteristic of the first-century CE Jewish community of Alexandria in which he lived. Indeed, I would argue that Philo more than hints that this is not the case. Rather, according to Philo, scripture's surface meaning is scripture's way of addressing the vast majority of Jews. I am not particularly interested in Philo's individual and perhaps idiosyncratic appropriation of scripture, or in Ezekiel the Tragedian's, or the like.

Second, without recourse to a Philo or an Ezekiel the Tragedian's writings that appropriate and interpret scripture, we must rely upon evidence that is largely indirect, episodic, and/or fragmentary about the place of scripture in the shared group identity and practice of Greco-Roman era diaspora Jewish communities. One often has to infer that place from passing remarks in literary evidence, much of it in writings of the early Church, in Roman edicts (some of which Josephus alleges to have accurately represented in *Antiquities* 14 and 16),[13] and in inscriptions and papyri. Or one must divine matters from other material remains of the Jewish community, such as the architecture and art of excavated synagogues.

Third, as tempting and as thick with detail as it is, evidence from early rabbinic literature should be used with great caution and, at the initial stages of analysis, mostly not at all. We have little evidence for widespread recognition of the authority of the early rabbis in the land of Israel before the fifth century at the earliest. And we have no evidence for such widespread authority among Greco-Roman diaspora Jews until much later still, so much later that I have no need to risk an estimate for present purposes. Methodologically, early rabbinic evidence might corroborate other testimonies, but it must be used rarely and very cautiously as an evidentiary basis. Given the limited confines of a chapter such as this, I mostly steer clear of it.

SACRED TEXT AS STORY, HOLY RELIC, AND AUTHORITATIVE SOURCEBOOK

Scripture's Stories and Shared Identity

That the shared group identity of Greco-Roman diaspora Jews, both before and following the Jerusalem temple's destruction in 70 CE, was based in the national-ethnic story of their ancestors as recounted in the biblical texts, just as it was for Jews in the land of Israel, is indisputable. Diaspora Jews self-designated as *Iudaioi*, which, if nothing else, is an ethno-national designation based on their self-professed origins in the land of Judah/Yehud (Latinized as "Judea"), the homeland's principal name from Achaemenid-Persian times onward. The narratives of the Judaic biblical scriptures provided the link between diaspora Jews' self-understanding as the progeny of their ancestral homeland, Yehud, and its capital, Jerusalem, given to their ancestors by their national god, YHWH, the creator and sole deity of the world, with whom the Jews/*Iudaioi* (lit. "the People of [the land of] Yehud) enjoy a unique relationship. Arguably, no source, other than the biblical scriptures, provided as compelling and as robust a basis for constructing such a myth of identity and origins for diaspora Jewry. For example, the probably mid-third-century CE frescoes painted on the walls of the synagogue discovered at Dura-Europas are replete with representations of biblical narratives, including the attempted sacrifice of Isaac by Abraham, Moses's infancy, the crossing of the Red Sea, the inauguration of the priesthood of Aaron (indicated by name in Greek letters), perhaps King David (depicted as an Orpheus-type musician), the liberation of the ark of the covenant from the Philistines, segments of the Elijah story cycle, perhaps the elevation of Mordechai as told in the Book of Esther, and more besides. Most of the frescoes' panels are unintelligible without reference to the scripture's narrative. And if there are common themes in what is depicted, they are that YHWH repeatedly intervenes to deliver his covenanted people, Israel, and has given them a means, the temple administered by the Aaronite priesthood, to serve YHWH and to seek atonement. These pictorial representations occur in the diaspora almost two hundred years after the Jerusalem temple's destruction.

Communal Study of Scripture as (Part of) Cultic Worship

The biblical scriptures themselves know of no institutionalized, regular, public, communal recitation of chapters from scripture as part and parcel of the cult of YHWH in the ancestral homeland. Certainly, *individuals* are said to have studied "the Torah [of Moses]" and its laws and to have enacted "public policy" accordingly. Josiah, King of Judah, Shaphan, Josiah's scribe, and Hilkiah, the royal temple's high priest, are depicted in 2 Kings 22 and 23 to have done so after the alleged discovery in the Jerusalem temple of scrolls attributed to Moses. Among the stated qualifications for Ezra's appointment as governor of the land of Yehud is Ezra's mastery of "the Torah of Moses" and its laws (Ezra 7:6, 10). Moreover, Ezra is said to have been charged by the Persian monarch to train a cadre of judges in same (Ezra 7:25). The book of Deuteronomy (17:14–20) charges future kings of the people of Israel to spend time making a copy of "this Torah [of Moses]," no doubt for the king's own edification and study needs, as a prerequisite for crafting national policy. Writing centuries later than the framers of the book of Deuteronomy, the Greek translator of the book of Ben-Sira (grandson of Ben-Sira himself) lists as the primary qualification of his grandfather the assiduous study of the books of "the Law (i.e., the Torah of Moses), the prophets, and [other sacred] writings."[14]

By contrast, the *public* reading of scripture is depicted *in biblical literature* as happening on distinctive, episodic, one-off occasions, usually in a narrative describing some sort of national, covenant-renewal event. Take for example the story recounted in Ezra-Nehemiah, where such a convocation is said to have been held, and the Torah (whatever text the term would have denoted at the time) is said to have been publicly read aloud *in its entirety* (Nehemiah 8:1–8) to the assembled population of Jerusalem and Yehud. Yet, sometime before the turn of the second century CE, the regular, *public* reading of scripture in local assemblies becomes commonplace. For example, by the time Acts of the Apostles was written,[15] it is apparent that part and parcel of the regular communal gatherings and ritual practices on sabbaths and festivals observed in the synagogues of the Greco-Roman diaspora is the reading (in Greek) of sections of scripture (likely from the Torah and Prophets). These institutionalized, regular, local public readings of scripture were followed by some sort of exposition of the meaning of the lections by a learned resident or guest sage. In Acts (e.g., Acts 17:2), Paul is said regularly to have exploited this apparently now-institutionalized feature of the diaspora-Jewish communal assemblies' ritual practice in order to attract some new followers for Christ from among synagogue attendees. How else would one better describe this regular practice of publicly reading and expounding upon sections of scripture than as communal, public study of scripture as worship of the God of Israel?

I do not deign to know when and where such a public ritual began. Some argue that its roots are in regular, local gatherings in the land of Israel in the late-Hellenistic and/or early-Roman periods. The argument tends to assert that the local Jewish communal assembly hall (synagogue) was a privileged site for education in scripture well before such assemblies were the loci of communal prayer. That may be so,[16] although it has little bearing on the claims made in this chapter. Certainly the Mishnah, tractate Megillah (c. 200 CE), assumes that the practice of regular, local, public readings of scripture (in Hebrew, interspersed with translation into Aramaic) as part of individual settlements' communal worship services is normal and ubiquitous. But this does not detract from the fact that sometime *before* the time of Acts, such a practice (in Greek translation) had become a staple in the Greco-Roman Jewish diaspora. What begs further consideration is the sheer oddity of ritualized, public reading/study of a sacred text as an act of cultic service of one's god. And it is to this issue that I turn after discussing the elevation of copies of scriptures (even in Greek translation) to the status of holy relics.

Scripture as Sacred Relic

Many biblical scholars, and certainly those who pioneered modern biblical scholarship, were the products of Christian (and occasionally Jewish) communities. For them, reading scripture as part and parcel of public worship of the deity seemed (and still seems) normal – a ritual practice the perceived legitimacy and importance of which was significantly enhanced in Christian congregations by the ideas of the Protestant Reformation. But from the perspective of the history of religions, this ritual practice is far from the norm. In the religious cults and observances of the Greco-Roman world, such a public, communal ritual would be perceived as quite abnormal. Many things rendered Jews and early Christians strange in the eyes of their Greco-Roman neighbours. But one of the things that certainly would have seemed odd would have been the public reading of scripture as cultic observance and worship. No Roman or Greek of the period would have regularly joined their fellows at their local temples on holy days to hear a book read aloud as an aspect of cultic practice and service to the gods. Among "pagans" in the Greco-Roman world, public worship overwhelmingly comprised sacrifices of produce and animals on altars situated in front of the god's sanctuary, in which stood a statue of the deity representing his or her indwelling presence. And it does absolutely no good to object that, other than Jews and Christians, no religions of the Greco-Roman world had sacred scriptures. Such an objection, if raised, just proves the point.

The "abnormality" of such a cultic practice, even by the standards of how Judaic scripture *itself* depicts public reading of scripture, raises an important question. What shared perceptions and notions among Greco-Roman diaspora Jews would make the regular public study of scripture in communal assemblies not only religiously edifying but also "worshipful" in formal communal gatherings on holy days as an effective means of connecting the community with its deity? The answer lies in evidence that points to a shared perception that individual editions of scripture (even in Greek) were *holy*, and this in addition to, and apart from, scripture's content. This is far more than to say that scripture is authoritative because it is revelation. After all, the content of the oracles of Delphi was conceived by those who sought them to be revelation. But no one receiving such oracles would normally have defined transcriptions of them to be holy and prescribed that such transcriptions be used in cultic rituals, even if the Delphi prophetess herself was deemed to be a holy person.

Several types of evidence point to this shared perception of the holiness of editions of scripture among Greco-Roman diaspora Jews and to what ends this holiness was put. Over the third, fourth, and fifth centuries CE, the renovations and expansions of ancient synagogues in the Near East, Levant, and Mediterranean basin often included the construction of ever more prominent and elaborate niches and receptacles in their main assembly halls. It is the overwhelming consensus of archaeologists that these niches and receptacles were used to house the scrolls of scripture.[17] Before this architectural trend, it would appear that the scrolls were housed in a much less impressive closet or in an adjacent room (a small library?). Renovations of ancient synagogue buildings not only gave more prominence to these closets and moved them into the main halls of the sanctuaries but also imbued the newly constructed receptacle with many symbolic features. For example, the niches were commonly designed with columned or faux-columned porticos, sometimes decorated with depictions of artifacts of the Jerusalem temple such as the menorah. And the renovators often added mosaic floors, the pictorial representations on which (1) were oriented to direct attention to the Torah niche and (2) themselves included images of temple paraphernalia and/or images of columned porticos. Clearly, then, both the design of the niches and the representations on the mosaic floors facing them were meant to recall the Jerusalem temple (even if they often bore a closer resemblance to the architecture of the local Greco-Roman pagan sanctuaries). The intended message of these architectural and artistic features appears clear, in my opinion. Through these porticoed niches is an alternative "holy of holies." Consequently, these niches are perceived to be efficacious portals to the deity, through which the praise and supplications of the assembled congregants may pass more readily to their intended recipient.[18] And what makes these niches such privileged gateways? The answer seems incontrovertible: the presence in them of the scrolls of scripture, whose holiness opens a local gateway to heaven. This makes the scrolls of scripture a veritable holy relic of what had been said to be YHWH's abiding presence in the temple.[19]

Is there literary evidence from the Greco-Roman era that confirms such a reading of the material evidence? Putting aside attestations in early Rabbinic literature (for reasons stated above),[20] explicit, contemporary, literary evidence affirming such notions comes, ironically, from Christian sources, and indeed from some of the most virulently anti-Jewish and anti-Judaic rhetoric of early Christianity: John Chrysostom, when he was still a presbyter in Syrian Antioch early in the second half of the fourth century CE. Late one summer and into the fall, Chrysostom composed a series of anti-Judaic sermons in an attempt to dissuade his gentile Christian congregants from attending the local synagogue assembly's early fall celebrations of their high holy days.[21] Evidently, regular or episodic attendance at and participation in synagogue assemblies, as well as recourse to the local synagogue's healers and arbitration courts, were common practices of many of the gentile Christians of Antioch in Chrysostom's time. Chrysostom's anti-Jewish sermons are notorious for espousing themes that for centuries thereafter informed the negative tropes of Christian antisemitic discourse: the Jews are in league with Satan; they are possessed by demons; their hospitality and readiness to be of service to and inclusive of Christians is feigned and is intended to snare unsuspecting Christians for Satan; their physicians heal Christians using demonic powers; and so on. But for Chrysostom, these tropes would not in themselves suffice to stop Antioch's gentile Christians from attending synagogue assemblies on Judaic festivals, almost all of which were rooted in the same scriptures that Christians too revered as revelation. Chrysostom must, in addition, counter-argue and refute the reasons his Christian parishioners gave him for going to the synagogue.

In *Homily 1: Against the Jews* (section 4), Chrysostom says that his Church's congregants tell him that they view the synagogue as a "holy place" because the scrolls of the Law, the books of the Prophets, and other Judaic sacred writing (all most likely in Greek translation) are there. These books are holy, and their presence in the synagogue makes the synagogue assembly hall holy. It is their holiness that makes the synagogue an efficacious place to commune with the God of Israel (who is, of course, also the Christian God).[22] In other words, the holiness of the scrolls of scripture present in the synagogue makes God (more) present in the synagogue too. And it is entirely reasonable to conclude that these views articulated by Chrysostom's recalcitrant congregants accurately reflected the shared perceptions of Antioch's Jews in the latter half of the fourth century. But if scripture's scrolls are the contents of the new "holy of holies" in the synagogue-assembly hall, how does one understand the sacrality of the Greek-language translations? All evidence strongly supports the claim that Greco-Roman diaspora Jews publicly read scriptures from Greek editions of the texts. The early rabbis' Mishnah insists that the communal reading of scripture take place in its original language, Hebrew,[23] even if the assembled community (in synagogues of the land of Israel) was also edified by recitation of an Aramaic translation. The early rabbis never permitted the public reading of scripture in Aramaic only (let alone in Greek) as part of the regular synagogue rites. But in the Greco-Roman synagogue assembly, the public, worshipful reading of scriptures took place in Greek from scrolls written in Greek.[24] The Greco-Roman diaspora community sacralized the Greek texts of scripture.

The most direct evidence for this sacralization is the pervasive myth propounded by Greco-Roman diaspora Jews about the origins of the translation (at least of the Torah). That myth is at least as old as the early second century BCE,[25] and it relates how the translation of the Torah was commissioned by Ptolemy II, who in the early third century BCE ruled Hellenistic Egypt. As the myth goes, seventy (or seventy-two) elders were chosen, at Ptolemy's request, by the high priest in the temple in Jerusalem to travel to Egypt to undertake the translation. Elements of the myth, as rehearsed in multiple versions from the second century BCE and thereafter, stress that these seventy (or seventy-two) elders were all independently guided in their work by one mind, that is, YHWH. The Greek translation, like the original Hebrew, is being acclaimed as revelation. Chrysostom's vitriol in *Homily I, Against the Jews* makes passing reference to the "myth of the translation of the seventy." He admits, as he must, that the Greek scriptures are indeed holy, but they no more make the synagogue a holy place because of their presence there than they made Ptolemy II's library holy by reason of their depositure in that building. In Chrysostom's vituperous "No!" one hears the echo of his congregants' emphatic "Yes!": the Greek editions of the scrolls of scripture are holy, and their presence in the synagogue makes the synagogue holy and (consequently) an efficacious place to commune with the God of Israel.

If many of Chrysostom's gentile Christians so perceive matters, all the more so would Antioch's Jews, who, Chrysostom maintains, infected his parishioners with such views.

So, the scrolls of scripture, housed in their temple-like niches in the synagogues of the Greco-Roman-era diaspora Jews are holy relics of YHWH. What does one do with relics? One venerates them and taps their power to provide conduits to heaven. Prayers go up through these conduits, and God's life-giving power comes down through these conduits.[26] Veneration of the relics helps activate them, or it motivates or psychologically prepares the congregants in some manner. The highly ritualized public reading of the scriptures in the synagogue assembly not only edifies those present, but it is also part and parcel of the collective ritual veneration of the scrolls.

Scripture as Authoritative Sourcebook

I reserve for the end of this section what at first glance seems the most problematic issue. I have indicated that many or most of the prescriptions and proscriptions of the Torah were a dead letter in a diaspora context because their practise required ready access to the Jerusalem temple. That temple, before its destruction in 70 CE, was not immediately accessible to diaspora Jews (even though every year thousands of them made pilgrimage to Jerusalem). After 70 CE, the temple cult was defunct altogether. Yet, on the eve of the temple's destruction, these scriptural regulations (together with a body of supplementary norms) constituted the warp and woof of the *practice* of a shared, distinctively Judaic, national, religio-cultural identity. Shared identity is not only constructed from the mythopoeic narratives in our minds; shared identity must also be constructed from commonly practised norms and common social institutions. It is easy to understand that distance from the temple before 70 CE and the temple's destruction in 70 CE posed *existential* challenges for Judaic identity, which, by then, had become irrevocably grounded in the scripture for (1) an identity-constructing national narrative and (2) norms for Judaic life and cult. I have already discussed the former; now let us consider the latter.

Greco-Roman diaspora Jews addressed the "dead-letter" problem of scripture's regulations by "cherry picking" what could be practised without recourse to the Jerusalem temple's cult. It appears to be the case that, by the late first and the second centuries CE, there was a fairly broad consensus among Greco-Roman diaspora Jews about what core elements constituted the "picked cherries" (leaving aside the matter of local variation in how precisely each community practised this core). We know this broadly shared core existed because evidence from Jews, Greek and Latin "pagan" writers, and early Christian authors all seem to agree on what its elements were.[27] The main elements constituting the core were: exclusive worship of YHWH; veneration of revealed scriptures; distancing from pagan cults; circumcision of males; endogamy; avoidance of foods forbidden by scripture (including foodstuffs in the marketplace that were resales of pagan cultic offerings); refraining from work and from lighting fires on sabbath and on scripturally prescribed festivals and holy days; gathering as a community in synagogues for worship and reading of scripture, in particular on sabbaths and other holy days; ritual immersion in cleansing pools; fasting on prescribed days; establishment of arbitration courts based in the synagogue; establishment of poor funds and "soup kitchens" administered by and in the synagogue; and the annual levy of a head tax sent to the Jerusalem temple (until its demise in 70 CE).

To be sure, some of these elements might be said to parallel functions of Greco-Roman urban associations. And so much the better that they do: because diaspora Jews not only faced the challenge of constructing a distinctively Judaic group identity, they also had to manage the challenges of fitting into, and gaining acceptance within, urban life in the Greco-Roman period. That said, specific scriptural prescriptions and proscriptions provide warrant for the items on the list, with few exceptions. And this is key, even if scripture's authors could not have imagined (and would not have sanctioned) the manner in which these scripturally based norms were practised by diaspora Jews.[28] In sum, I believe that it is legitimate to speculate that diaspora Jews of the Greco-Roman world understood their shared identity and its practices as grounded in, and as faithful observance of, scripture, notwithstanding the fact that, with respect to the latter, diaspora Jews had of necessity to be highly selective in picking and choosing from among the scriptural injunctions. One might say that, for these Jews, the observance of *part* of scripture counts for the observance of the *whole* of scripture.

THEORETICAL AND CONCEPTUAL CONSIDERATIONS

Our survey of the place of the Judaic scriptures in the lives diaspora Jews lived together in the Greco-Roman world spotlights two phenomena:

1 Jews not only accepted the content of scripture as authentic revelation, they also perceived the physical copies of scripture to be powerful sacred objects of veneration. They thereby actuated

efficacious conduits between heaven and the community. Among other acts of veneration, I would include the regular, public reading of portions of scripture in the synagogue assemblies as worshipful acts, to be distinguished from the study of scripture privately or in educational institutions.[29]

2 In the diaspora and post-70 CE context, only a subset of scripture's teachings was still operable. So what the (pen-)ultimate framers of the Pentateuch intended to be taken and practised as a whole could only be observed in a piecemeal, selective manner by Greco-Roman diaspora Jews. Moreover, there seems to have been a fair degree of consensus among diaspora Jews about what selection of elements were to form the core of a life lived in accordance with scripture. These include a shared identity shaped by scripture's narrative and a select subset of rules and norms enjoined by, or understood to be based in, scripture.

From these specific observations about a particular group of communities and the place of scripture in their group lives, what may we say more generally about the academic study of "lives lived in accordance with scripture," to paraphrase W.C. Smith?

First and perhaps most obviously, the academic study of scripture ought to seek and analyze instances in which material copies of scripture are treated as sacred objects. In so doing, scholars may better understand the full range of ways scripture forms a part of religiously constructed cultures and communities. Second and arguably less obvious, in addition to those questions about scripture that tend to drive the lion's share of biblical scholarship, the academic study of scripture might consider the place, meaning, and use of scripture at further removes (geographically, temporally, and culturally) from its original or near original settings. Earlier in this chapter, I state that many of the most important contributions of modern biblical scholarship have derived from a focus on texts' and their constituent sources' original or near-original settings. But, to be blunt, these are short-lived moments in historical time and in social and cultural space. Once scriptures are deemed by a community to be authoritative, they almost immediately are removed from or move beyond the original settings in which and for which they were produced. Texts' new settings may differ from the original ones in either significant or relatively insignificant ways. We should devote more time to studying such instances, if we are truly to grasp the role scripture plays in the lives of religiously informed communities. And we should, as soon as we are able, move from the study of such instances to theorizing about them. Based on the case at hand, then, I heuristically proffer some elements that might form part of the bare bones of such theorizing.

What one observes in the case of Greco-Roman diaspora Judaism is the attempt to reconfigure the perception of their received scripture so that the result fits or is homologous with their Judaic-ly constructed lives together in their diaspora setting. They cannot (or, more accurately, can no longer) do this by editing the text since to do so to a canonical text risks its perceived immutability as revelation, undermining its authority. And the community requires that authority to remain intact. So, the community effectively "edits" their scripture *perceptually* without *actually* editing the text, and thereby reestablishes the homologous fit between their scripture and their lives. The actual text remains whole, but the effectively *perceived* text is a body of bits and pieces that were not rendered dead letter in a diaspora setting.

The determinants and importance of shared perceptions of reality in religiously informed cultural systems, which perceptions may differ from readily observable empirical facts, have been discussed for more than half a century in anthropology. In the mid-1960s, when Clifford Geertz described religions as cultural systems,[30] he proposed that religious beliefs and rituals, and social narratives, norms, and institutions, interact to elicit "strong sentiments" among community members that serve to reinforce their shared cultural systems, identity, and social organization. I take Geertz to mean (1) that these powerful sentiments are one requisite of maintaining cultural systems that are experienced by the community or society as particularly valid and cogent, and (2) that what I have called the fit among the elements of the system is, to some significant degree, what elicits these sentiments. It would follow, to my mind, that maintaining group perceptions, even obviously counterfactual ones, so as to maintain that fit is important. And indeed, this is what Mary Douglas proposes. Douglas writes about socially constructed, shared perceptions of reality, even with respect to naturally occurring, empirically verifiable, and obvious phenomena.[31] She documents instances in which critical elements of a group's social structure and system radically affect their shared perception of the most obvious aspects of their physical environment, such as when in the year the hot season occurs (a matter easily verifiable by a thermometer, if not by sense perception). She maintains that such shared perceptions of the world are determined and shaped so as to better fit the social system of the group. If social requisites can shape shared perceptions of natural, easily observable phenomena, while the natural phenomena remain unchanged, why should the same not occur with the shared perceptions of sacred scriptures, which cannot or should not be altered, so that the mutually reinforcing fit between scripture and the group's life is maintained? The community might not (indeed probably does not) deny the presence of the dead-letter aspects of scripture; rather, they have tacitly agreed to direct attention away from those aspects, *as if* they did not exist. To dwell on these aspects would undermine the role scripture plays in fitting their social and cultural identities. Such a solution would probably not suffice for ancient philosophical theologians, who would seek "to rationalize these inconvenient bits away" for other philosophically and theologically trained co-religionists.[32] But it does seem to suffice for the community at large.

Near the outset of this chapter I state that the Judaic scriptures travelled with the Jews to the diaspora, but those scriptures did not travel well. Now, I would revise that claim somewhat. Sacred texts, like the Judaic scriptures, are *always* on the move beyond their original or near-original social and cultural settings. This is normal. We should expect, look for, and analyze how sacred scriptures are re-perceived by their respective communities in order to continue to play their roles in the lives of their devotees in these new settings, while not a single word of the text is changed and the copies of these scriptures are revered and venerated as holy objects providing a conduit to heaven.

NOTES

1 Much of what I say about the AAR and SBL applies (mutatis mutandis) to the Canadian Society for the Study of Religion (CSSR) and the Canadian Society of Biblical Studies (CSBS), including the history of my personal association with the latter two. That said, it is my experience that the CSBS's interests differ from those of the SBL in important respects, the significant and many-decades-long openness to interdisciplinarity being one of them.

2 A self-referential time frame, as it is the length to date of my academic career.

3 In the interests of being above board about my own allegiances, I became a member of the AAR at the outset of my academic career and later joined the SBL and allowed my membership in the AAR to lapse. My affiliations with the CSSR and CSBS followed the same pattern.

4 Daniel Boyarin, *A Travelling Homeland: The Babylonian Talmud as Diaspora* (Philadelphia: University of Pennsylvania Press, 2015), i.

5 As a matter of personal observation, the sessions in which these papers have been presented and discussed have tended not to attract larger audiences at the AAR or SBL, except when they were crafted to shed light on early Christianity. In this particular respect, the CSBS differs significantly from the SBL. It is my experience that, over the years, research papers on the Greco-Roman period and post-biblical Judaism and its literature have been consistently integrated into other

topical sessions and multi-year seminars, for example, on religious associations in the Greco-Roman period, to name just one. In my view, this has produced significantly different and more innovative scholarship than what typically has emerged from SBL sessions (or the AAR, for that matter). This has happened for two reasons. One is demography. The CSBS's membership is diminutive in comparison to that of the SBL. As a result, CSBS members with different research specializations have had to talk with one another or they would have had very few people to talk with at all. The other, not unrelated, reason has to do with personalities: several prominent members with new ideas for scholarly programming at the CSBS have had significant influence in the organization. One of these is the late Stephen Wilson, to whose memory this book is dedicated.

6 It is worth keeping in mind that most of the prominent founding figures of both modern biblical studies and the modern academic study of religion emerged from schools of theology, and W.C. Smith is a case in point. In North America two quite distinct approaches to the modern academic study of religion developed in the mid-twentieth century, the "Comparative Religions School" (principally associated with Harvard) and the "History of Religions School" (principally associated with the University of Chicago). W.C. Smith was associated with the former.

7 This chapter cannot provide anything like a comprehensive or even summative account of the unity or diversity of diaspora Jewish identity and institutions. For a more thorough account, see Jack N. Lightstone, *The Commerce of the Sacred: Mediation of the Divine Among Jews in the Greco-Roman World* (New York: Columbia University Press, 2006); Lightstone, "Roman Diaspora Judaism," in *A Companion to Roman Religion*, ed. Jörg Rüpke, Blackwell Companions to the Ancient World 9 (Oxford: Blackwell, 2007), 345–77; Lightstone, "Is It meaningful to Talk of *a* Greco-Roman Diaspora Judaism? A Case Study in Taxonomical Issues in the Study of Ancient Judaism," in *Introducing Religion: Essays in Honor of Jonathan Z. Smith*, ed. Willi Braun and Russell McCutcheon (London: Equinox, 2008), 267–81. There is a rich body of modern scholarship on diaspora Jews and Judaism in the Greco-Roman era, including: Erich S. Gruen, *Diaspora: Jews Amidst Greeks and Romans* (Cambridge: Harvard University Press, 2003); Alf Thomas Kraabel, "The Roman Diaspora: Six Questionable Assumptions," *Journal of Jewish Studies* 33 (1982): 454–64; Kraabel, "Unity and Diversity among Diaspora Synagogues," in *Diaspora Jews and Judaism*, ed. J. Andrew Overman and Robert S. MacLennan (Atlanta: Scholars Press, 1992), 21–33; Kraabel, "The Diaspora Synagogue: Archaeological and Epigraphic Evidence since Sukenik," in *Aufstieg und Niedergang der Römischen Welt. Band 19/1. Halbband Religion (Judentum: Allgemeines; palästinisches Judentum)*, ed. Wolfgang Haase, 477–511; Lee I. Levine, *The Ancient Synagogue: The First Thousand Years*, 2nd ed. (New Haven: Yale University Press, 2005); Martin Hengel, "Proseuche und Synagoge: Jüdische Gemeinde, Gotteshaus und Gottesdienst in der Diaspora und in Palästina," in *The Synagogue*, ed. Joseph Gutmann (New York: Ktav, 1975), 27–54; Mark Nanos,

"Life in the Diaspora Synagogues: An Evaluation," in *The Ancient Synagogue from its Origins to 200 CE*, ed. Birger Olssen, Coniectanea Biblica, New Testament Series 39 (Stockholm: Almqvist & Wiksell International, 2003), 208–18; Tessa Rajak, "Synagogue and Community in the Graeco-Roman Diaspora," in *Jews in the Hellenistic and Roman Cities*, ed. John R. Bartlett (London: Routledge, 2002), 22–38.

8 The temples to YHWH at Elephantine (in the late Assyrian and Achaemenid-Persian periods) and at Leontopolis/Heliopolis (in the Ptolemaic-Hellenistic and early Roman era) are two notable exceptions that do not disprove the rule that sacrifices to YHWH were to take place only at the Jerusalem temple. To be sure, it may be argued that many of the prescriptions and proscriptions contained in the Pentateuch have their origins in religious law and practice that predate the successful centralization of the cult of YHWH in Jerusalem. Nevertheless, when the extant texts of the Hebrew Bible, and especially the Pentateuch, assumed their more or less final forms sometime in the Hellenistic and Hasmonean periods, that centralization was, and had long been, de rigueur.

9 For example, Philo of Alexandria says (*Flaccum* 46 and *Legatio* 281–2) that Jerusalem is the "mother city" of all Jewish settlements in the Middle Eastern and Mediterranean lands, which settlements he characterizes as colonies of Jerusalem. *Colonia* has a specific social, cultural, and especially legal connotation in the late republican and early imperial Roman context. Rome established such *coloniae* around the "Roman world," often to settle therein retired military personnel. Citizens of a *colonia* had Latin rights, even if they did not previously have Roman citizenship, and the administrative and legal systems of *coloniae* were modelled on those of Rome, as guaranteed in each city's charter. In borrowing such terminology, Philo is implying (1) that the laws of Jerusalem, based on the Torah, ought to and do apply in Jewish diaspora communities, and (2) that Rome ought to recognize and acquiesce to this since it is similar to the relationship between the city of Rome and its *coloniae*. That Rome would have deemed this a convincing argument is doubtful. But it is understandable that Jewish luminaries such as Philo would have chosen to self-define this way and to promote such a view to their non-Jewish neighbours. See Torrey Seland, "'Colony' and 'Metropolis' in Philo: Examples of Mimicry and Hybridity in Philo's Writing back from the Empire?" *Études Platoniciennes* 7 (2010): 11–33; Sarah Pearce, "Jerusalem as 'Mother-City' in the Writings of Philo of Alexandria," in *Negotiating Diaspora: Jewish Strategies in the Roman Empire*, ed. John Barclay, Library of Second Temple Studies 45 (New York, T & T Clark, 2004), 19–37.

10 For W.C. Smith, "canonical criticism" as pursued by biblical scholars tends to tack closest to his own interests in how scripture functioned in the lives of religion-based communities.

11 Although papers on the latter would certainly have a home in conferences and journals of associations of Jewish or Judaic studies. That, in my view, says something in itself.

12 See Lightstone, *Commerce of the Sacred*, 119–30; also Christine Hayes, *What Is Divine about Divine Law? Early Perspectives* (Princeton: Princeton University Press, 2015), 105–36. See Erwin R. Goodenough, *An Introduction to Philo Judaeus* (New Haven: Yale University Press, 1940), 1–223, for an interpretation of Philo as proponent of a Platonic philosophical-mystical Judaism, the practices of which were understood to be "mystery rites." Goodenough became convinced that Philo reflected a more general religious ideology and practice among Jews of the Greco-Roman diaspora. Accordingly, he began to interpret other evidence, in particular material evidence, from Greco-Roman diaspora Jews in light of this conviction. See Goodenough, *Jewish Symbols in the Greco-Roman Period* (New York: Bollingen, 1965), 12:1–217. There is no evidentiary warrant for such a generalization to diaspora Jews at large. *If* Goodenough's interpretation of Philo as a proponent of a philosophical-mystical interpretation of Judaism is correct, then such a Judaism is Philo's personal religious philosophy and (perhaps) influenced his students (although we know of none who has left us writings). Philo in fact admits that the plain-sense understanding of scripture is intended for the masses of Jews. For a scholarly critique of Goodenough in these respects, see Morton Smith, "Goodenough's *Jewish Symbols* in Retrospect," *Journal of Biblical Literature* 86 (1967): 53–68.

13 See Claude Eilers, "The Date of Augustus' Edict on the Jews (Jos. AJ 16.162–165) and the Career of C. Marcius Censorinus," *Phoenix* 58 (2004): 86–95; Evanthia Polyviou, "Caesar's Jewish Policy according to Flavius Josephus (*Jewish Antiquities* XIV, 190–222)," *Anistoriton Journal* 14 (2014–15): 1–11, http://www.anistor.gr/english/enback; Tessa Rajak, "Was There a Roman Charter for the Jews?" *Journal of Roman Studies* 74 (1984): 107–23.

14 See the prologue to the Wisdom of Ben Sira. This, by the way, is clearly a reference to what by the late second century BCE was an emerging, normative notion that the Judaic biblical scriptures were comprised of three collections of texts of differing levels of authority.

15 See Alf Thomas Kraabel, "Traditional Christian Evidence for Diaspora Judaism: The Book of Acts," *Society of Biblical Literature Seminar Papers* 122 (1986): 644–51.

16 The position articulated by those who hold this view is that regular, local, communal, public prayer in the land of Israel did not develop while the Jerusalem temple still functioned, and it only developed (in Judea?) in the aftermath of the temple's destruction in 70 CE. One indication, among others, that this claim, whether warranted or not, has no bearing on our discussion of ancient synagogue functions and practices in the diaspora comes from pre-70 CE inscriptional and literary evidence from and about Jews in Egypt in Hellenistic and Roman times (see Philo's *Flaccum* and *Legatio*). Jews in Egypt seem unique in calling the local Jewish community's assembly hall a *proseuche*, a "house of Prayer." I do not find convincing the argument that a *proseuche* was a roofless or outdoor place of prayer habitually used by Egyptian Jews in distinction from their synagogues. Far more likely is that before 70 CE *proseuche* was the preferred term among Egypt's Jewry

for what Jews elsewhere in the diaspora and the land of Israel called a "synagogue." Alternatively, the terms were simply interchangeable in Egypt, with *proseuche* being the more common usage. Either way, one may conclude that Jews in the diaspora gathered for communal prayer well before the Jerusalem temple's destruction in 70 CE.

17 Levine, *Ancient Synagogue*, 313–80.

18 See the discussion of portal imagery in ancient Judaic art in Bernard Goldman, *The Sacred Portal: A Primary Symbol in Ancient Judaic Art* (Detroit: Wayne State University Press, 1966).

19 See my discussion of the synagogue institution in the diaspora in Lightstone, *Commerce of the Sacred*, 78–86. See also Levine, *Ancient Synagogue*, 313–80.

20 For instance, one may point to Mishnah, tractate Megillah 3:1, which, like several other pericopae in Mishnah, proffers lists of objects, persons, places, or states of affairs of increasingly higher levels of purity (or impurity) or sacredness. In ascending order Megillah 3:1 lists: the town square, the synagogue, the ark in the synagogue (for housing scrolls of scripture), cloth wrappings for scrolls of scripture, scrolls of the Prophets and Writings, and scrolls of the Torah. This Mishnah passage presents a "Russian-doll" perception of holy place and holy objects at the local level and apart from the Jerusalem temple (destroyed approximately 130 years before Mishnah's production c. 200 CE in the land of Israel). This perception squares with what John Chrysostom's Gentile Christian parishioners in fourth-century CE Antioch say about why they perceive the local synagogue to be holy.

21 I discuss this evidence extensively elsewhere: see Lightstone, *Commerce of the Sacred*, 87–97. See also Wayne A. Meeks and Robert L. Wilken, *Jews and Christians in Antioch in the First Four Christian Centuries*, SBL Sources for Biblical Studies 13 (Missoula: Scholars Press, 1978).

22 Much of what immediately follows in Chrysostom's *Homily 1: Against the Jews* is devoted to counter-arguments to this view. His plan of attack is simple. Yes, the scrolls of scripture are holy. But the Jews, who are in league with the Devil, have perverted the meaning of scripture because they refuse to see in them the foretelling of Christ's advent, identity, and mission. Therefore there is nothing holy about the Jews, their assemblies, or their synagogue assembly halls, even if the scrolls there remain holy. God has rejected the Jews.

23 Mishnah tractate Yadayim 4 specified that copies of scripture are holy ("make the hands unclean if touched") only when copies of scriptural books are in the Hebrew language (Aramaic sections of Daniel and Ezra-Nehemiah excepted) and written in "Assyrian script" (as opposed to the several scripts that modern scholars identify as paleo-Hebrew script). For the authors of the Mishnah, copies of translation of the scriptures into Greek or Aramaic are not holy, and the early rabbis seem particularly to have disparaged the translation(s) of the Hebrew scriptures into Greek.

24 Later, in the mid-sixth century CE, Justinian issues an edict (*Novella* no. 146 from 553 CE) forbidding the public reading of the Hebrew text of scriptures in the synagogue liturgy. He orders that the rite continue exclusively in Greek. Justinian's motivations (or the motivations of the Christian clergy who pressed him to issue this edict) are not altogether clear to me. To be sure, there was an element of anti-Judaism in this initiative. Justinian's *Codex Iuris Civilis* and his addendum of *Novellae* have a number of edicts or rescripts on "Jewish matters," and some of these undoubtedly are intended to limit the potential appeal of Judaism to Christians as well as to limit any influence and authority individual Jews had over Christians. That said, I have long suspected that another factor in banning the use of Hebrew texts of scripture in the public worship services of synagogues has to do with a resistance to the "Hebraization" of the synagogue liturgy. My suspicion (and it is only a suspicion at this point) is that opposition came from members of the established leadership of the diaspora Jewish communities themselves. Many, I suspect, were resistant to this development. I further suspect that in issuing the edict in question, Justinian and Christian clergy were supporting the hand of the resisters because it seemed to them the better course to support the status quo. So, who would have pushed for "Hebraization" of the synagogue rites, and specifically for the public reading of scripture in Hebrew? Again, I do not know, but I have my suspicions. I am of the view that during the sixth century CE we may discern the first inklings of the attempted exercise of Rabbinic authority in parts of the diaspora. I suspect that rabbis coming from the land of Israel were advocating for the adoption of liturgical practices in the diaspora that accorded with what had long been their teachings about appropriate practice in the land of Israel. Of course, several centuries later the rabbis got their way.

25 I refer to the *Pseudo-Aristaeus* (*The Letter of Aristaeus to Philocrates*). Thereafter this myth became ubiquitous in Jewish, as well as in early Christian, circles. It is also clear to me that the author of *Pseudo-Aristaeus* is not the original creator of the myth since the elements of the myth as recounted there provide the *occasion* for the author to fashion the main body of the composition, which is about the philosophical dialogues portrayed as having taken place between the elders and Ptolemy II.

26 Lightstone, *Commerce of the Sacred.*

27 Ibid.; Lightstone, "Roman Diaspora Judaism"; Lightstone, "Meaningful."

28 To be fair, the same qualifying clause may be applied to Judaic practice by Jews living in the land of Israel in the century or two preceding the temple's destruction.

29 Of which Ben Sira's scribal school would be one example (see Sirach 39:1; 51:23–8).

30 Clifford Geertz, "Religion as a Cultural System," 87–125, in *The Interpretation of Cultures: Selected Essays*, 3rd ed. (New York: Basic Books, 2017).

31 Mary Douglas, "Self-Evidence," 252–82, in *Implicit Meanings: Essays in Anthropology*, 2nd ed. (London: Routledge, 1999).

32 The early rabbis simply viewed the inoperable bits of the Torah of Moses as temporarily inoperable, that is, until some future redemption, however distant in time. Their rationalizing took the form of a (non-militant) messianism. Philo sees many of the rites enjoined in scripture as symbolic acts anyway. Early Christian theologians and apologists who developed Paul's approach to the Law in articulating an emergent Christian orthodoxy adopted other rationales to do away with most of *their* scripture's prescriptions and proscriptions, rejecting approaches such as that of Marcion.

18

Response: Practice and Identity

Alicia J. Batten

The authors of the six chapters in this section of Religious Inventions examine a diverse range of practices and/or issues concerning identity that the study of the ancient Mediterranean world has prompted them to explore. Although each contribution has its own focus, they all demonstrate that questions of group identity are not separate from practice. Indeed, practice, whether highly specific and specialized or more discursive, is a central component of identity construction. The same is likely true for today, at least with regard to personal identity, as contemporary philosopher Hilde Lindemann argues.[1] In addition, and as is widely acknowledged in current scholarship, the analysis of religious "ideas" or "doctrine" has often been at the expense of attending to what people actually *do* when they participate in some sort of "religion," as well as how they articulate their identity.[2] Such negligence is not a characteristic of the chapters found here.

Before examining some of the practices explored here, however, it is important to observe that several of these chapters have done the service of sorting out the ways in which particular categories or concepts have developed within the history of scholarship, developments that have sometimes occluded the ability to perceive elements within ancient materials. These chapters illustrate in disparate ways that the clarification, deconstruction, or disentanglement of concepts is necessary if the goal is to gain a clearer picture of what might be happening in the extant texts from Mediterranean antiquity as well as what might actually have been happening on the ground.

Adele Reinhartz engages most explicitly in this work as she places the concepts of "identity" and "hybridity" under the microscope. She provides a brief but fascinating history of some of the ways in which scholarship has used these terms. Although Reinhartz does not think it necessary to toss out such concepts, she calls for more clarity on the part of interpreters as to why and how notions of identity and hybridity are analytically useful. Sensitivity, as well, to the emic and etic dimensions of description are requisite as the manner in which ancient groups or individuals might describe or understand themselves can be vastly different from the way in which an outsider, such as a modern scholar, might imagine them. Reinhartz's chapter is a lucid and convincing reminder of the importance of the scholarly virtues of clarity, specificity, and self-awareness.

Both John Van Maaren and Kimberly Stratton do address this thorny question of identity in their respective chapters, and they each proceed carefully, with attention to particularity and awareness of the complexity of the concepts of "Jewishness," as is the case with Van Maaren, and "Christian," as in Stratton's discussion. As anyone who studies ancient Judaisms or Christianities knows, the categories of "Jew" and "Christian" are fraught. What did it mean to be a Jew in antiquity? How and when did the notion of "Christian" emerge? Van Maaren engages the question of "Jewishness" by applying an ethnic boundary-making model developed in the field of ethnic studies. Rather than using one of the binaries of "religion" or "ethnic group," he attends to the multiple ways, proffered by the model, in which people can create an identity. When applied to *Jubilees*, one observes that a strong boundary between Jew/non-Jew is apparent in the text as, for example, is evident in the prohibition of exogamy. Unlike the Hasmoneans, however, for whom Jewishness was more of a national identity, the writer of *Jubilees* identified Jewishness with the notion of "race," to use, as Van Maaren indicates, a modern term. The author of *Jubilees* did not have access to political means of boundary making. He rewrites the history of the Jews such that genealogy figures centrally. Thus, the writer of *Jubilees* contributes to the formation of what he understands to be Jewishness, which is quite different from how his contemporaries, the Hasmoneans, perceived and constructed their notion of what it meant to be Jewish.

Kimberly Stratton deals with a later context, focusing her chapter on Justin Martyr's *Dialogue with Trypho.* Here, Stratton pays careful attention to the stages of the argument and the terms used. She points out that at a certain point in the dialogue, Trypho, for example, perceives Justin and his associates as Judeans who should have upheld Judean law, while Justin does not indicate that there is a new "religion" of "Christians" but that Jesus has replaced the law. Importantly, this means that, so far in the discussion, there is no notion of *Christian* as a separate religious category. It is only when Justin eventually describes what unites all followers of Jesus, and indicates that they are to forget their ancestral customs, that "Christian" appears to indicate a new and different identity over against a "Judean." This adoption of a common identity emerges, argues Stratton, in order to include gentile Jesus people and to confront Trypho's charge that Justin and his community have done away with Torah and angered God. Stratton is in no way claiming that this particular debate and set of circumstances is ultimately responsible for the "parting of the ways." She is demonstrating, however, how attempts to make meaning out of historical events could lead to arguments, which, in turn, can contribute to the development of a particular identity – an identity reflected in a new name and set of practices. Rather than assuming all sorts of things about the meaning of "Christian" in Justin's *Dialogue*, she attends to the specificity of how, why, and when it is used within a debate. In this case, then, there is a dialogic quality to the formation of identity.

The value of specificity and the other virtues implicit in Reinhartz's chapter continues throughout the other chapters as well. For example, William Arnal critically reviews some of the distinctions between "religion" and "magic" that New Testament scholars have made over the years. Historically, the argument has tended to focus on whether or not we can classify Jesus and other figures, such as Paul, as magicians. Certainly, the awareness that, historically, some scholars have been heavily invested in *not* describing Jesus as a magician must be acknowledged. Such perspectives, as Arnal illustrates, can impede a fair assessment of what magic is. Building from Marcel Mauss's definition of magic as "unauthorized ritual," Arnal underlines how magic is not a static phenomenon, but fluid, and can apply to a number of practices, people, and claims. With careful and clear attention to the texts, Arnal demonstrates that, while figures such as Jesus and Paul practise "magic" as mobile ritual specialists, their activities effectively localize, transfer, or extend the temple's operations over against the work of other ritual specialists or "magicians" such as the Pharisees in Mark, or Simon Magus in Acts. By thinking about magic more precisely as a set of varied practices within specific and changing contexts, therefore, some of the dynamics within these literary accounts become more apparent.

Purported distinctions between religion and magic have also influenced other categorizations within biblical studies. Ryan D. Schroeder narrates how the perdurance of the magic/religion divide has historically contributed to downplaying the significance of oracular consultation in the Hebrew Bible. However, now that many scholars seriously question or squarely reject that magic/religion binary, there is greater acceptance that the Hebrew prophets were not doing something unique, as earlier scholarship would have it, but were participating in divination, which was so widespread throughout antiquity. A new paradigm of prophecy, argues Schroeder, fosters a reimagining of what oracular consultation might look like. No longer is prophecy solely at the initiative of the deity but can involve solicitation by the prophet. Spontaneous prophecy still appears in the texts of ancient Israel, but, as Schroeder explains, the "spontaneous" element of these prophetic writings is especially amplified by the editorial work of Second Temple scribes. The reasons for such amplification include both theological and social motivations that can serve to set Israel apart from other nations. Without considering Israelite prophecy within the overall category of divination, however, this feature of Second Temple scribal activity may have been more difficult to perceive. How scholarship categorizes and conceptualizes practices therefore makes a difference to what we are able to illuminate by critical textual analysis.

Most of these chapters deal with varying types of practice, whether these practices are performed by figures within the literature or by those who wrote and edited the texts. As already mentioned, under discussion here are ritual activities, divination, boundary making, scribal editing, examples of debate, and attempts at meaning making. Jack Lightstone's chapter also centres on practice, but, in this case, it is not so much what the texts say as how they are used. Lightstone explores the role of scriptures in post-biblical Judaism outside of the land of Israel. Although he acknowledges the importance of analyzing how and why these texts were created, and what they meant, Lightstone stresses the need for biblical scholarship to study how scriptures were subsequently employed. The *use* of scriptures, he argues, contributed to identity formation just as the perceived *meaning* of the scriptures did. He examines a variety of uses, most notably the function of scriptures as sacred relics. A range of evidence, including the remains of niches and receptacles, and, ironically, the texts of writers such as John Chrysostom, supports the claim that scriptures were placed in special locations within synagogues, where they were objects of veneration. This veneration included the reading of scripture within worship. Moreover, among Greco-Roman Jews, not all of scripture could be followed; these Jews had to be selective. Yet they did not change scripture, for to do so would be to question its authority, but edited it "perceptually" such that the scriptures remained the source of authority and a path to the divine. Thus with Lightstone's chapter we have an example of how the use of scriptures, including as objects of veneration, played a significant part in fostering and maintaining the identity of diaspora Jews outside of Israel in the early centuries of the common era.

Collectively, how do these studies of ancient Mediterranean texts and peoples help us think about the study of religion? First, to my mind the authors here indicate and provide clear evidence that the development, articulation, and maintenance of ancient Jewish and Christian groups must begin with a focus on their particular types of practice. Θρησκεία, for example, means "practice"; to translate it as "religion," which is the usual translation of Jas 1:26–27, is misleading. By studying activities, including scribal undertakings and dialogues, one is better positioned to observe not only how different groups might share particular identities and names but also how they may have very different understandings of what it meant to be, for example, a "Jew/Judean" or a "Christian."

What is clear, as well, is that these practices are always in a particular social and political context, and will vary depending upon who the competitors, interlocutors, opponents, and perhaps supporters are. These are shifting and changing activities, influenced by historical and environmental factors. Practices could change depending upon where and when a particular individual or group was living. For example, as Joshua Schwartz asks: "How common … was the wearing of *tzitzit*? Was practice the same in both Palestine and Babylonia and the rest of the Jewish Diaspora?"[3] One cannot assume that practices were identical across geographic regions or consistent among the people who identified with a particular group or who used the same name to describe themselves.

In addition, many people throughout the ancient world shared some of the practices described in these chapters, not just "Jews/Judeans" or "Christians." As scholarship has learned over the past century or so, we risk describing practices badly when we insist that these figures, groups, and texts are so different from their contemporaries. As these chapters demonstrate, how one classifies groups and practices matters. This is not to say that there were no differences; of course there were. However, I think that these chapters show that it is better to begin from the ground up, without assuming that there were always vast distinctions between groups, and with careful and critical attention to the categories and concepts employed, such that we can describe these practices in all of their particularity.

In sum, the contributions here provide not only constructive critique, they also stimulate new ideas and offer new possibilities for moving forward as we think about life in the ancient Mediterranean world. In addition, I think that these chapters furnish methodological caution and provide insight into the classification and understanding of what today we refer to as "religion."

NOTES

1 See Hilde Lindemann, *Holding and Letting Go: The Social Practice of Personal Identities* (New York: Oxford University Press, 2014).

2 See Talal Asad, *Genealogies of Religion: Discipline and Reasons of Power in Christianity and Islam* (Baltimore: Johns Hopkins University Press, 1993), 27–54.

3 Joshua Schwartz, "Clothes Make the Jew: Was There Distinctive Jewish Dress in the Greco-Roman Period," in *Dress in Mediterranean Antiquity. Greeks, Romans, Jews, Christians*, ed. Alicia J. Batten and Kelly Olson (London: Bloomsbury/T & T Clark, 2021), 251.

SECTION FOUR

Comparison

The five chapters in this section focus on the possibilities and perils of comparison in the study of ancient religions. Chapter 19 looks at contemporary Chinese spirit mediums as potential comparative evidence for making sense of ancient Mediterranean freelance religious experts. Chapter 20 shows how a comparison of Clement of Alexandria's exegetical techniques with those of Philo has in some ways inhibited our understanding of the real context of Alexandrian intellectual activity. Chapter 21 also deals with the nuances and dangers of comparison, in this case, comparisons of Christian ideals about benefaction with contemporary parallels, both literary and inscriptional. Chapter 22 makes a case for human universals residing in shared human biology, though without discounting the role of cultural specificity. Chapter 23 explores the concept of spirit possession as a kind of generality that allows comparisons across cultures but that avoids universalistic claims. A response to these contributions (chapter 24) concludes the section.

19

The Enchanted World of Antiquity: On Incommensurability, Religion, and Comparison

Heidi Wendt

INTRODUCTION

This chapter reflects on how ethnographies of contemporary polytheistic societies stand to improve our reconstructions and analysis of ancient Mediterranean religion. The last decade has witnessed several challenges to the applicability of a modern concept of religion to antiquity as well as to other cultures that lack equivalent emic concepts or terms. Many critics argue that, in such cases, "religion" is imagined or retrojected onto pasts or places for which it is ill suited. From here, some scholars of antiquity then take the position that ancient and modern societies are incommensurable with respect to matters concerning the gods.

Were this a valid premise, there would be little to recommend the sort of comparison I propose below. However, I follow critical realists in maintaining that a reflective concept of religion can be applied appropriately and productively to those social practices by which ancient Mediterranean peoples engaged in mutual relations with divine beings. This stance encourages comparisons that, among other gains, offer an important corrective to the unchecked tendency towards overly romantic or exoticizing fantasies about the reality of inhabiting an ancient world "full of gods."[1] Consideration of contemporary cultures with similar epistemologies about and interactions with their gods calls into question automatic disclaimers about the peculiarity of that world, while also disabusing scholars of antiquity of notions that would receive greater scrutiny were they advanced about modern rather than ancient subjects.

To demonstrate the utility of ethnographies of polytheistic religion for studying Greco-Roman religion, I apply the framework of freelance religious expertise that I developed in earlier work to similarly self-authorized Chinese figures, known in English as "spirit mediums" for their ability to channel gods and spirits. Much could be said about the value of such case studies for thinking about ancient religious experts, but at present I am interested in two prominent themes in scholarship on Chinese spirit mediums and Chinese popular religion more generally.[2] The first is the ease with which mediums creatively take up discursive materials – particularly discourses and texts associated with alien, dominant cultures in contexts of differential power relations – to individuate and signal the prestige of their religious programs. The second is the challenge, if not futility, of trying to slot these figures into existing religious categories by the discourses they adopt, adapt, or exapt.[3]

As figures who often cultivate exoticism and insist upon their own novelty, spirit mediums, who are an ordinary feature of Chinese popular religion, ought to caution scholars of antiquity against credulous readings of our evidence for freelance religious experts as well as common practices – mystery initiation, divination, exorcism, and so forth – with which they were linked. Moreover, the example of Chinese spirit mediums also invites critical reflection on scholarly efforts to develop definitions for ancient *religions* since the plasticity, innovation, and competition so central to this form of religious activity render somewhat arbitrary the selection and application of definitional criteria. Even more so when, in the Roman period, similar experts were responsible for much of the discursive and institutionalizing labour that brought into existence concepts or entities that resemble modern *religions*. To proceed from a predetermined category that then includes these figures at the margins, by some criterion of resemblance to more central actors or phenomena, thus gets things exactly backward.

"RELIGION" IN ANTIQUITY?

The last two decades have witnessed great interest in the question of whether religion is an appropriate concept for study of antiquity, with many scholars registering objections. Their criticisms are not limited to the classical world but arise from wider debates about whether religion is a coherent object of study or has any independent status apart from academic discourse. For many, "the concept of 'religion' is manufactured, constructed, invented, or imagined, but does not correspond to an objective reality, 'out there' in the world."[4] Or, in the oft-quoted words of J.Z. Smith, "*There is no data for religion*. Religion is solely the creation of the scholar's study. It is created for the scholar's analytic purposes by his imaginative acts of comparison and generalization."[5]

While other strains of Smith's theoretical work complicate stark interpretations of his statement,[6] the construal of "religion" as *merely* a heuristic device has engendered a distinct "anti-realist" strain in the academic study of religion. Critics have rightly highlighted the liabilities of assigning religion an objective character – irrespective of time, place, or cultural milieu – that is then the scholar's task to discern and excavate. Such an approach universalizes a historically contingent concept, even though some cultures to which it is applied have no linguistic or conceptual equivalents. Indeed, Greek and Latin lack terms that map easily onto the modern concept of religion,[7] while the notion that religion occupies a distinct sphere is alien to a society in which practices involving the gods were distributed through every area of social life.[8] Moreover, critics note, since "religion" had its genesis in the age of European imperialism it cannot be culturally neutral. Applied to antiquity, then, the concept is flawed not only because it essentializes and homogenizes but also because it exports characteristics that are anachronistic and Christo-centric.

Versions of this position enjoy many advocates. Greg Anderson, for example, identifies radical points of disjuncture between the ontological premises of modernity and those of the ancient worlds that historians seek to reconstruct.[9] For him, ancient societies were isolated ontological worlds whose premises passed into oblivion once one culture sharing a holistic scheme of epistemological commitments evolved into another with its own.[10] With respect to religion, Anderson situates moderns, who inhabit a thoroughly disenchanted real world, at an irrevocable distance "from peoples who took it for granted that countless non-human agents and subjects were always out there, imminent in earth, sky, rivers, and seas, making all human life possible."[11] Since "religion" only makes sense in our modern Western world, it is without value for describing one in which "prayers, oaths, and offerings to the gods accompanied almost every human activity and event" and "engagements with divinity were ubiquitous and continuous."[12] Hence to speak of religion in Attica, his example, is to impose an artificial secularism on a culture whose interactions with the gods are fundamentally incommensurable with ours and, therefore, unintelligible today.[13]

Those who protest the uncritical use of religion in scholarship on the ancient world rightly identify potential hazards, particularly when the concept is employed descriptively rather than as a second-order category. However, most frame the problem in such a way that permits only one of two solutions: either ancient people engaged in practices and held beliefs that fit a *modern concept of religion*, with its baggage, or they would have recognized no such concept, and we cannot speak of their "religion" without transforming our ancient sources into reflections of contemporary practice and institutions.

But we are not beholden to only these two possibilities in determining whether Mediterranean relations with divine beings might count as religion. The linguistic argument that a concept cannot exist in cultures lacking native terms for it[14] confuses emic conceptualization – how humans experience and describe the world in their own language and categories – with the characteristics of some underlying social reality that is independent of human experience.[15] Maintaining this crucial distinction between epistemic and ontological objects of inquiry allows us to identify and examine distinctive social practices that occur trans-historically and cross-culturally, regardless of whether all the periods and cultures in question would recognize them in terms that match modern concepts. In our case, any social practices that involve the imagined participation of divine beings – gods, demi-gods, spirits, the dead, and so on, along with their practitioners and the institutions that maintain such practices – can be identified and redescribed as religion in the ontological sense.[16] Critical realism not only allows for but also demands relentless critical reflection on one's own conceptual tools, in no small part, through detailed comparative work.[17] Where Greco-Roman religion is concerned, I propose that comparison guards against a recurring flaw in the premise of antiquity's incommensurability.

Most critics of "religion" as a concept for antiquity over-correct, albeit in different ways, for potential category distortions by disallowing *any* continuity between how ancient and modern peoples imagined and engaged with divine beings. The language of enchantment (or disenchantment) is commonplace and ideologically central to such claims yet it is inadequately theorized, if theorized at all. "Enchantment" is invoked somewhat indiscriminately to capture such features as the materiality of divine beings and their intimate entanglements with all areas of human existence, over and against the abstract and removed notion of divinity ascribed to the modern West. But the self-evident fashion in which this language is employed results in what might be described as the *over-enchanting* of antiquity. For while such characteristics are often presented as erstwhile and uniquely ancient Mediterranean, they persist, mutatis mutandis, in many polytheistic regions.

In India, for instance, a profusion of temples, shrines, altars, and other sites of religious practice produces, as Edward Watts writes, "a passive and unconscious acceptance of their necessity."[18] Likening the sacred landscape of the Roman Empire to the pervasive religious infrastructure that one encounters in modern Indian cities – from major temples with dedicated attendants to smaller shrines lacking regular staff to the diminutive altars erected beside trees or maintained in households and places of business – Watts proposes that their abundance and visibility communicated the physical ubiquity of the gods while facilitating regular interactions with them.[19] The comparison is apt: ethnographies of polytheistic religion reveal a comingling of human and divine affairs – portrayed in much classical scholarship as a bygone condition – to be more ordinary than talk of antiquity's enchantment would suggest. Applied to modern peoples, this language would also sound concerning notes of Orientalism or essentialist fantasy: the exoticization of a culture's practices on a premise of extreme otherness.

A critical realist ontology of religion thus facilitates comparison between Mediterranean practitioners and other populations that engaged, or still engage, in the activities that constituted the bulk of the former's interactions with divine beings: sacrifice and other offerings, prayer, cursing, healing, divination, initiation, purification, honouring ancestors, and so forth. Ethnographies of modern polytheism offer an important check on problematic notions about ancient religiosity, which suffers for lack of the norms and stringent ethical policing required for studying living human subjects. While social practices involving the gods were inflected by the diverse ecologies of the ancient Mediterranean, as are social practices in any period and place, I am unconvinced that they are radically at odds even with comparanda in the modern West, let alone in contemporary polytheistic cultures. To the contrary, if practices, understandings, interests, and dynamics that were pervasive in antiquity can be redescribed profitably as "religion," then, thus redescribed, our interpretations of the ancient evidence stand to benefit from ethnographies of cultural areas whose interactions with divine beings seem to operate according to a similar logic.

FREELANCE RELIGIOUS EXPERTISE AS A CROSS-CULTURAL CATEGORY

The preceding section suggests a general advantage to recognizing religion in antiquity: that doing so enables the kind of comparative work that disabuses our historical reconstructions of problematic assumptions with a view to improving them. I also flag a foundational set of assumptions about the character of ancient Mediterranean religion – its enchantment and incommensurability – that, in my view, require sustained critical attention. In my own work, ethnographies of the Chinese popular religion that has persisted throughout Southeast Asia and resurged more recently in parts of China have proven highly conducive to such critical reflection on the religious history of the Roman Empire. While comparisons of this sort invite a more ambitious reimagining than present space allows, I would like to sketch some of the insights gleaned from thinking about a particular Mediterranean phenomenon – the religion of self-authorized or "freelance" experts – in relation to ethnographic studies of similarly self-authorized religious actors in Southeast Asia and China. This example is apropos of my earlier point about the over-enchantment of antiquity since these figures have been highly prone to incredulity and exaggeration in both comparanda, yet ethnographers have been far more diligent in rooting out problematic assumptions about them.

In previous work, I charted the Roman-period expansion of the religion of "freelance" experts, whereby I intended to capture any purveyor of specialized religious teachings, texts, rites, or adjacent services – often combinations of many such things – whose displays of skill and learning compensated for the types of recognition and legitimacy more typically drawn from affiliation with an existing religious institution (e.g., a temple, a priestly college) or a well-defined tradition.[20] Over the first two centuries of the Roman Empire, these would-be experts in religion grew increasingly influential, more diverse with respect to the skills or methods in which they claimed expertise, and more global in the ethnic coding of their wisdom and practices. *Religious* experts, in the sense defended above, intersected with similarly self-authorized specialists in philosophy, medicine, and *paideia*. The boundaries between these putative areas were highly porous and less significant than the deeper dynamics that all experts negotiated. Here, I have in mind such factors as the challenges of constructing and defending one's authority; rife competition, particularly among rivals claiming related specialty, and, in some cases, the same traditions (e.g., the wisdom of Orpheus, Pythagoras, Hystaspes, Mithras, Hermes Trismegistus) or texts (Sibylline, Chaldean, Judean oracles); and vulnerability to charges of charlatanry, pseudo-intellectualism, and profit-mongering, among other discrediting tactics.

My aims in developing this framework of freelance religious expertise were twofold, one historical and the other comparative. Regarding the former, I aimed to theorize a form of religious activity that cut across the boundaries of *our* flawed categories – foremost Judaism, Christianity, magic, and mystery cults – to explain the emergence of Christ phenomena as an unexceptional constellation of possibilities to arise from it. My secondary objective was to isolate a recurring feature of many religious landscapes across time and cultural milieu that intensifies, especially, under conditions of significant inter-cultural encounter and demographic change, which usually precipitate a collision of unfamiliar divine beings, religious practices, and theological vocabularies as well as (now) novel religious or philosophical texts. Such conditions, in antiquity and other periods, are usually byproducts of empire or complex colonial situations. Hence my overarching ambition was to redescribe Roman-period religious experts in a manner that promotes comparison with similar figures operating in religious landscapes that resemble those of the Roman world in key respects, for the sake of bilateral conceptual refinement.

Ethnographies of religious actors who seem to fit my category of freelance expertise were vital to how I conceptualized it, ferreting out several assumptions primed by the ancient sources and prior scholarship. It is rather easy to fall into the experts' own traps by simply granting the novelty and exotic allure that many cultivated diligently to their own advantage. Since our knowledge of them depends almost entirely on ancient literature – accounts that negatively caricature their activities – and, less often, their own writings, elements of distortion, to their benefit or disadvantage, are always prominent in the evidence. However, comparison reminds us not only that freelance experts are entirely ordinary – and are sometimes even the predominant religious authorities – within polytheistic societies but also that depictions of them as marginal, exotic, unique, implausible, and so forth are highly interested and have their own incentives for masking the ordinariness of this form of religiosity. Colonial conditions tend to compound the latter impressions by heightening demand for the religion of freelance experts while multiplying exponentially the forms it might take. Freelance experts are hardly the only religious actors affected by these conditions, but their institutional independence and rivalries enable (or require) them to adapt more freely to new discursive inputs and popular enthusiasms.

Specialists who fall under the rubric of Chinese popular religion furnish particularly evocative case studies in so far as they have been prominent for generations among overseas Chinese throughout the richly diverse regions of Southeast Asia.[21] Notwithstanding this diversity, there is great cultural continuity across Chinese populations in Malaysia, Indonesia, and Singapore stemming from common patterns of immigration from Mainland China, where popular religion was pervasive prior to China's Communist Revolution in 1949.[22] As scholars of Chinese religion consistently note, the bulk of popular religion unfolds outside formal institutional structures in ways that are familiar to scholars of antiquity: through prayer and the presentation of offerings to local deities; through the impromptu constructions of private shrines and temples; through the organization of local festivals; through networking between specialists, shrines, and temples; through the sponsorship of Chinese operas and other performances dedicated to gods; and through the veneration of deceased ancestors, which entails adorning a gravesite and burning there paper replicas of money, basic amenities, and prestige items before dedicating a special meal to be consumed later by the family.

In addition to these practices, which require only intuitive knowledge about how to perform or otherwise participate in them, spirit possession is central to Chinese popular religiosity; it interfaces with nearly all permutations and also coexists (perhaps not always comfortably) with more highly institutionalized forms of religion, including Buddhism, Daoism, Hinduism, and Islam."[23] Mediums are consulted regularly and provide myriad religious services that range from healing and exorcism to forging protective talismans to divination, often to discern auspicious dates or lottery numbers. Some are also teachers who draw on "a deep tradition of popular literature and the textual works of the Three Doctrines (*Samkao, Sanjiao*), Daoism, Confucianism, and Buddhism," among other sources, to devise proprietary cosmologies and ethical programs.[24] Regardless of their profiles, mediums serve as conduits for a variety of divine beings: usually Chinese gods, ancestors, and military heroes, but also on occasion for non-Chinese gods, saints, spirits, or protectors encountered in local environments. In Malaysia and Indonesia, for instance, Chinese mediums are regularly possessed by Malay spirits known as "datuk," who signal their presence through behaviours and preferences, acted out by the medium, that accord with a putative Muslim affiliation.

The multiethnic Malaysian island of Penang – established in 1786 as a British entrepôt for Chinese trade that was a major hub second only to Singapore on the sea route between India and China – serves as a veritable laboratory for the religious creativity that can incubate in such a cultural ecosystem. The island's population consists in significant numbers of (typically Muslim) ethnic Malays and East Malaysian indigenous peoples, Chinese "immigrants" from multilingual regions of China, and Indians, a diversity that is reflected in what is often described as the "eclecticism" of Chinese popular religion there.[25]

In Penang, religious experts operating within different cultural idioms both rival and network with one another, so that a Chinese spirit medium might view as potential competitors or collaborators not just other Chinese mediums but also Thai, Tibetan, Malay, and Indian actors boasting similar religious services. Moreover, Chinese mediums can channel Malay spirits, Muslim saints, or Indian gods, while their Indian counterparts become possessed by Chinese gods in addition to Hindu ones.[26] The conspicuous "ethnic coding" of certain skills and specialty allows for even more complexity. For example, Thai "black magic" is acknowledged to be more powerful than Chinese animating forces and thus widely feared, even though some Chinese mediums claim to have mastered its powers so that they are able to subvert or transform them. Despite their capacity for innovation, most

Chinese mediums root their religious programs in a common cosmological framework and discursive vocabulary that is transmitted through the literary traditions of Daosim, Buddhim, and Confucianism. Therefore, what gives them some cogency in the face of great potentiality is their indebtedness to a common literary repertoire or, at least, to language, concepts, and representations drawn from these texts.

Mediums typically operate in pavilions that occupy the front rooms of modest houses or apartments, although highly successful ones can acquire dedicated spaces or even construct proper temples for the gods whom they channel. Their possession commences in a neutral state: the medium typically meditates while waiting for one of the gods with whom he or she has a relationship to respond to an environmental lure – the fragrance of burning incense, clanging cymbals, beating drums – at which point the god enters the medium. Since most mediums maintain relationships with somewhere between three and five divine beings, the one who has taken possession must then indicate its identity by directing the medium to don a suitable costume and accoutrements while manifesting distinctive behaviours. A general god will strike militant postures, while those known for wisdom may adopt a more formal register of speech and deliver impromptu teachings. Gods even have distinct preferences about beverages, and may, upon assuming human form, request rice wine, French brandy, or Guinness Stout.[27] Mediums often "enact the god's transcendence and the antiquity of their historical age by making their language obscure or opaque; sometimes they speak in a glossolalic register in which no meaning is attached to the sounds produced."[28] Such cues are instantly recognizable to bystanders since they accord with standard ideas about the gods that are transmitted through multimedia representations and a range of performances. The authenticity of a possession is usually confirmed further by acts of self-mortification, during which the medium, now under the command of the being who inhabits him or her, experiences no pain or even the usual physiological effects that the act would produce.

Although Chinese spirit mediums, like other kinds of religious experts, offer multiple and overlapping religious services, most develop reputations for particular skills that are determined in part by environmental factors. A revealing instance of local conditions contouring the roles of religious specialists is found in how Chinese mediums who migrated to Indonesia and Malaysia in the same waves from the same regions of Mainland China interface with the healthcare systems of each country. Mediums in both countries offer healing services, often in the form of "prescriptions" that a possessing god writes either in vermillion ink – in Daoist alchemy, a potent ingredient with connotations of immortality – or with invisible characters on a piece of yellow paper (the paper is then boiled for the ailing person to consume as a tea).[29] In Indonesia, where healthcare is costly and uneven in quality, spirit mediums are among the primary medical resources for ethnic Chinese – not only local inhabitants but also some emigrants who return to Indonesia from more developed countries to seek local healing. Hence one encounters great diversity there in healing methods and performances, with some mediums achieving global reputations for efficacy in specific medical conditions. Efficacy can be communicated in any number of ways, as Adam Yuet Chau shows for mediums in Mainland China. Some attain considerable fame as healers and diviners, largely thanks to clients who spread tales of their skills. The fame of a medium is also measured by the business of consultation sessions; by the distance people travel to seek help, especially when they come from outside the medium's local sphere of activity; and how many sedan cars, which signal rich patrons, line up outside the medium's home.[30]

In Malaysia, however, where the healthcare system is superior on account of the country's longer durée as a British colony, mediums discriminate unequivocally between physical and spiritual causes of illness, insisting that people consult doctors for the former as they diagnose and tend in a complementary fashion to spiritual disturbances less amenable to modern medicine. In Penang, if an illness does not follow a normal course, the patient might consult a medium about underlying spiritual afflictions while continuing medical treatment.[31] The rise of Western psychology has even lent legitimacy to this binary approach to treatment. As Jean DeBernardi explains, "Spirit mediums are aware that modern scientific medicine poses a competitive threat, but they also know that modern medicine is not always effective in treating spiritual disturbances, which Western scholars tend to regard as psychological in origin and therefore internal to the individual, but which spirit mediums diagnose as having an external source."[32] This important distinction between how mediums in Indonesia and Malaysia operate in relation to other forms of healthcare holds even for the island of Borneo, whose territory is divided between the two countries.

Spirit mediums – along with the broader constellation of religious practices that constitute Chinese popular religion as defined by scholars such as DeBernardi and Chau – are placed at the margins of categories such as Daoism or Buddhism, often with the qualification that they are a "folk" instance thereof. Such designations are misleading, however, even when there is evidence of self-identification to support them. In Southeast Asia, apparent acts of affiliation are often the product of residents being required to declare membership with one official religion among a predetermined set of options on a government identity card; in practice, people's actual religious entanglements do not map neatly onto a single category or conform to a normative formulation thereof. The misalignment is pronounced for spirit mediums, who, as we have seen, adapt discourses and artifacts or channel divine beings across religious categories (Buddhism, Hinduism, Islam, Christianity) or ethnic idioms (Chinese, Malay, Thai). Hence, even in cases of putative religious affiliation, the dynamic sampling that occurs with few constraints among spirit mediums calls into question any efforts to categorize them in relation to a well defined and institutionalized religious tradition.

While comparisons between similarly self-authorized experts in Chinese and ancient Mediterranean religion could be conducted along several lines, for theorizing earliest "Christianity," it is especially evocative to consider the impact that variables such as new or foreign intellectual practices and discursive materials (religious tracts, moral handbooks, philosophical texts, etc.) – had on the religious programs of would-be religious experts in the former context. The colonial histories of places such as Penang and Singapore are essential for understanding the spectrum of possibilities available to religious experts there.[33] While their regular flow of Europeans may have waned, the material legacy of past interactions remains in everything from architecture to the presence of global religious institutions and literatures to contemporary educational priorities. These postcolonial settings have much in common with the complex negotiations of local, Greek, and, later, Roman culture that characterized the Hellenistic and Roman eras of the Mediterranean world, as do the global networks, population hybridity, linguistic diversity, reflection upon religious difference, and intellectual exchange that occurred under all the imperial situations in question.

For scholars of antiquity, DeBernardi's case studies of intellectualizing spirit mediums – often men who assumed these roles after receiving advanced Western educations and working as teachers or in comparable roles – are especially evocative. Whereas most mediums she documents refrain from dispensing robust moral teachings (at least, not beyond generically exhorting their clients to be good charitable people, to abstain from evil, and so forth) these examples developed complex moralizing discourses rich in exegesis of classificatory and ethical terms deriving from Daoist, Buddhist, and Confucian texts.[34] Drawing on language and concepts recognizable from these traditions, they profess elaborate, systematized cosmologies that either finely parse different classes of divine beings and their relations and ranks vis-à-vis one another or else synthesize concepts drawn from multiple religious lexica to arrive at universal precepts.[35] Intellectualizing mediums are also more likely to affiliate with some human master in addition to the gods they channel: Chinese wisdom teachers but also Theravada Buddhist monks and Indian gurus.[36] Moreover, the gods they mediate tend not to be ones who commonly possess mediums in Penang but divine beings with more abstruse origins in ancient texts or vernacular religious literature. This novelty affords considerable latitude for fleshing out their aspects and purviews.

Mediums with such profiles formulate teachings from an incredibly diverse range of literatures, including the Bible and the teachings of Socrates. They also resort to symbolic interpretations of well-known texts or stories about the gods, explaining that these are merely parables designed to inspire respect for their own authority and the veracity of their teachings. One man, known now as Master Lim, studied for the Cambridge exams with the Bible as his special subject and, after failing those, spent twelve years teaching art in one of Penang's most elite English-language schools.[37] After heeding signs of his own spiritual insight, he gained renown as a spirit medium with transcendent powers and a universalist philosophy.

Master Lim's practices were far simpler and less performative than those of other mediums; his skills and authenticity lay instead in intellectual demonstrations.[38] He also preferred to distinguish his spiritual practice and teachings not from those of local rivals but, rather, from those of Sai Baba, an Indian guru with a worldwide following.[39] He did not confine himself to the teachings of a single tradition but cited as his principal influences a Sinhalese Theravada Buddhist monk and books by two Western authors who had travelled East to study Hinduism and Buddhism. In his autobiography, he also admits to having attended meetings of the Penang Theosophical Society; indeed, he imparted lessons in Buddhism using the English theosophist Edwin Arnold's epic poem, *The Light of Asia*. Like Master Poh, a medium who had immigrated to Penang during the mid-century persecutions of mediums in China, Master Lim "insisted that *real* religion," understood in a universalist sense, "should be distinguished from dogmatic sectarianism, and that there are many paths to salvation."[40] Both mediums advocated ascetic cultivation and moral self-mastery as the means of escaping the unending cycle of death and rebirth.[41]

Consideration of the audiences for these more intellectualizing religious specialists also holds interesting possibilities for the ancient world. In cosmopolitan regions of Southeast Asia, religious practitioners are awash in and regularly sample religious activities associated with another ethno-religious idiom. "Chinese religious practitioners," DeBernardi explains, "are often self-consciously syncretic, combining elements that practitioners identify as Daoist, Buddhist, Confucian, and even sometimes Christian. Indeed, *practitioners regard syncretism as evidence of their tolerance and universality*."[42] Sometimes the "syncretism" in question is framed or understood not as something new and innovative but as a revitalization of highly *traditional* cultural forms in light of new historical circumstances.[43] While similar priorities obtain across social strata, certain kinds of people gravitate towards religious activities with a conspicuous intellectual profile.

Master Lim's clientele and temple committee consisted foremost of English-educated and socially aspirational members of the Chinese middle-class – including a medical doctor, a professor, and a stock analyst – who would meet regularly with their master for esoteric instruction and didactic expositions of classic texts such as the *Daodejing* and *Yijing*. Master Lim not only adapted these to Penang's social landscape to bridge the gap between cultural and linguistic traditions but also regularly juxtaposed their material with lines from the Bible or English poems, adducing congruent or parallel messages across the texts. Whereas the clientele of most spirit mediums consult them on an occasional, as needed basis, his followers conceived of themselves foremost as students and cultivated a strong sense of group membership by virtue of their communal instruction in and revelation of esoteric wisdom. Textual interpretation, philosophical discourses, and other scholastic activities were essential to realizing this collective social formation and the strong sense of common identity held by its members.

For figures such as Masters Lim and Poh, affinities between their practices and specific *religions* is largely a matter of which writings inform their exegetical activities, to say nothing of which discourses or activities an outsider might glimpse at any given moment. While it is not inconceivable that their groups could become sufficiently well defined to seek official recognition by an established religious organization, to label them thus without attention to nuance raises questions about the impetus to thus categorize them at all. Such creativity is most apparent at the level of entrepreneurial experts and the various social formations with which they are linked: scholastic circles, initiatory groups, occasional consulting relationships, and so forth.

It is tempting to describe these figures as bricoleurs of the various traditions from which they sample, and, in many respects, this is an apt characterization of their relationship to other religious social formations. However, in the ancient Mediterranean context, at least, it is rather *the traditions* that seem to have emerged from this sort of religious activity, whereupon they continued to interact with freelance actors to complex effect. In the case of Christianity, there are strong indications that unaffiliated religious experts were responsible for the initial diffusion of varied Christ phenomena and then for a few centuries of institutionalizing initiative before a particular version of such phenomena achieved the status of *a* religion through a combination of a well-defined discursive tradition and civic enfranchisement.[44] Other *religions* such as Judaism and Manicheism seem to have come into being through similar processes.[45] Likewise, scholars of Chinese religion document many inventions of "tradition" presented and understood as acts of revitalization, here too often at the behest of freelance experts. Once *religions* possess their own integrity, the institutions, customs, and writings that support them become points of reference for freelance experts. This dialectic is most apparent for figures who assume intellectualizing postures and affiliate selectively with recognized traditions by adopting domain-specific language, concepts, or texts.

The ethnographic evidence for Chinese spirit mediums appears to fit the corrigible framework of freelance religious expertise that I developed for the ancient Mediterranean world. Indeed, Giovanni Bazzana's recent study of spirit possession and exorcism in earliest Christianity ably demonstrates the utility of approaching these practices and their epistemological premises as cross-cultural phenomena.[46] I have identified other prospective angles for sustained comparison: tactics of self-authorization and institutionalization; the recognition and appeal of different kinds of experts to particular audiences; the ethnic coding of religious wisdom and practices; the profusion of texts and objects that occurs in imperial contexts, and the exponential innovation these support; and the emergence of putative religious groups from the institutionalizing labour of freelance experts and their followers, among others. Situated within this broader framework, studies of self-authorized religious experts in Chinese popular religion contribute rich data for further expansion, refinement, and the continuous conceptual reflection upon our reconstructions of the ancient Mediterranean world that critical realism advocates.

CONCLUSION

My primary goals in this chapter are to affirm and gesture towards the explanatory potential of treating ancient Mediterranean social practices involving divine beings as commensurable with and, therefore, comparable to other cultures in history where there is evidence for practices predicated on the existence of such beings or super-empirical realities.[47] Embracing this commensurability lays a path for detailed comparative work of the sort that holds our redescriptive efforts to account. As Kevin Schilbrack writes, "This work is asymptotic, never finished, always in a hermeneutic circle from one's initial descriptions and then back to critical reflection on one's conceptual tools. One cannot improve one's account of the past if one does not move into the reflective mode."[48] Claims of incommensurability masquerade as a form of critical reflection but have the opposite effect: of reinforcing caricatures of ancient peoples and social life that would be more amenable to critique were they placed in regular dialogue with comparanda for which they simply could not stand. As much ethnographic literature makes plain, there is nothing altogether extraordinary about inhabiting a world full of gods.

NOTES

1 Thalles (no. 91), in G.S. Kirk, J.E. Raven, and M. Schofield, *The Presocratic Philosophers: A Critical History with a Selection of Texts* (Cambridge: Cambridge University Press, 1984).

2 Indeed, Giovanni Bazzana's study of spirit possession in earliest Christianity (Giovanni Bazzana, *Having the Spirit of Christ: Spirit Possession and Exorcism in the Early Christ Groups* [New Haven: Yale University Press, 2020]; and see chapter 23 in this volume), published shortly after I presented this chapter as a paper at the 2019 meeting of the Canadian Society of Biblical Literature, is a wonderful illustration of how nuanced engagement with ethnographic accounts of this practice can clarify the epistemology undergirding its mentions and depictions in New Testament literature.

3 As Stanley Stowers writes ("Mythmaking, Social Formation, and Varieties of Social Theory," in *Redescribing Christian Origins*, ed. Ron Cameron and Merrill P. Miller [Atlanta: Society of Biblical Literature, 2004], 494): "A social exaptation would be a cultural artifact that in some sense originated in one social formation and environment but that came to serve a different use and function in another population, environment, and social formation." Social exaptation is useful for thinking about selective acts of "preservation" (often revitalization) involving archaic forms of writing, texts, and so forth.

4 Kevin Schilbrack, "Religions: Are There Any?," *Journal of the American Academy of Religion* 78 (2010): 1112.

5 Jonathan Z. Smith, *Imagining Religion: From Babylon to Jonestown*, Chicago Studies in the History of Judaism (Chicago: University of Chicago Press, 1982), xi (emphasis in original).

6 Stanley Stowers, "The Ontology of Religion," in *Introducing Religion: Essays in Honor of Jonathan Z. Smith*, ed. Willi Braun and Russell T. McCutcheon (London: Equinox, 2008), 435; Kevin Schilbrack, "A Realist Social Ontology of Religion," *Religion* 47 (2017): 173–5; Schilbrack, "Imagining Religion in Antiquity: A How To," in *Theorizing "Religion" in Antiquity*, ed. Nickolas P. Roubekas, Studies in Ancient Religion and Culture (London: Equinox, 2019), 59–63.

7 For example, Brent Nongbri, *Before Religion: A History of a Modern Concept* (New Haven: Yale University Press, 2013), 25–38; Carlin A. Barton and Daniel Boyarin,

Imagine No Religion: How Modern Abstractions Hide Ancient Realities (New York: Fordham University Press, 2016), 123–34.

8 Brent Nongbri, "Dislodging 'Embedded' Religion: A Brief Note on a Scholarly Trope," *Numen* 55 (2008): 440–60.

9 Greg Anderson, *The Realness of Things Past: Ancient Greece and Ontological History* (New York: Oxford University Press, 2018); Anderson, "Retrieving the Lost Worlds of the Past: The Case for an Ontological Turn," *American Historical Review* 120 (2015): 787–810.

10 Anderson, "Retrieving the Lost Worlds," 789, 795, 807. How such ruptures occur or where their edges lie in this segmented view of history is unclear.

11 Ibid., 792.

12 Ibid., 795.

13 Ibid., 800.

14 For example, Nongbri, *Before Religion*, 22–4; Barton and Boyarin, *Imagine No Religion*, 2–9.

15 Schilbrack, "Religions," 1123–6; Schilbrack, "Imagining Religion in Antiquity," 69–71.

16 Stowers, "Ontology of Religion"; Schilbrack, "Imagining Religion in Antiquity."

17 Schilbrack, "Imagining Religion in Antiquity," 74.

18 Edward J. Watts, *The Final Pagan Generation* (Oakland: University of California Press, 2015), 17.

19 Ibid., 19–26.

20 Especially Heidi Wendt, *At the Temple Gates: The Religion of Freelance Experts in the Roman Empire* (New York: Oxford University Press, 2016).

21 For a theorization of Chinese popular religion, see Adam Yuet Chau, *Miraculous Response: Doing Popular Religion in Contemporary China* (Stanford, CA: Stanford University Press, 2005), 44–58; Adam Yuet Chau, ed., *Religion in Contemporary China: Revitalization and Innovation* (London: Routledge, 2011), 1–4.

22 Jean DeBernardi, *The Way That Lives in the Heart: Chinese Popular Religion and Spirit Mediums in Penang, Malaysia* (Stanford, CA: Stanford University Press, 2006), 4–10, sketches a topography of Chinese mediums that includes Southern Min-speaking communities of Fujian Province, Taiwan, and the Southeast Asian diaspora: northern mainland Southeast Asia, the Malay peninsula, and island Southeast Asia, in particular, the Indonesian islands of Sumatra, Sulawesi, and Borneo. The practice of spirit possession is widespread even in state-controlled societies that nominally adhere to a single religion, of which Indonesia and Malaysia are prominent Muslim examples. As a social practice and performance frame, it is also based on assumptions the Chinese share with other Southeast Asian and South Asian populations. For the suppression of popular religion in China under the radical anti-traditionalist policies of both the Republican and Communist regimes, as well as the more recent "revitalization" of religious traditions, see Chau, *Religion in Contemporary China*.

23 DeBernardi, *Way That Lives in the Heart*, 13.

24 Ibid., 121.

25 I qualify "immigrants" because many of these people's ancestors immigrated to Southeast Asia generations ago yet retain a sense of Chinese cultural differentiation through the preservation of non-standardized (Mandarin) dialects, among other markers.

26 DeBernardi, *Way that Lives in the Heart*, 12–13. DeBernardi also (ibid., 123) documents an instance of a medium named Mr Lim being possessed by the spirit of a Thai ancestor on his grandfather's side, which suggests that one's own ancestry might furnish opportunities for innovative performances of mediumship.

27 Ibid., 127.

28 Ibid., 142.

29 Ibid., 112. Pauline scholars might sense in such suppositions a potential comparandum for the joint material-mental dimensions of the lord's dinner in 1 Cor 11:29–30, wherein Paul explains how one who participates in this meal without discerning Christ's body (μὴ διακρίνων τὸ σῶμα) in the consumption of otherwise ordinary food and drink – acts which he has previously assigned pneumatic and, therefore, material and transformative significance (1 Cor 10:1–4) – risks illness and even death.

30 Chau, *Miraculous Response*, 55–6.

31 DeBernardi, *Way that Lives in the Heart*, 106.

32 Ibid., 111.

33 As DeBernardi explains (ibid., 20):

> The ethnic, linguistic, and religious landscape of the Straits Settlements and colonial Malaya was extraordinarily diverse, and as early as 1836 the curious onlooker could observe "the rites of most of the religions of Asia" in cosmopolitan Penang and Singapore. In multicultural Penang, some of these religions were universal, salvific, and evangelical, and others were ethnically defined. By the mid-nineteenth century, Christian evangelists also were a force in the region, circulating tracts and religious books in an extraordinary range of languages as they sought to create diverse, multiethnic communities of like-minded believers. Their tracting is testimony to the diversity of peoples flowing through the port cities of Penang and Singapore: to sailors they distributed tracts in English, French, German, Italian, Swedish, Danish, Dutch, Greek, Spanish, Portuguese, and Russian; to the local people they offered tracts in Chinese, Malay, Tamil, English, Urdu, Gurmuki, Persian, Arabic, Portuguese, and Thai. In Brethren Assemblies in Singapore and Penang, English sailors and Chinese converts together underwent baptism by immersion in the sea.

34 Ibid., 205.

35 Ibid., 85.

36 Ibid., 145.

37 Ibid., 222–3.

38 As DeBernardi observes (ibid., 236), "the simplicity of his practice confirmed his transcendent powers, distinguishing him from the spirit mediums possessed by lower, more malevolent gods."

39 Ibid., 242.
40 Ibid., 223 (emphasis in original).
41 Ibid., 224.
42 Ibid., 173 (emphasis added).
43 Ibid, 222.
44 William Arnal, "The Collection and Synthesis of 'Tradition' and the Second-Century Invention of Christianity," *Method and Theory in the Study of Religion* 23 (2011): 193–215; Heidi Wendt, "The Gods and Other Divine Beings," in *Religion in the Roman Empire*, ed. Jörg Rüpke and Greg Woolf, Die Religionen der Menschheit 16.2 (Stuttgart: Kolhammer, 2021), 141–65; Wendt, *At the Temple Gates*.
45 For example, Stowers, "Ontology of Religion"; Daniel Boyarin, *Borderlines: The Partition of Judaeo-Christianity* (Philadelphia: University of Pennsylvania Press, 2004); Jason BeDuhn, "Mani and the Crystallization of the Concept of 'Religion' in Third Century Iran," in *Mani at the Court of Persian Kings: Studies on the Chester Beatty Kephalaia Codex*, ed. Iain Gardner, Jason BeDuhn, and Paul Dilley, Nag Hammadi and Manichaean Studies 87 (Leiden: Brill, 2015), 247–75.
46 Bazzana, *Having the Spirit of Christ*; and see chapter 23 in this volume.
47 Stowers, "Ontology of Religion"; Schilbrack "Imagining Religion in Antiquity," 74.
48 Schilbrack, "Imagining Religion in Antiquity," 74.

20

Comparison and (Dis-)Continuity: The Case of Philo and the Alexandrian Christians

Jennifer Otto

INTRODUCTION: PHILO AND CHRISTIAN ORIGINS IN EGYPT

The origins of Christianity in Egypt have long had a reputation for being murky.[1] While Walter Bauer famously proposed that earliest Alexandrian Christianity was dominated by "heretical" teachers,[2] a rival stream of scholarship has accounted for the silence of early sources by claiming that Jesus-devotion remained a subset of Judaism in Alexandria, rather than a distinct and separate religion, until well into the second century.[3] This theory is conjectural; no text survives that explicitly claims to have been written by an Alexandrian Jewish Jesus-follower.[4] The possibility of continuity between Alexandria's Jewish community and later Christian groups in the city is thrown further into question by the seeming end to organized Jewish life in the city in the aftermath of the Jewish revolts in Egypt and Cyrenaica against Roman rule in 115–117 and 130–131 CE.[5] By the middle of the second century, Christian teachers, including Basilides and Valentinus, are attested in the city, but their writings survive only in fragments preserved by their opponents.[6] It is only with the writings of Clement in the late second century CE that the image of Alexandrian Christianity comes into sharper focus.

One possible sign of continuity linking Clement's Christian community to first-century Alexandrian Judaism is the substantial use he makes of the writings of Philo of Alexandria, the prolific Jewish philosopher and scriptural exegete (c. 20 BCE–50 CE). Ronald E. Heine suggests that "one of the more obvious traces of the continuing imprint of [the Alexandrian church's] early Jewish-Christian origins is the acceptance and use of the works of Philo in a segment, at least, of the Alexandrian Christian community."[7] Similarly, while

Ilaria L.E. Ramelli admits that "the link between Philo and the Early Christian community in Alexandria" is "historically unfounded," she contends that it "reflects however the probable Jewish roots of Alexandrian Christianity."[8]

In the late 1990s, Annewies van den Hoek and Gregory Sterling published influential essays that proposed reconstructions of the chain of transmission that enabled Clement to access Philo's works. Since Clement does not explicitly say how Philo's writings came into his possession, their reconstructions are admittedly speculative.[9] As we shall see, although these transmission theories differ in their details, both cast Clement and his successors among the Alexandrian Christians as the heirs of a single continuous school tradition that passed Philo's writings and his allegorical hermeneutic from Jewish to Christian hands. As I aim to show below, however, this hypothetical chain of transmission is not necessary to account for Christian access to Philo's texts. That Christians came to know and cite Philo's writings is not as clear an indication of the Alexandrian Church's Jewish roots as Heine, Ramelli, and others have suggested.

I begin this chapter by reviewing the evidence that van den Hoek and Sterling cite to support a chain of transmission that locates the reading and citing of Philo's texts in a tradition that begins within first-century Alexandrian Judaism and ends among Alexandrian Christians. I aim to show how this reconstruction reinforces a narrative of Christian origins in Alexandria that casts Christians as the legitimate heirs of a form of Hellenized Judaism that reaches its apex in Philo's writings. I argue that this narrative relies on the assumption that, as adherents of exclusive "religions," Jews and then Christians formed closed discursive communities. Philo's writings would only have been of interest to other Jews, and non-Jewish Christians like Clement could only have come to know of Philo's texts via the mediation of Jews who converted to Christianity or "Jewish-Christians."

In the second part of this chapter, I draw on a recent wave of research that situates Philo together with second-century Christians, including Clement, but also non-Alexandrians, including Justin Martyr and Tatian, within broader circles of intellectuals that included participants of diverse ethnic backgrounds and philosophical affiliations.[10] Their writings are considered alongside those of figures including Celsus, Plutarch, and Numenius of Apamea who sought "a re-definition of that very Greek discipline of philosophy that was spacious enough not only to accommodate non-Greek wisdom, but even to privilege it as the ancient and true wisdom of which Greek philosophy is but a later elaboration or copy."[11] I propose an alternative, and admittedly still speculative, transmission theory that suggests that Clement read Philo's writings not as part of an inherited exclusive Jewish-Christian exegetical tradition but within a network of textual exchange that included many diverse conversation partners. By placing Philo and his Christian readers within a wider circle of comparators, the continuity linking Philo's Jewish community to the Alexandrian Christians becomes less clear.

THE ALEXANDRIAN JEWISH-CHRISTIAN SCHOOL TRADITION

In "The Catechetical School of Early Christian Alexandria and Its Philonic Heritage," Annewies van den Hoek sketches lines of possible continuity between Philo and the Alexandrian church of the late second century described by Eusebius in his *Ecclesiastical History*. Following Eusebius's claim that "by ancient custom a school of sacred writings had been established among [the Alexandrians]," van den Hoek argues that a "catechetical" school under the supervision of a bishop already existed in Alexandria in Clement's day. This idea has been met with scepticism by some scholars, who think it more likely that Clement was one of a network of loosely connected independent Christian teachers.[12] Van den Hoek, however, cites as evidence for her argument her earlier study of Clement's borrowings from Philo in the *Stromateis*. In this work, she demonstrates that Clement had copies of Philo's treatises open in front of him as he wrote – treatises from which he borrowed liberally.[13] The lack of similar borrowings in writings Clement composed after leaving Alexandria suggests to van den Hoek that he accessed the works of Philo, and of other Jewish authors, in an organized library that housed texts to support the catechetical and liturgical functions of the Christian community in Alexandria.[14]

While admitting that "one cannot answer the question of how the Philonic corpus and other Jewish texts ended up in Christian libraries,"[15] van den Hoek suggests two possible paths of transmission: "One among a multitude of possibilities is that some hellenized Jewish groups who studied the scriptures and Jewish-Greek writing in general could have 'converted' to Christianity, while keeping their 'ancestral' scrolls."[16] Alternatively, "during or after the suppression of the Jewish revolt, Christians (among them Jews and non-Jews) might have appropriated or rescued (depending on the perspective) existing book collections."[17] Van den Hoek ends her essay by emphasizing the continuity between Philo and Alexandria's Christian catechetical school: "Philo and the Christian school are closely related and, in a sense, they are inseparable. The Philonic corpus owes its preservation to the Christian tradition of Alexandria and its extension via Origen in Caesarea. The link with Philo was no longer with a living Jewish tradition but with a literary heritage. One might never have known any of Philo's works were it not for the Christian Alexandrian tradition, but then again, one might never have heard of a Christian Alexandrian tradition were it not for Philo."[18]

The question of continuity between Philo and later Christians is answered somewhat differently in Gregory Sterling's "The School of Sacred Laws: The Social Setting of Philo's Treatises."[19] Rather than locating Philo's treatises in the library of a catechetical school under the supervision of a bishop, Sterling proposes that the scrolls changed hands via a succession of independent teachers. He begins by theorizing the setting of Philo's own teaching activities. Rejecting the idea that Philo taught in a synagogue, he suggests "that Philo had a private school in his home or personally owned structure for advanced students which was similar to schools of higher education run by individuals throughout the Greco-Roman world."[20] The philosophical schools of the ancient Mediterranean world were typically small and informal, best understood as circles of students who attached themselves to a teacher.[21] It is in a school of this nature that Sterling locates Philo's pedagogical activities.

Sterling continues by proposing that Clement's access to Philo's corpus was mediated through a continuous succession of teachers and students. If "Philo had a school," he reasons, "his students would have kept the library."[22] Due to hostilities between Jewish and Greek communities in Alexandria in the mid-first century CE, Sterling thinks it unlikely that Philo's writings would have been preserved by non-Jews.[23] That they survived the Jewish uprising under Trajan in 115–117 CE indicates to Sterling that Philo's scrolls had by that time become the property of a Christian. "There are two possibilities," he contends, to account for this transfer: "one, a student in the school was either a Christian or became one and made arrangements for the Christian community to obtain copies of the manuscripts; or, a later disciple who became the head of his own school converted to Christianity and brought the library with him." Admitting that "we will probably never know what actually took place," Sterling concludes that "the theory that his library was preserved by a school of disciples appears the most reasonable explanation of the evidence. Either a student or a head of a subsequent school converted to Christianity and brought the library." Via this succession of teachers, Philo's exegetical method "began to move in Christian circles" and "continued its unofficial and informal life until it reached Clement and Origen."[24] Sterling clarifies that he is not suggesting that Philo's school itself eventually evolved into the Alexandrian catechetical school; rather, he proposes "the passing of the hermeneutic and its library from one private school to another." Nevertheless, he concludes, "I think that it is in this sense that we may speak of Philo's 'school of sacred laws' as the forerunner of the later Christian *didaskaleion* at Alexandria."[25]

While van den Hoek's transmission theory grants a greater role to an organized, institutional church in Alexandria than does Sterling's, both share several assumptions. Although they admit the possibility that Philo may have been deemed sufficiently "famous" or "significant" for his writings to have found a place in official libraries, neither thinks that his writings circulated widely.[26] Both presume that Philo's writings would have interested only a very limited readership of Jews, Jewish converts to Christianity, or "Christians (among them Jews and non-Jews)."[27] Philo's treatises are thus presented as travelling along a circumscribed continuum of progressively-less-Jewish readers, being preserved first by Jews, then by "Jewish-Christians," before being finally – and decisively – rescued (or appropriated) by Christians.[28] This transmission theory reflects and reinforces a narrative of Christian origins as a gradual emergence out of Hellenistic Judaism, making Clement and his Christian school heir to Philo's Jewish community.

PHILO AMONG GREEKS, ROMANS, AND BARBARIANS

If Philo's treatises didn't reach Clement via a gradually-more-Christian chain of transmission, how could they have come into his possession? I echo the caveat that we cannot answer this question with certainty. But I suggest that we return to the earliest source to narrate the Christian encounter with Philo – book 2 of Eusebius's *Ecclesiastical History* – for suggestions of an alternative. In this text, Eusebius first introduces Philo as follows:

> Κατὰ δὴ τοῦτον Φίλων ἐγνωρίζετο πλείστοις, ἀνὴρ οὐ μόνον τῶν ἡμετέρων, ἀλλὰ καὶ τῶν ἀπὸ τῆς ἔξωθεν ὁρμωμένων παιδείας ἐπισημότατος. τὸ μὲν οὖν γένος ἀνέκαθεν Ἑβραῖος ἦν, τῶν δ' ἐπ' Ἀλεξανδρείας ἐν τέλει διαφανῶν οὐδενὸς χείρων, περὶ δὲ τὰ θεῖα καὶ πάτρια μαθήματα ὅσον τε καὶ ὁπηλίκον εἰσενήνεκται πόνον, ἔργῳ πᾶσι δῆλος, καὶ περὶ τὰ φιλόσοφια δὲ καὶ ἐλευθέρια τῆς ἔξωθεν παιδείας οἷός τις ἦν, οὐδὲν δεῖ λέγειν, ὅτε μάλιστα τὴν κατὰ Πλάτωνα καὶ Πυθαγόραν ἐζηλωκὼς ἀγωγήν, διενεγκεῖν ἅπαντας τοὺς καθ' ἑαυτὸν ἱστορεῖται.
>
> At this time [i.e., during the reign of Gaius Caligula] Philo was famous, a man most renowned not only among our people but even among those keen on outside learning. He was a Hebrew by race, inferior in excellence to none of the distinguished men of Alexandria, and that he worked long and hard studying the divine and ancestral

> teachings is in fact evident to everyone. And that he was so greatly accomplished in philosophy and the liberal studies of outsiders it is not necessary to say, for he was so zealous in his study of the Platonic and Pythagorean traditions that he is reported to have surpassed everyone of his time.[29]

We do not have to assume that Eusebius's testimony is entirely accurate – or entirely innocent – to note the following key features of this description. First, Philo is presented as a famous person among the distinguished men of Alexandria and as renowned not only among Eusebius's own people but among outsiders as well. Second, the reason for Philo's fame is his intellectual accomplishments in the study of "the divine and ancestral teachings" as well as the study of "Platonic and Pythagorean traditions." While we may suspect Eusebius of exaggerating in his claim that Philo's philosophical learning "surpassed everyone in his own time," the picture that he presents is of a well-known and well-regarded scholar who achieved at least some degree of notoriety among the philosophical adepts of the Greek-speaking Roman world.

This description aligns with the portrayal presented in Maren Niehoff's recent *Philo of Alexandria: An Intellectual Biography*, which casts Philo as a participant in a "lively intellectual exchange in Rome" parallel to other ambassadors known to have engaged in "cultural activities" while in the capital.[30] Niehoff contends that approximately half of Philo's literary output, including the *Exposition of the Law* as well as the historical and philosophical treatises, can be dated to the period after his Roman embassy. She argues that these writings, unlike the *Allegorical Commentary* and *Questions and Answers* treatises composed in Alexandria earlier in Philo's career, were aimed at Roman audiences, "most likely cultural salons," and that Philo may have counted Seneca among his conversation partners.[31]

Niehoff's description of Philo as a participant in the intellectual life of Rome suggests that he intended his texts to find an audience beyond a small circle of students. Based on a lack of early citations and internal cross-references, James R. Royse concludes that it is doubtful that Philo's writings were published in the sense of being widely circulated beyond his immediate circle of acquaintance. He allows, however, that Philo wrote books aimed at a variety of audiences, including some dealing with philosophical issues, contemporary political events, and others with broadly apologetic purposes. "Is it plausible," he asks, "that he would have written all of these diverse books for the private use of himself and his circle of students and colleagues?" Royse concludes, "again, we are left, I regret, with something much less than clarity or certainty."[32]

In two more recent articles, Gregory Sterling has himself suggested two plausible readers of Philo's writings beyond his own students. Answering the question, "Did Josephus Know the Writings of Philo?," Sterling concludes that "it appears to me very likely that Josephus had not only read but drew from *On the creation of the cosmos* and *The Life of Moses*. He may have read some of the other treatises in the *Exposition of the Law*, especially *On the virtues*. It is also possible that he read some of the *Questions and Answers on Genesis and Exodus*."[33] He suggests two possible places where Josephus may have come across Philo's writings: Alexandria, a city that Josephus visited, and Rome, his eventual home: "Philo's works were certainly extant in Alexandria when Josephus visited and some of them may well have been in Rome when the historian lived in Vespasian's former house."[34] In a 2015 article, Sterling takes up the question of Philo's possible influence on the second-century Pythagorean Platonist, Numenius of Apamea, whose work survives only in fragments preserved by Christians. Sterling considers Philo and Numenius to "share a common outlook," considering both together with Plutarch and Chaeremon, the Egyptian priest and Stoic philosopher, in a "larger tradition that brought sacred Eastern texts into alignment with Greek philosophical thought through allegorical exegesis."[35] Although no explicit citations of Philo are found in any of Numenius's surviving fragments, on the basis of the similarity of their thought, Sterling judges "that minimally it is possible that Numenius knew some of Philo's works and maximally it is probable that he did."[36] Neither Josephus, the Judean general transplanted to Rome, nor Numenius, the Syrian disciple of Pythagoras, fit the profile of a Jewish(-Christian) teacher in Alexandria. If they indeed knew Philo's writings, it would suggest that Philo enjoyed a wider readership beyond the circumscribed chain of teachers and students than Sterling previously proposed.

Justin Jeffcoat Schedtler has recently described how private libraries facilitated the exchange of texts among intellectuals across the Mediterranean world. "Though privately owned," he writes, "these libraries are in many ways indistinguishable from 'public' or institutional libraries, e.g., in terms of the size of the collections, the contents of the collections, and their use as centers of scholarship for those in the wider community."[37] Alexandria was particularly noted for its book trade. Ronald Heine describes Alexandria as "a city of books outside those in the great libraries … People living outside Alexandria ordered books from booksellers in the city."[38] David Lincicum has shown that Philo himself likely possessed a private library of moderate size that included not only Jewish and Biblical texts but also many of Plato's works as well as texts by Empedocles, Heraclitus, Posidonius, and Zeno.[39]

On the basis of his study of Greek works cited by Philo, Erkki Koskenniemi concludes that Philo "undoubtedly" had a library and that "it is not too bold to claim that he enjoyed its treasures with his friends, i.e., learned fellow Jews and Gentiles leaning to Judaism."[40]

If Philo's writings found a place in the libraries of intellectuals of the Roman Empire, then there is no need to posit one single chain of transmission, nor one single decisive act of conversion, that marked the passage of Philo's scrolls from Jewish to Christian hands. Philo's writings could have been bought, borrowed, consulted, or copied by different Christians at different times via different intermediaries, not all of whom may have been Jews. That Clement himself did not primarily associate Philo with a continuous Jewish-Christian school tradition is suggested by the fact that he refers to him, twice, as a Pythagorean.[41]

The discovery of a fragmentary codex containing eight known and at least one lost Philonic treatise at Oxyrhynchus provides additional tantalizing, albeit uncertain, evidence of a wider audience for Philo's works. The fragments, which have been published as *P.Oxy.* 9.1173, 11.1356, 18.2158, 82.5291, *PSI* XI 1207, and *P.Haun.* 8, are dated to the third century CE on paleographical grounds, indicating that Philo's works were being read four hundred kilometres south of Alexandria around the same time that Clement was at work on the *Stromateis*.[42] The precise circumstances of the codex's discovery by Bernard Grenfell and Arthur Hunt is not clear, but the inventory numbers and handwritten notes on the fragments suggest that they were found during the fifth season of their excavation, 1905–06. That winter, Grenfell and Hunt identified three distinct concentrations of numerous literary papyri. The excavators believed, and subsequent scholars have concurred, that the literary papyri in each concentration most likely came from individual ancient book collections that were disposed of together.[43] Each of the three collections contain a mix of well-known authors (Homer, Hesiod, Callimachus, etc.) as well as obscure and otherwise unknown works. In a 2007 article, George W. Houston includes the Philo codex in the third major concentration, a collection that contains, among other works, Plato's *Timaeus*, *Phaedrus*, and *Gorgias*, but no identifiably Jewish or Christian texts.[44] In 2014, Houston changed his mind, noting that the largest surviving fragments of the Philo codex were published in *P.Oxy.* 9 and 11, volumes that contain no other documents from the third concentration. "It would appear," Houston reasons, "that a few small fragments became detached from the codex and came to rest near the concentration … but are not a part of that concentration."[45] Without more precise information about the codex's discovery, it is impossible to conclude with certainty whether this edition of Philo's works was part of the collection.

CONCLUSION

It is certainly correct that Clement and other later Christian allegorists read the works of Philo, employed similar exegetical methodologies, and explicitly adopted some of his hermeneutical moves. They did so, however, within social, intellectual, and literary contexts that included many other diverse conversation partners. The positing of a continuous "Judeo-Christian" exegetical tradition emphasizes the similarities between these two groups but imposes unnecessary limits on the possible variety of contributors – Pythagoreans, Platonists, Stoics, and Christian "heretics" – to the exegetical tradition in which the Alexandrian Christians worked. The invention of a continuous Alexandrian Jewish-Christian school tradition dislocates both Philo and his later Christian readers from their immediate social contexts, obscures the diversity of their conversation partners, and reinforces the teleological idea that Christianity evolved out of – and superseded – Hellenistic Judaism.

NOTES

This chapter extends arguments that I develop in chapter 2 of Jennifer Otto, *Philo of Alexandria and Construction of Jewishness in Early Christian Writings* (Oxford: Oxford University Press, 2018), making use of new research that has appeared since its publication.

1 The dearth of sources for early Alexandrian Christianity was lamented already by Adolf von Harnack, *Mission and Expansion of Christianity in the First Three Centuries*, trans. and ed. James Moffatt, 2nd ed. (New York: Putnam, 1908).

2 Walter Bauer, *Orthodoxy and Heresy in Earliest Christianity*, trans. and ed. R.A. Kraft and G. Krodel (Philadelphia: Fortress Press, 1971).

3 This position is defended in Colin H. Roberts, *Manuscript, Society and Belief in Early Christian Egypt* (London: The British Academy, 1979); Helmut Koester, "Egypt," 658–76, in *History and Literature of Early Christianity*, vol. 2 of *Introduction to the New Testament*, 2nd ed. (Berlin: De Gruyter, 2000); Birger Pearson, "Earliest Christianity in Egypt: Some Observations," in *The Roots of Egyptian Christianity*, ed. Birgen Pearson and James E. Goehring (Philadelphia: Fortress Press, 1986), 132–59; and, recently, Benjamin Schliesser, "Jewish Beginnings: Earliest Christianity in Alexandria," in *Alexandria: Hub of the Hellenistic World*, ed. Benjamin Schliesser, Jan Rüggemeier, Thomas J. Kraus, and Jörg Frey (Tübingen: Mohr Siebeck, 2021), 369–97.

4 Alexandrian provenance has been proposed for several New Testament texts, including the Gospel of John, Hebrews, Jude, and 2 Peter, none conclusively. Jörg Frey, "Locating New Testament Writings in Alexandria: On Method and the Aporias of Scholarship," 345–65, in *Alexandria: Hub of the Hellenistic World*, 364, proposes an Alexandrian provenance for two noncanonical texts, the *Apocalypse*

of Peter and the *Gospel according to the Hebrews*, but admits, "the conundrum of the earliest expressions of Alexandrian Christianity remains."

5 The extent of Jewish presence in Alexandria after the revolts remains debated. William Horbury, *Jewish War under Trajan and Hadrian* (Cambridge: Cambridge University Press, 2014), 234–5, represents the majority view that "the papyri from the Egyptian *chora* and the Fifth Sibylline book allow the suggestion that an Alexandrian Jewish remnant survived under Hadrian … Yet not until the third century, probably, did an Alexandrian Jewish community begin to regain any considerable prominence."

6 Recent scholarship has resisted an earlier paradigm that categorized Basilides and Valentinus as "Gnostics." See Karen L. King, *What Is Gnosticism?* (Cambridge: Belknap Press, 2003); Ismo Dunderberg, *Beyond Gnosticism: Myth, Lifestyle and Society in the School of Valentinus* (New York: Columbia University Press, 2008); David Brakke, *The Gnostics: Myth, Ritual, and Diversity in Early Christianity* (Cambridge: Harvard University Press, 2010).

7 Ronald E. Heine, *Origen: Scholarship in Service of the Church* (Oxford: Oxford University Press, 2010), 31.

8 Illaria L.E. Ramelli, "The Birth of the Rome-Alexandria Connection: The Early Sources on Mark and Philo, and the Petrine Tradition," *Studia Philonica Annual* 23 (2011): 78.

9 The problem has been recognized by Tobias Nicklas, "Jews and Christians? Sketches from Second Century Alexandria," in *Jews and Christians: Parting Ways in the First Two Centuries CE? Reflections on the Gains and Losses of a Model*, ed. Matthias Konradt, Judith Lieu, Laura Nasrallah, Jens Schröter, and Gregory E. Sterling (Berlin: De Gruyter, 2021), 357: "we have to fill a gap of several decades in which there must have been a time where Philo's writings made it into the hands of people we call 'Christians' today."

10 Recent studies that take up the concept of the Christian "intellectual" include Kendra Eshleman, *The Social World of Intellectuals in the Roman Empire: Sophists, Philosophers, and Christians* (Cambridge: Cambridge University Press, 2013); Anders Klostergaard Petersen, "Dissolving the Philosophy-Religion Dichotomy in the Context of Jewish Paideia: Wisdom of Solomon, 4 Maccabees, and Philo," in *Second Temple Jewish Paideia in Context*, ed. Jason M. Zurawski and Gabriele Boccaccini (Berlin: De Gruyter, 2017), 185–204; Lewis Ayres and H. Clifton Ward, ed., *The Rise of the Early Christian Intellectual* (Berlin: De Gruyter, 2020); Heidi Wendt, "Christians as and among Writer-Intellectuals in Second-Century Rome," in *Christian Teachers in Second-Century Rome: Schools and Students in the Ancient City*, ed. H. Gregory Snyder (Leiden: Brill, 2020), 84–108; Jared Secord, *Christian Intellectuals and the Roman Empire: From Justin Martyr to Origen* (University Park: The Pennsylvania State University Press, 2020).

11 Winrich Löhr, "Modelling Second-Century Christian Theology: Christian Theology as *Philosophia*," in *Christianity in the Second Century: Themes and*

Developments, ed. James Carleton Paget and Judith Lieu (Cambridge: Cambridge University Press, 2017), 161.

12 See Roelof van den Broek, "The Christian 'School' in Alexandria in the Second and Third Centuries," 38–45, in *Centers of Learning: Learning and Location in Pre-Modern Europe and the Near East*, ed. Jan Willem Drijvers and Alasdair A. MacDonald (Leiden: Brill, 1995).

13 Annewies van den Hoek, *Clement of Alexandria and His Use of Philo in the Stromateis: An Early Reshaping of a Jewish Model* (Leiden: Brill, 1988).

14 Eusebius, *Ecclesiastical History* 5.10.1.

15 Annewies van den Hoek, "The 'Catechetical' School of Early Christian Alexandria and Its Philonic Heritage," *Harvard Theological Review* 90 (1997): 84.

16 Ibid., 84.

17 Ibid., 85.

18 Ibid., 87. David T. Runia has advanced the yet bolder thesis that Philo's works were preserved "in the so-called Catechetical school of the Christian diocese of Alexandria, perhaps through the special efforts of its first 'director' – (to use a modern term) – Pantaenus." See Runia, "Witness or Participant? Philo and the Neoplatonist Tradition," in *Philo and the Church Fathers: A Collection of Papers*, ed. David T. Runia (Brill: Leiden, 1995), 191.

19 Gregory Sterling, "The School of Sacred Laws: The Social Setting of Philo's Treatises," *Vigilae Christianae* 53 (1999): 148–64. Sterling reaffirms this reconstruction in "The School of Moses in Alexandria: An Attempt to Reconstruct the School of Philo," in *Second Temple Jewish Paideia in Context*, ed. Jason M. Zurawski and Gabriele Boccaccini (Berlin: De Gruyter, 2017), 166: "It is likely that one of his prize students inherited his library and the school. Eventually, this appears to have become the property of Christians who learned how to think theologically from Philo."

20 Sterling, "School of Sacred Laws," 150. See also David T. Runia, "Philo of Alexandria and the Greek *Hairesis*-Model," *Vigilae Christianae* 53 (1999): 117–47.

21 Ibid., 151, 159.

22 Ibid., 163.

23 Ibid., 164.

24 Ibid., 163.

25 Ibid., 164.

26 van den Hoek, "Catechetical School," 81; Sterling, "School of Sacred Laws," 161.

27 On the scholarly construct of "Jewish Christianity," see James Carleton Paget, "The Definition of the Term 'Jewish Christian'/'Jewish Christianity' in the History of Research," in *Jews, Christians and Jewish Christians in Antiquity*, ed. James Carleton Paget, (Tübingen: Mohr Siebeck, 2010), 289–324. For a recent critique, see Matt Jackson-McCabe, *Jewish Christianity: The Making of the Christianity-Judaism Divide* (New Haven: Yale University Press, 2020).

28 van den Hoek, "Catechetical School," 85.

29 *Ecclesiastical History* 2.4.2–3. I follow the translation in Eusebius of Caesarea, *The History of the Church: A New Translation,* trans. Jeremy Schott (Oakland: University of California Press, 2019).

30 Maren Niehoff, *Philo of Alexandria: An Intellectual Biography* (New Haven: Yale University Press, 2018), 14.

31 Ibid., 18.

32 James R. Royse, "Did Philo Publish His Works?" *Studia Philonica Annual* 25 (2013): 100.

33 Gregory Sterling, "Did Josephus Know the Writings of Philo?" *Studia Philonica Annual* 25 (2013): 112.

34 Sterling, "Did Josephus Know the Writings of Philo?" 112.

35 Gregory Sterling, "The Theft of Philosophy: Philo of Alexandria and Numenius of Apamea," *Studia Philonica Annual* 27 (2015): 80.

36 Sterling, "Philo of Alexandria and Numenius of Apamea," 84.

37 Gregory Sterling, "The Theft of Philosophy: Philo of Alexandria and Numenius of Apamea," *Studia Philonica Annual* 27 (2015): 71–85, citing Fabio Tutrone, "Libraries and Intellectual Debate in the Late Republic," 124–36, in Jason König, Katerina Oikonomopoulou, and Greg Woolf, *Ancient Libraries* (Cambridge: Cambridge University Press, 2013).

38 Heine, *Origen*, 22.

39 David Lincicum, "Philo's Library," *Studia Philonica Annual* 26 (2014): 113.

40 Erkki Koskenniemi, *Greek Writers and Philosophers in Philo and Josephus: A Study of Their Secular Education and Educational Ideals* (Leiden: Brill, 2019), 131.

41 See Jennifer Otto, "Philo, Judaeus? A Re-Evaluation of Why Clement Calls Philo 'the Pythagorean,'" *Studia Philonica Annual* 25 (2013): 115–38.

42 The known Philonic treatises included in the codex are *Legum allegoriae I and II, De ebriatate, Quod deterius potiori insidari soleat, De sacrifiis, De providentia* I and II, and *De posteritate Caini*. On the contents and condition of the codex, see James R. Royse, "The Oxyrhynchus Papyrus of Philo," *Bulletin of the American Society of Papyrologists* 17 (1980): 155–65.

43 George W. Houston, *Inside Roman Libraries: Book Collections and Their Management in Antiquity* (Chapel Hill, NC: University of North Carolina Press, 2014), 31.

44 George W. Houston, "Grenfell, Hunt, Breccia, and the Book Collections of Oxyrhynchus." *Greek, Roman, and Byzantine Studies* 47 (2017): 343.

45 Houston, *Inside Roman Libraries*, 287.

21

Euergetism in Comparative Perspective: Did the "Ideal Benefactor" Exist in Christ Groups?

Rebecca Runesson

INTRODUCTION

The aim of this chapter is to question whether the concept of an "ideal benefactor" as defined by the work of Stephan Joubert manages to accurately describe the realities of euergetism in association contexts. This is an important question because Joubert constructs the ideal benefactor using elite Greco-Roman literary texts and applies it to early Christ groups, but we need to consider whether the socio-institutional context of early Christ groups allows for the application of this literature as reliable comparative material in this case. To test this, I investigate whether Joubert's categories make sense in an associative setting, which has been argued by a number of scholars as the most likely institutional context for the early Christ cult.[1] My investigation focuses on: (1) the terminology of euergetism, (2) Joubert's distinction between patronage and benefaction, and (3) whether or not associative evidence corroborates Joubert's categories. I conclude that Joubert's categories are not supported by associative evidence, which in fact indicate that little to no benefaction went without reciprocation. The only discernable distinction associations made between different types of donors was whether they were internal or external to the group. If we wish to understand Christ groups within their proper socio-historical context, we need to use comparative material that is able to accurately reflect their socio-economic and institutional setting.

THE TERMINOLOGY OF EUERGETISM

Patronage/benefaction is a notoriously difficult concept to define. Joubert, and others following him, wish to distinguish between patronage, on the one hand, and benefaction, on the other. Before delving more deeply into the validity – or lack thereof – of the distinction, I want to first focus on defining the concept behind these terms. Richard Saller, who works with the term "patronage," defines it as "an exchange relationship between men [*sic*] of unequal social status."[2] Further, Saller's definition, building on Geller, states that it "involves the *reciprocal* exchange of goods and services. Secondly, to distinguish it from a commercial transaction in the marketplace, the relationship must be a personal one of some duration. Thirdly, it must be asymmetrical, in the sense that the two parties are of unequal status and offer different kinds of goods and services in exchange — a quality which sets patronage off from friendship between equals."[3] Millet adds a fourth component to Saller's definition, namely, that "the relationship was conducted along lines largely determined by the party of superior status,"[4] which could enable the exploitation of the party with the lower status. Saller convincingly illustrates that a number of terms were used to characterize and describe the patronal relationship, including *amicitiae (amicus), officium, beneficium, meritum,* and *gratia.*[5] Therefore, the patronal relationship was not defined by the usage of the terms *patronus* or *cliens* but, rather, by the existence of a reciprocal exchange, something that Saller points out as central to all descriptions of patronage, regardless of terminology.[6] Saller deals exclusively with Latin evidence (mainly literary), and even though my own analysis focuses on Greek evidence (mainly epigraphic), Saller's discussion of the terminology of patronage is still relevant, not in the least since there was considerable overlap between the Greek- and Latin-speaking world during the first century CE.[7] In addition, the diversity of terms noted by Saller is mirrored in Greek epigraphy (I return to this below).[8]

Saller's definition places patronage firmly in the category of general reciprocity,[9] since it hinges on the unequal status of the individuals engaged in the exchange.[10] Technically, what a patron gives to a client can never be identified as a "gift" since true gifts in antiquity could only be exchanged within the limits of a balanced reciprocity, whereby both interlocutors were of equal status and therefore able to reciprocate each other's gifts with material of equal value.[11] Here Saller's discussion of the diversity of patronage terminology again proves itself invaluable, since *gratia,* χάρις, and δωρεά could be used in ancient sources to describe exchanges that occurred within a general reciprocity, even though the material exchanged within such a reciprocity cannot be categorized as a gift but must, rather, be seen as a benefaction.[12] Thus, we cannot base our evaluation of a possibly patronal ancient relationship on the terminology used to describe it since the language of balanced reciprocity (i.e., the language of friendship) was often used in antiquity to "mask" patronal relationships (i.e., general reciprocity).[13] Instead, we need to follow Saller's lead and begin by identifying which type of reciprocity is at work within the relationship.

JOUBERT'S DISTINCTIONS BETWEEN PATRONAGE AND BENEFACTION

Now we know how to define patronage — but what of benefaction? The truth is that many scholars use the terms synonymously.[14] Scholars who do see a distinction between the two often take patronage to represent distinct Roman approaches to the concept and use benefaction to refer to Greek understandings of the same concept.[15] Stephan Joubert argues that the main distinction to be made between patronage and benefaction is that patronage was necessarily prone to exploitation since it occurred on a smaller, personal scale (between individuals, patrons and associations, emperors and client-kings, etc.) whereas (collective/civic) benefaction (which he calls *euergetism* and which he identifies as a Greek concept – despite, as Zeba Crook points out, using Seneca as his main source to describe it[16]) occurred on a larger, impersonal scale (from wealthy givers to larger groups where individual identity was irrelevant) and therefore was not prone to the same risk of exploitation.[17] Based on Joubert, Alicia Batten builds on the idea of this distinction and finds that the "ideal benefactor" is often described through the use of friendship diction.[18] Although Batten states that friendship diction is *also* used to describe relationships that Joubert would categorize as patronage, she sees friendship diction in such cases as a "mask" hiding the exploitative patron.[19] Although I agree with the latter assertion, the method of discernment by which some friendship diction can be categorized as a "mask" and some can be seen as evidence of Joubert's ideal benefaction remains somewhat unclear to me, particularly in light of Onno van Njif's work on the "make-believe" of benefaction in the Greek East. Van Njif argues that that friendship diction and the language of civic benefaction (cf. Joubert's *euegertism*) was often used in cases of patronage to make it appear as though no reciprocation was necessary, when actually it was, since the honorific inscription itself was the reciprocation.[20] In addition, Saller's compelling analysis of *amicitiae* strongly suggests that many Greco-Roman *amici* were actually engaged in relationships firmly anchored in a general reciprocity where one *amicus* inevitably came to function as *patronus* and the other as *cliens*.[21] In my view, this represents a cause for critical reflection before using friendship diction as a measure to determine the type of reciprocity at work in a relationship since the evidence itself, particularly in the case of epigraphy, is at times actively engaged in a public façade, the goal of which is to portray cases of general reciprocity as balanced reciprocity by using the language of friendship and civic benefaction. The end goal of Joubert's argument is to show that there existed in antiquity an "ideal benefactor" who, despite being of unequal status with the recipient(s), gave benefactions without expecting reciprocity.[22] Since he mainly utilizes elite literature, like the works of Seneca on benefaction, to construct this ideal benefactor, it is worthwhile to ask whether or not such benefaction was actually historically lived out in associations of middling to lower socio-economic status.

EVIDENCE FROM ASSOCIATIONS

If we wish to discover whether the "ideal benefactor" existed in association settings, we must look for distinctions between different types of "giving" in honorific inscriptions produced by associations. This is a justified approach since, as Saller rightly notes, the language of euergetism is starkly different in elite literary sources than in epigraphic sources,[23] perhaps because euergetism was viewed and/or functioned differently within the different social locations behind each *corpus* of material. Generally, elite literary sources represent the perspective of the patron/benefactor, while honorific inscriptions represent that of the client/recipient. Therefore, my aim here has to be emic as I try to determine how euergetism was viewed and functioned from the perspective of association members.

Due to the nature of association epigraphy, we primarily have access to honorific inscriptions.[24] The majority of these inscriptions are dedicated to donors and individuals who in some way benefitted the associations in question. Honorific inscriptions bestowed public honour and, as such, were a valued commodity in antiquity; they are useful for our purposes here because they are our primary source of evidence for patrons/benefactors in associations. In relation to Joubert, the first thing that must be noted is that they do not distinguish between large-scale and small-scale benefactions in terms of reciprocity demand.[25] For example, in *IEph* 727 = AGRW 171, a guild (συνεργασία) of wool-workers in Ephesus honoured "the founder of the city of the Ephesians," P. Vedius Antoninus, with the same type of reciprocation form – a public honorific inscription – as the association of fellow-sacrificers (συνθύται) in Boeotia used to honour the founder of their association (SEG 53 [2003], no. 457). According to Joubert, benefactions given from an individual to a city constituted a form of what he calls *euergetism* and, as such, did not require a clear reciprocation from anyone, unlike benefactions from an individual to an association, which he classifies as "patronage." In the case of these two inscriptions (and others like them),[26] the benefaction is the same: both honoured men are founders, but the scale and closeness of contact of the benefactions varies considerably. Clearly, however, both benefactions required the same reciprocity form, namely, public honour. Thus, it does not seem that associations always distinguished between large-scale, impersonal benefactions and those given on a more personal, smaller scale.[27] Both types of giving were seen to require the same form of reciprocity.

The focus on honour here is key. Associations typically reciprocated benefactions with public honour, which created a sort of balance between donors and recipients since donors were partly dependent on the public honour bestowed upon them by the recipients of their "giving." Onno van Njif and Anna Heller argue that the currency of public honour could be at least partly controlled by the community awarding it,[28] and thus the powerlessness that Joubert associates with patronage could be questioned. Just because a benefaction required reciprocation did not mean that the recipient had no power in the exchange, something highlighted by the fact that the Greek word for both "honour" and "price" is actually the *same*: τιμή; the materials exchanged on both sides are equated by the Greek language itself. This is exemplified by a number of interesting association inscriptions. Take IProse I 40, where an assembly of "United Farmers" (συναγωγής των συγγεώργων) in Psenamosis (Egypt, Berenike *nome*) honours a man named Paris for extensive donations to the group. After listing Paris's various good deeds towards them and describing the lavish way they plan to honour him for it, they write "for it is right that honour from us all should be given to those who are generous towards the association; and if he, being ambitious, should leave something else to the association, another day will be observed for him in the city."[29] Clearly, the United Farmers felt that they had the power to entice Paris, and others who might read the stele, to continue to act as patron for them, despite the fact that Paris's gifts were of such value that there could never be a balanced reciprocity between him and the farmers. This problematizes Joubert's assertion that patronage left clients with little to no power in antiquity. Another inscription, IG II^2 1342, provides us with an excellent example of what van Njif calls the "make-belief of benefaction." The inscription was set up by a group of *Soteriastai* to honour their founder Diodorus son of Sokrates of the Aphidnai *deme*. The *Soteriastai* describe how Diodorus hosted the members at "no little cost" to himself but, in the same sentence, also take care to emphasize that he did this "without love of money" (ἀφιλαργύρως). The "make-believe of benefaction" references the habit in honorific inscriptions of using language that masks the nature of the exchange. The *Soteriastai* describe Diodorus as having no love of money, and yet the exchange they are trying to mask with this term remains clear: Diodorus financially funds a number of their activities and in exchange they give him public honour. The "make-belief of benefaction" suggests that language indicating equal exchange cannot be taken at face value in this kind of data.

Where does this leave us? First, associative data do not support Joubert's distinction between patronage and benefaction (*euergetism*). Second, the reciprocity demand in patronal relationships between associations and wealthy individuals required public honour to be doled out in exchange for material and financial resources. Public honour was such a valued commodity in antiquity that associations could actually use their ability to distribute it as a way of balancing out an otherwise unequal exchange, giving them as clients more power than Joubert's characterization of patronage allows. Third, the "make-believe of benefaction" problematizes the assertion that we can in some cases use friendship and civic benefaction diction in order to identify an "ideal benefactor" in Christ groups. It might very well be true of the elite literary sources from which Joubert constructs his ideal benefactor, but in the case of associations there is little evidence that the diction of an equal exchange was ever used as more than a mask.

Despite what my analysis at this point might suggest, I do not believe that there were *no* distinctions between different types of giving in associations. In an otherwise relatively universal pattern of reciprocating benefactions of varying types with public honour and acclaim, associations tended to note whether the giver in question was internal (i.e., a member) to the group. For example, in *IG* II^2 1261 = *AGRW* 14, a certain Stephanos was honoured with a crown and public honour due to his excellent administration of the association's affairs during his time as the society's supervisor (ἐπιμελητής). While the reciprocation form does not differ from the type of honours bestowed on some external givers (cf. the crown/inscription combination in *IDelos* 1520 = *AGRW* 224 and *IG* XII, 1 937), the fact that internal functions/favours are singled out as the reason for the honour is significant.[30] It strongly suggests that the internal hierarchy of these associations was such that a balanced reciprocity could not always exist between those occupying internal offices and general members. In addition, it tells us that internal functions/favours could be viewed as benefactions to the association, thereby enabling what could be generally called "internal euergetism."

John Kloppenborg notes the existence of what he calls "peer benefaction" within associations.[31] According to Kloppenborg, such benefaction consists of "the peer/member who contributed to the operation of the association through lesser administrative functions."[32] He rightly notes that inscriptions honouring such "peer benefactors" are actually just as common as those honouring external, elite givers.[33] Based on Kloppenborg's observations, Richard Last emphasizes the importance of these honours for "peer benefactors" with regard to encouraging other members to take administrative roles and contribute to the association themselves.[34] Although this in itself does not distinguish internal giving from external giving in terms of the wish to create rivalry,[35] it does indicate two different target audiences. The general reciprocity element is the same in both types of euergetism since both are reciprocated in the form of public honour.[36] This suggests that internal euergetism/peer benefaction was not "more equal" than external euergetism, which problematizes Joubert's argument that the Jerusalem Collection was not an exploitative case of patronage or less hierarchical because it was internal. "Peer benefactors" may have been "peers" in that they were likely (but not necessarily) of similar socio-economic status as general members, but they were certainly in possession of more symbolic capital than a general member,[37] and thus "peer benefaction" should not be seen as creating greater group equality than external euergetism.[38] Both types of euergetism create a socio-institutional hierarchy; in the case of internal euergetism, the individual given higher status was constantly present in the group whereas many external donors only attended special functions, and thus it could even be argued that the elevated status of external donors was less conspicuous than that of internal donors, who were constantly present.

CONCLUSIONS

Where does this leave Christ groups? First and foremost, it leaves us in a position where we must pause for critical reflection before we apply Joubert's concept of ideal benefaction to activities in early Christ groups. If Joubert's concept of ideal benefaction existed in antiquity, it did not leave a discernible footprint in the world of ancient associations, of which the early Christ cult was a part. If we want to think about the possibility of different types of giving in early Christ groups, we might instead think in terms of internal or external euergetism, but we should be careful not to assume that internal euergetism/peer benefaction would have led to greater group equality. Of course, the kind of comparison upon which my study rests can only ever be heuristic,[39] but the same is true for Joubert's study, and, as I hope I have demonstrated, the elite literary sources Joubert uses as comparative material are not representative of association life in antiquity.

APPENDIX I

The following table provides inscriptional evidence that the only distinction made by associations in honorific epigraphy was the internal or external location of the giver in relation to the group. Everything else, including the reciprocation form, is, as the chart below illustrates, difficult to differentiate.

Table 21.1
Benefactions and honours in association inscriptions

Inscription (honours)★	*Type of gift*	*Relationship of giver(s) to association (based on emic description)*	*Reciprocated honour form*	*External or internal?*
IG II^2 1261 = *AGRW* 14 (Attica, 301/300 BCE)	Administering of the association's affairs, ambitious on behalf of the association, conducting of a procession (internal functions/favours)	An epimeletes of the association (koinon)	Crown of olive wreath, 10 drachmas, honorific inscription	Internal
IG II^2 1262 = *AGRW* 15 (Attica, 300/299 BCE)	Sacrificial duties, responsibilities towards the association (internal functions/favours)	*Epimeletai* of the *koinon*	Crowning with olive wreaths, provided with votive plaques worth 20 drachmas, honorific inscription	Internal
IG II^2 1263 = *AGRW* 16 (Attica, 300/299 BCE)	Excellent and honest carrying out of treasury duties (internal functions/favours)	Secretary (*grammateus*) in charge of treasury	Crowning with a votive plaque worth 50 drachmas (plaque placed in public place to inspire ambition)	Internal
IG II^2 1327 = *AGRW* 20 (Attica, 178/177 BCE)	Treasury duties carried out with excellence etc. (internal functions/favours)	Treasurer (*tamias*) of the association	Image of individual set up in temple & crowned at every sacrifice, honorific inscription	Internal
IKosPH 382 (Kos, III BCE)	Sacrificial duties, arrangement of reception for members, zeal/eagerness	Monthly elected officers (*epimenoi*)	Crowning with ten gold crowns, honorific inscription	Internal
IEph 727 = *AGRW* 171 (Ephesus, mid-second century CE)	Founding the "city of the Ephesian"	Founder of the city in which the association (*synergasia*) was located	Honorific inscription near the civic council building	External
IHeirapJ 41 = *AGRW* 157 (Heirapolis, Phrygia, third century CE)	Unclear. "Honour-loving director of contests, civic commander, secretary of the temples that are in Asia, benefactor of the homeland."	Unclear. Probably external benefactor.	Honorific inscription	External

IRhodPerBlümel 110 (Caria, Asia Minor, imperial period)	Twice serving as leader (*archon*) in a "friendly manner" and rebuilding the meeting hall (*andron*)	"resident alien" in a neighbourhood (*ktonia/ptonai*) association, unclear if *archon* is symbolic here or not	Crowned with olive wreaths, honorific inscription	Internal
IPessinous 18 = *GRA* I 151 (Galatia, 180–200 CE)	Goodwill and virtue towards the association	Benefactor and friend (*philon/ evergeten*)	Honorific inscription with his many accomplishments listed	External
SEG 36 = *AGRW* 181 (Miletos, Ionia, late second century CE)	"because he (an athlete) granted freedom from disturbances during the athletic contests"	"voluntary benefactor" of the homeland	Honorific inscription by the association of linen-weavers in the section of the stage (of a theatre) which the athlete built	External
ISmyrna 652 = *AGRW* 189 (Smyrna, Ionia, first century CE)	Displaying love of honour in serving as director of contests	Director of contests (civic?)	Honorific inscription, public (base of a grey marble column)	External
IDelos 1520 = *AGRW* 224 (Delos, 149/148 BCE)	Donating to renovate the association's meeting hall (*oikos*), promise of future benefaction	Benefactor	(perpetual) Crowning, statue/ portrait, honorific inscription	External
CIG 3422 (Lydia, Asia Minor, after 212 CE)	Financial gifts for many associations (not only the one issuing the honours)	Benefactor	Honorific inscription	External
IG XII, 1 937 (Aegean Islands, I CE)	Financial help in relation to lawsuits and renovations of meeting place(s?)	Benefactor (mentioned with his wife: both are honoured)	Crowned with gold crowns, publicly proclaimed by the association (*koinon*), honorific inscription	External
IBerenike 17 = *AGRW* 306 (Berenike, Cyrenaica, 24 CE).	Good, calm leadership in his provincial governing duties that were beneficial for the Judeans of Berenike	Roman provincial official who had some interactions with the association	Crowned at each gathering and new moon and an honorific inscription in a public place (amphitheatre)	External

Table 21.1
Benefactions and honours in association inscriptions (cont.)

Inscription (honours)★	*Type of gift*	*Relationship of giver(s) to association (based on emic description)*	*Reciprocated honour form*	*External or internal?*
IJO II 36 = *AGRW* 105 (Kyme, Asia Minor, third century CE)	Donated money to build an open-air enclosure from her own resources	Unclear. Perhaps member given reciprocation form.	Gold crown and the right to sit in the front seats (*proedria*)	Unclear
CIG 3422 (Lydia, Asia Minor, after 212 CE)	List of donations given to other groups and to civic events, nothing specific to the association behind the inscription is listed	Benefactor	Public honorific inscription (with a long list of benefactions, not only to assc. in question)	External
IPhrygR 534 = *AGRW* 146 (Akmoneia, Phrygia, 98–117 CE)	Unclear	Benefactor (*euergeten*)	Public honorific inscription	External
IDelos 1796 (Delos, Asia Minor, 153–88 BCE)	Being head of the society (*archithiasites*) and priest (*hierus*) respectively (2 benefactors listed) (internal function/favour)	Benefactor (*euergetou*), society leader, and priest	Public honorific inscription	Internal
SEG 53 (2003), no. 475 (Boeotia, Greece and Macedonia, I–II CE)	Founding the association of fellow-sacrificers (*synthytai*)	Benefactor and founder	Public honorific inscription	Internal
IG II^2 1293 (Attica, Greece, ca. 250 BCE)	Unspecified benefaction	Benefactor	Public honorific inscription, olive crown, and inscription of name on a *stele* in the Temple	External

Inscriptions were selected based on two criteria: (1) that they are honouring an individual and (2) that the honoured individual has given a gift (an euerg- /xar- type gift, or internal function/favour) of some kind to the association.

NOTES

1 John S. Kloppenborg, *Christ's Associations: Connecting and Belonging in the Ancient City* (New Haven: Yale University Press, 2019); Kloppenborg, "Collegia and *Thiasoi*: Issues in Function, Taxonomy, and Membership," in *Voluntary Associations in the Graeco-Roman World*, ed. John S. Kloppenborg and Stephen G. Wilson (London: Routledge, 1996), 16–30; Philip A. Harland, *Associations, Synagogues, and Congregations: Claiming a Place in Ancient Mediterranean Society* (Minneapolis: Fortress Press, 2003); Richard Last, *The Pauline Church and the Corinthian Ekklesia*, SNTSMS 164 (Cambridge: Cambridge University Press, 2016); cf. Markus Öhler, "Gründer und ihre Gründung. Antike Vereinigungen und die paulinische Gemeinde in Philippi," in *Der Philipperbrief des Paulus in der hellenistisch-römischen Welt*, ed. J. Frey and B. Schliesser (Tübingen: Mohr Siebeck, 2015), 121–52. On the use of association epigraphy as comparative data for Christ groups, see John S. Kloppenborg, "Disciplined Exaggeration: The Heuristics of Comparison in Biblical Studies," *NovT* 59, no. 4 (2017): 390–414.

2 Richard Saller, *Personal Patronage under the Early Empire* (Cambridge: Cambridge University Press, 2009), 8. Cf. Alicia J. Batten, *Friendship and Benefaction in James*, Emory Studies of Early Christianity 15 (Atlanta: SBL Press, 2017), 58; John S. Kloppenborg, "Patronage Avoidance in James," *Teologiese Studies/Theological Studies* 55, no. 4 (1999): 771; Carolyn Osiek, "The Politics of Patronage and the Politics of Kinship: The Meeting of the Ways," *Biblical Theology Bulletin* 29, no. 3 (2009): 143–52. Note that the generic masculine used in Saller's definition actively mutes the fact that many women are attested by epigraphic evidence to have acted as patrons, not in the least in Asia Minor, where female patrons and internal leadership seem to have been commonplace (see Paul Trebilco, *Jewish Communities in Asia Minor* [Cambridge: Cambridge University Press, 1991], 104–11; cf. *IJO* II 168 = *AGRW* 145, *TAM* V.2 972 = *AGRW* 129, *IJO* II 36 = *AGRW* 105, *IJO* II BS5 = *AGRW* 86).

3 Richard Saller, "Patronage and Friendship in Early Imperial Rome: Drawing the Distinction," in *Patronage in Ancient Society*, ed. A. Wallace-Hadrill, Leicester-Nottingham Studies in Ancient Society 1 (London: Routledge, 1989), 49; cf. E. Gellner and J. Waterbury, ed., *Patrons and Clients in Mediterranean Societies* (London: Duckworth, 1977), 1 (emphasis in original).

4 P. Millet, "Patronage and Its Avoidance in Classical Athens," in Wallace-Hadrill, *Patronage in Ancient Society*, 16.

5 Saller, *Personal Patronage*, 11–22.

6 Ibid., 22.

7 The overlaps between Greek and Roman culture are well known in scholarship, but Ulrich Gotter provides an interesting example of just how important the cross-cultural contact was for the development of certain concepts (in Gotter's case "power," in our case, "patronage") in both cultures' spheres. See Ulrich Gotter, "Cultural Differences and Cross-Cultural Contact: Greek and

Roman Concepts of Power," *Harvard Studies in Classical Philology* 104 (2008): 179–230.

8 Note Saller's discussion of the difference in patronage terminology between literary and epigraphic sources (see Saller, *Personal Patronage*, 9–11). Saller explains the fact that literary sources never explicitly refer to clients using *cliens* (*patronus* is also rare) whereas such terms are common in the epigraphic evidence if one points to the social location of the authors of most literary sources. Pliny, Tacitus, Seneca, and others whose literary work we rely on generally occupied the role of *patronus*, whereas the epigraphic evidence originates from individuals occupying the role of *cliens*. While the explicit referencing of someone as a *cliens* was seen as rude among the "patron class," this was not the case among the "client class." Thus, the social location of those describing their patronal relationship will determine how they describe it.

9 By "general reciprocity," I am referring to Marshall Sahlins's categories of reciprocity. See Marshall Sahlins, *Stone Age Economics* (New York: Aldine, 1974).

10 I follow the Stegemanns' reconceptualization of Marshall Sahlins's classic categories of reciprocity. Instead of selecting kinship distance as the modifier of reciprocity type, as does Sahlins, the Stegemanns argue that, in Antiquity, it makes more sense to select status distance as the modifier of reciprocity type (see Ekkehard Stegemann and Wolfgang Stegemann, *The Jesus Movement: A Social History of Its First Century*, trans. O.C. Dean, Jr [Minneapolis: Fortress Press, 1999], 35–7). Cf. Zeba Crook, *Reconceptualising Conversion: Patronage, Loyalty, and Conversion in the Religions of the Ancient Mediterranean* (Berlin: de Gruyter, 2004), 56–9. This is especially prudent when analyzing associative epigraphy, where (fictive) kinship language is often employed (see Philip A. Harland, *Dynamics of Identity in the World of the Early Christians* [London: T & T Clark, 2009], 63–80, 81–96; cf. *IBosp* 1283 = AGRW 92).

11 Crook, *Reconceptualising Conversion*, 58. Cf. Stegemann and Stegemann, *Jesus Movement*, 36.

12 Crook, *Reconceptualising Conversion*, 58. See IG XII, 736, where a gift from a patron is identified as a δωρεά; cf. Saller, *Personal Patronage*, 21–2, on the usage of *gratia* within patronage, and Crook, *Reconceptualising Conversion*, 132–3, 139–44, for an analysis of χάρις in patronal context.

13 Kloppenborg, "Patronage Avoidance," 768–71.

14 Even Crook, who *does* see a slight difference between patronage and benefaction, chooses to use the terms synonymously. See Crook, *Reconceptualising Conversion*, 66.

15 For example, see Stephan Joubert, *Paul as Benefactor: Reciprocity, Strategy and Theological Reflection in Paul's Collection* (Tubingen: Mohr Siebeck, 2000).

16 Crook, *Reconceptualising Conversion*, 62.

17 Joubert, *Paul as Benefactor*, 51–4. Cf. Crook, *Reconceptualising Conversion*, 61.

18 Batten, *Friendship*, 74.

19 Ibid., 58.

20 Onno van Nijf, *The Civic World of Professional Associations in the Roman East* (Amsterdam: J.C. Gieben, 1997), 119.

21 Saller, *Personal Patronage*, 11–15.

22 Joubert, *Paul the Benefactor*, 46, 68; Batten, *Friendship*, 71–4; Alicia J. Batten, "God in the Letter of James: Patron or Benefactor?" *New Testament Studies* 50, no. 2 (2004): 261. Cf. James R. Harrison, *Paul's Language of Grace in its Graeco-Roman Context* (Tübingen: Mohr Siebeck, 2003), 131–3.

23 Saller, *Personal Patronage*, 9–11. See also note 5 above. Cf. Harland, who notes that, in general, epigraphic and archaeological sources should not be interpreted in light of literary evidence (Harland, *Associations*, 18).

24 Harland, *Associations*, 17.

25 See Joubert, *Paul the Benefactor*, 36–7, 51, 58.

26 See *IHeirapJ* 41 = AGRW 157 and IKosPH 382; *IPessinous* 18 = GRA I 151 and *IRhodPerBlümel* 110; *IG* II^2 1293 and *IG* II^2 1261 = AGRW 14.

27 *Contra* Crook, *Reconceptualising Conversion*, 64.

28 Anna Heller and Onno van Njif, ed., *The Politics of Honour in the Greek Cities of the Roman Empire*, Brill Studies in Greek and Roman Epigraphy 8 (Leuven: Brill, 2017), 5–7.

29 My translation.

30 Cf. *IHeirapJ* 41 = AGRW 157 and SEG 6 no. 167, where the specific benefaction is not mentioned at all, suggesting that associations were not obligated to specify the benefaction being honoured.

31 John S. Kloppenborg, "Greco-Roman *Thiasoi*, the *Ekklesia* at Corinth, and Conflict Management," in *Redescribing Paul and the Corinthians*, ed. Ron Cameron and Merrill P. Miller (Atlanta: SBL Press, 2011), 212–13. See also Last, *Pauline Church*, 150–2.

32 Kloppenborg, "Greco-Roman *Thiasoi*," 212.

33 Ibid., 213.

34 Last, *Pauline Church*, 151.

35 Harland, *Dynamics*, 149.

36 In addition to this, it is important to keep in mind that association members honoured for their services in various leadership functions were not of equal status with association members not currently occupying an office (cf. the Stegemanns' identification of status distance as the modifier of reciprocity type: see Stegemann and Stegemann, *Jesus Movement*, 35–6 and Crook, *Reconceptualising Conversion*, 56–9). As Last has convincingly shown, elected officers/leaders in associations held greater status than did those without an office. Since the occupation of these leadership positions was fluid, the status of the members fluctuated constantly based on which offices they currently occupied (see Last, *Pauline Church*, 201–4).

37 Pierre Bourdieu, "Social Space and Symbolic Power," *Sociological Theory* 7, no. 1 (1989): 14–25; James S. Coleman, "Social Capital in the Creation of Human Capital," *American Journal of Sociology* 94 (1988): 95–120.

38 As argued by Nancy J. Vyhmeister, "The Rich Man in James 2: Does Ancient Patronage Illumine the Text?," *Andrews University Seminary Studies* 33 (1995): 283; Batten, *Friendship*, 156–70.

39 Kloppenborg, "Disciplined Exaggeration."

22

Is It Culture All the Way Down?

Colleen Shantz

Why do we flinch at that word, "universal"? Why do we so resist similarity, even sameness? What intellectual immunological responses have we inherited from our teachers and academic ancestors?

Jeffrey J. Kripal[1]

Steve Wilson demonstrated two tensive impulses in his scholarship. Within the academy, he routinely brought people together: initiating ongoing seminars to coordinate the collective work of his colleagues, editing volumes to share that work and celebrate others, and scheduling dinners to coordinate convivial company on the eve of the annual Canadian Society for Biblical Studies meeting. At the same time, in his own scholarship he often explored lines of division: intergroup competition, defection, and in-betweenness. Of course, I've created a false dichotomy in depicting these contributions as contrasting because, as his work and collegiality show, nuance and openness characterize both spheres. In the case of the focus of this volume, drawing from the seminar initiated by Steve, the creative back-and-forth inheres in the exchange between the discipline of religious studies, in general, and the study of ancient Mediterranean cultures and movements that are typically called religions. More specifically, this chapter considers phenomena in the earliest generations of the Christ movement – phenomena that have been thoroughly described in their particularity as cultural artifacts but may, at the same time, express patterns that are ubiquitously human.

In this chapter I aim for a Wilson-worthy dinner party of exchange and collegiality in considering the potential interplay of these two approaches that seldom sit down together. On one side of the table is the exacting attention to the particularities of specific historical moments and cultural transmission of human ideas and behaviour, while seated across from it are the purportedly universal patterns in human behaviour that depend on evolved biological features. Laid out between them is a set of questions made possible by their shared presence. Currently – at least when religion is on the menu – culture dominates the conversation, in part because cultural analysis has produced important insights that do not reduce to claims of singularity or flat-footed associations of empirical study with objectivity, for example. Coincidentally, the idea of religion as a natural kind has depreciated during this time, especially (and perhaps ironically) within the field of religious studies. So, both the legitimacy of religion as a thing in the world and its basis in other sorts of universally human or natural patterns have been actively countered or have simply withered through neglect. In my estimation, this theoretical adjustment now teeters on the edge of overcorrection and it is an opportune time to more effectively theorize the interplay between biological givens, which are ubiquitous across human populations, and the influence of culture.

THE GUEST LIST

I take Russell McCutcheon as exemplary of one set of guests at the virtual dinner table: those who actively resist claims to universals in the study of religion. McCutcheon argues that position in, for example, an article subtitled "On Making a Shift in the Study of Religion,"[2] in which he describes a mounting dissatisfaction early in his teaching career with the format and content of his department's core course on world religions. The crux of his disquiet lay precisely in the sense that, whatever differences in behaviour were observed in the ethnographic record, they were presented as "but a poorly phrased/poorly interpreted expression of some prior, pristine, universal inner sentiment … in which – or so Cantwell Smith, like so many others, would have argued – an inner faith motivates and thereby grounds outward tradition."[3] In his revisionist efforts, McCutcheon reports undertaking a "steady shift from religion(s) to 'religion'" in the design of the course but doing so not in order to heighten the sense of a shared universal object of study. Rather, in as much as one might describe McCutcheon advocating for a category of universal significance, that category was rhetorical, ideological, and reflexive. He began to represent religion as a product of discursive efforts to create identity, showing that, for academics and laypeople alike, claims that something is religious/religion were just another line in the sand separating an asserted Us and a constructed Them. Or, in McCutcheon's own words, his revised curriculum involved "the shift … from seeing our object(s) of study, whatever it/they may be, as unique, set apart, and thus obviously and irreducibly religious, to instead seeing it/them as exemplary and thus illustrative of more general human practices, leading to scholars with other training learning something applicable to their own field by reading us writing about issues in our own."[4]

In the context of my simulated dinner party, McCutcheon's contribution (and he is exemplary of others at this virtual table[5]) complicates the concept of universals, for he does indeed posit a universal but does so precisely for the purpose of defusing religion as a natural (and hence universal) kind except in its contemporary currency as a rhetorical tool. In short, for McCutcheon, the use of normative labels is universal, religion per se is not; rather, religion is one of many discursive labels through which human beings distinguish in-group from out-group, as they are universally wont to do. Other guests in this set include those who dispute claims of a universal matrix for phenomena like religious ecstasy[6] or human emotion,[7] for example. For this set of dinner guests, such elements are irreducibly motivated, constituted, and interpreted by cultures. We might describe these contributions as culture-maximalist.

Representing the second broad category of intellectual guests at the table are Francisca Cho and Richard King Squire.[8] They identify religion as a *complex dynamic system* and, as such, a real kind in the world. Like family resemblance models, systems theories consider numerous elements in their object of study, no one of which is conclusive in defining it as an example of the larger category. But distinct from family resemblance theory, systems theory understands the relevant phenomenon (in this case religion) to arise only in the *interaction* of its elements. Key features of religion that are not fully present in any of its component elements nonetheless originate from the combination of those elements. In short, religion is an emergent phenomenon. The aphorism that "the whole is more than the sum of its parts" expresses a folk awareness of emergence, and a murmuration of starlings provides one of the most readily accessible examples. In the case of religion, emergent features like altruism and its adaptive character in the face of contextual changes have been studied.[9] Theorized in this way, religion as a natural kind subsists in its recurrent and ubiquitous patterns beyond the specificity of cultural variation. Some individual features that are considered religious are also theorized in this way – especially supernatural ideation,[10] ritual structure,[11] and religious experience.[12] For convenience, we might generalize the interests of this group of scholars as *psychobiological*.

Interest in universal claims thrives in some academic quarters but rarely in religious studies where discussions of universals have fallen out of favour. As a result, culture theorists and ideological critics, on the one hand, and those with an interest in theories that are staked in universal psychobiological claims – cognitive, evolutionary psychological, and biological theories – on the other, have tended to work independently of one another in the study of religion.

Perhaps surprisingly, given his association with thick, culturally attentive description, Clifford Geertz worried about just such a segregation of approaches. Early in his career, Geertz warned against the self-reinforcing power of cultural detail and the difficulty of moving from that specificity to theoretical abstraction. "The besetting sin" as he put it, of such rich collections of specific detail "is that they tend to resist, or to be permitted to resist, conceptual articulation and thus to escape systematic modes of assessment." Thick description "is presented as self-validating, or, worse, as validated by the supposedly developed sensitivities of the person who presents it; any attempt to cast what it says in terms other than its own is regarded as a travesty – as … ethnocentrism."[13] This methodological concern remained at the end of Geertz's career, receiving further impetus from the postmodern debates of that time: "Unable to embrace either relativism or absolutism – the first because it disables judgment, the second because it removes it from history – our philosophers, historians, and social scientists turn toward the sort of we-are-we and they-are-they *imperméabilité* Lévi-Strauss recommends."[14]

The concern of imbalance, of specificity hardening into impermeable difference, pertains equally to the study of religion where it has developed for its own reasons. Consistent with Geertz's description, historians of ancient Mediterranean social worlds specialize in the collation of exacting detail about their subjects. Further, when our subject is Christian origins, critical scholarship requires additional vigilance about presentist readings and ingrained anti-Jewish hermeneutics – both of which are more likely to encourage projection of false universal claims onto the text. Critical scholarship about Christian origins has also practised heightened vigilance about reconstructions that rely on sui generis claims that uncritically feed confessional agendas. So too the association of empirical study with absolutist claims has left a bad taste in the mouths of many critical theorists – despite the important (and decades-old) work on the false dichotomy between scientific and humanities epistemologics.[15] Each of these factors has contributed to suspicion about universals in the study of formative Christianity. But in what way do they, or should they, continue in force?

THE PROOF OF THE PUDDING

It's about time to serve up a plate of case study at our imagined symposium, and the history of interpretation of Rom 7:14–25 offers much that we might want for the occasion. First, and generating some heat, is its purported investment in the distinction between incipient Judaism and Christianity, a focus that depends on the conceptualizing of religious groups and boundaries between them. Second, the passage is a classic, having been an active site of critical debate for the last sixty years and of more naïve interest for centuries before that, producing a correspondingly satisfying selection of interpretations. Third, and most significantly suited to this occasion, its main interpretive knot is tangled up with the question of whether it addresses a fundamentally universal claim about human nature or is fully explained as a cultural debate of its time.

"I do not understand my behaviour [κατεργάζομαι]," Paul writes. "For I don't do what I intend/desire but [instead] the thing that I devalue [μισῶ], this I do" (Rom 7:15). From the early reception of the letter onward, interpreters have noted the artifice of the first-person speech in Romans 7 and pondered the degree to which the I-speech conveys either (or both) a condition that is ubiquitously human and felt more keenly in some circumstances than others or some specific account of Paul's own experience of a fragmented sense of intentions. Yet, by 1963, the year that Krister Stendahl published his watershed essay on Romans 7,[16] representations of cultural difference dominated the interpretation of the passage. Misrepresentation of Judaism and law as a psychological burden gradually infected this passage, particularly among those who read the I-speech as Paul's autobiographical description of his life before and after a conversion. Although others before him attempted to correct the misrepresentation of second temple attitudes,[17] Stendahl intervened explicitly with his own arguments about cultural difference – in this case, between Paul's culturally conditioned "robust conscience" and the culturally Western introspection and self-scrutiny that drew in part on Luther's moral scrupulousness. Stendahl argued that the point of the I-speech was a defence of the law and that it should be interpreted with that intention as its key. In other words, Paul "is not primarily concerned about [the human person's] or his own cloven ego or predicament."[18] He suggests, rather, that Paul "acquits" the self of the speech by identifying it fully with the good intentions while attributing the negative actions to sin as an independent agent that inhabits the person. As Paul puts it, "It is no longer I who enact it but the sin that inhabits me" (Rom 7:17). In a similar vein, Stendahl opines that the ego's tension is nothing but "the rather trivial observation that every man knows that there is a difference between what he ought to do and what he does."[19] Stendahl concludes that "Paul happened to express this supporting argument so well that what to him and his contemporaries was a common sense observation appeared to later interpreters to be a most penetrating insight into the nature of [human beings] and into the nature of sin." In short, the I-speech should not be read (as by Augustine, Jerome, Luther, and his peers) as an expression of the troubled conscience of the I-speaker since Paul's comments in other letters demonstrate the opposite at every point in his life: a robust sense of guiltlessness relative to legal requirements.

Stendahl's intervention realigned much that was awry in the history of interpretation so effectively that he helped to shift the course scholarship on Paul and Judaism. He did so both by attending to the misrepresentation of second temple nomism and by illuminating unexamined assumptions about sameness. At the same time, he signalled a second shift, this one concerning the significance of the human dilemma performed in the I-speech. Stendahl's reading insulated the fragmented-I of the passage from consequential interest in human fragmentation in general. In his reading, the passage was (merely) rhetorical and discursive. What started as an argument against "a subjective conscience struggle" on Paul's part hardened somewhat into the partitioning of concepts into cultural holding cells.[20] Stendahl extrapolates from his reconstruction of Paul's robust conscience to a claim about human experience in Judaism generally and, to quote Geertz, initiates a *we-are-we* (contemporary Westerners) and *they-are-they* (Second Temple Jews) approach to the passage.

After Stendahl, scholarship on this passage maintained its interest in more responsible readings of Judaism and also began to identify Graeco-Roman cultural parallels to its content and form. A more subtle change that accompanied this shift of attention was the reinforcement of culture as the key to interpretation. No longer was the fragmented-I caused by Judaism, but Graeco-Roman philosophy may have been to blame. This scholarship, in effect, defamiliarized the passage relative to the present by coordinating it with philosophical thought of antiquity. We see some of this, for example, in the work of Stanley Stowers, Troels Engberg-Pedersen, and Emma Wasserman on this passage, spanning two decades of scholarship.[21] Each of the authors adduces the Graeco-Roman philosophical concept of *akrasia* (lack of self-governance) as crucial for the passage, arguing in various ways for its explanatory power in Romans 7. In an essay on the reception of Graeco-Roman culture in the New Testament, Engberg-Pedersen begins with a straightforward assumption of the centrality of *akrasia* to Paul's ideas, despite the absence of the term in the passage.[22] He describes the interjection of Rom 7:24a ("Miserable person that I am, who will rescue me") as functioning "exceedingly well to give expression to the acratic experience" and glosses it further as "the whole, basic situation of recognizing something in oneself from which one feels strongly dissociated and which one is nevertheless forced to allow as a genuine part of oneself."[23] I have been emphasizing cultural constructivism, but here the description sounds quasi-universal; in fact, that definite article – "*the* acratic experience" – tilts towards a psychological norm. Interestingly, Engberg-Pedersen does not take a comparative tack with the evidence; instead, he concludes with a catalogue of similarities between Aristotelian and Stoic treatments of *akrasia* and features of the I-speech, asserting that the former account for the latter, without offering any mediating explanation for the transfer of culturally defined epistemology. To argue, as Engberg-Pedersen does, that philosophical concepts were in the air is not unreasonable and it is certainly common. Regarding the conversation between particularities of cultures and psycho-biological universals, he seems to have it both ways: everyone feels *akrasia*, but only philosophical schools articulated it for us, thereby bringing it to our attention.

By contrast, Stowers and Wasserman attend more explicitly to how culture influences the construction of distinct worldviews. For his part, Stowers defamiliarizes the passage by arguing that the embedded notion of "self-mastery" does not equate even to the contemporary concept of self-discipline "because ancient and modern conceptions of the person and society differ so greatly."[24] Correspondingly, Wasserman notes that the import of the passage relies on "notions of self or personality" and that, because such concepts are mutable, the ideas in the passage must be contextualized historically.[25] So far, so good. Both authors announce their commitment to historicized readings and critique the ease with which readers slide into presentist – and hence implicitly universal and generally ahistorical – assumptions about the psychology of the passage.

They also practise what they propose. Each of them reviews the writing of middle-Platonic figures like Galen and Philo to consider how these thinkers constructed the problem of motivational fragmentation. Insightfully, Stowers notes the synchrony between the psychology of an embattled ego and "the organization of society. Just as intense competition characterizes social life, so a violent competition within [the individual] characterizes those who aspire to moral excellence and self-mastery."[26] The point is subtle and worthy of focused attention: social structures reconfigure psychological responses. Building on that observation of "mirroring" inner and outer worlds, he draws a culturally maximalist conclusion: "If one can believe the impressive amount of Greco-Roman literature [that is] in one way or another concerned with mastery of the body and passions, many ancients must have experienced the basic dynamics of their society as inward psychological realities. Perhaps psychology is a reflection of social structure in all societies."[27] In short, the sociocultural generates the psychological. The flow of influence is one-way, with human psychology imprinted with the pattern of its host society.

Wasserman's culturally maximalist reconstruction applies details from ancient philosophical writing to fill in silences and narrow down the metaphorical potentials in the passage. Drawing on Platonic tradition, she proposes that the I of Romans 7 is not a person, even a fictive one, but a personification of the mind/reason discussing personified sin and the death of the soul. Thus, the human psycho-biological agent disappears entirely and the I persists as a cultural construct all the way down. She argues that sin functions analogously to the personified passions that play the role of bad guy in some Hellenistic philosophy. For Wasserman, Paul's purported dependence on these philosophical traditions indicates that the target of the passage must likewise be borrowed from that tradition, namely, "a type of extremely wicked Gentile."[28] As with Stowers, Wasserman's examples are relevant, but she surpasses him in asserting their direct influence on the details of Romans 7, including the pattern of its metaphors.[29] At this point she describes sameness rather than comparability. Parts of her reconstruction are not self-evident on the surface of the text of Romans, especially given the lack of shared technical language (no mention of *akrasia*, for example) and Paul's distinctive use of a marriage metaphor as the source of his talk of death. Still, her proposal would shift from possible to probable if no other reasons for the similarities could be adduced.

I am interested in the other viable reasons. For instance, there is ample evidence that fragmentation of motivation and other internal tensions are inextricable from human biology and, thus, might appear in texts independently of direct cultural influence. Take, for example, the case of sexuality (which happens to be the context to which some early interpreters applied the I-speech of Romans 7). Human beings have evolved with three separate biological clusters of sexual motivation, each of which provided its own adaptive advantage in discrete sets of circumstances that are not always easily reconciled with one another. The three modes are typically labelled *lust*, *attraction*, and *attachment*, and each comprises a distinctive set of motivations, behaviours, and associated hormones and neurotransmitters.[30] The *lust system*, or sex drive, maximizes mating opportunities, straightforwardly increasing the odds that the genes that carry this characteristic will be passed on at higher rates. Lust proved evolutionarily adaptive when the prospects for sex were limited by a shortage of fertile partners or other circumstantial factors because it maximized the motivation for mating opportunities. Estrogen and testosterone are key components of this cluster. By contrast, *attraction*, now associated with romantic love, proved adaptive when the number of possible partners was more abundant and mating success was facilitated by greater commitment to securing the best mate among the available options. This mode is characterized by "focused attention on a preferred mating partner" along with "feelings of exhilaration, 'intrusive thinking' about the love object, and a craving for emotional union with this partner."[31] It is marked by increased levels of dopamine and norepinephrine and lowered levels of serotonin, a combination associated with stress and reward conditions,[32] and it confers the adaptive advantage of more efficient mating success, both by centring on a single desired partner and by doing so with single-minded attention. Third, the *attachment* mode in both human and non-human animals is marked by "mutual territory defense and/or nest building, mutual feeding and grooming, the maintenance of close proximity, separation anxiety, shared parental chores, and other affiliative behaviors." Its emotional tone, associated with oxytocin and vasopressin, is characterized by social comfort, calmness, and feelings of closeness.[33] The adaptive value of this mode is its contribution to the survival of offspring that are produced through the cooperation of both parents in feeding and protection of the young, again ensuring that related genes survive and are passed on.

These three systems are just one example of the motivational fragmentation of the sense of a single, acting self. They stabilized within human populations because they each addressed a distinct challenge to genetic survival and, while there is evidence that the three interact in complex ways in the processes of mating and reproduction, their potential for conflict is obvious. For example, because of the effectiveness of the lust system an individual can be sexually aroused by someone whose character they find repugnant. Similarly, the obsessive and anxious character of the attraction system and its accompanying emotional zing sits uncomfortably in the cozy nest of attachment. The three modes vary in intensity among individuals and seem to be predictably sexually dimorphic to some degree, but they are generally available across the species and, despite differences in their cultural expression, they are recognizable in all human populations. They surface at the felt level of bodily sensations of pain, pleasure, innate attention, and motivation. Language helps to shape one's experience of them, but so too do they constrain which linguistic expressions will be successful and which social challenges will be most salient.

Furthermore, sexual motivation is but one example of the way that, at the level of bodily stimulation or suppression and accompanying feelings, human beings can desire conflicting goals at the same time. At any given moment, intangible value commitments (like heart health) are not reinforced biologically with the same intensity as are more immediate pleasures (like Cheetos). The success of the former requires proxy mechanisms such as the pings and affirmations that are built into fitness apps, for example. Or, as a project deadline approaches, the biopsychological mechanisms of reward pull in the opposite direction to those of anxiety and uncertainty, with each set of motivations based in distinct sets of neurological arousal.[34] Likewise, self-interest and group-interest, both of which are also evolutionarily supported, are not equally salient at every moment and are sometimes even at odds. Each of these motivations also interfaces with consciously held reasons that are culturally derived and maintained. Many ancient writers (and modern ones) identify processes of attending to those reasons as rationality, distinguishing that conscious awareness from other bodily processes that are entangled with norms, values, and social schemas. Some cultural constructions of self are more effective than others in managing such motivational fragmentation, but the tensive force of competing motivations exceeds those cultural concepts. And it is felt in human populations ubiquitously. It may be culture all the way down but only when culture is in a deep embrace with biology.

BACK TO THE CUTTING BOARD

It should come as no surprise by this point that the discussion has been moving towards something like a both-and resolution between cultural and psychobiological approaches. But that phrase cheapens the currency of both bodies of knowledge. The potential of an attentive conversation between cultural particularity and biological universals requires a more deeply interdisciplinary conversation than we typically engage, but it begins by recognizing that culture is not the only epistemological source at the table of human movements and phenomena. Stowers is surely correct that aspects of social structure can colonize personal psychology; yet influence in the other direction is equally relevant, and our efforts should lie in discerning the character of the interaction between modes.

With these nuances in mind, one more round of analysis of the influence of culture in Romans 7 is in order. Motivational fragmentation is a sufficiently salient and ubiquitous psychobiological experience that Euripides portrayed it in *Medea* centuries before Seneca or Galen applied the term *akrasia* in their analyses of that play. So, why would we imagine that Paul cannot discuss conflicting impulses without imitating philosophical discourse (particularly when the key term is absent from the passage)? Instead of *akrasia* and the passions, Paul attends to another form of cultural regulation – the law – and another inhabiting dynamic – sin. The opportunity in the case of Romans 7 to make better use of the ingredients at hand lies in the leverage we gain through comparison. Here, the consistency of psychobiological disruption becomes a shared point of concern between Pauline and broadly Platonic or Stoic representations (or denials) of the fragmented self. Each group wields a cluster of cultural tools for their distinct purposes. What might we learn by considering the patterns of overlap and distinction between Paul's Sin and the philosophers' Passions as personified players in the drama of self? Might material circumstances of class differences help to explain Paul's pessimism, relative to that of philosophical writers, about the possibility of surmounting motivational fragmentation?

A second relevant category – emotion – poses one of the most interesting examples of inflation of cultural influence because emotion is both manifestly visceral, and hence biological, and yet frequently analyzed as though linguistic categories define its boundaries. So, for instance, the fact that no word in the cultures of Mediterranean antiquity translates tidily to "emotion" is often taken as evidence of an essential incomparability between contemporary and ancient affect.[35] (The current proliferation of blog posts and memes that catalogue allegedly culturally exclusive feelings provides popular support for this tendency.) Indeed, both points are relevant.

I illustrate the point with another historian whose work I respect. With his typical close reading, David Konstan concludes that Greek offers no specific word for erotic jealousy and that this absence of a cultural construction corresponds to constraints of behaviour and expression among ancient authors. In short, whatever they may feel, it is not expressed as erotic jealousy, the implication being that Hellenistic culture did not structure relationships in such a way that the erotic in one person belonged to their partner. It is a compelling and fascinating point about the power of culture to constrain experience. Konstan applies it to that fascinatingly early, emotionally fraught work *Medea* in which marital infidelity results in Medea's murderous spree. He further excludes Medea from feeling erotic jealousy because her motivation is "anger at Jason's violation of his oaths."[36] At the same time, Maria Sassi shows that, whatever Euripides's explicit account of Medea's feelings, the play itself is also replete with "vivid metaphors that are common in classical literature for describing erotic passion (stings, bites, twisting of the bowels), not to mention the references made by all the characters to the empty bed, betrayed or abandoned (the bed being an obvious metonymy of marriage and/or sex), for a total of thirty-six, more than in any other preserved tragedy."[37] This list of somatic features shows how attention to the biological universals of affective stimulation actually interrupts undertheorized constructions of emotion. The lines of speech that Euripides composes for Medea remain (as per Konstan) within the confines of culture, but the descriptions provided by supporting figures like the nurse and the chorus (as per Sassi) describe the bodily experience that exceeds those confines and coordinates with the phenomena displayed in other times when words for the fixation of romantic attachment do exist. Euripides observes both in his own way, and that alone is a compelling observation.[38]

A number of other spheres are amenable to bio-cultural insights. Cognitive linguistics is already in use because of its utility in the analysis of texts.[39] The theory is built on the dependency of language on embodiment – experiences of moving through space with a human body that stands upright and patterns of cognition that fluidly organize and associate the affordances of elements in a metaphor. In this case, this universal cognitive patterning helps to explain the myriad innovations of language non-reductively. The analytical partnership between biology and culture is a happy one. The study of ritual patterning is further along, aided by the use of animal studies. Still, the most intriguing potential for biocultural analysis may be the study of religion in itself rather than religious elements within it. If religion is a natural kind, it is surely so as a complex dynamic system that coordinates available cultural tools with the givens of human biology within specific contexts. But this is work that requires sustained conversation among a wide range of academic disciplines well beyond the metaphorical intimacy of a dinner party.

NOTES

1 Jeffrey J. Kripal, "Foreword," in *The Routledge Companion to Ecstatic Experience in the Ancient World*, ed. Diana L. Stein, Sarah Kielt Costello, and Karen Polinger Foster (Abingdon: Routledge, 2022), xix.

2 Russell T. McCutcheon, "Critical Thinking Begins at Home: On Making a Shift in the Study of Religion," *Implicit Religion* 22, nos 3 and 4 (2019): 349–72.

3 McCutcheon, "Critical Thinking," 361.

4 McCutcheon describes this theoretical shift in "Critical Thinking," 359–64. The quotation is from p. 362.

5 Jonathan Z. Smith is the intellectual/spiritual progenitor of this family of thought. Within his oeuvre the collection of essays in *Relating Religion: Essays in the Study of Religion* (Chicago: University of Chicago, 2004) provides an apt sampling of his theorizing. Currently noteworthy among those advocating this view is Brent Nongbri, *Before Religion: A History of a Modern Concept* (New Haven: Yale University Press, 2013). Before him, Timothy Fitzgerald made a more strident case against religion as a natural kind in *The Ideology of Religious Studies* (New York: Oxford University Press, 2000) and *Discourse of Civility and Barbarity: A Critical History of Religion and Related Categories* (New York: Oxford University

Press, 2007). See also Talal Asad, *Genealogies of Religion: Discipline and Reasons of Power in Christianity and Islam (Baltimore: Johns Hopkins University Press, 1993).*

6 This work was especially active a generation or two ago, during the cultural turn, and is exemplified by Wayne Proudfoot, *Religious Experience* (Berkeley: University of California Press, 1985), and Steven T. Katz, "The 'Conservative' Character of Religious Experience," 3–60 in *Mysticism and Religious Traditions* (New York: Oxford University Press, 1983). More recent work tends to focus on the unresolvable complexity of experience. See, for example, Robert H. Sharf, "Experience," 94–116, in *Critical Terms for Religious Studies*, ed. Mark C. Taylor (Chicago: University of Chicago Press, 1998).

7 David Konstan is exemplary for his important and attentive descriptions of the cultural specificity of emotion in ancient Greek and Roman contexts. See, for example, Konstan, *The Emotions of the Ancient Greeks: Studies in Aristotle and Classical Literature* (Toronto: University of Toronto Press, 2006).

8 Francisca Cho and Richard King Squier, "Religion as a Complex and Dynamic System," *Journal of the American Academy of Religion* 81, no. 2 (2013): 357–98. More recently, Richard Sosis and colleagues have been exploring religion as a dynamic system: Connor Wood and Richard Sosis, "Simulating Religions as Adaptive Systems," 209–32, in *Human Simulation: Perspectives, Insights, and Applications*, ed. Saikou Y. Diallo, Wesley J. Wildman, F. LeRon Shults, and Andreas Tolk (Cham: Springer International, 2019); and Candace S. Alcorta and Richard Sosis, "Ritual, Emotion and Sacred Symbols: The Evolution of Religion as an Adaptive Complex," *Human Nature* 16, no. 4 (2005): 323–59.

9 Wood and Sosis, "Simulating Religions," 215–16. Similarly, altruism (self-sacrifice for the sake of others in the in-group) is higher among members of religious groups. See Jordan Kiper and Richard Sosis, "The Roots of Intergroup Conflict and the Co-Optation of the Religious System: An Evolutionary Perspective on Religious Terrorism," in *The Oxford Handbook of Evolutionary Psychology and Religion*, ed. James R. Liddle and Todd K. Shackelford (New York: Oxford University Press, 2021), 265–81; and Scott Atran, "The Devoted Actor: Unconditional Commitment and Intractable Conflict across Cultures," *Current Anthropology* 57, no. S13 (2016): 192–203.

10 Representative of this focus are Pascal Boyer's theorizing of supernatural ideation in *Religion Explained: The Evolutionary Origins of Religious Thought* (New York: Basic Books, 2001); and work on representation of gods and its relationship to social expansion and moral behaviour in Ara Norenzayan, *Big Gods: How Religion Transformed Cooperation and Conflict* (Princeton, NJ: Princeton University Press, 2013) and John Teehan, "Religion and Morality: The Evolution of the Cognitive Nexus," in *The Oxford Handbook of Evolutionary Psychology and Religion*, ed. James R. Liddle, and Todd K. Shackelford (online edition, Oxford Academic, 2021).

11 For examples in this category see Joseph A. Bulbulia, "Ritual and Cooperation," in *The Oxford Handbook of Early Christian Ritual*, ed. Risto Uro, Juliette J. Day, Rikard Roitto, and Richard E. DeMaris (New York: Oxford University Press,

2018), 94–114; Jonathan A. Lanman, "The Importance of Religious Displays for Belief Acquisition and Secularization," *Journal of Contemporary Religion* 27, no. 1 (2012): 49–65. As the title suggests, Lanman (and others) understand ritual to be essential to all human systems, not only to religion.

12 For this category see, for example, Patrick McNamara, *The Neuroscience of Religious Experience* (New York: Cambridge University Press, 2009); Colleen Shantz, *Paul in Ecstasy* (New York: Cambridge University Press, 2009); and Nina P. Azari, John Missimer, and Rudiger J. Seitz, "Religious Experience and Emotion: Evidence for Distinctive Cognitive Neural Patterns," *International Journal for the Psychology of Religion* 15, no. 4 (2005): 263–81.

13 Clifford Geertz, "Thick Description: Toward an Interpretive Theory of Culture," 3–30, in *The Interpretation of Cultures* (New York: Basic Books, 1973), 24. As Geertz notes, the concept originated with Gilbert Ryle.

14 Clifford Geertz, *Available Light: Anthropological Reflections on Philosophical Topics* (Princeton, NJ: Princeton University Press, 2012), 72. Cho and Squier's article drew my attention to this thread in Geertz's thought ("Religion as a Complex," 357–9).

15 Exemplary of such critique is Donna Haraway's "Situated Knowledges: The Science Question in Feminism and the Privilege of Partial Perspective," *Feminist Studies* 14 (1988): 575–99; and Edward G. Slingerland, *What Science Offers the Humanities: Integrating Body and Culture* (Cambridge: Cambridge University Press, 2008).

16 Krister Stendahl, "The Apostle Paul and the Introspective Conscience of the West," *Harvard Theological Review* 56, no. 3 (1963): 199–215. Interestingly, the piece was originally written as an address to the annual meeting of the American Psychological Association.

17 On this point, Stendahl credits Werner Georg Kümmel, *Römer 7 und das Bild des Menschen im Neuen Testament: Zwei Studien*, Theologische Bücherei, Bd. 53 (München: C. Kaiser, 1974 [1929]); and George Foot Moore, *Judaism in the First Centuries of the Christian Era: The Age of the Tannaim*, vol. 3 (Cambridge, MA: Harvard University Press, 1930).

18 Stendahl, "Introspective Conscience," 211. Regarding the law as the point of this section of Romans, Stendahl is indebted to W.G. Kümmel, *Römer 7 und das Bild des Menschen im Neuen Testament*, TBü 53 (Munich: Kaiser Verlag, 1929).

19 Stendahl, "Introspective Conscience," 212. Stendahl grants that fragmentation of motivation is a generally human phenomenon but also trivializes the significance of such experiences. I note that he did so from the vantage point of someone who lived with a high degree of coherence between the circumstances of his life and the social valuation systems of his society. Among the several other signs of that coherence are his appointments as a bishop, a professor, and a dean. The scope to bring motivations and intentions into alignment is far greater for someone with access to the avenues afforded by those positions than for many other members of society. But that is a discussion for another paper and does not diminish the generous use Stendahl made of his relative privilege.

20 Stendahl, "Introspective Conscience," 213.

21 Stanley Kent Stowers, *A Rereading of Romans: Justice, Jews, and Gentiles* (New Haven: Yale University Press, 1994), especially 44–82; Troels Engberg-Pedersen, "The Reception of Graeco-Roman Culture in the New Testament: The Case of Romans 7.7–25," 32–57, in *The New Testament as Reception*, ed. Mogens Müller and Henrik Tronier, JSNT SS 230 (London: Sheffield Academic Press, 2002); and Emma Wasserman, "Paul among the Ancient Philosophers: The Case of Romans 7," 69–84, in *Paul and the Philosophers*, ed. Ward Blanton and Hent de Vries (New York: Fordham University Press, 2014). I have chosen these three authors not because of some deficiency in their writing but because of the influence of their work and their investment in critical historiography – especially attention to the context of Graeco-Roman culture for Paul's letters. Wasserman has published several studies of the chapter, so my treatment here is representative rather than exhaustive. Further, I am not considering another swath of scholarship that has continued to read Romans 7 as universally relevant without critically reconsidering the basis for a ubiquitous human experience of self-fragmentation.

22 Although Paul knows and uses the term *akrasia* (1 Cor 7:5) he does not introduce it explicitly anywhere in Romans 7. Rather than speaking about self-control he speaks of the conflict between desiring (θέλω) and despising (μισῶ) and various sorts of "laws." It is a different argument.

23 Engberg-Pedersen, "Reception of Graeco-Roman Culture," 53.

24 Stowers, *Rereading Romans*, 42. He states more pointedly: "The difficult task of imagining a reading possible for readers in Paul's time must preclude Christian assumptions and readings that make sense only in epochs later than Paul's."

25 Wasserman, "Paul among the Ancient Philosophers," 70.

26 Stowers, *Reading Romans*, 48. He proceeds with an astute analysis of the asymmetries of self-mastery in a culturally structured context of unequal power and social dominance.

27 Stowers, *Rereading Romans*, 49.

28 Wasserman, "Paul among the Ancient Philosophers," 79.

29 Ibid. She notes, in particular, the use of "death as a metaphor for domination" (76).

30 Mads Larsen, "Untangling Darwinian Confusion around Lust, Love, and Attachment in the Scandinavian Modern Breakthrough," *Evolutionary Studies in Imaginative Culture* 5, no. 1 (2021): 41–56.

31 Helen E. Fisher, Arthur Aron, Debra Mashek, Haifang Li, and Lucy L. Brown, "Defining the Brain Systems of Lust, Romantic Attraction, and Attachment," *Archives of Sexual Behavior* 31, no. 5 (2002): 413–19, 413.

32 Andreas Bartels and Semir Zeki, "The Neural Correlates of Maternal and Romantic Love," *NeuroImage* 21, no. 3 (2004): 1155–66; Bartels and Zeki, "The Neural Basis of Romantic Love," *Neuroreport* 11, no. 17 (2000): 3829–34; and Krishna Seshadri, "The Neuroendocrinology of Love," *Indian Journal of Endocrinology and Metabolism* 20, no. 4 (2016): 558–63.

33 Fisher et al., "Defining the Brain System," 413–14; Seshadri, "Neuroendrocrinology of Love."

34 Ian McGregor, Kyle Nash, Nikki Mann, and Curtis E. Phills, "Anxious Uncertainty and Reactive Approach Motivation (RAM)," *Journal of Personality and Social Psychology* 99 (2010): 133–47.

35 See the discussion by Juanita Feros Ruys, Michael W. Champion, and Kirk Essary, "Introduction," in *Before Emotion: The Language of Feeling, 400–1800* (New York: Routledge, 2019).

36 David Konstan, "Before Jealousy," 7–28, in *Envy, Spite and Jealousy: The Rivalrous Emotions in Ancient Greece*, ed. Keith Rutter and David Konstan (Edinburgh: Edinburgh University Press, 2003), 22.

37 Maria Michela Sassi, "The Medea Syndrome," *Philosophical Inquiries* 5, no. 1 (2017): 91–106.

38 Exciting research under way in the Swiss Center for Affective Sciences in the Université de Genève is making inroads by refining a model through cross-cultural testing. The theory manages to identify recurrent universal patterns of assessment that are inherently attuned to context – a synergistic blend of biology and culture.

39 Two recent (and related) examples are Frederick S. Tappenden, *Resurrection in Paul: Cognition, Metaphor, and Transformation*, Early Christianity and Its Literature 19 (Atlanta: SBL Press, 2016); and Kai-Hsuan Chang, *The Impact of Bodily Experience on Paul's Resurrection Theology*, Library of New Testament Studies 5655 (New York: T&T Clark/Bloomsbury, 2021).

23

The Universality of Spirit Possession Revisited

Giovanni B. Bazzana

The question at the centre of the colloquium for which the present contribution was originally written could have been formulated (in a rather simplistic way) as "are there universals"? Of course, there is little doubt that providing an answer for such a question would not need much of a discussion: the most recent developments in philosophical and epistemological research have established that "universals," in the traditional and positivistic sense in which such a category is often taken, do not and cannot exist. However, in part from the conversations conducted in the above-mentioned colloquium, it became clear that a much more interesting and potentially productive way to reformulate the initial question would be to switch our focus away from matters of ontology and instead pay more sustained attention to the significance of universals in epistemology. The present chapter thus focuses on a slightly different question: "Do we need some form of universal categories in order to understand phenomena and, in particular, given the nature of the volume in which the present contribution is included, phenomena that have to do with the study of religion?"

In the course of this treatment, it also becomes evident that, at least in the mind of the present author, the matter of "universal" categories is closely related to the issue of the comparative method. Interestingly, methodological discussions around the legitimacy and the feasibility of comparison, which seemed to have definitively disappeared until a decade ago, have seen a significant resurgence over the course of the last few years, especially in relation to the study of religion. It has even been argued (as discussed below) that the comparative method constitutes the *proprium* of the study of religion. For these reasons, the present discussion of universals entails a good deal of engagement with their construction through and for the comparison of religious phenomena. Finally, it seems that such points can be argued appropriately only by way of a concrete exemplification. The length of a chapter such as this, of course, does not allow for a full-fledged case study. However, in order to offer at least a relatively coherent examination, my contribution ends with a case study, presented out of necessity and in a rather summary fashion. Its subject is "possession," which is appropriate given that this religious phenomenon has been approached with a very diverse array of methodological and theoretical tools both by anthropologists and by scholars of religion.

* * *

Before delving into the discussion of universal categories and their potential role in comparison, it is worth adding a few more introductory words. For starters, while it is unquestionable that, as mentioned above, universals are no longer viable(especially in the substantive and positivistic sense in which they have dominated modern Western thought[1]), recent years have witnessed a significant resurgence of interest in them, particularly outside the ontological and epistemological debates that constitute my main subject matter. A major stimulus seems to come from current political events. At least from a European vantage point, it appears clear that the worrying success of so many right-wing movements all over the continent is driven by a potent desire to revivify ideas that the process of European unification seemed to have eliminated but that, in fact, are very much alive in the concrete world of power relationships under the labels of "nation," "land," and "blood."[2]

Besides that, however, there are also other pieces of evidence that, while indicating that the epoch of categorical deconstruction that we have gone through over the least couple of decades is at an end, may hint at the return of universals whose influence could be more beneficial than those just mentioned. It may suffice to think about the enormous success of something like the rightly celebrated "1619 Project," whose impulse reaches strongly and effectively even into the study of the ancient world (which only a few decades ago one could have believed almost immune from concerns like racecraft or enslavement[3]). It is difficult to imagine a clearer statement that any resistance to the "grand narrative" in historiography is at this point outdated. As some of the other contributors to the present volume illustrate in their chapters, in this context great attention should now be paid to cognitive studies. The latter are quite clearly (perhaps more evidently in their more successful – and better funded – iterations in Europe than in North America) a means to rethink and repurpose "humanity" as a universal category and as a basis from which to address the crucial and contested issues of rights and inequality.[4] It is even possible that something as neglected as "class struggle" may be dusted off in North America, where the joint effort of neoliberal discourses and Althusserian or Derridean "reshaping" of Marxian theory had seemed to erase this other revolutionary universal from consideration.[5]

* * *

Are universals back, then? As we have just seen, the answer to such a question cannot be neatly expressed as a simple yes or no. On the one hand, there is no doubt that going back seamlessly to the ontological reality of universals that was romanticized by European positivism in the second half of the nineteenth century would be a very serious and dangerous mistake. As illustrated recently and compellingly by Stefania Consigliere, fascism feeds precisely on the feelings of nostalgia for safety and uniformity that are foundational to a reconstructive project of this type.[6] On the other hand, it becomes more and more clear that humans have (at the very least on an epistemological level) a need for categorical and conceptual constructs that may have some claim to be "general" (leaving aside the term "universal" since it seems to be too fraught to be viable[7]). The brief remarks presented above highlight the fact that such a demand not only meets a need for appropriate academic tools but also goes well beyond that in responding to the human desire to establish communication and to organize communal life.

At the risk of sounding overly simplistic, it seems quite obvious that even basic communication, let alone scholarly understanding or political strategizing, would be impossible without some generalizing categories upon which to build. This is readily apparent, for instance, when one considers translation, something with which most of the readers of this chapter are probably very familiar since many scholars of religion (and especially those working on the ancient world) spend the majority of their time dealing with materials that are preserved in textual forms and that are generally written in languages that they do not speak. Theorists of translation are pretty much all in agreement that a perfect correspondence between source and target languages is, by definition, impossible.[8] This is in part due to the fact that words (and their attendant mental concepts) are not universals: even when they look (or sound) identical across languages (and sometimes even within them) they always maintain an irreducible space of difference and untranslatability. However, as noted above, humans always need translations not only to communicate but also to engage in scholarship, political action, and so on. Thus, translators face a task that may, at first sight, appear basic but that is actually sophisticated and comparative, as is well known to anyone who has lived for an extended period of time in a foreign country. Translators must create correspondences and patterns of correspondence between words stemming from different languages. In practice, this involves the creation of "universals" (or, better, "general concepts"). A closer examination of this process of creation reveals two important features that are also common to any category that is employed in other types of scholarly work.

The first feature is fairly uncontroversial: these "generalizing" categories are most certainly constructed by translators and other scholars. As such, they should never be taken as having ontological reality but, rather, as the products of epistemological and heuristic opportunity.[9] The second feature is that these general categories can and should be modified according to the different goals and projects for which they were originally constructed and mobilized.[10] From this perspective, it is of paramount importance that whoever makes use of universal or generalizing categories should be as transparent about and critical of their goals and their strategies as is possible.

* * *

This chapter is directed towards an audience that has some experience with the theories involved in the study of religion. Since I have just concluded a paragraph by issuing a call for methodological transparency in constructing generalizing categories, it seems appropriate that I should also declare that what I outline in the following pages is greatly indebted to the masterful and seminal work of Jonathan Z. Smith. The latter is of course an author who is well known and duly controversial, among other things, for his theoretical contributions to the use of comparison in the study of religion. In recent years comparative work has become slightly out of fashion in academic circles (for reasons that are significant but that are impossible to discuss here as fully as they deserve), and one has the feeling that Smith's work has been progressively relegated to the section on comparison in our theories and methods syllabi.[11] However, it can be argued that the potential inherent in Smith's theoretical contributions may be more far-reaching and more productive than is usually assumed. One may indeed argue that, with regard to the study of religion, comparison is not and cannot be treated as just one method among others.

First, comparison is in fact the very foundation for every kind of human communication. Even though we tend to take this aspect of our work for granted, we perform comparative moves every time we formulate an intellectual problem. I have already mentioned the case of translation, which perhaps presents the most obvious application of a comparative methodology, but such observations also apply to disciplines that do not work with textual materials. At a simplistic level, would it be possible for an archaeologist to identify types of artifacts or architectural structures without performing some kind of comparison? Or would it be possible for scholars of the ancient economy to speak, for example, about inflation in the Roman Empire in the third century CE without making some kind of comparison?

The foundational role of comparison is acknowledged even by Bruce Lincoln in his rightly celebrated "Theses on Comparison." In this short text, which is otherwise severely critical of comparison, the third thesis is: "all generalization depends on comparison, although the latter is usually pursued in ways inadequate to the task. Still, the only alternatives are (a) a discourse whose generalizations remain intuitive, unreflective, and commonsensical, i.e. without basis, rigor, or method, and (b) a parochialism that dares speak nothing beyond the petty and the particular."[12] The contradiction between the necessity of comparison and its shortcomings is characteristic of Lincoln's most recent thinking on this subject and is re-examined later in this chapter, but it clearly highlights the role that comparison plays in building any form of human knowledge.

In a recent and very effective intervention relating to comparison in the study of religion, Oliver Freiberger observes its pervasiveness in all academic disciplines.[13] Insightfully, Freiberger also notes that most scholars (including, at this point, those working on religion) tend to minimize, if not to deny altogether, the role it plays in shaping their research. The reasons behind such a stance are sketched above and it is not possible to deal with them in full here. However, it is worth mentioning Freiberger's diagnosis that these scholars want to convey the idea that "their research questions exclude comparative efforts that go beyond a specific, contextually-limited data set."[14] Such a starting point can only produce scholarship of the type that Lincoln emphatically describes as speaking "nothing beyond the petty and the particular." In any event, with Freiberger I would argue that comparison plays an even more crucial role in the study of religion than it does in the study of the formation of human knowledge. In the following section I look at how Jonathan Z. Smith's reflections shed light on the comparative method.

* * *

It should be clear to everyone with even a superficial acquaintance with Smith's work that it offers significant insights and guidelines, even though these are not free from pitfalls. One of these is certainly the notorious fact that Smith was not a systematic theorist. Thus, his theoretical observations are scattered in episodic studies that, from time to time, he deemed worthy of his attention. But any reader familiar with Smith's body of work can easily pick up a recurring pattern governing his comparisons. These should, more appropriately, be designated as "redescriptions," to use the terminology that

Smith adopted later in his career. In any event, while we return below to the topic of redescription, it is worth stressing that Smith's terminological change does not seem to have been accompanied by a corresponding change in his theoretical or practical attitudes towards comparison.[15]

One can find a systematic illustration of Smith's comparative process in a few pages of *Drudgery Divine*, located in chapter 2, which is appropriately entitled "On Comparison."[16] Smith begins by stating that comparison brings together similarities and differences "within the space of the scholar's mind for the scholar's own intellectual reasons."[17] This bringing together of similarities and differences (or "comparison," or "redescription," in his oft-changing terminology) is the first step on the way to the construction of those "generalizing categories" (or "universals") mentioned earlier. Importantly, Smith underscores the fact that these intellectual activities do not bring any ontological reality into being; rather, they are part of the scholar's mind, an epistemological and heuristic necessity. On this basis, Smith goes on to say that it is not only insufficient to say "*x* resembles *y*" but also unethical since such a statement hides the fact that comparisons and the generalizations built on them are always formulated as "*x* resembles *y* more than *z* with respect to … "The latter part of this statement ("more than *z* with respect to … ") is too often either left unmentioned or not fully discussed. This is a problematic oversight as this formulation gestures towards the scholarly agenda and goals that undergird any comparative enterprise and that must thus always be disclosed and discussed.[18]

* * *

There is no need to spell out Smith's methodological theorization in fuller detail since one can safely assume that it is well known to most, if not all, readers of this chapter, but it is worth explicitly stating the points mentioned above because they are foundational to considerations made in what follows. From this point on, I concretize these reflections by moving on to the topic of "spirit possession." I employ this test case as a convenient tool to exemplify how, on the basis of Smith's theorization, one can configure the benefits and pitfalls of comparison as well as of those generalizations that can are derived from it.

"Possession" has a long and controversial history in scholarship, both in religious studies and in anthropology. As a topic, it lends itself to theoretical reflection because it has been analyzed (in both disciplines) through of a panoply of methods, and this has yielded a gamut of results that are, in turn, interesting to compare and contrast. In the interest of keeping the present discussion reasonably short and focused, I present only two opposing cases. These have been selected because they map quite well onto the binary between incomplete and complete modes of comparison sketched by Jonathan Z. Smith.

First, I examine an instance of comparison and consequent generalization involving possession that produces problematic results. Subsequently, I offer an alternative case, which arguably provides a better outcome for the comparison (a case that may be characterized as a "redescription"). Before presenting these two test cases, however, it is necessary to say something about the word "possession." It cannot be denied that this choice of terminology is already a product of comparison and generalization. "Possession" is far from an innocent label, and it has done a good deal of intellectual work since it became established as a scholarly term in ethnographic and theological writing in the early modern era. That being said, it is important to underscore that conducting a comparative study of possession is in no way different from conducting any other comparative exercise. The selection of comparanda and of the terminology through which they are brought together is never and can never be a completely "fresh" start. Scholars always begin to formulate problems and initial hypotheses on the basis of disciplinary training, institutional background, and even personal experiences. Any other scenario is unthinkable, but this does not negate the scholar-centred approach to comparison sketched in the previous paragraph. The already mentioned Oliver Freiberger argues this point quite convincingly.[19] While comparisons are initially the product of scholarly discourses, the very performance of comparison enables scholars to step back from initial categorizations and, for all intents and purposes, to produce redescriptions, which can sometimes be very deep reformulations of the initial scholarly discourse itself.

Choosing to make possession the subject of a comparative exercise must be understood in these terms. At the outset, however, it is worth stressing that I define possession in a very broad way: it is taken to indicate any "hold exerted over human beings by external forces or entities more powerful than them." Tellingly, this is a definition that does not come from the study of religion or from New Testament studies; rather, it is the product of anthropological research.[20] I hope that the advantages inherent in adopting such a definition (as well as its disadvantages) become clear in what follows.

* * *

A convenient starting point for this discussion is to take a quick look at how a long-standing scholarly tradition uses comparison to study possession within biblical studies. For instance, it is not uncommon for scholars to draw instances from ethnographic studies of non-European cultures in order to compare them with the exorcism narratives attributed to Jesus in the canonical Gospels.[21] Such comparative analyses are most certainly built on an understanding of possession as a general (if not a universal) human phenomenon. Usually in the most recent of these studies, both ethnographic materials and, even more important, their interpretive patterns are drawn from a very influential book, *Ecstatic Religion: A Study of Shamanism and Spirit Possession*, written by the famed anthropologist Ioan M. Lewis in 1971. Lewis was a student of Evans-Pritchard and thus his description of possession across several different cultures and societies is decidedly functionalist character: phenomena of possession are seen as social "venting valves," through which oppressed and marginal groups and individuals – for the most part women – find ways to "get back" at their oppressors. But within this framework, possession is a means of manifesting marginalization that leaves the basic social structure intact.

Thus described, in these studies possession is compared to the narratives of Jesus's exorcisms encountered in the Gospels. Since possession, understood as a universal human phenomenon, has been categorized as a symptom or a reaction to some sort of oppression, then Jesus's "healings" may be seen as providing a better, more effective solution (through exorcism) to such unwelcome and painful symptoms. In the classical German exegetical tradition (informed by a traditional reading of Paul's theology of salvation), the plight of these possessed individuals becomes (rather allegorically, one must note) "sin," from which Jesus provides liberation through exorcism (representing "grace").[22] In more recent (usually North American) readings, the oppression is no longer sin but Roman imperialism and colonization (especially in the case of the demon called Legion in Mk 5:1–20), but Jesus again provides a spiritual liberation that is much more effective than any actual anti-imperial revolt.[23]

In terms of Smith's formula for comparison presented above (*x* resembles *y*), we can express these readings as asserting that "ethnographic cases of possession resemble demonic possession in the New Testament." This may be fine, but it is worth remembering that Smith also notes that such formulations are deceptively and problematically incomplete. One must expand them into the form of "*x* resembles *y more than z* with respect to … " Importantly, the issue is not that these comparisons do not *have* the second half of the formula (more than *z* with respect to …), but that this second part (which is by definition always present) is hidden. So, it is worth asking, how can one fill in the missing pieces for these well-established and traditional readings?

From what has been noted above, it is clear that, for authors like Hollenbach, the resemblance between possession in the New Testament and possession encountered in ethnographic reports has to do with the social "function" performed by this phenomenon. It is a little more difficult to figure out what *z* could be in Smith's formula of comparison. I submit the hypothesis that the unspoken and hidden *z* is something that may be described as "the operation of the divine spirit in the Christian church." So, our formula could be phrased as follows: "ethnographic cases of possession resemble demonic possession in the New Testament *more than the operation of the divine spirit in the Christian church.*"

Readers will note that, for Smith to be satisfied, this formulation needs another piece: "with respect to what?" Answering this question goes a long way towards clarifying why it is important that the "operation of the divine spirit" not resemble the "possession produced by demons" or those instances of possession encountered by ethnographers. To arrive at an answer, one needs to attend to the history of theological reflection on possession and demons from the beginnings of Christianity down to the modern era. Here it suffices to say that, starting in the second and third century CE, early Christian theologians began to systematize demonological and angelological taxonomies and that this resulted in the creation of a sharp conceptual distinction between good and bad spirits. At a basic terminological level, such a shift is evident in the creation of a distinction between good "angels" on one side and bad "demons" on the other. This is a significant departure from the tradition of Mediterranean cultures that had, until then, envisaged a cosmos populated by a host of morally ambiguous "spirits."[24] This development took another decisive turn in modern times, with the colonial encounter between Christianity and peoples who practised rites that Christian missionaries and European ethnographers promptly classified as "possession." As in many other cases, the initial definition of categories employed in anthropology and in the study of religion was profoundly influenced by concepts and ideas derived from Christian theology. As a result, a "bad" type of possession, entailing a loss of individual free will and the need to be "healed" through exorcism, was attributed to non-Europeans and to their religious traditions. On the contrary, (North) Europeans were thought to be fundamentally immune from the risk of possession since their individual self was understood to be "buffered," in full control of its will, and not "porous" and thus prey to external influences.[25] As a consequence, non-European and colonized peoples were open to possession, which became a signifier of their inferiority as well as of the legitimacy of their bodies being "owned" by other, superior races.[26]

So, our formula of comparison for possession phenomena could be expanded, according to Smith's guidelines, to: "ethnographic cases of possession resemble demonic possession in the New Testament more than the operation of the divine spirit in Christian churches with respect to the social function of this phenomenon." Thus the ideological work performed by the traditional comparative exercises applied to the cases of possession in biblical studies becomes evident. On the one hand, this arrangement cordons off the activity of the divine spirit in Christianity from instances of "bad" possession (and so the Holy Spirit brings about a kind of possession that can be taxonomically distinguished as "good").[27] On the other hand, this form of comparison ensures the correspondence between Christianity and modern European hegemonic conceptions of the human self. For the reasons that have just been presented, this mode of comparison is problematic and unsatisfactory. That being said, it is important to underscore that the problem is neither in the attempt at generalization via comparison per se nor in the fact that this comparative work serves specific ideological goals (which is true for all comparisons and all generalizations).

* * *

The problem with the comparative exercise described above and with the resulting concept of possession emerges when one looks closely at the historical material that we have at our disposal. This is a complicated matter and may be illustrated here only by way of a couple of crucial questions. To begin with, is it really true that the distinction between "good" and "bad" forms of possession (with their attendant spiritual agents) is supported in the texts, for instance, of the New Testament? It is enough to mention two very interesting and very well-known examples to see that this is not the case. First, when Jesus is baptized by John at the beginning of the Gospel of Mark, we are told (in Mk 1:10) that "*the* spirit" (with no other more specific qualifications) goes "*into* him."[28] How different is this phenomenon from what happens to the demoniacs whom Jesus will meet later in the book? Second, what is going on with Paul's statements concerning the relationship between himself and Christ? For instance, at a crucial juncture of his letter to the Galatians, the apostle says: "I have been crucified with Christ; and it is no longer I who live, but it is Christ who lives in me" (Gal 2:19–20).[29] Could there be a more explicit expression of possession by a stronger entity with the consequent loss of individual autonomy?

It seems that these pieces of evidence (and others that could be added to them) demand a revision of the formula of comparison presented in the preceding section and, consequently, a revision of the notion of possession. Such a revision (and the comparison as a whole) is significantly reframed when one employs another set of anthropological and ethnographic materials – one that pushes our understanding of the phenomenon beyond the functionalist paradigm deployed by Lewis. The contributions of scholars like Janice Boddy, Michael Lambek, and Diana Espírito Santo show that one should not conceive of possession merely as a reaction to oppression or as a "venting valve."[30] While these elements are not absent in some cases of possession, these more recent studies also highlight the "positive" and constructive side of the phenomenon. Thus, possession is not only a painful and traumatic experience but also (and often at the same time) a highly creative and flexible cultural event through which individuals shape their subjectivity and develop their ethics, and through which groups reflect critically on their past and on their identities. These features are all present in the New Testament and in other early Christian texts, as long as one applies a broad definition of possession (like that of Boddy, noted above). Such a definition includes the complex relationships between Jesus and the divine spirit or Paul and the spirit of Christ – relationships that are too often treated like puzzling oddities in New Testament studies.

In light of these considerations, one may come up not only with a new (and more "neutral") definition of possession but also with a revision of the formula for comparison – one that more adequately matches Smith's criteria. One could say that "with respect to the cultural work performed through this phenomenon, possession, as it is employed in other religious traditions, resembles early Christian possession more than its dogmatic systematization in Christian theological thought." This revised formulation has the advantage of more adequately fitting the historical materials at our disposal. That being said, I would add that the new formula of comparison produces another attendant benefit: it enables one to see how the religious experience of early Christ groups was not that different from those of other people throughout the world.[31] It thus significantly erodes the fantasy of Christian European exceptionalism and (perhaps even more important) underscores the general conclusion that human subjectivities are far from "buffered." They are instead porous and radically open to external forces and influences, and not only those of a religious or spiritual nature. Indeed, through such an exercise in comparison one may be alerted to the opportunity of extending ontological categories to include other-than-human beings, whether spirits or animals or even the earth itself. Such a reorientation is extraordinarily important when, for instance, confronting the consequences of climate change demands that ethical choices be made in full cognizance that the stakes go well beyond the modern conception of humanity.[32]

* * *

This chapter shows that, while universal categories are epistemologically and ontologically impossible, generalizing categories play a foundational role in any form of human cognition and action. In particular, generalizing categories carry weight in the study of religion and should be constantly revised and reframed through the application of methodologically sound comparative analysis. I discuss this theoretical point by using "spirit possession" as a case study. Traditional comparative exercises that focus on early Christian phenomena designated as possession display a reductionist understanding of possession and an ideological approach influenced by Christian and modern European exceptionalism. Building on Jonathan Z. Smith's understanding of the goal of comparison as "redescription,"[33] I conclude by proposing a different comparative frame for "possession" – one that stresses the "positive" cultural work this phenomenon performs in refashioning individual subjectivities and group identities.

NOTES

1 It suffices to mention the by now classic indictment of Bruno LaTour, *We Have Never Been Modern* (Cambridge: Harvard University Press, 1993).

2 For a subtle analysis of these phenomena focused on the Italian case, see Stefania Consigliere, *Favole del reincanto: Molteplicità, immaginario, rivoluzione*, Habitus Environmental Humanities 3 (Roma: Derive Approdi, 2020).

3 https://www.nytimes.com/interactive/2019/08/14/magazine/1619-america-slavery.html.

4 Not so much in North America, but at this point cognitive approaches are a well-established subdiscipline within religious studies. See Justin L. Barrett, ed., *The Oxford Handbook of the Cognitive Science of Religion* (New York: Oxford University Press, 2022).

5 https://twitter.com/aoc/status/1213210234732371968?lang=en. See also Roland Boer and Christina Petterson, *Time of Troubles: A New Economic Framework for Early Christianity* (Minneapolis: Fortress Press, 2017); and G. Anthony Keddie, Michael Flexsenhar III, and Steven J. Friesen, eds., *The Struggle over Class: Socioeconomic Analysis of Ancient Christian Texts* (Atlanta: SBL Press, 2021).

6 Consigliere, *Favole*, 62–79.

7 Along with the "universal," I also set aside the ontological. The following remarks focus only on epistemology.

8 See, for instance, Lawrence Venuti, "Translation, Community, Utopia," in *The Translation Studies Reader*, ed. Lawrence Venuti (London: Routledge, 2000), 468–85. Naturally, such a basic observation gives rise to a number of divergent theories regarding which translation technique may be more suitable to the goals of effective communication and community building mentioned above.

9 To fail to recognize such a state of affairs runs the risk of replicating the mistakes of modern positivism with all its attendant problems, which, in turn (and as noted above), can be envisaged as the first stepping stone for the resurgence of fascisms in Europe and beyond.

10 In this perspective, the analogy with translation theory is interesting and productive because, quite some time ago, theorists of translation noted that a universally "right" translation for any given speech or text is an impossibility. On the contrary, practitioners of translation must always remain aware that the appropriateness and effectiveness of their chosen tools should be constantly measured against the nature of the target audience and the communicative goals for which said tools are developed and selected. See a seminal reflection along these lines in Hans J. Vermeer, "Skopos and Commission in Translational Action," 219–230, in Venuti, *Translation*, 221–31.

11 In this regard, it is interesting to note how Bruce Lincoln, in the introduction to a recently published collection of his essays on comparison, describes his first student encounter with Smith in 1971. Apparently, the already quite well-established Smith responded to Lincoln's request for advice on comparison with a harsh: "Comparison is over. You need to get serious and specialize" (Bruce Lincoln, *Apples and Oranges: Explorations in, on, and with Comparison* [Chicago: University of Chicago Press, 2018], 4–5). Of course, as noted by Lincoln retrospectively, this was also the moment when Smith was beginning to work on a systematic critique of Eliade's method.

12 The essay was originally published in 2012 but is quoted here from Lincoln, *Apples*, 25.

13 Oliver Freiberger, *Considering Comparison: A Method for Religious Studies* (New York: Oxford University Press, 2019), 7–44.

14 Ibid., 24.

15 Such a point is illustrated in a clear and helpful way in Christopher I. Lehrich, *Jonathan Z. Smith on Religion* (Abingdon: Routledge, 2021), 49–74.

16 Jonathan Z. Smith, *Drudgery Divine: On the Comparison of Early Christianities and the Religions of Late Antiquity*, Jordan Lectures in Comparative Religion 14 (London: SOAS, 1990), 50–3.

17 The centring of the scholar in this phrase is noteworthy and it clearly resonates with the delineation of "a scholar-centered approach to comparative methodology" advanced in Freiberger, *Comparison*, 109–10.

18 In rereading this well-known *Drudgery Divine* passage for the purpose of the present discussion, I noticed that Smith adds a few interesting lines: "religious studies, with its bias towards the 'unique' and the 'total,' expressed methodologically through its deep involvement in morphology, phenomenology, and, more recently, in a morality of regard for local interpretations, has been a discipline profoundly and not unsurprisingly of the 'right.' The comparative endeavour herein described is relentlessly an affair of the 'left.'" The political resonances and the mention of "local interpretations" may have a very different

(and problematic) meaning thirty years after the original formulation, but there is no space here for a full discussion of the point.

19 Freiberger, *Comparison*, 104–9.

20 The definition is a slight adaptation of Janice Boddy, "Spirit Possession Revisited: Beyond Instrumentality," *Annual Review of Anthropology* 23 (1994): 407.

21 Two often-quoted and recent examples of such an approach can be found in Bernd Kollmann, *Jesus und die Christen als Wundertäter: Studien zu Magie, Medizin, und Schamanismus in Antike und Christentum*, FRLANT 170 (Göttingen: Vandenhoeck & Ruprecht, 1996); and in Paul W. Hollenbach, "Jesus, Demoniacs, and Public Authorities: A Socio-Historical Study," *Journal of the American Academy of Religion* 49 (1981): 567–88. Many of these works draw the ethnographic material for their comparisons from the enormously influential contribution of Ioan M. Lewis, *Ecstatic Religion: A Study of Shamanism and Spirit Possession*, 3rd ed. (London: Routledge, 2003), a masterpiece of functionalist anthropology of religion.

22 See a classic example in Franz Annen, *Heil für die Heiden: Zur Bedeuunbg und Geschichte der Tradition von besessenen Gerasener (Mk 5,1–20 parr)*, Frankfurter Theologische Studien 20 (Frankfurt am Main: Joseph Knecht, 1976).

23 As examples of such interpretive moves, see, besides Hollenbach's article mentioned above, Warren Carter, "Cross-Gendered Romans and Mark's Jesus: Legion Enters the Pigs (Mark 5:1–20)," *Journal of Biblica Literature* 134 (2015): 139–55.

24 The initial stages of this intellectual process are illustrated by Heidi Marx-Wolf, *Spiritual Taxonomies and Ritual Authority: Platonists, Priests, and Gnostics in the Third Century CE* (Philadelphia: University of Pennsylvania Press, 2016). Later stages (and their contradictions) are well represented in David Brakke, *Demons and the Making of the Monk: Spiritual Combat in Early Christianity* (Cambridge: Harvard University Press, 2008); and Ellen Muehlberger, *Angels in Late Ancient Christianity* (New York: Oxford University Press, 2013).

25 That this was of course a fantasy has always been clear (to echo the famous provocation of LaTour, mentioned above). See, for instance, the subtle analysis of the great debates in early modern Catholicism (on the subject of possible possession of the body only or of the soul as well) provided by Moshe Sluhovsky, *Believe Not Every Spirit: Possession, Mysticism, and Discernment in Early Modern Catholicism* (Chicago: University of Chicago, 2007).

26 On this point, see the very thoughtful reflections of Paul Christopher Johnson, "Toward an Atlantic Genealogy of Spirit Possession," in *Spirited Things: The Work of "Possession" in Afro-Atlantic Religions* (Chicago: University of Chicago, 2014), 23–45.

27 Emblematic, in this perspective, is the interpretive struggle to understand whether Jesus's alleged possession by Beelzebul should be characterized as "bad" or "good." See Giovanni B. Bazzana, *Having the Spirit of Christ: Spirit Possession and Exorcism in the Early Christ Groups* (New Haven: Yale University Press, 2020), 24–59.

28 Emphasis added. For a summary of the complex discussion concerning the text-critical nature and translation of this Greek phrase, see Adela Yarbro Collins, *Mark: A Commentary* (Philadelphia: Fortress Press, 2007), 150.

29 For a more detailed discussion, see Bazzana, *Spirit*, 134–66.

30 Janice P. Boddy, *Wombs and Alien Spirits: Women, Men, and the Zâr Cults in Northern Sudan* (Madison: University of Wisconsin Press, 1989); Michael Lambek, "How to Make Up One's Mind: Reason, Passion, and Ethics in Spirit Possession," *University of Toronto Quarterly* 79 (2010): 720–41; and Diana Espirito Santo, "Imagination, Sensation, and the Education of the Attention among Cuban Spirit Mediums," *Ethnos* 77 (2012): 252–71.

31 Defamiliarization is also indicated as one of the most important goals of comparative work by Freiberger, *Comparison*, 35. This should be understood within the confines of the ethical and political program sketched by Dipesh Chakrabarty, *Provincializing Europe: Postcolonial Thought and Historical Difference* (Princeton, NJ: Princeton University Press, 2008).

32 Denise K. Buell, "The Microbes and Pneuma That Therefore I Am," in *Divinanimality: Animal Theory, Creaturely Theology*, ed. S.D. Moore (New York: Fordham University Press, 2014), 63–87.

33 This important benefit of comparative work is also emphasized by Freiberger, *Comparison*, 35, using the same terminology of "redescription."

24

Response: Comparison

Maia Kotrosits

For a section that includes scholars with such dense connective tissue of shared ethos and intellectual background, I was surprised to find so little agreement on "big issues." And while each chapter brings generous insight and nuance to a variety of historical points (of which I am glad to be a beneficiary), I am drawn most, by virtue of the theme of this section, to respond to the questions posed by these "big issues" and the significant theoretical tensions across the chapters since these tensions reverberate across the field.

For Shantz and Wendt, for instance, the strong critiques of "religion" over the last two decades or so have overshot the mark, and they see religion, even with its flaws, as an enabling category for expressions of human experience across time and place. While for Otto, on the other hand, the scholarly reliance on religion as a category has warped representations of the social lives of Alexandrian intellectuals and produced supersessionist Christian historical pictures. For Bazzana, the notion of universals of any kind is a non-starter, tied inevitably to European and Christian exceptionalism and nationalist aspirations, and he prefers the smaller, much more modest "generalities" to universals. Shantz, by contrast, offers the biological and cognitive sciences as ground for a less apparently ideological universalism. If there can be any small agreement between these chapters, it would seem to be that all their writers subscribe to, or at least endorse, a chastened comparative methodology.

But what might be said about all of the chapters, whatever their actual position on the aforementioned terms, is that they are worried by the prospects of knowledge production after modernity. In other words, they are responding to the state of crisis, if not the critical collapse, of the foundational aspirations of the discipline of religious studies: namely, that it become a secularized, scientific discipline. The question animating them is: Can the elements of those foundational aspirations be retrieved, be made useful? Can we reclaim the beloved and central elements of a thoroughly modern discipline – comparative studies, universalism, religion? And to what extent would doing so be a reclamation of modernity itself?

Biblical studies came late to the religious studies game. But the prospects of the integration were promising: it offered a deliverance, so it seemed, from the exegetical, dogmatic, and ethical readings of biblical texts that not only dominated the field but also disrupted the potential for proper social, cultural, and intellectual history. That is, religious studies offered biblical studies a new chance to become, at least by association, a properly modern, secular field of study. In one way, the hopes placed in religious studies echoed the (now deflated) hopes placed in historical criticism: once deeply unsettling to pietistic and confessional interests, a promise to make biblical studies more thoroughly part of the discipline of history and the work of the humanities at large – historical criticism ultimately became (whatever its purveyors imagined about it) an unmarked instrument of liberal Protestant interpretation.[1]

But religious studies' epistemology and history is not a comfort. Tomoko Masuzawa's *The Invention of World Religions* (2005) gives us a genealogy of each of these central elements of the study of religion. Indeed, each of these three terms – comparison, universalism, and religion – are historically entangled with one another. The making of comparative religions, Masuzawa demonstrates at length, is founded on an assumption that religion is a universal (and, at the same time, some religions are "more universal" than others), thus producing a certain kind of cultural equivalence in order to enable comparison. On what terms? Of course, it was always Christianity that was the mould and model for what counted as "religion." What's more, Masuzawa writes, "the modern discourse of religion and religions was from the very beginning – that is to say, inherently, if also ironically – a discourse of secularization; at the same time it was clearly a discourse of othering."[2]

One of Masuzawa's more striking chapters shows the source of some of this irony: fully and genealogically embedded in the making of comparative religion as a science was the much more obviously pietistic enterprise of nineteenth-century comparative theology, which was explicit in its colonial Christian supremacy. Figures such as Charles Hardwick and Frank Field Ellinwood, for instance, who were some of the earliest scholars of comparative religion, represent not a departure from confessional investments for the sake of more balanced study but a "collusion" between the "scientific and the evangelical."[3] For some, like Robert Flint, it was actually Christianity's supremacy that *allowed* (in his mind) impartial, objective comparison: "It alone raises us to a height from which all the religions of the earth may be seen as they really are."[4] The fact that all of this might sound counter-intuitive says as much about our trained expectations of science as it does about nineteenth-century scholarship.[5]

Masuzawa recalls these figures in order to produce a fuller, more critical history, and a less romantic narrative, of the discourse of religion and of comparative religions. What her work implies, however, is that the question of whether we can "retrieve" these terms and epistemologies (universalism, comparison, religion) with less sinister implications, if we do our due diligence, is sort of beside the point. It is not really about how carefully we use such terms since the discourse is not ours. The terms continue to use us, to condition what it is that we search for and what we crave from history. And no amount of scholarly care will save us from our desire. In fact, if there are any lessons in the wake of modernity, surely a striking one is that "scholarly care"/rigour has long been an alibi for all kinds of exorbitant desires to possess and master via knowledge.

Indeed, it seems to me, following Masuzawa, that we should not, as we might be tempted, approach such "embarrassing" figures in the history of the field as cautionary tales or aberrations from a course of progress – figures from whom to differentiate ourselves. Such a move would only support an idealized understanding of ourselves within that history, and an idealized version of the field. We should rather consider such figures as spectres whose desires haunt our own since, as participants in the field of their making, we are in fact living (or at least working) in the house that they built. If we listened, what could they tell us, these garrulous ghosts, about what we want out of the analytical frames we ostensibly choose? Or better: What could they tell us about what history wants out of us?

NOTES

1 Paul Michael Kurtz, "A Historical, Critical Retrospective on Historical Criticism," in *The New Cambridge Companion of Biblical Interpretation*, ed. Ian Boxall and Bradley C. Gregory (New York: Cambridge, 2022), 15–36.

2 Tomoko Masuzawa, *The Invention of World Religions* (Chicago: University of Chicago Press, 2005), 20.

3 Ibid., 100.

4 Robert Flint, *Faiths of the World* (Edinburgh: William Blackwood and Sons, 1882), 392, as quoted in Masuzawa, *Invention of World Religions*, 102.

5 See Loraine Daston and Peter Galison, *Objectivity* (New York: Zone Books, 2007), 17. In the nineteenth century, objectivity itself, as we understand it, was

still being worked out, and it was only during this time that the notion of objectivity and subjectivity as antitheses even congealed, objectivity becoming equated not only with a strenuously performed ascetic ethical posture but also with knowledge that "bears no trace of the knower."

Contributors

WILLIAM ARNAL is professor of religious studies at the University of Regina. His research interests revolve around early Christian writings, both canonical and non-canonical, and theoretical issues in the study of religion. His most recent publications include articles on the textual transmission of the *Gospel of Thomas* (JECS) and the presentation of power in *Hypostasis of the Archons* (*Asdiwal*).

ALICIA J. BATTEN is professor of religious studies and theological studies at Conrad Grebel University College at the University of Waterloo. She has a variety of research interests, including ancient material culture, the social history of early Christ groups, and, more specifically, the Letter of James.

GIOVANNI. B. BAZZANA is Frothingham Professor of the History of Religion at Harvard Divinity School. Bazzana's research and teaching focus chiefly on the critical study of the early Christ movement and of early Christianity in the context of Second Temple Judaism and of ancient Mediterranean history, religions, and material cultures. Bazzana's writing is centred on gospels and apocalypses (both those that became canonical and those that were ultimately excluded from the canon). His latest book, *Having the Spirit of Christ: Spirit Possession and Exorcism in the Early Christ Groups* (Yale 2020), starts from the observation that the earliest Christian writings are filled with stories of possession and exorcism, which were crucial for the activity of the historical Jesus and for the practice of the earliest groups of his followers.

WILLI BRAUN is professor emeritus of religion in the Department of History, Classics, and Religion at the University of Alberta in Edmonton, Canada. His research and publications have been preoccupied with topics dealing with the formation of early Christianity and theories of religion.

ESTHER GUILLEN is a PhD candidate in history at McGill University. Her dissertation ("Let the Wisdom in: Epistemological Realms in the Gospel of Matthew") explores the author's construction of interpretive authority through their presentation of supernatural wisdom.

JOHN S. KLOPPENBORG holds the rank of university professor at the University of Toronto and is a fellow of the Royal Society of Canada. He has published widely in the field of synoptic studies, Q, social history of Mediterranean antiquity, and the Letter of James.

MAIA KOTROSITS works at the intersections of ancient Christian studies, the study of religion, contemporary cultural studies, and classics. Her most recent books are *The Lives of Objects: Material Culture, Experience, the Real in the History of Early Christianity* (Chicago, 2020) and *Theory, History, and the Study of Religion in Late Antiquity* (Cambridge, 2023). She is a visiting scholar at the University of Toronto.

JACK N. LIGHTSTONE is professor emeritus, history (Brock); and distinguished professor emeritus, religion (Concordia). He melds historical, literary, and social-scientific approaches in the study of early Judaism. His recent books are *In the Seat of Moses* and *What Were the Early Rabbis?* (both by Cascade).

HEATHER MACUMBER is associate professor of biblical studies at Providence University College. Her most recent publications engage with monster theory and include *Recovering the Monstrous in Revelation* published with Lexington Books/Fortress Academic.

CHRISTINE MITCHELL is professor of Hebrew Bible and academic dean at Knox College, Toronto School of Theology. She is writing a commentary on 1-2 Chronicles for Oxford University Press.

MATTHEW W. MITCHELL is originally from northeast Saskatchewan but now resides in Buffalo, New York, having completed a JD at the University at Buffalo School of Law in 2024. He was the recipient of multiple awards for both teaching and scholarly research, publishing in New Testament,

Hebrew Bible, Patristics, and popular culture. He was also named the 2020 Scholar of the Year for Arts and Sciences at Canisius College. His unexpected exit from academia mere months later is chronicled in part in the AAUP's 2021 sanction of Canisius College.

JENNIFER OTTO is associate professor of religious studies at the University of Lethbridge. She is the author of *Philo of Alexandria and the Construction of Jewishness in Early Christian Writings* (Oxford University Press, 2018).

ADELE REINHARTZ is Distinguished University Professor at the University of Ottawa, where she teaches in the Department of Classics and Religious Studies. She is also a research fellow at the University of the Free State, South Africa. Her most recent books are *Cast Out of the Covenant: Jews and Anti-Judaism in the Gospel of John* (2018) and *The Bible and Cinema: An Introduction* (2nd ed., 2022).

REBECCA RUNESSON is a PhD candidate in the Department for the Study of Religion at the University of Toronto. Her research focuses on early interactions between the Christ cult and the Roman military. Recent publications include "Centurions in the Jesus Movement? Rethinking Luke 7:1–10 in Light of the Gaianus Inscription at Kefar 'Othnay,'" *Journal of Biblical Literature* 142 (2023).

COLLEEN SHANTZ is associate professor at St Michael's College, University of Toronto. Her research and publishing explores the interplay of biology and culture in Christian origins, as, for example, in her recent co-edited volume, *Social and Cognitive Perspectives on the Sermon on the Mount* (Equinox, 2021).

RYAN D. SCHROEDER (PhD in religious studies, University of British Columbia) is a scholar of religion specializing in the Hebrew Bible (a.k.a., "Old Testament") and ancient West Asian prophecy. His forthcoming monograph is entitled, *Let Us Go to the Seer! Prophecy, Scribal Culture, and the Invention of Hebrew Scripture* (De Gruyter).

DANIEL A. SMITH is dean of theology and the Clark and Mary Wright Professor of New Testament Theology at Huron University in London, Ontario. He is the author of *Revisiting the Empty Tomb: The Early History of Easter* (Fortress, 2010) and is currently working on a commentary on Jude and 2 Peter for the International Critical Commentary series (Bloomsbury).

STANLEY STOWERS taught at Brown University for thirty-one years and is now professor emeritus of religious studies. He has worked in early Christianity, ancient philosophy, Greek religion, and theory of religion. Two new books appeared in 2024, *Christian Beginnings: A Study in Ancient Mediterranean Religion* and *History as the Study of Religion: The Ancient Mediterranean as a Test Case.*

KIMBERLY B. STRATTON is associate professor in the College of the Humanities at Carleton University. She is currently working on a series of articles and a book that consider the role of trauma and meaning-making in the origins of Judaism and Christianity.

JOHN VAN MAAREN, University of Vienna, has recently written on the great multitude of Revelation 7:9 (*Harvard Theological Review* 2024), the Gospel of Mark's relation to Paul (*Journal of Biblical Literature* 2024), and how New Testament texts might be described as versions of Judaism (*Zeitschrift Für Die Neutestamentliche Wissenschaft Und Die Kunde Der Älteren Kirche* 2023).

ERIN K. VEARNCOMBE is an assistant professor, Teaching Stream with the Institute for the Study of University Pedagogy, University of Toronto Mississauga. She was the lead author on the 2021 book *After Jesus before Christianity*. Her research in the academic study of religion focuses on dress as an embodied social reality in writings of early Jesus groups.

HEIDI WENDT is associate professor of religion in the Greco-Roman World, jointly appointed in the School of Religious Studies and the Department of History and Classical Studies at McGill University. She is the author of *At the Temple Gates: The Religion of Freelance Experts in the Roman Empire* (Oxford, 2016) as well as several articles and essays on topics dealing with the New Testament, early Christianity, and ancient Mediterranean religion. With Ryan Schellenberg, she also co-edited the *T&T Clark Handbook to the Historical Paul* (Bloomsbury: 2022).

JASON YUH is assistant professor at Redeemer University. His research interests are based on the New Testament and early Christianity. His publications include an application of interdisciplinary studies to Galatians (*Journal for the Study of the New Testament*), the *Epistle of Barnabas* (*Harvard Theological Review*), Hebrews (*Journal of Biblical Literature*), and the *Didache* (*Journal of Ethnic and Cultural Studies*).

Index

GENERAL INDEX

INDEX OF TEXTS

Hebrew Bible

Rabbinic Works

EARLY CHRISTIAN WRITINGS

Inscriptions

Papyrological Sources